# The Psychology
# of Rigorous Humanism

# THE PSYCHOLOGY
# OF RIGOROUS HUMANISM

Joseph F. Rychlak

Purdue University

A Wiley-Interscience Publication
JOHN WILEY & SONS
New York/London/Sydney/Toronto

**Library of Congress Cataloging in Publication Data:**

Rychlak, Joseph F
  The psychology of rigorous humanism.

  "A Wiley-Interscience publication."
  Bibliography: p.
  Includes index.

  1. Psychology—Methodology.  2. Humanistic
psychology.  I. Title.  [DNLM: 1. Psychology.
2. Philosophy.  BF41 R991p]
BF38.5.R93        150        76-54838
ISBN 0-471-74796-3

Printed in the United States of America

10 9 8 7 6 5 4 3 2 1

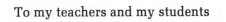

To my teachers and my students

# ACKNOWLEDGMENTS

Acknowledgment is made for permission to reprint the following materials:

From *Principles of Behavior Modification* by Albert Bandura. Copyright © 1969 by Holt, Rinehart and Winston, Inc. Reprinted by permission of Holt, Rinehart and Winston.

From *B. F. Skinner: The Man and His Ideas* by Richard I. Evans. Copyright © 1969 by Richard I. Evans. Reprinted by permission of the publishers, E. P. Dutton & Co., Inc.

From *Structure of Scientific Revolutions* by Thomas S. Kuhn. Copyright © 1962, 1970 by The University of Chicago. Published 1962. Second Edition, enlarged 1970. Reprinted by permission of The University of Chicago Press.

From *Existential Foundations of Psychology* by Adrian van Kaam. Copyright © 1966 by Duquesne University. Reprinted by permission of Duquesne University Press.

From *Cognitive Psychology* by Ulric Neisser. Copyright © 1967. Reprinted by permission of Prentice-Hall, Inc.

From *About Behaviorism* by B. F. Skinner. Copyright © 1974 by Alfred A. Knopf, Inc. Reprinted by permission.

From *Purposive Behavior in Animals and Men* by Edward Chace Tolman. Copyright © 1967 by Meredith Publishing Company. Reprinted by permission of Irvington Publishers, Inc.

# CONTENTS

# TABLES

# FIGURES

# The Psychology
# of Rigorous Humanism

# INTRODUCTION

Psychology has always been a difficult area of study to define—particularly if one were trying to place it within the family of the sciences. Advocates have called it an art in the sense of a healing activity which seems to promote intrapersonal and interpersonal strength in some inexplicable way. Others see it as related to man's spiritual needs, taking the place of ancient moral codes and religious myths in today's so-called materialistic world. When psychology is tied to science it is commonly labeled prescientific—a propaedeutic science which promises to become more worthy of the name in the future.

For those who are willing to call psychology a legitimate science in the present, the outcome is no clearer; for conflicts over whether this is a science of behavior or of the person seem inevitable. The advocate on the right wing of behaviorism or S-R psychology is likely to be called a mechanistic reductionist who distills human behavior into an arid substrate of meaningless motion. The advocate on the left wing of phenomenology or existentialism is likely to be called a neospiritualist, too emotionally caught up in his desire to rescue the human image from the precisions of experimental control to stand as impartial observer for the science of psychology.

It is the writer's belief that due to the underlying polemic in psychology's evolution, the undergraduate and graduate students who study or eventually take up careers in this profession sense—however unconsciously—a fundamental demoralization. Either they view their field from one of the polarized perspectives mentioned above, or they fumble along in near cynicism about what they are studying or actually practicing. They know full well of their second-class standing in the sciences, but they lack the arguments and the technical analyses to raise their morale and put them on the track for the status goals they rightfully deserve. This makes them particularly vulnerable and likely to acquiesce to the first theory having the "sound" of natural science. The hope is that this book will help provide these corrective arguments and analyses.

1

Though other sciences also have their areas of basic disagreement and vigorous misunderstanding, there does seem to be a core of issues in psychology that distinguishes its problems from those encountered elsewhere. The position of this book is that these unique factors have to do with the nature of the data studied by psychologists. There can be no doubt but that psychology's recurring problems stem from its entanglement in the *human* situation—whatever that means, and what *human* means is what this book attempts to answer.

Several other positions that purport to humanize the science of psychology are being advanced in the literature. In the writer's view, most of these approaches take the form of an attack on the methodology of modern science—as if the problems of a nonhumanistic behavioral account must necessarily emanate from the methods of science used by psychologists. The reader will find that in the present approach no changes are called for in the basic logic of scientific methodology as practiced today. The human image that is advanced will be buttressed by almost a full generation of experimental research in verbal learning. More than 50 data collections have been gathered by the author and his students in that time—the total of which presents a scientifically sound humanistic account of verbal behavior. Hence, rather than pointing a finger to methodological weaknesses, the problem of humanism and science is seen to flow from the theories used by psychologists to describe those "facts" they see fluctuating lawfully before their eyes. Psychology *must* remain a vigorous experimental science relying upon the same type of evidence employed in all other sciences.

What is needed, therefore, is greater emphasis on theory construction in the education and professional practice of psychologists. If we could match the sophistication of empirical methodology currently realized in the training of psychologists with a sophistication in the nature of theory construction, there would be fewer misunderstandings and hard feelings than we find today. To reject theory construction as philosophical and thus out of the realm of psychology is just as detrimental to the advance of our profession as is the tendency to reject experimental methodology because it does not now reflect a properly human image of the person. We shall never have complete agreement in the theories of psychology, just as in the physical sciences there will never be a single "true" account of reality. But we can have a single truly clear language on the basis of which we explicate our differences. If we merely turn to history and see how we came to the present, a considerable advance will be achieved by way of this retrospective analysis. Where we go from here is up to us, and most assuredly the path into the future will not be the same.

This volume provides the signposts along which this voyage into the future might take place. The first four chapters present an historical survey of how the humanism-mechanism dichotomy, which now bedevils us, came about. In Chapters 5 and 6 we take up the question of the changes that could be made to revolutionize psychology and set us on the right path. In Chapters 7 and 8 we get down to the specifics of a humanistic psychology, and in Chapters 9 and 10 we survey a program of research that was based on this theoretical approach. The book closes with a retrospective summary of the complete argument, takes up the most common criticisms made of it, and lays down the tenets of a rigorous humanistic psychology. There are summaries at the end of each chapter, and a glossary of important terms has been placed at the end of the book for ready reference (especially important for terminology introduced beginning with Chapter 7).

If one had to summarize the purpose of this book in a single phrase, it would be "an attempt to show that current scientific methodology is consonant with humanistic theoretical formulations." Psychology need never be torn apart on the basis of its methods, although its theories will continue to express divergent meanings. But that too is the nature of meaning in a *human* context.

# CHAPTER ONE

## An Historical Survey
## and Its Lessons

All fields of knowledge achieve distinctiveness based on the objects or events to which they are descriptively applied and the manner in which their resultant conceptualizations are tested for legitimacy. We might be tempted to say that even the objects or events described are theoretical constructions, but this would presume an idealistic interpretation of knowledge. The realist prefers to believe that objects and events exist independent of a theorist's conceptualization, and the challenge is to find accurate representations for what is "really there" in experience. Both realists and idealists must accept the fact that knowledge is impossible without a knower—an organism that processes descriptive information, tests it, and then expounds on what is true or what is inaccurate. Psychology's challenge is to know the knower, and there are surely many pitfalls in this descriptive effort.

To begin such a study a proper first step might be to survey the descent of Western thought, selecting from among its leading thinkers those who seem to have most influenced the ideas that were in existence at the beginning of the twentieth century, when psychology was newly emerging as a scientific discipline. What would such a survey reveal about the knower, the human being on whom our interests ultimately focus? One cannot be strictly empirical in such a survey, of course, because recorded history is not based on samplings from a parameter. Furthermore, if an historical comparison of thinkers (theorists) is to make any sense, we have to employ an organizing scheme. Because schemes prearrange (bias) what we have to say about things, the reader must be assured that the orienting scheme selected here was not arbitrarily concocted by the writer to prove a point from the outset; it has been woven into the fabric of history that we are unfolding.

The writer has employed precisely such a scheme in other contexts, based on Aristotelian terminology, which involved organizing the meaning of theoretical terms under four *causes*, or conceptual frames, having nonoverlapping meanings (see Rychlak, 1968, 1969, 1970, 1972, 1973). Though Aristotle assembled these meanings into four metaconceptions and named them he did not "think them up." We see these meanings in the earliest philosophical accounts. Aristotle did not even limit his framing of causes to the four meanings we review below. (For example, he suggested that change and spontaneity might be thought of as additional "chance" causes of events.) We are in no way committed to Aristotelian philosophy simply because we employ an aspect of his theory of knowledge as a starting point for our survey of Western theoretical history.

The first cause is a *material* cause, which we take to be the substance that comprises a thing. Theories of substance vary, but in general there is some assumption made about an underlying matter, or universal palpability, which lends the essential meaning to an object or event in experience. As further evidence that we are not using "pure" Aristotle in our historical scheme, we should note that he distinguished between primary and secondary substances. Primary substances were viewed as underlying entities that went as potentiality into the construction of all that is. Secondary substances, however, were the more recognizable species of beings, such as a man or a horse. The form (outline, shape) of the latter objects gave their substantial essence additional significance. According to our scheme, Aristotle thus added a formal-cause term to his material-cause account when he defined the secondary substance. When we equate substance with material cause we establish an independence from strict Aristotelian theory.

The second cause is the *efficient* cause, which gets at the *impetus* of or in events—for example, the push, thrust, flow, bringing-about-in-motion aspect of experience. The usual phrasing indicates that an antecedent event invariably and necessarily causes a consequent event, which is called an effect. Thanks to natural science, most people immediately think of *this* meaning of *cause* when we use the term. We often find this efficient cause-effect tandem used in opposition to some other term (e.g., *spontaneity or transcendence*) which lacks the meaning of an invariant antecedent-to-consequent push across the face of time.

The third cause in our scheme is the *formal* cause, which refers to a pattern, shape, outline, or recognizable organization in the flow of events or in the way that objects are constituted (*formed*, as in

Aristotle's secondary substance). Natural objects and behavioral sequences are clearly patterned outlines, recognizable styles of this or that significance to the viewer, who comes to know them as much by these features as by their substantial nature (material cause) or the fact that they are assembled (efficient cause). The very meaning of abstraction or construction in theorizing or in logico-mathematical reasoning comes down to some such patterning of our conceptions into recognizable, albeit abstract, designations. Without a pattern we are adrift and rudderless on the sea of knowledge.

The fourth cause is the one Aristotle specifically coined and made central to his physics, even though the concept of a cause as a reason for behavior had already been employed by Socrates. Aristotle said that before we had fully explicated the nature of anything, we had to state—if possible—its *final* cause. This is best defined as *that, for the sake of which* something happens or comes about. Is there a reason, purpose, intention, or premising meaning that acts as *that* for the sake of which a substance is formed into some recognizable shape, or a line of efficient causation leads to some end result? The emphasis on the direction, goal, or end of events is why theories that employ final-cause meanings are called telic or teleological descriptive accounts (from the Greek word *telos*, meaning end).

This brief introduction of the four causal meanings will suffice for now. Because we make extensive use of these terms throughout the following chapters, they will become increasingly familiar to the reader. Our purpose is not to work out a way of describing human behavior in terms of the causes lying at its root. We must not hypostatize these conceptual categories. Any two theorists might lay equal emphasis on the same cause yet differ dramatically in what they have to say about things. However, the causal scheme as a metaconception permits us to array historical figures for comparison, and it also allows us to diagnose the basic differences that exist in theories of human behavior across varying disciplines.

## A Survey of
## Western Intellectual History

A survey was conducted following three rules: (1) Select approximately 100 recognized thinkers from across the centuries (we included 104 individuals); (2) analyze one or more constructs of each thinker in terms of the four causes; (3) avoid psychologists *per se* (the history of psychology is discussed in Chapters 3 and 4), although William James and John Dewey had to be considered for their roles in philosophy. The concepts selected were all representative of the person in question. They made possible insightful comparisons among the individuals selected for historical consideration.

The reader will find the names and concepts of the thinkers arrayed in Table 1 (pp. 8–31). This table is organized from left to right as follows: (a) name and life dates of an historical figure; (b) construct(s) or general idea for which he is recognized (numbered consecutively if more than one); (c) definition of the construct or brief description of the idea (numbered consecutively in matching order to the constructs listed); (d) causal meaning(s) employed in the construct designated by an X under the headings Material, Efficient, Formal, and Final. Because more than one causal meaning can be used in a single construct, each X placed under a causal designation is numbered from one through four. Thus, if a theorist's construct employed the meanings of two or more causes, by examining the subscript the reader can get some idea of the predominant meanings employed. For example, in Aristotle's substance conceptions discussed above, primary substance would be given an X *only* under the Material Cause heading of Table 1. However, secondary substance would receive an $X_1$ under the Formal and $X_2$ under the Material Cause headings, because Aristotle was using the formal cause meaning as a major emphasis here.

The following sources were used in doing the research for Table 1: Alexander and Selesnick (1966), Becker and Barnes (1952), Burtt (1955), Edwards (1967), Eves (1969), Forbes and Dijksterhuis (1963), Frazer (1959), Kondo (1969), Magill and McGreal (1961), Russell (1959), Sarton (1968), Schwartz and Bishop (1958), Wiener and Noland (1957), and Wightman (1951).

## Discussion of Table 1

Note that the most frequently checked cause in Table 1 is the *formal*. This is doubtless due to the fact that one cannot speak about *meaning* without thereby implying a form, pattern, or organization in whatever is being referred to. Letters are patterns, and combined into various words, they acquire symbolic value in meaning expression. The same is true for numbers, and we cannot overlook the logical proposition and syllogism in which a discernible pattern (Wittgenstein's propositional variables) is to be noted. When we see objects (Avicenna), their recognition value (meaningfulness) hinges upon the degree to which the form perceived in nature matches the form we already have in mind (continued on p. 32).

Table 1  A Survey of Western Intellectual History

| Name and Life Dates | Construct | Definition | Causes | | | |
|---|---|---|---|---|---|---|
| | | | Material | Efficient | Formal | Final |
| Thales of Miletus (c. 640–c. 546 BC) | Water | Universal substance, making up all things and on which the world floats. | X | | | |
| Anaximander of Miletus (c. 611–c. 547 BC) | Boundless | Undifferentiated matter entering into the constitutive nature of everything in the world. | X | | | |
| Pythagoras (?–c. 497 BC) | Order | In nature, as reflected in numbers; indeed, "things are numbers!" | $X_2$ | | $X_1$ | |
| Heraclitus (c. 540–c. 480 BC) | Logos [rationale] | Rational order in universe, so events follow a discernible [lawful] pattern [incl. "reason"]. | | | $X_1$ | $X_2$ |
| Parmenides (c. 515–c. 456 BC) | Change is illusion | All appearances of change and motion are illusions. Reality is eternal and indestructible. | X | | | |
| Anaxagoras (c. 500–c. 428 BC) | Mind | A "thin and pure" form of matter, which orders other matter into what "is." | $X_1$ | | $X_3$ | $X_2$ |
| Empedocles (c. 493–c. 433 BC) | 1) Four roots | 1) Earth, air, fire, and water, as constituent elements out of which everything in the world is made. | X | | | |
| | 2) Motion | 2) Due to the interaction of love and strife. | | $X_2$ | | |
| Hippocrates (c. 460–c. 377 BC) | Four humors | Blood, black bile, yellow bile, and phlegm; combine to determine a person's temperament. | X | | $X_1$ | |

| Philosopher | Concept | Description | C1 | C2 | C3 | C4 |
|---|---|---|---|---|---|---|
| Democritus (c. 460–c. 370 BC) | 1) Atom | "Uncuttable"—i.e., indestructible substrate, differing in shape; atoms move and collide. | X₁ | X₃ | X₂ | |
| | 2) Nonrandomness | Because of rationale order, events and motions are never random; mechanical actions also take place. | | X₂ | X₁ | |
| Socrates (c. 470–399 BC) | 1) Eidos | A single unequivocal designation in mind; hence an "absolute form" or essence; a universal! | | | X | |
| | 2) Good | Purpose or intention of an act. | | | | X |
| | 3) Cause | Reason (grounds, premises, etc.) an action is carried out. | | | | X |
| | 4) One and many | Participation of universals in particulars. | | | X | |
| Plato (427–347 BC) | 1) Forms | Universal (a la Socrates); immaterial and eternal, signifying the "real nature" of things. | | | X | |
| | 2) Idea | That which is apprehended by intelligence. | | X₁ | | |
| | 3) Pleasure | Instrumental; unrelated to the end sought. | X₂ | X₁ | X₂ | |
| Aristotle (384–322 BC) | 1) Syllogism | Sequencing of proofs in reason—i.e., logic. | X₂ | | X₁ | |
| | 2) Soul | Living potentiality and actuality, incl. mind. | X₂ | X₃ | X₁ | |
| | 3) Good | That at which all things aim [telos or "end"]. | | | X | |
| | 4) Theory of causes | Material, efficient, formal, final. | X | X | X | |

**Table 1** A Survey of Western Intellectual History (*cont.*)

| Name and Life Dates | Construct | Definition | Causes | | | |
|---|---|---|---|---|---|---|
| | | | Material | Efficient | Formal | Final |
| Euclid (c. 300 BC) | Axioms | Definitional premises of a geometrical system, based on abstract order and common sense. | | | $X_1$ | $X_2$ |
| Epicurus (c. 342–270 BC) | Pleasure | Physical standard by which "good" is always to be judged. | $X_1$ | | $X_2$ | $X_3$ |
| Archimedes (287–212 BC) | Applied mathematics | Empirical demonstrations of mathematical reasoning, as in law of lever, body density, etc. | | | $X_1$ | $X_2$ |
| Lucretius (c. 96–55 BC) | Atomic materialism | No purpose in events, as all motions are due to the palpable flow of atoms, bumping into each other. | $X_2$ | $X_1$ | $X_3$ | |
| Marcus Aurelius (121–180) | Freedom | From the human's capacity to assent or dissent in life's requirements. Virtue is self-control. | | | $X_2$ | $X_1$ |
| Galen (130–200) | Vital and animal spirits | God-created enlivening forces that interact with the ebb and flow of blood to stimulate life. | | $X_2$ | | $X_1$ |
| Ptolemy (2nd Century) | Geocentric universe | The earth is immobile and at the center of our universe. | | | $X$ | |
| Origen (c. 185–c. 254) | Biblical fall of divine powers | Malignant powers of evil arose by free choice, in opposition to the good which God had created. | | $X_3$ | $X_2$ | $X_1$ |

| Philosopher | Concept | Description | (1) | (2) | (3) | (4) |
|---|---|---|---|---|---|---|
| Plotinus (c. 205–c. 270) | Soul | More perfect than body; lends meaning to sensations of body, organizing them via [Platonic] forms. | | | $X_1$ | $X_1$ |
| Saint Augustine (354–430) | 1) Evil | Absence of good. | | | X | |
| | 2) Holy Trinity | Three divine persons in "one" God. | | | X | |
| | 3) Free will | A self-cause; man must will to act. | | | | X |
| Avicenna (980–1037) | Imagery | Possible only when the form perceived by a mental faculty matches the form manifested in matter. | $X_3$ | | $X_1$ | $X_2$ |
| St. Anselm of Canterbury (1033–1109) | First cause proof of God | All efficient effects have antecedent causes; hence, there must be a First Cause (i.e., God). | | X | | |
| Peter Abelard (1079–1142) | Predication | A precedent meaning, lending meaning to other things known (e.g., a genus to a species) [Aristotelian]. | | | $X_1$ | $X_2$ |
| Averroës (1126–1198) | Unmoved Mover | Pure intelligence, outside of time, but within which motion occurs; both first and final cause of things. | | $X_3$ | $X_2$ | $X_1$ |
| Maimonides (1135–1204) | 1) Metaphorical meaning | Grasping inexact symbols through a sense of preliminary conviction (i.e., faith). | | | $X_2$ | $X_1$ |
| | 2) Negative theology | Description and coming to know God by elucidating His negative attributes (i.e., what He is not). | | | X | |
| Roger Bacon (1214–1294) | Experimentation | Empirical experience provides facts, which are far superior to reasoned explanations. | $X_2$ | $X_3$ | $X_1$ | |

**Table 1** A Survey of Western Intellectual History (cont.)

| Name and Life Dates | Construct | Definition | Causes | | | |
|---|---|---|---|---|---|---|
| | | | Material | Efficient | Formal | Final |
| Saint Bonaventura (1221–1274) | Mystical transcendence | Mind is self-reflexive: It turns back on senses to contemplate them rationally and turns back on rationality to fix attention on God mystically. | | | $X_2$ | $X_1$ |
| Saint Thomas Aquinas (c. 1225–1274) | 1) Argument from order | 1) A divine intelligence must have been necessary to work out the order and purpose in nature: God. | | | $X_1$ | $X_2$ |
| | 2) Truth | 2) The final end of the universe, which is telic. | | | | X |
| | 3) Evil will | 3) Due to erring reason. | | | $X_2$ | $X_1$ |
| | 4) Last, fixed end | 4) Never goods of the body or humanly created good, but only the vision of the Divine Essence. | | | $X_2$ | $X_1$ |
| John Duns Scotus (c. 1265–1308) | 1) Simplicity in explanation | 1) Unity of conception is to be preferred to plurality, which is never to be posited needlessly. | | | X | |
| | 2) Being | 2) As matter, which is more fundamental than form. | X | | | |
| | 3) Contingent cause | 3) An efficient cause made dependent upon an act of will, and therefore not a necessary action. | | $X_2$ | | $X_1$ |
| William of Ockham (c. 1300–c. 1349) | Razor | 1) An explanation involving fewer assumptions than an alternative is to be preferred at all times. | | | X | |

... (cut off) puts of sensory experience.

| | | 1 | 2 | 3 | 4 | 5 |
|---|---|---|---|---|---|---|
| | cognition | | | | | |
| | 3) Abstractive cognition — 3) Mental reflections on experience, but comes only after intuitive cognition is input. | | $X_3$ | $X_4$ | $X_2$ | $X_1$ |
| Copernicus (1473–1543) | 1) Heliocentric universe — 1) Sun is immobile and planets rotate in our universe. | | $X_2$ | $X_3$ | $X_1$ | |
| | 2) Gravity — 2) The result of matter, forming into spheres. | | $X_1$ | $X_2$ | $X_3$ | $X_1$ |
| Niccolo Machiavelli (1469–1527) | Imitation — Patterning one's behavior on another, by design. | | | | $X_2$ | |
| Vesalius (1514–1564) | Human vs. animal anatomy — Empirical demonstration of similarities and differences, running counter to Galen's ratiocinations. | | $X_1$ | | $X_2$ | |
| William Gilbert (1540–1603) | 1) Force — A magnetic or electrical field of attraction and/or repulsion. | | $X_2$ | $X_1$ | | |
| | 2) Experimental method — Patterned on a machine analogue, in which the efficient cause played a major conceptual role. | | $X_2$ | $X_1$ | | |
| | 3) Gravity — A reflection of the "force of attraction." | | | $X$ | | |
| Francis Bacon (1561–1626) | 1) Scientific explanation — Must be confined exclusively to efficient and material cause meanings. | | $X_2$ | $X_1$ | | |
| | 2) Proof — Inductive always preferable to deductive. | $X$ | | | | |
| | 3) Simple natures — Nature has a limited number of forms, and every body can be understood as a compound of these. | $X_1$ | $X_2$ | | | |
| Galileo (1564–1642) | 1) Law of uniform acceleration — Bodies of unequal weight fall the same distance in the same period of time. | | $X_2$ | $X_1$ | | |

**Table 1** A Survey of Western Intellectual History (cont.)

| Name and Life Dates | Construct | Definition | Causes | | | |
|---|---|---|---|---|---|---|
| | | | Mate-rial | Effi-cient | Formal | Final |
| | 2) Law of inertia | 2) Moving bodies, free of friction, will move until deflected by something else. | X₂ | X₁ | | |
| | 3) Proof | 3) Mathematics esteemed as a "new rationalism," but often empirical experimentation must supplement. | | | X | |
| Johannes Kepler (1571–1630) | Planetary motion | As elliptical, hence not conforming to the "perfection" thesis of circular motion. | | X₂ | X₁ | |
| William Harvey (1578–1657) | Blood circulation | Did not "ebb and flow" as Galen had claimed, but was pumped through body mechanically by heart. | X₁ | X₂ | | |
| Thomas Hobbes (1588–1679) | 1) Motion | 1) The central factor in life. | | X | | |
| | 2) Thought | 2) Computation—i.e., adding and subtracting ideas. | | X₂ | X₁ | |
| | 3) Scientific method | 3) Find [efficiently caused] effects in the movement of events. | | X₁ | X₂ | |
| | 4) Geometry | 4) The most abstract science of motion. | | X₁ | X₂ | |
| | 5) Proof | 5) A hypothetico-deductive procedure. | | | X | |
| | 6) Time | 6) The "phantasm of before and after in motion." | | X | | |
| | 7) Hard determinism | 7) Denial of contingency causation. | | X | | |
| | 8) Association of ideas | 8) Lawful and capable of determination as one aspect of motion. | | X₁ | X₂ | |

| Thinker | Concept | Description | | | | |
|---|---|---|---|---|---|---|
| René Descartes (1596–1650) | 1) Proof | Via reason (deduction), not senses or imagination. | | | X₂ | X₁ |
| | 2) Idea | Whatever the mind perceives directly. | | | X₁ | X₂ |
| | 3) Innate idea | As the idea of perfection, which by definition is beyond man; hence, placed in reason by God. | | | X₁ | X₂ |
| | 4) Free will | Judgment in the sense of assent or dissent. | | | | X |
| | 5) Reality | Like classical mechanics, with matter not needing to exist (except in God's eye); a machine world. | | X₃ | X | |
| | 6) Animals vs. humans | Humans have souls, which are not machine-like but teleological; animals lack souls and are machines. | | X₃ | X₂ | X₁ |
| Blaise Pascal (1623–1662) | 1) Thought | Independent from the body. | | | | X |
| | 2) As if . . . | Doubters in God's existence can act "as if" He does exist, and profit in this "wager." | | | | X |
| Thomas Sydenham (1624–1689) | Empirical medicine | Complete commitment to the empirical approach of Bacon and Locke; "rational" discourse is abjured. | X₂ | X₁ | X₃ | |
| Robert Boyle (1627–1691) | Pressure and volume in gases | Boyle's Law: At a given temperature, pressure is inversely proportional to the volume of a gas. | X₂ | X₁ | X₃ | |
| Christian Huygens (1629–1695) | 1) Centrifugal force | Due to the circularity of motion in planets. | X₂ | X₁ | X₃ | |
| | 2) Light | "Matter in motion;" waves of force that can summate to gain impact. | X₁ | X₂ | | |

**Table 1** A Survey of Western Intellectual History (cont.)

| Name and Life Dates | Construct | Definition | Causes | | | |
|---|---|---|---|---|---|---|
| | | | Material | Efficient | Formal | Final |
| Benedictus de Spinoza (1632–1677) | 1) Will | 1) Not free, but reason's ability to see a true idea. | | | $X_1$ | $X_2$ |
| | 2) Emotion | 2) In body, not mind, a passion that is ill-defined because we can have no clear idea of feelings. | X | | | |
| | 3) Intelligible extension | 3) Only ideas can be known certainly, not physical things—e.g., 3×3=9 must follow in rationality. | | | $X_2$ | $X_1$ |
| John Locke (1632–1704) | 1) Idea | 1) Comes exclusively from sensations (inputs). | $X_2$ | $X_1$ | $X_3$ | |
| | 2) Hierarchy | 2) Ideas begin as simple and combine quasi-mathematically to form higher-level more complex ideas. | | | X | |
| | 3) Mind | 3) Begins *tabula rasa*, but can reflect on inputs and thereby mediate knowledge. | | $X_1$ | $X_2$ | |
| | 4) Knowledge | 4) Perception of the agreement or disagreement of two ideas; dependent on frequency and contiguity. | | $X_2$ | $X_1$ | |
| | 5) Reality's qualities | 5) Primary qualities reside in object (solidity, extension), and secondary qualities reside in mind (color, odor). | $X_1$ | $X_2$ | | |
| | 6) Intuition | 6) Direct associative perception of agreement or disagreement of any two ideas; results in knowledge and furthers mental mediation [re. Ockham]. | $X_1$ | $X_2$ | $X_3$ | |

...sively on inanimate materials, functioning with mathematical precision and without regard for teleological or aesthetic considerations [except, in his informal theory of the world as perfection due to its functioning "within God"].

| Concept | Description | | | |
|---|---|---|---|---|
| 2) Absolute time & space | An anchoring point against which motion and change could be conceptualized mathematically. | | $X$ | |
| 3) Motion | A mathematical fiction based on Cartesian geometry. | | $X$ | $X$ |
| **Gottfried Wm. von Leibniz (1646–1716)** | | | | |
| 1) Free will | A willful act is not necessary, because its opposite does not involve a logical contradiction; hence, contingent causation is possible. | | $X$ | |
| 2) Preestablished order | That God's plan and man's (free-willed) volition should coincide was predestined. | | $X$ | |
| 3) Mind | Not *tabula rasa* but like a block of marble, with innate veins that experience must accomodate. | | $X_2$ | $X_1$ |
| 4) Apperception | "Active" perception, in which humans must bring to bear an intellectual effort in order to "see" or otherwise grasp sensory input [contra-Locke]. | | $X_2$ | $X_1$ |
| 5) Monad | A substance, analogized from logical predication. Indivisible and complete; cannot be explained by reference to other substances. Due to preestablished order, monads combine to make up matter. Are also purposeful, according to Divine Plan. | $X_1$ | $X_2$ | $X_3$ |

**Table 1** A Survey of Western Intellectual History (cont.)

| Name and Life Dates | Construct | Definition | Causes | | | |
| --- | --- | --- | --- | --- | --- | --- |
| | | | Material | Efficient | Formal | Final |
| Giovanni Battista Vico (1668–1744) | 1) Man, as measure of all things | 1) Whenever men can form no idea of unknown things, they judge them by what is familiar and at hand. | | | $X_2$ | $X_1$ |
| | 2) Cultural stages | 2) Age of Gods, heroes, and then man. | | | X | |
| George Berkeley (1685–1753) | Being | Is "being perceived." Contra-Locke, if mind fashions secondary qualities, it also fashions primary. | | | $X_2$ | $X_1$ |
| Joseph Butler (1692–1752) | Hierarchical order of human nature | Impulses, passions, and desires at base, with self-concern at higher level and conscience at the apex. | | | X | |
| Jonathan Edwards (1703–1758) | Will | Always determined by the greatest apparent good. Good essentially means "whatever draws the will." | | $X_3$ | $X_2$ | $X_1$ |
| Julien Offray de La Mettrie (1709–1751) | All animals are machines | Humans as well as lower animals are machines, differentially modified throughout the universe. | $X_2$ | $X_1$ | | |
| David Hume (1711–1776) | 1) Attraction | 1) Principle of association: Ideas attract each other due to similarity, contiguity in time, etc. | | X | | |
| | 2) Habit as cause | 2) Contiguous experience united in imagination by habit leads to our impression of cause-effect. | | X | | |

| Philosopher | Concept | Description | | | |
|---|---|---|---|---|---|
| | | be in contiguous relation with another. | | | |
| | 4) Determined judgment | Nature determines all of man's judgments, just as it determines his breathing and feeling. | $X_1$ | $X_2$ | |
| | 5) Value | Utilitarian view: That has value which ends in pleasure. To ask why pleasure is sought is absurd (i.e., nontelic). | $X_1$ | $X_2$ | |
| Thomas Reid (1710–1796) | 1) Cause in reality | Every event in material reality is efficiently caused. | | $X$ | |
| | 2) Reason | As influenced by final causes, incl. truth, duty. | | | $X$ |
| Jean Jacques Rousseau (1712–1778) | Social contract | The basis of society; the contract transforms man and makes him intelligent. | $X_1$ | | $X_2$ |
| Adam Smith (1723–1790) | Sympathy | Putting oneself in imagination in the place of another to experience his feelings. | $X_1$ | $X_2$ | |
| Immanuel Kant (1724–1804) | 1) Synthetic a priori | A truth due not to definition (analytic) or to facts (a posteriori); necessary because no sense experience can confute them—e.g., mathematics. | $X$ | | |
| | 2) Categories of understanding | Twelve dialectically framed dimensions, which lend meaning to sensation (i.e., input). | $X_1$ | $X$ | |
| | 3) Knowledge | Begins in experience, but does not arise from experience; categories make this possible. | $X_2$ | | $X_1$ |
| | 4) Intuition | A form, applied to sensory input, organizing it into a perception. | $X$ | | $X_1$ |

**Table 1**  A Survey of Western Intellectual History (cont.)

| Name and Life Dates | Construct | Definition | Causes Material | Effi- cient | Formal | Final |
|---|---|---|---|---|---|---|
| | 5) Sensation | Would be meaningless unless framed by space-time factors in perception. | | | X | |
| | 6) Noumena (thing-in-itself) | Substantiality, outside space and time, accounting for objectivity in perception among human beings. | X | | | |
| | 7) Phenomena | Appearances of things, made possible through perception and understanding. | | | $X_2$ | $X_1$ |
| | 8) Faculty | Those aspects of mind that are active (e. g., reason and understanding). | | | $X_1$ | $X_2$ |
| | 9) Judgment | Faculty of thinking the particular as contained under the universal [see predication, above]. | | | $X_2$ | $X_1$ |
| | 10) Will | Cause that acts in accordance with concepts. | | | $X_2$ | $X_1$ |
| | 11) Concept | Contains its purpose within its form. | | | $X_1$ | $X_2$ |
| | 12) Purpose | Concept of an object insofar as the concept is regarded as the cause of the object. Human reason provides the purpose in active conceptualization. | | | $X_2$ | $X_1$ |
| Antoine Lavoisier (1743–1794) | Table of chemical elements | Substrate elements of oxygen, hydrogen, azote [nitrogen], sulphur, phosphorous organized as substrate building blocks in the Lockean fashion. | $X_1$ | $X_2$ | $X_3$ | |

| Philosopher | Concept | Description | | | | |
|---|---|---|---|---|---|---|
| Jeremy Bentham (1748–1832) | 1) Principle of utility | All actions of men are directed toward pleasures or away from pains. | $X_2$ | $X_1$ | | |
| | 2) Disposition or choice | The sum of motives, drawing man in different directions. One's will is his motive(s). | $X_2$ | $X_1$ | $X_3$ | |
| | 3) Intention | Consists of motivation (will) and knowledge of the consequences of an act. Only consequences are properly good or evil. | $X_2$ | $X_1$ | $X_3$ | $X_4$ |
| Johann Gottlieb Fichte (1762–1814) | 1) World as self-construed | Rejection of noumenal construct of Kant; the world is an unconscious self-created construction. | $X_2$ | | $X_2$ | $X_1$ |
| | 2) Self [or ego] | Posits [premises] own existence, then dialectically posits nonself as a "world of experience." | $X_2$ | | $X_2$ | $X_1$ |
| Georg Wilhelm Hegel (1770–1831) | 1) Ground | Allows for unity because it provides relational contrast to self; hence, "not-self." | | | $X$ | |
| | 2) Spirit | Opposite to matter; freedom in essence; self-reflective and seeks to know and actualize. | | | | $X$ |
| | 3) Alienation | Creations stand free in meaning from creator. | $X_2$ | | $X_2$ | $X_1$ |
| | 4) Actualization | Makes mere possibility a reality; creation. | | | $X$ | |
| | 5) Historical stages | History moves in stages, like individual life. | | | | $X_1$ |
| Arthur Schopenhauer (1788–1860) | 1) Causation | Because the world is man's idea, all causal relations are formed by his understanding. | $X_2$ | | $X_2$ | $X_1$ |
| | 2) Will | A force, making things what they are—e.g., our body is "objectified will." It lacks purpose and is desire personified (yearning, striving, etc.). | $X_2$ | $X_1$ | $X_3$ | |

**Table 1** A Survey of Western Intellectual History (cont.)

| Name and Life Dates | Construct | Definition | Causes | | | |
|---|---|---|---|---|---|---|
| | | | Material | Efficient | Formal | Final |
| Michael Faraday (1791–1867) | Field | An altered space, containing moving lines of electrostatic force. | $X_3$ | $X_2$ | $X_1$ | |
| Auguste Comte (1798–1857) | Historical stages | History moves through theological, metaphysical, and positive stages. | | | X | |
| Peter Gustav Lejeune Dirichlet (1805–1859) | Function and variable concepts | Variable y is function of x when value assigned arbitrarily to latter automatically assigns value to the former. The x variable is thus "independent" and the y variable is "dependent" by (ratio) definition. | | | X | |
| John Stuart Mill (1806–1873) | Canons of logic | Agreement, residue, difference, and concomitant variation. Helped elucidate efficient causes in events. | | $X_1$ | $X_2$ | |
| Charles Darwin (1809–1882) | Natural selection | Nontelic, accidental principle in organic evolution. | $X_2$ | $X_1$ | | |
| Søren Kierkegaard (1813–1855) | 1) Existence | 1) A subjective predication in that life must be created through individual's decision and choice. | | | | X |
| | 2) Choice | 2) A dialectical either/or in existence. | | | | X |
| | 3) Authenticity | 3) Passionate self-commitment in the face of alienation (i.e., severance from past and future). | | | $X_2$ | $X_1$ |
| | 4) Truth | 4) A mode of existence; engagement, earnestness. | | | X | |

| 5) Individual | 5) All that there is; humanity does not exist. | | | | |
| --- | --- | --- | --- | --- | --- |
| Rudolph Hermann Lotze (1817–1881) | "From within" vs. "from without" | Behavior viewed "from within" is purposive; viewed "from without" it is mechanical. | | $X_2$ | $X_2$ | $X_1$ |
| Karl Marx (1818–1883) | Class struggle | An inevitable clash between alienated groups, defined by the internal contradiction of dialectical materialism unfolding in history. | $X_1$ | $X_3$ | $X_3$ | $X_1$ |
| Herbert Spencer (1820–1903) | Evolution | Change, from indefinite to definite, confused to ordered and equilibrated. | | $X_2$ | $X_1$ | |
| Louis Pasteur (1822–1895) | Disease | Empirically shown to be due to micro-organisms. | $X_1$ | $X_2$ | | |
| Thomas H. Huxley (1825–1895) | Life | Like a game, in which happiness depends upon knowing the rules; nature is amoral. | | | $X$ | |
| Ernst Heinrich Haeckel (1834–1919) | Biogenetic law | Ontogenesis is a brief and rapid recapitulation of phylogenesis. No teleology is involved. | $X_3$ | $X_2$ | $X_1$ | |
| Ernst Mach (1838–1916) | Phenomenological physics | The world consists solely of sense impressions. Scientific concepts are useful fictions, acting as names for complexes of phenomena. | $X_3$ | | $X_1$ | $X_2$ |
| Charles Sanders Peirce (1839–1914) | Mind | Irritation, arising from indecisiveness, causes a sensed uneasiness until a mode of action is settled on. | $X_1$ | $X_4$ | $X_2$ | $X_3$ |

**Table 1** A Survey of Western Intellectual History (cont.)

| Name and Life Dates | Construct | Definition | Causes | | | |
|---|---|---|---|---|---|---|
| | | | Material | Efficient | Formal | Final |
| Eduard von Hartmann (1842–1906) | Evolution of consciousness in history | Telic; working from instinct to intelligence, to higher and higher levels of consciousness —i.e., from out of unconsciousness to consciousness. | | | | X |
| William James (1842–1910) | 1) Faith | 1) Acting as premising [predicating] hypothesis, can make a possibility "come true." | | | | X |
| | 2) Tough-minded theorists | 2) Sensationalists and mechanists. | $X_1$ | $X_2$ | | |
| | 3) Tender-minded theorists | 3) Rationalists and free-willists. | | | $X_2$ | $X_1$ |
| | 4) Truth | 4) Working, permitting believer to have satisfactory relations with experience; "cash value" of an idea. Meaning is true if it leads to observable consequences. Ultimately, tied to sensations. | $X_3$ | | $X_1$ | $X_2$ |
| | 5) Free will | 5) Humans have; involved with chance and possibility, concepts that determinisms do not handle well. | | | $X_2$ | $X_1$ |
| Friedrich Wilhelm Nietzsche (1844–1900) | 1) Life | 1) In command of oneself; will to power. | | | | X |
| | 2) Will to power | 2) Expansive, assimilating, positive, value-creating tendency in existence. | | $X_2$ | | $X_1$ |
| | 3) Cause | 3) A fiction—i.e., used by thinkers to account for things, but not necessarily in nature. | | | $X_2$ | $X_1$ |

| | | | A₁ | A₂ |
|---|---|---|---|---|
| | non-truth<br>...knowledge than are true ideas. | | | |
| | 5) Human nature | Basically valuational, even though absolutes no longer exist. (God is dead!) | X | X |
| Jules Henri Poincaré (1854–1912) | Reality | Mathematical laws held to represent the sole objective reality for science. | | |
| Henri Bergson (1859–1941) | 1) Duration | Succession of qualitative time changes, melting into each other with no clear outline. | X₂ | X₁ |
| | 2) Self | Pure duration, including contradictions such as "caused" and "free." Dynamic and not static. | X₂ | X₁ |
| | 3) Freedom | Relation of the self to the act it performs. It is a quality of the act, recognized that if same antecedent is enacted, same consequent follows. | X₂ | X₁ |
| | 4) Intuitive method | Intellectual sympathy, whereby one understands an object by placing oneself within it [incl. people!]. | X₂ | X₁ |
| | 5) Élan vital | Telic life force. History is a record of life trying to free itself from domination by matter. | | X |
| Edmund Husserl (1859–1938) | 1) Noeisis | Act of perceiving; essentially intentional. | | X |
| | 2) Noema | That which is perceived. | X | |
| | 3) Phenomenology | Study of immediate spontaneous experience. | X₁ | X₂ |
| | 4) Suspension of natural bias | To apprehend things spontaneously "as they are." | | X |

**Table 1**  A Survey of Western Intellectual History (cont.)

| Name and Life Dates | Construct | Definition | Causes | | | |
|---|---|---|---|---|---|---|
| | | | Material | Efficient | Formal | Final |
| John Dewey (1859–1952) | 1) Freedom | When a person acts through planning, he can vary the plan to meet changing conditions and has a conviction that choice and desire are involved. | | | $X_2$ | $X_1$ |
| | 2) Human conduct | Can be understood only in terms of purpose. | | | | X |
| | 3) Art | Nature, organized; clarifies by intensifying experience for the human being. | $X_2$ | | $X_1$ | $X_3$ |
| | 4) Scientific method | Based on controlled change and observation of the effects in an empirical context. | | $X_1$ | $X_2$ | |
| George Santayana (1863–1952) | 1) Preferences | Nonrational; things are good because we prefer them. | $X_2$ | | | $X_1$ |
| | 2) Reason | Order in nature. | | | X | |
| | 3) Beauty | Positive, intrinsic, objectified pleasure, attributed to things by a person as if it were a quality of the thing observed. Form is a major feature of beauty. | | | $X_1$ | $X_2$ |
| | 4) Matter | Changes, but beauty in form does not. | $X_1$ | | $X_3$ | |
| George Herbert Mead (1863–1931) | 1) Meaning | Found in significant symbols, which emerge objectively in social relations. We need not be aware of these meanings in social relations. | | $X_2$ | X | |
| | 2) Idea(s) | Anticipations of future expected actions, made possible via use of significant symbols. | | | $X_1$ | $X_2$ |

| Philosopher | Concept / Term | Description | X₂ | X₁ | X₂ |
|---|---|---|---|---|---|
| | 3) Role | Reflected appraisals that others define for us. | | X₁ | |
| | 4) Self | Not unique, but a role defined via others. | | X | |
| Harold Henry Joachim (1868–1938) | Coherence theory of truth | An idea is true if it fits in with other ideas to form a coherent whole. | | X | |
| George Edward Moore (1873–1958) | Common sense | The sense of knowledge as experienced by the ordinary man, as embodied in his use of language. | | X | |
| Bertrand Russell (1872–1970) | 1) Mathematical truths | Are tautologies, having nothing to do with the "facts" of reality. Purely formal in nature. | | X | |
| | 2) Primitive propositions | Undefined presumptions to which a proof must be reduced. Ultimate truths are impossible because everything is grounded in self-evidence. | | X₁ | X₂ |
| | 3) Self-evidence | Not "merely" psychological factors, but at heart a special case of the tautology. | | X₁ | X₂ |
| | 4) Tautology | Propositions in opposition to empirical propositions. We know these without appeal to experience. | | X | |
| | 5) Correspondence theory of truth | Defined by events, not percepts. Truth of a proposition is established by its verifier (i.e., independently established evidence corresponding to the proposition). | X₂ | X₁ | |
| | 6) Logic | In pure mathematics the only constants—giving relations between terms—are logical constants. Hence logic and mathematics are one! | | X | |

27

**Table 1**  A Survey of Western Intellectual History (cont.)

| Name and Life Dates | Construct | Definition | Causes | | | |
|---|---|---|---|---|---|---|
| | | | Material | Efficient | Formal | Final |
| Ernst Cassirer (1874–1945) | Knowledge | Emerges as mind discriminates between external and internal senses and between sense contents and affective tones. | $X_3$ | | $X_2$ | $X_1$ |
| Martin Buber (1878–1965) | 1) I-Thou | A living relation in the "filled present." | | | X | |
| | 2) Love | A sense of responsibility of an I for a Thou. | | | | X |
| | 3) Encounter | The total accepting relationship between I and Thou. | | | $X_2$ | $X_1$ |
| Albert Einstein (1879–1955) | 1) Relativity | There are no constants or absolutes in time, space, or motion. These concepts must be measured in relation to reference frames, which in turn can be arbitrarily assigned or presumed [predicated]. | | | $X_1$ | $X_2$ |
| | 2) Principle of equivalence | Tautological principle, allowing identities in conceptualization; hence gravitation is inertia, matter is energy, and gravity is curved space. | | | $X_1$ | $X_2$ |
| Curt John Ducasse (1881–1969) | 1) Freedom | Of choice, consists in awareness of alternatives of choice being determined by one's preferences. | | | | X |
| | 2) Volition | Determined by the circumstances facing a person, the consequences he judges that volition to have. Freedom of will is "freedom of efficacy" and not necessarily freedom to act. | | | $X_2$ | $X_1$ |

| | | | X₂ | X₁ |
|---|---|---|---|---|
| Karl Jaspers (1883–1969) | Consciousness | A relationship of man to the world of ideas. Ideas are permanent and timeless (within time). | X₂ | X₁ |
| Percy W. Bridgman (1882–1961) | Operational definition | The concept studied is synonymous with the corresponding operations. | X | |
| Paul Tillich (1886–1965) | Ontological reason | The structure of mind that enables it to grasp and thereby to shape reality. | X₂ | X₁ |
| Martin Heidegger (1889–1976) | 1) Phenomenon | 1) That which shows itself in primitive disclosure. | X | |
| | 2) Dasein | 2) Commitment to life, concerned about existence. | X₂ | X₁ |
| | 3) Authenticity | 3) Choosing for the whole of one's past, present, and future being-in-the-world (i.e., Dasein). | | X |
| Ludwig Wittgenstein (1889–1951) | 1) Atomic facts | 1) Incapable of analysis into more elemental facts. | X | |
| | 2) Reality | 2) Totality of atomic facts. | X | |
| | 3) Modeling | 3) Logical picture of a fact (a proposition). | X | |
| | 4) Language | 4) Cannot express anything that contradicts logic. | X | |
| | 5) Tautology [contra-Russell] | 5) Fails to say anything about the world, for it is true of all possible states of affairs (e.g., "It is raining, or it is not raining"). | X | |
| | 6) Logical necessity | 6) Is the only form of necessity that does not "exist" in the world. | X | |
| | 7) Words | 7) Tools. They do not "stand for" objects. | X | |

**Table 1**  A Survey of Western Intellectual History (cont.)

| Name and Life Dates | Construct | Definition | Causes | | | |
|---|---|---|---|---|---|---|
| | | | Material | Efficient | Formal | Final |
| | 8) Language games | Rules of procedure, having no necessary base in reality. | | | X | |
| | 9) Meaning | The use of a word in a language; words do not reflect a mental activity. | | $X_2$ | $X_1$ | |
| | 10) Propositional variable | The form of a proposition, which remains constant even though the word content changes. | | | X | |
| Rudolph Carnap (1891–1970) | Meaningful languages | Either logic and mathematics (analytical propositions) or science (empirically verifiable synthetic propositions). Logical analysis is logical syntax. | | | X | |
| Karl Barth (1896–1968) | 1) God | Always subject and never object. God cannot be known to reason, but only when the Divine Subject reveals Himself and wills a human response. | | $X_2$ | $X_1$ | |
| | 2) Christ | Because God regards man through Christ, only in Christ can man understand himself. To understand is to be as Christ. | | | $X_1$ | $X_2$ |
| Jean-Paul Sartre (1905–  ) | 1) Other | Affirms his freedom by rendering us as an object. We assert our freedom by doing the reverse. | | | $X_1$ | $X_2$ |
| | 2) Will | The manifestation of man's primordial freedom. | | | | X |

| Alfred Jules Ayer (1910– ) | 1) Verification principle | 1) Asserts that something has meaning only if the thinker can say what observations would lead to a verification of his concept. | | X | $X_1$ |
| | 2) Self | 2) A " logical construction" out of the sense experiences that constitute the actual and possible sense history of the individual. | $X_2$ | | |

Even beauty (Santayana) has been interpreted as a distinctive arrangement of preferential features of the environment, bringing pleasure to the beholder because of the resultant order—or the contrast of disorder!

We would be mistaken to check *every* construct in Table 1 under the formal cause simply because each thinker relied upon the patternings of language to express his ideas. We must not confound the meaning of the construct with the meanings of the words used to convey this construct. A similar problem arises with formal causation when we discuss teleologies. Although we have examples of "pure" final causation in Table 1, such as Socrates' conception of the good, or Aquinas' idea of truth, to think of a line of telic *behavior* in which the formal cause meaning is not included is virtually impossible. This is because the *that* in the "that for the sake of which" phrasing invariably comes down to some plan, scheme, mathematical assumption, frame of reference, analogue, and the like—all of which take meaning from formal causation. The major premises of syllogistic reasoning are therefore likely to be most readily subsumed under formal causation, but the fact that an organism reasons "for their sake" is what brings the final cause meaning into play.

The scheme we have employed in Table 1, for example, defines a pattern of interrelated meanings and is applied consistently across several different realms of knowledge. Yet it cannot be said to have a purpose as a useful frame of reference. There is a purpose for the scheme to fulfill as an end to *our* reasoning, but the scheme itself has no way of coming to an end—that is, *intending* its purpose. It can only "be" our purpose, as a metaconception. Thus Aristotle properly added the fourth cause to his scheme, because he could see that simply being a schematic pattern, or being part of a schematic pattern, did not necessarily mean that the object under description is behaving for the sake of this pattern.

Although Table 1 purports to present Western intellectual history, it contains important thinkers from the Middle Eastern world such as Avicenna and Averroës because of their acknowledged influence on Western thought. Had we included Oriental thinkers in Table 1 the scheme would have worked perfectly (Fehl, 1964). For example, the *Tao Te Ching* (author unknown, possibly Lao Tzu, c. 600 BC) makes reference to the *tao* (the "way" to various ends, combining formal and final cause meanings) as well as to the *yin-yang* principle (complementary forces of passivity and activity, implying formal and efficient cause meanings). Confucius' (c. 551–c. 479 BC) thought was heavily laden with formal cause meanings—for example, in his concept of *jen* (ideal human relationship) or *li* (rules of propriety). King-Sun Lung (c. 330–250 BC) had a formal-cause conception of universal names very similar to the Platonic-Socratic conceptions. And Han Fei (c. 280–c. 233 BC) had a Bentham-like utilitarian view of human behavior—that is, under the "two helms" of punishment (pain) and reward (pleasure) (implying material- and efficient-cause meanings). Space considerations prevent us from including many Oriental thinkers, but this restricted sampling should be enough to demonstrate that our scheme is viable in Eastern as well as Western thought. We now turn to four distinct lessons Table 1 has to teach us about the nature of theory and method in our intellectual history.

### The Concern for Precedents

A significant number of constructs in Table 1 were aimed at finding the possible functioning of precedent assumptions, essences (God), definitions, and the like, "for the sake of which" other beliefs, existences, or necessary implications thereby followed. It is almost as if a common recognition occurs that to know anything demands a background fundamental of some sort. Philosophy is often characterized as a search for some such list of universals or first principles, which enter into all that can be known for all time. This search begins in the ordered universe of a Pythagoras or Heraclitus. We see it in the realm of Being postulated by Socrates and Plato, where Universals or Forms resided in a timeless existence to lend meaning to the round of lived days called Becoming. Related ideas occur in Aristotle's concern with the basic premises of syllogistic reasoning, in Plotinus' conception of the soul as organizer of meanings; and it is most helpfully defined for us in the *predication* construct of Peter Abelard, as adapted from Aristotle. This meaning has remained with us, suggesting that in all arguments or lines of thought a predicate frame must be presumed for meaningful extension to take place. The scheme of Table 1 acts as such a predication in this volume.

In the medieval period theologians commonly contended that life must be predicated on a creation by some Divinity, who could thus bring existence into being but was not Himself subject to creation (predication). This Supreme Being was called an Unmoved Mover (Averroës) or a First Cause (St. Anselm) because His existence was based on an efficient-cause "proof" which suggested God as the *first* precedent to all existence, who got the string of cause-effects underway. A claim often made in medieval times was "The First Principle does not fall under a Genus." That is, God cannot be subsumed by some overriding conception lending meaning to Him, because He *is* the Beginning (the Word). So unfathomable was this Creator that one could not directly stipulate His nature, but rather must resort to a *negative theology* (Maimonides, St. Bonaventura, St. Thomas Aquinas) to approximate an account (i.e., say what God *is not*). In more recent times the elevation of the Creator construct to the highest most active meaning-endowing position possible is to be seen in Barth's claim that God is always a subject and never an object.

Concern for basic assumptions is also to be seen in the descent of mathematics. Pythagoras took a mystical view of numbers as constituting reality in some inscrutable fashion, but Euclid's approach was quite straightforward in its preoccupation with the axiomatic assumptions one need presume for other meanings to follow sequaciously. Archimedes then applied this knowledge to the world of events, and later mathematicians built this "language" into a major descriptive tool. Ptolemy and Copernicus made different assumptions concerning the universe and employed mathematical language with equal success to support their respective views. Galileo's assumptions about motion and the consequent empirical checks he made were also to be supported with mathematical commentary, as were the proofs of Newton and others who followed in the rise of modern science. When Mach, Einstein, and others made even more dramatic changes in the predications of science, a truly revolutionary view of familiar reality was brought about. In this realm of mathematical reasoning we must not overlook Russell's discussion of primitive propositions, which also seem ever to "be there" as precedent assumptions in the reasoning of a logician or a mathematician. One literally can *never* reach back far enough to reason mathematically without making some primitive assumption!

This idea of underlying meanings which are ever "there" has reflected itself in the debates over the human image, and what we can or cannot know as human beings *from birth*. Sometimes a theological point is being made. For example, the innate-idea concept was employed by Descartes and Leibniz to say that certain life assumptions are compelling yet clearly beyond man's true understanding. How could man know that something like perfection was the case, unless a (perfect) God had put this idea into man's *imperfect* mentality. Another form of the innate idea was simply a mathematical proof. This ability to work out—entirely within reason—mathematical consistencies by what Spinoza called intelligible extension was proof enough for some thinkers that human intelligence was innately endowed with ideas (or ideations). The term *idea* becomes vague here, because it is as much the *process* of proving a point as the finished product of this process which is being referred to. Kant's categories of the understanding are pictured more in this "process" sense; though they are not precisely ideas, they do represent supposed innate capacities of the human mind to order sensory input and thus create meaning, which would include mathematical proofs.

Not all thinkers who held that mathematical reasoning was fundamental to human intelligence agreed that mind *qua* mind created anything. Both Hobbes and Locke believed that human thought was essentially identical to mathematical calculation, but this did not suggest a creative intelligence. The human intellect was said to be *tabula rasa* at birth; though it could calculate influences from out of the past as probabilities for the future, it could not be said to in any way conceptualize knowledge from birth. Poincaré's reality, as consisting of mathematical laws, is seen to function within human reason to influence the course of mind as much as it functions lawfully within inanimate events. The meaning-endowing role for mind is almost lost in the modern analyses of Wittgenstein, Carnap, and Ayer, who suggest that a word is not an expression of anything until that meaning is observed functioning, as an empirically demonstrable tool, preferably with a mathematically predictable regularity.

## Teleologies Prompt
## Introspective Theoretical Descriptions

When we speak of assumptions an "assumer," who predicates his line of argument or reasoning with some such precedent meaning, naturally follows. By focusing on the actual process of this precedent assumption to sequacious inference, deduction, induction, implication, and the like we necessarily tilt our theoretical account to a *first person* exposition. A theory written from the slant or point of view of the object of this theory (i.e., the "data" needing explanation) can be said to be written from an *introspective* theoretical perspective (Rychlak, 1968, p. 27). However, a theory can be written from the slant or the point of view of an observer, looking outward in *third person* terms, about "that, over there." In this case, we can speak of an *extraspective* theoretical perspective (*ibid.*, pp. 27–28).

When we speak about the philosopher's quest for universals, our theoretical reference draws us to the introspective perspective. A human being is making this intellectual effort to find the universal *that* for the sake of which mankind can know anything. But when we speak about the *fruits* of such intellectual effort, we may or may not be speaking about constructs in an introspective sense. Euclid's axioms, for example, are framed to show how the mathematician's line of reasoning may correctly proceed. Granting *this* (for the sake of this), *that* will follow. Each time the mathematician proceeds "for the sake of" such axioms, he may indeed begin a line of teleological reasoning, leading to newly created insights. However, because the axioms and the principles and proofs that can be drawn from these assumptions can be written down and listed for memorization by students of geometry, we can speak of them in third-person or extraspective terms. The product of what seems accurately described in final-cause terms (mathematical reasoning) becomes a nontelic formulation. We have shifted over to that nontelic reliance on formal causality, which is what happens in the theories of Wittgenstein, Carnap, and Ayer. This "double-duty" capacity of mathematics has led to considerable ambiguity in the formulations of so-called hard scientific theory.

Teleological description thus prompts us to employ an introspective perspective. The theological accounts of a Divine Power (efficient cause), creating the palpable world (material cause) to meet some predicating Divine Plan (formal cause) forces us to look for a Divine Intention (i.e., the introspectively viewed end of God's purpose). Though the theologians of history do not presume to speak for God, they clearly choose to see his purposes *in* events. What is the *intent* of sexual intercourse? If the modern theologian sees in this act *only* a Divine Intention for species procreation, any use of contraceptives would represent a subversion of "God's Will." If, however, the theologian can see in the sexual union an alternate Divine Intention —possibly the highest expression of love among human beings—he will be more likely to accept a contraceptive device as consonant with God's Plan, just as he has already accepted the use of the menstruation cycle as a "natural" form of contraception.

Our point here is not to weigh the respective merits of such theological debates, but to demonstrate that invariably a teleological account reaches for the introspective perspective. This is what Lotze meant when he noted that behavior viewed "from within" (introspectively) could be purposive, although "from without" (extraspectively) it might be described in a mechanical fashion. Aristotle (1952a) felt it was important to include in one's science the end to which events moved as telic causes (p. 500). He therefore theorized that leaves exist for the purpose of providing shade for the fruit on trees, and thus that "nature is a cause, a cause that operates for a purpose" followed (1952b, pp. 276–277). Nature had the good intelligence to fashion leaves for the sake of shading fruit. This was, of course, backed up by a God-in-nature view, but even in his discussion of motion and gravity we find Aristotle's telic formulations giving a sense of intelligence to inanimate events (what was later to be called animism, or the anthropomorphization of nature). For example, he explained the motions of objects as due to internal urges by all bodies to seek the places "proper" to them in the world design. This could be interpreted as the movements within a pattern we referred to above—that is, as lacking a true "that for the sake of which" intentionality. Newton's extraspectively framed theory of gravity retained this formal-cause meaning of objects moving within a mathematized space entirely without intentions. However, Aristotle lent a decidedly anthropomorphic (introspective) quality to his theory of gravity when he suggested that something like Newton's "falling apple" would be *seeking* its natural state—union with the earth from which it had sprung.

This (introspective) self-seeking or self-directing side of behavior is what free-will advocates have tried to capture over the centuries—not without some confusion. We can see in the constructs of Marcus Aurelius, Descartes, Ducasse, and William James the common view of human nature as being capable of self-control through assent or dissent. If there are predications in life, presumably one can either affirm or deny certain of these precedent environmental demands. Human beings are not simply efficiently caused, said John Duns Scotus, but rather behave according to *contingent* causes, which are actions determined by the foreseen consequences of a preselected action. In other words a final cause *is* a contingent cause. The behavior carried out depended on what the individual preferred to have follow "this" way or "that" way in the future course of his behavior.

Origen's account of the fall of divine powers suggested that these identities or beings could exercise a choice by dissenting from the God-created goodness of life. This dissenting capacity proved an embarrassment to theological teleologies because if God permitted dissent He must have indirectly allowed for or created evil. Yet how could the Ultimate Goodness (i.e., God) create evil? The strategy since this time in history has been for theologians to remove God as having a direct active tie to the creation of evil. For example, St. Augustine claimed that evil was the *absence* of good—that is, it was not an active principle but the absence of a God-created active principle. St. Thomas Aquinas claimed that an evil will was due to

erroneous reason. If a man had all of the correct information (truth)
and was reasoning properly, he could not do otherwise but end up
in life where God would have wanted him if He had made the succession of choices for this man.

This common end of man's and God's decisions has led to difficulty in final-cause theory about the meaning of free will. It is com-
plicated by the fact that since the time of the Greeks good has been
presumed to be that toward which all acts intend (Socrates, Aristotle). The teleologist is therefore erroneously presumed to be speaking about good ends when he introduces his final-cause terminology.
This has served theology well, of course, because the intention is to
raise the likelihood of morally correct behavior in the human being.
But if man is frozen into a Divine Plan, so that his free-will decisions
must ever end up where God would have him end up, how can we
speak of true behavioral freedom? Is this behavior not simply another
one of those formal-cause within-the-design eventualities lacking in
true purpose? Leibniz tried to resolve such questions by suggesting
that a preestablished order existed, in which both man's volitional
course of free action and God's divine ends happened to coincide.
The problem of free will is yet to be solved to everyone's satisfaction.

There are a number of introspective telic accounts (see Table 1)
that do not call for a necessary tie of decision-making to "good" outcomes. Machiavelli's patterning of the self on the actions of others
does not imply that a good outcome is guaranteed, either for the self
or for those manipulated as a consequence of this often "selfish"
patterning. Vico's man as measure of all things, opting for the sake
of what is already known to understand what is still possible to
know, does not preclude a mean and harmful teleological outcome.
Kant's conception of judgment allowed for the weighing of selfish
and evil alternatives, although Kant tried to explicate more altruistic
grounds for the sake of which behavior ought to proceed in his *categorical imperative*. Nietzsche's transvaluation of values made clear
the idea that humans could opt for the very opposite of the traditional good. Santayana's preferential judgment suggested that reason
may never be fully rational, and Sartre's teleological image of man
is not dependent upon the concept of a "higher" nature.

Even so, introspectively framed teleologies are more likely to be
theories aimed at retrieving the dignity of man than at painting him
in the darker hues of existence. We see this in Adam Smith's concept
of sympathy, which is the assured basis for equity in human relations, and in Buber's concept of encounter, in which by taking the
feelings and outlooks of a "Thou'" into consideration, a truly loving

relationship is achieved between people. As a general philosophical point of order, existentialism has underscored the harm that is done when we fail to appreciate the individuality of others. Kierkegaard and Heidegger wrote extensively on the need for people to be genuine, authentic, and self-responsible in interpersonal relations, taking the introspective slant of the other into account at all times. If one views the other as a third-person "object" of manipulation, he effectively turns the other into a freedomless being (Sartre). This is the great danger of extraspective conceptualization, and it can be seen as an ominous likelihood in natural-science models.

The Rise of
Extraspective Theory in Science

If there is a tie uniting ancient to modern thought in science it has to be the rationalistic heritage of mathematics—a realm of knowledge that we have already said can be described either introspectively (in the mental activity of a Euclid) *or* extraspectively (in his finished system). Historians commonly refer to prescientific or nonscientific philosophies as rational philosophies or simply as rationalism. The theological arguments about God's necessary creation of the good would represent such rational philosophies. However, we must distinguish between philosophical rationalism and mathematical rationalism, because the same style of intellectual speculation and conviction through self-evidence functions in both realms. Evidence of this is to be seen in the fact that very often the same individual made significant contributions to both realms of knowledge.

The origins of rationalism can be seen in Pythagoras' and Heraclitus' assumptions of an ordered universe. Pythagoras saw everything as made up of numbers, and Heraclitus provided the initial justification for a belief in natural law by speaking of a *logos* or the rationale in events. Thus, from these early days rhyme and reason in nature was presumed; usually it was said to be due to the creations of the Deity. This belief in natural lawfulness (*logos* or numerical regularity) then permitted subsequent thinkers such as Democritus and Lucretius to say there is no chance happening in the universe. Though Aristotle referred to chance as one type of cause, a chance event would not follow a fixed or predictable pattern (formal cause); hence, if one holds to a rationale order, chance as illusory follows. This concept of 100% predictability in events because of a Divine Plan was to represent a major tenet of both the philosophical and the mathematical rationalist for centuries. Hard determinisms therefore actually began in the teleological presumption that order in the universe is perfect due to its creation by a Perfect Being. As an informal tenet, even Newton held to this view (see Table 1). The other source of a belief in 100% determinism stems from the material cause. For example, if one sculpts the form of a human person from a block of marble, one will have a statue of a "marble person." The same goes for human beings giving birth to offspring of comparable flesh and blood and so forth.

Concepts of perfection have always preoccupied thinkers as one aspect of their concern for precedents. The Platonic realm of Being was a mental sphere housing perfect forms called universals. When Plato speculated on the nature of the universe he suggested that planets must move in a circular orbit, for this is the most perfect of all geometrical forms. Here was a case of uniting the precedents of philosophical with mathematical rationalism. God was a Perfect Mathematician, so why should he not construct a world in which the most perfect of geometric forms was prominently displayed? This tendency for scientific explanation to assume a world of geometric elegance and simplicity was to predominate for centuries; when Kepler eventually proved that the paths of planets were in fact elliptical, he had to confront severe criticism. Leibniz was also a rationalist in both the philosophical and mathematical sense. We do not scoff at his unquestioned mathematical brilliance (mathematical rationalism), but when he concluded that this was the best of all possible worlds because as a Perfect Being the God who made it could not settle for *less*, we find his philosophical rationalism humorous (as did Voltaire).

Yet from presuming the shape of a planet's orbit or the perfection of a universe is but a short step to the mathematical proof of a Pythagorean theorem or a law of gravity. Rational self-evidence is at play in both realms, and the sense of conviction achieved is psychologically identical. Another offshoot of philosophical rationalism stems from attacks made on this style of theorizing, as employed by the Scholastics. Both Duns Scotus' call for simplicity in explanation and Ockham's razor were aimed at denigrating such rational proofs of God as the First Cause (St. Anselm) or the argument from order (Aquinas), not to mention the irrationalisms of negative theology (Maimonides, Bonaventura, and Aquinas). The only basis for a belief in God, said Ockham, was faith based on *empirical* revelations (miracles). Hence fanciful rational arguments amount to nothing by comparison.

This empirical attitude in theology was a reflection of the historical mood, for a growing dissatisfaction with verbal argumentation in philosophy and the emerging sciences was evident. Roger Bacon had called for empirical experimentation as early as the thirteenth century, and by the turn of the seventeenth century there was a firmly established scientific method and *attitude* on the rise. One could no longer sit in his library and reason his way to the proof of a deity, a world of circular orbits, and a perfectly fixed finite heaven put there for the edification of mankind. The methodological procedures of William Gilbert and the telescope of Galileo were changing the ground rules for knowledge.

We should not naively assume that all rationalism had been forsaken at the birth of science. Mathematical rationalism continued and grew in importance, becoming, as we have already seen, the exclusive "language" of modern science (Poincaré, Carnap). The mystical side to Pythagoras had been dropped, but the world as mathematical reality became one of those monumental precedent assumptions that moved man's thought along to new and exciting implications. Although he was an empiricist, Galileo felt an experiment was essential only when mathematical reasoning failed to end in a clear-cut answer to some problem.

In construing the world as mathematical the early scientists were not trying to account for their own reasoning. The double-duty feature of theoretical perspective in mathematics becomes particularly important in this context. What we find is an *externalization* of the formal-cause properties of mathematics without worrying about the mathematician *qua* human being who is doing the reasoning, making the assumptions, drawing the implications, and so forth. The resultant extraspective perspective meshed beautifully with the machine analogue on which Gilbert was to base the scientific method. We observe "that," in its regularity, and track the effect some antecedent manipulation has on a consequent. This is the spirit of the new science, and Sir Francis Bacon was to give it philosophical justification.

Bacon led the attack on teleological description in natural science. He pointed to Aristotle's erroneous assumptions and the fallacious physical accounts that resulted. There were no reasons for why leaves existed on trees or why bones held up muscles on the frames of bodies. To speculate on these matters was to ensure a dead end for science, which could never hope to establish a (God's) purpose in nature through empirical investigations. Teleological factors are simply unscientific considerations, and such descriptive accounts of things must be confined to aesthetics and ethics (including religion) but never mixed into science. By this time in history the Inquisition had provided Bacon and others with sufficient grounds for separating science from religion—which is another way of saying science from teleology! Though other factors were involved, the burning of Bruno at the stake in 1600 was a terrifying example of what can happen when theology and science clash on an empirical question (in this case the finitude or infinitude of the universe). If one considers Bruno a poor example of the scientist, there was Galileo's unhappy experience with the Inquisition to ponder as well.

Teleology was definitely on its way out of scientific description in the seventeenth century. William Harvey's empirical studies in blood circulation, Boyle's work on gases, and Huygens' speculation on centrifugal force did not require a "that for the sake of which" phrasing. At least in their formal role natural scientists since the seventeenth century have discounted questions of why (the end or purpose in patterns) in preference for questions of how (the mechanism of patterns). Bridgman's operationism is the modern heir of Ockham's razor, and the verification principle of Ayer and other logical positivists is also aimed at avoiding anything that might circumvent a purely efficient or material cause explanation of experience.

British Empiricism enveloped the human image in mechanism, aided by the view of mind as mathematical—as in Hobbes' contention that "thinking is reckoning [calculating]." The British revived the "atomic" model that Democritus and Lucretius had first propounded. This interest in the elements that might go to make up anything has been a continuing preoccupation with thinkers across the ages. In one sense this tactic is really a variation on the search for precedent factors discussed above. Plato looked to universals (Being) which supposedly lent meaning to particulars (Becoming), and Democritus looked to particulars (atoms) which then constituted general things (all in the universe). There is a decided similarity here in the concern for what precedes what, with one side conceptual (Plato) and the other constitutive (Democritus). But in moving from conceptual to constitutive explanations, a necessary shift takes place in the theoretical account.

Whether we think of Thales' water, the boundless of Anaximander, the roots of Empedocles, Hippocrates' humors, or the atoms of Democritus and Lucretius, the descriptive perspective we necessarily assume is third person! We describe what "that" is made up of, even though we may include ourselves in this extraspective designation. The "that" of a final cause is not third person. As a premise, we must necessarily take the meanings of the "that" into consideration as we come at life to behave "for its sake." But in theories of elements—including the periodic table of Lavoisier—the account is entirely extraspective. We lose a sense of intelligence in the commentary that only the final-cause meaning can capture, as it moves our explanation to an introspective slant.

John Locke's model of human reason is the most complete phrasing of this third-person constitutive explanation of behavior. We make considerable reference to Locke in the succeeding chapters of this volume, but the point for now is that he viewed ideas as input copies of an immutable reality. Ideas were like water, filling a glass. The mind at birth was *tabula rasa* (no innate ideas), and only after several mental glasses had been filled from experience, did a combination of such simple ideas begin to form into more complex ideas. Mind was thus constituted in this hierarchical sense, with meanings contained therein having been input at the base of the hierarchy (Ockham's intuitive cognition). Talk of a Platonic universal lending conceptual structure (meaning) to some particular makes no sense at all in the Lockean view. Mind is not conceptual. It is a constituted organization of meanings, "associated" together based on principles of contiguity and the frequency of certain occurrences in the life history of an individual.

David Hume was to build on this conception of behavior, reducing telic considerations to efficient-cause repetitions (practice), worn into Lockean habits by way of pleasurable consequences. Bentham's principle of utility then completed the picture of human behavior as entirely mechanical, moved along by pleasurable motives calculated mathematically to result in "so much" satisfaction, assuming that such and thus were to be done. Judgment is relegated to an (efficiently caused) effect on this model, and behavior is presumed to flow with a sort of Heraclitian pattern of complete predictability. Human existence amounts to being a pattern, because there is no way to break out from the hierarchy as shaped by input factors. An exclusive formal causality has replaced final-formal causality. The modern cybernetic image of behavior is the epitome of British Empiricistic thought.

There were those who demurred from this efficent-cause image of human reason. Descartes drew a distinction between human behavior, which he claimed was capable of judging via a free will, and the behavior of lower animals, which he held to be without a soul and hence completely machinelike. (La Mettrie subsequently rejected this distinction). All of the free-will advocates discussed above can be taken as opponents of the mechanistic image of man. Undoubtedly the most sophisticated counter to British Empircism was Kant's. Continuing in the line of descent stretching back to Plato, in which something precedent (universal form) is assumed to lend conceptual meaning to something following (particulars of life), Kant argued that mind is *not* a *tabula rasa* or empty-container process to be etched upon or filled with experience in a fundamentally passive sense. The mind takes raw materials from sensation and, using certain innate categories of the understanding, lends meaning to this meaningless input. We return to a more detailed consideration of the Lockean-Kantian models of mind or behavior in Chapter 2.

Although the actual founders of the new science were not all committed to the machine analogue for human behavior (Gilbert is a prime example), the evolving explanations of nature combined with the empirical style of providing evidence for scientific arguments led to a significant confusion taking place. We now turn to this aspect of Table 1.

## A Confounding of Theory and Method

There is no more significant development in Western thought than the rise of modern natural science. Let us review the essentials of this scientific revolution. We have said that it involved the dropping of philosophical rationalism, and the retaining of mathematical rationalism. Science also represents a strategy of logical steps to be taken in proving something to be the case, one that *must* end in an empirical demonstration of the claims on knowledge being made. This empirical test thrusts the attention of the scientist outward, so that to think of his observations in extraspective rather than introspective terms is considerably easier. As an observational frame we have noted that Gilbert employed a machine analogue. Machines are the quintessence of efficient causality, in which some antecedent factor moves or brings about a consequent factor over time. The basic meaning of an efficient cause involves this cause-effect occurrence over time. One cannot have an efficient cause explanation outside of a time frame. But this is not true of a logical proof, in which circles are readily drawn within circles (the "this-is-a-man" circle is drawn within the "all-mortal-beings" circle) and a *necessary* conclusion is visualized immediately, *within time* (a man in the inner circle *must* be a mortal being). There is no antecedent force bringing about this evidence as a consequent over time. If this be true, as we look outward to track events across time via Gilbert's method, is the proof we seek always and only of an efficient-cause nature (e.g., that a certain temperature level causes ice to melt), or could we be engaged in a *logical* line of evidential development as well?

This question is extremely important, because if we overlook the fundamental contribution of *nonefficient*-causality in our methodological verifications, possibly we may misinterpret that very evidence on which we claim the rigor of our science depends. Surely we appreciate that not every idea a scientist has is *true,* simply because he has experienced or formulated it. This holds for all reasoners, of course, but by stating the obvious here we underscore the fact that a distinction exists between one's theory and the means or manner whereby he establishes a sense of acceptance or conviction in the truth of his theory (recognizing of course that "truths" are never fixed for all time). This sense of conviction obviously requires a second step, an activity by the theorist that is not precisely theorizing but more on the side of proving or providing evidence in support of or against the theoretical statement he has framed (hypothesized, suggested, thought up, etc.).

Therefore we must distinguish between *theory* and *method* in knowledge accural. A *theory* is the uniting of meaningful relations between designated terms (constructs, abstractions), often framed as propositions or hypotheses (Rychlak, 1968, p. 42). Theoretical statements can be framed with great seriousness or purely fancifully and playfully, without regard for the actual truth-value of the speculation. Theoretical propositions are eventually tested, however, and the *methods* by which they are assessed take us into our second step. There is a purely cognitive method that can be used, entirely within mind, as typified by the rational tests of both philosophical and mathematical rationalism. The evidence suggested in such cognitive tests we have called *procedural (ibid.* p. 74), for it allows thinking to go forward by steps of plausibility and common sense. Joachim's presentation of the coherence theory of truth (Table 1) defines procedural evidence for us as a formal-cause conception. We test our ideas against the internal consistency of other ideas, and then, because of the plausibility afforded by the common sense of the totality, we proceed in thought with confidence if not conviction. The search for ultimates and related assumptions discussed above is an effort based on procedural evidence. The power of mind to know self-reflexively seems a compelling truth, although in recent philosophies (Wittgenstein, Carnap, Ayer) this has been stated as the power of mind to know language rules.

Natural science was to call for more stringent evidence. It did not drop reliance on procedural evidence, of course, because this is what mathematical rationalism relies on. Since, as Russell has taught us, logic and mathematics are at one level identical enterprises, we must appreciate that logical analysis is also based on procedural evidence. But what science called for was an extension, a development beyond complete reliance on procedural evidence to the employment of a *research* method. The experiment was a "trial run" in which the theory as framed might be put into an extraspective frame and tested for its capacity to meet empirical reality. Philosophical rationalism could retain those theories of geometric simplicity and perfection in the heavens only because the reasoners in this tradition blinded themselves to the opportunity of looking "out there, to the evidence of observation." Rather than logically arraying or controlling his alternative explanation of things and then, based on such clearly stated premises, making a prediction to the facts of empirical reality, the philosophical rationalist (Scholastic) made arguments "from definition" much as we have done above in the example of logical reasoning (with the circles and the necessary conclusion of *a* man's mortality). Thus granting a Perfect Being as architect, perfect figures in planetary motions *must* follow. Hence all empirical observations to the contrary are erroneous.

This new form of evidence that science ushered in is best called *validating;* it is based on the prearrangement of events taking place in a prescribed succession and based on the predicted and subsequently observed outcome of this succession, either supporting or failing to support the prediction (hypothesis) made (*ibid.*, p. 77). The prescribed succession of events we recognize as our experimental design (trial run) and the phrase *control and prediction* is well suited to describing the essential features of validating evidence. Russell's discussion of the correspondence theory of truth (Table 1) encompasses validation, because one's hypothesis (prediction) must correspond with the subsequent outcome of his experimental paradigm. Of course a scientist often stumbles onto a discovery he has not predicted. In this case he is usually working on some hypothesis that provides the Nietzschean negative value of contrast, for what he sees is not what he expects to see. Dropping the incorrect hypothesis, he then pursues the new discovery in the more typical fashion of controlling and predicting over several studies (called *cross-validation* of scientific findings).

We thus have *three* terms to consider in the generation of scientific knowledge: *theory, procedural evidence* (via cognitive method), and *validating evidence* (via research method). Having distinguished these terms, we can now analyze an historical development that blurred the distinction between what was a theoretical- and pro-cedural-evidence-based proof and what was a validation in the con-trol-and-prediction sense across a time span. It begins in the recog-nition that mathematical proofs are no more dependent upon time than are logical proofs. Russell has shown that mathematics and logic are identical ratiocinations. We can have mathematical assump-tions made about time, of course, as in Newton's (absolute) mathe-matical time (Wightman, 1951, p. 116). But the sense of conviction of a mathematical or logical proof does not wait on the prescribed suc-cession of events to generate "data" in support of one's contention, as is the case in validation.

When Russell tells us that, in the final analysis, all of mathemat-ics (as well as logic) reduces to tautologies he is saying that this is a procedural-evidence form of truth, one that functions outside of time flow. Though we take time to "figure out" or to diagram a mathe-matical proof, the role of time itself in this proof, as in the sense of conviction that follows, is nonexistent. Tautologies are immediately apparent (once perceived), true by definition, and analyzable into a repetition of the inherent "given." They cannot be efficiently caused because they are like internally consistent patterns, which are only to be recognized and not brought about or made to happen. Mathe-matical proofs are therefore always coherence theories (procedural evidence), relying on the internal consistency of a tautology to bring conviction rather than on their correspondence with externally (effi-ciently) caused events.

Even so, thanks to Newton, the machinelike methodology of Gil-bert, the laws of motion proposed by Galileo, and the efficient-cause emphasis of Francis Bacon were all brought together into a formid-able coalition that was to make Newtonian formal causes into nat-ural-science efficient causes. What Newton did was to take the more dynamic approach to geometry that Descartes had begun and apply it as a model to the description of the universe. Cartesian geometry was no longer a Euclidian study of the innate properties of given shapes, for it had acquired dynamic moving propensities. A circle for Euclid was a plane figure, bounded by a line, all of whose points are equidistant from a given point called the center. For Descartes the circle became a plane figure, bounded by a line formed by the *motion* of a point moving in such a way to be always at a constant distance from the center point. Hence when Newton looked at the universe, he, following Galileo's lead, fixed on the *moving* parts—literally the motion—which were then mathematized (*ibid.,* pp. 88–89).

   Although we are still in the realm of mathematics when we speak
about the motion of points in a line, the implication here is easily
drawn that movements are taking place *across time,* particularly
because subsequent predictions made from the mathematical theory
and proof (procedural evidence) were seen to take place in the time-
bound world of real events. When Newton's law of gravity not only
explained the motions of known planets and stars but also predicted
the existence of stars that were not yet seen (only their presumed
gravitational fields were seen to operate on the gravitational fields of
observable stars), the impact of this purely mathematical conception
on our interpretation of moving reality was inestimable. Numbers
were coming to life! To presume that Newton's *formal-cause* proofs
(theoretical speculations outside of time and based on procedural-
evidence) were actually *efficient-cause* proofs (validation by way of
empirical study within actual time) was an easy misunderstanding.
   When we look at Newton the man (introspectively) and attempt
to describe *his* behavior what do we see? Based on the plausibilities
and tautologies of mathematics, Newton works out a *fiction* called
gravity to account for certain mathematical relations that hold between points in motion (or one point in motion relative to a fixed
point). The fictionalized construct is *not* theorized as somehow created by antecedent events, generated within matter, bursting forth to
push consequent events across the face of time. Motion is happening
as a given in mathematical space, which means all at once in a formal-cause complex of theoretical mathematical relationships, tested
on the basis of tautological self-evidence (procedural evidence).
Whether gravity *is* happening in the real world or not is irrelevant to
Newton's mathematical ratiocinations. Unless we are prepared to say
that the firing of neurons (material-efficient causes) in Newton's
brain "caused" the style (formal cause) of his mathematical reasoning, an efficient-cause explanation of Newton's law of gravity is
absurd. Newton personally appreciated that he was not speaking
about efficient or material causes in his entirely mathematical law
of gravity. He once noted in a letter to a colleague Richard Bentley:
"You sometimes speak of gravity as essential and inherent to matter
[as a material-efficient cause construct]. Pray do not ascribe that
notion to me; for the [material-efficient] cause of gravity is what I do
not pretend to know" (*ibid.,* p. 101)).
   Of course we do not wish to suggest that Newton was in any way
an idealist in his recognition of a difference between the events that
mathematical theory accurately tracked and the reality itself. He was
most assuredly a realist, who put his trust more securely in the effi-

cient-cause regularity of natural lawfulness as Deity-based (see Burtt, 1955, p. 289) than he did in the formal-cause regularities of mathematical reasoning (ibid., p. 214). As fundamentally more empirical than Galileo (see above), Newton looked to Gilbert's experimental methods as the ultimate source of truth. So long as a scientist could empirically demonstrate natural lawfulness—helping the effort along the way through mathematics—he was doing his job properly. He was in the empirical realm of how things really happened even though admittedly (and properly!) he could not always say in his formal theory why these predictions held up in the world of palpable events. Though admirably empirical, this Newtonian brand of "natural" science actually survived on the blurring of a necessary distinction in the generation of knowledge.

Newton's concept of gravity was purely formal, a mathematical prediction of moving points in timeless mathematical space. But, thanks to the efficient-cause machine paradigm of Gilbert's scientific method and the call for efficient (and material) cause description in natural science by Bacon, a confounding took place between what was method (Gilbert) and what was theory (Bacon, Newton). There were two general results of this confusion: (1) Only efficient causes were assumed to be involved in the Newtonian explanation of gravity (motion, movement, then force); and (2) Observations of natural phenomena made through experiments were given an exclusively efficient- (and material-) cause explanation. Although presumptions of natural lawfulness and mathematical regularity had nothing to do with the efficient-cause meaning, a "natural scientist" looking (extraspectively) out to the "facts" could take these unnamed presumptions in his approach and report back nothing but the flow of efficient cause across time. His method confirmed his presumptions again and again, for it could not do otherwise. For him to see other than efficient causes in events that took place over time was impossible in principle. As Burtt so marvelously expressed it, the Newtonian physicist thereby succeeded in making "a metaphysics out of his method" (ibid., p. 229).

Further evidence of the confusion of (formal-cause) theory with (efficient-cause) method can be seen in the altered interpretation of the statistical "function" that has taken place in our time. Leibniz adopted the convention of referring to a stipulated relationship between two numerical values as a functional relationship. This was a mathematical (formal-cause) term, and when Dirichlet subsequently enlarged on the meanings of an independent and a dependent variable in this functional relationship, he in no way departed from formal- and final-cause phrasing. Thus, as noted in Table 1, an independent variable (x) is one to which the mathematician assigns a value *at will,* and the dependent variable (y) is thereby automatically given a value thanks to the functional (ratio) definition existing between variables.

When this mathematical conception was analogized to the machinelike sequence of validation, in which an experimenter *does* lay his hands on an antecedent "variable" to (efficiently) cause a predicted effect on a consequent "variable" over time, the confusion between formal- and efficient-cause terminology was furthered. The convention in experimentation has since been to call the antecedent variable the *independent* (the one the experimenter manipulates) and the consequent variable the *dependent* (because it supposedly records the effects of an antecedent efficient-cause). Here again, though the mathematical definition of a function is the "relations among numbers occurring *all at once,* by definition" (outside of time factors), the definition of an experimental function is the "impact of an antecedent event on a consequent event." Because experimental data are not only conceptualized but tested in terms of statistical theory (mathematics), the ironic fact is that with each formal-cause proof of this sort the "empirical" observer believes that he is finding further evidence for a universe of *only* efficient causes.

The confounding of methodological with theoretical meanings in science was not serious so long as descriptive accounts were limited to inanimate or subhuman descriptions. But when La Mettrie and others took the mechanistic ideology to the extreme of claiming that human beings were *proven* to be machines, a counterforce began to take place in the history of thought. Kierkegaard and Nietzsche pointed to the subjectivities of life, noting the importance that such ephemeral, often unprovable, and telic factors have on the meaning of life as actually lived. Bergson and Husserl attacked the methods of science, claiming that an alternative method along intuitive lines must be fashioned if human nature was to be properly circumscribed. Such criticisms have merit, although the solutions proffered are not always helpful. We will have our own recommendations in the following chapters. For now, we simply observe in consonance with such critics that when a method precludes the testing of teleological hypotheses it forgoes the claim of being an objective vehicle for the exercise of evidence. A method that dictates acceptable terms for theory is as repressive as a theory that dictates terms for a method. The notorious Inquisition made the latter error; one must hope that modern science will not repeat history by making the former error.

Concluding Suggestions for an Objective Psychology

We must surely be impressed with the common efforts expended by the thinkers listed in Table 1. Across all areas of knowledge we see the search for precedents, the concern with rational orders, and the call for increasingly convincing evidence. We cannot escape the suggestion that there is a common humanity reflected in the intellectual preoccupations of the individuals surveyed. Analogizing to Wittgenstein's "propositional variable," we might say that the form of human nature reflected in Table 1 remains constant although the intellectual content of our thinkers has varied. Yet looking at the major approaches to descriptive explanation in the *science* of psychology today, the conceptual tools now in use would not seem to permit an accurate and fair presentation of the totality of Table 1. As a supposed "natural" science, psychology has committed itself to only *certain* of the Table's contents. How *objective* has this commitment allowed psychology to be in the description of human behavior?

No suggestion is made here that psychology need answer problems framed by theology, or art, or critical philosophy. Harking back to our double-duty feature of mathematics, we can now appreciate the important distinction between the problems as put and then solved *and* those who put such problems for solution. The introspective theorist can see a commonality across all members listed in Table 1 because he is thinking in terms of the *people* sampled there, working as identities to ask and then to answer questions. Is not the greatest form of objectivity to begin our quest in the description of man by looking at all men? We cannot study like a natural scientist if we are studying *the* natural scientist and find his ground rules tripping us. We have to rethink the rules of scientific description, fully appreciating the problems a seventeenth-century scientist faced, but arraying these alongside our twentieth-century problems, arrive thereby at a plausible resolution for our time that will meet the needs of both yesterday and today.

The common themes of Table 1, of which we have only scratched the surface, serve as continuing guidelines for the approach to psychology that is developed in detail in the next several chapters and more generally in later chapters in this volume. We follow this procedure on the assumption that there is nothing in Table 1 that is undeserving of our interest and attention. These are our "data" calling for description, and we return to them whenever appropriate as ready examples for the reader's edification. All of the constructs mentioned in Table 1 are products of a *human* mentality; and in that spirit of complete objectivity which typifies the genuine scientist, we hope to suggest needed conceptual changes so that psychology might more accurately describe the kind of individuals who populate Table 1.

## Summary

A survey of 104 outstanding individuals in the history of Western thought is described in Chapter 1. Major conceptions were taken from these thinkers and arrayed into a table, in which definitions and an analysis of these constructs into material, efficient, formal, and final cause meanings were accomplished preliminary to the drawing of certain conclusions regarding the descriptive terminologies surveyed. Study of this table revealed a general concern for the precedent assumptions or premises made in all areas of thought. Thus, whether a theologian or a mathematician, the outstanding thinker of history has devoted considerable attention to the predications of his speciality. Teleologists have formulated theories from an introspective slant, whereas the rise of modern natural science, which has been in principle opposed to telic description, has tilted this frame of reference to an extraspective slant. Efficient-cause and material-cause accounts are invariably extraspective in nature, whereas final-cause description demands an introspective theoretical statement. The formal-cause meaning is used most often by thinkers, undoubtedly due to the fact that "to conceptualize" involves patterning and organization—for example, in the idea or the image of a mental content.

The rise of modern science is shown to parallel a shift in the demands for evidential support in accruing knowledge. Rather than resting his case with the plausibilities of procedural evidence (coherence theory of truth), the modern scientist demands that an additional step be taken to validate theories experimentally (correspondence theory of truth). Although the theories are what attract our interest, the fundamental issue dividing science from other realms of knowledge has to do with *methodological* factors. Though science employs procedural evidence in the mathematical justification it gives to observed events, the translation of such purely formal proofs into experimental designs has caused scientific evidence to appear to support *only* efficient- or material-cause "findings." The formal-cause basis of mathematics, as well as the final-cause reasonings of the mathematician, are rendered incomprehensible in this blurring of distinctions between theory (what human behavior is like) and methodological proof (cognitive methods of the scientist as well as research methods of science). The psychologist more than any other scientist must not let his thinking be prejudiced by the historical remnants of a seventeenth-century struggle between theology (telic accounts) and natural science (mechanistic accounts). The goal is set for a psychology to be unfolded in this volume in which all of the concepts expressed in the historical survey are readily subsumed and taken seriously as "data" reflecting the human condition.

## References

Alexander, F. G., & Selesnick, S. T. The history of psychiatry: An evaluation of psychiatric thought and practice from prehistoric times to the present. New York: Harper & Row, 1966.

Aristotle, Metaphysics. In R. M. Hutchins (Ed.), Great books of the western world (Vol. 8). Chicago: Encyclopedia Britannica, 1952. Pp. 499–626. (a)

Aristotle. Physics. In R. M. Hutchins (Ed.), Great books of the western world (Vol. 8). Chicago: Encyclopedia Britannica, 1952. Pp. 257–355. (b)

Becker, H., & Barnes, H. E. Social thought from lore to science (2 vols.). Washington, D.C.: Harren, 1952.

Burtt, E. A. The metaphysical foundations of modern physical science. Garden City, N.Y.: Doubleday, 1955.

Edwards, P. (Editor in Chief), The encyclopedia of philosophy (8 vols.). New York: Macmillan and Free Press, 1967.

Eves, H. An introduction to the history of mathematics (3rd ed.). New York: Holt, Rinehart & Winston, 1969.

Fehl, N. E. History and society. Hong Kong: Chung Chi College Publication, 1964.

Forbes, R. J., & Dijksterhuis, E. J. A history of science and technology (2 vols.). Baltimore: Penguin Books, 1963.

Frazer, J. G. (abridged by T. H. Gaster). The new golden bough. Great Meadows, N.J.: S. G. Phillips, 1959.

Kondo, H. Albert Einstein and the theory of relativity. New York: Franklin Watts, 1969.

Magill, F. N., & McGreal, I. P. (Eds.). Masterpieces of world philosophy (2 vols.). New York: Salem, 1961.

Russell, B. Wisdom of the west. Garden City, N.Y.: Doubleday, 1959.

Rychlak, J. F. A philosophy of science for personality theory. Boston: Houghton Mifflin, 1968.

Rychlak, J. F. Lockean vs. Kantian theoretical models and the "cause" of therapeutic change. Psychotherapy: Theory, Research and Practice, 1969, 6, 214–222.

Rychlak, J. F. The human person in modern psychological science. *British Journal of Medical Psychology*, 1970, **43**, 233–240.

Rychlak, J. F. Communication in human concordance: Possibilities and impossibilities. In J. H. Masserman & J. J. Schwab (Eds.), *Man for humanity: On concordance vs. discord in human behavior.* Springfield, Ill.: Charles C Thomas, 1972. Pp. 91–101.

Rychlak, J. F. *Introduction to personality and psychotherapy: A theory-construction approach.* Boston: Houghton Mifflin, 1973.

Sarton, G. *Introduction to the history of science* (4 vols.). Baltimore: Williams & Wilkins, 1927. [Reprinted 1968]

Schwartz, G., & Bishop, P. W. (Eds.), *Moments of discovery: The origins of science.* New York: Basic Books, 1958.

Wiener, P. P., & Noland, A. (Eds.), *Roots of scientific thought.* New York: Basic Books, 1957.

Wightman, W. P. D. *The growth of scientific ideas.* New Haven: Yale Univeristy Press, 1951.

# CHAPTER TWO

## On Meaning and Models in Human Behavior

### The Meaning of Meaning

Meaning as a Relational Concept

In beginning the historical survey in Chapter 1 through the employment of four causal meanings we put off a question that must be confronted: What do we mean by the meaning of anything? This question and the issues it generates recur throughout many of this volume's topics, but we must now deal with it in a preliminary way as one of those predication investigations that so preoccupied the historical thinkers listed in Table 1. If we were to follow the procedures employed in Table 1, the term *meaning* would be listed as primarily a final-cause designation, with probably a second check for the formal cause. The word *meaning* has Anglo-Saxon roots in "to wish" and "to intend." This suggests a directional pointing or inference whereby some "given" heralds "something else," joining the two factors into a patterned totality. Language expressions are framed in this way in that words act as patterned instrumentalities for the meaning extensions a speaker or writer is intending to convey. Meanings therefore always reach beyond the specific and suggest, imply, connote, or clearly signify something beyond simply the given. This means that a *relation* or *relationship* is being emphasized whenever we speak about the meaning of anything. Most experts in this area of study are prone to call meaning a *relational* term, though what is meant by this varies considerably among them (see Creelman, 1966).

There are several ways of speaking about the relations involved in meaning, but we can best organize theories of meaning into two broad classifications based on our introspective versus extraspective distinction. Extraspective relations can be seen in what we have called the tie between a given and the something else to which it points. We might call the former an *item* and the latter its *referent*. Thus, a word like *dog* or *chein* can be termed an item bearing a stipulated relationship to the animal referent we recognize in perceptual imagery as "a certain kind of four-legged creature." The reason we call this relation extraspective is because it is formulated in third-person terms, so that whether or not the person understands French we have a clear tie of "that" collection of letters (*chein*) to "that" image of a canine animal. In this sense language terms are purely formal designations, patterned signs that—strictly speaking—lack a purpose as all formal-cause designs lack purposes. Even so, because there *is* a relational tie here and because many students of language in psychology refer to these extraspective relational ties as reflecting meaning, we have to consider them as such. Let us refer to such theoretical usages as being *sign meanings*. A sign is merely a surrogate image or collection of letters, numbers, and so on, that stand for something else (Cassirer, 1944, pp. 80–84). A sign meaning is therefore important to the process of conveying meanings, but it takes no active, creative, or expressive role in this process.

Turning now to the introspective view of meaning, we might consider the plight of an English-speaking person who does not understand French. Though he knows the word [item] *dog*, as well as its referent, canine image, he does *not* find meaning in the word *chein* (aside from idiosyncratic meanings that he might ascribe to the word in an autistic sense). In this case we are viewing a slightly altered relationship between the individual in the *process* of understanding or conveying meanings and the items he has available (or that he can fashion) in this active process. We learn, therefore, that an item can be related to introspectively just as it can be tied to extraspectively. The heuristic scheme of four causes employed in Chapter 1 is a perfect example of this multiple relatedness in all meanings. We began by defining the four causes as sign meanings (pp. 5–6). These relational ties of four items to four different referents stand whether or not a person is employing the causal terms as a sort of premising meaning for his theoretical conceptions. But when we now look at the thinking of 104 outstanding individuals we find that the relation between a premising or predicating causal meaning and the specific concept that each thinker actually framed makes the *distinctive* difference in what is being meaningfully expressed. Even when the thinker coins an original expression, it is framed through our highly abstract metaconstructs of the four causes.

There is still a meaning relation here, of the sort one finds between the major and minor premises of a syllogism, with the flow of meaning-extension developing from the former to the latter. Using the signs as instrumentalities, this active extension of meaning takes place in the thinker's (introspective) cogitations. Let us refer to this usage as dealing with *symbolic meanings*. A symbol is never a mere surrogate, but is framed to mean something itself and in a new, unique, or idiosyncratic way (Langer, 1948, p. 46). Symbolic meanings *are* teleological in that they *do* intend something or purport to express something. We say "they do" when in fact the action must always be found introspectively in the framing of a symbol *by a person*. Symbolical expression is therefore by definition an introspective theoretical account of meaning. For example, when the number 7 is used by people as a surrogate for *seven things*, this shorthand notation serves a purely sign function. However, when 7 is taken by the individual as representing *luck*, there is a new meaning emerging in the use of this number that was not initially defined as a referent of this item. Of course, in time the numeral 7 can be employed for *luck* by others routinely, who do not really believe (intend that) luck follows this item as an inevitable referent. But at this point in time we would say that the symbolical meaning has given way to a sign meaning. In this sense Jung (1956) has accurately observed how true symbols must "come alive" in the telic activity of a person (or a people).

We might now define meaning as follows: The word [item] *meaning* refers [relates] to the relations between items and their referents as well as to the relations between a user of such meaningful ties and the items he employs for the understanding of experience. An *item* can be a verbal language term (letter, word, sentence, etc.) or a purely sensory image (visual, auditory, etc.). Its relation to a referent signifies [points to] something of importance, relevance, or general understanding to the person involved or to an aspect of his personality. The proviso *to an aspect of his personality* is added because we do not wish to foreclose on the possibility of unconscious symbolical expressions developing, which express significant meanings that are not consciously understood. The term *meaningfulness* can be used to describe the extent of significance, import, or general understanding that an item has for an individual. *Meaningfulness* is thus a measure or metric of the extent of meaning—i.e., clarity, centrality, import, value—the item holds for the individual or part-personality structure.

Extraspective formulations of meaning are framed so that all individuals can learn their relations. We can think of this as an objective meaningful relation between items and their referents. The more generally understood an item is among members of a specified group (language system, culture, civilization, etc.), the more objective is that item. However, when we now look at the introspective application of meanings we can see that people often use items (which the culture has defined) quite incorrectly or as colored by their peculiar (symbolical) connotations. Because two people use the same word does not mean that they are expressing the same meaning. As meanings become idiosyncratic and difficult for all members of a specified group to understand, they can be termed *subjective* (Rychlak, 1968, pp. 22–27). Newly created terms are thus born in the subjective meaning-realm of an individual who strives to say something that cannot yet be stated in the language terms made available by the culture in which he lives. He thus coins a new term, often through a precedent analogy or root-language term. In time, through use of examples and by explicating the concept he has in mind, the individual can make his subjective notions known, and to that extent they become objective. If he cannot, although they continue to have subjective meaning for him, they fail to become objective items for the rest of us.

In speaking of meaning as a relation we are forced to think about the polar factors involved in this relation—what we have to this point called the item (one pole) and its referent (a second pole). Is this tie between the polar ends of a relation something that comes about through the joining of separate and distinct *unipolarities*? Or is the seeming conjoining of unipolarities illusory in some cases, so that what seems to have been "joined" parts into a totality is actually a totality from the outset, now drawn out into intrinsically related parts? In short, can meaning be—at least sometimes—a bipolarity (or multipolarity) in which implicit relations between terms exist *by definitional implication*? The conceptualization one has of language expression, thinking, and human behavior in general will vary depending upon whether he views the relations of meaning as always unipolar identities brought together into a relationship, or whether he views at least certain of these ties as essentially discriminations between bipolarities having intrinsic unity.

A unipolar theorist would claim that we have an item [word] *dog* as a unipolar designation, joined through association or practice by the individual to an image of a canine animal as a unipolar referent. These unipolarities have been joined definitionally by the culture "to mean" something, and this is all any meaning-relation can amount to—a tying together of unipolar designations. A theorist who would favor the bipolar view of meaning would question the universality of such unipolar bondings and point to word relations such as up and down or left and right. Can we truly learn what up is without necessarily understanding what down is? Is this really just an associative bonding of unipolarities, or is there something implicit in the relational tie of at least certain bipolar meanings in language usage (as well as in perceptual imagery, because one image can often bring to mind its opposite quite spontaneously—for example, in a dream or a reverie). In a sense the unipolar theorist of language fixes on the poles per se, whereas the bipolar theorist keeps his attention focused on the relation per se; and because there are these two sides to meaning, we cannot say which theoretical emphasis is more correct. Indeed, we are back to precedents, and as with all such predicate assumptions, we find that they have a history.

*Dialectical versus Demonstrative*
*Theories of Meaning: The Beginnings.*

The first *recorded* philosophical debate of history stemmed from our unipolarity-versus-bipolarity issue (Magill & McGreal, 1961, pp. 1–2). Thales had begun philosophical explanation by claiming that all things originated from water.[1] His student Anaximander felt that such a unipolar substance, having infinite existence, would have made impossible the multiplicity of what we now call elements to have arisen in the universe. His concept of the boundless was substituted as a kind of neutral undifferentiated stuff that was no more wet than dry nor no more hot than cold. But such identities as this *did* exist in life, and hence Anaximander argued that they were held together by an opposition within the very nature of things—for example, air is cold, fire is hot, water is moist, and so forth. The boundless could exist as a sea of opposition because it served a relational or "in-between" role in this theory of substantial reality.

This theme of opposition as a bonding agent was carried further by Heraclitus, who added the idea that opposites were fundamentally in strife, and therefore life was a dynamic affair. Heraclitus liked to point out that we could not grasp certain meanings unless these meanings were oppositionally united. For example, *justice* is meaningless unless we also recognize that injustices exist. Stressing that the totality of dynamic events to be seen within the rationale

---

[1] The names and theoretical constructs mentioned in Chapter 2 without specific life dates or book citations are taken from the historical survey of Table 1 (pp. 8–31).

could not be unipolar and clear, Heraclitus observed: "Things taken together are wholes and not wholes; being brought together is being parted; concord is dissonance; and out of all things, one; and out of one, all things" (Magill & McGreal, 1961, p. 13). We see here the widely cited one-in-many or many-in-one thesis. The celebrated universality of the Graecian intellect was in part due to this capacity to see interlacing meanings in all things (Becker & Barnes, 1952, ch. 4). A comparable thesis had arisen even earlier in the philosophies of India and China (Nakamura, 1964). There is no evidence of direct cultural transmission here, but none is required because, as with the causal usages discussed in Chapter 1, the question of unipolar versus bipolar interpretations of meaning confronts any thinker— Eastern or Western—once he begins to contemplate this intricate subject. The one-in-many thesis doubtless had separate origins in the history of thought.

Introduction of the term *dialectic* to represent the bipolar emphasis in theories of meaning is proper at this point. There is no one definition for this term, as there is no one school of dialectical usage (see Rychlak, 1968, 1973, 1976 for other treatments of this topic). In the present context a dialectical formulation of meaning would always look to the *relations* between things (items and their referents) or to the opposite of what was being pointed to as *the* referent of a word, and so on. This kind of reverse emphasis to what is being expressed naturally results in a Heraclitian dissonance and confusion from time to time. The dialectical side to meaning is always *implied* by the fact that some given meaning is being affirmed in a statement or proposition. In the example of Heraclitus given above, to stipulate *justice* implies *injustice*. He also spoke of *up* implying *down*. We say *implying* here, but of course the dialectical thesis holds that justice-injustice and up-down are literally one (and also many, considered separately). When a unipolar designation is made, as in the case of a noun such as *tree*, for example, the bipolarity would occur on the question of its existence; in this case the opposite implication would be *nontree* or *no tree*.

There is a fluid quality about opposite meanings in this sense, because we cannot stay with a single "what-is" item without thereby suggesting literally any number of "what-is-not" items. We can ignore alternatives as implied opposites of other opposites, of course. But the inkling and the potential for meanings to "move on" to something else is always there. This motile side to dialectical meaning-generation was used by Heraclitus and Empedocles to say that change itself depended upon the clash of opposition. Empedocles narrowed this clash down to love and strife, which he felt caused all motion in the world through a kind of running confrontation in events (leading some modern thinkers to suggest that he had anticipated the Freudian eros-versus-death instinct theories). The concept of dialectic has altered in this treatment. It has been given a motivating-power role in explanations of life, and a sort of "thrust" quality of efficient causation has therefore been added to the purely formal-cause meaning of opposition within a totality (rationale).

Running counter to the dialecticians of early Greece, the philosophy of Parmenides emphasized the clear and the certain over the multiplex and the dissonant. Although he proffered several arguments favoring the view that nothing changes (itself a kind of unipolarity or fixedness in events), Parmenides is more respected for his beginning efforts toward the founding of what is now called formal logic. Starting his philosophical career as a Pythagorean and much drawn to the clarity and unipolar certainty of numbers, Parmenides framed what might be seen as an early version of Aristotle's Law of Contradiction. Parmenides was attacking the dialecticians when he observed that we can never prove that what-is-not is, because a nothing cannot be a something. Aristotle was later to prove the major force in formal logic, and he stated this unipolar rule of thumb as, "A is not not-A." Note that the focus has again shifted, for now we are considering the matter of *proof* in relation to dialectical meanings.

The early Greeks were much taken with this question of how to know truth in the generation of knowledge. Modern science takes root from their efforts. When Socrates and Plato came onto the historical scene a group of teacher-philosophers had formed called the *sophists*. These men were dedicated to instruction, the pursuit of knowledge, and in a more practical vein, often served as what today might be called lawyers before the courts in service of a client. Facile and clever, if a little superficial, the sophists relied on a procedure of questioning others to extract desired admissions from them in debate or during court appearances. The cunning placement of certain questions enabled a sophist to establish some point he had set out to prove or to teach to a student. This procedure of questions-and-answers was termed dialectical discourse or the dialectical method, and it is said that as a young man Socrates was once befuddled and made to look the fool by the crafty questions of a sophist who had the young man's head spinning, answering affirmatively to points with which he did not agree. Though he found the dialectical procedure of questioning useful in his subsequent philosophical activities, Socrates more than anyone else helped to make the word *sophist* stand for a specious, insincere, or fallacious reasoner (debator).

The sophists had perverted dialectic, said Socrates, by pointing it unidirectionally (unipolarly) toward a predetermined end, whereas the essence of true dialectical discourse is to be open to *any* direction as the meanings being explored unfolded. The participants need have no idea of where their discourse would take them at the outset. Even if they were to begin in error, through a continuing question-and-answer procedure in which questions were prompted by the meanings opposite to the answers "just given" by the student, Socrates felt that he could come to know truth; for were not truth and error *one* (many-in-one thesis)? If the student took position A, following Socrates' first question, as questioner he defended position not-A; if the student had answered with position not-A, Socrates would have gone to position A. It was all the same in this procedure of intellectual inquiry. Plato later showed how this procedure occurred in the thinking of a single person, thus removing the absolute necessity for two people in the dialectical effort. When we wrestle with a problem calling for creativity, mulling things over in an internal examination of the factors concerned, we behave very much like the Socratic exploration carried on by two people. Through an internal dialogue of opposition we gradually stumble upon a "possible" then "likely" then "certain" course of knowledge. Plato held that we could reason our way from the lived realm of *Becoming* (our normal life experience) to the realm of *Being* (where the universals, pure truth or forms resided) by way of such a dialectical procedure.

Unfortunately, in recording the Socratic dialogues for posterity, Plato has given many individuals today the attitude that Socrates was himself a sly questioner who manipulated his counterpart in the discussion through clever questioning in order to end up at a predetermined point in the discussion. The step-by-step frozen quality that Plato's account gives us of the dialogues reads like a scenario that had been written and then enacted. The clearest example of this would be in the questioning of Meno's ignorant slave boy, who comes, through Socrates' leading questions, to construct a difficult geometrical proof. The reason Socrates conducted this exercise of leading questions was to show Meno that the boy, who had no idea of what direction to take in this problem solution, could find a proof if only the proper questions were raised for him in an intellectual inquiry. The questioning is not so oppositional in this case, because the various "dead ends" that a completely open dialectical discourse would engender are obviated as a kind of "shortcut" effort. In his preliminary remarks before the demonstration, Socrates makes clear that in the case of a newly created discovery he would be as ignorant as the slave boy. His partner in the dialectical questioning process would also be ignorant of the needed directions to take, but because the dialectic is open to *all* implications and each statement suggested in the discourse can be evaluated as it emerges, in time a gradual progression to truth would be accomplished. To interpret Socrates as using questions like prongs to extract what he desired from a counterpart in the discursive exchanges he so loved is therefore quite improper.

Aristotle (1952) gave the most sophisticated counter to dialectical examination as a proper method of true science (p. 142). He felt that the dialecticians were falling into the same specious argumentation that the sophists had engendered. He could not see how mere talk could alter the fact that two individuals were floundering in error "from the outset." To clarify his criticism, Aristotle proposed a scheme for describing how all human beings reason. This is the well-known syllogism, in which thought is said to move from a major premise (e.g., all men are mortal) through a minor premise (e.g., this is a man) to a conclusion (this man is mortal). In the tradition of Parmenides, Aristotle was trying to work out some formal rule of how such syllogistic steps might be taken without erroneous conclusions being drawn. We might emphasize here that the discussion of meaning at the opening of Chapter 2 is relevant to the structure and sequencing of propositions in the syllogism. That is, meaning continues to be seen as a relational term. Within a proposition (statement), there is the relation of an antecedent (men) to a consequent (mortality) term. There is also the relation of one proposition (premise) to a second, culminating in the implied meaning-enrichment of man as mortal in the conclusion. Meaning-relations take place within and across propositional statements, just as they take place between a single item (word) and its referent.

Having outlined the syllogism as a model for human reason, Aristotle next distinguished between two ways in which thinking might proceed, basing his distinction entirely on how a person comes to believe in the meaning(s) of his major premise(s). This is where all reasoning must begin, and what meanings are to be furthered necessarily flow from the meanings with which one begins as a major premise or "predication" (a term Aristotle as well as Peter Abelard helped fix into our vocabulary). In contrast to Socrates, Aristotle now states that any discourse that *begins* in error *ends* in error. As in his elucidation of the law of contradiction, Aristotle effectively draws a unipolar distinction between truth and error (i.e., these two meanings are *not* intrinsically related).

When we reason *dialectically*, said Aristotle, we begin a line of meaning-extension by posing an alternative to a partner in discourse (or to ourselves, in that Platonic sense of internal dialogue mentioned above). Based then on what the partner selects as a meaningful alternative, the discourse proceeds to some eventual conclusion even if the opening question (which delimits the area of study) as well as its answer are entirely specious. To ask a question may appear to legitimatize the area of investigation, but this is not necessarily true—as it was not in the case of the notorious query drawn from the Middle Ages of "how many angels can dance on the head of a pin?" Aristotle therefore argued that dialectical examination rests on *opinion* rather than primary and true major premises. When Socrates asked a student some opening question such as What is the nature of honesty? there is no necessary reason to suspect that his fumbling answer will put the discourse on the road to truth. The student's answer might encompass truth but it could just as well embody error; and according to the rules of the syllogism, an erroneous major premise (all men are honest) must of necessity result in erroneous conclusions.

Fortunately, as a counterweight to the dialectical pattern of reasoning, Aristotle contended that we also have a *demonstrative* reasoning capacity. This more ironclad premising of the syllogism is possible because we can delimit our predications to a unipolar designation. Aristotle called such premises "primary and true," and there are two general cases of this type: a truth by tautological definition —for example, when we state "All bachelors are unmarried males" —or a truth that states the "facts" as empirically (demonstrably) known. Centuries later Kant (1952) called the former analytical propositions and the latter synthetical propositions (p. 16). An analytical proposition's truth value can be determined through analysis of the meanings of its antecedent and its consequent terms. The meaning of bachelor thus embraces the meaning of unmarried male tautologically. A synthetical proposition must be shown to be true empirically because the antecedent and consequent terms are not tautologically related in this fashion. For example, claiming that firstborn children make excellent community leaders in adulthood is a synthetical tie of birth order to community leadership. We cannot find the truth here by an examination of concepts, but must go to empirical experience and prove our claim through some form of validation.

Aristotle recognized that dialectical examination helped in determining the truth value of analytical statements. He specifically noted that everyone—including the scientist—must resort to dialectical strategies when major premises could not be established as "primary and true" at some given point in time. But he adamantly denied that a dialectical examination of synthetical propositions had merit. Why? Because such examination relied exclusively on what we have called procedural evidence—or the coherence theory of truth (Joachim). As one of the first tough-minded philosophers of history, Aristotle's theory of knowledge is pitched at the need for validating evidence— or the correspondence theory of truth. One's statements had better meet the facts, said Aristotle, or all he knows for certain is that a subjective and opinionated view is making sense for the present. But the work of knowledge has not yet been completed. It is significant in light of modern developments to note that Aristotle's commitment to methodological rigor did not dissuade him from describing events teleologically. He founded a science of biology but also assigned purpose to nature.

Dialectical versus Demonstrative Themes
in Western Thought

We can now employ Aristotle's terminological distinction to retrace our steps across history, pointing to the various uses thinkers have made of either a dialectical (bipolar meanings, reasonings) or a demonstrative (unipolar meanings, reasonings) formulation of events.

In general the mathematicians of history have served to elevate the role of demonstrative reasoning, especially since about the time of Descartes. But a mathematical inclination was not always anathema to a dialectical outlook on the nature of things. The "father of mathematics," Pythagoras, who held to the view that the world was comprised of numbers (as reflections of universals), *also* believed that all things were comprised of opposites and nothing in nature was therefore simple and unmixed (atomic or unipolar) (Untersteiner, 1954, pp. 19–26). Pythagoras was simply reflecting the widely held one-in-many thesis of his age, and though he had many so-called mystical thoughts on the role of numbers in life, his mysticism invariably drew from a dialectical rationale (a fact that is true of all mysticisms). The general belief is that the revival of (neo-) Pythagoreanism in Italy during the fifteenth century influenced Copernicus, in the idealistic sense of the universe conforming to a series of mathematically precise (unipolar) laws (see Burtt, 1955, p. 42). Unfortunately, by this time the dialectical side of Pythagoras had been lost to history. Mathematicians, like all natural scientists, now wanted to explicate what "is" and not what oppositionally "might be" (is not).

There are other indications of a dialectical emphasis in mathematics. The word *algebra* derives from the title of an Arabic treatise (about 825 A.D.) on the subject by *al-Khowarizmi*, which translates "the science of the reunion and the opposition" (Eves, 1969, p. 195). We use the more familiar and equally correct translation "transposition and cancellation" today, but there is a decided implication here of the one-in-many thesis, with the view that mathematical reasoning harmonized the totality through joining the many subparts by oppositions. Today we do not conceptualize the numbers flanking an equation sign as reflecting bipolarity, because the sign represents a tautological identity between the two values. Though identical, there are many ways of viewing the "same" (unipolar) equation by way of moving values about in opposition (bipolar) to each other. We might ponder at this point whether this facility would really be possible in an organism that could reason *only* demonstratively.

The concept of a substrate unity that in turn might constitute all things is to be seen in the atomic conceptions of Democritus and Lucretius. Along with unity in mathematics, this atomic notion has been of immense historical importance to the rise of demonstrative concepts and reasonings. Here we have a belief in the reducibility of all things to a certain unipolar substrate (i.e., atom as the uncuttable or indivisible hence unipolar unit), which in turn formed into complex assemblages of things, reflecting as a consequence (efficient cause) of this assemblage an overriding pattern of recognizable order. Though Heraclitus had seen his rationale (order) as a mixture of clashing oppositions, Democritus and Lucretius changed this multipolar conception to one of a concatenation of unipolar items, joined fixedly into a hierarchy of determinate order. By determinate in this case we mean unidirectional. Events moved as they did because they were "made" to work in that way "and that way only" (law of contradiction). Both Democritus and Lucretius were easily led into a hard-deterministic position based on their demonstrative interpretation of the rationale. This perfection in the rational order was subsequently buttressed by theologians who ascribed things to a "Grand Mathematician" (God).

Of course, this did not mean that theology could rest with a demonstrative tactic. Anyone who studies religious theory will be impressed by the frequent dialectical formulations of many theologians. The foremost dialectician of the Roman Catholic Church is undoubtedly Saint Augustine. He not only called for the free use of dialectical argumentation to buttress our faith in God's existence (even if this amounted to sophistry!), but he also resolved some problems in theological conceptualization through dialectical constructs. The Holy Trinity is the most celebrated of these solutions (Jaspers, 1962, pp. 196–197). Negative theology is also a dialectical formulation.

Theologians and others frequently rely on dialectical formulations to deal with the question of free will. Origen's concept of the fall of divine powers was of this sort. The good—as created by God—would have no meaning without its opposite evil as a potentiality. It was simply a question of time before the opposite possibility was affirmed by Divinities who had this option open to them as dialectical beings. A similar theme is seen in the philosophy of Marcus Aurelius. He argued that the nature of life demanded that each person either affirm (assent) or deny (dissent) certain directions in which meaningful events were unfolding. Life events are not unidirectional, but they call for a contribution from the individual in this sense; this self-initiated affirmation or negation is at the root of human freedom. In the seventeenth and eighteenth centuries we see this theme in the writings of Leibniz. How different this is from the unidirectional determinisms of Democritus and Lucretius! Once we begin our line of thought with a dialectical rationale, there is room in conceptualization for the inconsistencies, the turn of events, the so-called indeterminate features of life (Rychlak, 1976).

Throughout the Medieval period and into recent times the concept of dialectic was also cultivated in the practices of oratory, polemics, and disputation. Rhetoric as a skillful use of speech in persuasion has generally been interpreted as a form of "acceptable" sophistry, much to be admired in individuals who have such abilities (propaganda and modern advertising are further steps down this often sophistical path). In the evolution of law and courtroom procedures a form of questioning arose to counteract such rhetorical manipulations—especially as pressed by a witness before the bar. The witness in today's courtroom is therefore not given the freedom of an open dialogue with the attorney who is putting questions to him in quasi-cybernetic fashion. Witnesses are instructed by the court to behave demonstratively—to answer questions with a unipolar statement of meaning. The questioner must make this possible by limiting his questions to relevant (unipolarly precise) points. Equivocation, qualification, and related human practices of a more dialectical nature arise in the courtroom only through the exchanges of the opponent attorneys, each of whom is out to manipulate the proceedings to reach their predetermined ends of guilt or innocence (amounting to a form of Socratic sophistry when viewed from either end). The jury should weigh whatever evidence is presented; make allowances for the sophistry in the advocacy procedure; and through a more open colloquy, arrive at a reasoned affirmation of guilt or innocence.

The theories of history which we are prone to call "mystical" because we have no way of conceptualizing them via customary logic, often come down to a variant of the dialectical theme. For example, Jung (1953) found that the alchemists believed every form of matter contained within its identity an inner antithesis (p. 268). Lower identities therefore contained the potentials for higher manifestations of their being. As in the transubstantiation of a lower matter (bread and wine) into a higher matter (body and blood of Christ) in the rites of the Catholic Mass, the alchemists tried to convert lead into gold as a concrete proof of God's existence. At least the earliest alchemists tried. In time the symbolical meanings of the alchemical investigations were lost to posterity and the essentially spiritual practices of the founders were eclipsed by purely materialistic efforts (symbols into signs). Another example of mysticism is to be seen in the introspective religious practices of Bonaventura, who theorized as follows: Man can obviously turn back on his senses and contemplate rationally what he receives from vision, hearing, and so on. He is therefore no slave to illusion. But if he can turn back on the senses, why can he not *also* turn back on his rationality and fix thereby on the nonrational? This is possible, said Bonaventura, and he asked that the effort be made to turn inward and away from the rational to a mystical communion with God, a Being so fantastic that He transcends all rational insight in any case.

Saint Thomas Aquinas cast a jaundiced eye at the excesses of dialectical formulations. Though he gave some credence to negative theology and held, as Aristotle had, that all people reason both demonstratively and dialectically, Aquinas did *not* feel it was proper to give free vent to dialectical speculations. In this he countered the more Platonic tradition of Saint Augustine. Aquinas sought to reason from premises that were primary and true (analytical) to the indubitable conclusion in support of God's existence. Arguments from the first cause, order, and purpose in nature represent his efforts in this regard. This intellectual approach was to be called Scholasticism, and it became a form of philosophical rationalism that was eventually to conflict with the rise of natural science in the seventeenth century.

The Age of Science was already presaged in the thirteenth- and fourteenth-century theologies of John Duns Scotus and William of Ockham, both of whom were instrumental in raising the stature of *empirical* demonstration in religious debate. Duns Scotus opposed Scholasticism and belittled the role of analytical philosopher in theology. Explanations must end in simplicity and unity, said Duns Scotus; intricate and subtle accounts of God's existence are therefore suspect on the face of things. Ockham was highly suspicious of the power of mind to know anything about God's existence that was not directly perceived in experience as a miracle (the only legitimate proof, for it was empirical). He distinguished between the *intuitive cognition,* which takes in such empirical information from the environment, and the *abstractive cognition,* which deals with such information mentally after it has been acquired. All knowledge is therefore grounded in experience, outside of mind; hence no amount of introspection or fanciful argumentation concerning God's existence can equal the weight of one empirical demonstration (miraculous happening). All else is and must remain based on faith. A more modern rephrasing of this theme occurs in Karl Barth, who denies that God can be known through human reason and looks to Christ as a corporeal manifestation of proof. Ockham's contention that all knowledge is extramental was to provide an important justification for the school of thought known as British Empiricism, of which he must be seen as a precursor if not an actual founding father.

The denigration of mind reflected in the theologies of Duns Scotus and Ockham did not extend to mathematics, which in the sixteenth and seventeenth centuries was making great strides. Dialectical reasoning was obviously in jeopardy when a great dialectical effort like Descartes'—in which he opened his examination with the question How do I know that I exist? and went on from there in the style of a Platonist—could be completely misunderstood and unappreciated by the man who made it. Descartes (1952) felt that dialectical logic was completely devoid of meaning (p. 17). Though he accepted free will and spoke of assent and dissent in the style of Aurelius, he like most mathematicians—with notable exceptions like Pascal (see Cassirer, 1944, p. 27)—did not think of such mental judgments as due to reasonings by opposition in meaning. Descartes would be placed on the tougher side of the line of descent stemming from Aristotle through Aquinas, because he really was not rejecting the possibility of a dialectical reasoning capacity in man; it was not in principle impossible to reason in this fashion, but when carried out it was without objective meaning. When we move on to the mathematicians of British Empiricism, the *very possibility* of an organism that can reason dialectically drops from view.

The preliminaries for a demonstrative image of human behavior were put down by Bacon and Gilbert, both of whom placed Ockham's intuitive cognition uppermost in defining science as an inductive procedure. The scientist must ever seek to find what "is" in experience as "truth" and avoid what "is not" as an "error." An error is thus basically *nothing*. Only truth has existence. Copernicus and Galileo now add to this strategy the extraspective utility of mathematical reasoning, which is in this sense the quintessence of demonstration. A mathematician may reason dialectically in thinking through his proofs, but as sketched on the blackboard there is no more beautiful example of demonstrative reasoning than a mathematical derivation (recall our double-duty role for mathematics, p. 36). Thomas Hobbes was to take this conception and apply it directly to human reason. Thinking, said Hobbes, is nothing more than "reckoning"—that is, the addition and subtraction of ideas. This meant *all* thinking, so that demonstrative reasoning was no longer just one of at least two ways in which human beings might employ meanings. Man's stomach and liver functioned in only one way, and his brain or mind *also* worked in but one way! John Locke gave us the clearest statement of this demonstrative image of man. Because we use the Lockean model as prototype for all of the demonstrative theories across history we forego further consideration in the present context and take it up in detail below (pp. 86–88).

From this time forward in history there was a growing conviction that all things scientific can be dealt with through demonstrative formulations. Newtonian science is a prime example of this attitude. The fact that Newton dabbled in alchemy for years and subscribed to a religious view of the universe does not alter the fact that he, more than anyone else, gave credence to the view that a science must not only be demonstrative in methodological approach, but scientists must deal with and think in terms of demonstrative theoretical meanings alone!

The most sophisticated counter to this image of man embodied in British philosophy was given by Immanuel Kant, but since we also discuss him below (pp. 88–92) as a prototype model in opposition to Locke, we overlook his approach in the present context. Suffice to say that Kant picked up on Bonaventura's thesis about mind turning back on itself and accounted for such transcendent capacities by way of what he called the transcendental dialectic. Though he put the dialectic back into man's image, Kant was as suspicious of its extensive use as Aristotle and Aquinas had been (yet not so pessimistic as Descartes). Johann Gottlieb Fichte had no such compunctions. Fichte was a subjective idealist, who believed that as selves we first posit our own ego and then through an innate dialectical capacity posit the world of experience. This meant that he reversed the order of merit in Ockham's two realms of cognition. Sensations could not be the source of knowledge, said Fichte, because they were nothing more than phenomenal constructions, projected onto so-called reality rather than taken from it.

G. W. F. Hegel then so dominated dialectical theory in the late eighteenth and early nineteenth centuries that today one can hardly use the term *dialectic* without one's listeners presuming that this is the historical precedent to which one is referring. Some have claimed that every twentieth-century philosophical movement is either a continuation of the Hegelian philosophy in modified form (e.g., Marxian theory) or a reaction against it. Hegel's dialectical formulation takes us back to Heraclitus and Empedocles, because he used it as a rationale for the flow of history. Hegel referred to this as a dynamic unfolding of successive clashes between the opposites of a thesis and an antithesis, resolving itself into a synthesis, which in turn acts as a new thesis to an antithesis, and so forth. What was unfolding here was the mind of a God, coming to self-consciousness as a final "negation of a negation." (In the case of Hegelian theory, it occurred in the balance of an enlightened Prussian monarchy.) Once the divine spirit of this pantheism had achieved self-consciousness, the historical march of the dialectic ended. It is as if Plato's individual, dialectically mulling things over in his mind's eye, trying to work through a problem of some sort, had finally solved the complex riddle and no longer sensed the inner turmoil of creation. Note that this is an introspective formulation of history. History is the reflection of an individual God's dialectical mullings, with the clash of civilizations and the alternations of national characters to be seen among different people of the earth acting as "way stations" along the evolutionary course to divine self-consciousness.

This tendency to view a resolution of thesis-antithesis into a synthesis suggests to many dialecticians *prima facie* evidence that an advance or a development has occurred in events over the three-step process. A synthesis is assumed not to have occurred unless the best of both sides (thesis-antithesis) were fused into one, indicating thereby that an improvement (development, maturation) over the initially contradictory or inconsistent circumstances had taken place. The dialectical conception of change is considerably different from demonstrative conceptions, and we defer for a later topic more detailed consideration of this difference (see ch. 6, pp. 240–241). But in the present context we should note that neo-Hegelian interpretations of the dialectic borrow this suggestion of a developmental advance across stages or levels of either psychological or physical development. A modern example of this use of dialectic can be seen in Riegel's (1973) theory of development.

Hegelian philosophy was idealistic, viewing the material products of a culture as the result of its ideology or the spirit of its age—what Herder had called the *Geist* or *Zeitgeist* (Becker & Barnes, 1952, pp. 487–490). Marx reversed this by turning the Hegelian dialectic to say that ideas always flow from the material realities of a culture's economic forces. Ideas are class linked, and they always reflect the justifications and rationalizations of a group seeking to gain advantage in the dialectical class struggle. This use of the dialectical conception is *extraspective*, putting the thesis, antithesis, and synthesis into the fabric of reality as what Marx and Engels called dialectical materialism. Like Hegel, the Marxian dialectic is also seen to end in the so-called classless state which flows from the final negation of a negation in the realities of socioeconomic evolution. The founders of communism were quite aware of how their conception of events countered the typical demonstrative world views then in ascendance. Marx (1952) pointed out how the logic of dialectics continually upset the doctrinaire professors of his time, who swept its truths under the carpet at every turn and refused to give it legitimacy (p. 11). Engels (1966) noted how dialectical conceptualizations befuddled the Newtonian physicists, who seemed to feel that what they could not understand must necessarily be erroneous (pp. 201–202). Whether or not we favor their economic theory, the observations of these two eminent champions of the dialectic are *surely* correct. An impartial survey of history must convince us that the dialectic as a useful heuristic scheme of animate as well as inanimate nature has been drummed out of natural science.

Dialectic is employed in certain religious formulations, however, as well as in the more humanistic psychologies and philosophies of our time—sometimes without being named as such. The religious critic and founder of existentialism, Søren Kierkegaard, employed a concept of the dialectic which was personal and subjective. This was quite in contrast to the sweeping conception that Hegel employed, but Kierkegaard specifically wanted to put the turmoil and personal decision between opposites back into the individual human being rather than claim that humans were mere pawns in the pantheistic evolution of a divine consciousness. His subjective dialectic has lent the humanistic psychologies of our time a rationale for their concepts of personal action, authenticity, and commitment in life. We see here modern reflections of the Origen-Aurelius-Leibniz line of descent. Continuing in this vein, Paul Tillich's religious theory is dialectical in essence, stressing the need for a self-affirmation on the side of being or nonbeing. Martin Buber's I-Thou concept of encounter is also clearly dialectical in meaning.

Another founder of existentialistic philosophy, Friedrich Nietzsche, was drawn to the tactic of looking at the other side of our most hallowed values and scientific truths. Demonstrative theories of knowledge are fixed only on what is true and not on what is false, but Nietzsche stressed that the value of an idea cannot always be measured by its truth. If man is a telic animal, he can—as Socrates would have said—learn from the reverse of facts. If this were not the case, people would be unable to turn what "is not" into what "is" by way of telic commitment to creation, change, and innovation. The one-sidedness of demonstrative reasoning worried Nietzsche, for he feared that man's valuational capacities could be weakened by the unwillingness to commit oneself to a value judgment in science (an issue that has returned to haunt us in the modern age of atomic physics). Man is a valuing animal, yet natural science has taken away this (final-cause) side of his description as well as fostered an attitude of "who can say?" on moral questions.

This question of valuation is central to dialectical judgment, because clearly if there are two or more meaning-implications in any given situation facing the individual he is forced to find some grounds for the sake of which (final cause) his behavior ought to proceed. George Santayana contrasted the demonstrative physical sciences, which deal with unipolar facts, and the dialectical sciences, which deal in bipolar ideas. Art was viewed as one such dialectical science, in which the objective grounds for a judgment of beauty were constantly under study. As with ethical or religious decisions, the judgment of beauty in art must be actively affirmed (symbolical meaning) for it to come about. Beauty is the antithesis of a sign meaning, for no one could possibly have an esthetic experience if an art object were nothing more than a sign. Rather than coming in through the senses by way of Ockham's intuitive cognition, beauty must be created through an evaluative act. This stems from a dialectical effort made by the individual, who must judge and thereby objectify the grounds for the sake of which one object can be said to be more beautiful than another.

The humanistic philosopher, Henri Bergson, took the Heraclitus-Empedocles-Hegel line of dialectical theory further in his teleological conception of mankind. Rather than supraindividual, the dialectic was said to function within each person (*a la Kierkegaard*) as a vital force (*élan vital*) which dynamically and creatively evolved in nature by way of contradictions. Life and matter were seen as the inverse of each other, even though they had a common origin in an energic reservoir (one-in-many thesis). Following a Hegelian line, Bergson claimed that history was the telic account of life (formal-final causation) trying to free itself from the domination of matter (material-efficient causation) and thereby to achieve self-consciousness. Although he did not give his dialectical conceptions this evolutionary emphasis, the theories of Edmund Husserl retained the self-created and subjectively unique emphases of Bergson, Nietzsche, and Kierkegaard.

The spirit of our age (*Zeitgeist*) is surely not in tune with such dialectical formulations. Societies that embrace dialectical materialism are ironically unsympathetic to minority and divisive ideas. In the philosophies of our time there is little fascination expressed with error, confusion, or inefficiency. Pragmatism (William James), pragmaticism (Charles S. Peirce), instrumentalism (John Dewey), and logical positivism (Rudolph Carnap, Alfred Jules Ayer) are all on the side of demonstrative reasoning. Mathematical and related formal-logic positions (Bertrand Russell, Ludwig Wittgenstein) are similarly construed. The greatest strides in human reason these past four centuries (the Age of Science) have been made with the clear recognition that demonstrative strategies have been employed. But there is a stunning ignorance of the comparable role dialectical conceptions have *also* played in this advance. One of the purposes of this volume is to underscore the forgotten and overlooked side to reason—the one that capitalizes on the bipolarities of meaning and *also* must be elucidated if we are to have a well-rounded picture of the *human* situation.

Dialectical versus Demonstrative Themes
in Eastern Thought

In Chapter 1 we stressed that the causal meanings were to be seen in Eastern as well as Western theories of knowledge and that therefore the image of humanity we were reviewing was not culturally regional in nature. Our dialectical-versus-demonstrative distinction can also be seen in Indian and Oriental thinking. To characterize a whole civilization as predominantly one way or the other is risky scholarly business, but we would not be too far from the truth to state that whereas Western thought was to hone the edges of demonstrative reasoning to a fine point, Eastern thinkers have given equal care to the refinement of dialectical thinking (see Kuo, 1976, for additional evidence on this point). This comes as a great revelation to many Western modernists, who see in the Eastern philosophies an almost superhuman magical alternative to their own world views.

The role of Buddhism in shaping Eastern thought is often stressed by scholars, who characterize the peculiarities of Indian, Chinese, and Japanese thought by the ways in which these peoples have assimilated Buddhistic concepts (see, e.g., Nakamura, 1964). Buddhism was founded in its first form in India, of course. The view is generally accepted today that Buddhism was an offshoot of the Upanishadic philosophies of the Vedic literature (Raju, 1967, p. 44). This Hindu philosophy gives a major emphasis to our one-in-many thesis (Saksena, 1967, p. 31). The predominant theme running through both the Hindu and Buddhistic philosophies of India is the necessary search for a oneness in nature, the breaking down of false dichotomies, and a unity in the totality of experience that results in liberation (moksa) or nirvana. The Brahman (Hindu) or Buddha (Buddhistic) constructs are both views of a universal soul to which we must relate by way of an internal search. This inward effort is reminiscent of the Platonic dialectic at work (Raju, 1967, p. 52). The Buddhists seem to have been the first great synthesizers of history, and the Indian mind in general is said to be less analytical than synthetical (ibid., pp. 44 and 62). But this does not mean that synthetical relations are studied empirically, in demonstrative fashion; rather the Indian synthesis is achieved by adoption of a dialectical attitude that suggests that all theories of knowledge are equally correct "from their particular point of view" (Moore, 1967a, p. 14). Hence any ultimate truths must of necessity be a "one" of the Heraclitian sort, in which inner contradictions will naturally exist. Or a further insight might emerge in which what were initially taken as contradictions would be found to be noncontradictions after all.

Buddhism has thus been a philosophy based on the theory of negation as the proper means for arriving at truth: "Accordingly, all the Buddhist schools which rested chiefly on some dialectic arguments can be designated as those of negative Rationalism, the static nature of 'Thusness' [ultimate truth] being only negatively arrived at as the remainder" (Takakusu, 1967, p. 87). We can see a Bonaventura-like tendency to deny rather than affirm as a method for coming to truth in the Eightfold Negation of the great Indian Buddhistic philosopher, Nāgārjuna (c. 100–150 AD). He denied or negated the world of phenomenal experience through four paired oppositions: neither birth nor death, neither permanence nor extinction, neither unity nor diversity, and neither coming nor going (ibid., p. 112). We have a variation here of that negation of negation theme noted in Western thought, so that the Buddhistic monk achieves the middle path (nirvana) by slipping into the totality of existence that is ever rent apart by the tensions of opposition. The dichotomies Nāgārjuna rejected have in a sense set him free of this tension as he effectively becomes one within these many sides to experience.

In contrast to the Western demonstrative presumption that perception is unipolar—for example, we see what is "there" or we see nothing at all (law of contradiction)—the Indian mentality has it that man sees nonexistence just as clearly as he sees existence: ". . . looking at the table, we can say that there is no cat there, just as we can say that there is a book there" (Datta, 1967, pp. 129–130). Even in the Hindu approach to meditation, where the goal is to focus attention on the nondual Brahman, the steps to be taken follow a dialectical path (Nikhilananda, 1967, p. 147). We come to Brahman by the dialectical steps of dismissing ideas of body, senses, mind, and ego which are oppositional to his identity. Once our focusing on Brahman is complete, we find the nodal point of perfect harmony and unity—as a kind of enlightenment by way of removing the irrelevancies from our awareness. Considered in the logic of dialectics, we again have that negation-of-a-negation principle that both Hegel and Marx wove into their conceptions of society as enlightened monarchies or classless states. The golden mean of Greece or the middle path of India are identical notions when looked at through the strategy of dialectical reasoning.

In Chinese thought a comparable synthesizing tendency is seen with great emphasis placed on the one-in-many thesis (Moore, 1967b, pp. 6–7). There arose in China a clear parallel to the demonstrative versus dialectical counterplay we have found in Western history. The renowned Chinese text, the Tao Te Ching (c. 600 BC, probably of multiple authorship) is replete with dialectical conceptions, the most famous of which is the yin-yang principle (see Chapter 1, p. 32). The yin force or element is pictured as passive, receiving, and meek (on the face of things); yet like the female or mother, yin represents the potential for infinite creation in the world. In this sense, *yin* is closer to *tao* or the "way"—that is, the universal principle underlying all things as an ultimate pattern of growth (formal-final cause meaning). The *yang* force is more active and bold, reflecting its power overtly in a more masculine sense. Harmony as a kind of dialectical balance between *yin* and *yang* is most desirable, although the Chinese Sage, who is closer to *tao* than others, refuses to display his powers openly and thus appears overly passive to the Western intellect.

In contrast to this dialectical text, the school of thought that devolves from Confucius (551–479 BC) is clearly demonstrative in tone. Confucius was a pragmatic man, more oriented to innovation and change in the world of affairs than to the rejection of this world in contemplation of an inner life. He was critical of the rulers of his time, whom he felt were disdainful of the humanity of their citizenry. He wanted to change things, and the strategy of innovation he followed was to gain the lines of control in the society, either directly by trying to get a position of great authority (at which he was not successful) or indirectly through placing his students in positions of bureaucratic influence. Having taught these men in a way that would ensure their character, Confucius believed that their education would translate into better conditions for the people. His sayings are still quoted as guidelines for the right, proper, and humane way in which to live. He taught respect for tradition and parental authority. He believed that there *is* a right and a wrong way in which to behave. The demonstrative flavor of this style of thought is clear, and therefore we are not surprised to learn that there is no dialectical side to the classical philosophy of Confucius (Kuo, 1976).

Confucius was not alone in his concern for people. Chinese thought has always been humanely oriented (Chan, 1967a, p. 26). Much of the philosophy recorded in China has dealt with the problems of good government, cordial relations between people, family life, and so on. In the fifth century BC Mo Ti (c. 470–391 BC) presented a challenge to Confucianism and at the same time helped found what has since been called the Dialectician School in Chinese philosophy. The dates of his life span are almost identical to those of Socrates (who lived c. 470–399 BC), a remarkable parallel in the history of dialectical conceptualization. Mo Ti's definition of the dialectic brings together humanistic with more purely abstract considerations, for he defined it as an effort to distinguish right from wrong, good from bad government, similarity from difference, name from actuality, benefit from harm, and certainty from uncertainty. These various oppositions cover much of what we have seen con-

sidered in the descent of Western dialectical thinking. Mo Ti's outlook on life was more pedestrian and egalitarian than that of Confucius (as was his personal geneology). He stressed the basic
equality of all men and rejected the Confucian acceptance of fate—
a unidirectional, demonstrative conception—holding instead that
every person must have an equal opportunity to influence his own
destiny. He was particularly harsh in criticizing the Confucian fascination with ritual. Mo Ti's attitudes remind us of the revolutionary
inclinations of a Marx or a Nietzsche, not to mention the individual-
istic focus of a Kierkegaard.

A notable difference between the demonstrative philosophies of
the West and those of China was that the former were invariably
realisms, whereas neo-Confucianism evolved at least one idealism,
thanks to Mencius (c. 372–c. 289 BC). Confucius encouraged man to
be humane toward others so that society would be peaceful; Mencius
encouraged man to be kind to others because that was man's innate
propensity, but one which needed cultivation. Man must practice his
innate "senses" (propensities) to humanity, or they will wither away
as does a limb that is never exercised. Hence goodness (humaneness)
is something which is idealistically created in each individual lifestyle, rather than something that is shaped by the realities of the
external (real) environment. The good man acquires an all-pervading
force (ch'i) by practicing the principles of humanity and morality.
He must constantly subject his sense perceptions to the control of
mind, cultivating his innate tendencies to be humane and thereby
come to know Heaven in his lifetime. Although idealistic and spiritual, there is no dialectical formulation in this philosophy. Mencius
is not as distinctively demonstrative as Confucius, but his stress on
the good as innately given (primary and true) hence knowable to all
who make the effort is surely in this general direction.

Not all Confucians accepted this idealistic strain, of course. Han
Fei (c. 280–233 BC) was educated a Confucian but took a more
realistic position on the nature of reality. He was a social philosopher
with an extremely materialistic, even Machiavellian, outlook on
things. Nothing interests man, said Han Fei, except the material
advantages he can gain in life. Men are controlled, not by Mencius'
assumption of an innate goodness needing cultivation, but by the
external sanction of laws that are backed by the power of a ruler.
The effective ruler must maintain a strong state by extending rewards
to those who help his sovereignty and using punishment for those
who fail to submit to his control. Punishment and reward are the
"two helms" that guide man's behavior, and they do so from without
in the extraspective sense we have seen employed in the utilitari-

anism of British Empiricism. Han Fei is thus a demonstrative spokesman for the ruler, whereas Confucius had in a sense been the spokesman for those who are ruled (at least the middle-class members of this society). Both Han Fei and Confucius perceive the lines of control in the society as unidirectionally devolving from a position of authority. Neither is a revolutionary thinker, but each seeks to work within the constraints of the power structure to make things happen by way of this unidirectionality.

But the more characteristic spirit of Chinese thought is dialectical, focused on the individual, and directed inwardly. The rise of Buddhistic philosophy was an instrumental factor in this world view. Chuang Tzu (c. 370–c. 285 BC) wrote a famous theory of the equality of all things; he liked to point out that right is only right because of the existence of wrong (Chan, 1967b, p. 54). Kung-Sun Lung (c. 330–250 BC) devoted considerable effort to an explication of what we in the West call the Socratic-Platonic universals. He was a leader of the dialecticians, held to the one-in-many thesis, and formulated many intricate philosophical arguments, some of which are considered sophistical. The founding of Zen Buddhism in China (c. 600 AD) was to give even greater prominence to dialectical formulations. The transfer of Zen to Japan in the twelfth and thirteenth centuries was to exert an immense influence on the philosophical outlook of that country.

It is said that in ancient Japanese philosophy there was very little argumentation or dispute (Nakamura, 1964, p. 539). A kind of practical acceptance of events was characteristic of these early thinkers, who had a one-in-many view that the phenomenal reality as known by each person was tantamount to reality. Concern over differences or the existence of an independent reality to which everyone's conception must conform simply made no headway in early Japan. Nakamura has shown how the forms of expression in the Japanese language are oriented more to emotional factors than to the truth value of a demonstrative logic (ibid., p. 531). Hence Zen Buddhism and the dialectical outlook on which it depended found a ready intellectual atmosphere when in 1227 Dogen (1200–1235) brought the Sōtō Zen sect of Buddhism to Japan. We find in his writings the paradoxical statements so typical of this philosophy. Muso (or Soseki, 1275–1351) followed, and the general style of master-student instruction in Zen was perfected under his leadership and example.

A comparison of the dialectical exchanges of the Zen Buddhists to the exchanges carried on by Socrates in the dialogues is interesting. In the latter case Socrates as teacher always initiated and kept the exchanges going through a series of questions that were suggested as the dialogue unfolded. The teacher takes an active (yang) role and seems to be the one who is leading the way to a discovery of knowledge, although he does not pretend to have information stored in his head for transmission to the student's head. The Zen master, however, is always pictured in a passive (yin) role, and invariably the student must take the initiative by asking the opening question. When the student does this, his teacher responds in a most unusual manner. He might give an answer that is completely unrelated to the question asked; he might simply raise a finger or a fist as a kind of reply; or he might pick up a small stick and throw it at the student. Often he remains silent. If the student prods for a question from the Zen master long enough, he might be treated by what is—on demonstrative grounds—a totally meaningless query; the most popularly cited example is "What is the sound of one hand clapping?"

In the literature of Zen one commonly reads of students going from one master to another, trying various questions on them, getting assorted replies or queries of the type cited, all the while suffering a sense of almost unbearable frustration. Suzuki (1962) tells the classic tale of a student physically striking his teacher for the latter's seeming obtuseness, but to no avail because a conventional answer was still not forthcoming (p. 40). Socrates at times frustrated his students, but this was the result of a sense of confusion due to the many interlocking issues on which his questioning touched. The Socratic dialogues did not always end in clear-cut solutions, and occasionally they led to unexpected paths that created more problems for the student than they solved. But the Zen student's irritation stemmed from the frustration of "not even getting started" on his road to knowledge. The Zen master, of course, was not refusing to aid in the student's education. His paradoxical or non-sequitor answer was an answer; even his silence said something in reply. He was essentially suggesting to the student that in the act of framing questions we create meaningless problems for ourselves. All questions regarding nature must necessarily disrupt the totality of nature, because they focus on the bits and pieces of experience in order to be answered. Even if a question can be answered, that the answer is worthy of expression does not follow—particularly because all it can lead to is a further question, hence more unnatural dichotomization and destruction of the totality that is life.

By answering questions in a seemingly ridiculous fashion the Zen master therefore teaches the student that a senseless question, which can lend no lasting satisfaction to the seeker of enlightenment, must be answered in kind. The posing of a self-contradictory question about the sound of one hand clapping is simply the reverse of this. People who put questions must learn that their precedent conceptualizations are already foisting onto the answering party an arbitrary scheme that might well distort the very thing they are seeking to understand. There is also the implication through all of this that in a final all-encompassing sense the *end* of knowledge is to lend an air of satisfaction and contentment to the educated or enlightened person. By focusing on the ultimate of knowledge, arriving there more through denial or negation of the question–answer dichotomies of life than through the temporary possession of "answers," the Zen master is hoping to exemplify a higher truth for his student.

When he achieves Perfect Enlightenment the student resigns himself completely to what *is*. He no longer raises questions about life and death, truth or falsehood, beauty or ugliness, and so on, because he now appreciates that these are *all* Buddha. He has no anxiety about such questions, for there is nothing to fear in a realm of totality. As the trees do not analyze the clouds and there is no night *versus* day in the earth's rotation, he does not draw oppositional dichotomies to split up nature in some arbitrary fashion. Rather, he slips into the totality that is nature and exists with contentment, having now made the journey that Buddha made and coming to the end at which Buddha arrived. Of course we are making enlightenment appear to be solely an intellectual understanding when in fact the effort of introspective study and contemplation associated with the quest for wisdom in Zen Buddhism must be seen as important *per se*. That is, the student must in effect rediscover the same— highly subjective—experience Buddha had lived through as he made his way to liberation. As Suzuki (1962) notes: "The Buddha's experience of Enlightenment . . . could not be understood by referring it to the intellect which tantalizes but fails to fulfill and satisfy" (p. 84). Hence there is an ineffable, highly personal, and subjective side to the achievement of Buddhahood—the oneness in spirit with humanity—taking us beyond the scope of the present book. Even so, it is not improper to have shown that the *logic* of this so-called mystical school of thought is our familiar brand of dialectical reasoning and conceptualization.

## Conclusions and Implications

What are we to conclude from our review of meaning? There is probably little new for the reader to learn in the overview of demonstrative interpretations of meaning. We are educated in the West to think clearly and rigorously in our mathematics and logic classes, not to mention in our personal affairs. We think of science as clear and explicable, whereas art or religion is considered inscrutable and personal, more a mystery than something that can be understood through the objective methods of science. Knowledge has been equated with scientific knowledge so that everyone believes that what is "really factual" will be circumscribed by science someday, whereas all the other business will remain nonscientific, hence weaker or cheaper, by comparison. The harmful effect of this great valuation of demonstrative reasoning is that if we, as human persons, now behave inconsistently or fail to see only one set of "facts" in an event, we are made to feel somehow "outside the pale" of respectable conceptualization as rationalizers, illogical beings, or simply stupid—as if we are not living up to some underlying characteristic of our natures.

Yet anyone who has taken the time to familiarize himself with dialectical logic can immediately make sense of much of this diversity and inconsistency in the error variance of a scientific investigation on human behavior. Error becomes as active a principle in his outlook as accuracy, and he no longer feels responsible for only the manageable (predicted) portion of his observations. More to the point, how can we as students of humanity overlook the centuries of evidence which make abundantly clear that a dialectical logic is at work in the conscious (nonillusory) efforts of human beings to make sense of their experience? To found science on one of two opposing traditions and then dismiss the other as nonexistent or as unimportant simply because it cannot be subsumed by its opponent is a circular argument at best and an intellectually lazy solution at worst. We in scientific psychology must carefully examine and come to some position on that aspect of behavior we now forego completely —the dialectic!

What, then, can we say the dialectic is? In answering, we must surely conclude: There is no one definition of the dialectic (see Rychlak, 1976, Chapter 1). Anyone who claims to speak for the dialectic is either poorly informed or playing the sophist. The only common characteristic of dialectic is the point we began this chapter with— the use of bipolar meanings in the theoretical account as a central emphasis. To speak of the dialectic without such opposition would be impossible. Following this, all kinds of theoretical developments flow. We can emphasize the opposition per se and speak of the dynamic clash, strife, class struggle, internal tension, and so on or harmonize this opposition and see it as a one-in-many developmental synthesis, advance, or rationale. The dialectic can be thought of extraspectively, as moving across history in the material substance of the universe as a world principle, or it can be placed introspectively as an individual's peculiar way of coming at life through the affirmation of opposites, hence alternatives, open to him. Strictly speaking, all alternatives begin in the poles of opposition when we view them introspectively (as opposites of opposites *ad infinitum*).

We can limit our talk of dialectic to the fact that "a" concept has more than one meaning-implication; or we can speak of the flow of this meaning-implication as an extension of one, the other, or both of the polar references concerned. When we use the dialectic as a single-identity construct—for example, in Saint Augustine's Holy Trinity conception—the bipolarity is limited to a fixed "something." We do not have to speak of the dialectic as a dynamic flow of meaning-extension in reasoning or as a series of developmental stages. However, this dynamic step is easily taken, particularly when our singular conceptions are framed introspectively (which the Holy Trinity is not). This brings us to a significant point concerning the type of logical statement that flows from one or the other of our two views of meaning.

We noted in Chapter 1 that mathematics served a double duty in that it could be employed as a conceptualization with equal facility both extraspectively and introspectively. Mathematics is simply one example of demonstrative reasoning, and therefore this double-duty feature holds for *all* forms of demonstrative reasoning—for example, classical or so-called Aristotelian logic with its use of the syllogistic frame to capture the steps of accurate (truthful) reasoning. But how often do people begin a line of *their* reasoning from premises that are "primary and true?" Though *in principle* we might all be capable of this, few of us actually do so in our routine thinking. Hence, as a theoretical statement of what people introspectively actually do in life, the demonstrative conception is probably a rather poor reflection of the human reality.

However, this does not detract from the fact that demonstrative reasoning is a supreme example of what human thought could be— and sometimes is—particularly when we frame it extraspectively, as perforce on a blackboard. If we systematically record a planned sequence of life steps, or if we design a scientific experiment by putting down our thoughts in writing this way, anyone who understands our language symbols can see immediately what is being projected sequentially. Anyone other than us could therefore *predict* what must be done to comply with the extraspectively-framed steps recorded on the blackboard. In fact another person could even enlarge upon what obviously was called for in the *unidirectional* logic progression. The steps of this logic are necessarily there in the Aristotelian manner.

The sequential flow of dialectical logic, however, proves difficult if not impossible to capture in exclusively extraspective terms. For example, let us contrast the extraspective world principle used by Marx (dialectical materialism) with the introspective world principle of Hegelian dialectical theory. The Hegelian formulation (on which the Marxian was based) comes off much clearer and true to form. This is so because in dialectical reasoning we are always concerned with the premise *eventually* taken and never simply with the implications to flow from this opening affirmation. As Aristotle correctly stated, in the logical progression of dialectic you never know what direction will be followed until *after* it has been selected. There is no point in graphing a dialectical syllogism extraspectively by beginning with, "Now, in the major premise we have 'this' affirmation acting as predicate-assumption, which in turn calls up 'that' opposition" because *no one can say* what is to be initially affirmed or what the opposite as conceptualized will be! In fact, there may be a succession of oppositions so that after reasoning from an opposite to an opposite to an opposite, when the syllogistic steps are undertaken the meanings under extension could well be far from where we had begun. This means that the essential strategy of analysis in dialectical logic is *post hoc*. We retrace our steps and try to look at the dialectical proceedings from *within* the (first person) cogitations of an individual who is approaching some problem with the attitude, "Now, let's see, just what is going on here, what are the possibilities, what is this all about?"

Hence the most accurate representation of how a dialectical logic flows is to be seen in introspective formulations, and the analysis on which we must of necessity rely is "after the fact" of having set a course of meaning-extension. Hegel's view of history was correctly *post hoc* in this fashion, retracing its steps to determine what premises the Divine Spirit affirmed as He moved historical events along. After all, who can foretell what a God will do? All we can assess is what He *did*. This search for His premises pushes our account to an introspective perspective. Although Marx retained this *post hoc* tendency in his efforts to reinterpret history, the rational counterplay in events was lost to his theory. Dialectical materialism has become less the active principle in events than the step-by-step rationale for the energies expended in the class struggle. Hegelian dialectic was teleological, with God making the *free* decision to halt events—each of which might have gone otherwise—at that point when He had achieved a level of Self-consciousness to His satisfaction. The Prussian monarchy was God's choice, now made actual in reality and therefore seen by Hegel through *post hoc* examination. Though the Marxian dialectic leads to a certain end (classless state), it has lost this telic character as it was made just another "predetermined" force of nature. Harking back to Socrates, we might say that Marx used the dialectic sophistically. He tried to make it predict events to a foregone conclusion. But one cannot simply draw the course of the dialectic on a blackboard and say where it must necessarily end.

Since the direction taken is *not* predetermined in free dialectic, the direction *actually* taken can be evaluated vis à vis the options open to the identity affirming one way or another at the outset. Finding the grounds for this selection is what interests the artist (Santayana) as well as the religious thinkers of history. We might characterize the logic of dialectic as a *logic of implication*. And though such implications often create "decision problems" and related devisiveness in the topic under consideration, the dialectic as a one-in-many thesis permits us to see how such articulated differences are again brought together. There is almost a reverse implication of "maybe these are the same?" or "maybe there is something identical about these?" based on the initial affirmation of "these are all different."

Dialectical machinations are also well suited to theoretical speculation, but they leave something to be desired in the realm of method, which in this case must ever remain cognitive due to the reliance on *post hoc* analyses. Demonstrative strategies are quite amenable—indeed we might say that they provide the backbone—to research methods of experimentation. Dialectical accounts are thus heavily laden with procedural evidence. Problems arise when, because of this, a scientist thinks that he cannot devise some demonstrative experiment that would support the *fact of* dialectical meanings or reasonings functioning among human beings. This is, of course, quite absurd, and in Chapters 9, 10, 11 of this book we review a decade's work on one such dialectical conception. To appreciate that one might not always predict the course of a dialectical meaning-extension does not mean that we are unable to show the effects of a dialectical intelligence on the course of learning. We must first entertain the possibility that this (dialectical) side to behavior exists before we can begin to design experiments that might test predictions (meaning-extensions) which flow therefrom.

## Lockean versus Kantian Models

We can now bring the essentials of the nature of meaning and its uses together into two models of explanation (though the term *paradigm* as employed by Kuhn [1970] would be equally applicable). We can think of these as prototypes for all demonstratively inclined (Lockean) models and dialectically inclined (Kantian) models—with the proviso that we mean "in relation to human description." That is, an impersonal world principle of the Marxian sort cannot be subsumed by what we will term the Kantian model, though Hegel's view is somewhat consonant with this model because he had a personlike identity (God) in mind as one aspect of his world-principle formulation. History does indeed repeat itself, and although certain refinements in the basic pattern of a metaconception might change over the centuries, there is enough fundamental meaning in all human thought styles to justify the coining of two prototypes. Hence we can correctly refer to philosophies that predated Locke's and Kant's lifespan—even in an altogether different culture—as Lockean or Kantian formulations. We use these individuals as symbols of the thought styles we have observed across both Eastern and Western history (for alternate discussions of these models see Rychlak, 1968, pp. 274–283, and Rychlak, 1973, pp. 8–13).

### The Lockean Model

John Locke's conception of the human mentality was totally demonstrative—a constitutive model that begins in the atomic theories of Democritus and Lucretius and is carried forward in time to its most thorough phrasing in British Empiricism. Drawing on the precedents of Bacon and Hobbes, Locke held that the contents of mind could only be those (primary and true) items that came into this repository of sensory input "from the outside." Each mental content (unipolar meaning) was embodied in its own discrete unit or a combination of such "idea units" (comparable to the "uncuttable" concept of the atom). At the base of experience we have the *simple ideas* which embody inputs from an independent reality and etch a mental imprint upon what Locke called the *tabula rasa* intellect (a term Aquinas had used in another context). At birth the mind is like a smoothed (blank) tablet and all that comes into mind is put there by the inputs from experience.

Note that the initiative here in meaning generation is put onto the exterior environment. Meanings devolve from outside to inside, and therefore a realistic thesis is highly compatible with the Lockean model. The real world exists "out there," sending inward certain information by way of what Ockham had called the intuitive cognition. *After* this input has been registered on the smoothed-tablet mind we then can see mental operations taking place in terms of what Ockham had called the abstractive cognition. Locke (1952) therefore held that insofar as mind has any power of creation, it is the power to deal with past inputs (i.e., occurring since birth) through memory and by thus recalling ideas, comparing them, affirming or suspending their import for our lives, a contribution of sorts is made to our sequence of behavior (p. 200). This is as active as mind can get in the Lockean view. There is no possibility for mental conceptualization at the point of birth, no organizing or construing potential in the idea whatsoever

The unipolar inputs from reality initially etched onto mind (i.e., simple ideas) are analogical to the lowest whole number (unity) in mathematics, except that a simple idea cannot itself be further subdivided. In other words, at the base of experience an idea is a discrete unit (atomic) having an either-or characteristic mapping reality accurately or inaccurately by way of sensory inputs. The mind records and then recollects this most basic of all information input, combining it in time via a quasi-mathematical (demonstrative) form of reasoning into higher and higher levels of information units called *complex ideas*. Complex ideas *are* divisible, of course; they are similar to complex numbers—for example, when we add three ones and then multiply this by the total of two ones to get six, and so forth. Harking back to Democritus and Lucretius, the simple idea is like an atomistic building block, which combines *in the beginnings* of thought with other atomistic bits of information to constitute a mathematical totality as the mind stores more and more information. These combinations of ideas were called habits or habits of association by Locke, but they were determinate habits based on an analogy to the "thinking-is-reckoning" suggestion of Hobbes. In this sense all meanings issue "from below," from the substrate reality which is the source of input-information. Locke specifically said that the mind could not invent or frame one new simple idea, nor could it subdivide or destroy those simple ideas which have already entered (*ibid.*, p. 128). Quite obviously, no dialectician could agree that "a" simple idea was indivisible by nature because he would see two meaning implications, ready for bifurcation, in many if not all of these so-called simple ideas.

Dialecticians would also disagree on the question of how meanings are input. According to Locke, the meaning *left* enters mind as a simple idea and the meaning *right* enters as a completely different simple idea; in time through frequent (habitual) association of left to right in our experience we learn the concept of directionality as a complex idea. This input frequency is thought of in purely efficient-cause terms (after Bacon). Both the input and the associative tie to other ideas occur purely as efficient-cause connections. Because the input information is conveyed by a sensory apparatus, we find that the Lockean model also makes good use of material-cause description. We can even view the patterning of more and more complex ideas as a kind of formal cause. However, the pattern *qua* pattern is never the source of meaning; it does not organize what is developing meaningfully below, but is merely the determinate end-result (effect) of the coalescing of the lower-order inputs (efficient-causes). Because the pattern does not endow things with meaning, there is no way possible to express human thought as behaving "for the sake of" this organization. Hence a final-cause conception does not enter into this model at all.

How might Locke account for dialectical machinations such as doubt, distrust, rejection, disbelief, wavering between affirmation and negation, conjecture, the concoction of possibilities, and so on? He would claim that such subjectively felt experiences, which we take to be the operations of our active intellects, were actually due to the kinds of frequency distributions of inputs on either or both sides of a question. Moderate or considerable input on "this" side of a point is sensed as opinion, belief, or conviction; fairly equal inputs on both "this" and "that" side of a point result in so-called indecision, or doubt; little input on either side of the point would constitute negation or disbelief and so forth (*ibid.*, p. 369). A possibility is simply a complex idea that has been calculated out of the memory storage of individual inputs, indicating a statistical probability or likelihood that certain events will flow if certain steps are taken.

### The Kantian Model

Immanuel Kant aimed much of his commentary at the British empiricist and philosophical skeptic, David Hume, whose writings are in the Lockean tradition. For example, concerning the supposed power of mind to act on experience Hume (1952) observed: ". . . all this creative power of the mind amounts to [is] no more than the faculty of compounding, transposing, augmenting, or diminishing the materials afforded us by the senses and experience" (p. 456). We recognize the spirit of Ockham in this quote as well as the quasi-mathematical view of thought promoted by Hobbes and Locke. Kant favored a conceptual model of mind, one in which meaning devolved from above, framed in by certain inborn capacities that actively function to endow experiences with meaning. We see here a philosophical predilection that stretches back to Plato and Socrates, whose realm of Being within which the universals (forms) resided is a parallel conception to the model of mind that Kant embraced. Kant considered himself a critical realist, but he sounded a note for idealism just as Plato had done centuries earlier. We could easily consider this a Platonic model, just as we might call its contrast a Lucretian or Democritan model.

Kant agreed that there were two sides to knowledge—one having to do with sensation and the other with something more mental—but he disagreed with the passive input view of these activities that the British had proposed. Was sensation, for example, really an outside-to-inside input, or were there certain frames of reference that had to be applied to this process for a meaningful understanding to take place? Ockham had made intuitive cognition seem a completely unstructured or unorganized affair, when actually, Kant argued, sensations are always framed in terms of both time and space. Space and time factors are not *in* the input but are placed onto the input messages to provide them with a meaningful organization. Kant was putting his opening emphasis on a formal-cause usage in countering the strictly efficient- and material-cause usages of the Lockean model.

But this capacity for organization is even more important when we consider the higher mental processes, such as reasoning and understanding. We have mental ideas at both these levels, and particularly in pure reason we have ideas that *transcend* sensory experience entirely (Kant, 1952, p. 115). Knowledge can begin in experience, as organized by sensory factors, but it does not always arise out of experience because in pure reason—completely free thought—ideas are possible that were never input and bear no conceivable relationship to experience. This can occur because of the functioning of a *transcendental dialectic* in mind (dialectical reasoning), permitting us to concoct fanciful and highly distorted versions of that which we perceive daily through reasoning by opposites and the opposites of opposites, until we have removed ourselves from the realm of familiar events and known "facts." Sometimes these fantasied distortions result in workable ideas, which are innovated and put into experience by the person so that a creation comes about. If the head of a man and the body of a lion are combined into a sphynx symbolizing certain things about its originator, can we say in truth that this mixing of man-animal, lower-higher, strength-frailty, and so on is due to input influences alone? Who has ever seen such a figure in nature? Or could it be that a human intelligence is doing something to the input in a way only *it* can manage and that the patent reality of the sphynx is material evidence of this dialectical human capacity? Kant would have held to the latter interpretation.

The emphasis in Kantian thought on the formal cause as lending meaning to—rather than being constituted of—input items in experience is seen in his distinction between the noumenal and the phenomenal aspects of experience. External reality or a "thing in itself" cannot be known directly because of the sensory barrier that comes between us and the palpability of matter. This physical substrate Kant called the *noumena*. What we know of the noumenal realm comes through the combined orderings of our sensations and our cognitive understandings of it via mind. This latter organization of noumenal inputs into meaningful understanding Kant termed *phenomena*. Man cannot escape the fact that his only knowledge of the external world is through his sensory and cognitive shield of phenomenal understanding. Kant called himself a (critical) *realist* because, though he was aware of the drawbacks in speaking about how reality supposedly determined mental behavior, he did accept on faith that the noumenal world really existed.

If we were to describe the phenomenal realm as Lockeans, we would say that the simple ideas became, through repetitions, complex ideas of an habitual nature that provided a kind of higher-order pattern through which subsequent life events might then be interpreted. But this was not Kant's view. He said that just as sensation was organized along space and time lines, so too was the higher understanding organized by *a priori* "categories" which lent meaning to experience *from birth*. Although we need not detail these categories of the understanding that Kant felt all humans had as an aspect of their innate equipment "to know," the observation that he formulated these conceptions in a dialectical fashion is interesting. For example, modality was said to involve possibility-impossibility, existence-nonexistence, and necessity-contingency. Quantity was framed in terms of unity, plurality, and totality. Kant's view of mind was greatly influenced by dialectical metaconceptions. He effectively reversed the Ockham-Lockean line by suggesting that far from being the *source* of all knowledge, intuitive cognition is *meaningless noumenal noise* without the organizing function of space and time at the level of sensation and the categories of the understanding at the level of cognition (knowing). In the Kantian model, rather than an "after" function, abstractive cognition becomes a necessary pre- liminary activity to the accrual of knowledge. Mind is not *tabula rasa*, but *pro forma*.

With the capacity to reason dialectically in free thought (pure reason) we have quite a contrast to the Lockean model. Kant's model subsumes the meaning of final causation, because the idea here is not a determinate effect of some unidirectional (efficient) cause. Be- cause of the transcendental dialectic in mind, we can even turn back on the evidence of our senses or deny the validity of our categories of reason. We must not think that Kant felt one could not rise above the focusing propensities of the phenomenal realm. When Einstein later challenged our popular conceptions of space and time he did some- thing Kant felt any person could do—that is, "in principle" look to the other side of any designatable meaning-affirmation and thereby propose an alternative. This would not mean that the way in which the organism spontaneously experienced events would necessarily change. Einsteinian theory may be true although the average person is little affected by the fact that there is a relativity to his natural sensations of time. But no person is frozen into his conceptual equip- ment one way because he can always think to the opposite of what this portends—and to the opposite of this opposite *ad infinitum*.

Though we use the metaphor of a smoothed tablet or a blank sheet to think about Locke's concept of mind, in some ways the metaphor of the water glass is better. Locke thought of each idea as a glass of water in which the water contained therein had been poured in from the outside world. This means that whatever idea is in mind had been put there. If Kant now wants to speak of meanings like modality or quality, Locke would ask him: "Where do these ideas come from if not from the environmental input? How can you speak about such *innate ideas* of things without telling us how they got into mind?" Locke's challenge makes great sense if we view ideas the way he did.

Kant's idea construct was different from a unit of water filling a discrete glass unit, which might then also combine with other glass units of water to form complexities in thought. Kant's idea metaphor was more like a pair of spectacles through which the individual must look to see what is "out there." Our side (as wearers) of the specta- cles is the phenomenal realm, and the other side (with which we can never come in contact) is the noumenal realm. The organizing power of these spectacles is never and *never has been* input, anymore than our memory capacity (on which the Lockean model relies) has been input.

In describing our natures we have words for things. We can speak of our memory capacity. There are also words for something we call a possibility or an impossibility as an aspect of what we might call modality. But the only thing that is input about concepts such as possibility-impossibility (modality) is the particular letter collections (words) we employ as items for the referents to which we allude. Kant did not say the words *possibility* and *impossibility* were innate, but rather that the implicit understanding of something like "that can happen" or "that simply cannot happen" are *applied to* experience rather than obtained from it. For example, the child reaches for the moon and then learns that it is not possible to grasp it. But, is the conception of impossibility learned here or the *fact* of what is or is not possible to attain? Kant would contend the latter is input but the former is innate! In time this child will also learn the meanings of the words *possibility-impossibility*; but he will by that time *already know* and indeed can only learn the meanings of these words because he has conceptually experienced what these words refer to. The child has a kind of beginning capacity to organize experience, to contribute something to it *from birth*, and then he builds on this organizational capacity to bring more and more knowledge to bear in an ever-expanding intellectually active sense.

One final point on Kant and the dialectic: Do not conclude that he favored the free use of dialectical speculation. To speculate wildly was perfectly all right, but in science we must take our thoughts a step further and validate them in the most rigorous manner possible. Kant was thus very much in the tradition of Aristotle and Aquinas on the question of dialectical argumentation.

**Summary**

In Chapter 2 we took up the question of how to interpret meaning *per se*, a concept that was taken for granted in the survey of causation in Chapter 1. As a relational term, meaning can be interpreted as the conjoining of unipolarities or, as a bipolar relationship, within knowledge from the outset. It can also be a combination of both unipolarities and bipolarities. We then suggested that unipolar interpretations of meaning are based on demonstrative conceptualizations, and bipolar interpretations of meaning are based on dialectical conceptualizations. These two approaches to meaning were then traced in the history of both Western and Eastern thought. As in the case of the four causes, this ubiquitous dichotomy is seen to have manifested itself in a number of different areas of knowledge, among all peoples of the earth. By and large, Western thinking has given greater attention to demonstrative and Eastern thought to dialectical strategies and formulations. The rise of mathematics and natural science in the West has virtually eclipsed the dialectic as a conceptual scheme in modern times.

If psychology is to be a science that is representative of the human condition, an appreciation of the dialectical side to behavior must be made. This recognition need not detract from the rigor of the science of psychology. No one theorist can speak for the dialectic, because there are numerous interpretations of the concept with its major emphasis at some point that an oppositional bipolarity in meaning must be presumed by the theoretician in question. Although both forms of conceptualization can be framed from either theoretical perspective, dialectical constructs lend themselves to introspective meanings and demonstrative constructs lend themselves to extraspective meanings. Chapter 2 closes with a discussion of the Lockean and the Kantian models. These metaconceptions nicely subsume the factors discussed in Chapters 1 and 2. The Lockean model is demonstrative, extraspective, prone to the use of material and efficient causation, and fundamentally constitutive in expressive style. The Kantian model is dialectical, introspective, prone to the use of formal and final causation, and fundamentally conceptual in expressive style.

## References

Aristotle. *Posterior analytics.* In R. M. Hutchins (Ed.), *Great books of the western world* (Vol. 8). Chicago: Encyclopedia Britannica, 1952. Pp. 95–137.

Becker, H., & Barnes, H. E. *Social thought from lore to science* (2 vols.). Washington, D.C.: Harren, 1952.

Burtt, E. A. *The metaphysical foundations of modern physical science* (rev. ed.). Garden City, N.Y.: Doubleday, 1955.

Cassirer, E. *An essay on man.* Garden City, N.Y.: Doubleday, 1944.

Chan, W.-T. Chinese theory and practice, with special reference to humanism. In C. A. Moore (Ed.), *The Chinese mind: Essentials of Chinese philosophy and culture.* Honolulu: University of Hawaii Press, 1967. Pp. 11–30. (a)

Chan, W.-T. The story of Chinese philosophy. In C. A. Moore (Ed.), *The Chinese mind: Essentials of Chinese philosophy and culture.* Honolulu: University of Hawaii Press, 1967. Pp. 31–76. (b)

Creelman, M. B. *The experimental investigation of meaning: A review of the literature.* New York: Springer, 1966.

Datta, D. M. Epistemological methods in Indian philosophy. In C. A. Moore (Ed.), *The Indian Mind: Essentials of Indian philosophy and culture.* Honolulu: University of Hawaii Press, 1967. Pp. 118–135.

Descartes, R. *Rules for the direction of mind.* In R. M. Hutchins (Ed.), *Great books of the western world* (Vol. 31). Chicago: Encyclopedia Britannica, 1952. Pp. 1–40.

Engels, F. *Dialectics of nature.* Moscow: Progress, 1966.

Eves, H. *An introduction to the history of mathematics* (3rd ed.). New York: Holt, Rinehart & Winston, 1969.

Hume, D. *An enquiry concerning human understanding.* In R. M. Hutchins (Ed.), *Great books of the western world* (Vol. 35). Chicago: Encyclopedia Britannica, 1952. Pp. 446–509.

Jaspers, K. *The great philosophers.* New York: Harcourt, Brace & World, 1962.

Jung, C. G. *Psychology and alchemy.* In H. Read, M. Fordham, & G. Adler (Eds.), *The collected works of C. G. Jung* (Vol. 12, rev. ed.). Bollingen Series XX.12. New York: Pantheon Books, 1953.

Jung, C. G. *Symbols of transformation.* In H. Read, M. Fordham, & G. Adler (Eds.), *The collected works of C. G. Jung* (Vol. 5). Bollingen Series XX.5. New York: Pantheon Books, 1956.

Kant, I. *The critique of pure reason.* In R. M. Hutchins (Ed.), *Great books of the western world* (Vol. 42). Chicago: Encyclopedia Britannica, 1952. Pp. 1–250.

Kuhn, T. S. *The structure of scientific revolutions* (2nd. ed.). Chicago: The University of Chicago Press, 1970. (1st ed., 1962).

Kuo, Y. Chinese dialectical thought and character. In J. F. Rychlak (Ed.), *Dialectic: Humanistic rationale for behavior and development.* Basel, Switzerland: S. Karger AG, 1976. Pp. 72–85.

Langer, S. K. *Philosophy in a new key.* New York: Penguin Books, 1948.

Locke, J. *An essay concerning human understanding.* In R. M. Hutchins (Ed.), *Great books of the western world* (Vol. 35). Chicago: Encyclopedia Britannica, 1952. Pp. 85–395.

Magill, F. N., & McGreal, I. P. (Eds.) *Masterpieces of world philosophy* (2 vols.). New York: Salem, 1961.

Marx, K. *Capital.* In R. M. Hutchins (Ed.), *Great books of the western world* (Vol. 50). Chicago: Encyclopedia Britannica, 1952. Pp. 1–393.

Moore, C. A. Introduction: The comprehensive Indian mind. In C. A. Moore (Ed.), *The Indian mind: Essentials of Indian philosophy and culture.* Honolulu: University of Hawaii Press, 1967. Pp. 1–18. (a)

Moore, C. A. Introduction: The humanistic Chinese mind. In C. A. Moore (Ed.), *The Chinese mind: Essentials of Chinese philosophy and culture.* Honolulu: University of Hawaii Press, 1967. Pp. 1–10. (b)

Nakamura, H. *Ways of thinking of Eastern peoples.* Honolulu: East-West Center Press, 1964.

Nikhilananda, S. Concentration and meditation as methods of Indian philosophy. In C. A. Moore (Ed.), *The Indian mind: Essentials of Indian philosophy and culture.* Honolulu: University of Hawaii Press, 1967. Pp. 136–151.

Raju, P. T. Metaphysical theories in Indian philosophy. In C. A. Moore (Ed.), *The Indian mind: Essentials of Indian philosophy and culture.* Honolulu: University of Hawaii Press, 1967. Pp. 19–40.

Riegel, K. F. Dialectical operations: The final period of cognitive development. *Human Development,* 1973, *16,* 346–370.

Rychlak, J. F. *A philosophy of science for personality theory.* Boston: Houghton Mifflin, 1968.

Rychlak, J. F. *Introduction to personality and psychotherapy: A theory-construction approach.* Boston: Houghton Mifflin, 1973.

Rychlak, J. F. (Ed.), *Dialectic: Humanistic rationale for behavior and development.* Basel, Switzerland: S. Karger AG, 1976.

Saksena, S. K. Relation of philosophical theories to the practical affairs of men. In C. A. Moore (Ed.), *The Indian mind: Essentials of Indian philosophy and culture.* Honolulu: University of Hawaii Press, 1967. Pp. 19–40.

Suzuki, D. T. *The essentials of Zen Buddhism.* New York: Dutton, 1962. [Edited and with an introduction by B. Phillips.]

Takakusu, J. Buddhism as a philosophy of "thusness." In C. A. Moore (Ed.), *The Indian mind: Essentials of Indian philosophy and culture.* Honolulu: University of Hawaii Press, 1967. Pp. 86–117.

Untersteiner, M. *The sophists.* New York: Philosophical Library, 1954.

# CHAPTER THREE

## The Beginnings:
## Lockean and Kantian Themes
## in European Psychology

A thesis of this book is that a running exchange between Lockean and Kantian themes in the image of mankind has permeated the history of psychology, which was to be resolved in the American schools as a victory on the side of Lockeanism (see Chapter 4). In this chapter we begin a documentation of this historical thesis, starting with a consideration of the intellectual climate that had developed in science before psychology's nineteenth-century legitimization in the universities and then carrying forward through the views of important figures in the founding of academic psychology. In a closing section we consider Sigmund Freud's attempted resolution of the same Lockean-Kantian theoretical issues.

### Before Psychology:
### The Scientific Heritage

Psychology as a formal scientific discipline is usually dated from some point in the latter half of the nineteenth century. The immensely influential historian Edwin G. Boring (1950) has succeeded in fixing the year 1879 as the year in which "the very first formal psychological laboratory in the world" was founded (pp. 323–324). Robert Watson's (1971) historical research would suggest that Wundt's lab—to which this refers—was not actually formalized at the University of Leipzig until later, possibly not until 1894 (p. 272). In basing the birthdate of experimental psychology on such administrative—even bureaucratic—decisions Boring had some justification. He was, after all, addressing himself to the literal place (physical plant) in which experimental research was to be conducted. We know that others (including William James here in America) conducted experiments of a psychological nature before 1879, even in university settings. But this did not mean quite the same thing as being legitimized by a university table of organization. So we can accept Boring's grounds for experimental or "laboratory" psychology, but unfortunately, due to his influence this date has been singled out as the birthdate of all psychology (or all "scientific" psychology). One can easily take issue with such a claim.

A newly formalized science does not arrive on the scene without having to adapt its conceptions to sciences that have already staked out proprietary rights. There are certain paradigmatic assumptions (Kuhn, 1970) made by the established sciences that must be conformed to if a fledgling discipline in the university setting hopes to be given its official stamp of creditation. Four tributaries joined at the confluence of scientific thinking predominant in the last quarter of the nineteenth century. We survey these four sources before going on to a detailed consideration of the origins of European psychology per se.

The Medical Model

Psychology purports to study the human being, and medicine has traditionally combined fundamental scientific questions with an interest in the total functioning of the human being. The "family of the sciences" rests on the assumption that there are more and less basic disciplines at work within the totality, one resting upon the other and in principle reducible one to the other. Parallels are easier to draw between medico-biological or physiological concepts and human behavior than between chemistry or physics and behavior, and indeed, many of the early figures in laboratory psychology were physicians (e.g., Fechner, J. Müller, Helmholtz, Hering, Wundt).

A basic constitutive emphasis is to be seen in the medical model, as in the humoral theory of Hippocrates who is often called the "father of medicine."[1] Blood, phlegm, black and yellow bile, all served to combine in various portions to make up a person's temperamental and disease proclivities. There was no teleology in such a conception, but Galen was in time to propose that certain "vital" animals spirits also intermingled with the ebb and flow of blood to

[1] As in Chapters 1 and 2, when names appear in Chapter 3 without life dates or concepts are given without specific book citations the reader can locate them in Table 1 (pp. 8–31). Historical figures not listed in Table 1 are given life dates in the text.

stimulate behavior in living creatures. This was seen as a reflection of God's intention, and Galen's immensely influential anatomical studies of lower animals were conducted as a supposed proof of the Divine Plan. We find, even today, that a tough-minded scientist is likely to accuse the teleologist of wishing to reintroduce vital spirits or vitalism back into science in his talk of intentionality or related final-cause conceptions.

Vesalius later wrote a purely empirical anatomy that used Galen's insights but without the theology. Building on Hippocrates' conception of harmony or homeostasis among bodily fluids (humors), Vesalius' medical model was an essentially mechanical conception of organ systems, structurally interlacing and working without the benefit of a directing vital spirit. Thanks to such nontelic description, Vesalius (as Galileo after him) fell from grace with Church officials and ended his days removed from basic scientific pursuits.

Harvey's discovery that the blood did not "flood and ebb" through the body as Galen had claimed—based on an even earlier analogy drawn by Egyptian physicians to the actions of the Nile River—further advanced the mechanical conception of bodily functioning. The heart acted as a pump, which automatically circulated blood through vessels to nourish the cells of the body. Viewing the bodily cell (or its constituent elements) as something akin to the atomic units (uncuttables) of Democritus or Lucretius was now easy. Little indivisible things entered into and constituted bigger things in all aspects of bodily anatomy and physical functioning. Thomas Sydenham then stripped the last vestige of Galenic religious dogma from medicine in what he called his empirical approach to medicine. Subsequent developments in the medical model incorporated the chemical elements of Lavoisier and others, and the microorganisms of Pasteur's work. Each of these conceptions can also be cast in the building-block or atomic substrate formulations of the classical medical model.

Natural Science

In Chapters 1 and 2 we outlined the rise of natural science, so there is no need to retrace these steps in the present context. Suffice to say that we find a comparable development in physics, astronomy, chemistry, and so on to the evolving extraspective, material-efficient cause models unfolding in medicine. Whether basic or applied, a scientist was increasingly thought of as one who searched for the underlying substrate of factors that went to make up (atoms) or hold together (gravity, chemical union, etc.) the world of palpable (observed) reality.

## Mathematics

Although we have already devoted space to a consideration of mathematics in Chapters 1 and 2, we should focus on this historical development in more detail. In doing so we refer to several leaders in the founding of natural science, because obviously mathematics has been taken to be a major ingredient of the scientific ideology.

Recall that Pythagoras adapted a Heraclitian logos-conception of number to the universe, concluding thereby that things are numbers. Based on this assumption of nature as consisting of numbers, Democritus could then suggest that the flow of events was determinately fixed. This tendency to confound a formal cause (mathematics) and an efficient cause (the push of determinate events over time) is a recurring item in the history of thought (see Chapter 1, pp. 41–43, for a somewhat different reflection of this same question). Euclid's axioms have also been thought of as mechanical or efficient causes, particularly because Archimedes was able to put such principles into reality via his law of the lever and concept of body density. If numbers are things, axioms and mathematical laws are the even more refined things of which numbers themselves are constituted. When Ptolemy effectively applied mathematics to the world of experience in his (since discredited) geocentric universe conception, he made the Pythagorean dream a reality.

Roger Bacon's efforts were directed at combining mathematical certainty with the certainty of research experimentation. Bacon was more the advocate of empirical and mathematical study than he was an actual practicing scientist in the sense of propounding researched knowledge *per se*. He helped identify mathematics and research procedures as related aspects of science. Of course not all of the mathematicians of history were enamored with literal experimentation—and *vice versa*! Galileo believed research evidence necessary only when two lines of mathematical reasoning could not solve the problem facing a scientist. Newton's view was the opposite. Even so, there has been a coalescing of roles so that the dream of a perfectly mathematized empirically proven world of reality has been one of the major assumptions of classical experimental science since the time of Roger Bacon.

Burtt (1955, p. 53) has noted that Copernicus owed much to the rebirth of Pythagorean mathematical philosophy engendered by

Roger Bacon, Leonardo da Vinci, Nicholas of Cusa, Bruno, and others in the later Medieval period. Though he reformulated Ptolemaic theory in his heliocentric conception of the universe, Copernicus' victory was still won in the realm of mathematical proof. That is, he did nothing to weaken the grip a mathematized world view had on the imaginations of the budding natural scientists of the seventeenth century. The work of Galileo and Kepler also served to wed the conceptions of mathematics to nature. Descartes frequently put the evidence of mathematical proofs on the side of innate ideas (inspired by God's creation), feeling as he did that this ability to reason abstractly is what distinguishes the higher organisms (humans with spirits) from the lower organisms (animals without spirits) in nature. Newtonian physics construed nature as a mathematized regularity by way of Cartesian geometry. In addition to his purely chemical researches, Antoine Lavoisier next devised a mechanical apparatus for measuring linear and cubical expansions; and before long his friend Pierre Simon Laplace (1749–1827) was speaking exuberantly of the universe as a kind of immense clock, wound to a preset rate of movement, in which "a superhuman intelligence acquainted with the position and motions of atoms at any moment could predict the whole course of future events" (*ibid.*, p. 96).

A major mathematical event of the nineteenth century occurred when James Clerk Maxwell (1831–1879) wrote the mathematical formulae for Michael Faraday's epic experimental achievement of turning magnetism into electricity. Not only stars but the physical phenomena of magnetism and electricity could now be seen to obey mathematical "laws." The role of one "force" on another was effectively thought of as comparable to the impact of the independent variable upon the dependent variable following Dirichlet's refinement of the Leibnitzian function construct. Mathematical certitude was taken to be "in" nature, so that Henri Poincaré could state that in natural science mathematical laws represent the sole objective reality.

## Evolution

The final source of influence in the nineteenth century stemmed from the concept of an evolution in nature. It is easy today to think of evolution as a development or forward progression of events. But this idea of a rising progression did not come easily in the history of thought (see Becker & Barnes, 1952). The early Greeks, for example, believed that they had descended from a Golden Age of demigods and heroic figures, and the theological views of a Garden of Eden or a fall of divine powers (Origen) were also not conducive to the picture of an evolutionary advance. Gradually over the ages a dawning of the idea of progress developed, to parallel the advances in scientific and mathematical thought we have already discussed. The distinction Descartes drew between the lower and the higher forms of animal life sounded an early note for an ordering of nature. Giovanni Battista Vico proposed one of the earliest theories of evolution, suggesting that mankind moves through the ages of gods, to heroes, and thence to man—a sequence that is still more or less at the heart of modern theories of social development.

The march of civilization bears the implication of a directed movement, and one of the recurring issues we see raised in discussions of evolution is whether this movement through stages is teleological. Much of the zeal and optimism expressed by the founders of science as to the predictability of events stemmed from their assumption of a perfect order which had been put to design and operation by a Perfect Being. Even when the rationalistic theologian, Joseph Butler, tried to base an ethics on reason rather than exclusively on revelation (in contradistinction to Ockham) the arguments he advanced rested on a conception of man's "higher nature." Man's behaviors were cast in a hierarchical frame, with his impulses and passions at the base and his self-concerns above these, arching ever upward to the highest levels where altruism and conscience were said to rest at the apex of a kind of triangular hierarchy.

Of course not everyone thought of such hierarchies as fundamentally telic. Basing his view of the organism on a Lockean habit conception, Julien Offray de La Mettrie argued that Descartes' distinction between lower and higher organisms was untenable. All behavior is mechanically habituated, and the human being is simply a more complex machine than the subhuman animal. Though such formulations disparaged theological conceptions of free will, the view of organisms as developing from less to more complex mechanical structures, including higher-order reasoning capabilities, was consonant with the idea of evolutionary advance. A growing complexity need not be intelligently aimed to improve from the outset. Fortuitous complexity could, after all, simply "happen" serendipitously.

By the close of the eighteenth century evolutionary concepts were taking rather firm hold in Western thought. Georg Wilhelm Hegel's theory was telic, suggesting that a God was coming to consciousness across dialectical steps in the march of historical events. August Comte took a Vico-like view of history, suggesting that human societies typically move through the three stages of theology, metaphysics, and thence to a "positive" stage of science. The emphasis here was clearly on advance, improvement, and the rising of culture to greater fulfilment under the aegis of empirical science.

The nineteenth-century theory was to crystalize all earlier fumblings into a grand scheme of *physical* evolution, brilliantly uniting the medical model and the budding conceptions of modern natural science as it did so. We refer of course to the theory of organic evolution proposed by Charles Darwin and variations on this theme proffered by Jean Baptiste de Lamarck (1744–1829). The impact of Darwinian thinking on the closing decades of the nineteenth century cannot be overstated—and we mean here on *all* aspects of human knowledge. But its reflections in psychology are striking. Darwin began his studies with some personal inclination towards a telic account of nature, but of course he ended with a decided nontelic or natural-selection view of organic development. He also made use of Herbert Spencer's conception of survival of the fittest which could explain how improvements in animal or plant life might take place without intention or planning. The species that survived weather and the attack of predators could thereby live and multiply. Weaker species must ever succumb to the ravages of the elements and predators. The net effect is an unplanned progression, an improvement in the totality of nature which itself moves blindly. The biogenetic law proposed by Ernst Heinrich Haeckel was also brought into evolutionary theory, suggesting a kind of natural reenactment of evolution by organisms developing *in utero*. The phrase "Ontogeny recapitulates phylogeny" was to capture the imagination of scientists in the closing decades of the nineteenth century.

## The Tie That Binds

Is there any tie binding these four root influences on the thinking of an aspiring scientist in the last third of the nineteenth century? Quite obviously they all are easily subsumed by a Lockean conceptualization, stressing as they do the constitutive nature of things. The medical model has cells adding up to larger tissues and bone structures, and beneath this cellular integration level it presumes even more refined chemical and mineral constituents. Though stemming primarily from mathematical calculations, the structure of Newtonian physics is similarly Lockean in conception. As this theory of reality was developed, an image of atomic structures, wound into the very fabric of physical reality, pushed events along according to a Laplacian determinateness. The ultimate source of all things was thus energic, and the core of this energy was to be found in the substrate of atomic structure. The "language of science" (mathematics) was spoken in exclusively demonstrative tongues. This unidirectional style of meaning-extension was also true of evolutionary theory, as a kind of multiplication of lower organisms into higher organisms. Of course one does not claim that a fish "times" a bird "added to" a monkey "makes" a man. But the unidirectional trend line of calculation and constitution from lower to higher organism is clearly in line with the Lockean formulations of our other three sources of influence. And, indeed, we cannot deny that Darwinian biology (eugenics, selection probabilities, etc.) rests on a completely statistical account of transmission and change.

These influences were all conceptualized extraspectively. Science was based exclusively on extraspective theory before the advent of psychology. To the extent that an aspiring scientist of the period considered himself in the mainstream of scientific thought he would be formulating his conceptions in third-person terms. He would hope, if not to work directly with some form of (brass) instrumentation giving immediate evidence of the phenomenon of interest, at least to be able to submit his scientific data to statistical test. In line with the extraspective premise, he would also hope to deal with something palpable—a physical substance that might be dissected, analyzed, or entered into various relationships with other substances leading to clearly discernible outcomes or effects. If he could not work on a "more complex" animal, there was always the opportunity of dealing with "less complex" animals. This strategy was furthered by the Darwinian-Lockean implication that studying simpler organisms was a good first step to the understanding of the more complex organism. This tactic was the reverse of reductive explanation and therefore quite in line with good scientific procedure.

Probably the most comforting aspect of all of this was that, as our well-trained scientist of the late nineteenth century moved about the halls of a first-ranked university, he could expect a *uniformity* in presentation across his classroom lectures and textbook readings. Though the study material changed—from anatomy to mathematics to physics—the model subsuming these various disciplines did not! In time there would be a change taking place in the budding physical theories of Mach, Hertz, Duhem, and eventually Einstein, Bohr, and others (Cassirer, 1950, Ch. 5), but these more Kantian styles of explanation had not yet made their impact on natural science. Psychology emerged at the height of extraspective Newtonian-Lockeanism, and as we now attempt to show, came up against those age-old *intro-spective* and *telic* problems of mind or spirit which had been successfully dropped from this style of explanation. This resulted in a body-mind (-spirit, -soul) confrontation that has to the present day never been satisfactorily conceptualized much less resolved, though it has surfaced regularly under many guises over psychology's brief history. What is not properly grasped in this confrontation is that it is fundamentally a Lockean-Kantian paradigmatic clash!

## European Psychological Science

Gustav Theodor Fechner

If we were to name a "father" of experimental psychology based on the design of experimental research instruments (so-called methods) rather than on the founding of a recognized laboratory, Gustav Theodor Fechner (1801–1887) would in all likelihood be our first choice. After an early career in physics, in which he earned a reputation for his work on the quantitative measurement of direct electrical current (Ohm's law was reported in 1826), Fechner turned his attention to the study of consciousness. He was a daring thinker, who believed that mind and matter are merely two ways of speaking about the same thing hence to suggest a mental life for animals or even plants was not a foolish speculation in Fechner's scientific outlook. The problem was one of technique—that is, how can we measure something like the mind scientifically? Ernst Heinrich Weber (1795–1878) had earlier suggested that the perception of a change or a "just noticeable difference" in any stimulus is dependent upon the relationship of this change to the intensity of the stimulation. Adding one candle to two is easily noted, but more than one candle is required to see a change in brightness when a dozen candles are already lighted.

Fechner was to work out a precise mathematical statement of this phenomenon—today often called the Weber-Fechner Law (see Boring, 1950, pp. 287–288)—and he went on from there to devise the psychophysical methods. These experimental devices (average error, constant stimuli, etc.) were his way of proving that mind could be subject to empirical study with as much precision as matter. Fechner considered the mathematization of Weber's speculations and experimental proof in its support (which we now know holds only for a narrow range of stimulation) as sufficient justification that a mind *and* body sphere of experience was true of human behavior. One side (matter, body) worked according to absolute units of energy, but the other side (mind) did not. The mental recognition of a difference is thus *not* one-to-one with the physical stimulus change, but bears a relativistic or ratio function.

According to Boring, Fechner's clearly humanistic interests in founding a "psycho (mind)-physics (body)" area of study were prompted by the fact that he suffered through a period of physical and mental illness (*ibid.*, pp. 275–283). Yet even before his breakdown Fechner delighted in poking fun at the medical model in his satirical writings, under the *nom de plume* of Dr. Mises. Fechner's style is clearly Kantian. We see this in his distinction between inner and outer psychophysics. The question arose: Did the Weber-Fechner ratio hold between a stimulus value in the environment and the raw sensations in the body (outer psychophysics), or did it hold between these bodily sensations and the mind (inner psychophysics)? A Kantian would of necessity take the inner-psychophysics position because of his belief that the sensations entering from the environment were organized according to space-time considerations and then brought into conceptual meaningfulness by the categories of the understanding. Fechner left no doubt that he favored the theory of an *inner* psychophysics, developing arguments to suggest that human beings have a limen of *consciousness* (mentality) rather than a limen of sensory excitation (submentality). Fechner liked to point to the example of dreaming, where there are surely sensations taking place but the dreamer's limen of consciousness has been crossed.

It is prophetic that Fechner should be given historic notice for his experimental techniques even as his teleological theories have been dismissed as misguided spiritual aspirations brought on by mental illness. Invariably experimental designs aimed at validating humanistic theories are subsumed by mechanistic accounts of what supposedly took place in the experimental apparatus (see especially Chapters 4, 5, and 6). Also, each time a theorist has dared to employ final-cause description he has left himself open to the *ad hominem* form of counter which Boring uses in relation to Fechner's telic interests. Obviously, so long as proper techniques are designed to test a humanistic hypothesis, where a theorist's interest springs from in the formulation of this hypothesis makes no difference. Theistic interests are no more suspect than nontheistic interests. But the modern humanist can take heart in the fact that the man who is probably more deserving of the title "father of experimental psychology" than any other was an indominable teleologist, relying on the tactics of a Kantian model to make his case.

## Bell versus Müller

The first notable Lockean-Kantian confrontation having implications for an experimental psychology took place even before Fechner's work. In 1791 Luigi Galvani (1737–1798) had proven that nerves were conductors of electrical impulses. In 1811 Sir Charles Bell (1774–1842)—and Magendie in 1822—proved anatomically the dorsal-ventral arrangement of the sensory-motor nerves. This specialization of nerves according to function is also to be seen in the doctrine of specific nerve energies, which Johannes Peter Müller (1801–1855) subsequently proposed, suggesting that not the mode of stimulation but the particular nerve stimulated accounts for the type of sensation a given sensory receptor conveys. Though we have similar anatomical and experimental "facts" cited here about the body's nerve structures, the way in which Bell and Müller theoretically explained these valid findings differed significantly.

As a Lockean, Bell took the position that a person's mental knowledge is the product of dorsal-route sensory inputs, going electrically up nervous pathways to the brain where they are stored as (efficiently-caused) effects to be used in ventral route outputs at the proper times. As Bell said: "All ideas originate in the brain: the operation of producing them is the remote effect of an agitation or impression on the extremities of the nerves of sense" (Boring, 1950, p. 86). Müller, however, held that: "External agencies can give rise to no kind of sensation which can not also be produced by internal causes, exciting changes in the condition of our nerves" (ibid.). This is essentially what Fechner meant by inner psychophysics. Müller also noted that the mind has a direct influence on sensation, imparting intensity to sensory receptors by way of focusing attention on one or another. His model is Kantian, in opposition to the Lockean formulations of Bell.

## Helmholtz versus Hering

Our next decidedly Lockean-Kantian confrontation in the rise of psychological science was between Hermann von Helmholtz (1821–1894) and Ewald Hering (1834–1918). Helmholtz was educated as a physician but achieved his major reputation as a physicist, an interest he pursued after leaving medical school. His feat of timing the electrical nerve impulse extended the Galvani-Bell-Magendie line of theory. Helmholtz also helped further the constancy principle (first proposed by the physician, Robert Mayer, in 1842) as a style of explanation in physics. This principle held that there is a tendency for energies in a closed system to redistribute themselves (conservation of energy), and hence this force of redistribution could account in an efficient-cause sense for the observed behavior of natural objects. We can see in the following quote from Helmholtz a tendency both to do what Newton found distasteful—that is, reify mathematics into a concept of "force in things" (see Chapter 1, p. 48)—and also to put such forces forward as necessary reductive steps in all physical explanations:

The appointed . . . task of physics is thus to refer natural phenomena to unchangeable attractive and repulsive forces, whose intensity depends upon distance.[2] . . . The work of science will have been completed only when phenomena have been traced back to the simple forces, and when it can be shown also that the given account is the only possible one admitted by the phenomena. Then this would have been proven to be the necessary way of interpreting nature, and it would be the one to which objective truth should be ascribed (Cassirer, 1950, p. 86).

This reductive (and realistic) theory of scientific explanation is completely Lockean in spirit. An energic redistribution of forces amounts to a blind determinism of efficient causes. A role for mental conceptualization (pro forma) drops out of such scientific theories in principle, because a mental conception would itself represent a kind of "mobilization of forces" blindly uniting into an idea-unit that has flowed into mind rather than been pressed onto awareness by mind. Of course no possibility for dialectical reasoning would exist on this exclusively demonstrative model. Arguing in a decidedly nondialectical fashion, Helmholtz can say in his famous paper on physiological optics:

[2] This Newtonian translation of mathematical space into physical reality provided the rationale for "associationistic" principles of learning in psychology. The widely heralded Principle of Contiguity was therefore not simply "discovered" in laboratory settings. It was taken as a paradigmatic assumption based on analogy to the Newtonian principle of gravity! That is, the closer two idea inputs are together "in mind" and the more associatively "large" these congeries of inputs might be, the stronger is the associative bond between them. See Chapter 4 for a discussion of the frequency and contiguity theses in psychological theories.

My conclusion is, that *nothing in our sense-perceptions can be recognized as sensation which can be overcome in the perceptual image and converted into its opposite by factors that are not demonstrably due to experience. . . . Whatever, therefore can be overcome by factors of experience, we must consider as being itself the product of experience and training* (Helmholtz, 1961, p. 96).

If mind has an influence on itself by way of perceptual under- standing of events, the altering of a current perceptual image is pos- sible only because of former inputs (sensations), which now act as modifiers of ongoing sensation. This procedure followed a kind of unnamed logical premising that Helmholtz referred to as "uncon- scious conclusions" (*ibid.*, p. 83) or "inductive conclusions" (*ibid.*, p. 115) (also translated by Boring, 1950, p. 308, as "unconscious inference"). In the realm of vision these learned inputs were recorded as "local signs" which—through subsequent unconscious inference— provided the individual with grounds for depth perception and the like. Helmholtz was aware of the Lockean-Kantian questions in- volved, for during the decade of the 1860s in which he carried on his debate with Hering, he specifically mentioned the commitment his opponent had to Kantian theory (Helmholtz, 1961, p. 102). Helmholtz called his theory empirical because he supposedly did not go beyond the observed data, and he termed Hering's position "intuition theory" because it supposedly concocted undemonstrable hence unparsimoni- ous innate mechanisms to account for the data of perception (*ibid.*, p. 101).

Hering argued and presented evidence in support of the view that each retinal point has three innate "local signs," one for height, one for the right-to-left position and one for the depth of the visual field. In consonance with Kant he placed a formal-cause notion into the mind structure from the outset of life, claiming that sensation is organized in this fashion without the benefit of input learning. Prac- tice or experience perfects this capacity to see depth and so on, but it does not *cause* it in an efficient-cause sense to come about initially (Boring, 1950, p. 353). Hering's theoretical strategy of bringing a fixed frame to bear in ordering perception is the root of all subsequent phenomenological theories in psychology (gestalt, existential, etc.), although the topics of interest have shifted from vision to cognitive questions of how human beings come to know anything. Helmholtz (1961) admitted that his differences with Hering could not at that time be resolved through experimentation (p. 102), but he implied that systematic data collections would in time clarify things one way or the other. We shall have occasion to question the soundness of this (unconscious or otherwise) inference in the later chapters of this volume.

## Wundt and Brentano

We come now to a more mixed-model form of confrontation, in which the protagonists are not so easily aligned as strictly Kantian or Lockean in theoretical outlook. Because it is the most frequently cited confrontation of psychology's history we will go into it in some detail. One of these men finished a major work of his with the following statement:

And this accords with the fundamental character of mental life, which I would have you always bear in mind. It does not consist in the connexion of unalterable objects and varying conditions: in all its phases it [mental life] is *process*; and *active*, not a passive, existence; *development*, not stagnation. The understanding of the basal laws of this development is the final goal of psychology.

If we were to have as multiple choice identifications of this quote Wilhelm Wundt (1832–1920) or Franz Brentano (1838–1917), most psychologists today—having accepted Boring's (1950, p. 385) opposition of Act to Content Psychology—would probably choose Brentano. Yet these lines are the closing statement of Wundt's *Lectures on Human and Animal Psychology* (1907, p. 454).

Wundt's portrayal by Boring (1950) as the father of experimental psychology is not always consonant with statements we read in Wundt's actual writings. For example, Boring claimed that Wundt's view of method held that we must (1) analyze consciousness into elements, (2) determine the manner of connection of these elements, and (3) determine the laws of these connections.

The goal of psychology is the analysis of mind into simple qualities and the determination of the form of their ordered multiplicity. The method, Wundt thought, is adequate to the problem except in the case of the higher processes, where analysis fails and we are reduced to the comparative observation of social phenomena, as when we use the study of language as the key to the psychology of thought (*ibid.*, p. 333).

Wundt (1961) did indeed call for the study of "national units as wholes" (p. 69) through the use of statistics. In fact he seems clearly to have *preferred* such study (*völkerpsychologie*) to physiological experimentation, which he called a "second tool" (p. 70), and not a totally effective one at that. To say, as Boring (1950) does, that

"Wundt fixed the notion of elementism upon psychology" (p. 333) is perplexing when we read again and again in Wundt of the *impossibility* of reducing mind to body and of the many problems involved in such elementary self-analysis in any case. For example, in 1862 Wundt (1961) said:

The psychology based on self-observation, which preferred to designate itself *empirical* [i.e., Brentano's] psychology, must therefore limit itself to an unsystematic juxtaposition of the facts of the consciousness; and, since it is unable to discover an inner connection between these facts, it splits up those components which belong together into a large number of dissociated details (pp. 57–58).

Later, after he had come to define introspection as "internal perception" (Wundt, 1907, p. 245) in which the individual confronts mind (as consciousness) *directly*, Wundt was never convinced that all of the reasons for behavior could be discovered in this way. For one thing, ideas are never completely unique. Ultimately our ideas are subject to cultural influence, and one must therefore look to this supraindividual source for the meanings that enter into behavior (the culture was termed a "collective will"). But even more fundamentally, there was a serious flaw in the method of introspection *per se* (*ibid.*, 1961, p. 427). Introspection permits us to look "at" consciousness, and, if properly trained, we can delineate our emotional and ideational perceptions through this procedure. As such, we can offer scientific accounts of our sensory apparatus in efficient-cause terms (Wundt called these "natural" causes). But when it comes to a complete accounting of behavior as volition or will, introspection must *fail*:

The motives which determine the will are parts of the universal chain of natural causation [i.e., efficient causes]. Nevertheless, the personal character, which alone can constitute volition, cannot be assigned a place in this causal nexus. We cannot therefore decide immediately and empirically that personality in its inmost nature, the source and origin of every difference that exists between individuals and between communities, is itself subject to natural causality (Wundt, 1907, p. 434).

We see reflected in this quote both Wundt's reluctance to reduce character to efficient causes (he claimed that ultimately, personality "is always a riddle," *ibid.*, p. 433) and his acceptance of traditional science which forced him to admit *in principle* that the root source of all behavior is in the efficient causes of nature. Thus an elementism can be inferred in his approach, as it can in all Lockean constitutive models. Yet Wundt believed that reducing mind to body would imply some quasi-material substance that acted like mind yet could never be conceived of in a truly mental fashion:

We conclude, then, that the assumption of a mental substance different from the various manifestations of mental life [as directly perceived internally] involves the unjustifiable transference of a mode of thought necessary for the investigation of external nature to a sphere in which it is wholly inapplicable; it implies a kind of unconscious materialism. . . . What can this "substance" do for us, a substance devoid of will, of feeling, and of thought, and having no part in the constitution of our personality (ibid., p. 453)?

So here we have the generally acknowledged "father of experimental psychology" casting doubts on both efficient (natural) and material (substance) causation as proper descriptive terms for mind. Wundt was in time to be rejected as "mentalistic" by the behavioristic psychologists of this century. He proved an outspoken critic of the "anglo-American utilitarianism and materialism" of his time (Wundt, 1973, p. 17). How is it, then, that we can so readily view him today as an apostle of tough-minded nontelic psychology? Because in his *basic technical position* Wundt fell back on the Lockean models by accepting the "going" definitions of scientific description, statistics, and especially the Darwinian evolutionary models as major heuristic devices. He was influenced by Helmholtz at one point. And we cannot forget the role of Titchener, Wundt's student, who probably did more than any other person aside from Boring (who was Titchener's student) to bring out these fundamentally Lockean themes in Wundt's thought as if they were the only ones held to by the founder of our first psychological laboratory.

The record is gradually being corrected, thanks not in the least to Wundt's son (see Max Wundt, 1944) as well as to some excellent efforts on the part of others (e.g., Blumenthal, 1975; Mischel, 1970). Sometimes Wundt is made out to be almost Kantian in theoretical predilection, which is apparently the course his school took after the Americans had left Leipzig to establish shop in America (see especially Blumenthal, 1975). The position taken in the present analysis is that Wundt was a mixed-model theorist who, for certain technical reasons when he put on his psychologist's cap (i.e., walked across the hall from his philosophical duties), construed experimental research in a way that cemented him to natural science as framed by British Empiricism although as a theoretician he was unhappy with associationistic and mechanistic formulations. This rigorous methodological side to Wundt was the side that Titchener elevated and translated into a supposed Wundtian theoretical outlook for Boring to write into the history books (see Mischel, 1970).

Brentano was not a simple or uncritical Kantian theorist. He owed his greatest inspiration to Aristotle and was critical of Kantian philosophy per se (Brentano, 1973, pp. 10–11). Yet there is little doubt but that his fundamental technical stance, and the outlook his famous students Carl Stumpf and Edmund Husserl took from him, was Kantian (in the sense that we have been using this term). Rancurello (1968) notes that Brentano's psychology is fundamentally nativistic (p. 55)—on the order of Hering's view—for he accepted the position that our sensations are by nature spatially organized (a Kantian theme). And who would doubt that Husserl's phenomenology is but a further development of Brentano's Kantian-model concepts of mental life?

Wundt and Brentano both believed in the immediacy of a reality "in mind," making psychology a somewhat different kind of science than the other sciences. Brentano said that sciences like physics must deal with experience indirectly, employing as "data" items that take on indirect significance only as they stimulate and hence cause certain reactions in human beings. Thus color exists only because a perceiving subject reports such an awareness to the physicist. In his early theorizing Brentano insisted that the color experience was real, although it existed as an "object" only in the mental cogitations of the person who was having this color-sensation at the moment (called intentional in-existence). Actually, any object in experience bears this kind of reality, as something "immanently objective" or, in other words, something that actually existed only in the mental act (called a presentation) (Brentano, 1973, pp. 19–20).

Brentano was therefore contending that physical science must deal with assumed realities, because these realities were supposedly in the noumena (i.e., free of mind per se), yet all the physicist has to go on in his work is the phenomenological data reported by a person. Psychology, however, works exclusively at the level of phenomena, meaning it acquires as its subject matter directly relevant data! Mental acts do not stand for anything else, as the phenomenal must stand for the noumenal in physics. Though he intially felt it necessary to insist on the reality (in mental substance) of the "point" of a mental idea (called the terminus or that to which the subjective idea relates as an object), by 1911 Brentano had dropped this realistic position as when he noted: ". . . the thinker is the only object [whose existence is] demanded by the psychical act. The terminus [object] of the so-called relation does not have to be given in reality" (Rancurello, 1968, p. 18).

To call Wundt an evolutionary theorist would not be incorrect. He used this form of theoretical explanation to say that language developed from primitive gestures (Wundt, 1973, p. 148), reflexes were habitual repetitions retained by evolving organisms (ibid., p. 227), emotions were evolutionary remnants of feelings (ibid., p. 387), impulses were developmental precursors of voluntary acts (ibid., p. 423), and mind evolved in parallel fashion to the body from simple associations to a highly complex consciousness (ibid., p. 366, p. 443, p. 451, and p. 454). In drawing out the latter theory, Wundt said that originally man was unaware of himself as a thinking organism. His thought lacked self-reflexivity at an early evolutionary stage, so that man's ideas were taken literally as an object existing in reality much as anything else literally exists (Titchener, 1972, p. 100). The idea was not referential but taken itself as an actuality. As man evolved to a higher stage he gradually became aware of the fact that his ideas were referential (i.e., they made reference to something else), and these latter contents were not therefore necessarily an actuality. This means, of course, that the external reality (say, a given color hue, as measured by objective instruments) and the internal idea of this reality (the actual color hue sensed) need not be entirely in accord. Titchener said this disparity was at the root of the so-called stimulus error. To confuse the object as seen "out there" with the experience actually had "in here" is to commit the stimulus error.

At this point Wundt put forward arguments reminiscent of Brentano. Not only must the physicist himself conceptualize in order to know objective reality, but he must of necessity rely on the indirect evidence proffered by other people about this or that item of information. The psychologist, however, can turn his gaze inward and, through internal perception or introspection, gaze directly at the idea as a process and a content (Wundt, 1907, p. 245). The idea is a content in the sense that it makes reference to some form of perceived referent (a tree, a color, etc.). Though mind is parallel to body, Wundt believed that every idea that occurs to us has, at some level, a connection to the physical realm by way of sensation (ibid., p. 445). This assumption of a mind paralleling the body by way of sensory contact was to provide the introspectionist with a justification for the study of two-point thresholds in touch, visual color differences, and so forth. One side (mind) essentially "tracked" the other's (body) actions (psychophysical parallelism). Titchener and Boring referred to the contentual findings of introspection (internal perception) as the elements of Wundt's so-called content psychology. This is a questionable one-sided interpretation of Wundtian psychology.

However, the basic view Wundt took of scientific explanation probably ensured that something like a reductive content psychology would flow from his laboratory in time. The most celebrated example here is his dispute with Brentano's student, Carl Stumpf (1848–1936). Wundt's students had found what they took to be evidence that melodies were actually constituted of elemental sounds, so that a tune was the product or combination of these substrate "contents" of sound. Stumpf pointed out that certain of these so-called scientific findings contradicted what a trained musician's ear would find important to the melody (Boring, 1950, p. 365). Stumpf therefore rejected these findings as simply not reflective of what the musical experience actually entailed. A heated debate with Wundt followed, in which Stumpf argued in the Kantian vein for the total experience and Wundt argued stoically for the "reductionistic" findings of his laboratory students. Two of Stumpf's students were Köhler and Koffka, cofounders along with Wertheimer of the gestalt psychology approach (see Chapter 4). This exchange over the nature of melody can be thought of as a bona fide manifestation of the Lockean-Kantian confrontation.

Though Wundt and Brentano began from a point of agreement on the direct nature of psychological investigation, they ended in a decidedly different psychological account of what was to be seen there. In the interpretation of the facts to be gleaned from the method of psychology we can find our classic difference in outlook taking hold. Wundt drew a firm distinction between the realms of science (pursuit of observed facts) and the philosophical examination of basic tenets (as used by the scientist in beginning his quest or as found by him empirically). Wundt admitted that his acceptance of a psychophysical parallelism created conceptual problems. How are we to think of these two realms relating to each other? Though he thought this was a worthwhile question that required an answer, Wundt did not feel it was one that the psychologist need worry himself over (Wundt, 1907, pp. 450–451). So long as the psychologist in *fact* found a mind-body dualism in human behavior he must proceed on the basis of such observations without concern (just as he must accept evidence that contradicts the practices of musicians in his study of the melody). It was the philosopher who must confront the subtle implications of a psychophysical parallelism! Far from demeaning such philosophical examinations, Wundt believed they were essential to the advance of psychological science because they complemented the work of empirical investigation. In a sense the empiricist led the way and reported the findings that in time the philosopher helped to clarify. But it would be dangerous to confound these two roles.

Brentano was more ready to consider such inscrutable questions, philosophical assumptions, points of view, and so on as the direct province of *psychological* investigation. He had even planned to take up the question of immortality in his formal psychological work (Brentano, 1973, p. 26). One can see Brentano framing a role for such quasi-philosophical study in his distinction between *genetic* and *descriptive* psychology (*ibid.*, pp. 28–29). Genetic psychology is psychophysical; it can take evolutionary themes into consideration, accrue inductive data, and submit such explicit findings to mathematical formulation and test. Descriptive psychology is *not* inductive but seeks to find those abstract presumptions and outlooks of a more deductive nature which cannot be observed or tested with mathematical precision. Indeed mathematics itself rests on such assumptions (axioms, basic concepts). Wundt would find the examination of these and similar world-assumptions in the province of logic and philosophy. Wundt was major professor to 70 doctoral students in philosophy as well as to 116 doctoral students in psychology (Watson, 1971, p. 277). He also *opposed* the tendency, which so many of his American psychology students favored, of removing themselves from Departments of Philosophy to found separate Departments of Psychology (*ibid.*, p. 273). Clearly his concept of the human sciences included equal and cooperative status for psychology and philosophy.

This divergence in professional-role definitions can be seen influencing how Wundt and Brentano talked about *introspection* (Wundt's term) or *inner perception* (Brentano's term). Looked at simply and overtly, both proponents seemed to be doing something alike in that they focused on the sensations and perceptions of mind directly. But the interpretation of what was going on here differed dramatically. For Wundt (1907), introspection was a strictly controlled experimental procedure of "internal perception" (p. 245) in which one presumed that a trained person could observe the functioning of mind (including such things as the awareness of color, the emotional reactions to stimuli, etc.). The steps of this method were taken as replicable and as sensitive to the nuances of changing sensation as was the measurement procedure employed by a physicist (Watson, 1971, p. 269). The only difference is that the introspectionist looks "in here" rather than "out there." Brentano (1973) accurately called Wundt's approach "inner observation" (p. 29) because it seemed to be transferring the empirical attitude of the physicist inwardly.

One of the characteristics of [Brentano's] inner perception is that it can never become [Wundt's] inner observation. We can observe objects which, as they say, are perceived externally. In observation, we direct our full attention to a phenomenon in order to apprehend it accurately. But with objects of inner perception this is absolutely impossible. This is especially clear with regard to certain mental phenomena such as anger. If someone is in a state in which he wants to observe his own anger raging within him, the anger must already be somewhat diminished, and so his original object of observation would have disappeared. The same impossibility is also present in all other cases. It is a universally valid psychological law that we can never focus our *attention* upon the object of inner perception (*ibid.*, pp. 29–30).

To account for internal study Brentano suggested that every mental act is dual, having some object external to it as referent for a primary consciousness, but also a *secondary* act of consciousness in which there is an awareness of itself (*ibid.*, p. 153). Hence, ". . . every mental act, no matter how simple, has a double object, a primary and a secondary object. The simplest act, for example the act of hearing, has as its primary object the sound, and for its secondary object, itself, the mental phenomenon in which the sound is heard" (*ibid.*, pp. 153–154). The upshot here is that every idea is itself a self-presentation, an act of cognition which can be perceived via this secondary act of perception. Brentano rejected unconscious mental acts on the grounds that this would demand a *nonrelation* between an idea and its referent—something that is impossible on the face of things! This is not the same interpretation of the unconscious the Freudians were later to use. Brentano believed that every idea *must* include its terminus, or referent (that to which it meaningfully points). To be conscious therefore meant to be "conscious of something else." Secondary acts of consciousness thus had as their terminus the primary ideas (e.g., seeing items in the environment, having hopes for the future, feeling an emotion, etc.).

Lacking this two-pronged view of internal study, Wundt's method (introspection) amounted to a turning inward of the physical-science approach. As Wundt (1961) suggested in 1862: "As soon as the psyche is viewed as a natural phenomenon and psychology as a natural science, the experimental methods must also be capable of full application to this science" (p. 70). Now, when we turn the natural science approach inward, drawing a direct analogy between the approach dedicated to extraspective study and the approach dedicated to "internal" study, what is likely to happen? Our internal theoretical account will probably be cast in extraspective terms. And this is what actually happened. Though it rests on a so-called introspection, *Wundtian psychology is extraspective in its theoretical account!* Brentano's psychology, however, takes on a more introspective formulation, because he is constantly trying to speak about experience from the slant of the thinking feeling human being. He is "within mind" rather than "looking inward at mind" as introspection was wont to do. Invariably this resulted in a telic account, for Brentano's interest centers on how the person is "coming at life" (in his primary consciousness) rather than in how he is being moved about by the stimuli enervating his sensory apparatus "from without." This is why Brentano placed intentionality at the center of his psychology.

Wundt, who served as an assistant to Helmholtz at the University of Heidelberg, accepted the necessity of science to account for phenomena by reducing the descriptive account to a "simple force" (principle of constancy). Even in 1907, long after he had separated from Helmholtz's direct influence, Wundt could say this about acts of volition: ". . . in giving an account of the particular causes which determine volition, we shall only recognise as *determinate* motives those which give it a definite direction, and which act like simple forces, incapable of further analysis" (Wundt, 1907, p. 231). Indeed, because a force must of necessity act on something that is itself not a force in order to be recognized as such, Wundt's conception of adequate scientific description went beyond the Helmholtzian when he noted, "We must trace every change back to the only conceivable one in which an object remains identical: motion" (Cassirer, 1950, p. 88).

We can see the functioning of forces in the motions of substantial objects. For this reason Wundt did some of his earliest work on the temporal extent of ideation in thinking, bringing him into the "personal equation" phenomenon noted among astronomers (Wundt, 1961, p. 70). Mind takes time to work, because fundamentally it is moved along by efficient causation, even though to isolate "the" causes of behavior is very difficult (Wundt, 1907, p. 434). One can see Wundt making special efforts in his theorizing to bring the idea of a motion into his accounts. For example, an emotional expression was said to be a movement acting as a sign in primitive forms of communication (Wundt, 1973, p. 73), or the instinctive drive was said to act as a motion that propelled impulsive behavior (*ibid.*, p. 147). If he could bring his account down to a motion of some sort, Wundt presumed that he had rendered a full and satisfactory scientific description of events.

Undoubtedly this acceptance of reductive science prompted Wundt's students and interpreters to suggest that he wanted to reduce the mind (psyche) to the body (physical). Furthermore, Wundt's theory of mind simply failed to deal with the teleological issues that a mind construct always raises. He spoke of a parallelism and criticized simplistic efficient- and material-cause accounts of mind, but we do *not* find a satisfactory formal-final cause account issuing in his basic formulations. Wundt suggested that a voluntary action is one in which the "thought of the end to be realised accompanies or precedes it" (Wundt, 1907, p. 387). But this could involve impulsive actions as well, and emotional behaviors were for him *complex* impulsive actions. In fact a volitional act was said always to presuppose a *feeling* acting as antecedent to the behavior that flowed from it (*ibid.*, p. 229). Choice was said to be a complex volition (*ibid.*, p. 228), but there was no freedom of a will to contemplate these choices and select thereby a preferred alternative. The preferred alternative was fixed *first* in the sequence of behavior based on the feelings (emotions, instinctual drives) as follows:

Feeling is not independent of volition . . . impulse is not a process which can be distinguished from will, still less opposed to it; and desire is not the uniform antecedent of will, but rather a process which only appears in consciousness when some inhibition of voluntary activity prevents the realisation of volition proper (*ibid.*, p. 225).

One can see in these beginning theories of behavior a motivation-to-behavior sequence that will someday be formalized in the Lockean drive-to-stimulus-to-behavioral-response style of theorizing that ʌmerican learning theories were to adopt.[3] There is no way of conceptualizing a truly free choice on this efficient-cause model, because as Wundt observed in the quote cited above: "The motives which determine the will are parts of the universal chain of natural causation [i.e., efficient causes]" (Wundt, 1907, p. 434). Without a dialectical rationale Wundt, like all demonstrative thinkers of history, was forced to concede what Brentano (1973) felt he would be forced to

[3] Blumenthal (1975) places Wundt in the camp of the modern cognitivist or information-processing theorist. This may be correct; however, as discussed in Chapter 5, modern cognitive theory is *still* founded on a Lockean model.

concede—that is, the functioning of mind internally is precisely identical to the functioning of physical events externally (p. 49). Wundt found in his extraspective studies (his theoretical accounts of what he "did") a nontelic albeit highly complex mental machine. Phenomenologists since his time, beginning with Brentano and furthered greatly by the latter's student, Husserl, have tried to call attention to the particular assumptions the Wundtian introspective method makes. But each time the phenomenologist raises one of these most fundamental of all questions, the Lockean thinker in the Wundtian tradition (or is it Titchenerian?) cries, "Foul!" because such questions are for philosophers and not psychologists to answer.

Brentano saw mind as meaning-inducing in that typically Kantian sense—that is, similar to categories of the understanding infusing sensory input with a structure of meaning before anything external can be understood internally. His difficult concept of intentional inexistence gets at precisely this notion of one substance (mind) relating meanings outward to another totally different substance (physical reality) that lacks this conceptualizing facility. Mind is by nature referential, pointing through meaning-extension (ideas) to something (a terminus) other than itself (*ibid.*, p. 97). When it does so it gives this terminus immanent objectivity—that is, although one could not find the terminus of the idea "in reality" it can be located as truly existing "within mind." The existence is "in" mind, we might say, for mind-substance has this capacity intentionally to "inexist" (create extant referents by intending that they exist). As a nonconceptualizing substance that cannot process meanings in this fashion, the physical realm can never, even in *principle*, account for the mental realm. What this calls for then is a reintroduction of formal and final cause description at the level of mind, because the material and efficient causes of natural science's physical reality will *never* prove satisfactory. Brentano turns his back on the natural science which Wundt was only too ready to embrace.

Though more complex than earlier confrontations, the basic and unresolvable differences between Wundt and Brentano stemmed from their respective reliance or emphases on the Lockean and Kantian models.

Ebbinghaus versus G. E. Müller

Another manifestation of our historical confrontation took place in the contrasting ways in which Hermann Ebbinghaus (1850–1909) and G. E. Müller (1850–1934; no relation to Johannes Müller) studied the phenomenon of memory. Ebbinghaus initiated this study, single-handedly devising a method and using himself as subject (following the precedent of introspection here). In searching about for an experimental design to study memory—and in partial reaction to Wundt's belief that higher mental processes could not be brought into the laboratory—Ebbinghaus used as his prototype the method of "natural science," adding:

We all know of what this method consists: an attempt is made to keep constant the mass of conditions which have proven themselves causally connected with a certain result; one of these conditions is isolated from the rest and varied in a way that can be numerically described; then the accompanying change on the side of the effect is ascertained by measurement or computation (Ebbinghaus, 1964, p. 7).

The reference here to causal connection and the strategy of varying an antecedent to note its measurable effect on a consequent are entirely on the side of efficient causality. Equating mathematical (formal) causation with the independent-dependent (efficient-cause) variable sequence Ebbinghaus could next suggest: "A numerical determination of the interdependent changes of cause and effect appears indeed possible if only we can realise the necessary uniformity of the significant conditions in the repetition of our experiments" (*ibid.*, p. 11). A great stress was therefore put on the constancy of experimentation, with strict procedures that involved memorizing a string of (inappropriately named) meaningless nonsense syllables. These were assembled through random combination of a vowel flanked by two consonants, totaling roughly 2300 syllables that were employed in various lists and put to memory. Ebbinghaus laid great emphasis on the importance of a statistical test of the data that issued from his well-controlled procedures.

Every effort was made in the learning trials to avoid fitting nonsense syllables into some prearranged and familiar pattern: "There was no attempt to connect the nonsense syllables by the invention of special associations of the mnemotechnik type; learning was carried on solely by the influence of the mere repetitions upon the natural memory" (*ibid.*, p. 25). This requirement of the method ensured that statistical treatment of the data would be more clear-cut and compelling. All of the precautions taken by Ebbinghaus ensured that a frequency conception of memory, with its length and strength of retentive capacity, would follow statistical summative lines. As such, the methodology is shot through with Lockean presumptions and biases.

G. E. Müller began his theorizing on memory from a more introspective slant. Rather than adapting his theory of retention exclusively to third-person numerical counts and statistical distributions, he encouraged subjects to introspect after they had achieved learning criterion in order to suggest how it was that they had mastered the task (Watson, 1971, p. 298). Müller felt that Ebbinghaus had made the memorial process appear more mechanical than it actually was. By allowing his subjects to be interviewed in the learning process and to introspect (more in the Brentano sense than the Wundtian), he found that all kinds of already established patterns of meaning were brought to bear by the subjects to organize and hence retain their learning assignments. Subjects looked for meanings in the nonsense materials and *found* them; they fell back on rhyming procedures, used those personalized mnemonic tricks that Ebbinghaus was so careful to avoid in his own case, and so forth. Müller's theory of memory held that the principles of frequency and contiguity could not in themselves account for the nature of learning and memory. He took a decidedly Kantian approach, emphasizing the conceptualizing features the individual manifested in preference to the mechanical forces of repetition and reorganization after the input had been banked in memory.

## The Wurzburg School of Imageless Thought

From 1900 to approximately 1909 a series of studies was issued from the University of Wurzburg under the leadership of Oswald Külpe (1862–1915). This work has been referred to collectively as the Wurzburg School of Imageless Thought. Important students and collaborators in this work included Ach, Bühler, Marbe, Mayer, Orth and Watt. Külpe had studied under both G. E. Müller and Wundt, but he followed in the former's Kantian footsteps. In fact Külpe published a short volume, revised twice, on Immanuel Kant's thought, and he published philosophical works of his own dealing with the doctrine of categories. The Wurzburgers did not set out to be a school of "imageless thought." This title devolved on them because of their research findings.

Beginning with the premise of Brentano that it *was* possible—through a kind of secondary consciousness—to examine one's own thought processes, Külpe and his students began to study introspecting subjects. When we introspect in this self-reflexive fashion, subjective factors such as the flow of certain images in free thought begin to intrude themselves in our associations—a fact that Freud was also to find in working with therapeutic cases. Bakan (1954) has even suggested that one of the main reasons Külpe's finished system lacked a proper treatment of thought was that he and his associates balked at doing what Freud was prepared to do: overcome resistances and plunge into the deeper reaches of mind that come alive because of the kind of free associations upon which the Wurzburgers had stumbled.

What all of this highly personalized recollection by their subjects *did* suggest to the Wurzburgers was that memory was hardly quantitative. There were qualitative, and to that extent, nongeneralizable statements to be made about human memory when people were allowed to be themselves in a methodological procedure. Furthermore, Marbe was to find that subjects who are instructed to judge which of two weights is heavier did not require a *conscious*—analyzable—act of judgment to complete the experimental instruction. This conscious attitude was therefore imageless, and hence the title of the school was born. Watt was to name this conception of the upcoming task *aufgabe*, and the resulting unconscious (imageless) attitude to complete experimental requirements he called *einstellung* (set). Ach referred to this as a *determining tendency*, but all of these concepts come down to the same thing.

The theory is clearly akin to a Kantian category (formal cause) which in turn frames and lends meaning to the task that follows. For Watt, *aufgabe* meant "to behave for the sake of the intended task at hand"—it referred to the subject's *intention* as he came at the experimental procedure. Though Ach was not so clearly telic in his determining-tendency construct, the parallel is clearly there. There was much criticism of the rigor and objectivity of these researches, with Wundt directing the fusillade; but surely we cannot look back from today's perspective and fail to be cognizant of what theory-construction factors were *also* at play.

## Galton and Morgan

There is no clearer representative of British Empiricism and its Lockean theory than Sir Francis Galton (1822–1911). His psychological diletantism was characterized by a stress on the statistical investigation of large numbers of individuals. He had no particular theory of behavior to promote, although he did study mental imagery and association through so-called self report techniques. He was also greatly committed to evolutionary theory, due in part to the fact that he was a cousin of Charles Darwin (Watson, 1971, p. 311). He also relied heavily on hereditary transmission concepts so that he was an active proponent of all four of the Lockean precursors mentioned at the beginning of this chapter.

C. Lloyd Morgan (1852–1936) was also a prime advocate of Lockeanism, proposing a famous canon which is similar to Ockham's razor (Chapter 1, p. 12) in that it suggests: "In no case may we interpret an action as the outcome of the exercise of a higher physical faculty, if it can be interpreted as the outcome of the exercise of one which stands lower in the psychological scale" (Boring, 1950, p. 474). This canon meshed nicely with the Helmholtzian and Wundtian reductive conceptions of proper scientific description. It amounts to a denigration of all formal-final cause description in favor of material-efficient cause description. Morgan is usually cited in the history books for having explained the seemingly telic behavior of lower animals *without* relying on final causation. The opprobrious example in this regard is John Romanes (1848–1894) who, relying also on evolutionary theory, held that animals possessed in rudimentary form a self-directive capacity suggesting intelligence. His accounts of animal intelligence were highly anthropomorphized telic accounts, and Morgan's criticisms of this approach were widely disseminated among psychologists who had a commitment to natural science.

### Sigmund Freud and the Lockean-Kantian Models

During the nineteenth century the field of applied psychology or psychiatry like the academic centers was faced with problems concerning our historical models. Because he is probably more misunderstood on this question than most, we review the theoretical usages Sigmund Freud (1856–1939) employed to bring together a clinical practice which invited Kantian formulations and a conception of science that demanded Lockean translations. There were three early (pre-1900) sources of pressure on Freud to take a Lockean position on the nature of human behavior and mental illness.

### Brücke

The first Lockean influence on Freud was that of Ernst Brücke (1819–1892), his beloved physiology professor at the University of Vienna. Freud attended the lectures of Brentano at this university, and he even translated J. S. Mill into German for Wundt's protagonist (Boring, 1950, p. 358). However, there is no evidence to suggest that Freud was influenced by Brentano, whereas Brücke clearly did have an impact. Of course, as Freud was himself to exemplify, a student does not always follow the complete outlook of his teacher. This seems to have been the case for Brücke, who along with classmates Carl Ludwig, Emil du Bois-Reymond, and Hermann von Helmholtz, failed to adopt the Kantian inclinations of their teacher, Johannes Müller. Whereas Müller would have been open to a telic account, in 1845 these four gifted students—all of whom would achieve recognition in science—formed a pact to fight against vitalism in scientific explanation (ibid., p. 708). Because vitalism is one type of telic account, the humanistic theorist who would like to think teleologically might be excused if he senses considerable prejudice on the part of those scientists who—like these four quite dispassionate empiricists—look at his efforts as a regression to Galenic medievalism. The constancy principle (conservation of energy) was greatly favored by Brücke, who gave the following version in his published lectures:

Organisms differ from dead material entities in action—machines—in possessing the faculty of assimilation, but they are all phenomena of the physical world; systems of atoms, moved by forces, according to the principle of the conservation of energy discovered by Robert Mayer in 1842, neglected for twenty years, and then popularized by Helmholtz [as the constancy principle]. The sum of forces (motive forces and potential forces) remains constant in every isolated system. The real causes are symbolized in science by the word "force." The less we know about them, the more kinds of forces do we have to distinguish: mechancal, electrical, magnetic forces, light, heat. Progress in knowledge reduces them to two—attraction and repulsion. All this applies as well to the organism man (Jones, 1953, p. 41).

This Lockean constitutive, hence reductive, formulation of behavior followed Freud throughout his career after he left Brücke's laboratory. Though he was to have his fallings-out with many associates over the years, Freud carried a fond affection for Brücke's memory. Trained as a physician, Freud aspired to the role of scientist; in later years he could admit that he was never a doctor in the proper sense of putting cure above understanding of the neurosis (and behavior) (see Rychlak, 1968, pp. 169–191). Freud lagged behind his medical school class a full three years, and even after taking the M.D. degree in 1881, he worked for 15 unrecompensed months in Brücke's Institute, doing anatomical and microscopic studies on lower animals. Brücke helped Freud arrange a post-degree travel grant to study with Charcot in Paris. Freud also had great admiration for Jean Charcot (1825–1893), but this was only a brief contact of one year. Though Freud did probably learn from the French that a purely psychogenic explanation of behavior (without reducing behavior to underlying forces) *could* be highly instructive, he did not identify himself as a follower of Charcot.

## Breuer

The second Lockean influence on Freud stemmed from his collaboration with Josef Breuer (1842–1925) (Breuer & Freud, 1955). Breuer, who also had attended Brücke's lectures, put much more stock than Freud did in the constancy principle to account for hysterical disorders. For example, the concept of *strangulated affect* as a kind of bound energy that required working-over in order for it to dissipate is Helmholtzian in tone and clearly the favored view of Breuer (*ibid.*, p. 8). The process by which this energy was unbound or redistributed involved taking the patient back in hypnosis to a reconstruction of the unhealthy circumstance in which the emotion had been strangulated (bound) (*ibid.*, p. 17). Reliving such a pathognomic situation after the fact through verbal report was termed an *abreaction* (*ibid.*, pp. 8–11). Freud seems to have accepted this formulation in general terms, but when the collaborators broached the question of the cause of such strangulations of affect, a parting of the theoretical ways proved inevitable.

Breuer fell back on the traditional medical model and said the proclivity to split consciousness and hence to strangulate as hysterics do was traceable to an inborn condition, which he called the *hypnoid state* (Breuer, 1955, pp. 235–236). Freud, however, began to find in his cases a form of defensive avoidance that seemed to trigger the condition without any underlying physiological reason. In discussing one such early case Freud observes: "I was repeatedly able to show that *the splitting of the content of consciousness is the result of an act of will on the part of the patient*; that is to say, it is initiated by an effort of will whose motive can be specified" (Freud, 1962a, p. 46). The reasons motivating such splitting of consciousness into repressed (unconscious) ideas versus active acceptable ones were, of course, to wait on Freud's self-analysis, the sexuality thesis, and so forth. But for appearances sake, the collaborators acknowledged two different forms of the mental disorder—hypnoid hysteria (Breuer's etiology) and defense hysteria (Freud's etiology).

Freud's theory is clearly a departure from the time-honored medical model. His formulation did not even demand that an energic reduction be made. The defense and "wish" defended against were more akin to logical (and especially dialectically logical) maneuvers rather than the running off of an energy to some new redistribution in a closed system. In short, Freud's account has taken on teleological overtones. By looking at the motives of his patients he was moving to the introspective perspective and finding the Kantian formulation of things increasingly meaningful. Breuer was a conventional Lockean thinker, seeing people as constituted of certain genetic structures, influenced by these factors no matter what they might do as human beings to bring things about in life. Intention or will had no place in this completely extraspective account.

If we trace Freud's handling of the hypnoid-state theory, we find a neat demolishment taking place. He begins the process with rather faint praise in 1895 by observing:

I regard this distinction [hypnoid versus defense hysteria] as so important that, on the strength of it, I willingly adhere to this hypothesis of there being a hypnoid hysteria. Strangely enough, I have never in my own experience met with a genuine hypnoid hysteria. Any that I took in hand turned into a defence hysteria. . . . In short, I am unable to suppress a suspicion that somewhere or other the roots of hypnoid and defence hysteria come together, and that there the primary factor is defence" (Freud, 1955, p. 286).

In an 1896 paper on "The aetiology of hysteria" he notes that "there are often no grounds whatever for presupposing the presence of such hypnoid states" (Freud, 1962b, p. 195). He adds that if one only searches deeper into the psyche he will find a repressed defense in time. Finally, in a 1908 paper entitled "Some general remarks on hysterical attacks," Freud reduces the phenomenon of a hypnoid state to the physiological sensation of a protracted pause following a climax of intense sexual release (Freud, 1959, p. 233).

Fliess

Wilhelm Fliess (1858–1928) was a successful nose–throat specialist who practiced in Berlin and with whom Freud, who lived in Vienna, carried on a correspondence between the years 1887 and 1902. Breuer had introduced the two men. By Freud's (1954) personal estimate, Fliess was his "only audience" (p. 337) during the difficult years of the 1890s while he was conducting his self-analysis and putting together his thoughts into the *Interpretation of Dreams* (Freud, 1953). We cannot overestimate the importance Freud attached to Fliess's friendship and encouragement. No other professional relationship in his life was to have more significance, not even the subsequent contact with Jung. Intermingled with the personal features of the Freud–Fliess relationship was the fact that one man (Freud) had telic leanings as a theoretician and the other (Fliess) was an uncompromising physical determinist, who argued that men as well as women were governed by "periodic cycles" of either 23 or 28 days (like the menstrual cycle) which accounted for both physical and psychological diseases.

Fliess seems to have nagged Freud for physicalistic descriptions of behavior, because there are several points in the correspondence where Freud challenges his friend to suggest how they might in some way explain things physiologically or organically (Freud, 1954, p. 169, p. 265). We have to guess at much of this because Freud did not preserve Fliess's letters; in fact he tried to have the remaining correspondence and drafts destroyed unpublished—more for personal reasons than anything else. Fortunately, he did not succeed, and one quite remarkable document remains called the *Project For A Scientific Psychology* (Freud, 1966b, pp. 283–387). Freud began work on this unfinished psychology on the train while he was returning from a September meeting with Fliess in 1895. We can surmise from the correspondence that Fliess' prompting got the work underway, and Freud worked on it almost feverishly until October of that year, at which point he sent off three parts of a projected book. But by November 1895—one month later—he could say to Fliess in a letter: "I no longer understand the state of mind in which I concocted the psychology [the *Project*]" (Freud, 1954, p. 134). Though he did make a few fitful returns to this work in response to Fliess' urging, he never completed it and, as we have noted, tried to have it destroyed altogether. In the opening lines of the *Project* we read the following:

The intention is to furnish a psychology that shall be a natural science: that is, to represent psychical processes as quantitatively determinate states of specifiable material particles, thus making those processes perspicuous and free from contradiction. Two principal ideas are involved: (1) What distinguishes activity from rest is to be regarded as Q, subject to the general laws of motion. (2) The neurones are to be taken as the material particles (Freud, 1966b, p. 295).

This is (1) the most beautiful Lockean phrasing in *all* of Freud's writings; (2) this is the *only* Lockean phrasing in *all* of Freud's writings. The style here is clearly Helmholtzian; it reveals the fact that Freud knew very well how to take a demonstrative view of behavior, reducing psychological factors to a substrate of efficient (motion) and material (neurones) causation. The fact that he could not complete the *Project* is a mute testimony. It teaches us that this extraspective effort, in which Freud really tries to frame behavior "over there, in the physical functioning of the body" rather than "in here, within the various levels of mind" misfired completely. This was simply *not* the way in which Freud reasoned.

From his very first paper (Freud, 1966a) in which he attempted to explain neuroses without the Lockean interventions of Breuer, Freud proved to be a sagacious *dialectician*. He framed this first in terms of *antithetical ideas*, each generated by the same person at the same time—for example, when we aspire to win but also recognize that we might lose just as readily. In certain instances such negatively framed ideas actually reach the light of day, and the result is an hysterical neurosis (*ibid.*, p. 121). The recognition here is that meanings and meaning-expressions are *bipolar*! Intending more than one thing at the same time is *not* impossible. Yet, in the quote from the *Project* above we have Freud embracing the Law of Contradiction— a most unFreudian affirmation!

The dialectical side to Freud's thought, which enables him to make telic commentary, is patently clear in the Fliess correspondence. Freud learned that antithetical ideas were often the other side of consciously stated intentions precisely because the individual had initially toyed with them as his "true" attitude. They were frequently self-reproaches, voiced by individuals suffering from guilt (a judgment made of one's worth "for the sake of" or on the basis of some principle). In 1896 he could say to Fliess: "Indeed, it appears as though the whole psychical complex—recollection and self-reproach —is conscious at first. Later on, without anything fresh happening, both of them are repressed, and in their place an *antithetic symptom* is formed in consciousness" (Freud, 1954, p. 149). Freud should have named the symptom a synoptic, or synthesized, symptom, for this was the feature of the dialectic he was to arrive at, as have all dialecticians since the beginnings of thought.

What happens when there are two ideas, each antithetical to the other? The dialectician finds that invariably these seeming opposites can be shown to imply a new alternative, or at the very least, they can be brought together in a more or less unhappy alliance for a period of time. And so it was to dawn on Freud that symptoms were compromises! The symptom thus always reflected what Freud was to call the repressed wish (formerly the antithetic idea) and the repressing wish (formerly the intention). A wish is surely a final cause, a hoped-for or merely expected state of affairs toward which the individual feels himself drawn—often, in spite of himself (e.g., Freud would say one can *wish* for punishment). With this new development Freud could now weave the most shocking dialectical twists for Fliess, as in the following:

It turns out, for instance, that hysterical headaches are due to a fantastic parallel which equates the head with the other end of the body (hair in both places—cheeks and buttocks—lips and labiae—mouth and vagina); so that a migraine can be used to represent a forcible defloration, the illness thus again standing for a wish-fulfillment (Freud, 1954, p. 273).

The migraine patient could have her psychic cake and eat it too. Her repressed wish (to be seduced or raped) might be accomplished even as the repressing wish for punishment (the pain of headache) could be satisfied as well. In an alternative case mentioned to Fliess, Freud theorizes that hysterical vomiting in a female patient is to be seen as emanating from an unconscious (repressed wish) to be pregnant—even from an imaginary lover—while also becoming emaciated and undesirable sexually in response to the moral indignation the woman feels (repressing wish) for her lustful sexual phantasies (*ibid.*, p. 277).

Freud thus evolved a model of illness in which the personality structure sought a certain adjustment level, with the ego as the "man in the middle" seeking a balance between the unacceptable intentions (wishes) of the id and the socially more appropriate intentions (wishes) of the superego. These specific constructs were worked out after the turn of the century, of course, but the line of thought is presaged in the correspondence in the all-important period of the 1890s. Considering the oppositional character of mental intentions (due to the bipolarity of meanings), if some form of stalemate were possible, one could speak of mental health. If for any of a number of reasons the personality structure deteriorated and the stalemate was broken, neurosis or psychosis was the result. In Freudian psychology there is a fine line between what is neurosis (illness) and what is simply character (personality structure). In modifying the medical model as he did, Freud put teleology back into the human condition. It was not illness that acquired a final cause, not disease which gained a mentality, but rather the "personality" about whom a judgment of mental normality was being made.

Of course such talk of dialectical twists and wishes bringing about illness fell on unsympathetic ears. Fliess had mental illness springing from a kind of broken biological clock, which distorted the rhythm of the periodic cycles. It was the Breuer theory all over again, a variation on the traditional medical model. He never appreciated the Freudian thought style, and at their final meeting in Achensee in 1900 there was a vitriolic scene in which Fliess called Freud a "thought reader" who projected his own ideas onto clients (a charge that is still made against psychoanalysis) (*ibid.*, p. 324). Freud's bitter response to this assessment left Fliess with little motivation to continue their relationship. There were a few letters after this (Lockean-Kantian) argument, but by 1902 Freud and Fliess no longer corresponded. Thus personal considerations did not prevent Freud from sticking to his theoretical guns. But he did feel the need to give his new psychology a "sound" that might be more harmonious to the natural scientist's ears.

The Freudian Compromise: Libido Theory

Sigmund Freud must be seen as a transitional figure in the history of science, one of those eminent thinkers who have a predilection of what is needed, but yet who strive to retain what they take to be the merits of the older conceptualizations. Much was taking place on the Continent in the closing decades of the nineteenth century, the period when Freud was to mature and put forward his initial views (see, e.g., Feuer, 1974). A "new physics" was being written at this time, drafted from a more Kantian phenomenological frame of reference as exemplified by Ernst Mach (1838–1916) (Cassirer, 1950, p. 93). The emphasis here was on how the physicist himself—as a conceptualizer—might perceive his data, the assumptions made in doing so, the consequent "reality" observed, and so forth. Looked at psychologically, here was a view of science that might have underwritten Freudian thought beautifully. Freud could have jettisoned not only the traditional medical model, but the traditional Newtonian model of science as well!

   But this is not how things went. Doubtless out of reverence for Brücke and possibly also out of a certain guilty concern over the "thought reader" charge, Freud viewed the theories of Mach as anathema to science. Indeed Freud apparently avoided the social philosopher Josef Popper-Lynkeus, a man he admired, because the latter had Mach as a friend. He did not want to bestir the waters in his relations with Popper-Lynkeus, who could somehow cultivate a social life with the "intellectual nihilist" Ernst Mach (Rieff, 1959, p. 26). Thus Freud missed an opportunity to move into the stream of a changing physics, a more Kantian physics, as reflected in the thought of men like Mach, Hertz, and Duhem (Rychlak, 1968, p. 116).

In place of this invitation to phenomenological science, Freud reverted to a Lockean reductionistic strategy and raised a mental energy conception to the forefront of his theory. Freud never even mentioned *libido* until late in the Fliess correspondence, and his handling of the construct was strange, to say the least. Though he had other instincts in mind during various formulations of his theory, the energy of the sexual instincts is the only one he ever named. He assigned no name to the energy of the self-preservation instinct (earlier theory) or the death instinct (later theory). Freud sought a continuing focus on sexuality. *Libido*, a term physicians used to refer to sexual promptings, allowed him to keep this focus and also to give his theory the look of natural science. As late as December 1909 Jung could ask Freud in a letter: "I should like to pump you sometime for a definition of libido. So far I haven't come up with anything satisfactory" (McGuire, 1974, p. 270). Freud responds in the same month: "[In answer to] . . . your difficulty regarding 'my' libido. In the first sentence of the *Theory of Sexuality* there is a clear definition in which I see nothing to change: The analagon to hunger, for which, in the sexual context, the German language has no word except the ambiguous '*Lust*'" (*ibid.*, p. 277). This is as explicit as Freud would become, even when speaking informally with a friend and ally. There is absolutely no need in a dialectical account to reduce intentions or wishes (formal-final causes) to energies (material-efficient causes), but Freud seems to have felt he would be afforded scientific status if he did so.

There is a certain irony in the fact that a man who began his conceptualizations entirely at the level of intentional analysis, and thereby not only explained but cured neuroses *without* an energy notion, should end up as apostle for instinctive drives and mental energies. A reasoned overview of Freud's intellectual development must surely convince us that libido theory is a superfluous—really metaphorical—account of the workings of mind. It is the remnant of a constancy-principle strategy, but one that is badly distorted and in fact misplaced. There would be nothing uniquely Freudian in viewing mental energies as forces that propel the organism when they rise (bound) and cease this propulsion as they fall off in volume or level (unbound).

What *is peculiar* to Freud's mental energies is the fact that in his theoretical formulations drive power *always* issued from a dialectical ploy, oriented teleologically for conflicting ends, and then rephrased in energy terms *after* the implications were clear. Not merely the instinctual drive or its (efficient cause) energy provided the dynamics of motion; the energy as stimulated and then opposed by another oppositional (antithetical) energy required a resolution or synthesis in repression, projection, sublimation, or whatever. Energies that run to their expenditure in physics are never manipulated with strategies (formal causes) "for the sake of which" (final causes) one side of the mind (id) makes itself known through a devious parapraxis despite the vigilance of an opposing side of mind (ego, superego). In the Freudian unconscious there *is* trickery and deceit, ploy and counter-ploy, until one's head is set spinning from trying to keep up with the machinations supposedly going on. Each client is a marvel of intricate detail and fascinating motivation.

This is not to say that Freud employed a dialectical strategy consciously, nor that he would in any way have liked to be considered a dialectician—which to him meant sophist (Rychlak, 1968, p. 323). The "thought reader" charge was to haunt Freud throughout his lifetime. Nor did Freud clearly appreciate the addition of final causes in his presentation. He seems to have simply presumed that anyone who rejected his views did so on the basis of their sexualized content. As late as 1915 he freely admitted that his libido theory depended more on an analogy to biology than on the direct evidence of psychoanalysis (Freud, 1957, p. 79). He could always present explanations of the neurosis in *either* psychological (formal-final causal) *or* libidinal-energic (material-efficient causal) terms. As he grew older he even seems to have used the libidinal phrasing more and more, but the basic style of Freudian thought was to remain dialectical and telic. However, Freud must be viewed as a mixed-model theorist. Those who feel he was a physicalistic theorist in the classical medical-model sense would do well to read *The Freud/Jung Letters* (McGuire, 1974) where there are numerous examples of Freud and Jung rejecting traditional medical explanation (see especially pp. 115–116).

## Summary

Chapter 3 begins with a discussion of the conceptual forces that served to define natural science for the nineteenth century, the period in which psychology emerged as an independent science. The medical model, Newtonian mechanism, rise of mathematics, and Darwinian evolutionary theory are shown to merge in a fundamental Lockeanism which was to exert an overwhelming influence on natural-science theory. But the founders of psychological science were not all committed to a Lockean model. We surveyed several important figures and found that there always was much sympathy for a more Kantian formulation of human behavior. This was true of Fechner, who because he first devised experimental procedures is probably more deserving of the title Father of Experimental Psychology than is Wundt.

The Bell–J. Müller differences in interpreting nerve functions and mentality are seen to encompass a Lockean-Kantian difference, as did the Helmholtz-Hering disagreement on the nature of visual perception. Helmholtz popularized the constancy principle in psychology, which demanded that for a full scientific account to be rendered the theorist must bring his psychological theory down to underlying physical simple forces. This traditional Lockean form of explanation was also embraced by Wundt, who added that we must explicate these forces in terms of the motions (efficient-causes) within which they are manifested. A detailed comparison of Wundt and Brentano then revealed that the Lockean-Kantian issue defines their differences, albeit in a somewhat more subtle way because there are indications of a leaning toward a mixed model on both sides. Wundt's basic commitment to scientific procedure is what stamps him as predominantly a Lockean, although he was more inclined to make room for humanistic (as opposed to mechanistic) theories than our leading historians have given him credit for. An important conclusion derived from this comparative study is that, whereas Brentano's "inner perception" resulted in *introspective* theory, Wundt's "internal perception" (introspection) resulted in *extraspective* theory. Ebbinghaus (Lockean) and G. E. Müller (Kantian) are seen to take different positions on the historical confrontation of our models in the theories of memory and learning they each advocated. Similar contrasts can be seen between the Wurzburgers (Kantian) on the Continent, and the British psychologists, Galton and C. L. Morgan (Lockean).

Though he refused to think in strictly Lockean demonstrative terms despite pressure to do so from Brücke, Breuer, and Fliess, Freud *did* embrace a form of Lockean reductionism in his libido theory. Though he might have based psychoanalysis on the newly emerging physics of his time, Freud demurred and returned to the Helmholtzian strategy of reducing *psychic* events to *psychic* simple forces. The resultant libido theory is a Lockean-Kantian compromise of major proportions and one of the least viable aspects of psycho-analytical thought. Ultimately libido theory rests on a dialectical and telic rationale, though it has succeeded in convincing many people that Freud was a demonstrative theorist and a biological determinist.

## References

Bakan, D. A reconsideration of the problem of introspection. *Psychological Bulletin*, 1954, **51**, 105–118.

Becker, H., & Barnes, H. E. *Social thought from lore to science* (2 vols.). Washington, D.C.: Harren, 1952.

Blumenthal, A. L. A reappraisal of Wilhelm Wundt. *American Psychologist*, 1975, **30**, 1081–1088.

Boring, E. G. *A history of experimental psychology* (2nd ed.). New York: Appleton-Century-Crofts, 1950.

Brentano, F. *Psychology from an empirical standpoint*. New York: Humanities, 1973.

Breuer, J. Theoretical selection, section III. In J. Strachey (Ed.), *The standard edition of the complete psychological works of Sigmund Freud* (Vol. II). London: Hogarth, 1955. Pp. 185–251.

Breuer, J., & Freud, S. On the psychical mechanism of hysterical phenomena: Preliminary communication. In J. Strachey (Ed.), *The standard edition of the complete psychological works of Sigmund Freud* (Vol. II). London: Hogarth, 1955. Pp. 1–17.

Burtt, E. A. *The metaphysical foundations of modern physical science* (rev. ed.). Garden City, N.Y.: Doubleday, 1955.

Cassirer, E. *The problem of knowledge*. New Haven: Yale University Press, 1950.

Ebbinghaus, H. *Memory: A contribution to experimental psychology*. New York: Dover, 1964.

Feuer, L. S. *Einstein and the generations of science*. New York: Basic Books, 1974.

Freud, S. *The interpretation of dreams*. In J. Strachey (Ed.), *The standard edition of the complete psychological works of Sigmund Freud* (Vols. IV & V). London: Hogarth, 1953.

Freud, S. *The origins of psycho-analysis, letters to Wilhelm Fliess, drafts and notes: 1887–1902*. New York: Basic Books, 1954.

Freud, S. The psychotherapy of hysteria. In J. Strachey (Ed.), *The standard edition of the complete psychological works of Sigmund Freud* (Vol. II). London: Hogarth, 1955. Pp. 254–305.

Freud, S. On narcissism: An introduction. In J. Strachey (Ed.), *The standard edition of the complete psychological works of Sigmund Freud* (Vol. XIV). London: Hogarth, 1957. Pp. 67–102.

Freud, S. Some general remarks on hysterical attacks. In J. Strachey (Ed.), *The* standard edition of the complete psychological works of Sigmund Freud (Vol. IX). London: Hogarth, 1959. Pp. 227–234.

Freud, S. The neuro-psychoses of defence. In J. Strachey (Ed.), The standard edition of the complete psychological works of Sigmund Freud (Vol. III). London: Hogarth, 1962. Pp. 41–61. (a)

Freud, S. The aetiology of hysteria. In J. Strachey (Ed.), The standard edition of the complete pyschological works of Sigmund Freud (Vol. III). London: Hogarth, 1962. Pp. 182–221. (b)

Freud, S. A case of successful treatment of hypnotism. In J. Strachey (Ed.), The standard edition of the complete psychological works of Sigmund Freud (Vol. I). London: Hogarth, 1966. Pp. 115–128. (a)

Freud, S. Project for a scientific psychology. In J. Strachey (Ed.), The standard edition of the complete psychological works of Sigmund Freud (Vol. I). London: Hogarth, 1966. Pp. 283–397. (b)

Helmholtz, H. von Treatise on physiological optics. In T. Shipley (Ed.), Classics in psychology. New York: Philosophical Library, 1961.

Jones, E. The life and work of Sigmund Freud: The formative years and great discoveries (Vol. 1). New York: Basic Books, 1953.

Kuhn, T. S. The structure of scientific revolutions (2nd. ed.). Chicago: University of Chicago Press, 1970. (1st ed., 1962.)

McGuire, W. (Ed.), The Freud/Jung letters. Bollingen Series XCIV. Princeton, N.J.: Princeton University Press, 1974.

Mischel, T. Wundt and the conceptual foundations of psychology. Philosophical and Phenomenological Research, 1970, 31, 1–26.

Rancurello, A. C. A study of Franz Brentano. New York: Academic, 1968.

Rieff, P. Freud: The mind of the moralist. New York: Viking, 1959.

Rychlak, J. F. A philosophy of science for personality theory. Boston: Houghton Mifflin, 1968.

Titchener, E. B. Systematic psychology: Prolegomena. Ithaca, N.Y.: Cornell University Press, 1972.

Watson, R. I. The great psychologists. Philadelphia: Lippincott, 1971.

Wundt, M. Die Wurzein der deutschen Philosophie in Stamm und Rasse. Berlin: Junker und Dunnhaupt, 1944.

Wundt, W. Lectures on human and animal psychology (4th ed.). New York: Macmillan, 1907. (1st ed., 1894.)

Wundt, W. Contributions to the theory of sensory perception. In T. Shipley (Ed.), Classics in psychology. New York: Philosophical Library, 1961.

Wundt, W. The language of gestures. Paris: Mouton, 1973.

# CHAPTER FOUR

## A Lockean Victory:
## The Americanization of
## Scientific Psychology

Because most of the early influential American psychologists had taken advanced degrees in Europe—or at least had spent some time in study there—the issues discussed in Chapter 3 were naturally alive in the academic circles of the United States in the late nineteenth and early twentieth centuries. However, an Americanization of scientific psychology was to take place in relatively short order as the lead in this discipline shifted from Europe to the United States. In Chapter 4 we underscore a few of the predominant themes in psychology's historical development, showing thereby how they solidified into an *institutionalized* outlook on the nature of proper scientific psychology.

### Functionalism Versus Structuralism

Caldwell, Titchener, Calkins, Angell

In 1897 Professor William Caldwell (1863–1942) traveled from Northwestern University in Evanston, Illinois, to Ithaca, New York, where the American Psychological Association was holding a December meeting. Caldwell disagreed with the psychology then being advocated by E. B. Titchener (1867–1927), Wundt's student and foremost advocate in America. Indeed, as we suggested in Chapter 3, much of what we know and understand about Wundtian psychology in America derives from Titchener's interpretations of his mentor's outlook (aided and abetted by the writings of Boring, who was the protégé of Titchener). Caldwell presented a small paper at the Ithaca meeting, which was later published in the *Psychological Review*

(Caldwell, 1898). Though he was not aware of it at the time, this brief "point of order" raised by Caldwell was to touch off a major confrontation in early American psychology.

Caldwell's complaint centered on the fact that in his book *An Outline of Psychology* Titchener (1897) chose to speak for *all* of psychology when he held that there was no evidence for mind in the findings of experimental psychology. When Titchener spoke of experimental psychology he was stressing the introspective method, but he also included the work of Ebbinghaus (see Titchener, 1961, p. 231). Titchener viewed the *self* as the total of conscious processes that run their course under the conditions laid down by bodily tendencies (Caldwell, 1898). Based on his own introspective investigations, Caldwell objected to these blanket statements and argued: "There is in us a feeling consciousness of selfhood, or the realization of (as Aristotle puts it) an inward operative (formal or final) purpose which is not expressed by his biological self, his 'sum of tendencies' [a phrase used by Titchener]" (*ibid.*, p. 403).

Based on *evidence* using the same methods proposed by Titchener of internal perception, Caldwell felt that he had observed a "mind or 'will' working from within outwards, conditioning mental process" (*ibid.*, p. 402). Stout (1860–1944) also found this natural tendency for an attitude of mind, utilizing schematic apprehensions in an *active* fashion (*ibid.*, p. 405). Mind is passive when it must confront sensations from without, yet it *also* can be proven introspectively that it is active, schematizing, conceptualizing, and so on. However, "Titchener will not call it both active and passive; he insists that it is passive, consisting merely of sensation and affection" (*ibid.*, p. 405). In this "active" criticism leveled at Titchener Caldwell was to frame for the first time a major distinction in our history when he observed: "Titchener surely separates the 'content' from the 'activity' of attention" (*ibid.*, p. 404).

This seems to be the first explicit statement opposing content (Lockean) to act (Kantian) psychology. Though such differences existed in the outlooks of Wundt and Brentano, the former did not consider himself a content psychologist and the latter called his approach empirical psychology. The point of Caldwell's criticism is that in the Titchenerian-Wundtian use of introspection, what resulted was an *extraspective* formulation of elements—excitations contained in the physical apparatus—totaling "over there" into behavior. As an introspectionist in the tradition of Brentano, Caldwell felt that this account denied the *objective fact* that something like a self-identity brought forward a contribution to experience *in addition to* the simple taking in and collating of such sensation-contents in the physical apparatus of the body to summate or "make up" behavior.

Just as Ebbinghaus had tried to perfect his experimental methods to accomodate a mathematical theoretical formulation (see Chapter 3, p. 120), so too did Wundt and Titchener make every effort to train their introspecting subjects to *avoid* questions of selfhood in the effort. Becoming aware of one's self-identity in the process could contaminate the findings, and introduce subjectivity (recall the Wurzburgers!) hence unreliability, into the procedure. Therefore evidence for selfhood could not be attained in the Titchenerian model of introspection as method. There is also clear evidence that Titchener did not wish to entertain anything smacking of teleological theory. Caldwell even observed that Wundt was more accepting of the mind as an active agent in life than was Titchener (*ibid.*, p. 406). In support of his findings on the self he noted that a physiological text of the period "refers to an ultimate tendency of living matter to act from within outwards, to act in a way that cannot be explained by mechanical or reflex action. There is a self-preservation *nisus* in the life of a biological organism which may be said to constitute its unity, to make it more than the mere sum of tendencies" [One in Many Thesis!] (*ibid.*, p. 406). The entire talk is a beautiful example of a humanistic theorist, leveling his Kantian guns at a leading Lockean thinker of the period.

Caldwell's name is not found in today's major psychology history texts, but his unsung role must not be forgotten, because in charging that Titchener was losing the human person in the assemblage of elements he called a self, Caldwell prompted Titchener to write his famous 1898 paper "The Postulates of a Structural Psychology" (appearing in the *Philosophical Review*, and reprinted in Shipley, 1961, from which we take quotations). In his quasi-reply—where reference to Caldwell is made only in footnotes—Titchener (1961) bases his case on an analogy to biology where the division between morphology, or structure, and the function these various structures serve to the economy of the organism is commonly made (p. 224). The structural approach in psychology is then identified as experimental psychology, and the functional approach is likened to what Titchener called Brentano's descriptive (nonexperimental) psychology. Titchener added a third aspect having to do with the changes in structure or function over time—implying a developmental form of psychological study as an extension of either or both of the basic approaches. No real discussion of this third alternative is carried out.

Titchener employed the structure-function dichotomy in two

ways. The first and major use was to suggest a "pecking-order" distinction in psychology, relegating functionalism to a second-class standing—for example, when he noted: "The methods of descriptive psychology cannot, in the nature of the case, lead to results of scientific finality" (*ibid*, p. 228). That is, in simply describing how things happen the psychological scientist does not base his account on the firm underpinning of a structure; hence, he cannot be a first-rate scientist. Titchener drew no real distinction between functionalism, act psychology, descriptive psychology, and even faculty psychology (*ibid*., p. 228). All of these approaches settled on explanations that were insufficient and often spurious. We must never forget that "function presupposes structure" (*ibid*., p. 227). A physical apparatus is required to do the behaving in all behavior! This is especially important for a science of psychology, because: "There is, further, the danger that, if function is studied before structure has been fully elucidated, the student may fall into that acceptance of *teleological explanation which is fatal to scientific advance* . . . [italics added] (*ibid*., p. 229).

The second use of the dichotomy takes root from this attack on teleological description. Titchener tried to identify all functionalists as teleologists, and vice versa. This included an effort to make this dichotomy a rephrase of what *he now called* the content-act confrontations of his student days. Thus he referred to Brentano's difficult phrase of immanent objectively (see Chapter 3, p. 112) as "language of function, not of structure" (*ibid*., p. 232) and added: "The 'psychology from an empirical standpoint' is a systematization of mental 'activities,' *i.e.*, of the mental functions of the human organism" (*ibid*., p. 232). He went on to place William James (1842–1910) in the functionalist camp because of the latter's concept of the "fiat of the will" (*ibid*., p. 241) and even underscored the Aristotelian and Kantian features of all functionalist psychologies (*ibid*., p. 242).

The actual postulates of a structuralist psychology amount to three or four points: that sensations (*ibid*., p. 233) and affections (*ibid*., p. 234) are the elements of mind, that these are underivable, one from the other (*ibid*., p. 236), and that they are subject to determination by the factors of intensity and quality (*ibid*., p. 236). The question of *time* in the workings of mind was also emphasized because Titchener could not conceive of an affective or sensational process that was free of duration (*ibid*., p. 238). Titchener ends his paper by observing that structuralists are more in agreement with what their approach to psychology involves than are the functionalists (*ibid*., pp. 241–242).

Caldwell (1899) was to write a rebuttal to Titchener in which he admirably reaffirmed his charges and defended a telic interpretation of selfhood. Subsequently Mary Whiton Calkins (1863–1930) (1906), in her 1905 Presidential Address to the American Psychological Association, also took up the question of a much needed self-construct in psychology. Calkins called for a union of functionalism (her theoretical outlook) and structuralism, with *both* sides accepting as a "basal fact" (*ibid.*, p. 68) the reality of a self in human behavior (based on the evidence of introspection). Calkins directed her commentary primarily at James Rowland Angell (1867–1949) and only secondarily at Titchener. Angell, who was at the University of Chicago at this time (along with John Dewey until 1904, at which time Dewey left for Columbia University), was becoming a leading spokesman for the (more accurately, "a") functionalist outlook. In 1902, during the Decennial celebration of the University of Chicago, Angell delivered a talk on the nature of structural versus functional psychology. In 1903 he published a paper on the relations of structural and functional psychology to philosophy (Angell, 1903). The Chicago School of psychologists (Dewey, Angell, later Carr and others) were conducting experiments on both humans and lower animals. They employed introspection as well as other strictly empirical strategies that we now identify as "the" approach to experimental psychology. Though this would seem to be the province of structural psychology *a la* Titchener, these men at Chicago were calling themselves functionalists!

Understandably Caldwell and Calkins were dissatisfied with structural or content psychology. They were humanists, wanting to see a role for intentionality by way of self-direction in the psychology of their time. Calkins (1906) even charged that Angell had gone over to a structuralist position in his stressing the necessity of providing a physical basis to behavior (p. 71; see Angell's discussion, below). But what the structuralists at Cornell (Titchener's university) and the functionalists at Chicago (Dewey, Angell, Carr) had to argue about is considerably more difficult to appreciate. This was surely a most unusual debate. The humanists, Caldwell and Calkins, soon fell from view in this exchange (relegated to footnote mention by the apparently more eminent protagonists). When he was elected President of the American Psychological Association in 1906, Angell (1907) used the occasion to spell out in detail what he considered was "The Province of Functional Psychology." We will take a close look at this historic rebuttal [sic] to Titchener's 1898 paper.

Angell organizes his presentation around three basic characteristics of the functional outlook, although he notes that there are variations on each of these themes. The first point confronts directly the Wundtian-Titchenerian use of introspection, for it suggests that functionalists hope to "discern and portray the typical *operations* of consciousness under actual life conditions, as over against the attempt to analyze and describe its elementary and complex *contents*" (*ibid.*, pp. 62–63). Angell does not speak of act or of an active mind conceptualizing events; he sees the functionalist as tracking the *operations* of mind, a term which he soon uses interchangeably with *function* (*ibid.*, p. 66). The functionalists at Chicago do not go along with the Wundtian thesis of a "direct observation of inner experience" (see Chapter 3, p. 112). They find this artificial, a *post hoc* examination of consciousness: "As a matter of fact many modern investigations of an experimental kind largely dispense with the usual direct form of introspection and concern themselves in a distinctly functionalistic spirit with a determination of what work is accomplished and what the conditions are under which it is achieved" (*ibid.*, p. 65).

A second characteristic of the functionalist approach is its commitment to the Darwinian theory of evolution (*ibid.*, p. 62). The functionalist would like to study "mental activity as part of a larger stream of biological forces which are daily and hourly at work before our eyes and which are constitutive of the most important and most absorbing part of our world" (*ibid.*, p. 68). Combined with the move away from introspection, this has resulted, said Angell, in a "quasi-biological field which we designate [as] animal psychology" (*ibid.*, p. 69). One studies lower animals to gain thereby "the longitudinal rather than the transverse view of life phenomena" (*ibid.*, pp. 70–71). This does *not* mean the anthropomorphization of lower animals. The modern functionalists' observations are "in the spirit of conservative non-anthropomorphism as earlier observations almost never were" (*ibid.*, p. 70). Indeed, Angell insisted that most behaviors are formed through repetitions into a regularity "approximating physiological automatism" (*ibid.*, p. 72) so that when we contemplate the role of consciousness in life it is actually a form of "accommodation to the novel" (*ibid.*, p. 72). The novel, once put into habitual routine, becomes the automatic. But what is the "operation" by which this routinizing of behavior is made possible? Angell observes:

In the execution of the accommodatory activity [i.e., mental activity] the instincts represent the racially hereditary utilities, many of which are under the extant conditions of life extremely anomalous in their value. The sensory-algedonic-motor phenomena represent the immediate short circuit unreflective forms of selective response. Whereas the ideational-algedonic-motor series at its several levels represents the long circuit response under the influence of the *mediating effects of previous experience* [italics added]. This experience serves either to inhibit the propulsive power intrinsic to the stimulus, or to reinforce this power by adding to it its own dynamic tendencies. This last variety of *action* [italics added] is the peculiarly human form of mediated control. On its lowest stages, genetically speaking, it merges with the purely immediate algedonic type of response. All the other familiar psychological processes are subordinate to one or more of these groups. Conception, judgement, reasoning, emotion, desire, aversion, volition, etc., simply designate special varieties in which these generic forms appear (*ibid.*, p. 74).

The term *algedonic* refers to the pleasantness-unpleasantness dimension of hedonic physiological experience. By linking sensory-algedonic-motor phenomena into the overall concept of a response, Angell was pointing to the reflex-arc concept which had by this time been widely discussed in America. But in speaking of the mediating effects of previous experience on such reflex activity Angell was anticipating in striking fashion the line of development behaviorism was to take. We return to this point below in our discussion of the wedding of behaviorism to functionalism.

Although Angell speaks of *action* in the above quote, note that this has nothing to do with what Brentano (or Caldwell or Calkins) would have meant by the term—i.e., as a conceptualizing effort of mind to confront and exert an influence on experience. For Angell, the action of mind is exclusively as an instrumentality: "Mind [is] conceived as primarily engaged in mediating between the environment and the needs of the organism" (*ibid.*, p. 85). Angell lumped actions with functions, and these concepts in turn were both viewed as aspects of control in behavior—a term that issues from the third characteristic attributed to functional psychology.

This has to do with "determining the relations to one another of the physical and mental portions of the organism" (*ibid.*, p. 80). Functionalism takes on a psychophysiological coloring at this point because it does not rest easily with Wundtian psychophysical parallelism (see Chapter 3). It begins with the premise that the bodily side of experience has some *necessary* tie to the mental side. This is what Calkins rebuked in Angell's position, believing that it was proper for psychology to deal exclusively with the workings (Brentano-like acts) of mind *qua* mind. Angell's functionalism had no real appreciation for the phenomenal realm of experience, except as the possible effect of purely physical causes. As he said of human volition:

. . . if one considers the usual accounts of the ontogenesis of human volitional acts one is again confronted with intrinsically physiological data in
which reflexes, automatic and instinctive acts are much in evidence . . . .
volition cannot be understood either as regards its origin or its outcome
without constant and overt reference to these factors (ibid., p. 81).

Though Titchener would have the functionalist resorting to telic
formulations, there is absolutely nothing but efficient causation in
this theoretical treatment of volition.

A vital adjunct to this functionalist interest in the relations of
body-mind involved what might be termed an "argument from
method" rather than from theory in the settling of all scientific disputes. This harks back to the first characteristic of functionalism,
having to do with a discarding of introspection in favor of more "lifelike" studies. Rather than looking inward (introspection a la Wundt),
the functionalists at Chicago wanted to look outward to study things
the way any natural scientist studies them. Angell felt that in so
doing they shifted the question of mind-body relations from the
realm of theoretical opinion to that of methodological verification.
Hence he said: "The position to which I refer regards the mind-body
relation as capable of treatment in psychology as a methodological
distinction rather than as a metaphysically existential one" (ibid.,
p. 83).

In other words, what was defined as "mind" in an experimental
format and what was defined as "body" depended upon the data an
experimentalist focused on in the design of his study. If confusion
between the two realms of explanations occurred, the proper context in which to resolve such differences is the methodological and
not the theoretical. This strategy of looking for answers to all problems of knowledge in a methodological rather than a theoretical context was important to functionalism—so important that Angell
termed it a "functionalistic metaphysics" (ibid., p. 84). In shifting
all questions of knowledge over exclusively to the side of method
Angell began a long line of arguing from the circumstances (later
called the antecedents) under which behavior takes place rather
than from the mental acts people are (introspectively) aware of while
they are behaving. This action of mind came to be known as consciousness, and here is how he framed this still popular functionalistic argument:

They [the functionalists] urge further that the profitable and significant
thing is to seek for a more exact appreciation of the precise conditions

under which consciousness is in evidence and the conditions under which it retires in favor of the more exclusively physiological. Such knowledge so far as it can be obtained is on a level with all scientific and practical information. It states the circumstances under which certain sorts of results will appear (*ibid.*, p. 84).

Wundt and Brentano (Chapter 3) would have considered this an indirect form of mind-study, for it leaves things up to an observer *other than the subject under observation* to name (induct, presume, deduce, etc.) those circumstances under which consciousness may or may not be said to enter into experimental findings. Indeed this observer need not even ask the subject what *he* thinks is at play in the succession of "observed events" which have been pre-arranged entirely at the convenience of the experimental observer in the first instance. This is a vital question in any research done on human beings, one Angell did not foresee arising but which was to be resurrected generations later in the history of experimental psychology as an embarrassment of major proportions (see Chapter 6). We must consider what a subject might be consciously contributing to the experimental procedure because Angell equated all "circumstances" under which behavior—both mental and physiological—takes place with *controls* on behavior. He noted that any account of mind had to deal with the "manner in which mental processes eventuate in motor phenomena of the physiological organism" (*ibid.*, p. 86). Only when consciousness eventuates in bodily action can we state with scientific assurance that there is such an operation as mind. Mind is therefore a controlling factor in behavior:

The functionalist's most intimate persuasion leads him to regard consciousness as primarily and intrinsically a control phenomenon. Just as behavior may be regarded as the most distinctly basic category of general biology in its functional phase so control would perhaps serve as the most fundamental category in functional psychology, the special forms and differentiations of consciousness simply constituting particular phases of the general process of control (*ibid.*, p. 88).

This word *control* was to become a premiere construct in experimental psychology, albeit a frequently misunderstood one. Angell is confident that mind controls behavior (body) and that we can study such factors empirically. But what if, in studying the mind "indirectly" (to quote Wundt and Brentano), the empirical observer finds that he can personally *predict* what the subject will or will not do in an experimental context based on the observer's knowledge of most famous of which is the yin-yang principle (see Chapter 1, p. 00). the antecedent circumstances that also face the subject? Following Angell's prescription to let the empirical methods answer questions of knowledge, would it not then be more accurate to say that the circumstances controlled consciousness (mind) than vice versa? Angell did not anticipate such a ready reversal of his confident belief in the mind as controlling agent, but as we shall see below, because of his denigration of a role for *theory* in knowledge-accrual, this is what actually happened with the advent of behaviorism. He spoke of ethics and logic as a means of controlling behavior (*ibid.*, p. 89) and ended with a summary statement of the functionalist's aim: "to see the mind which he analyzes as it actually is when engaged in the discharge of its vital functions" (*ibid.*, p. 90). In a few years his student, John Watson, would drop the mind (consciousness) construct altogether.

There was no immediate reply by Titchener. Though he returned to the topic of functionalism in his *Systematic Psychology: Prolegomena* (1972; first published in 1929), Titchener did not feel that the dispute needed furthering. He analyzed the functionalism of George Trumbill Ladd (1842–1921), who was cut from the Brentano mold (see Boring, 1950, p. 526), placing him in opposition to the more biological approach of Angell. He then placed C. H. Judd (1873–1946) between these two extremes, as a theorist who tried with little apparent success to preserve both the physical basis of behavior and the self as a "possessor of knowledge" (Titchener, 1972, pp. 159–160). But Titchener had little heart for continuing the debate. His closing views on the subject were as follows:

"Structural" psychology, as its name implies, recognized the existence of a correlative psychology of function; it isolated itself only to the degree that it demanded equal rights for content and activity, and by so doing protested against the autocracy of function. In the "biological" atmosphere of its time the phrase did good controversial service. If the view of my book [*Systematic Psychology: Prolegomena*] is accepted, both "functional" and "structural," as qualifications of "psychology," are now obsolete terms (Titchener, 1972, p. 178).

## A Misfired Polemic

Much to psychology's detriment, the humanistic polemic advanced by Caldwell was *never* aired properly, nor given clear acknowledgement in the history books. As a result the significant role teleological questions have had to play in the historical development of psychology has been submerged. Boring (1950, p. 555) suggests that Titchener raised the structural-functional issue as an angular jab at Dewey (who is mentioned once in the article). Hilgard and Bower (1966) go so far as to suggest that Titchener "attacked Dewey's position" (p. 298). Titchener was actually prodded into action by Caldwell, and then he made a first effort to align sides in terms of the same distinctions he felt were at play in his student days between Wundt and Brentano. He skirted the telic theoretical question by disclaiming it as a nonscientific concern, and in the ensuing emphasis on proper scientific procedures he lost the initiative to an even more vigorous approach.

Titchener properly aligned Caldwell and Brentano and then, characterizing these approaches as essentially nonscientific descriptive psychologies, tried to equate his view with the natural-science tradition of experimentation (the "pecking-order" intimidation referred to above). Translating the issue into theory-construction terms, we can see that for him structure meant the material-cause apparatus of the nervous system and so on, and content meant the stimulus complexes (sum of excitations) that were carried by these structures. As nonexperimentalists, Caldwell and Brentano were characterized as likely to speculate telically, falling back on the formal-final cause tandem in accounting for behavior.

If the debate could have been sustained with a leading teleologist (Caldwell did not qualify), Titchener might have succeeded in his alignment of sides—with "his side" being "the" scientific community and the opponents "something else." But a satisfactory opponent to speak for teleology was not forthcoming. Ladd's 10 years in the ministry probably disqualified him (Boring, 1950, pp. 524–526), and by this time in the eyes of American psychologists James had become more the philosopher than the leader of a spirited defense of teleological psychology. And as if to bedevil Titchener or challenge his lead, we have the Chicago group taking the wrong name from his scheme to identify themselves as "the" scientific community! The move from Wundtian introspectionism to overt experimentation proved a boon to psychological science. Its Darwinian justification of animal psychology led to a host of highly instructive experiments. A body of objective knowledge began to accrue having great heuristic value as well as practical implications for the control of human behavior.

Hence, Titchener found himself engaged in two somewhat different arguments: one aimed at the familiar Brentano-like psychologists who wanted to view human behavior as telic, framed introspectively around a self, and one aimed at the Chicago brand of psychologists who were nontelic, extraspective, and just as dedicated to experimental psychology as he was. The former confrontation was a classical Kantian-Lockean one, but the latter was a *Lockean-Lockean nonconfrontation!* Although the question of proper scientific method separated Cornell from Chicago, even this is not without certain qualifications. Because Titchener *did* include the work of Ebbinghaus as an example of structural psychology, the criticism suggesting that he refused to study lifelike researches or that he was committed *only* to introspection did not hold in the broader sense. Furthermore, the Wundtian methods of introspection —which, as we noted in Chapter 3 (p. 117), resulted in extraspective theoretical accounts—even advanced the study of physiological processes or functions (a fact Titchener always stressed).

The oft-cited historical confrontation between functionalism and structuralism was no confrontation at all in one aspect and a misfired polemic in another. It was begun by a humanist, who found the Newtonian interpretations of science brought to this country by Wundt's students lacking in something vital to man's conceptualization. Titchener lost the totality (the one) in the constitutive total of basal elements (the many), and yet this self-organizing principle of mental life is most characteristic of the human experience. Rather than a full airing of the introspective-versus-extraspective *theoretical* slant implied, what developed was a temporary quibble over the rules of *methodological* procedure. There was an implicit assumption held to by Cornell *and* Chicago which Angell made explicit: All problems of a theoretical (philosophical) nature could be answered in time through methodological refinements. The data gathered in psychological science would answer all questions about selves and consciousness and minds, so why play at the role of philosopher in these matters? Get on with the accrual of scientific evidence, which in turn meant (extraspectively) *observe behavior.* The stage was set for a new development.

## The Wedding of Behaviorism to Functionalism

The Lockean Advocates:
Watson, Tolman, Hull, Skinner

Although we do not need to go into their work to make the point of this section, we should mention Edward L. Thorndike (1874–1949) and Ivan Petrovich Pavlov (1849–1936) because of the importance of their respective law of effect and reinforcement principles to the development of behaviorism. Every psychologist knows that John B. Watson (1879–1958) formally established behaviorism as an approach to psychology in his classic 1913 paper "Psychology as the Behaviorist Views It." The groundwork for behaviorism had already been presaged in Angell's brand of functionalism. Watson was Angell's student in psychology at the University of Chicago, where he earned a doctoral degree in 1903 (with the physiologist Donaldson as co-major professor) and then stayed on as a member of the faculty. Boring (1950) suggests that what may have set Watson off on his own path was a 1907 monograph he authored on the kinaesthetic and organic sensations of the white rat in the learning of mazes:

The rule of functional animal psychology of that date was that, when you have finished your observations of behavior, you use the results to infer the nature of the animal's consciousness and then show how those processes function in the animal's behavior. Watson rebelled at lugging consciousness in, after he had adequately described the animal's functional behavior (p. 556).

There are three important points entailed in this adjustment made by Watson. First, when he rebelled at lugging consciousness in he was making a *theoretical* shift in emphasis (i.e., selecting which constructs he would use to account for the data). There is *never* anything explicitly in the data of experimentation to dictate for the observer what one and *only* one theoretical explanation must be used to account for the fact pattern under observation. In dropping consciousness Watson was taking the prerogative of an extraspective observer —that is, to employ only the theory which is necessary to account for the data under observation *that interests him!* Second, in giving his *reasons* why he needed to drop consciousness Watson in that typical functionalist way begun by his mentor (Angell), held that the data *compelled* him to do so. In other words, he leveled the argument from method we mentioned above. Because all one can "see" in the T-maze apparatus is a white rat running about in response to certain observed environmental circumstances and other presumed internal circumstances (drives), why impute a consciousness of these circumstances to the rat? This lack of parsimony is unbecoming to science. Why not be *truly* scientific and remain with only that which is observed?

Third, in predicating his argument in this fashion Watson could go on to the *next* issue in the above quote and say: If behavior is a function of environmental (and internal) circumstances, it is *itself* an effect and not a cause. It is under control rather than controlling.

Consciousness is simply the remnant of a medieval mythology about the supposed control that mind has on behavior (this is a repudiation of Angell; see above, p. 144). Because he was of the opinion that his methodological observations and not his theoretical stance is what forced him to limit his descriptions to the behavioral functions at play before his eyes, Watson had no real alternative but to use the language of *efficient causality* (with a secondary emphasis on the material cause to account for internal stimuli). The upshot is that he did what other natural scientists were doing: confounding his theory of functionalism with the supposed functional relationships of antecedent events impelling consequent events in that independent variable-dependent variable (IV-DV) sequence we know of as an experimental procedure. In speaking of this sequence theoretically he took the language of stimulus-response (S-R), a familiar antecedent-consequent succession due to the reflex arc concept that had been given wide consideration by psychologists. Both the IV-DV and S-R conceptions were used in the sense of efficient causality. Watson (1913) was therefore in the position of drawing a startling parallel: "Psychology as the behaviorist views it is a purely objective branch of natural science. Its theoretical goal is the prediction and control of behavior" (p. 158).

The response is a function of the stimulus; some stimuli exist internally and others exist externally in the environment. When a given response is made in reasonable proximity to a given stimulus, and especially if this association is repeated frequently, the resultant S-R regularity persists as a *habit*. Internal responses can be thought of as implicit, and external responses are overt and hence rather than reflecting mental consciousness, human thought is *implicit responding* (Watson, 1924, p. 15). It is controlled and not controlling. So to carry out his program, the "rule, or measuring rod, which the behaviorist puts in front of him always is: Can I describe this bit of behavior I see in terms of 'stimulus and response'" (*ibid.*, p. 6)? Because the stimulus always controls the response, a sagacious behaviorist in time should be able to work out the complete (efficiently) causal network of events of which behavior "is a function" (Watson, 1913, p. 167).

The phrase *control and prediction* has become a rallying cry for rigorous psychologists ever since. Introductory texts often define psychology as "the science of behavioral control and prediction" or a like definition. Mixed into this abstract formulation of a professional goal are the meanings of both a theoretical sort (what kind of determinism is presumed in this word *control*?) and a methodological sort (is not this a standard for validating evidence, and no more?). Many psychologists would prefer to restrict the phrase to the side of our methodological procedures in accruing evidence, because they do not feel that psychology should have as a professional aim the control of the lives of people. To meet such objections we have to spend some time on the theoretical side of knowledge, using our conceptual facilities (procedural evidence) to clarify our directions. But Watson failed to appreciate the theory-method distinction because all there is to life is behavior. Ultimately, behavior is a response that is a motion (reminiscent of the Wundtian reduction; see Chapter 3, p. 110), flowing along as a function of implicit and overt stimulation. He placed his psychology on the confident grounds of Newtonian-Laplacian science. There is probably no clearer call for mechanistic psychology in the literature than Watson's request of his generation: *". . . let us try to think of man as an assembled organic machine ready to run"* (Watson, 1924, p. 216).

Before long this simplistic version of "S to R to habit"—analogized from the reflex-arc cycle—was found wanting as a theoretical statement, although Watson's efforts were paying dividends. Psychology was building a distinctive body of scientific knowledge. Edward Chace Tolman (1886–1961) felt that a refinement was needed in the input-output mechanism of Watsonian behaviorism. Tolman spent time with the gestalt psychologist Kurt Koffka, and although he was not influenced sufficiently to take a more Kantian view of things, he *did* come away believing that behaviorism had to broaden its explanatory range. In his classic work *Purposive Behavior in Animals and Men* (1967; first appeared in 1932), Tolman begins his argument for a revised behaviorism as follows: "It will be contended by us (if not by Watson) that 'behavior-acts,' though no doubt in complete one-to-one correspondence with the underlying molecular facts of physics and physiology, have, as 'molar' wholes, certain emergent properties of their own" (p. 7).

The joining of behavior to act excites our interest, suggesting that Tolman was cognizant of the terminological and conceptual disputes of his predecessors. But by *act* Tolman did not mean anything other than responsivity in the typical behavioral sense. His reference to emergent properties in molar behavior relates to the gestaltist emphasis on the one (gestalt) over the many (elementalism). This formal-cause theme is what Tolman brought to behaviorism to "account for behavior," as the saying now goes. Tolman here initiates a theoretical proclivity that has been cultivated by all subsequent behaviorists. The strategy is essentially to try to explain humanistic terms in other than telic fashion. Of course it is put more professionally than this, as "try to account for all behavior using 'scientific' terminology." Graduate students in psychology soon learn to express—and in time, unfortunately, to think—this way, which comes down to "exclude final causation from your speculations!"

Yet Tolman is known for his founding of a purposive behaviorism (a phrase William McDougall used to describe his work and which Tolman then adopted). He was critical of Watson for wanting to limit the description of behavior to muscle twitches or aimless motions. Behavior has molar properties which emerge to give it a unique quality (the gestaltists had spoken of form qualities). If one looks at these molar patterns, he invariably finds them to be goal oriented. Behavior is always a question of "getting-to or getting-from a specific goal-object, or goal-situation" (ibid., p. 10). And this persistent striving toward or away from goals itself takes on "a specific pattern of commerce-, intercourse-, engagement-, communion-with such and such intervening means-objects, as the way to get thus to or from" (ibid., p. 11). If behavior is thus aimed at ends by its very nature, surely one should be able to observe the course of such actions and to see if a purposive effort is made to improve on the performance vis à vis some (equally observable) goal. Hence:

The doctrine we here contend for is, in short, that wherever a response shows docility [i.e., teachableness, improvability] relative to some end—wherever a response is ready (a) to break out into trial and error and (b) to select gradually, or suddenly, the more efficient of such trials and errors with respect to getting to that end—such a response expresses and defines something which for convenience [italics added], we name a purpose (ibid., p. 14).

We have italicized the phrase for convenience in the above quote to (1) emphasize that this is what we mean by the extraspective theorist describing events "over there" (third person) as he sees fit—that is, for his convenience and not for the convenience of the subject—and also to (2) provide another example of the tendency to account for a telic phenomenon in other than telic terms. Tolman is not saying that he is presenting evidence here of what the teleologists of history have meant by purpose. He is saying that to view behavior as purposive seems reasonable, although in truth we can never hope to "see" palpable purposes as we can see a rat's leg, flexing in behavior; but maybe we can use the term anyhow, relating it to the improvement in performance that a rat might show in running the maze, and in this way broaden behaviorism as we "account for" what the teleologists have been wanting us to consider but in a more scientific fashion! Tolman was quite aware of this strategy of explanation. He took special pains to distinguish his data-based view of purpose from other more traditional telic accounts, as in the following discussion of William McDougall:

> . . . for us, purpose is a purely objectively defined *variable* [italics added], which is defined by the facts of trial and error and of resultant docility; for Professor McDougall, purpose seems to be an introspectively defined subjective "somewhat," which is a something other, and more than, the manner in which it appears in behavior; it is a "psychic," "mentalistic" somewhat, behind such objective appearances, and to be known in the last analysis through introspection only. This difference between our point of view and McDougall's is fundamental and . . . complete . . . " (*ibid.*, p. 16).

This remarkable passage continues the argument from method which we saw Angell initiate. Note that Tolman here refers to purpose as a *variable*! It is not a theoretical construct, something that is framed by the psychologist and then put to test in a methodology calling for IV-DV regularities and the attendant controls that result in validation or fail to do so. Purpose is itself a "variable" to be captured in the facts of experimental observation. There is a blatant confound here of method-talk with theory-talk. Tolman speaks as if all he were disparaging is the introspective *methods* of the earlier psychologies. Actually, he is also disparaging the *theoretical* constructions a psychologist such as McDougall might have hoped to put to test in the experimental methods of functionalism or behaviorism. McDougall, the humanist, is pictured as a kind of "swami," playing with psychic unobservables, which comes down to nonentities hence nonscientific methodological formulations.

Had he been more circumspect concerning his total procedure as a scientist, Tolman could have seen that he was *not* rejecting McDougall's position on the basis of data—that is, the findings of experimentation! He was defining (or ridiculing) it away exclusively on theoretical grounds. He and behaviorists before and after him made it appear that something like a purpose, in the telic sense of a "that for the sake of which" (theoretical account), could not be put to scientific test. Of course even Angell would have seen the docility of behavior in Tolman's rat-runs as evidence for *consciousness!* And a psychological theory *could* view it as evidence for a genuine "that for the sake of which" characteristic in the rat's behavior. If the steps of control and prediction in validation were followed, there is nothing intrinsically impossible with testing a theory of *teleological* behavior in the IV-DV sequence, so long as we keep clearly in mind what is our *theory* (of purpose in behavior) and what is our *method* of validation. By placing his definition of purpose on the side of method—as a variable to be seen fluctuating in the IV-DV sequence —Tolman effectively negates the possibility of *ever* proving empirically that final causation exists in behavior. Why? Because the IV-DV sequence is taken *by definition* as an efficient-cause sequence of events.

If purpose is a variable, which variable might it be—the independent or the dependent? As a manifestation of behavior it is a response, and therefore clearly it must fall on the side of a dependent variable. Hence, it is by definition an efficiently caused effect and *no purpose at all*, if we mean by this term what the common sense of humanity has meant by it. Tolman wanted to correct the aspect of the humanistic-mechanistic debate on which behaviorism had been vulnerable. He tried to give behaviorism a more relevant formulation, one that would speak more directly to an extrapolation to man's behavior. To "account for" the fact that animals and humans might indeed contribute something to their course of behavior and not simply "muscle twitch" their way through life Tolman next proposed what might be called the *mediation thesis:*

The behaviorism here . . . presented will contend that mental processes are most usefully to be conceived as but dynamic aspects, or determinants, of behavior. They are *functional variables* [italics added] which *intermediate* [italics added] in the causal equation between environmental stimuli and initiating physiological states or excitements, on the one side, and final overt behavior, on the other (*ibid.*, p. 2).

A variant statement bringing in the word *response* follows:

Our system [purposive behaviorism] . . . conceives mental processes as *functional variables intervening* [italics added] between stimuli, initiating physiological states, and the general heredity and past training of the organism, on the one hand, and final resulting responses, on the other. These *intervening variables* [italics added] it defines as behavior-determinants (*ibid.*, p. 414).

This formulation obviated having to name whether purposes were independent or dependent variables. Purposes were *neither*. They "functioned" between a host of stimuli on the one side, and a number of responses on the other. In coining the term *intervening variable* (Int. V) Tolman legitimized the practice of mixing method-talk with theory-talk in experimental psychology. Behavior was now said to involve "S-Int. V-R" or "S-O-R" (with the O standing for organism, as Robert S. Woodworth [1869–1962] was to conceptualize the mediational sequence). What role did such intervening functions have in learning? Tolman suggested: "The process of learning any specific maze is thus the building-up of, or rather a refinement of and correction in, the expectations of such specific (*sign, significate and signified means-ends-relation*)-wholes, or, as we may hereafter call them, *sign-gestalts*" (*ibid.*, p. 136). The sign-gestalt (sometimes called a cognitive map) acts as a mediational aid, and the process is self-corrective so that:

. . . after learning has brought about the . . . changes in the expected sign-gestalts, such changes are going to react upon and modify the "readinesses" to sign-gestalts which the animal is going to carry with him to subsequent problems. The effect is one of reinforcing the propensities for certain types of means-objects as "probable" ways to given types of goals and weakening it for others (*ibid*, pp. 151–152).

We shall have much to say of the mediation model in the remaining pages of this volume. For now a note is sufficient that it makes no difference to a *theory* of behavior as efficiently caused whether we say "today's behaviors (responses) are a function of today's stimulations" or whether we say "today's behaviors (responses) are a function of yesterday's (mediated) stimulations *plus* today's stimulations." The latter account, which is what Tolman (and Woodworth) proposed, adds former efficient causes, but the basic meaning of a quasi-knee-jerk impetus to *all* behavior remains! The individual cannot on this theory opt against the experience he has had in the past. He is unable to go against these probabilities or to circumvent the layout of the sign-gestalt until subsequent experience intrudes and changes his purpose for him. Tolman has built on Angell's mediation idea to strengthen the behavioristic line of theory, but he has failed completely to "account for" what we know of as a purpose in that Brentano sense of reasoning "for the sake of" intended meaning-extensions. As the historical survey of Table 1 has taught us, one cannot say final cause when one really means yesterday's efficient cause.

The next major figure in this line of descent was Clark Leonard Hull (1884–1952). Hull (1943) elaborated on the concept of reinforcement, bringing in drive-reduction as a major explanatory principle. This remained within the material-cause type of formulation. He kept the mediation concept alive, and to "account for" seemingly telic behavior of the sort Tolman would have called purposive, he coined the term *fractional, antedating goal reaction* (later called *anticipatory goal response* by Neal Miller). It was not that an animal was making purposive moves in improving his responses toward the goal. One could see the rat gradually edging along the wall in the direction of the turn he would be making in the T-maze. It may have looked like a purposive maneuver, an intended preparation coming before the actual goal response of eating the food in the goal box, but it was not! What the animal had been learning via his repeated trials in the T-maze is a response of run-turn-eat. As he became more proficient through the practice trials (combining Watsonian frequency with drive reduction), the animal might reflect a "fraction" of the total goal reaction even before it had reached the point in the maze where its reward would be found.

The unique feature of this account is that Hull was to turn responses into stimuli here. That is, the actual stimulus for a fractional antedating goal reaction was the *responses* an animal was making in reaching the eventual goal. A fraction of the behavioral output generated a new kind of "intervening" input, which Hull termed the *pure stimulus act*. These stimuli were pure in the sense that their only role was to guide the course of behavior along the route to eventual reinforcement. They could not result in drive reduction via a consummatory response being made to them directly. Based on such a line of explanation, Hull (1952) developed his more extended theories of secondary reinforcement, habit-family hierarchies, and so on. Our point here is not to give a full presentation of Hullian learning theory, but simply to demonstrate that mediation theory was greatly expanded in the descent of behaviorism and this expansion was *not* an affair of method but rather of theoretical development. Tolman's claims of observing purpose methodologically were simply not defensible. Purpose is a *construct*, entertained theoretically by the observing experimentalist, who obtains empirical evidence favoring his conceptualization or fails to do so.

As Tolman did not reject McDougall based on evidence, Hull did not drop Tolmanian purpose based on evidence but rather on theoretical predilection. All of Tolman's evidence was simply reinterpreted! Hull was trying, in the best traditions of behaviorism, to give behavior a scientific (nontelic) appearance. The great advantage that he enjoyed, as all modern behaviorists enjoy, is the fact that the efficient- and material-cause conceptions are easily moved up and down the levels of abstraction we employ in describing anything (see Rychlak, 1968). The efficient cause in particular is the most multiordinal conception we have available to us. Literally *anything* can be seen in terms of its constitution (material cause) or those motions that have brought it about (efficient cause). Because plans of action must be drawn up by someone, rather than focusing on the pattern of behavior resulting (the formal-cause aspects) one can stress the motions that went into this planning by the individual who used a pencil to do (behavior) the drawing (planning). If a person seems to be putting his plans into effect (final-cause behaviors "for the sake of" plans), focus on the motion in behavior rather than on the strategy under presumption. Behaviorism's claim is that the motion *causes* the plans to come about, as well as the eventual intended actions in lieu of the plans. The *reverse* explanation is considered mentalistic, anthropomorphic, and probably spiritual as well.

The final person we wish to mention in this section is Burrhus Frederic Skinner (1904–       ). Because Skinner's thought is examined in detail in other sections of this book (see especially Chapter 6, pp. 255–270), we do not delve deeply into his outlook at this point. Suffice to say that Skinner (1938) *reverses* the classical S-R construct to a kind of R-S regularity in events. A behavioral response is not elicited by fixed stimuli, but rather is emitted as a kind of acting-upon operation. Responses are operators, or *operants*, which bring about changes in the contingent circumstances resulting in positive reinforcements (which are in this case stimuli for the next occasion). This does not mean that Skinner has foresaken the language of mediation. He once said: "As a determinist, I must assume that the organism is simply mediating the relationships between the forces acting upon it and its own output, and these are the kinds of relationships I'm anxious to formulate" (Evans, 1968, p. 23). Once again, clearly in the theoretical realm do we find Skinner eager to make formulations, although to hear him argue the case all of his views would seem to have been pressed on him by the weight of observational evidence (see, e.g., Skinner, 1956).

The Kantian Dissenters:
James, McDougall, Gestaltists, Rogers

William James (1842–1910) did not participate in the debate over functionalism versus structuralism (claiming on one occasion that he did not understand it), but we must surely accept him as an impor-

tant historical figure who would have resisted the trend functionalism was to establish in psychology. He would have considered this
an automation theory of behavior, and he specifically rejected this
point of view (see James, 1952, p. 90). James would have to be considered a mixed Lockean-Kantian theorist. His philosophy of Pragmatism has definite intonations of Lockeanism, in the sense of a
Yankee empiricism and practicality. He also gave the concept of
habit considerable emphasis, and his psychology is heavy with
physiological descriptions. But his fundamental efforts in the description of behavior were to account for it introspectively and,
above all, to include telic factors in the description. His celebrated
distinction between tough-minded (Lockean) and tender-minded
(Kantian) approaches to psychology reflected our historical confrontation. He claimed to have taken a middle position on this dimension, and we agree with that assessment.

  The first major spokesman for teleological psychology in America
was probably William McDougall (1871–1938). Though he was to
wage an essentially losing battle, McDougall clearly saw the developing trends of a functional psychology and what this could only mean
for a humanistic image of man. For example, he saw the inevitable
divergence that a mechanistic account of behavior stressing efficient
causes would engender vis à vis the more literary descriptions of
human experience (McDougall, 1922, p. 8). Literary psychology demands formal-final cause phraseology, and to be viable our science
must be capable of embracing such descriptions without distortion.
Watson's psychology was being typified as pure science in the 1920s,
but McDougall feared that this form of purification was distilling the
human constants from the behavioral equation.

  Though he used the language of instincts in his theories, McDougall saw these as inborn potentials for making self-contributions to
one's behavior, allowing for a true "that for the sake of which"
framing of human experience. The organism does not have to be
taught its instinctive potentials, although through experience such
nativistic tendencies were modified in maturation. But the way in
which these instincts were modified over life was not through what
Watson called the shaping of behavior. Only an efficiently caused
behavior can be shaped. Instincts were purposive sequences. Purpose was an introspectively conceived (theoretical) telic account of
the organism "coming at" the world with a self-directed contribution
to that course of methodological events under Tolmanian observation. McDougall astutely underscored the newly emerging tendency
in the 1920s for behaviorists to "account for" telic meanings in their

use of terms such as: "motor sets . . . trends . . . drives . . . [and] determining tendencies, all of which are terms of the Purposive Psychology, thinly disguised" (McDougall, 1923, p. 288). He was a committed humanistic psychologist, whose vision of psychology was too broad to be encompassed in the tightening grips of the antecedent-consequent vise that was closing in on psychology.

The next group of dissenters, who also fought a somewhat losing although brilliant battle with the rising functionalism *qua* behaviorism, were the gestalt psychologists: Max Wertheimer (1880–1943), Wolfgang Köhler (1887–1967), and Kurt Koffka (1886–1941). The Kantian-Lockean lines of the gestalt-behaviorism disagreements were more apparent than they had been in the cases of James and McDougall. Köhler (1961b) reiterated one of the central themes of the present volume when he observed:

The psychologist no less than other people has learned to see the world through the eyeglasses of natural science. What he beholds in this manner seems to him so obvious, he is so little aware of his eyeglasses, that any other view will appear to him as a distortion of the genuine aspect of the world (p. 207).

As we know, the gestaltists were to popularize these Kantian spectacles as the *phenomenal field*, which functioned as a gestalt one to organize the many features within its frame of reference. To suggest that we might be able to "account for" the intellectual life of man in terms of the "intrinsically blind, connection of mere facts" according to the frequency thesis or principle of contiguity was to fill Köhler (1961a) with "a mild, incredulous horror" (p. 11).

The gestaltists based their counter to behaviorism on researches conducted in sensory modalities, particularly vision, and they extended their views by way of analogy to explanations of higher mental processes (Wertheimer, 1945), personality (Koffka, 1935), and social behaviors of all types (Marrow, 1969). They were sophisticated concerning the rise of the "new physics" in Europe at the turn of the twentieth century and took from this more dynamic conception of science a series of terms to help convey their approach to psychology—terms such as *field, vector, force,* and so on. Although not thought of as a strict gestaltist, Kurt Lewin (1890–1947) must surely be considered in this light as well (*ibid.*). What the gestaltists actually did in theory-construction terms was to add the formal cause to the hopper of scientific description; in fact they gave it primary emphasis! This did not mean they *also* welcomed final-cause description. Though we can at points see what are clearly telic leanings in their writings (e.g., Wertheimer, 1945, p. 215), there are also significant disclaimers, as in the following:

To say: a certain process occurs because it is biologically useful, would be the kind of explanation we have to guard against. For the biological advantage of a process is an effect which has to be explained by the process, but the former cannot be used to explain the latter. A process must find its explanation in the dynamics of the system within which it occurs; the concept of biological advantage, on the other hand, does not belong to dynamics at all. And therefore teleological explanations in terms of biological advantage have no place in gestalt theory (Koffka, 1935, pp. 599–600).

This limits things to biological description, but it is difficult specifying what the gestaltists believed about man's ability to be free from unidirectional controls emanating in the stimulations of the environment or from the "functioning" (as Wertheimer, 1945, liked to call it) of the physical brain processes. The gestaltists were basically realistic in theoretical persuasion. They tried to bring behavior into a uniformity with its biological side or counterpart, but *not* in the Lockean sense of trying to point to the determinate substrate or the substantial constituent of behavior. Rather, the claim was made that a gestalt *identity* (isomorphism!) existed between the molar organization of the (proximal) stimulus as input from the (distal) environmental stimulation *and* the "motion of the atoms and molecules of the brain" (Koffka, 1935, p. 62). Though we have succeeded here in supplanting the efficient-cause (Lockean) building blocks "from below" by the organizing gestalt (Kantian) spectacles "from above," there is no more clear role for the "that for the sake of which" phrasing in the latter than in the former theoretical account. The final cause has been left out of both views.

Although the gestaltists had much to say about the organization of the proximal stimulus of the phenomenal field by way of various principles (figure-ground, closure, good continuation, proximity, etc.), they did not employ the dialectic in their descriptions. The bodily processes on which they based their explanations were best suited to demonstrative terminology, so that what was psychological and what was physical became united through a formal-cause emphasis without the benefit of a bipolar conception keeping the former potentially independent from the latter (at least to some extent!). Meaning for the gestaltist is always organization or structure. (Of course, this has nothing to do with Titchenerian structuralism.) Thinking (hence behavior) must be seen to take place in the layout of the pattern facing a person. As Wertheimer (1945) put it: "When one grasps a problem situation, its structural features and requirements set up certain strains, stresses, tensions in the thinker. What happens in real thinking is that these strains and stresses are followed up, yield vectors in the direction of improvement of the situation, and change it accordingly" (p. 195).

To describe the organization of a phenomenal (proximal) stimulus on the retina according to gestalt principles is one thing. But when we now equate such organizations with the brain material itself (isomorphism) and go on from there to explain thinking as due to the stresses, strains, and tensions of a phenomenal field, definite problems develop for the teleologist. We might now ask the gestaltists: What role does the *person* play in this structural organization and reorganization of the phenomenal field as the tensions are resolved and then reactivated? To say that a person as an ego or self is an "organized portion of the field" (Koffka, 1935, p. 520) does not answer the question, because as we noted concerning the scheme of Table 1 (p. 32) or the organization of letters into words (p. 56), simply being a part of a pattern does not mean that one behaves "for the sake of" this pattern. To speak of "patterns of energies" playing themselves out to a new level of gestalt organization is no more telic than to speak of efficiently caused (S-R) reflexes tying into a chain of associated habits. Though the flavor of each theory is distinctive, neither explanation has the individual-as-contributor active in the flux and flow of behavior.

A similar problem arises in the theorizing of our last major historical dissenter: Carl Rogers (1902–    ). Rogers and Skinner (1956) were to have a series of important debates that helped clarify the incompatibilities of mechanism and humanism. Although he tried to emphasize the person's organization of his *own* (subjective) phenomenal field, Rogers (1951, 1961) took most of his theoretical terminology from neogestalt theories and wound up with some of the same drawbacks to a full and rich humanistic formulation of behavior. There can be no doubt on the commitment Rogers has had to a teleological image of man. Speaking of the Skinnerian world view, Rogers (1961) once said:

I do . . . have strong personal reactions to the kind of . . . world which Skinner explicitly (and many other scientists implicitly) expect and hope for in the future. To me this kind of world would destroy the human person as I have come to know him in the deepest moments of psychotherapy. In such moments I am in relationship with a person who is spontaneous, who is responsibly free, that is, aware of this freedom to choose who he will be, and aware also of the consequences of his choice. To believe, as Skinner holds, that all this is an illusion, and that spontaneity, freedom, responsibility, and choice have no real existence, would be impossible for me (pp. 390–391).

Much as one might agree with Rogers here, the problem for a theoretician is to say how this freedom comes about. Lacking an appreciation of the dialectic as a theoretical tool, Rogers had to base his theory of personality on the *feelings* people have as they organize their phenomenal fields. Feelings teach us about what we value, and our values in turn reflect the organization of our phenomenal fields. If one is psychologically congruent with his feelings, the rest of his phenomenal experience will fall into place. In a sense Rogers holds that an isomorphism between bodily feelings and psychological values is not only possible but is the natural state of human beings. Only when we deny or distort these feeling-based values do we run the risk of personal maladjustment (incongruence). Rogers eventually built this view of man into what might be termed a naturalistic ethic, bringing to the fore again his teleology but in a different context:

Instead of universal values "out there," or a universal value system imposed by some group—philosophers, rulers, priests, or psychologists—we have the possibility of universal human value directions emerging from the experiencing of the human organism. Evidence from therapy indicates that both personal and social values emerge as natural, and experienced, when the individual is close to his own organismic valuing process [i.e., a feeling-based process]. The suggestion is that though modern man no longer trusts religion or science or philosophy nor any system of beliefs to give him values, he may find an organismic valuing base within himself which, if he can learn again to be in touch with it, will prove to be an organized, adaptive, and social approach to the perplexing value issues which face all of us (Rogers, 1970, p. 441).

This feeling-based organismic valuing process is therefore culture free, based on the assumption that any human being, anywhere in the world, at any point in history, would opt the same way as any other person, given only that he would openly and honestly contemplate the circumstances in light of how he felt about them as a human being (congruence) (*ibid.*, p. 440). Though an interesting thesis, the theory leaves unstated how a physical process (the feeling!) can evaluate or be the basis for an evaluation that can go "either way." That is, when an emotion is underway it does not appear to be open to alternatives. The feeling is definite and one-sided; though it can be in opposition to what is transpiring in experience, this is as an adamant opposition—often characterized as an unreasoned ("emotional") prompting. To judge, an organism must align that which is to be assessed "in relation to" some independent standard, and "for the sake of this comparison" arrive at a valued course of action. If the feeling is not the act of assessment, it must be the standard.

But this leaves the account unfinished, for it must surely be true that subhuman animals rely on such direct emotional reactions, yet we do not consider them valuing organisms. Human beings are considered higher animals because of what man has done in relation to his emotional standards, how he has been able to use or—as Rogers' theory points out—not use the emotional base as standard against which to assess his course of action. The concept of *feeling* takes its meaning from the material- and efficient-causes, and we might add, a formal-cause meaning in the sense of a patterning of emotions. But to speak of a *value* is to go beyond such considerations and impute some capacity on the part of an organism to evaluate (reason "for the sake of"). Behaviorists describe a value as either some kind of secondary reinforcement, which has presumably "rubbed off" from basic drive reductions, or an (efficiently caused) input via cultural influence now serving a mediating role in the succession of behavior. Rogers feels that this takes the humanity out of behavioral description, and he tries to present us with an alternative. Yet the same difficulties that confronted the behaviorists stymie Rogers: We cannot *say* one thing (feeling, as a material-efficient cause) and *mean* another (value, as a final cause).

## Functionalism's Heritage

In the remaining pages of Chapter 4 we review five points that are still relevant to modern psychology as the heritage of functionalism.

### Arguments from "Scientific" Method

The functionalists quickly adopted the "argument from method" which permitted them to require empirically demonstrable "facts" *before* they would entertain the likelihood of a given theoretical suggestion. This began as an attack on the "nebulous" humanistic conceptions of ego, spirit, or consciousness (Weiss, 1919) but soon spread to any form of teleological explanation (Kuo, 1928). The use of statistical tests (Calverton, 1924) brought mathematics into the functionalistic approach, and in time a theory of meaning was embraced that took operationalism (Stevens, 1935) as a kind of prerequisite for the possible employment of constructs. What was not operationally definable was, in effect, nonexistent. Hull's (1937) hypothetico-deductive method ensured that theory would not stray too far from the hard facts of observation.

This quarter often contended that mentalistic conceptions were anathema to the necessary determinism a scientific method had to presume for such knowledge to accrue (Boring, 1946). Behavior was just one more item of scientific manipulation in the pursuit of rigorous knowledge (Bergmann & Spence, 1941). To speak of mentalistic phenomena was to speak of the chimerical. Thought is not reality, said the functionalists, and all we can observe to validate is behavior as a palpable reality. Theory, as a product of thought, was not to be cultivated *as* theory. Better to deal in the intervening (methodological) variable than in the hypothetical (theoretical) construct (Meehl & MacCorqoudale, 1948). To contend that the scientist, himself a human being, needs accounting for in some reasonable fashion that may not be readily experimented on is to miss the point. Such speculations on human nature are best done in the nether regions of the arts, not at the hard frontiers of objective science (Spence, 1948). Indeed, a properly worked-out science would not require *any* theoretical speculation whatsoever (Skinner, 1950). Observed reality is before us, and experimental manipulations are predictable. Why then concern ourselves with archaic notions about human nature? We know what science is. Let us practice it!

From the other side, humanism, there came a steady counter to such developing functionalistic positions. Fernberger (1922) suggested that psychology might split into two wings, one devoted to the study of behavior (efficient causes) and the other to the study of consciousness (final causes). A decade later Yerkes (1933) reintroduced this notion of calling for a division between psychology and psychobiology. Although an eminent researcher himself, Yerkes freely admitted that he was never a psychologist in the true sense of the word (*ibid.*, p. 211). Adams (1928, 1937) made many fine arguments in favor of a concept of mind in psychology. Skaggs (1934) noted that the contrived laboratory procedures being used by psychologists bore little relation to life outside the laboratory. And Winter (1936) pointed to the outmoded Newtonian physics on which behaviorism was basing its approach to science. There was much concern expressed over the "mechanicomorphizing" of human behavior (Waters, 1939, 1948) and the overidealization of science (Allport,

1946, p. 132). Miller (1946) emphasized that proof is open to many interpretations, and the control-and-prediction sequence of scientific validation did not always result in complete understanding of the phenomenon studied in any case. Finally, Bakan (1953a, 1953b) uncovered many informal assumptions in behaviorism, assumptions the scientist permits himself to make yet fails to attribute a comparable intellectual facility to the persons under his description.

The unhappy outcome of this steady barrage of humanistic counters to functionalism is that it served to further the very tender-minded stereotype the behaviorists were advancing as characteristic of all teleologists. In donning the mantle of Spokesman and Defender of Science the functionalistic psychologists stole the initiative from the humanists, who were now put in the intolerable position of seeming to argue *against* rigor each time they raised a point of philosophical dispute. The behaviorist *always* begins his line of commentary from what can be observed, or from the hard data, as he calls it. This makes it appear that his arguments are always factual and without interpretations of these facts. In challenging such naiveté, the humanist—even though he is correct—comes off looking the tender-minded critic of science in the process. He could not hope to win in this polemical stance, and surely by mid-twentieth century he had not won much in the way of an innovation to psychological science. The behaviorists have succeeded in making the choice appear to be either *their* rigorous views or the mushy views of arty types who are incapable of conducting proper empirical investigations.

### Arbitrary and Miniature Theorizing: The "Accounting For" Argument

A second heritage of functionalism involves the tendency we have already emphasized above, of "accounting for" certain concepts in a supposedly more scientific fashion (see Dollard & Miller, 1950, p. 6, for a typical claim of this sort concerning Freudian theory's translation into S-R terminology). We noted this tendency above—for example, when Tolman suggested that *purpose* was a methodological term or when Hull framed this intentionalism as a supposed fractional antedating goal response. The great stress on operational definitions early in psychology's existence probably hurt more than it helped (Stevens, 1935; Bergmann & Spence, 1941). This "canon" made it appear that by simply defining a conception in terms of the operations required to measure it *always clarified* the meaning of this construct. It also implied that errors in meaning could not be promulgated for any length of time, because everyone would immediately see what is transpiring and the confusions generated would be made plain. Neither of these assumptions are correct.

In fact quite the reverse has *usually* taken place. Rather than taking the responsibility to frame clear theoretical positions and *then* moving to an operationalization (or occasionally reversing this sequence), psychologists have felt that their job was finished if they could simply point to a reproducible "empirical" effect. The trouble is that our theories do not always get translated into research designs clearly, so the observed data really are meaningless unless understood in light of the assumptions which generated them. Operational definitions and empirical observations are *never* free of theoretical interpretations.

For example, in their book *Social Learning and Imitation* Miller and Dollard (1941) defined *stimulus* and *response* as follows: "A response is any activity within the individual which can become functionally connected with an antecedent event through learning; a stimulus is any event to which a response can be so connected" (p. 59). Quite obviously, unless we knew a lot about what psychologists had been considering a stimulus and a response beforehand, this definition would not help us very much. The definitions given in their later effort, *Personality and Psychotherapy*, are not much clearer: "We shall call anything a stimulus that seems to have the functional properties of a stimulus and anything a response that seems to have the functional properties of a response" (Dollard & Miller, 1950, p. 69). Though both definitions have a functionalist rationale, they fail to reflect the broad history of purely theoretical assumptions made by those individuals who "operationalized" the stimulus and response constructs in the first place. We shall see in the next section how this led to a confounding of methods with theories. For now we simply want to stress that the functional properties of stimuli and responses are *not* that easily observed.

Consider the pupillary observations introduced to the literature by Hess (1965) and subsequently elevated into an important experimental topic called pupillometry. If a person looks at a picture of something he likes, as opposed to something to which he is indifferent or dislikes, we can often observe his pupils dilating. According to Dollard and Miller's operational definitions, the liked picture would be a stimulus and the dilation of the pupil would be a response. Though a reasonable (extraspective) theory, this is *all it is!* We are not empirically observing dilations as responses and pictures as stimuli here. We are witnessing the conceptualizations of a particular line of *theory* (stimulus and response are theory terms) being put to methodological test. A teleologist might conceptualize the identical observations differently, so that the pupil dilation does not come out a response to the picture; it is a preparatory, hence *stimulating act* in the tradition of Brentano (see Chapter 3). Attention is being mobilized "for the sake of" an interest, and this mobilization is *not* responsive but prospective—literally stimulating the organism to extend interest and meaning rather than respond to anything.

The teleologist might therefore hold that the picture is merely an instrumentality, conceptualized essentially as a response to the projected interest pattern of the individual now looking at something that he likes. This more Kantian interpretation of the dilation is just as reasonable a(n) (introspective) theory as the one currently accepted which ever frames the pupillary dilation as a response. But the point is that nothing in the observations made can decide which of these two interpretations we take is the "real" one, or even the "best" one. The only reason we take the conventional interpretation is because it is readily grasped by all, and it has the sanctions of our institutionalized paradigm. But there is a price paid for this agreement, because although it is easier to see one's theory directly in one's apparatus than in having to keep these two realms separate, the tendency is to stick with rather mundane theoretical conceptions—variations on not only common but *dull* themes. Irwin [1971] has said this about as well as it could be said: "Identification of the meaning of psychological terms with experimental manipulations may once have had corrective value against extreme looseness of conception, but it has also had the effect of sanctifying dull and superficial work and making thought stop short where it is most needed" (p. 25).

The very ease with which we can become confused about what the "operations" mean forced the functionalists to bring their theoretical commentary closer and closer to the experimental design actually followed in the study. Phrases such as "for the purposes of this experiment, construct X is operationally defined as Y and Z" seemed to meet the criticisms of detractors who felt that the translation of a concept into operations often distorted the meaning as framed. By limiting one's claims to one specific experiment we of course end up focusing our attention on what was actually functioning in the experimental design *per se. Functionalism* came to mean study carefully whatever seems functionally relatable in an experimental format (see, e.g., Woodworth & Sheehan, 1964, pp. 57–58). It has been defined as follows:

Functionalism is empiricist rather than systematic. It eschews inference for established experimental relationships between demonstrable variables. Its laws are quantitative, directly descriptive of data. There is a healthy respect for data, and there is a commendable urge to state issues specifically in a form subject to test (Hilgard & Bower, 1966, p. 330).

Although this definition is aimed at functionalism as merely one school of thought among many, the present argument holds that literally *all* of modern experimental psychology has this value system. The earlier behaviorists—men like Tolman, Hull, Guthrie—tried to explain things systematically. They were the system builders, with Hull achieving the heights of this explanation style. Since his time we have witnessed the rise of so-called miniature theories (*ibid.*, pp. 332–333), supposedly less ambitious but more precise efforts to clarify a delimited area of study. But the truth is, such narrow-gauged theorizing was *inevitable*, once the exclusive focus on method had taken place. Miniature theorizing is the justification given to the fact that we are not permitted to reason (theorize) very much beyond the experimental apparatus *per se*. We find the experimenter saying the same things in various sections of his report—introduction, method, and discussion of results—so that the design becomes the common denominator because this is where the functioning of variables actually took place.

This leaves no room for telic theory, of course, because the paradigm of scientific method is properly devoid of intentional manipulation. The purpose of validation is to remove the plausible rules on which procedural evidence is dependent. Even the most rudimentary theoretical or metatheoretical examination of the course of scientific investigation establishes this fact. But when one expects to learn all there is to know from methods of this sort, methods that have *intentionally* been stripped of intentionality, then through a kind of Ebbinghaus-circularity (see Chapter 3, pp. 119–121) it is impossible in principle to establish the easily discernible role of telic factors in the behavior of human beings—subjects *or* scientists! In the style of Titchener, criticisms of this circular approach were relegated to philosophy by our leading functionalists—an especially telling relegation because unlike Wundt these psychologists saw no use for philosophy at all! There was a rush to data, and anything that might be circumscribed operationally was taken as worthy of study, especially if this empirical definition suggested a simplified version of behavior. Animal study was popular because of the implicit Dar-

winian view that it could provide insights into rudimentary laws
going to make up all forms of behavior.

The Lockean assumption was made that someday these bits and
pieces of "well-controlled research" could then be put together and
say something meaningful. But this putting together of a data puzzle
is *not* a methodological problem in any case. It is a theoretical effort,
one that will require some overriding suggestions that cannot be seen
directly in any one (or more) experimental design(s). Even if this be
true, the functionalist is likely to say that to base one's theory on
well-controlled data is better than to speculate from fuzzy conceptions before the facts are gathered. This sounds plausible and is
based on the realistic assumption that facts are like apples—fallen
from the tree of knowledge. But facts are never quite this palpable
or meaningfully discernible, even when we define our experimental
terms operationally and test our findings statistically. Indeed, as the
next section demonstrates, the functionalists did not even keep
clearly in mind what was their *theory* and what was their *method*. In
a situation of this sort a call for "the" facts is surely gratuitous.

Confounding Method with Theory

A method is the means or manner employed to advance evidential
support for one's theoretical speculations, hunches, predictions, and
so on. There are two general cases of method: the *cognitive* method,
in which procedural evidence is employed as a test of truth value,
and the *research* method, in which validating evidence is taken as
the standard for belief in the theory espoused. Experimental evidence is of the latter variety, in which the scientist designs a "trial
run" (an experiment) to test his thoughts or simply arranges circumstances so that he cannot *intentionally* tamper with how they might
eventuate and watches to see what happens without any particular
idea as to what this might be. This control of circumstances and the
possible prediction of an outcome is what we mean by experimental
validation or research evidence. Ordinarily, if a scientist begins his
research by simply watching for an outcome, he tries to crossvali-
date whatever knowledge he has accrued by doing his more formal
predicting in a follow-up study (usually, a series of studies).

As operational definitions do not always clarify a meaning as
originally expressed (recall Tolman's redefinition of purpose), so too
validation in an experimental context does not always answer what
we want to know. That is, sometimes we can observe a controlled
sequence of events (experimental design) and even predict its even-

tual outcome without understanding what is taking place, how it achieves its predictable outcome, or why it should work under certain circumstances and not others. Functionalists believe that because they might literally observe the antecedents to behavior and, in conjunction with these, the consequents of behavior, the conceptual requirements of understanding will necessarily issue during the experimental course of events. Sagacious observation *per se* will provide explanations for what is empirically known. But this is simply untrue, and it has been untrue for all other sciences in the history of thought.

As the eminent philosopher of science Philipp Frank (1957) has shown, scientific findings (validated predictions or observations) *outstrip* the common sense understanding of them, taking us back to that condition earlier in history where we could control and predict without knowing why, what, or how such regularities in events were really brought about. Man predicted his course of travel under the stars, controlled the crops through practical know-how, and cured himself of certain diseases centuries before there was anything like a scientific account of these beneficial outcomes. With the birth of science, and especially with the advent of modern physics, the kinds of predictions that were possible from the thinking of an Einstein or a Bohr did not make "common sense," although they were found observationally to be valid. In truth the earlier folk theories of stars as baubles, hung in the sky above a flat terrain by a God so that man could find his way about were more plausible than, for example, the notions of gravity *as* inertia, or electrons making quantum leaps.

The obvious lesson is that science is not only a methodological endeavor. Constant attention must be given to theoretical considerations—or, as they might be called, metatheoretical or philosophical considerations. The cognitive test of procedural evidence is all that can be hoped for here, but there is always the counterbalancing requirement in science to return to validation whenever possible. One side need not be ignored in preference to the other, as has happened too often in the history of thought. Recall from Chapter 1 how the medieval theorist, relying exclusively on procedural evidence, came to anthropomorphize nature. Later, in Newtonian science, the uncritical acceptance of empirical data without sophisticated study of assumptions led to a "theorization" of scientific method—that is, the assumptions of the method were projected onto the world as a *necessary* characteristic and then "proved so" by the results of this very same method (Burtt, 1955, p. 229). Though functionalists like to

point to the former circumstance as an inevitable outcome of teleology in science, they constantly fall into the errors of the latter
variety by confusing what is their methodological commentary with
what is their theory of explanation.

This confounding was easy to make because both stimulus-
response (S-R) theory and the independent variable-dependent variable (IV-DV) sequence of experimentation can be construed in
exclusively efficient-cause terms—even though the IV-DV sequence
was introduced as a mathematical formal cause (see Chapter 1, p. 50).
Because the functionalists eschewed philosophical analysis as not
sufficiently empirical for science to worry about, the almost shocking
confounding of terms that was to result went unnoticed in the arbitrariness and practicality of their research efforts. We now turn to
an historical documentation of these charges.

In his opening call for behaviorism John Watson (1913) set as his
goal the "working out [of] a systematic scheme for the prediction and
control of response in general" (pp. 162–163). As we have just reviewed it, the phrase control and prediction defines validating evidence. But Watson was not saying that the experimentalist performs
this activity to support or refute his theoretical hypotheses, which in
turn might account for the observed data. He was controlling not an
independent variable, but a "stimulus" (ibid., p. 163) so that he might
efficiently cause the organism's movements to go the way he wanted
them to go. Rather than validated knowledge, behaviorism sought
lawful ties of stimuli to responses: "In a system of psychology completely worked out, given the response the stimuli can be predicted;
given the stimuli the response can be predicted" (ibid., p. 167).

Tolman was next to confound theoretical with methodological
terminology, and he did so while expressly trying to "cognize" the
simplistic efficient-cause approach of Watson. Watson had removed
the organism qua thinker from the succession of events called behavior, but Tolman reintroduced a modest role for mentality in
behavior, as a kind of "middle term" in the efficient-cause sequence.
Returning to the quote cited above (p. 153), we find Tolman (1967)
saying: "Our system . . . conceives [of] mental processes as functional variables intervening between stimuli, initiating physiological
states, and the general heredity and past training of the organism, on
the one hand, and final resulting responses, on the other. These
intervening [italics added] variables it defines as behavior-determinants" (p. 414). A variable, whether intervening or not, is a
methodological concept, referring specifically to the logic of experimental design. The status of a variable is achieved by translating our

theoretical construct into a measurable (demonstrable) factor in the experimental sequence, allowing for an IV-DV succession of events to take place with an hypothesized outcome. To put such evidential measurements into the central nervous system of people (or rats) is to make an unwarranted extension of what is or can be observed in the experimental design.

Stevens (1935) next crystallized an attitude in experimental theoretical description that has continued to the present: "Psychology regards all observations, including those which a psychologist makes upon himself, as made upon the 'other one' and thereby makes explicit the distinction between the experimenter and the thing observed" (p. 517). This should be recorded in the history of psychology as the *principle of extraspection!* Whereas Brentano had a secondary consciousness in his introspective method, observing the observer from an introspective slant, the Americans now assumed that whenever they observed the observation was extraspective. Even when they looked into their own activities as scientists they were describing events in an extraspective sense.

Hull (1937) defined the equation of method to theory for all time. The second rule of his hypothetico-deductive method called for what is effectively a tautological identity of theory (or postulate) and the test of that theory (in the experimental procedure). Bergmann and Spence (1941) then voiced a classic confounding of terms in their reiteration of the Watsonian dream when they observed, "Like every other science, psychology conceives its problem as one of establishing the interrelations within a set of variables, most characteristically between response variables on the one hand and a manifold of environmental variables on the other" (pp. 9–10). To speak of response variables is blatantly to preempt the possible theoretical account of why experimental variables might be said to bear an observed relationship. This paradigmatic preemption effectively *dictates* terms to the experimenter, who must now either see his dependent variable as a response or risk being considered nonscientific by his peers. Meehl and MacCorquodale's (1948) subsequent paper on the distinction between a hypothetical construct (theory) and an intervening variable (method) did nothing to check the developing terminological confusion. The point of this classic paper was to suggest that a methodological construct—the intervening variable—is somehow more meaningful (because it is part of the operations made in validation) than is a theoretical construct (which accounts for the observed data in a less real unobservable fashion).

By mid-twentieth century our leading psychologists easily slipped back and forth between terminologies. Though he does not consider himself an S-R psychologist (and with good reason), Skinner can say of himself: "As an analyst of behavior, I want to relate the probability of response to a large number of independent variables, even when these variables are separated in time and space" (Evans, 1968, p. 12). A scientist who believes he is observing "variables at play," which are efficient causes *only* in the experimental context, will have put himself in the position of being unable to see a role for teleology in behavior *in principle*, so long as he follows this experimental procedure! He will have defined himself into a mechanistic corner which even empirical evidence cannot bring him out of. This takes us into the next heritage of functionalism.

## Negating Proof for Teleology: The S-R Bind

Let us assume that a humanistic psychologist were to follow the strict canons of validation, putting his telic theoretical construct to test in an empirical research effort. He begins by designing an experiment that flows from his premising theory, properly controls the designated variables in consideration of his hypothesis, and then eventually makes the proper empirical observations which are tested statistically and found to be significantly different from a chance array of means in the direction of his predictions. Having found evidence for his telic construct, he drafts his empirical findings as a report and submits it to a leading journal of experimental psychology with appropriate theoretical commentary on the findings embracing the validity of teleological behavior. What does the typical toughminded referee say upon reading this manuscript? Does he reason as follows: "I'll be darned. There does seem to be grounds here for a belief in teleological accounts. Let's see how this theorist develops his thinking in light of his findings." From personal experience and knowledge of other humanists' experiences, the present writer can answer: *Hardly!* The preponderant odds are that his cogitations will run as follows: "There seems to be a behavioral (S-R) regularity in there, but until we delineate all of the antecedent variables controlling these measured responses the author seems to think are selfinitiated intentions, we are unable to say *what* is taking place. One thing for certain: this business about mental intentions and personal directions is unwarranted by the observations. We must find the antecedent determinants (S-R laws) of these mediating intentions. We need a more scientific account!"

The humanist can either change his theoretical account and do what functionalists always do—that is, repeat his experimental design as a pseudotheory in the discussion section—or he can resubmit the manuscript to another journal. But even in this eventuality, the editorial review will probably be the same. If so, are the journal referees proved *correct* in their assessment of humanistic research? Is not the humanist simply demonstrating in his carping about how evidence is to be interpreted what the functionalists have claimed all along? Humanists are unable to accept the judgment of their peers in an objective test of their theories. Nothing could be further from the truth!

The point here is that the *evidence* has been laid down in the original experimental design. Evidence must always be seen in the prediction and control of events *before* data are arrayed. In the demonstrative strategy one always moves from the meaning as originally formulated in theory *to* the predicted succession of events in methodological test. Having so confounded methodological with theoretical considerations, the reviewer honestly believes that the humanist's IV-DV (method) succession supports *his* (the reviewer's) S-R theory. Of course any form of efficient-cause theory would be the same here, such as input-mediation-output, and so on. Terminology changes across journal referees but the efficient causality remains constant, making it impossible *in principle* for a final-cause construct to be tested.

The concept of law in psychology is interpreted so that this efficient-cause empiricism is permitted to flourish. A law is, or should be, considered a stipulated and proven relationship between two or more variables, often expressed in mathematical terms. A law is therefore methodological terminology. When it is graphed or stated as a statistical value the law can be thought of as one of the Leibniz-Dirichlet functions (see Chapter 1, p. 22, and p. 49). But in psychology the confounding of method with theory has resulted in erroneous claims such as "S-R laws are discovered" rather than "lawful relations under methodological observation may be given S-R (efficient-cause) interpretations."

Even today too many psychologists take as self-evident that: (1) antecedent Ss determine consequent Rs in the cause-effect terms of efficient causality; (2) experimental IVs define Ss and DVs define Rs; (3) for all practical purposes IVs *are* Ss and DVs *are* Rs; (4) the relationship between these two "variables" are therefore determinate, as proven by the statistically significant evidence of a predicted outcome; (5) the extent of this efficient-cause determination of an antecedent-to-a-consequent can be expressed mathematically as a(n) (S-R) law or function; and (6) theoretical speculations going beyond such empirically observed facts are unwarranted, unless they make direct reference to further variables which can be concretely manipulated (i.e., efficiently caused to vary).

This functionalistic credo has fooled many into thinking that it is an *objective* approach to science, but ironically it is precisely the opposite. The writer has termed this style of theorizing the "S-R Bind," but it could just as readily be called an "efficient-cause bind," for what it reflects is a circularity in which, because of the confusion of theory and method, any evidence presented in the efficient-cause IV-DV methodological frame is seen, hence "proven," as the S-R theoretical frame (Rychlak, 1968, pp. 57–60). This literally precludes establishing a teleological construct as valid. Without consciously intending to do so, the functionalistic psychologists have devised an approach to science that is nonobjective and essentially repressive, because it cannot leave room for explanations that fail to meet its efficient-cause biases.

## Institutionalization of the Lockean Model

The final heritage of functionalism is a clear victory of the Lockean over the Kantian model. Because of Kuhn's (1970, 1st ed., 1962) analysis of the "scientific paradigm," much attention has been devoted to the question of psychology's having or not having a paradigm. We take up Kuhn's work in Chapter 5. For now we simply wish to note that it is commonly believed that psychology lacks a unifying paradigm of this sort. Robert Watson (1967) has argued that rather than functioning under a formal paradigm, psychology splits up into camps under the influence of a series of oppositionally framed "prescriptions," such as our historical functionalism-structuralism debate. Giorgi (1970, p. 165) has suggested that we may be in a preparadigmatic stage in psychology, for we surely have much disagreement over what sort of human image to embrace.

The present analysis holds that we *do* have a formal institutionalized paradigm in psychology, stemming from the confounding of method and theory discussed above. In large measure because of the rise of functionalism, which due to its eclecticism has become a kind of universal outlook among all empirical psychologists, the Lockean model has emerged victorious in the historic confrontation with Kantianism. The Yankee Spirit of hardheaded no-nonsense practicality has made this victory possible. Those psychologists who were

attracted to the simplicity and promise of clarity advanced by functionalism were also the individuals who populated the academic
centers of America. By stressing empirical data and going easy on
the question of theory a number of different viewpoints could be
brought together to prove that psychology was a science, like any
of the established sciences in the university setting. Lockeanism took
hold of psychology as an *officially sanctioned theory of behavior,*
even though it gained this status under the guise of scientific method.

This legitimizing of Lockeanism in experimentation ensures that
it will not be dislodged until psychologists take a completely new
look at what they are doing in the research context. Even if a modern
psychologist does not think of himself as an S-R theorist, when he
now describes what he is doing in the research context the weight of
procedural evidence implying a one-to-one correspondence of IV-DV
to S-R is overwhelming. As do the gestaltists, he feels that to speak
of "the stimulus" in a behavioral context is objectively correct. This
does not make him an S-R theorist. Of course, stimuli stimulate,
which means that next we are in the realm of responses. But responses do not have to be mechanical; they can simply be descriptions of behavior. Does not behavior move along? This means it is
constituted of responses, does it not? And so it goes. Before two
pages have been written, thanks to the paucity of *technical* terms
for a telic account of behavior, the modern psychologist finds himself slipping inevitably into the Efficient-Cause (S-R) Bind.

For the teleologist to retain the integrity of what he really wants
to say will require the fashioning of a new technical language in the
description of behavior. Above all, he will have to take a close look
at terms that in the past have been brushed over lightly, dismissed
as philosophical, or arbitrarily redefined to meet the needs of experimental design. In the remaining chapters of this volume we make
this effort and suggest a more useful terminology for telic description. We do not call for a complete rejection of Lockeanism in this
reexamination. Rather, we hope to restore its historical opponent
(Kantianism) to a more equal status in the ongoing activity of psychological science. We think this would be good for psychology,
bringing back the kind of dialectical confrontation that used to make
psychology a dynamic science but has in recent years been lost to
the succeeding generations of individuals who enter the profession.
There are still such clashes in the realm of basic-versus-applied or
clinical-versus-experimental psychology, but we hope to see it re-
stored "right in academia" between those rigorous psychologists
who consider themselves humanists and those who do not. In fact

we think that much of the necessity for clashes such as basic-applied or clinical-experimental would be removed if there were a viable Kantian alternative to the Lockeanism presently issuing from the psychological laboratory. The applied and clinical psychologists would then have perfectly rigorous psychological principles (laws, functions) of a *telic* variety on which to base their theories of human behavior.

## Summary

Chapter 4 carries the historical confrontations of the Kantian-Lockean models in psychology to America. It begins with a consideration of the structuralism-functionalism debate, showing how this historical confrontation was initiated by a humanistic criticism of the Wundtian-Titchenerian approach to psychology (more Titchener than Wundt, actually). Caldwell leveled this criticism and it was subsequently carried forward by Calkins, both of whom might be said to be Kantians in the style of Brentano. However, the major figures to emerge in this debate were Titchener and Angell. Titchener seems to have become embroiled in two different kinds of debate. Because, as the chapter demonstrates, *both* Titchener and Angell favored Lockean formulations, the Kantian-Lockean issue that triggered Caldwell's criticism was never satisfactorily resolved. What is worse, its humanistic theme was lost to the history of psychology. We conclude that the notorious structuralist-functionalist disagreement was in fact a Lockean-Lockean *non*confrontation, an insignificant quibble so far as the basic "image of man" issue is concerned.

We trace the rise of functionalism in America over the first half of the twentieth century, with specific attention given to behaviorism's role in this advance. Watson, Tolman, Hull, and Skinner are presented as major Lockean advocates of the functionalist metaphysics. The growing emphasis given to efficient-cause description in functionalism's rise as well as the tendency to redefine telic terminology to meet the needs of experimental design are underscored. James, McDougall, Wertheimer, Köhler, Koffka, Lewin, and Rogers are then reviewed as the major Kantian dissenters over the first half of the twentieth century. Some of the weaknesses of these latter positions are discussed.

The final third of Chapter 4 is devoted to a consideration of functionalism's heritage. We contend that modern American psychology is based on a functionalist metaphysics. The following characteristics are to be seen in this heritage: arguments from "scientific" method, arbitrary and miniature theorizing, the confounding of method with theory, arbitrarily negating proof for teleology, and the institutionalization of the Lockean model. Before psychology will be in a position to rectify its current one-sidedness, a study will have to be made of the technical language used to describe behavior. This can be achieved if the present Lockeanism is counterbalanced with a more viable Kantianism. Chapter 4 completes the historical background required to understand the revolutionary changes called for in the chapters that follow.

## References

Adams, D. K. The inference of mind. Psychological Review, 1928, **35**, 235–252.

Adams, D. K. Note on method. Psychological Review, 1937, **44**, 212–218.

Allport, G. W. Personalistic psychology as a science: A reply. Psychological Review, 1946, **53**, 132–135.

Angell, J. R. The relations of structural and functional psychology to philosophy. Philosophical Review, 1903, **12**, 203–243.

Angell, J. R. The province of functional psychology. Psychological Review, 1907, **2**, 61–91.

Bakan, D. Learning and the scientific enterprise. Psychological Review, 1953, **60**, 45–49. (a)

Bakan, D. Learning and the principle of inverse probability. Psychological Review, 1953, **60**, 360–370. (b)

Bergmann, G., & Spence, K. Operationism and theory in psychology. Psychological Review, 1941, **48**, 1–14.

Boring, E. G. Mind and mechanism. American Journal of Psychology, 1946, **54**, 173–192.

Boring, E. G. A history of experimental psychology. New York: Appleton-Century-Crofts, 1950.

Burtt, E. A. The metaphysical foundations of modern physical science (rev. ed.). Garden City, N.Y.: Doubleday, 1955.

Caldwell, W. Professor Titchener's view of the self. Psychological Review, 1898, **5**, 401–408.

Caldwell, W. The postulates of a structural psychology. Psychological Review, 1899, **6**, 187–191.

Calkins, M. W. A reconciliation between structural and functional psychology. Psychological Review, 1906, **13**, 61–81.

Calverton, V. F. The rise of objective psychology. Psychological Review, 1924, **31**, 418–426.

Dollard, J., & Miller, N. E. Personality and psychotherapy: An analysis in terms of learning, thinking, and culture. New York: McGraw-Hill, 1950.

Evans, R. I. B. F. Skinner: The man and his ideas. New York: Dutton, 1968.

Fernberger, S. W. Behavior versus introspective psychology. *Psychological Review*, 1922, **29**, 409–413.

Frank, P. *Philosophy of science*. Englewood Cliffs, N.J.: Prentice-Hall, 1957.

Giorgi, A. *Psychology as a human science: A phenomenologically based approach*. New York: Harper & Row, 1970.

Hess, E. H. Attitude and pupil size. *Scientific American*, 1965, **212**, 46–54.

Hilgard, E. R., & Bower, G. H. *Theories of learning*. New York: Appleton-Century-Crofts, 1966.

Hull, C. L. Mind, mechanism, and adaptive behavior. *Psychological Review*, 1937, **44**, 1–32.

Hull, C. L. *Principles of behavior*. New York: Appleton-Century-Crofts, 1943.

Hull, C. L. *A behavior system*. New Haven: Yale University Press, 1952.

Irwin, F. W. *Intentional behavior and motivation: A cognitive theory*. Philadelphia: Lippincott, 1971.

James, W. *The principles of psychology*. In R. M. Hutchins (Ed.), *Great books of the western world* (Vol. 53). Chicago: Encyclopedia Britannica, 1952.

Koffka, K. *Principles of gestalt psychology*. New York: Harcourt, Brace, 1935.

Köhler, W. Gestalt psychology today. In M. Henle (Ed.), *Documents of gestalt psychology*. Berkeley: University of California Press, 1961. Pp. 1–15. (a)

Köhler, W. Psychological remarks on some questions of anthropology. In M. Henle (Ed.), *Documents of gestalt psychology*. Berkeley: University of California Press, 1961. Pp. 203–221. (b)

Kuhn, T. S. *The structure of scientific revolutions* (2nd ed.). Chicago: The University of Chicago Press, 1970 [1st ed., 1962].

Kuo, Z. Y. The fundamental error of the concept of purpose and the trial and error fallacy. *Psychological Review*, 1928, **35**, 414–433.

Marrow, A. J. *The practical theorist: The life and work of Kurt Lewin*. New York: Basic Books, 1969.

McDougall, W. Prolegomena to psychology. *Psychological Review*, 1922, **29**, 1–43.

McDougall, W. Purposive or mechanical psychology? *Psychological Review*, 1923, **30**, 273–288.

Meehl, P. E., & MacCorquodale, K. On a distinction between hypothetical constructs and intervening variables. *Psychological Review*, 1948, **55**, 95–107.

Miller, D. L. The meaning of explanation. *Psychological Review*, 1946, **53**, 241–246.

Miller, N. E., & Dollard, J. *Social learning and imitation*. New Haven: Yale University Press, 1941.

Rogers, C. R. *Client-centered therapy*. Boston: Houghton Mifflin, 1951.

Rogers, C. R. *On becoming a person*. Boston: Houghton Mifflin, 1961.

Rogers, C. R. Toward a modern approach to values: The valuing process in the mature person. In J. T. Hart & T. M. Tomlinson (Eds.), *New directions in client-centered therapy*. Boston: Houghton Mifflin, 1970. Pp. 430–441.

Rogers, C. R., & Skinner, B. F. Some issues concerning the control of human behavior: A symposium. *Science*, 1956, **124**, 1057–1066.

Rychlak, J. F. *A philosophy of science for personality theory*. Boston: Houghton Mifflin, 1968.

Skaggs, E. B. The limitations of scientific psychology as an applied practical science. *Psychological Review*, 1934, **41**, 572–576.

Skinner, B. F. *The behavior of organisms: An experimental analysis.* New York: Appleton-Century, 1938.

Skinner, B. F. Are theories of learning necessary? *Psychological Review*, 1950, **57**, 193–216.

Skinner, B. F. A case history in scientific method. *American Psychologist*, 1956, **11**, 221–233.

Spence, K. W. The postulates and methods of "behaviorism." *Psychological Review*, 1948, **55**, 67–78.

Stevens, S. S. The operational definition of psychological concepts. *Psychological Review*, 1935, **42**, 517–527.

Titchener, E. B. *An outline of psychology.* New York: Macmillan, 1897.

Titchener, E. B. The postulates of a structural psychology. In T. Shipley (Ed.), *Classics in psychology.* New York: Philosophical Library, 1961. Pp. 224–243. Originally published in *Philosophical Review*, 1898, **7**, 449–465.

Titchener, E. B. *Systematic psychology: Prolegomena.* Ithaca and London: Cornell University Press, 1972.

Tolman, E. C. *Purposive behavior in animals and men.* New York: Appleton-Century-Crofts, 1967.

Waters, R. H. Morgan's canon and anthropomorphism. *Psychological Review*, 1939, **46**, 534–540.

Waters, R. H. Mechanicomorphism: A new term for an old mode of thought. *Psychological Review*, 1948, **55**, 139–142.

Watson, J. B. Psychology as the behaviorist views it. *Psychological Review*, 1913, **20**, 158–177.

Watson, J. B. *Behaviorism.* New York: Norton, 1924.

Watson, R. I. Psychology: A prescriptive science. *American Psychologist*, 1967, **22**, 435–443.

Weiss, A. P. The mind and the man within. *Psychological Review*, 1919, **26**, 327–334.

Wertheimer, M. *Productive thinking.* New York: Harper, 1945.

Winter, J. E. The postulates of psychology. *Psychological Review*, 1936, **43**, 130–148.

Woodworth, R. S., & Sheehan, M. R. *Contemporary schools of psychology* (3rd ed.). New York: Ronald, 1964.

Yerkes, R. M. Concerning the anthropocentrism of psychology. *Psychological Review*, 1933, **40**, 209–212.

# CHAPTER FIVE

## What Kind of Scientific Revolution Is Needed in Psychology?

We said at the close of Chapter 4 that psychology's institutionalized paradigm is in fact the Lockean Model. Chapter 5 clarifies what a paradigm is and what it means to say that we can revise or revolutionize this aspect of scientific practice. Because our view is that psychology can never be properly humanistic on an exclusively Lockean model, we must deal with this paradigmatic question. We begin with a clarification of the concept of scientific revolution.

### What is a Scientific Revolution? Kuhn versus Popper

Although novel ideas have always been called revolutionary, the popularization of this term for advances in science must surely be traced to Thomas S. Kuhn's *The Structure of Scientific Revolutions* (1970a; 1st ed., 1962), which has had a great influence on our thinking. Kuhn defines revolutions as "those non-cumulative developmental episodes in which an older paradigm is replaced in whole or in part by an incompatible new one" (*ibid.*, p. 92). If we ask what a paradigm is, the issue becomes clouded; for the term has a broad range of definitional convenience, and for good reason because it relates to the most abstract features of scientific reasoning as well as to the explicit steps to be taken in the observation and description of empirical phenomena. Masterman (1970) has suggested that Kuhn used this term in no less than 21 different senses, but Kuhn (1970a) believes that he had used it in only two general ways.

The first, or sociological, usage refers to the "entire constellation of beliefs, values, techniques, and so on shared by the members of a given community" (*ibid.*, p. 175). The second, which is a less encompassing usage, has to do with "the concrete puzzle-solutions which, employed as models or examples, can replace explicit rules as a basis for the solution of the remaining puzzles of normal science" (*ibid.*, p. 175). Rules are the more formalized, established viewpoints and preconceptions of a school of thought, which derive from paradigms to act as prescriptions for how to proceed in the experimental-design activity of science (*ibid.*, pp. 38–39). However, a paradigm can guide research in the absence of rules (*ibid.*, p. 42).

The heart of Kuhn's (itself revolutionary!) argument is that science does not proceed through the so-called principle of falsification *alone*, and indeed, one wonders if it ever follows this ideologically satisfying conception. One of the foremost spokesman for this view of how science is done, Karl R. Popper (1959), has defined this principle as follows: "*It must be possible for an empirical scientific system to be refuted by experience*" (p. 41). If a statement is put in such a way that it cannot be refuted, it is not a scientific pronouncement. The statement "It will or will not rain here tomorrow" is not scientific, for it cannot be refuted; but the statement "It will rain here tomorrow" can be refuted, hence it is properly scientific. Science can only work through a kind of negating procedure of *falsifying* claims put to nature by the theorist in question. As scientists, says Popper, we never really verify things but continually falsify—or fail to falsify—claims (theories, hypotheses, etc.) expressed by some investigator (recognizing, of course, that serendipitous findings occur as well). This is why the scientist always restates his hypotheses into the null form. Ultimately the reason we must falsify has to do with the logical fallacy of "affirming the consequent" of an "If [antecedent] . . . then [consequent] . . ." proposition.

This error in reasoning occurs as follows: Take the major premise "All men are mortal" (i.e., If a man, then a mortal). Assume we now affirm the antecedent of this proposition by pointing to an animal standing before us and say "man" (i.e., This is a man). Given our major premise it follows *necessarily* that "This man is mortal" (see Chapter 2, p. 63). In this case we have affirmed (in our act of pointing) the antecedent of an "If . . . then . . ." proposition. However, if we were to have affirmed the consequent (i.e., pointed and said "mortal") it would not have followed necessarily from our major premise that the animal standing before us was a man. Obviously there can be several other animals besides humans designated as mortal beings. The principle of falsification simply emphasizes that scientific statements are always of the latter type, because what we do in an experiment is say "If my theory X holds, then the following sequence of Y events (my experiment) will result in findings Z.

Following the sequence of Y events, Z *does* occur! Hence?" We like to think our theory has necessarily been verified, but Popper teaches us that it has not. There will always be, *in principle*, other ways of accounting for the observed data (the facts) than our preferred theory.

As a logician, Popper has devoted himself to clarifying issues such as these and to stipulating certain rules of procedure which he claims all scientists who are doing the work of science correctly will have to follow. He does not concern himself much with how scientists come to their major premises in actual practice, the actual reasons why they may take this or that point of view which is framed in their scientific statements such as "It will rain tomorrow." Popper's concern is therefore more with the *deductions* made by the scientist once he has put his statement (hypothesis) to nature. His opening sentences of *The Logic of Scientific Discovery* reveal this deductive interest of his as the tone of the volume is being established:

A scientist, whether theorist or experimenter, puts forward statements, or systems of statements, and tests them step by step. In the field of the empirical sciences, more particularly, he constructs hypotheses, or systems of theories, and tests them against experience by observation and experiment (*ibid.*, p. 27).

Popper is a great favorite of psychologists who consider themselves rigorous, for they see in his writings a parallel to Hull's (1937) hypo-thetico-*deductive* method [italics added]. When Popper (1959) says ". . . in my view there is no such thing as induction" (p. 40) (except for a possible mathematical induction), he aligns himself with the realistic theories of psychology which have taken the Lockean presumption that ideas are not put onto experience (induced), but obtained strictly through inputs from experience.

Kuhn has come along to challenge this idealized view of science that Popper has promulgated. Kuhn's study of history has convinced him that scientists are usually eager to support in their research efforts the meaning-presumptions made in their theoretical paradigms from the outset. In other words, the practice of science is more *inductive* than Popper has led us to believe. Scientists are seen to go along, defending their paradigmatic presumptions and continuing to do so until some anomaly develops in their findings or a new area of interest in science develops that does not fit these presumptions too well. At such "extraordinary" times in history we see a revolution coming about. Negative instances (falsifications) are at such revolutionary nodal points taken as evidence *against* a paradigm rather than simply as "puzzles," and the sympathies of many (especially the younger) scientists for the predominant paradigm of that period wanes. In these extraordinary times a new paradigm emerges, once again to capture the imagination and explanatory proclivities of the scientists who then further it.

The rest of the time we have what Kuhn calls normal science, and during such stretches the paradigm in ascendance is not really under threat. There is none of that disinterested rigorously deductive effort to disprove the paradigm which Popper believes occurs; at least there is remarkably little of it. What most scientists do during this normal period is to solve fairly limited puzzles generated by the background paradigm (Kuhn, 1970a, p. 82). Some of these are really new anomalies, taking shape gradually, but the "normal scientist" does not see them as such. To use Popper's terminology, he is more the verifier at this point than the falsifier. He designs his study to *support* and not to falsify the already accepted paradigm, although the logic of science still applies in the sense of affirming the consequent. He is a rule follower, doing what his forerunners have done with minor variations on their experimental designs (*ibid.*, p. 10). Sometimes the rules worked out actually hamper the discovery of new facts so that a shift in experimental techniques is required before a significant advance is achieved (*ibid.*, p. 59).

If we now hark back to the terminology of Chapter 1, we see that as an historian, Kuhn's interests are in the *precedents* of the scientific quest. He finds that scientists *do* have such precedent paradigms at play in their work, as overriding inductive inferences, and he cannot bring himself to accept the idealized Popperian view that scientists are interested *only* (or even primarily) in the evidence that may or may not falsify their theoretical statements. As he noted in direct colloquy with Popper, not only is evidence overlooked or reinterpreted out of the anomaly category into the unsolved puzzle category, but sometimes a theory is dropped (e.g., the Ptolemaic) even *before* it is put to satisfactory test (Kuhn, 1970b, p. 10). We cannot hope to judge a whole theory in the same way that we judge the outcome of a single experiment (*ibid.*, p. 12).

Saying "It will rain tomorrow" can easily be seen as true or false, but when we study the more abstract paradigmatic assumptions concerning the nature of rain (why it can be said to fall, for example) they cannot be falsified, nor can the theoretical statements derived from these assumptions. As Frank (1957) has noted, agree-

ment with observations and logical consistency cannot resolve differences in scientific outlook of such a high generality (p. 359).
Whether we call it a paradigm or a precedent makes no difference;
the point-of-view factor is *always* present because whatever one
*states* rests on some other given (as brought to bear "from above"
on the ladder of abstraction; see Rychlak, 1968, pp. 12–16). Thus
Kuhn has challenged the principle of falsification, stating that it is
not a logical rule but more an ideology and methodological rule reflecting one view of the scientific endeavor (Kuhn, 1970b, p. 15).
Summing up, Kuhn charges that Popper "has sought to solve the
problem of theory choice during revolutions by logical criteria that
are applicable in full only when a [precedent] theory can already be
presupposed" (*ibid.*, p. 19).

In his reply Popper (1970) admitted that something like Kuhn's
concept of normal science existed, but he denied that this was in any
way the normal activities of all or even most scientists. Indeed those
individuals who practice science this way had been "taught badly"
(*ibid.*, p. 52). Science, at any time in its history, ranges on a continuum between the Kuhnian poles of so-called normal and extraordinary scientific activity (*ibid.*, p. 54). No single paradigm ever has
the complete grip on a scientific specialty (biology, physics, etc.) as
Kuhn implies; at the very least in *certain* sciences there are one or
more such paradigms active at the same time. Furthermore, some of
the benefits to be accrued from scientific efforts devolve from the
interchanges between such competing paradigms. Popper criticized
Kuhn for suggesting that there can be no rational discussion between
such frameworks, leading to the necessity for a revolution in outlook
(*ibid.*, p. 57). Attesting to his belief in absolute, or objective, truth
(as opposed to the relativism implied in Kuhn's analysis), Popper
reaffirmed his belief that only in the test of empirical evidence will
such varied paradigms as are active in science be furthered or
dropped (*ibid.*, p. 56).

Despite Popper's belief in rational discussion across conflicting
paradigms, the writer has found that we are—as a science of psychology (applied settings not included)—under the unilateral direction of the precedent implications of a single paradigm, the advocates of which have not yet perceived what a minority of humanistic
psychologists view as glaring anomalies in their Lockean framework.
A change, if not a revolution, is surely called for; but before this is
possible, advocates on *both* sides of the question must be clearer on
just where the locus of a Kuhnian argument applies.

## Revolutions in Theory, Not in Method

If scientific knowledge combines both theory and method, it follows that paradigmatic influences devolve on both sides of the theory-method distinction. Further, to think of Kuhnian revolutions occurring on *either* side without necessarily affecting the other is quite possible. Thus we might revolutionize what we accept as the grounds for belief in a statement (i.e., method) without affecting the kinds of theories we put to test. Or we might alter the kinds of theoretical statements we make in relation to the methods we continue to employ in testing them. Where does Kuhn focus his argument in speaking of scientific revolutions?

That Kuhn (1970a) thinks of revolutions occurring in the *theoretical* realm is clear from many sources in his treatise (p. 7, pp. 17–18, p. 77, and especially, p. 182). Indeed even such a distinctive paradigm as quantum mechanics is said to be open to *various* interpretations by different groups within the science of physics (*ibid.*, p. 50). There are two instances in which Kuhn seems to be driving at method. First, there is the matter of rules, which encompass the "acceptable steps" to be taken in the design of experiments. Resting ultimately on the procedural evidence of an overriding paradigm, rules act as strictures. If the researcher does not follow the rules of proper science, ending in validating evidence, he is not going to be listened to. He also had better stay close to certain research designs, mix his chemicals in the prescribed fashion before conducting the test called for, and so forth. A second type of methodological issue can be seen in Kuhn's (1970a) reference to a preparadigm period in the history of science: "The pre-paradigm period . . . is regularly marked by frequent and deep debates over legitimate methods, problems, and standards of solution, though these serve rather to define schools than to produce agreement" (pp. 47–48).

Except for these two somewhat angular references to a concern over the evidential steps to be taken in the practice of science, Kuhn's emphasis is entirely on the question of what kind of theoretical position are we to take on the nature of our subject matter? The revolutionaries to whom he refers—Copernicus, Newton, Lavoisier, and Einstein (*ibid.*, p. 6)—*did not* revolutionize the paradigm on which rested the assumptions concerning strict research procedures or the need to control and predict events to validate one's claims on knowledge. Revolutions as paradigm confrontations arise purely in the sphere of theory (as buttressed, of course, by the cognitive testing of what is or is not plausible via procedural evidence). The essential ingredient is when a particular scientist is likely to call one man's puzzle—whether solved or not—his anomaly:

Copernicus saw as counterinstances what most of Ptolemy's other successors had seen as puzzles in the match between observation and theory. Lavoisier saw as a counterinstance what Priestly had seen as a successfully solved puzzle in the articulation of phlogiston theory. And Einstein saw as counterinstances what Lorentz, Fitzgerald, and others had seen as puzzles in the articulation of Newton's and Maxwell's theories (ibid., pp. 79–80).

At these subtle points in history an extraordinary scientific event is likely to take place. A paradigmatic shift at the level of theory occurs, and the findings that had stood before as evidence for theory X now fall nicely into place for theory Y (not to mention the entirely new things theory Y teaches us). This can always happen because of that affirming-the-consequent nature of experimental evidence we discussed above. There is frequently a shift in the instrumentation employed by the innovator as well. He does not follow the institutionalized rules of design any more than he has followed the institutionalized form of explanation. This does not mean he departs from validating evidence, of course. But so often our technical instruments, our stilted patterns of experimental design, keep us from seeing what could be shown to be valid simply because we fail to theorize beyond our fixed instrumentation. Kuhn (1970a) now asks:

Ought we [to] conclude from the frequency with which such instrumental commitments prove misleading that science should abandon standard tests and standard instruments? That would result in an inconceivable method of research. Paradigm procedures and applications are as necessary to science as paradigm laws and theories, and they have the same effects. Inevitably they restrict the phenomenological field accessible for scientific investigation at any given time (pp. 60–61).

This restriction of theory by method is what we have been driving at in emphasizing the confounding of the former with the latter. But when we are speaking of a Kuhnian revolution we are referring to dramatic shifts in the theoretical viewpoints of scientists. Indeed since the turn of the seventeenth century and the rise of modern science, though there have been a number of quite startling paradigm shifts in scientific theory, there has never been a paradigmatic shift in the theory of knowledge defining scientific method! There have been some attempts in this direction, primarily at the philosophical level (Kuhn's preparadigmatic efforts); but insofar as science *per se* has retained an identity, the ground rules for evidence have remained validation. One must of necessity begin with procedural evidence in cognitive tests—which includes mathematical reasoning—but the mark of a true scientist since Newton has been the recognition that ultimately his formulations would have to bear up under the control-and-prediction rule of objective empirical evidence.

## How Can a Rigorous Science Be Humanistic?

We are now prepared to understand how a humanistic science can be rigorous. The logic of scientific method need not be altered to achieve a humanistic science of psychology. What we must revolutionize is the way in which we construe the design of our experiments, the manipulations we apply to our independent variables, and the explanations we proffer for the observed changes in the dependent variables. We must recognize that the empirical test of control and prediction in validation is *never* the sole source of descriptive terminology which presumes to say what is going on within the apparatus. It was once believed to be so; for example, when Bergmann and Spence (1941) claimed: "All scientific terms are derived terms, derived from and retraceable to what one might call 'the hard data,' the 'immediately observable' or what Stevens calls the 'elementary operation of discrimination'" (p. 6). We must now say in no uncertain terms that *this functionalist ideology is wrong.* The concept of an elementary operation of discrimination is itself fraught with Lockean (simple-to-complex) presumptions and hence cannot be accepted without question. Psychologists derive their terms from all manner of sources, including analogies to philosophical models that have been woven into the very fabric of their metaphysical outlook "as scientists."

The only thing standing in the way of a rigorous humanistic psychology is the lack of recognition on the part of psychologists that such a theory of man is possible! Lacking this recognition, they do not frame their precedent hypotheses in terms of it, which means that studies are never designed to test this possibility, and evidence which might in fact support it continually goes unrecognized. We do not have to change our ground rules for validation to initiate a rigorous program of empirical research providing evidence for or against the thesis that human behavior is telic. This may occasionally call for some unique experimental designs, or we can go on using the same experimental designs that we have always been using, with the only change being that now we begin with the assumption that a telic animal is in the apparatus. What does this imply about the likely outcome, and how can we check our thinking against a purely mechanistic hypothesis? Starting at this level, researches can be conducted just as they are now except that the introduction and discussion sections of these reports will be more than simply rephrases of the procedure section (see our comments concerning this practice in Chapter 4, p. 167).

The adjustment called for in our revolution is purely technical. Humanism is the desire on the part of a theoretician to employ formal- and final-cause description. Humanists do not ask the functionalist question of how we can more scientifically *account for* what used to be called purpose (i.e., as an efficient cause), but seek to answer a question like how we can prove scientifically that purpose in human affairs actually takes place (i.e., as a final cause). As introspective theorists, humanists fall more naturally into the Kantian line of descent which places emphasis on the inductive capacity of mind to organize or influence its experience in some way *from birth*. Talk of phenomenal fields (Rogers, 1951), world views (Binswanger, 1963), and personal constructs (Kelly, 1955) fills their accounts—all of which are introspectively conceived Kantian spectacles, serving as the *that* (grounds) on the basis of which behavior is being carried out. But once such telic theoretical formulations are translated and verified in the research designs called for, they fall easy prey to the theory-method confound and come out as mediated efficient causes (see Chapter 4, pp. 168–172).

Feuer (1974) has argued persuasively that using *revolution* in speaking of paradigm change in science may be too strong a word, falsely analogized from social upheavals that occur when a class of people is actively repressed. After all, the scientific method is committed to the rule of evidence, so ultimately it must encourage revisions and additions to its knowledge (*ibid.*, p. 265). Sometimes the scientists using the favored paradigm even give credence to the newly emerging paradigm (*ibid.*, p. 275). This is hardly what one finds when we observe the machinations of a vested social class, working to preserve its advantages and actively repressing some disadvantaged class or classes "beneath them." Why then insist upon the more aggressive term when something like *revision* might do as well?

Although we agree with this argument in principle, there are still a few points we must consider before dropping revolution as a proper descriptive characterization of what is needed in psychology. First, as Feuer himself appreciates, there is undoubted merit to Kuhn's arguments concerning the reticence of scientists to accept empirical data that fail to support the precedent assumptions they make as a school of thought (ibid., pp. 330–334). Hence the provisions made in science for a self-correcting revision in outlook are not foolproof and at their best are exceedingly slow in allowing for an alternative idea to take shape. Second, and more to the point for rigorous humanism, *we have had very little need in the natural sciences to revolutionize the basic antipathy felt for teleological explanations.* Though science may indeed accept evidence and ultimately aid the revolutionary paradigm in its ascendancy, the rule-strictures on what is a scientific explanation remain. Whenever a telic commentary enters scientific discourse, it is framed as something other than legitimate science, or the scientist is speaking loosely and we are all quite aware that his references to intention or purpose in events are given *enquotes.*

If we now analogize between groups of scientists advocating telic theory versus natural-science theory and the bourgeoisie versus proletarian classes of Marxian theory, the parallel may not be so extreme after all. When as a young man of 24, Hermann von Helmholtz (see Chapter 3, pp. 123–124) formed a pact with his fellow students (including Brücke, later to be Freud's professor) to fight vitalism in science, he was reflecting the values of his class identity (Boring, 1950, p. 708). Though it is confounded with quasi-materialistic ideology, the vitalistic principle of explanation in physical science is fundamentally telic. By swearing oaths to repress such theory Helmholtz was surely not reflecting the disinterested spirit of a principle of falsification. That is, although Fechner specifically designed his research to test a mind-body question of this type (see Chapter 3, p. 105), the psychologists who followed Helmholtz's lead (including Wundt) were not seen to entertain such possibilities in their subsequent employment of the psychophysical methods. Helmholtz's opposition to vitalism was framed initially in the sphere of physical explanation. But as psychology was then modeled on physical theory, this antiteleology attitude was carried over to psychological explanation as well.

Returning to Feuer's admonition, though he is quite correct that scientific innovations are not generally akin to social revolutions, in psychology we feel the parallel is properly drawn. We do indeed require a scientific revolution in psychology. We hope that the resulting *synthesis* of a new theoretical paradigm with the old methodological paradigm will take the best from both sides. We wish to add telic theories while retaining the same, nontelic, empirical, purely mechanical ordering of events over time known as the *experimental design*. The advantages of objectivity to be gained in the latter procedure are what we feel must be retained. There will be no pacts in this revolution to fight mechanism. We need sophistication following our revolution, not further repression. Some psychologists find this modest suggestion too revolutionary, but others find it not revolutionary enough. There are hopes in certain quarters to revolutionize scientific method *per se,* and we now turn to a few of these views.

## Why Humanistic Methodologies Tend to Fail as Rigorous Science

Humanism is a growing movement in psychology and the call for humanistic methods is often heard from these quarters. An Association for Humanistic Psychology now exists, with an accompanying *Journal of Humanistic Psychology,* dedicated to the advancement of humanistic topics such as love, creativity, spontaneity, play, warmth, ego-transcendence, autonomy, responsibility, authenticity, meaning, transcendental experience, and courage (Bugental, 1963; Haigh, 1969; Maslow, 1961). The papers which appear in this journal do not necessarily follow the format of an experiment, with procedure sections and the statistical analysis of data, but are usually discursive surveys, case-history reports, or personal observations. Humanists like to cite Polanyi (1964), because this distinguished philosopher-scientist puts the intuition of the investigator above the validation of an experiment in any rank ordering of steps in the scientific enterprise. Others seek to find an alternative to control and prediction in validation by going to analytical or conceptual procedures such as cultural hermeneutics (Palmer, 1969) or Zen's enlightenment (Suzuki, 1962).

To attempt a survey of the many different strategies employed by humanists in their calling to question or outright rejection of scientific methodology would require a volume in itself. We therefore restrict our comments to two of the better-known and well-done efforts of this nature in the literature—the existentialistic critique of Adrain van Kaam (1969) and the phenomenological critique of

Amedeo Giorgi (1970a). Before turning to these specific presentations, we must clarify where the problems arise in most humanistic revisions of the scientific enterprise.

## The Steps in Science as a "Line of Development"

If we were to frame the general steps taken by a scientist in furthering knowledge, the following would be a fair approximation: (1) speculate theoretically at whatever level of formalization (i.e., from rough analogies through involved "systems" of explanation); (2) test the plausibility of such speculations cognitively (procedural evidence) and design thereby an experiment that can show the implications of this theory quite independently of the scientist *qua* theorist; (3) carry out the projected validation. Sharp distinctions between these three steps, especially 1 and 2, are not possible, but the general logic here suggests that only those who move through step 3 *at least some of the time* are participating in a scientific endeavor (see Chapter 1).

We call this sequence the *line of development,* because we recognize the fact that sheer validation is never meaningful in and of itself. There is and always must be some background assumption lending meaning to the findings as seen in the experimental sequence (apparatus, instrument, etc.). We take cognizance here of that affirming-the-consequent issue discussed above even as we raise the significance of theory and procedural evidence in the course of scientific "discovery." Of course not all human beings take our third step and actually validate impartially what they think could be validated if someone would but do the work involved. Hence, though we agree with Conant (1952) that scientists in the laboratory carry out habits of well-ordered inquiry that go back to the caveman (p. 40), we do not entirely agree with Kelly (1955) when he suggests that every man is a scientist (p. 5). The challenge of science comes in when we take our third step, and though potentially capable, not everyone is prepared or willing to do so.

Having now recognized that scientific investigation calls for a line of development, we can acknowledge further that it can be *stretched* somewhat in going from points 1 to 3. To conduct an experiment that was implied by some background theory at point 1 without having this complete theory ensconced in the experimental apparatus at point 3 is not a violation of parsimony. Indeed *in principle* we can never have all of the precedents which function as background factors to our empirical studies nestled in our experimental designs. There will always be some more abstract level from which a premise or paradigm or metaphysical assumption is taking root in our approach to knowledge. What is essential in this process is that we be. clear about what our background factors *are* and that we do the best job we can in logically developing these meanings into our eventual test of our thinking at point 3. In other words, some of the so-called control that becomes prominent at step 3 is already underway in the logical controls being developed across points 1 and 2.

As we hope to show in the examples below, the tendency for humanistic methods is either to stop somewhere around points 1 or 2, falling short of scientific validation altogether, or to go on to 3 with some loosely designed project, often boiling down to a discursive survey of some group of individuals. There is a rationale given for such efforts, but these justifications simply do not salvage the kind of tepid science that ensues. What is so disheartening about these efforts is that they pass by many fine opportunities to show humanistic features of behavior in the laboratory. There is no reason why humanistic constructs cannot be framed and put to test in the most rigidly controlled arid realms of laboratory science imaginable. All one need do is begin at point 1 with the proper assumptions and then, working carefully and rigorously, develop through a kind of extension of the meanings carried by these premises a program of empirical research that can be repeated by anyone who takes an interest in the problem. Rather than *a* final cause, or *an* aspiration, as construed in the theory at point 1, we end up at point 3 with some marks on a piece of paper made by subjects who have been put into an experimental design established to test the implications of our theory (at point 1).

One can easily sympathize with the dreams of those who hope someday to find a scientific method which is capable of capturing the richness of lived human experience. The scientific method is clearly aimed demonstratively at restricting and narrowing alternative factors down to the point that any *one* study is rather a thin soup. This is why paradigms need considerable filling in during what Kuhn (1970a) has called the phase of normal science (pp. 23–42). But this delimitation in each study proves discouraging to many humanists on two counts. First, there is the sense of artificiality that such controlled efforts lend to the theoretical account. It all seems a make-believe game, with either validation sought for some trivia already known or having no true relevance to the lived experience of the man on the street. Second, the humanist who considers himself existentialistic or phenomenological in orientation finds the variables designed for in the experiment to be so far removed from what the individual is actually experiencing at his end of the observer-subject continuum as to be a violation of scientific objectivity on the face of things. This charge of a distortion in the arbitrarily selected dimensions of study by the extraspectionist, who then forces his schemes onto his subjects with total disregard for their actual experience, is what we mean by the *purity criticism* (Rychlak, 1968, p. 390).

The extraspectionist in psychology has been accused of purposely neglecting his responsibility to capture the more introspectively framed account of life that we all live within, each day of our existence. Based on some misguided principle of natural science, the extraspectionist ignores purely spontaneous experience to perpetuate the illusion of a material- and efficient-cause theory of humanity as natural products. Although quite legitimately stated in psychology, the unhappy result of the purity criticism is that it tends to focus on the methods of science rather than on its theories. The nemesis of failing to distinguish proof from theoretical description or explanation continues to dog us. A typical derision of science is to be seen in the following quote from Boss (1963), who is commenting on his more humanistic approach to psychology (Daseinsanalysis):

. . . analysis of *Dasein* urges all those who deal with human beings to start seeing and thinking from the beginning, so that they can remain with what they immediately perceive and do not get lost in "scientific" abstractions, derivations, explanations, and calculations estranged from the immediate reality of the given phenomena (pp. 29–30).

What makes such derision unfortunate is that, if we survey the leading figures in science over this century—for example, Bridgman (1959), Bronowski (1958), Conant (1952), Eddington (1958), Einstein (1934), Oppenheimer (1956), Schrödinger (1957), and Whitehead (1958)—we find much more support for a humanistic theory of behavior than for a mechanistic account. Modern science has become more open to Kantian-like terminology because of its recognition that what one observes in the "hard reality" is due at least in part to what one presumes from the outset. This is clearly a recognition of the telic factors in the work of science or the scientist-human who does the work. A liberal approach to scientific theorizing is more current and appropriate than is the staid and lifeless form of Newtonian science that is still dreamed of in too many psychology departments. To provide our students with a humanistic outlook which is internally hostile to research design seems more harmful than helpful. Furthermore, we tend to attract students who are *in fact* disinterested in developing the necessary self-discipline and exerting the effort that a scientific career demands.

Two Examples of a Humanistic "Method:" Van Kaam and Giorgi

We turn now to two distinguished examples of psychological criticism that call for a humanistic approach to method: the existential view of van Kaam (1969) and the phenomenological critique of Giorgi (1970a). Our intention here is to look into each of these views in light of the claim that scientific method (validation, or step 3 above) need *not* be revised, much less revolutionized, to achieve the goals being sought by van Kaam and Giorgi.

In his book *Existential Foundations of Psychology* van Kaam (1969) levels a purity criticism in the opening arguments: ". . . human sciences will never present us with a full understanding of man so long as they are pure speculative knowledge or mere laboratory knowledge without reference to the real, lived world of man" (p. 25). The culprit is developed as more method than theory, with the suggestion that a phenomenological substitution is called for: "Phenomenology as a method in psychology thus seeks to disclose and elucidate the phenomena of behavior as they manifest themselves in their perceived immediacy" (*ibid.*, p. 29).

A distinction between *comprehensive* and *differential* psychological theories (van Kaam's term for theory here is *modes of existence*) is then drawn (*ibid.*, pp. 114–175). The point of this distinction is to say that science tends to discriminate and break down behavior from its totality into differential pieces (in our terms, a Lockean-model reduction), whereas a comprehensive psychological theory tries to retain the wholeness of lived experience. As such, comprehensive theory would retain teleological descriptions of human behavior (*ibid.*, p. 110). Though one might suspect that van Kaam's polemic is solely on the side of theory, when he speaks of his approach as *anthropological phenomenology* he brings in the factor of method as supposedly *also* changed: "Anthropological existential phenomenology is both an attitude [in our terms, theory] and a controlled method. It leads to a comprehensive understanding of intentional behavior as a structured whole which is differentiated in many patterns of behavior" (*ibid.*, p. 252).

Without *phenomenological explication* of scientific endeavors, a science of psychology can be sent scurrying about on meaningless endeavors:

Empirical observation, experimentation, measurement, and accumulation of data should be fostered in all differential psychologies. From the viewpoint of comprehensive psychology, however, much of this admirable effort is wasted if there is no phenomenological explication of *what* it is that is being observed, experimented upon, measured, correlated, and applied (*ibid.*, p. 303).

We can heartily agree with the need for phenomenological explication, *if* what this means is something akin to our steps 1 and 2— thinking about what sorts of speculations are worth making and, in light of this reflective assessment, a procedural-evidence testing of what one's scientific activity is "all about." This sort of preliminary activity is essential to a proper experimental design, and this preparatory effort seems to be what van Kaam is referring to. However, in the familiar style of purity critics he bears down rather severely on the scientific method of step 3 *per se*—for example, in the following excerpt where he is discussing the evidence of so-called differential (typical Lockean) psychology:

. . . the hypothesis that learning is based on a process of conditioning can be verified only by differential-scientific evidence; it cannot be validated directly by either spontaneous or comprehensive-scientific evidence. The evidences of differential psychologies are only indirect evidences. They do not make behavior itself manifest; they are deduced from spontaneous evidences by means of abstract scientific methods. The latter may consist of logical, mathematical deductions or of empirical inductions, the methods of which may differ in each differential psychology. To be sure, the conclusions of differential psychology possess their own type of evidence. Yet such scientific-differential evidences are always less reliable than naive self-evidences (*ibid.*, p. 275).

We learn in the next few paragraphs that what van Kaam means by *less reliable* is less constant or subject to change—for example, when a future scientific account based on new evidence alters our current thinking on some topic, such as human learning in behavior. People 50 years from now will have the same spontaneous phenomenal experience of learning that we have today. However, our scientific theories of the learning process, based on evidence accumulated over the next 50 years, may be vastly different from what it is today. Hence differential scientific evidences are less reliable than the naive commentaries proffered by living subjects (*ibid.*, p. 276). Note what has happened here: van Kaam has also confounded theory with method so that he is uncertain as to what is unreliable and what needs ever to be reliable in the scientific quest. Could not the style of accruing evidence have remained highly reliable over the

50-year span, even as the theories being put to test in this fixed strategy of accruing evidence changed? In fact these theories *could* have changed in the direction of greater congruence with the spontaneous phenomenal accounts of today and tomorrow (which is the revolution we hope to see take place!).

To say that a *method* (evidence source) is unreliable because it tests different theories over time is like saying an aging automobile is unreliable (or unfaithful) because it dependably carried a series of different owners over time. What van Kaam has stumbled upon here is the fact that scientific methods are *always* those last steps of our three-step sequence, which means they always have more than one theory that might account for them. Methods are those consequents we examined above, which are affirmed in the logic of scientific test and to that extent are *never* in one-to-one (necessary) agreement with their antecedent theoretical backgrounds. The empirical findings of scientific method are not unreliable; they are simply subject to change in theoretical description—over time, within time, any time! By confounding what is method with the theory accounting for the resultant findings, van Kaam, like so many humanistic critics, points his guns in the wrong direction.

What kind of actual study would be conducted if we used the phenomenological method? In the example cited van Kaam presents data on a survey of high school and college students who "explicated" their feelings—in writing on a form administered by the experimenters—when they were really "understood by somebody" (*ibid., p. 331*). The sample was then broken down into percentages of subjects expressing various positive reactions to being understood, such as that they felt relieved and satisfied, safe in the relationship, in experiential communion with the person, accepted, and so on (*ibid., p. 336*). How does this differ from *any* study conducted by a scientist who is going to follow the rules of validation at step 3? Clearly, for the sake of convenience, he would want to construct a scale following such prestudy, and after he had accumulated items dealing with the feeling of being "really understood by somebody" that reflected reliability of a test-retest variety, he would probably search about for other samples of people in order to extend the range of his knowledge about this theoretical construct.

For example, a group of prisoners would probably have a different sense of what it means to be really understood than high school and college students. Though the phenomenal experience is presented very positively, what about those times when we are caught in a lie or some other misbehavior and hence feel "really understood" yet hardly safe, at ease, or in experiential communion with the person or persons who understood us. The survey instructions (*ibid.*, p. 331) do not make such circumstances clear, and there was obviously a very positive demand characteristic or set in this study. But these are precisely the kinds of questions a sagacious investigator would next seek to answer if he is *scientifically* interested in his theoretical construct. This is why the paradigm continues to be filled in by normal science (Kuhn, 1970a). We do not wish to be unfair to van Kaam, because this study was presumably done merely as an example to show how his approach lets the subjects define the construct eventually to be used, rather than coming to them with a preconceived definition of the construct (*a la* the purity criticism); yet, in counterexample fashion we must at least point out that humanists are frequently criticized for the paucity and superficiality of their scientific work.

Giorgi (1970a) begins his critique with a sophisticated review of the tendency in psychology to press natural-science efficient-cause models onto the teleological human being. He argues that there was a kind of choice early in the game between a humanistic theory of man and a scientific methodological approach, with the result that "in the conflict between fidelity to scientific methodology and fidelity to the phenomena (in this case man), almost all early psychologists opted for the methodology" (*ibid.*, p. 92). Once again we find a leading humanist making scientific method appear by definition to be anathema to humanistic theories. Yet, as we demonstrated in Chapter 3, both Gustav Fechner (p. 105) and Johannes Müller (p. 106)—individuals who were important to the founding of experimental methods in psychology—took a clearly Kantian humanistic view of mankind. Only later, as the Lockean thinkers—Helmholtz in particular as well as Wundt—came on the scene was a confounding of efficient-cause method with efficient-cause theory accomplished. Rather than these Lockean scientists having an option in the matter, they were merely encouraged by the hard data being generated in the laboratory that complex human behavior was reducible to underlying simple forces and motions (Cassirer, 1950, pp. 85–91).

The purity criticism plays a central role in Giorgi's polemic:

Let us take, as an example, experiments designed to discover the threshold time for subjects to perceive how many dots are on a screen. This experiment is usually described as "perception as a function of time," meaning that the experimenter is interested in finding out how long it takes the subject to perceive what he (the experimenter) already *knows*. Thus, the subject must acquire knowledge and express an objective fact—x dots—and is usually not in any way instructed to relate how he experienced the phenomenon of tachistoscopic visual presentations. The latter factor is simply presumed and never taken into account (Giorgi, 1970a, p. 153).

The fault here would seem to lie in the exclusively extraspective and arbitrary *theory* of the experimenter, who selected the time dimension as a base-rate standard against which to claim learning was a function of (see our discussion of functionalism, Chapter 4, pp. 162–176). Yet Giorgi's continuing analysis places the fault on the side of the method used to validate such assumptions. He calls for a phenomenological technique of reduction (*ibid.*, p. 162), which means that we should try to clarify and delineate the presuppositions that define our perspective. By *perspective* is meant something akin to the Kantian spectacles that we bring to bear in formulating a precedent slant on things, a slant that in turn will determine sequaciously what we will say about them: "The fact of perspectivity is the main argument against all theories that posit absolute positions" (*ibid.*, p. 163). Once again this seems more a question of theory than method. But Giorgi also favors Merleau-Ponty's concept of *structure*, which is a conceptualized "whole" that is identifiable, analyzable, and transposable. When clarified or explicated it reflects the psychological meaning a person experiences in relation to it (*ibid.*, pp. 178–179). This formal-cause concept implies that a procedural-evidence-based examination of structure can be carried out, due to its Heraclitian order or internal consistency as a total (coherence theory of truth). Giorgi refers to this analysis of structure as a method (*ibid.*, p. 192), but in our terms this would represent a cognitive and *not* a research method (see Chapter 1, p. 46). Because it would stop short of our step 3, we could not accept it as a genuinely scientific method —adding, as Giorgi would doubtless want us to, "based on our definition of science!"

An experiment by Colaizzi (1967; see also 1973) is then cited by Giorgi (1970a) in which subjects in a memory task are interrupted after one trial and asked what they were thinking about at that time (p. 192). Rather than learning as a function of time, these subjects were actually becoming accustomed to the apparatus; some mentioned the unfamiliarity of the learnable materials, others gave their reactions to the instructions, and so forth. Here again the aim is to map the course of learning according to the (introspectively conceived) subject's actual experience rather than to the already known fact that *time* (practice, rehearsal, familiarization, repetition, etc.)

would be required to acquire the materials. Giorgi calls such experimental designs "human scientific procedures" (*ibid.*, p. 193) and adds that they are really not totally existent in modern psychology but that they are possible. Though they may not look scientific, they are just as scientific as any other approach to valid data.

As with our reaction to the van Kaam study above, we are moved to ask: How does this procedure differ from the standard control and prediction sequence? Obviously Colaizzi's design could be repeated, with the data found initially predicted to cross-validate. In fact Colaizzi's work is itself a kind of cross-validation of G. E. Müller's historic findings that (when asked!) subjects in memory tasks may be seen to be doing more than simply acquiring materials mechanically "as a function of time" (as Ebbinghaus might have had it). By asking his subjects, Müller found that they consciously organized their materials after the kinds of preliminary assessments Colaizzi reported taking place in the first few "look sees" of the task at hand had been completed (see Watson, 1971, p. 298). Clearly, there is no strike against the scientific method in Colaizzi's work. What we humanists need is *more of the same*: humanistic theoretical statements put to test in a continuing line of cross-validations, carried on within a *rigorous* experimental context. We actually do have a viable paradigm in the Kantian model. What we need is a core of humanists willing to carry on the work of normal science (Kuhn, 1970a).

Giorgi (1970b) seems to be aware of the theory-leaning basis of the phenomenologist's polemic and of the paucity of research that flows from this general outlook. He noted that after a phenomenological argument has been presented, a critic will generally rise in the audience and say, "There's a phenomenologist for you. They are always telling you what *ought* to be done instead of *doing* it themselves. When will they stop talking and start *doing* something" (p. 96). Admitting that there is a certain truth to this charge, Giorgi then observes that what the phenomenologist is calling for is "a new way of *conceiving* the problem" (p. 96). He then adds:

In other words, the break-through that is demanded [i.e., what we have been calling a revolution in psychology] is essentially a theoretical one—how to *conceive* of new ways of experimenting, or of new ways of looking at phenomena, etc. Thus, we [phenomenologists] are *doing* plenty, even if we are not collecting data. If "doing" is defined narrowly and only in terms of data collection—then our critic is right. But if thinking is a mode of behavior—and empirically oriented psychologists apparently think so, at least so far as experiments are conducted in thinking—then the effort to seek new ways of *conceiving* perennial problems cannot be dismissed as irrelevant (*ibid.*, pp. 96–97).

Although Giorgi and the writer would appear to be *in tandem* on the question of where psychology needs revolutionizing, in our exchanges at the 1974–1975 Nebraska Symposium on Motivation we had considerable difficulty getting together on the program of change called for (see Rychlak, 1975 and Giorgi, 1975). Giorgi continually sought an admission that there was a precedent to *every* meaningful term in the language and that there were—at least possibly—as many precedents as there were individuals thinking and talking and using conceptual language. Yet the facts of history and even of science suggest to the writer that at some point in our search for precedents —for the slants and subjective meanings of unique persons—we *just do* find a realm of objective understanding in the terminological meanings confronted. We have objectivities and we have subjectivities in the precedents to which *every* language term ultimately relates. This objective realm—where a term or conception is understood by more individuals than just the single (subjective) person using it—used to be discussed at the most abstract levels as the question of universals. This ancient preoccupation of thinkers across history (see Table 1) to secure universal verities is hardly *subjective,* because we see again and again those recurring issues of causation, one and many, demonstrative versus dialectical strategies in reason, and so forth, indicating that there is as much commonality as there is difference in the extant or even potential knowledge of mankind. The purity criticism has merit, but it cannot be used in *every* instance without *itself* becoming a universal.

All of this phenomenological or existential talk about revolutionizing the methods of science constitutes a *straw man* argument. There are no inherent conflicts between validation and humanism. Those approaches that profess to fall back on the wisdom of philosophy or on the knowledge to be gained from the arts have failed as science because of their need to rely exclusively on procedural evidence to support their theoretical points of view. This in no way denigrates the role of philosophy or art in existence, and one can often go directly from philosophy and art to a scientifically testable line of development. We must never forget that human beings can create or "think up" possibilities that are not now in existence but which they could indeed "make happen." To say that some experience is phenomenally true but unamenable to scientific validation might simply mean that it has not yet reached creation in overt behavior. This ability to create can of course be studied scientifically. But to expect a scientist to run after each person's phenomenal reality in hopes of capturing each possibility that might be subjectively concocted is surely unnecessary and a waste of time. We need philosophical analysis to clarify our thinking, and artistic creations to enrich our life alternatives. These theory-laden and procedural-evidence-based activities are necessary and important to science. Yet so is validation important to science because there can be no science without it. Science means a stand on evidence *not* a stand on the human image. If science dictates the human image, it is no longer science! But most assuredly, any so-called humanistic methodology that falls short of validation is doomed to failure. Humanists *must* take our third step.

## Why Mediational and Related Cognitive Theories Tend To Fail as Humanisms

A humanist making arguments of the sort being presented in this book is often confronted with the following objection:

You seem to be making the differences between humanism and mechanism insolvable by arguing against a behaviorism which no longer exists. Present day cognitive behaviorism or cognitive psychology handles all of the issues you raise about an active intellect and final causes. All we need do here is to acknowledge that the living organism surely *does* have certain processes that contribute to the stimulus input—literally *constructs* the stimulus— and then go on from there to build a more unified science of psychology. There are innumerable ways in which such processes mediate between sensation and behavior, possibly serving a feedback function or whatever. If you want to call these intervening processes (or the long-term memory of items stored in these processes) the "that for the sake of which" newer sensory inputs are constructed, that's your business. Why not say things this way and end all of this divisiveness in psychology by making it appear that humanism and mechanism are so incompatible when they are not!

This objection is actually a rephrasing of the "accounting for" argument discussed in Chapter 4 (p. 164), and it has beguiled psychologists for generations in the rise of the functionalist ideology. Though the writer would love to play the role of arbiter and resolver of psychological theoretical disputes like those of humanism-mechanism, the honest truth is that a mediational model—which is what the objector invariably calls for—simply *cannot* convey the meanings being expressed in the humanistic polemic. The reason for this theoretical intransigence is that we confront the meanings of efficient-formal causation (mechanism) here with the meanings of formal-final causation (humanism). Cancelling what is common to both ends of the confrontation we are left with the fulcrum issue: Can we rely exclusively on efficient causation to account for our data on human beings, or must we add the meaning of a final cause as well? Though it may deflate the scientific self-assurance of the objector to learn that we cannot reduce the meaning of final causation to an underlying efficient causation—that is, treat this matter via the institutionalized Lockean model—the fact will always remain that we *cannot* say one thing (efficient cause) and mean another (final cause).

To be more precise, one cannot do this in a demonstrative presentation, which is the posture taken by the scientist in this context. One could of course say one thing and mean another—for example, by informally analogizing from what is said but not meant to what is meant but not said. This would involve a dialectical maneuver and rely in large measure on sophistry (see Chapter 2). Because a rigorous science should not be based on sophistry or on informally framed analogical arguments in general, we would do well to clarify our thinking on just what is involved in the humanism-mechanism controversy that keeps it from being "handled" to the satisfaction of both sides. A good first step here is to focus on the terminology employed.

Cognitive Theory and Mediation Theory

Along with objections of the sort mentioned above, the humanist is likely to hear of various "new looks" developing in the learning theories or other forms of psychological theory at any given point in time. Colleagues or students are ever ready to reassure the humanist that his concerns over the grip of Lockeanism on psychology are no longer necessary. The most recent saviour theory seems to be a collection of views termed *cognitive* psychology. Because the term *cognitive* has a distinctive history in psychology, the psychologist who is mature enough to recall how prominently it was employed to describe approaches like those of Rogers (1951) in the 1940s and 1950s might be quite surprised to see what sorts of psychologists claim to be cognitive in outlook a generation later. Some even claim to be recapturing this earlier paradigm in their newer versions (e.g., Boneau, 1974). References to Kuhn are prominent in these approaches, and the general impression is usually given that we are on the brink of an extraordinary-science period with the dawning of a new paradigm in the rise of cognitive psychology (see, e.g., Solso, 1974, p. ix). A detailed look at these new theories convinces the writer that, except for intimations of a change in emphasis (to be discussed below), what they have to offer poses no threat to the Lockean model. Though advocates of cognitive psychology like to place themselves in opposition to S-R behavior theory (e.g., Dulany, 1968), on the critical point of *telic description* there is absolutely no difference between such views. Indeed there is about as much difference between modern cognitive and behavior theories as we found between American structuralism and functionalism (Chapter 4).

What does the term *cognition* mean? A dictionary search teaches us that it devolves from Latin roots meaning to become acquainted with or to get a knowledge of. The preferred meaning is "act or faculty of knowing," which suggests that there is a process of some sort going on in coming to know experience. When we get down to the details of describing this process, the point at which it is thought to occur, troubles begin to develop and our familiar divergence results. The British Empiricist (Lockean) interpretation of this process begins in William of Ockham's rules for proper theological debate (see Table 1). In rejecting what he took to be the fanciful theological proofs of the scholastics, Ockham distinguished between two kinds of knowing. Recall from Chapter 2 (pp. 69–70) that there is the *intuitive cognition*, which is tantamount to saying sensory input of experience through the organic structures of the body (eyes, ears, touch, etc.), and there is the *abstractive cognition*, which refers to the purely mental processing that man can accomplish based *solely* on the inputs of intuitive cognition. Proofs of God couched in the abstractive cognition are no better than those items of information that are made available through the intuitive cognition. As such they can never be a substitute for the empirical demonstration of miraculous occurrences—which are also input at the level of sensation. In the final analysis this empirical demonstration at the level of intuitive cognition is the *only* satisfactory evidence for the belief in God. This same question arose later in Locke's attack on the possibility of innate ideas (Chapter 2, p. 91). Mind is on the receptive side of knowledge, taking in rather than creating knowledge or having it stored innately to manufacture at will.

In opposition to this use of cognition, continental philosophy devolving from Kant took quite another view of the knowing process. As if to underscore the central nature of this difference, Kant (1952)

takes up the question in the very first paragraph of his first introduction to *The Critique of Pure Reason*. Kant admits that "all knowledge
begins with experience" (*ibid.*, p. 14), but adds that it does not necessarily follow from this that all knowledge arises out of experience:

> For, on the contrary, it is quite possible that our empirical knowledge is
> a compound of that which we receive through [sensory] impressions, and
> that which the *faculty of cognition* [italics added] supplies from itself
> (sensuous impressions giving merely the *occasion*), an addition which we
> cannot distinguish from the original element given by sense, till long prac-
> tice has made us attentive to, and skilful in separating it (*ibid.*, p. 14).

As we noted in Chapter 2 (p. 92), Kant had the level of intuitive
cognition *itself* organized by time and space, and then at the so-called
abstractive cognitive levels he brought in his concept of the categories of the understanding.

In essence the Kantian faculty of cognition returns to the scholastic model which Ockham was rejecting, because it suggests that
there is a unique reasoning potential in mind, one that could well
enter into the creation of knowledge *per se*. Kant was not trying to
wage theological debate, of course, but his concept of transcendence
via the *transcendental dialectic* permitted him to say that mind *qua*
mind was not always on the passive side of an intuitive-to-
abstractive cognitive course. The *faculty* concept was to become an
object of derision in psychology, whereby everything from the Kantian categories of the understanding to Gall's phrenological labels
were lumped into the same designation and then dismissed as "innate ideas" (Boring, 1950, p. 53). Those of us who recall using the
term *cognitive* to describe Rogerian theory circa 1950 are surely
thinking of this descriptive label in its Kantian sense. It was a neogestalt term at that time, having to do with the role that purely
phenomenal organizations had upon sensory input, not *after* input
had been affected, but coming at the same time or possibly even
before such input was sensed (see Koffka, 1935, pp. 78 and 382). The
distinction between distal (geographical) and proximal (phenomenal)
stimuli made by the gestaltists closely approximated Kant's distinction between the noumenal and the phenomenal in cognition. As
cognitive faculties the categories of the understanding operated completely in the phenomenal realm.

Having now pinpointed the current use of cognitive as some mixture of Ockham's intuitive and abstractive cognitions, we further
argue that there is really no difference here from what in Chapter 4

we outlined as the mediation view of behavior (p. 154). Though this formal designation has been used most often in S-R theories, the study of history teaches that it has always been a vital part of theories relying predominantly on the efficient cause to account for descriptions of behavior. Helmholtz' concept of inductive conclusions or unconscious inference was of this variety (Chapter 3, p. 108). Wundt later employed the concept of apperception in similar fashion: He meant that inputs after birth act in the present as habitual frames determining the actual perception of an object we see before us today (Boring, 1950, p. 329). Indeed John Locke (1952) himself referred to the role of earlier inputs (associated ideas) on later input propensities as "intellectual habits" (p. 250). Such habits of thought give us an illusion of determining our own conceptual understanding, but in actuality the frequency of inputs arraying themselves "this way or that" in our connected habit (mediational) systems are really the determining factors: "Probability upon such grounds carries so much evidence with it, that it naturally determines the judgment, and leaves us as little liberty to believe or disbelieve, as a demonstration does, whether we will know [cognize] or be ignorant" (ibid., p. 369).

This British Empiricist interpretation of cognition can be seen in E. C. Tolman's mediation conception (see Chapter 4, pp. 152–154). Tolman (1967) believed he could observe purposes and cognitions in behavior (pp. 12–13). These aspects of behavior necessarily went together (ibid., p. 13), because in a sense cognitions were the "carriers" of purposes (ibid., p. 27). As such, cognitions were said to be behavior-determinants, acting as intervening variables (ibid., p. 414). In his glossary of terms, Tolman defined cognition as:

A generic term for one of the two classes of immanent determinants . . . of behavior. A cognition (a means-end readiness . . . or an expectation . . .) is present in a behavior in so far as the continued going-off of that behavior is contingent upon environment entities (i.e., types of discriminanda, manipulanda, or means-end-relations) proving to be "so and so." And such a contingency will be testified to whenever, if these environmental entities do not prove to be so and so, the given behavior will exhibit disruption . . . and be followed by learning (ibid., p. 440).

Cognition thus referred to certain judgments and expectations which the organism had functioning as a mediator that "thus and such" would lead to "so and so," and following a purposive act of some sort, if this sequence of events failed to develop in the contingent circumstances, a disrupted pattern resulted calling for new learning to occur. This kernal idea of an organism mediating certain purposive or intentional *information* (the most common term employed) is what modern cognitive psychology has retained (e.g., see Broadbent, 1963). We turn now to two fine examples of such cognitive theories

## Two Examples of Cognitive Mediation Theories: Irwin and Neisser

Advocates of teleological theory may find encouragement in the patent efforts being made by modern cognitivists to employ terminology that is usually found in what Skinner (1971) has termed the "literature of freedom" (p. 30). On the surface such terms as *intention, purpose, active* or *constructive perception, optional behaviors, freedom* and *behavioral unpredictability* reassure us that we are moving to something different in psychological theory. In his statement of cognitive behaviorism Boneau (1974) even claims: "A humanistic version of the human individual emerges as a distinct possibility" (p. 308). However, when we look closely at what is being expressed in these views, we invariably find the unacceptable device of using a mediation concept to account for how the person comes today to employ these seemingly intentional behaviors.

The dateline of a theory's appearance in the literature is unimportant to the issues now being raised. These issues will have to be considered in *all* subsequent theories purporting to be cognitive or otherwise humanistic in nature, for they are not subject to the corrective influences of recently gathered data. In other contexts the writer has taken up the views of Boneau (Rychlak, 1975) and Mischel (Rychlak, 1976) on similar counts. The reader is simply being alerted by way of examples to what a humanistic theorist finds unacceptable in mediational efforts "to account for" telic considerations in behavior. Corrective measures are proposed in subsequent chapters of this volume.

In his *Intentional Behavior and Motivation: A Cognitive Theory* Francis W. Irwin (1971) acknowledges a neo-Tolmanian precedent and defines cognition as the knowledge an organism has of the situations and outcomes in which it finds itself (p. 104). His Situation-Act-Outcome (SAO) theory relies on an interlocked triad notion (ibid., p. 75). This triad consists of a preference ($oPO'$) and a pair of complementary act-outcome expectancies ($aa'Eo$ and $a'aEo'$). If an organism prefers one outcome to another ($o'$ to $o$ in this example) and perceives that one act-outcome expectancy will lead to this preference ($a'aEo'$) while also perceiving that another act-outcome expectancy will lead to a dispreferred outcome (aa'Eo), a choice will be made by the organism for the former alternative (i.e., a'aEo'). The *situation* is essentially a complex of stimuli (ibid., p. 13); the *act* is anything that an organism can be said "to do" (ibid., p. 17); and the outcome is the state of an organism's environment "some time after an act" (ibid., p. 20).

The teleologist would be likely to interpret an act as literally creating or bringing about the outcomes of life, but Irwin (1971) makes clear that an act cannot influence its outcome because the latter is still in the future when the act is initiated. The outcome of an act can affect only *later* occurrences of comparable acts (p. 58). We find here a first intimation of the pseudohumanistic usage of *act* which separates the teleologist from the mediational thinker. How then are we to conceptualize the fact that a later event over time can influence an earlier event? Irwin responds: "The answer of a 'cognitive' theory is that the organism prefers the outcome that it *expects* its act to produce; it prefers the actual outcome only if it coincides with this *expected outcome*" (ibid., p. 58).

Irwin emphasizes that concepts of expectation are central to cognitive theories (ibid., p. 70). His contribution to expectancy theory and what separates him from stimulus-response psychologies is said to be the fact that he employs *two* terms on the "act" side of things, whereas the S-R theories settle for one term (ibid., p. 72). Hull's fractional antedating goal reaction (see Chapter 4, p. 155) is thus a single response made to a stimulus complex, whereas in SAO theory the organism is viewed as formulating two complementary expectancies—one for the preferred and one for the dispreferred outcome. This is where both choice and intention enter: ". . . we take an act to be intentional if and only if its occurrence depends upon the existence of an interlocked triad in which the expected outcome of the act in question is also the preferred outcome and the expected outcome of the alternative act is also the dispreferred outcome" (ibid.; p. 78). A choice is the process that eventuates in one of the two alternative acts being carried out (ibid., p. 79). The act chosen is intentional, but even the rejected act is an intentional act (ibid., p. 84).

The upshot is that to speak of a choice on this model depends upon an act first occurring (ibid., p. 89). To speak of possible choices, which might or might not eventuate in overt behavior, has little place in this theory. Irwin keeps his theory close to research paradigms in which terms like choice become operationalized. He sprinkles his presentation with examples in which a subject already

*has* a preference or in which a preference or expectancy is established in earlier trials for a subject, who manifests it at some point,
and then we bring to bear SAO theory to account for the process of
selection *after* such preferential acts have been made *(ibid.,* p. 91).
When accounting for how preferences or expectancies arise initially,
Irwin falls back on a familiar theme. He says these are "acquired"
*(ibid.,* pp. 60, 103) or learned: "It may be remarked that the acquisition and modification of act-outcome expectancies, which is required
by our criteria, is obviously a form of learning . . ." *(ibid.,* p. 81).
How are we to conceive of this learning process? The mediation-
model strategy of this cognitive theory is never clearer than in the
following, where Irwin employs a theory-method confound to put his
central constructs between what we know as past inputs and present
outputs, acting now in succession as fundamentally *efficient causes:*

Preferences and expectancies are dispositional states of the organism, and
changes in such states, such as "learning," are processes. Psychology attempts to relate such states and processes to prior and concomitant variables, on the one hand, and to acts, on the other. In a logical sense, then,
they are *intervening variables* [italics added] (Irwin, 1971, p. 106).

   If we can relate such states and processes to prior and concomitant variables and if our variables of interest (preferences, expectancies) are intervening variables, of what use are such conceptions as behavioral *originators?* The behavioral determination
here is exclusively instrumental, which means fundamentally that
it has *itself* been efficiently caused by some antecedent event. Irwin's
dispositional states *do not* dispose from birth but are brought in as
theoretical analogues to the telic meaning of intentionality in that
typical "accounting for" fashion of the functionalist's argument (see
Chapter 4). No matter how often Irwin (1971) may use terms like
intentions, choices, and even freedom (p. 85), the SAO theorist cannot escape the S-R (efficient-cause) Bind because he is willing to see
in his experimental observations a variable mediating between other
variables, rather than a telic theoretical construct. Predicating all on
the Lockean *tabula-rasa* thesis, he must of necessity make behavior
a tail-end affair, under the direction of influences other than those
originating in the *pro-forma* possibilities of human creativity.
   Ulric Neisser's (1967) *Cognitive Psychology* ranges across the
broad discipline encompassed by this designation, but this excellent
volume also presents a preferred theory by its author. His many
assurances to the reader that, for example, "the world of experience

is produced by the man who experiences it" (p. 3) or that "perception is not a passive taking-in of stimuli, but an active process of synthesizing or constructing a visual figure" (p. 16) can lull one into believing that we have something other than the traditional Lockean-mediation model under development in this volume. Neisser apparently believes that his outlook is in the line of descent from Brentano's Act Psychology (*ibid.,* p. 10), and he makes several favorable references to the work of the gestalt psychologists (e.g., pp. 50, 90). However, he primarily bases his approach on the work of Bartlett (1932, 1958). His core definition of cognition would probably be "the flow of information in the organism" (p. 208; taken from Broadbent, 1963).

Neisser (1967) uses the word *mediation* throughout the text, but he does not seem to mean what we have been meaning in the sense of an efficient-cause sequence of events. He seems to use this concept in a more active sense, often equating it with the meanings of *construction* and *synthesis.* In speaking of his preferred outlook he notes: "The central assertion is that seeing, hearing, and remembering are all acts of construction, which may make more or less use of stimulus information depending on circumstances" (p. 10); yet this active contribution to the stimulus input is termed a *mediation* (p. 3), so that in effect "all knowledge of the world is mediated rather than direct" (p. 173). We therefore do not wish to make our case employing quotations from Neisser's writings in which he is employing the word *mediation* in his sense. But at the same time we *do* want to claim that Neisser *is* a mediation theorist in the meaning of our term—that is, having ultimately to fall back on the meaning of *yesterday's efficient causes.* Though he wavers somewhat, this seems clearly to be his *basic* theoretical stance, all humanistic-sounding assurances to the contrary.

Neisser's cognitive approach is more British than continental, a fact we quickly discern in his distinction between a cognitive and a dynamic account of cognition: "Asked why I did a certain thing, I may answer in dynamic terms, 'Because I wanted . . . ,' or, from the cognitive point of view, 'Because it seemed to me . . .' " (*ibid.,* p. 4). In a subsequent discussion, however, we learn that the processes of focal attention in cognition are "very much under the control of developmental and dynamic factors" (*ibid.,* pp. 103–104). Though this might suggest a greater stress on the telic features in cognition (the "wants" of people in knowing) Neisser's treatment of cognitive phenomena does not encompass much in the way of identity concepts—apparently because this is not specifically the province of cognitive psychology. This is especially noticeable in his discussion of the Hoffding function, which he views as primarily a question of "pattern recognition" (*ibid.*, p. 50). Koffka (1935) felt that this phenomenon underscored the active processes in recognition and immediately brought in an identity concept to account for it because "recognizing involves an object-Ego relationship" (p. 594). When Neisser (1967) turns his attention to an identity concept or executive, he does so by way of cybernetic or information-processing analogues (*ibid.*, p. 292), a strategy to which we return below. A good sense of Neisser's preferred theory is to be seen in the following, which is a summary of his figural synthesis conception:

If we allow several figures to appear at once, the number of possible input configurations is so very large that a wholly parallel mechanism, giving a different output for each of them, is inconceivable. To cope with this difficulty, even a mechanical recognition system must have some way to select *portions* of the incoming information for detailed analysis. This immediately implies the existence of two levels of analysis: the preattentive mechanisms, which form segregated objects and help to direct further processing, and the act of focal attention, which makes more sophisticated analyses of the chosen object. . . . This means that the detailed properties and features we ordinarily see in an attended figure are, in a sense, "optional." They do not arise automatically just because the relevant information is available in the icon [transient visual memory], but only because part of the input was selected for attention and certain operations then performed on it. . . . In this sense it is important to think of focal attention as a constructive, synthetic activity rather than as purely analytic. One does not simply examine the input and make a decision; one *builds* an appropriate visual object (*ibid.*, p. 94).

This is surely the core of Neisser's thinking, and he employs this conception of active synthesis or construction in several contexts (e.g., pp. 103, 212–213, 225, 235). We confine our comments to this style of theorizing in his treatment of the higher mental processes (memory, recall and thought). Neisser recognizes that the British Empiricists (Hobbes, Locke, Hume, and especially James Mill) popularized the so-called reappearance hypothesis in memory. This is "the notion that the stored information consists of ideas, suspended in a quiescent state from which they are occasionally aroused . . ." (*ibid.*, p. 281). We are challenged to learn that even the gestalt psychologists accepted this hypothesis, because they spoke of "traces" in memory (*ibid.*, p. 283). A recheck of Koffka (1935) finds him discussing how traces are altered through being assimilated to other patterns so that they frequently never reappear as initially perceived (p. 524). Koffka also reiterates the importance of ego-systems in this context, so that traces may even be actively kept from reappearing in awareness altogether (ibid., p. 525). This does not strike us as a simple reappearance hypothesis, surely.

To understand Neisser's (1967) strategy of explanation we must distinguish between construction (or synthesis) at the level of a sensory receptor (eye, ear, etc.) and construction at the level of the higher mental processes or, as we might call it, mind. Neisser seems to be a constructionist at the level of sensation—on the order of Kant's claim that sensory input is organized according to space and time—but at the level of mind he remains a traditionalist (a Lockean mediation theorist). He does not have a paralleling constructive role of mind qua mind as Kant did in his use of the categories of the understanding (see Chapter 2, p. 90). Hence, when we come to the higher mental processes, we find Neisser quickly foregoing his act-psychology stance to place a theoretical emphasis where Brentano would not have placed it. After noting that perceptual construction takes place, he observes that this requires a certain "raw material" on which to work (ibid., p. 284). Harking back to Kant's view of cognition (refer above, p. 204), we now wonder if this means that sensuous impressions as raw materials give cognition the occasion to act. But this is not the theory of cognition being advanced, for we next read: "Perception is constructive but the input information often plays the largest single role in determining the constructive process. A very similar role, it seems to me, is played by the aggregate of information stored in long-term memory" (ibid., p. 285). We have at this point clearly left the Kantian form of cognition and are now speaking of the influence of intuitive cognition on abstractive cognition in that sense of Ockham discussed above.

The unique feature of Neisser's argument, and where he departs from the reappearance hypothesis, is his claim that the nature of the information stored in long-term memory, which acts mediationally upon the inputs of "today," is not the "finished mental event" but rather the "traces of prior processes of construction" (ibid., p.285). All learning is response learning—that is, the learning to carry out some coordinated series of acts (ibid.). Neisser holds that the mental traces are not simply revived or reactivated by memory processes (recall) but that the recollection is of information concerning previous constructions used in the present to form new constructive acts. We always see and know more (ground) than the focal point of our attention (figure). When we first perceive or imagine an aspect of experience, the process of construction is never limited to the focal point in any case. We tend to build a spatial, temporal, and conceptual framework as well (*ibid.*, p. 287). Admitting that most of his text deals with the constructions in focal attention, Neisser then turns to a discussion of the *cognitive structures* to be found in higher mental processes:

> One easily forgets the *occasions* on which one learned how the local streets are oriented, what the Civil War was about, how to shift gears, or how to speak grammatically, but they leave a residue behind. Because these residues are organized in the sense that their parts have regular and controlling interrelations, the term "cognitive structures" is appropriate for them. (This definition is meant to leave the question of empiricism and nativism open. It is very possible that the form and organization of at least some cognitive structures, especially those for space, time, and language, are determined genetically, or otherwise, before any experience has accumulated) (ibid., p. 287).

Though at first blush this parenthetical disclaimer may appear to reflect proper scientific discretion, a moment's reflection will convince the reader that this is *precisely* the question on which Neisser should be taking a stand, for this is what *always* divides the Lockean from the Kantian. We cannot leave such questions open in the context of empirical research without assuring that a Lockean view of things will prevail due to the IV-DV, S-R confound (see Chapter 4, p. 173). Granting that information which has been input since birth plays a role in what a person brings to bear in life, does this mean the capactiy to know such information is *itself* a product of earlier information? If so, how was this earlier information made known? What is often unappreciated is that a Lockean is a nativist on the questions of long- and short-term memory. He makes no assumptions about memory being learned. Since we now find that memory is itself organized by the individual, the question becomes: Can such organizations of memory *also* be innate? To answer yes to this question calls for a somewhat too anthropomorphic formulation to suit the Lockean's empirical tastes. As we have seen with Neisser versus Koffka, for a thinker in this tradition to invoke ego identities as the "constructors" of events is difficult. Yet, cognitive structuring cannot simply "hang there" without some recognition that there is an executive role going begging. Neisser knows full well why modern tough-minded psychologists balk at postulating such executives in their cognitive theories:

They are afraid that a separate executive would return psychology to the soul, the will, and the *homunculus*; it would be equivalent to explaining behavior in terms of a "little man in the head." Such explanations seem to lead to an infinite regress, which must bar further research and frustrate theory. If the actions of the executive account for behavior, what accounts for those actions in turn? Does the ego have an ego (*ibid.*, p. 295)?

This shopworn argument is based exclusively on an efficient-cause premise as regards what "accounts for" behavior. Self-direction is being interpreted here analogously to an individual sitting in an automobile, determining where it will go and what it will do. The machine is nontelic, but the homunculus human being within "accounts for" the actions observed on the roadways. But if the person within is *also* a machine, we need another homunculus to drive this identity about, and then another for the machine within *ad infinitum*. The argument crumbles once we broaden our interpretation of causation to include the meanings of finality. Neisser does not do this, but retaining the essentially efficient-cause extraspective perspective, takes his lead from the instrumentation of modern computer technology:

It now seems possible that there is an escape from the regress that formerly seemed infinite. As recently as a generation ago, processes of control had to be thought of as *homunculi*, because man was the only known model of an executive agent. Today, the stored-program computer has provided us with an alternative possibility, in the form of the *executive routine* (*ibid.*, p. 295).

Modern psychologists often go to cybernetic or information-processing analogues of this nature. One is likely to see a flow chart in their presentations, consisting of a series of boxes arrayed from left to right, labeled with terms such as *selected filters, encoding, search units, sensory buffers, decision channels, long-term* and *short-term memory storages,* and there is likely to be a feedback loop or two in such characterizations before the input flows through the system to its "output" (see Solso, 1974, for some prime examples). Though there is a pattern in the design of this flow (that is, a formal-cause emphasis is given), the essential characteristic of such informational flow is that it is efficiently causal in nature. The machine never truly behaves "for the sake of" a premise (a "that") because it has no awareness (even in principle!) of the fact that it is reasoning according to predicate assumptions as framed in its program. Lacking a self-reflexive intelligence, its strategy of reasoning is exclusively mediational. In short the machine never really acts, never really constructs anything—if we mean by *active intellect* and *construction* a creative potential to conceptualize possibilities and thereby bring them to bear in actuality. This human prerogative is left to the programmer, and we are back to our question: 'Is he a homunculus or not?' Neisser's treatment of the executive factor in perception and cognition reflects his cybernetic-like theoretical resolution of the identity problem (that is, the synthesizer or constructor of knowledge):

> . . . when you see a friend across the street, you are not seeing only him. *He*, a person of a particular kind with a particular relevance to your life, is appearing *there*, a particular place in space, and *then*, at a certain point in time. Similarly, a spoken sentence is not just a string of words to be identified, but it has a particular meaning, is spoken by a particular person, at a particular time and place. These frames of reference can be thought of as a third level of cognitive construction. The preattentive processes delineate units, provide partial cues, and control simple responses; focal attention builds complexly structured objects or movements, one at a time, on the basis thus provided; the background processes build and maintain schemata *to which these objects are referred* [italics added] (*ibid.*, p. 286).

To the Kantian cognitivist, the schemata would be the very *starting* point, because meanings are said to devolve from above, rather than function as a frame of reference to which organized and structured objects from below are referred! Though we do have some changes of emphasis here, the fundamental institutionalized paradigm of psychology has gone essentially unscathed in Neisser's account. Whether we think of the cognitive hierarchy as consisting of focalized *items* or of *processes* makes no difference. So long as we are putting our emphasis on the source of knowledge as exclusively or primarily issuing from below, from the environmental input, which is *then* sequentially arrayed by way of one, two, or three organizational stages into a constitutive totality, we have the familiar Lockean model under espousal. Kantian formulations do not become those dreaded nativisms out of a love which their propounders have for innate mechanisms, but because Kantian theorists know full well that a mediation strategy must necessarily focus on the *processing* (the efficient-cause) of information as it flows from antecedent to consequent circumstance. There is no theory to date that has accepted mediation conceptualizations and avoided this necessary eventually. Some merely hide things better than others. The crux of the issue remains that *initial* capacity, ability, potential, of the organism to contribute something to the knowledge it acquires by way of experience without having "learned" to do so!

Hence we conclude that cognitive-mediational theories fail as humanisms because they simply do not capture the basic meaning of final causation. This inability to account for teleological behavior is also tied to the demonstrative nature of such theories. We have yet to see a cognitive theorist in the tradition of Ockham formulate a model that can subsume dialectical reasoning. However, Irwin's (1971) interlocked triad and his insistence on a complementary expectation, a rejected act to match the intended one, and so on, all suggest a quasi-dialectical formulation (pp. 75–77). Irwin seems to have employed these counterbalancing features primarily for reasons of logical symmetry, but dialectical formulations *could* have been introduced to his thinking at these specialized points of theory development. Neisser (1967) also moves into an area in which dialectical analysis is highly compatible when he begins speaking of the multiplicity of thought or the distinction between primary and secondary (Freudian) processes in thought (pp. 296–303). Neisser will have no little difficulty in accounting for the dialectical twists of dreaming and psychosis on an executive program fashioned exclusively along demonstrative lines.

Another drawback to the human image portrayed by these mediation conceptions is in their limited and simplistic treatment of choice. To see how a true choice is possible is difficult unless—at least some of the time—there is a truly arbitrary decision being depicted. Irwin's model of intentions leading to choices makes this process appear to run like clockwork, as indeed it can be made to do in a neatly devised research context. But is this the way choices arise in life? For example, can one choose an alternative going *against* one's preferences? Can we choose "for the devil of it?" Invariably such theories have choice fixed by the probability distribution of the information being mediated "this way" or "that way" on the question being pondered (not unlike Locke's use of probability quoted above, p. 205). Humanists find that this portrayal does not ring true, for people clearly *do* opt against the odds, standing against pressures, accepting the likelihood of death, taking the short end of a "long shot," and so forth. Is our only recourse to take a demonstrative posture and call all such behaviors illogical, or can we find an alternative logic on the basis of which people are behaving in these circumstances? Surely the humanist's position here is clear.

A further objection the humanist has to cognitive-mediational theories is their light treatment or highly inadequate treatment of *meaning*. No real distinction is made between what is a sign and what is a symbol in thought (Chapter 2). Constructive organizations are *always* seen as playing a sign function in the flow of information and never an expressive meaning-inducing role in the unfolding of events. *Meaning* is a relational term, and the nature of a relation is that it *does induce* an organization among the various elements being united. But cognitive theories fall back on mediated signs rather than on fundamentally expressive meanings in providing their accounts of what is supposedly going on in the experiment.

Putting together the points concerning the arbitrariness in behavior and the processing of meanings, we can see how mediation models find it impossible to capture the novel and the creative in behavior. To see the individual human being as creative we must take an introspective perspective and carefully elucidate what he contributes to the course of events going on within his lifeline. We cannot picture him extraspectively as a series of boxes with feedback loops, moving him along according to a set pattern based upon set input information now fixed into memory storages of various durations. There can be no originating source of control on such a model, in which the term *intention*, or *purpose*, may just as well be seen as a "code-X" carried by a feedback loop or storage box. There is no need for telic commentary on this model, because there is no true chance for creativity in the organism which is cybernetically conceptualized. Humanists prize these ascriptions, such as the person's creative potentials or peak experiences in living (Maslow, 1971, pp. 168–179). They simply cannot accept novelty as another one of those encoded behaviors that just happen to prove successful through serendipity or whatever, to a course of behavior.

We must also remember that the two views reviewed here as modern examples of psychological theory do not exhaust the varieties of mediation concepts presently employed. Space does not permit a thorough review of such *noncognitive* formulations as the admittedly S-R mediation theories or those Lockean formulations in which a physiological substrate is pointed to as the ultimate behavioral determinant. Obviously these mediation theories, many of which rely on drive reductions or genetic transmissions to say how it is that human behavior is determined, are totally unacceptable to a teleologist. The Skinnerian view is a special case, and we devote a full section to operant theory in Chapter 6 (pp. 255–270).

One final caution: We must not allow those who fail to see the retention of Lockeanism in mediational models to present themselves as the true innovators of our time. Although they act in a sincere belief that they are advancing psychology, the prophets of the "new look" of cognitive mediationism must be called to answer the arguments of the present chapter before we let them carry the revolutionary (or evolutionary) banner at our forefront. Mahoney (1974) is a case in point, as when he prepares his reader for the mediational models he is about to advocate following a very telling chapter on the weaknesses of so-called nonmediational (Lockean) models (pp. 35–39). He suggests to his reader: "We are long overdue for some evolutionary progress in our paradigm. The mediational models which we shall now examine may provide some adaptive conceptual mutations in our understanding of complex human behavior" (*ibid.*, p. 49). This seeming advance is a *trap*; it simply perpetuates the efficient causation of (nontelic) Lockeanism at another level of description; and far from being an evolutionary advance, it is an apology for the badly mangled but entrenched model of the academic establishment.

## Intimations of a Revolution in Psychology?

Significant changes do seem to be apparent in the thinking of rigorous psychologists in the last quarter of the twentieth century. Not everyone would agree with this assessment, of course. Kausler (1974) notes that the new look in cognition is actually the return to certain unsolved problems dating back to Ebbinghaus. Even so, because these are questions of *theory* and not of *method* (evidence), we have reason to look to the future of psychology with confidence that significant changes in theory will eventuate. The major stumbling block to teleology is proper terminology. The earliest most influential psychologists (including Ebbinghaus) simply refused to take seriously a psychology of telic description (Chapters 4 and 5). The time is now ripe for a serious reevaluation of our terminology in light of our experimental rules of data collection.

There is much talk of rules in modern cognitive psychology, stemming apparently from the writings of the logical positivists (see Table 1). Wittgenstein's influence in particular seems great, because his style of referring to language games and their attendant rules seems to have been adopted in a number of scientific theories, ranging from genetic codes to mathematical language systems. But the problem for psychology is that, although such rules (as all mathematics) are based upon *logic*, the mediation theorist seems to view logic itself as a kind of predetermined ordering that does not require a special "accounting for" in human behavior. Yet, as any logician knows, in the most fundamental of all logical efforts, *predication* (Table 1: Aristotle and Peter of Abelard), what is affirmed by the reasoner into a patterned meaning is *not* fixed and without arbitrariness at some point in the line of reasoning.

Logicians speak of "granting this, that follows" because they know full well the precedent-sequacious line of meaning-extension that human reason generates. And even if they are not dialecticians, they also know the reverse—that is, "granting that, this follows." Though we hear much about the ordering, organizing, and encoding of language terms according to rules from modern cognitivists, they are remarkably mute concerning *this* predicating or premising activity of logic. Logic is surely an ordering, and the resultant rules generated in cognition are most surely empirically demonstrable. But until we have some way of acknowledging that the cognizing individual literally *conceptualizes* (contributes to the form his logical reasoning will take), we will never capture what needs capturing in a psychology of the human being. Mediational models cannot help here because mediational organization always occurs as an *effect* of previous learning. Happily, there are growing signs that modern researchers are finding subject-induced organizations in learning tasks which are anomalous to a Lockean model.

For example, James J. Jenkins (1974) has done an excellent job of explicating the Lockean assumptions in traditional views of memory, assumptions which he notes are losing their grip on this field of inquiry. He and other psychologists have found the writings of Stephen C. Pepper (1970) to be of help in formulating theoretical alternatives to Lockeanism in psychology. Pepper distinguished a series of *world hypotheses*, which are root metaphors that thinkers of all types—from philosophers to scientists—employ in describing their areas of interest. Although the parallels here are not exact, the Lockean model relates to what Pepper calls the *mechanism* root metaphor (Jenkins, 1974, calls this "associationism" in psychology); and the Kantian model comes closest to his *contextualism* on certain crucial points (Pepper, 1970, Chapters 9 and 10). Pepper traces contextualism to the philosophies of Charles S. Peirce, William James, and John Dewey, but one could easily show that contextualism takes from these views the Kantian side of what in Chapter 4 we called a mixed Lockean-Kantian formulation in the philosophy of William James (p. 157).

To find a leading experimentalist of Jenkins' (1974) reputation calling for a shift to contextualism in the field of memory is of no small interest. He may well have named a significant trend in cognitive psychology, one begun in the work of Bousfield (1953) and Tulving (1962) and others, whereby the subject in a learning (memory) experiment is seen to organize his recall of words based upon certain categories—either those made available by the experimenter (for example, providing subjects with names of people vs. names of cities) or actually induced by a subject's idiosyncratic associative proclivities. Jenkins (1974) based much of his argument on a study of Bransford and Franks (1971), in which subjects were seen to *construct* (Neisser's term) complex sentences, which they believed with certainty that they had seen before *but had not*, out of shorter sentences, which were seen and which contained the meanings eventually inferred and organized into the longer sentences.

Thus evidence is accruing that for words (Bousfield, Tulving) and sentences (Bransford & Franks) a subject *does something* to the task at hand in terms of some organizational capacity he has to sort a task out in some way. Psychologists have undoubtedly known this for decades. They probably took this as one of those Kuhnian puzzles, rather than as an anomaly. Let us hope that we have a growing number of psychologists who are now considering the anomalies of a mediating animal which seems an actively organizing animal. Next question: Can this organization be shown to begin early in life, from birth or at least before any learning can be said to have taken place? If so, the mediation model as presently conceived must surely be modified significantly. This would doubtless be a genuine revolution in psychology, and it would be a revolution at the *level of theory*. The integrity of the scientific method would not be challenged.

## A Sensible Revolution For All Time

Though there will doubtless always be Kuhnian revolutions in psychology, just as there are in other sciences, we are proposing a single revolution *for all time* which will liberalize psychology on the side of theoretical description even as it keeps us within the bounds of rigorous science. Kantian theories will no longer be pressed into or "accounted for" by the linear strictures of a scientific methodology that itself sprang from Lockean precedents. We will retain the demonstrative rigor of this method even as we recognize the possibility that it can test *other* than Lockean theories. Dialectical and telic formulations will *not* be permitted to affect the strictures of validating evidence. *Rigor* will mean knowing where one comes from theoretically, carefully extending a line of development to the point of empirical testing and then, in the most demonstrative way possible, *proving* what we believe to be the case in the unmolested succession of events known as validation. Because we acknowledge the affirmation-of-the-consequent fallacy in this sequence, a healthy sense of modesty will characterize our claims concerning the facts we presume to discover in the empirical data at play before our eyes. The contribution theory makes to this sequence of events will never be forgotten.

We lose our theoretical way and become "method mad" when we fallaciously believe that theories arise only in the data. Theories, like cognitive structurings of the stimulus, have *other* sources of organization than that which patterns them in the noumenal reality. They have a source that is expressed variously but always comes back to that phenomenal awareness called *mentality*. That scientists behave as they do, according to the meaning-lending structurings of a precedent paradigm, is no mere accident. This is their course of activity because this is their very nature as human beings! We all *must* predicate our thinking on something other than the focal point of our concern. This is not a radical notion, but bears the weight of history as we discovered in Chapter 1 (see Table 1). The difficulty in furthering a revolution in psychology stems from the fact that we lack some appropriate *cognitive category* or *paradigmatic frame* within which to alert our senses to this side of behavior. Lacking this precedent, we cannot discover its effects even when they are involved in our studies, or we let them pass by as puzzles rather than catch them up as anomalies.

Kuhnian anomalies do not "spring forth" from the data, but are "put onto" such events in an empirical study. In the next three chapters of this volume we review a series of issues in an aim to clarify and then extend the terminology introduced to describe the nature of human behavior. In doing so we hope to be writing-in the precedents for a *sensible* revolution, one that will not unseat or repress *any* view on pseudoscientific grounds. We do not need to supplant the Lockean mechanistic model with the Kantian humanistic (contextualistic) model. Anyone who expresses interest in Lockean formulations should be encouraged and supported to continue his study just as he now does. But we hope that he would, if not be humbled, at least made contemplative by the recognition that his historical ties to the machine paradigm of scientific *method* are no longer mandates for a preferred position in the scientific *theoretical* hierarchy.

Telic theoretical accounts are no longer to be dismissed as lacking parsimony, or as departing from the data, or as reflecting a homunculus machine within a machine. No one who is unable or unwilling to take the theoretical viewpoint of another can claim objectivity in science. If the constructs being used are found wanting, they can easily be refuted *within the language realm* of the theory under espousal. But if a critic simply refuses to comprehend a telic theory and in some way claims the rights of preemption as a "genuine" scientist who "knows" what a proper scientific account must be like, something far more serious is taking place. In this case, rather than critical analysis, we are faced with *paradigmatic repression;* the only alternative here is to employ countermeasures to remove the repression. In this book we direct arguments counter to such repressions. If psychology is open to our revolution in theory *versus* method, there shall be no reason ever to repress an idea—that is, a theory or even a theory of knowledge. There *will* remain a repression of sorts on the side of method, because we insist on a validation by way of terminating the theoretical line of development in an objective repeatable experiment!

## Summary

In Chapter 5 we try to clarify what is meant by the phrase *scientific revolution,* and in light of this clarification, to propose the type of revolution called for in psychology. Kuhn's position is seen as reflecting more accurately what takes place in scientific work than does Popper's concept of the falsification of scientific theories. Scientists work to further the meanings of certain precedent paradigms to which they owe their very understanding of the area of study in which they are engaged. What is not generally appreciated, however, is that the Kuhnian concept of revolution is *exclusively* on the side of theory and not method. The scientific ground rules of validation are not what is being challenged in a scientific revolution, but rather the ways in which we conceptualize the findings of our empirical observations and experiments.

Indeed the very procedure of science as a line of development entails a necessary logical error—that of *affirming the consequent* of an 'If . . . then . . .'' proposition. This is not fatal to science, but it does signal that for any given fact pattern a series of (literally, N!) theoretical descriptions is potentially capable of accounting for the regularities observed. Psychology can be both rigorous and humanistic if we learn to use telic theories and then put them to test in typical experimental fashion, employing validating evidence. So long as we avoid confounding what is our theory with what is our method, such a rigorous humanism is possible.

We next discussed two kinds of views on how to solve the problems of a humanistic psychology by erring in opposite directions. First, there are the psychologists like van Kaam and Giorgi who indicate that we can derive a new methodology of science that will rectify the difficulties of writing humanistic theory by advancing something other than strict validation in their support. But when we come right down to what these alternative methods suggest, there is no difference between such practices and what would be expected from a more conventional scientific effort—particularly in an early stage of experimentation. So-called phenomenological and existential "methods" threaten to resolve themselves into an exclusively pro-cedural-evidence-based approach to science, and for this reason we cannot accept them as viable alternatives to the current rules of validation.

When we next turn to the cognitive approaches of Irwin and Neisser, which suggest to many psychologists that humanistic issues are now being "handled" adequately, a problem arises in the other direction. Although the rules of evidence are properly adhered to in these approaches, the actual theoretical constructs being put to test are simply *not* adequate to the explanatory task. Ultimately these theories are all mediational in tone and hence must—at the crucial point of behavior's earliest manifestations—accept a *tabula-rasa* rather than a *pro-forma* account of mentation. Mediation theory thus falls short of a genuinely telic theory on at least three counts: (1) Mediators (signs, rules, encoders, models, etc.) are input and hence are past "effects" rather than truly present "causes," which means that (2) a genuine "that for the sake of which" determination in the sequence of motion called behavior is *never* achieved (i.e., there is no arbitrariness in behavior); (3) resulting in exclusively a demon-strative way of describing the course of behavioral events.

A sensible revolution for psychology is to distinguish clearly between what is our theory and what is our method of validating these outlooks and to admit a broader range of theoretical formula-tions. Specifically, we need Kantian as well as Lockean theories of behavior. Neither outlook is to be given preferential status, and the telic formulations that invariably flow from Kantian models will only strengthen psychology as a science of human behavior.

## References

Bartlett, F. C. *Remembering*. Cambridge: The University Press, 1932.

Bartlett, F. C. *Thinking*. New York: Basic Books, 1958.

Bergmann, G., & Spence, K. Operationism and theory in psychology. *Psychological Review*, 1941, **48**, 1–14.

Binswanger, L. *Being-in-the-world*. (Translated and with a critical introduction by J. Needleman.) New York: Basic Books, 1963.

Boneau, C. A. Paradigm regained? Cognitive behaviorism restated. *American Psychologist*, 1974, **29**, 297–309.

Boring, E. G. *A history of experimental psychology*. New York: Appleton-Century-Crofts, 1950.

Boss, M. *Psychoanalysis and daseinsanalysis*. New York: Basic Books, 1963.

Bousfield, W. A. The occurrence of clustering in the free recall of randomly arranged associates. *Journal of General Psychology*, 1953, **49**, 229–240.

Bransford, J. D., & Franks, J. J. The abstraction of linguistic ideas. *Cognitive Psychology*, 1971, **2**, 331–350.

Bridgman, P. W. *The way things are*. Cambridge, Mass.: Harvard University Press, 1959.

Broadbent, D. E. Flow of information within the organism. *Journal of Verbal Learning and Verbal Behavior*, 1963, **2**, 34–39.

Bronowski, J. *The common sense of science*. Cambridge, Mass.: Harvard University Press, 1958.

Bugental, J. F. T. Humanistic psychology: A new break-through. *American Psychologist*, 1963, **18**, 563–567.

Cassirer, E. *The problem of knowledge*. New Haven: Yale University Press, 1950.

Colaizzi, P. F. An analysis of the learner's perception of learning material at various phases of a learning process. *Review of Existential Psychology and Psychiatry*, 1967, **7**, 95–105.

Colaizzi, P. F. *Reflection and research in psychology: A phenomenological study of learning*. Dubuque, Iowa: Kendall/Hunt, 1973.

Conant, J. B. *Modern science and modern man*. Garden City, N.Y.: Doubleday Anchor, 1952. (Originally published, New York: Columbia University Press, 1929.)

Dulany, D. Awareness, rules, and propositional control: A confrontation with S-R behavior theory. In T. R. Dixon & D. L. Horton (Eds.), *Verbal behavior and general behavior theory*. Englewood Cliffs, N.J.: Prentice-Hall, 1968.

Eddington, A. *The philosophy of physical science*. Ann Arbor: University of Michigan Press, 1958.

Einstein, A. *Essays in science*. New York: Philosophical Library, 1934.

Feuer, L. S. *Einstein and the generations of science*. New York: Basic Books, 1974.

Frank, P. *Philosophy of science*. Englewood Cliffs, N.J.: Prentice-Hall, 1957.

Giorgi, A. *Psychology as a human science: A phenomenologically based approach*. New York: Harper & Row, 1970. (a)

Giorgi, A. Toward phenomenologically based research in psychology. *Journal of Phenomenological Psychology*, 1970, **1**, 75–98. (b)

Giorgi, A. Phenomenology and the foundational problems of pyschology. In W. J. Arnold & J. K. Cole (Eds.), *Nebraska symposium on motivation* (Vol. 22). Lincoln: University of Nebraska Press, 1975.

Haigh, G. V. Letter to the editor. *Psychology Today*, 1969, **3**, 4.

Hull, C. L. Mind, mechanism, and adaptive behavior. *Psychological Review*, 1937, **44**, 1–32.

Irwin, F. W. *Intentional behavior and motivation: A cognitive theory.* Philadelphia: Lippincott, 1971.

Jenkins, J. J. Remember that old theory of memory? Well, forget it! *American Psychologist*, 1974, **29**, 785–795.

Kant, I. *The critique of pure reason.* In R. M. Hutchins (Ed.), *Great books of the western world* (Vol. 42). Chicago: Encyclopedia Britannica, 1952. Pp. 1–250.

Kausler, D. H. Continuity of processes across variants of recognition learning. In R. L. Solso (Ed.), *Theories in cognitive psychology: The Loyola symposium.* New York: Wiley, 1974. Pp. 45–75.

Kelly, G. A. *The psychology of personal constructs* (2 vols.). New York: Norton, 1955.

Koffka, K. *Principles of gestalt psychology.* New York: Harcourt, Brace, 1935.

Kuhn, T. S. *The structure of scientific revolutions* (2nd ed.). Chicago: The University of Chicago Press, 1970. (1st ed., 1962.) (a)

Kuhn, T. S. Logic of discovery or psychology of research? In I. Lakatos & A. Musgrave (Eds.), *Criticism and the growth of knowledge.* Cambridge: The University Press, 1970. Pp. 1–23. (b)

Locke, J. *An essay concerning human understanding.* In R. M. Hutchins (Ed.), *Great books of the western world* (Vol. 35). Chicago: Encyclopedia Britannica, 1952. Pp. 85–395.

Mahoney, M. J. *Cognition and behavior modification.* Cambridge, Mass.: Ballinger, 1974.

Maslow, A. H. Eupsychia, the good society. *Journal of Humanistic Psychology*, 1961, **1**, 1–11.

Maslow, A. H. *The farther reaches of human nature.* New York: The Viking Press, 1971.

Masterman, M. The nature of a paradigm. In I. Lakatos & A. Musgrave (Eds.), *Criticism and the growth of knowledge.* Cambridge: The University Press, 1970. Pp. 59–89.

Neisser, U. *Cognitive psychology.* New York: Appleton-Century-Crofts, 1967.

Oppenheimer, R. Analogy in science. *American Psychologist*, 1956, **11**, 127–135.

Palmer, R. E. *Hermeneutics.* Evanston, Ill.: Northwestern University Press, 1969.

Pepper, S. C. *World hypotheses.* Berkeley: University of California Press, 1970.

Polanyi, M. *Personal knowledge.* New York: Harper Torchbook, 1964.

Popper, K. R. *The logic of scientific discovery.* New York: Basic Books, 1959.

Popper, K. R. Normal science and its dangers. In I. Lakatos & A. Musgrave (Eds.), *Criticism and the growth of knowledge.* Cambridge: The University Press, 1970. Pp. 51–58.

Rogers, C. R. *Client-centered therapy.* Boston: Houghton Mifflin, 1951.

Rychlak, J. F. *A philosophy of science for personality theory.* Boston: Houghton Mifflin, 1968.

Rychlak, J. F. A humanist looks at psychological science. In W. J. Arnold & J. K. Cole (Eds.), *Nebraska symposium on motivation* (Vol. 22). Lincoln: University of Nebraska Press, 1975.

Rychlak, J. F. Is a concept of "self" necessary in psychological theory, and if so why? In A. H. Wandersman, P. J. Poppen, & D. F. Ricks (Eds.), *Humanism and behaviorism: Dialogue and growth.* Elmsford, N.Y.: Pergamon Press, 1976.

Schrödinger, E. *Science theory and man.* New York: Dover, 1957.

Skinner, B. F. *Beyond freedom and dignity.* New York: Knopf, 1971.

Solso, R. L. (Ed.), *Theories in cognitive psychology: The Loyola symposium.* New York: Wiley, 1974.

Suzuki, D. T. *The essentials of Zen Buddhism.* (B. Phillips, Ed.) New York: Dutton, 1962.

Tolman, E. C. *Purposive behavior in animals and men.* New York: Appleton-Century-Crofts, 1967.

Tulving, E. Subjective organization in free recall of "unrelated" words. *Psychological Review,* 1962, **69**, 344–354.

van Kaam, A. *Existential foundations of psychology* (Image Books ed.). Garden City, N.Y.: Doubleday, 1969.

Watson, R. I. *The great psychologists* (3rd ed.). Philadelphia: Lippincott, 1971.

Whitehead, A. N. *The function of reason.* Boston: Beacon, 1958.

# CHAPTER SIX

## Misunderstandings, Confoundings, and Oversights in Modern Psychological Science

The discussion of a revolution in the distinction between theory and method is continued in Chapter 6. We also underscore the role dialectic has *already* played in the rise of modern science, and give detailed consideration to what is frequently held up as a stumbling block to humanism—the concept of determinism in events.

### A More Rigorous Use of Terms That Can Mean Theory, Method, or Both

The arguments about the confounding of theory with method can best be documented by arraying a number of terms frequently used by psychologists under these designations in tabular form. We can then easily see that many of these meanings cross over in common psychological parlance. Table 2 pp. 228–229 contains such an array of terms. It has at the top different terms that refer to essentially the same thing whether framed in a *theoretical* (*model, contiguity, hypothesis*) or a *methodological* context (*design, frequency, prediction*). Near the midpoint of the table we begin to see several repetitions across the two arrays, sometimes with modest differences between theoretical usage (theoretical behaviorism) and methodological usage (methodological behaviorism). But at other times the identical word or phrase is used (*function of* or *law* or *control*). When identical words are used under each array they are in quotation marks.

Table 2 is not exhaustive, and the reader may not agree with all of the parallels drawn. But it can hardly be denied that something of this sort goes on regularly in psychology. Note an essential characteristic of this table: It lacks terminology which might refer to *dialectical* meanings. This is as it should be, for as we argued in Chapter 5, proper science calls for methods that are nondialectical. However, when psychologists consciously set out to *restrict* their range of theorizing to the conceptualizations of Table 2 in the name of rigor we find serious developments taking place. For example, Underwood (1975) has defined model as follows: "As I understand the strict use of the term *model*, it means that a set of empirical relationships developed in one area of discourse is applied to another area of research as a possible explanatory system" (p. 129). Clearly, if a psychologist were to follow this recommendation, he would have to confine his models (left side of Table 2) to analogues drawn from the right side of Table 2. This means that his models must necessarily remain demonstrative (an example of what we call below, p. 245, formal-cause determinism!).

Underwood goes on to recommend certain guidelines for satisfactory theory construction in psychology—the sort of thing one might teach to a student who has asked the question: How do you get a theory? (*ibid.*, p. 128). Two of the three recommendations stress that "The theory must assume at least two intervening processes, and these processes must interact in some way to relate the independent variables to the dependent variables;" and ". . . any assumed process [in the person's behavioral activity] must be tied to at least one independent variable" (*ibid.*, p. 131). We see here *precisely* the concern that humanists have regarding the likely outcome of psychological theory which is confounded with questions of proof. Using these guidelines, Underwood *must* teach his students to think about behavior in exclusively efficient-cause terms. He furthers the tradition of Bergmann and Spence (1941, pp. 9–10) and MacCorquodale and Meehl (1948, pp. 103–105), who taught us that the proper if not the *only* locus in which to consider the role of theory is *between* the independent and the dependent variables of an empirical investigation (i.e., the S-R bind).

Underwood is mistaken on several counts. There are just as many examples in the history of science where *unsuccessful* models have been resuscitated to solve problems as there are of successful models and designs doing so. Arago's proposal of the "crucial experiment" to test the corpuscular theory of light is a famous case in point. Though satisfactorily refuted in 1855, this corpuscular "model" was revived in 1905 by Einstein who employed its heuristic powers in modified form as the hypothesis of light quanta or photons (Frank, 1957, p. 31). To teach that theories serve heuristically only between observable and manipulable variables is simply *not true!* We have seen Kuhn's arguments to this effect in Chapter 5. Robert Oppenheimer (1956)

**Table 2**    Some Terms Employed in Psychology Having the Meaning
of Theory and/or Method

| Theoretical terminology | Methodological terminology |
| --- | --- |
| Model [paradigm] | Design |
| Facts | Data |
| Stimulus and response | Independent and dependent variable(s) |
| Antecedent [cause] | Independent variable |
| Consequent [effect] | Dependent variable |
| Contiguity | Frequency |
| Hypothesis | Prediction |
| Demonstration | Control |
| Parameter | Treatment |
| Hypothetical | Operational |
| Interpretation | Generalization |
| Individual differences | Variance |
| Relationship | Law (correlation) |
| Construct | Observation (variable) |
| Single | Idiographic |
| General | Nomothetic |
| Learning | Trials-to-criterion |
| Habituated | Reinforced |
| Association | Correlation (law) |
| Alternatives | Manipulations |
| Understanding | Evidence |
| Conviction | Confidence level |

once spoke about this directly to psychologists, pointing out how in
physics *analogues* as theoretical devices come into play even *before*
one sets about to identify what his variables will be. To believe that
models emerge from proven methods and that science is therefore
merely a question of extending these empirically derived frames of
reference to the further reaches of explanation is an injustice to the
human capacity for creativity. This is how psychology has come to
make an efficient-cause metaphysic of its efficient-cause method
(Burtt, 1955, p. 229).

Many readers can recall drafting research reports of the sort "The
effect of [variable] X on [variable] Y." Taken in this pristine methodological phrasing, no one can object to the meanings conveyed
which speak of evidential relationships between theoretical hypotheses now translated into operationalized variables. A related phrase
is the *functional relationship* between variables (see Chapter 4).
Combining as it does the meanings of empirical observation with that
of statistical analysis, this functional phraseology has an especially

**Table 2** Some Terms Employed in Psychology Having the Meaning
of Theory and/or Method (*Cont.*)

| Theoretical terminology | Methodological terminology |
| --- | --- |
| Consequence | Contingency |
| Descriptive | Actuarial |
| Reductionism | Operationism |
| Hypothetical construct | Intervening variable |
| Theoretical variable | Experimental variable |
| Theoretical behaviorism | Methodological behaviorism |
| Theoretical assumptions | Statistical assumptions |
| Theoretically determined | Statistically determined |
| "Effect(s) of" | "Effect(s) of" |
| "Function," "function of" | "Function," "function of" |
| "Dimension(s)" | "Dimension(s)" |
| "Findings" | "Findings" |
| "Results" | "Results" |
| "Influence(s)" | "Influence(s)" |
| "Law" | "Law" |
| "Norm" | "Norm" |
| "Determined" | "Determined" |
| "Mediate," "mediation" | "Mediate," "mediation" |
| "Generalization" | "Generalization" |
| "Control(s)" | "Control(s)" |
| "Contingent upon" | "Contingent upon" |
| "Interaction" | "Interaction" |
| "Condition(s)" | "Condition(s)" |
| Etc. | |

appealing sound to it, as when Kausler (1974) here argues for the
evidence supporting the continuity of learning processes across
experimental tasks: "In general, our confidence in continuity increases directly with the number of common functional relationships
that performance on the tasks in question bear with relevant independent variables" (p. 61). Looked at in one sense, all this conveys
is that our belief in a theoretical position is strengthened with increasing validating evidence in its support. But looked at in another,
there is the connoted suggestion that the performance of a subject is
functionally related to the independent variables—not to the theory
defining these variables, but to the variables *per se!* Kausler may
have meant it in either sense, but too many psychologists see in such
phrasings what they wish to see. A humanist can agree with the first
meaning, which merely emphasizes the role of evidence in research,
but he would object to the more theoretical efficient-cause connota-

tions of the second meaning. Although framed in a rigorous context of empirical research, this statement is *not* satisfactorily rigorous because it can be taken in different ways.

The use of certain phrases like *function of* or *effects of* in both a theoretical and methodological sense has given rise to ethical problems in psychology. Because one "sees" the dependent variable as a "function of" the independent variable and because, as an experimenter, one must "control and predict" the "effects of" the latter on the former it seems the purest of logic to conclude that psychology's mission is the "control and prediction of behavior" in general. The chief modern advocate of this view has been B. F. Skinner (1971), of course, but even such a biologically oriented psychologist as D. O. Hebb (1974) has spoken in favor of efforts to control people's behavior (pp. 71–72). If *control and prediction* means that psychology is a science relying on validating evidence, there can be no quarrel with it. This would merely state that all psychologists accept the same ground rules of evidence or proof in their empirical work (methodological usage). However, if this phrase means that psychologists in their professional role have literally to control and thereby predict the course of the lives of people or of social groups, quite another issue is being framed. In this case the language has shifted from purely methodological considerations to a theoretical or meta-theoretical question of values and ethics (see Rychlak, 1968, Chapter 6 for a more thorough discussion of this question). Not all psychologists value the role of applied scientist, actuarian, or social innovator; some even find the aspiration to the role of controller in human affairs unethical. Whether we agree with these values or not, once again a lack of precision in terminological usage has confounded and befuddled us all.

The high valuation placed on mathematics by psychologists cannot be overstated. A major feature of our history has been the rise of statistical methods, with names like Galton, Cattell, Spearman, Thorndike, Pearson, and Thurstone distinguishing the pages of our textbooks. Because of what we called in Chapters 1 (p. 36) and 2 (p. 83) the double-duty characteristic of mathematical reasoning, we can both speak about *our* statistical assumptions and at the same time refer to the statistical (functional) relationship of purely objective variables at play in research experiments. The former assumptive requirements can refer to the introspective theoretical perspective, because a reasoner makes such assumptions, whereas the latter commentary coalesces nicely with the extraspective theoretical perspective. Unfortunately, too many psychologists have forgotten the introspective features of mathematics and simply take as given that the world *is* a Pythagorean reality (see Table 1), functioning independently of man's puny intelligence but responding in certain ways to mathematical assessments.

This extraspective view of mathematics underwrites the frequent assertion by psychologists that they seek out variables to study in behavior. Statistical theory is based on the assumption of distinct parameters, existing as pools from which data can be sampled (albeit entirely in mathematical space). The plausible implication here is that literally *anything* that can be delineated, hence varied in some way (as to weight, patterning, intensity, etc.), *is* such an identity, drawn from a pool, parameter, base rate, and so on of identical variables. It follows from this implication that psychologists *must* be engaged in the study of variables. This reasoning is at the heart of a distinction currently drawn between so-called theoretical behaviorism and methodological behaviorism (not to be confused with Skinner's 1974 usage, pp. 13–16). This distinction asserts that *all* psychologists are methodological behaviorists because we all deal in observed behavior as variables in our (empirical) experiments, even when we disagree with the behavioristic theoretical accounts of such observations (e.g., disagree with conditioning theory). This distinction rests on the improper use of the word *behaviorism* in the methodological context. Observing behavior is not a behavio*rism*, which implies a doctrinaire adherence to a style of conceptualizing this behavior by all who engage in the methodological activity of validation. Because this is incorrect, the distinction is misleading—and unnecessary in any case.

Psychological scientists can no more study behavior without theoretically conceptualizing it in some fashion than they can study variables without such conceptualization. Saying that we in psychology study variables is method-lingo, correct enough in one sense but seriously overlooking the equally true statement that we make up these variables based on theoretical assumptions and paradigmatic predilections. Because variables do not drop like apples from the tree of knowledge, we never merely *study* variables. How and why have we delineated *this* particular variable to investigate? What is our understanding of *that* particular behavior in terms of causal description? Focusing on the end-state of our line of development from theory to test (see Chapter 5, p. 191) is surely a one-sided characterization of the scientific enterprise. Yet there are those in psychology who frame their complete outlook in terms of variables (method) as equivalent to constructs (theory). For example, Mischel

(1973) has distinguished between person and situational variables, combining these two into a kind of summative interaction as follows: ". . . to predict a subject's voluntary delay of gratification, one may have to know how old he is, his sex, the experimenter's sex, the particular objects for which he is waiting, the consequences of not waiting, the models to whom he was exposed, his immediately prior experience—the list gets almost endless" (p. 256).

When we frame the task of psychology as the prediction of a theoretical construct such as delay of gratification, we make this predicting of a multitude of variables, all "functioning" at once, appear to be what the psychologist must aspire to. Table 2 has the word *hypothesis* as the theoretical equivalent of the methodological term *prediction*. But Mischel is not saying here that we must study by way of a program of research the many hypotheses that seem plausibly related to his theoretical construct of delay of gratification. He is saying in the style of Underwood above that we must literally demonstrate the validity of such a prediction *all at once* by running the appropriately complex experiment. Cronbach (1975) subsequently noted that if such an experiment were actually designed and carried out it would involve 120 statistical interactions in the resulting factorial analysis of variance (p. 120). This complexity of data analysis obviously takes such an experiment out of the realm of possibility.

If we keep the distinction between theory and method before us, this problem vanishes in the recognition discussed throughout Chapter 5 that all scientific investigation affirms the consequent of an if . . . then . . . logical sequence. Unless one hopes to formulate a theory of how predictions are made, and so forth, the use of *prediction* as a theoretical statement of what we must know about the influences on delay of gratification *is simply inappropriate*. Predictions flow from hypotheses and serve as potential evidential supports for the theoretical outlook contained in these hypotheses. The hypothesis carries the antecedent belief (Age may be related to delay of gratification) *not* the prediction (Group A, being older, will delay more readily than group B). The hypothesis is a "may" statement, but the prediction is a "will" statement, and we should not be so ready to equate these two *different* formulations of things. And even if the prediction is sustained, the theory underlying the hypothesis must be held to in light of our affirmation-of-the-consequent limitations. That is, we must never forget that *other* hypotheses might *also* be sustained by the predictions made in validation. Cronbach seems to have appreciated that evidence never proves a theoretical hypothesis true for all time, but he ascribed this fact more to potential changes taking place in the actuarial universe or parameter than to the nature of scientific explanation *per se*. Accepting Mischel's (methodological) usage of "prediction" as proper, Cronbach discussed the changing fortunes of statistical prediction as follows:

The forecast of Y from A, B, and C will be valid enough, if conditions D, E, F, etc., are held constant in establishing and in applying the law. It will be actuarially valid, valid on the average, if it was established in a representative sample from a universe of situations, as long as the universe remains constant. When the universe changes, we have to go beyond our actuarial rule. . . . When we step outside the range of our experience, we have to use our heads (*ibid*., pp. 125–126).

Although we can "slip in" Mischel's variables into A, B, C, and so on, the theory under discussion here is purely mathematical, sustained by the plausibilities of procedural evidence (cognitive method) and used as an adjunct to the logic of validation (research method). But strictly speaking, we are not dealing in lived reality here anymore than Newton's mathematical conception of gravity was about forces inhering in real things (Chapter 1, p. 48). When we actually do an experiment and secure evidence in support of our delay-of-gratification theory, we are *not* dipping our hands into some existing "universe of situations" in randomly assigning subjects to experimental conditions. An observed experimental difference exceeding the .01 level of significance is based strictly on assumptions concerning the *single* sample we have dealt with, projected against statistical fictions of other samples that might have been selected *at this point in time* under identical conditions. We are in mathematical space *not* real space, so there is no proper expectation or reasonable guarantee that if 99 other samplings of these variables were done on successive days the observed (p.$<$.01) differences would be significantly identical 99 times out of 100. No one has ever conducted a series of 100 experiments in this fashion to see what would in fact eventuate for such an .01 level finding, except in computer simulations which are themselves "events" taking place in mathematical space and *not* reality!

And we should not be misled by the phrase *holding conditions constant*. This refers to a procedure for checking one's thinking, based on the logic of scientific method. Holding conditions constant is not something that we literally do in life, because conditions frequently cannot be handled this way. But we can still employ the *logic* of balancing off circumstances to observe a consistent variation. Returning to Cronbach's quote above, conditions *are what they are* once we assign theoretical constructs to our symbols A, B, C, and so on. If we can let these construed identities be what they "are" across our methodological group arrangements, while simultaneously requiring that some (usually one) consistent difference(s) across these groups exist(s), an evidential conclusion can be arrived at so long as we have predicted the outcome actually observed (validating evidence). But if we now believe that conditions in life must be held constant so as to increase the predictive power of this method *qua* theory, we not only delude ourselves as to our proper scientific role but also pose what is an impossible task.

We must therefore appreciate that holding conditions constant and making predictions to observed outcomes are purely methodological activities of the psychologist. Believing in these findings and carrying this line of theory forward to do further experiments—each of which is subject to the logical proviso of affirming the consequent —is predominantly a *theoretical* activity (sustained by procedural evidence, of course). We cannot overlook or denigrate this role of theory in science. Here is where our paradigms always come into play (Chapter 5).

Because Cronbach speaks of going beyond the actuarial rule in the above quote, he seems to have reserved a prominent place for the role of theory in his scientific outlook. This is unfortunately not true. He disputes with Suppes (1974), who has argued that a major duty of the psychologist is to theorize. After acknowledging that the theoretical stance one takes influences the prevailing view of man, Cronbach quickly adds: "But a point of view is not a theory, capable of sharp predictions to new conditions" (*ibid.*, p. 123). Cronbach, like Mischel and Underwood, thinks of theories as predictors—that is, he confounds method with theory-talk! Points of view *are* theories, and they not only permit us to isolate and define Cronbach's A, B, C, variables, but they provide the frame within which we must work when such universes change. How other than by the application of a theory can we find our way to new universes of relevance when old predictions crumble to insignificance? This is what *using our heads* means. If we could not delineate the universe of relevance, how sharp could our *methodological* predictions ever become? By continually referring to hypothetical theoretical activity as if it were predictive methodological activity, the leading psychologists of our time perpetuate the unfortunate denigration of theory which has plagued psychology for a century. Let us hope that in the last quarter of the twentieth century we will end this needlessly harmful practice.

Whether a psychologist is using a term in its theoretical or its methodological sense is not always immediately clear. But the writer has found that after moderate study of a written treatise or, if possible, discussion with the psychologist in question, *any* meaning can be clarified in the sense of our examples above. If leaning in the direction of descriptive explanation, we have a theoretical usage; and if leaning in the direction of proof or evidential support for such explanations, we have a methodological usage. Should this practice be made routine, introduction of dialectical theories into psychology would be far easier. As noted at the outset of this section, a science of psychology based exclusively on the meanings of Table 2 could never entertain dialectical theory. Yet dialectic has played a more prominent (albeit unnamed) role in psychological thinking than is now appreciated, and it has been given due recognition as a theoretical paradigm in the rise of physical science. We turn next to this frequently overlooked side of science.

## Dialectical Theory and the Rise of Modern Science

The program we have in mind for psychological science would emphasize demonstrative reasoning in the context of validation and allow *either* demonstrative or dialectical reasoning to flourish on the side of theory. So long as the psychologist would move to validate his theories "some of the time" we would accept his approach as scientific. This sequence of theory-to-test places the concept of prediction in proper perspective, because this is *not* something psychologists need do all the time! Psychologists do not have to become actuarians. As we now appreciate, events can be predicted without understanding *why* they occur as they do. Psychologists have a responsibility to fill in the understanding side of knowledge. Control and prediction is something we do in order to check our understanding by arranging circumstances or stipulating parameters for measurement, and so on, in the context of evidential support. The resultant data collections are often highly artificial in nature, not meant to be predicting life by any stretch of the imagination. If all theories must predict life, by definition a theory in favor of unpredictive life circumstances would be impossible. Yet, clearly, theories of the unpredictability of behavior are within the realm of possibility. The variance accounted for in our studies hardly outweighs the vast variance we *fail* to predict. Hence a theory might indeed speak for this *unpredictive* side to behavior.

One of the ironies of psychology is that there are and always have been dialectical theories underwriting its empirical investigations. These conceptualizations act as unnamed assumptions, and hence their influence goes unrecognized or at least unnamed in the *formal* statement of our "scientific knowledge." Beginning with Wilhelm Wundt, one of the fathers of experimental psychology (Chapter 3), we find that the outlines of his major theoretical contribution—a tridimensional theory of the emotions—are framed within the dialectical dimensions of pleasant-unpleasant, tension-relaxation, and excitement-depression. Mancuso (1976) has surveyed a number of areas in psychology which rely upon the unnamed presumption of a dialectically reasoning subject in experimental investigations. Continuing with the notion of acturial prediction, Mancuso shows how frequently the parameter, or variable, delineated by the statistically oriented psychologist is framed as a dimension within a bipolarity. The ends of the dimension framing a difference in value are opposites or require that the subject know oppositional meanings in order to be assessed, but no cognizance is taken of this fact. Scaling techniques employed by Thurstone (with Chave, 1929) and Sherif (with Hovland, 1961) as well as the *semantic differential* of Osgood's researches are shown to make informal presumptions of dialectical understanding in the subjects who are so assessed (Osgood, Suci, & Tannenbaum, 1957). The developmental psychology of Piaget (with Inhelder & Szeminska, 1964) is also shown to rely heavily on dialectical constructions, a fact to which Riegel (1973) has also pointed.

   One of the parameters often cited by the empirical psychologist is social-class level (lower, middle, upper), to which all manner of values, living styles, political attitudes, and so on, are functionally related. Yet the class consciousness or class identity that is simply presumed in framing these socioeconomic levels rests upon the delineation afforded by the social and economic theories of the great dialecticians Hegel and Marx (see Chapter 1). Class concepts are as the one and many, set in opposition (or contradiction) yet constituting a totality. This internal dynamic (force of opposition) provides the motives for social change, as a reorganization or synthesis of the old into the emerging new. Hegelian-Marxian themes of class consciousness have in recent decades been extended by analogy to relations between the races, the sexes, and even between age levels (youth versus aged). The debt owed to dialectical theory in social science is all the more remarkable because of the ignorance of social scientists in general about this style of reasoning and the consequent organization of human affairs that results.

   The reader may feel that showing dialectical theories at work in psychology and related social sciences is fairly easy but that no role for dialectic has been demonstrated in the "hard" sciences. This would be an erroneous conclusion, for there are several noteworthy examples of dialectic in the rise of physical science. The most basic rules of rigorous observation and discrimination are framed on a dialectical premise. For example, the Socratic-Platonic method of dichotomy (*Sophist*) holds that any grouping of the so-called genus in observation must be divided into two and only two subgroups: the logical species in which one is characterized by some feature (*differentia*) and the other is not. This rigorous classification scheme was subsequently refuted by Aristotle, who showed that no matter how carefully the differentiae are chosen, there is always overlap, so that *flying* would include some mammals and *not flying* some birds (Wightman, 1951, p. 365). But this general strategy of classification by way of opposition (Plato and Socrates *were* dialecticians!) was to be retained in the rise of science. We see it centuries later in John Stuart Mill's *Canon of Difference*, which was one of several such rules designed to aid a physical scientist in the elucidation of efficient causation (see Table 1). Mill's canon states that when cases in which a phenomenon occurs (A) differ from cases in which it does not occur (not-A) in only *one respect*, that respect, or its absence, is the effect or cause or part of the cause of this phenomenon (A). Mill's rigor is accepted by empirically oriented psychologists today, who reason out what is a stimulus and what is a response on precisely such bases as the Canon of Difference. But they fail to appreciate the underlying dialectical logic which makes such empirically observed regularities observably determinable.

Dialectical reasoning ends when its constructions are frozen into rigid "either-or" categories, of course. As noted in Chapter 2 (p. 85), the dialectician opposes the One and Many Principle to the demonstrative reasoner's Law of Contradiction. However, the ability to get such iron clad differences underway in thought doubtless stems from the human being's dialectical reasoning capacities. Oppositionality is extremely important to that *sine qua non* of demonstrative reasoning—mathematics! We do not always appreciate the fact that an equation sign unites two values in a relation of *identity* which are yet also *opposite* to each other so that it requires a change of sign to move numerical values across the balancing midpoint of $X + 2 = Y - 4$. As noted in Chapter 2 (p. 66)), the word *algebra* devolved from the title of a treatise by *al-Khowarizmi* which meant the "science of the reunion and the opposition" or "science of transposition and cancellation" (Eves, 1969, p. 195). We are more familiar with the latter terminology, but the obvious dialectical phraseology of the former is almost a rephrase of the One and Many Principle. Bakan (1953, 1956) has presented some excellent analyses of another clear reflection of dialectic in the mathematics of probability theory known as the Rule of Bayes. In opposition to the demonstrative frequency theories of probability—in which a distribution of events as "primarily and truly existing" is taken for granted—the Rule of Bayes finds its probability estimate in the comparison of two *opposite* likelihoods or possibilities. No assumption is made here about the reality of an independent frequency (see Rychlak, 1968, pp. 152–156, for a more thorough discussion of Bayes' theorem). Psychological statistics have been based predominantly on a frequency thesis.

Once the view is taken that there is a primary-and-true difference between events, a difference that is merely reflected as an opposite by the human awarenesss but is *not* fundamentally united by a one-in-many relational tie, we lose a dialectical to a demonstrative phraseology. The conceptualization of opposition here literally changes, and this change is often misleading because it appears on the surface that an "opposite is an opposite." Critics of dialectical theory invariably confound a demonstrative opposition with a truly dialectical opposition in this sense. When the dialectician is employing bipolarity or opposition he does not—or should not—suppose that this one distinction to which he alludes is the *only* one possible in the descriptive realm under consideration (see Rychlak, 1976). To think that an opposite is literally either-or is not to reason dialectically, but rather to reason cybernetically (demonstratively). Cybernetic machines reason according to such an either-or binary logic. Just as the machine takes its initial program "seriously" and hence cannot reason beyond what the program directs, so too is the machine frozen into a thinking pattern of unrelated either-or discriminations which are never simply arbitrary separations of the one into the many. A dialectical reasoner, however, is always conscious that other dichotomies can be drawn. His distinctions are made to elucidate the totality by way of oppositionality, *not* to break this totality up to state what is right or true or best and what is wrong or false or worst. C. G. Jung (1958) speaks as a true dialectician when he observes: "We name a thing, *from a certain point of view,* good or bad, high or low, right or left, light or dark, and so forth. Here the antithesis is just as factual and real as the thesis" (p. 305). Demonstrative conceptualizations are seriously wanting in the description of the ineffable in human experience: "Non-ambiguity and non-contradiction are one-sided and thus unsuited to express the incomprehensible" (Jung, 1953, p. 15).

Two kinds of dialectical themes are to be seen in the rise of modern mathematical physics. First, we have the stimulation provided by a thinker relying on dialectical alternatives who acts as a model and a spur for revolutionary conceptions. Einstein (1916) has acknowledged such an indebtedness to Ernst Mach (1893), who must surely be seen as a dialectically oriented theorist and the single person most influential in bringing about the separation of modern physics from classical Newtonian (Lockean) physics. Naming his outlook phenomenological physics, Mach insisted on recognizing the major role that the conceptualizing (theorizing) individual had on the description of nature. This critique was more than simply noting the selective biases in factual description that various physicists manifested. It got to the very core of how we think about reality, and in underscoring the alternatives possible in this conceptualization process, Mach used as examples the dialectical reversals and distortions of his dreams. He liked to show how either Ptolemy or Copernicus were correct, depending upon where one stood in assessing their explanations of the solar system—on the earth or on the sun. Mach rejected conventional views such as the immutability of time, atomic palpability, and the efficient-cause determinism of reality. As we noted in Chapter 3 (p. 130), although Mach readily embraced the speculative theories of Sigmund Freud, the father of psychoanalysis could not stomach what he took to be Mach's "intellectual nihilism" (Rieff, 1959, p. 26).

Feuer (1974) and others have argued that Einstein's willingness to shift his premises and to speculate daringly was influenced by this—what we now claim is a dialectical—style of Ernst Mach's theorizing. Feuer also notes that Einstein's personal friend during his student days, Friedrich Adler, was a Marxian philosopher-physicist who tried to unite Mach's phenomenological physics with the revolutionary dialectical theory of communism (*ibid.*, pp. 18–20). There is probably no better one-and-many phrasing than the following, where Mach is speaking of the primary role of the unifying *idea* over the multitude of isolated (factual) *observations:*

Guided by one's interest for the whole of things again and again one directs one's attention beyond the facts, whether these facts may be straight sensations or belonging to the domain of representations. . . . Then, one would, perhaps, in a happy moment, contemplate the simplifying and fertile thought (Frank, 1957, pp. 319–320).

A second more direct form of dialectical influence is to be seen in the rise of modern physical theory. Feuer (1974) presents a

fascinating argument in this sense for the translation of Kierkegaardian thought into the atomic physical theory of Niels Bohr (p. 138).
Bohr's professor and personal friend, Harøld Hoffding, had once
studied for the ministry before becoming estranged from the church.
The experience had brought him into contact with the philosophy
of Søren Kierkegaard. Like Mach, Hoffding took an interest in the
phenomenal conceptual schemes that physicists employed to explain
their data, speaking of these as various *analogies* which can be
sorted out through dialectical examination and then settled upon.
This type of dialectical examination was based on what Kierkegaard
had termed a *qualitative dialectic* in the psychic identity of human
beings.

   This more individualized interpretation of the dialectic was
opposed to Hegel's conception of a World Principle at play in historical events—a kind of objective dialectic that swallowed up the
unique individual (see Chapter 2). Kierkegaard's formulation was
more subjective than this, aimed at the idiographic course of life
each person must follow. He therefore gave his dialectic a developmental interpretation and used it to describe the qualitative changes
made in life as the individual moved from certain fixed stages in
living style (stadia) to other fixed points. Not all people traversed
the three stadia of life, but if they did so the movement followed
through *aesthetic, ethical,* and *religious* manners of spiritual (psychological) living. One cannot relate these stages to physical events,
and natural science is therefore unable to capture this entirely
spiritual development. Physical nature moves through gradations,
linear cause-effects, but the passage across life's stadia are abrupt
leaps or jumps. Kierkegaard, like Mach, was essentially rejecting the
natural scientist's penchant for explanation through efficient-cause
reduction. Rejecting this causal chain, Kierkegaard interpreted
change as dialectically generated through opposition; therefore the
direction taken was based upon a decision, a commitment to one
lifestyle over another, rather than through a uniform impulsion or a
seedling growth from the antecedent circumstance.

   According to Feuer, based on his study of Kierkegaard (*ibid.,*
p. 132) as well as his reading of the Møller novel *The Adventures of
a Danish Student,* in which dialectical themes are prominent (*ibid.,*
pp. 129–130), Niels Bohr fashioned a rationale for the inexplicable
leaps of the electron across the orbits of the atom:

The Kierkegaardian model of discontinuous leaps became part of Niels
Bohr's deepest emotional-intellectual standpoint. The atom in its "sta-

tionary state" was later like one of Kierkegaard's stadia of existence. And the leap of the electrons from one orbit to another was like the abrupt, inexplicable transitions of the self [across the stadia of life] (p. 136).

Bohr's theory of the atom thus departed from the Newtonian conception, in which the electrons around the nucleus could have traveled in any of an infinity of possible orbits; that is, any circular motion with any radius value would have been satisfactory. Bohr's conception held that only *certain* orbits with specific radii were admissible. Feuer quotes a remarkable passage from Bohr which should be contemplated by all modern psychologists who find telic commentary improper in the scientific context:

. . . the author [i.e., Bohr] suggested . . . that every change in the state of an atom should be regarded as an individual process, incapable of more detailed description, by which the atom goes over from one so-called stationary state to another. . . . We are here so far removed from a causal description that an atom in a stationary state may in general even be said to possess a free choice between various possible transitions to other stationary states (*ibid.*, p. 137).

This marvelous tie that dialectical conceptions have for what Jung called the incomprehensible is what attracts the humanist's attention to this style of reasoning. Other examples of dialectical influences in modern physical science could be noted. For example, Heisenberg learned from Plato's *Timaeus* that alternatives were as fundamental to human thought as were the forms of geometric figures—and such alternatives are born in the contrasting poles of dialectical opposition (*ibid.*, p. 173). But we want now to move ahead in the remainder of Chapter 6 to consider a topic of great concern for many social scientists: the question of determinism in events (including behavioral events). As we shall see, dialectical formulations permit us to justify a stand on behavior as *both* potentially free and yet always determined.

### The Meanings of Determinism and Some Applications of This Concept in Psychology

Assume that a man is driving along the highway in his automobile. Though he may not notice from the outset, gradually it dawns on him that more cars are passing his car than *vice versa*. Although he is obeying the posted speed limit, he is a relatively slow driver this day. As he mulls this fact over in his mind, he admits that this has always been the case. Whenever he takes a long trip and therefore has the time to take note of his driving style, he is struck by the high percentage of drivers who seem to be violating the speed limit to which he is holding. Soon the natural implication is suggested: Why not speed up? Because this suggestion is not totally satisfying, the man begins to wonder just what determines his behavior anyway? How could we answer this question?

As a first step we might assess whether his impressions are correct. Do more automobiles pass his vehicle than vice versa? This *observable event* can be tabulated from an extraspective perspective, and because we can extrapolate findings from earlier trips we could have predicted his rate of driving speed on this particular trip. But can we say that he is determined in behavior by the statistical probability which *we* assign to his driving rate? After all, even he knows that for his entire life he has driven at or below the legal speed limit. Surely we cannot believe that this statistical probability level determines his driving speed today. Maybe he has a physical reason for not propelling his car along at high speeds. He may have an inner-ear sensitivity that makes him uncomfortable when a vehicle is moving along too rapidly. He, more than the average person, senses the pitches and rolls of an automobile under high speeds.

Most psychologists would immediately suspect that this man's present driving rate "was a function of" (theory-method confound) his past experience in driving, whereby he had learned (been conditioned) to drive his car at a modest speed. One could even view the inner-ear sensitivity as an aspect of the reinforcement equipment that shaped this man into what is now a relatively slow highway driver. A reasonable hypothesis here is that he was taught to drive by a harsh parent or parent-surrogate, one who impressed on him the importance of driving within the limits of the law. The rigidity and moralistic overtones of such instruction doubtless emanated from a lifelong environment in which strict adherence to rules was required. The man may have been reared in an overly scrupulous religious home atmosphere. Once again we can think of this history of reinforcement in actuarial terms, postulating that if we had the proper observational opportunities of this man in *nondriving* situations, we still could have predicted through a *generalization-of-behavior* principle what would likely take place on the highway. This habitual pattern of behavior is not identical to the actuarial statistic that permits us to predict, of course. Presumably there is something carried by the man as an organism capable of learning to behave which is actually the determinant in this case.

But there is another possible determination of behavior we have not yet entertained. Left to his own devices, this man could well put it forward as follows: "I have thought all of the things over you mentioned. Surely I am not driving this way to maintain a statistic. The point about my inner-ear seems a bit farfetched because I have always been well-coordinated and enjoy rides at the amusement park such as a roller coaster. I suppose you could trace it to my religious instruction if you wanted to, but knowing this today why do I let this earlier influence go on determining me? When I *do* speed up just to show that I *can* do so it all seems very childish. No, the *real* reason I drive as I do today is because, after a careful examination of all these factors, I *choose* to do so. I don't need to save the few minutes or hours that speeding affords. I surely don't need the added tension of racing around other cars. My present rate is satisfactory in that it saves me fuel and that means money. Furthermore, an orderly society is to be preferred over one that lacks reasonable rules. So, all things considered and after careful reflection, I tell you straightout: I drive as I do because I want to!"

The reader has doubtless surmised that with this telic formulation we have covered all four of the causal meanings as they relate to the question of determinism in behavior. Psychologists rarely specify which of these meanings is involved when they refer to the determinations of behavior, but obviously this clarification is important.

## The Four Types of Determinism

The word *determine* has Latin roots meaning to set a limit on something. As applied to behavior, the limitations are usually thought of as alternatives that might be carried out in the course of events but are prevented from occurring. To refer to this setting of limitations in terms of the antecedent influences on consequent behavioral events is common in psychology. Antecedents go before consequents in time when we construe events in actual lived space. The puff of air is antecedent to the blinking of an eyelid. However, the definition of an antecedent also bears the meaning of a *precedent*, when applied to conceptual, logical, or grammatical usages. The antecedent of an *If . . . then . . .* proposition need not be thought of as occurring first in time. The total proposition is best viewed as a meaningful pattern, in which the antecedent term (*man*) does not efficiently or materially cause the consequent term (*mortal*) to come about determinately. The pattern (formal cause) of the totality ("If man, then mortal") bears the meaning completely free of time considerations.

244 The Psychology of Rigorous Humanism

The antecedent term in this case (man) does force the meaning of mortality into the pattern, but this conceptual necessity is a purely formal-cause eventuality. The precedent-sequacious line of meaning extension in this patterning is outside of time considerations. We have seen other examples of this extra-time feature of determinate relations—for example, in the necessity of mathematico-logical reasoning (Chapter 1, pp. 44–45) and in the use of the function construct in methodological validation (Chapter 1, p. 49 and Chapter 3, p. 100).

Our theory-method confound in psychology makes the introduction of time into every description of behavior easy; indeed to do so is quite necessary, for we have to "account for" the observed behavior of an IV-DV sequence *as* an antecedent-consequent flow of events. But even physical factors such as the inherited proclivity to inner-ear sensitivities can be viewed as antecedents to behavior which are not exactly functioning across time in that cause-effect fashion of the air puff and eyeblink. Thus, a malformed spine at birth is likely to limit the athletic skills of its bearer as a young adult; yet who would claim that the spine determined the restricted athletic ability in adulthood the same way that a foot race, run against a clock, determines our judgments of the athletic ability of even normal adults?

And what of our driver's reasons for proceeding as he does today? Are these not antecedents to his behavior, at least in the sense of precedents? We surely cannot think of the idea containing his reasons as pushing along the nervous impulses which synergistically enervate the muscles of his accelerator foot, efficiently causing it to relax. Mind-body dualisms arise in psychological theory because some of us feel it is desirable to capture this meaning of a determinate intention without identifying it with the actions carried out in its aim. Ideas encompass premises, frame meanings for the sake of which behavior is then carried out. But the carrying out in behavior is *not* the complete intentionality, says the dualist. The monist claims that all there *is* is behavior and hence to assign other causes to the sequence of motion we can observe is to depart from (Baconian) science. Are these views purely assumptive, or can we possibly hope to do research in psychology to settle the question of what determinate causes are at play in human behavior?

The thesis of this book is that we should be able *in principle* to cast light on this issue by way of rigorous empirical research, *after* we have clarified the issues involved, and hence what it means to see or not see telic factors in behavior. We state the proviso "in principle" because obviously to hope for a settled question is a vain and even naive anticipation. To crystallize the causal interpretations of determinism, Table 3 contains an array of the four kinds of antecedent determinants that may be said to arise when we emphasize one or another of these historic terms:

**Table 3**  Four Types of Antecedent Determinants, Arrayed According to Causal Description

| Causal Meanings | Nature of Determining Antecedent | Examples |
| --- | --- | --- |
| Material | A substance having certain qualities that set limits on behavior | Genes, drives as chemical agents, sensory experience, organic development, etc. |
| Efficient | A thrust, push, unidirectional action or necessary inducement limiting one line of behavior in regard to another | Stimuli, signals, cues, reflexes, motions, etc. |
| Formal | A pattern, form or style of behavior that limits what will be expressed, recognized, or expected | Type, order, paradigmatic frame, actuarial frequency distribution, norm, etc. |
| Final | A precedent "that for the sake of which" certain alternatives are limited in preference to others | Reason, premise, belief, assumption, bias, implication, conviction, etc. |

Granting each of the determining antecedents of Table 3, certain limitations are put upon the behavior to follow. The reader can easily think up examples of the consequents to flow from these antecedents. We must also note that any one line of behavior under description can contain several or *all* of the determinations. We do not mean to suggest that these are mutually exclusive designations, anymore than we felt that the causes of Table 1 were mutually exclusive as regards the theoretical constructs they entered into as descriptive meanings. The point of Table 3 is to dramatize the different uses we can make of the antecedent construct and the form of determinism that is then posited. We turn now to a number of issues having to do with determinism that have arisen in psychology.

## Laws and the Generalization of Behavior

There is no more familiar assertion in psychology than "behavior is lawful." This phrase is used as a rationale for prediction, because the assumption is that lawful behavior is under a determination of some sort and that therefore it generalizes across situations. Knowing the laws of one situation, we can predict to a subsequent situation of relative similarity. The problem is that we are not always certain precisely what form of determinism is going on in such predicted generalizations. Etymologically, the use of *law* has *not* meant an efficient-cause regularity. Laws as binding customs in a community were seen as claims put on peoples by a controlling authority. In religious circles this authority was a Supreme Being. This kind of law controls behavior because of final-cause determinism, as a binding premise, belief, or conviction among the loyal citizenry or the faithful. Laws in mathematics or in logic—for example, the Law of Contradiction (A is not not-A; see p. 61)—are similarly *not* determinate influences in an efficient-cause sense, but rather in a formal-cause sense. To be accepted such laws do not require validating evidence. They have a convincing quality based on their immediate expression (due to procedural evidence); once understood they are accepted and act as guiding assumptions which control behavior far more certainly than an antecedent based upon some thrust, push, or unidirectional action.

Levy (1963) observed that if we did not make the assumptions of lawfulness in behavior "there would be no point in performing any research; the results of any given study would have to be considered fortuitous and no generalizations would be possible" (p. 58). Statements of this sort are common in psychology, and they leave one wondering what is being generalized in a research finding. If we think of lawfulness as the relationship between an independent and dependent variable—the sort of thing one could graph and therefore give a mathematical statement of (recall Dirichlet's function construct, pp. 49 and 100)—clearly we should not expect this slope of line or its numerical equivalent to generalize. This is simply a shorthand notation for our empirical finding, which in turn reflects the theory we put to test. We are now using the term *law* in its proper *methodological* sense (Table 2). The *theory* not the law, always generalizes! Indeed the precise slope of line or the exact *p*-level of a lawful relationship between experimental variables are not expected to generalize *per se*. Occasionally the level of significance will even fall below an acceptable level without affecting the generalizability of the theory under test. Hence lawfulness *per se* has no direct tie to the generalizability of an empirical finding. Experimental findings will naturally be extended so long as these findings prove theoretically instructive to the scientist carrying on a line of investigation.

What sort of determination is involved in such theoretical generalizations? Obviously this is a question of formal (e.g., paradigmatic) and final (e.g., belief, conviction) causation. The scientist holds to his theory, filling in his very understanding of a subject matter in terms of such theoretical predilections. No modern scientist can overlook the role of theoretical determinism in his efforts. This point is what we referred to above (p. 234), in noting that though Cronbach was well aware of Mischel's unlikely program of methodological verification he (Cronbach) still felt it necessary to denigrate the role of theory in science. The statistically oriented psychologist is likely to do this because he has already accepted a theory, based on the plausibilities of formal- and (his) final-cause understanding. Mathematics is totally on the side of formal-cause determination, and when entertained by the reasoning intellect of a mathematician, the assumptions accepted thereby act as final-cause determinations of his behavior. Because the focus of attention is on data in these mathematically framed approaches, the psychologist so inclined finds it easy to take potshots at those *who do not* think of their professional role in life as that of a "sampler" of atheoretical data pools (parameters), which mysteriously change empirical definition from time to time, but which always fall neatly into line with statistical *theory*. Other theories are therefore excoriated quite regularly by these statistical "empiricists."

Of course, by keeping their attention focused on what they presume are atheoretical data items, picked from a bagful of natural laws called parameters, these empiricists are likely to end up in a theory-method confound. A case in point is Campbell and Stanley (1963), who after noting that researchers are often conditioned to avoid doing further research because of negative results in their earlier studies, go on to observe:

For the usual highly motivated researcher the nonconfirmation of a cherished hypothesis is actively painful. As a biological and psychological animal, the experimenter is subject to *laws of learning* [italics added] which lead him inevitably to associate this pain with the contiguous stimuli and events. These stimuli are apt to be the experimental process itself, more vividly and directly than the "true" source of frustration, i.e., the inadequate theory (p. 3).

In this quote Campbell and Stanley are not thinking of the *laws of learning* as methodological evidence for a theoretical position. They are using this phrase as a theory of behavior, accepting without question the traditional Lockean explanation of learning as efficiently caused habits, joined together *without* formal-final causa-tion as determinant antecedents. Antecedents and consequents get hooked up in contiguous fashion, and this is what a law is—a tend-ency to limit alternatives by way of fixing certain determiners (stimuli) to certain determinants (responses). We see here another example of the S-R Bind (p. 173). If psychologists would only dis-tinguish between what is their theory and what is their method, such statements would be judged in their proper light. The point is: It is wrong to present methodological findings as if they were theory free. Evidence *for a theory* can of course be presented, but it must always be understood as supportive of theoretical presumptions.

That this is not an isolated instance in the thinking of Campbell and Stanley is to be seen in their discussion of generalization, a con-cept equated with induction (*ibid.*, p. 17). They first distinguish be-tween internal and external validity. Internal validity refers to the predicted relationship between independent and dependent variables —for example, proving that practice on a verbal-memory task in-creases retention of the verbal items under memorization (*ibid.*, p. 5). External validity, however, refers to the applicability of such find-ings in contexts outside of the research laboratory—for example, in predicting the performance of subjects in an actual classroom (will the better memorizers in the lab also do well in the classroom?) (*ibid.*, p. 17). Problems of internal validity are satisfactorily handled through probability statistics, but generalizing to the classroom—external validity—is more difficult because: "Generalization always turns out to involve extrapolation into a realm not represented in one's sample. Such extrapolation is made by *assuming* one knows the relevant laws" (*ibid.*, p. 17).

Does a scientist make predictions based upon his actual or assumed knowledge of laws so that his inductive generalizations are solely or even primarily from past empirical findings? Doubtless once evidence has been accrued, and therefore lawful relations have been established, a scientist utilizes this evidence in support of the theory that generated the line of study in the first instance. But if scientists literally relied upon laws (methodological meaning) rather than upon a conviction that certain constructs when translated into variables could be shown to be lawfully related (theoretical mean-ing), there would be very little scientific advance. The history of science is replete with examples of men and women trying endlessly to bring forward evidence for something they believed theoretically to be the case but which could not yet be proven (Wightman, 1951). Believing something to be true—even when it is true!—and then *proving* it are two clearly different activities of the scientist. Saying that laws must be known rather than theories is surely a curious way of putting the scientific quest. Yet so great is their desire to avoid theory-talk that Campbell and Stanley (1963) suggest: ". . . we do, in generalizing, make guesses to yet *unproven laws* [italics added], including some not even explored" (p. 17).

To the psychologist who uses *law* in a methodological sense, speaking of unproven laws is a contradiction in terms. Laws *are* proofs—at least they are when we use this term in its scientific rather than in its logical or custom-bearing sense. Referring to laws which have not yet been explored is at worst a blatant reification of this construct or at best a poetic allusion to the scientific effort— rather like pointing to the remainder of our future as "unlived tomorrows." In the former case it is an efficient-cause theory of reality; in the latter it is a final-cause assumption on the part of the scientist which has no meaning until we fill in those variables that will be theoretically delineated and, when tested, constitute *a law* because of the proven relationship between them.

## The Behavioristic Concept of Freedom

A major tenet of humanistic psychologies is that the person is a contributing agent to his behavior; so behavioral style is *not* rooted solely in the patternings of the environment, but is patterned to some extent by the identity of the person. This self-induced pattern-ing of behavior is usually typified as *free will*, and as we have seen in the rise of mediation theory (Chapters 4 and 5), psychologists have attempted to account for this autonomy in strictly efficient-cause terms. In presenting his social-learning theory, Bandura (1969) states the typical mediational argument as follows:

. . . social-learning approaches treat internal processes as covert events that are manipulable and measurable. These mediating processes are ex-tensively controlled by external stimulus events and in turn regulate overt responsiveness. By contrast, psychodynamic theories tend to regard in-ternal events as relatively autonomous. These *hypothetical causal agents* [italics added] generally bear only a tenuous relationship to external stim-uli, or even to the "symptoms" that they supposedly produce (pp. 10–11).

As humanists we can easily see Bandura manipulating in his studies what we would prefer to call an independent variable, in order to observe the *effect* of this *stimulus* (his term) on what he calls the *response*, but what we would like to call the dependent variable. Having achieved the predicted outcome, Bandura, as all behaviorists, claims that *he* has determined the organism's behavior because the observed findings show this to be a fact. Humanists go on attributing hypothetical, nonscientific characteristics to behavior in their constructs of mind. Framing things in terms of scientific laws, Skinner (1974) expressed this same attitude as follows: ". . . pure mentalism . . . has dominated Western thinking for more than two thousand years. Almost all versions contend that the mind is a nonphysical space in which events obey nonphysical laws" (pp. 31–32).

Formulations like this characterize the humanist as a medieval cleric, clinging to supernatural beliefs of a spiritual realm without substance in which miraculous events violating natural laws occur. The truth is that when Bandura speaks of autonomous causal agents he is only referring to the autonomy of formal and final causes from merely material and efficient causes in the determination of behavior. This is all that Skinner's comments actually refer to. Formal-final cause constructs are nonphysical because they capture something the Baconian prescription specifically kept out of "natural" science. As we noted above in speaking of dualism, mentalistic positions arise *not* out of any desire on the part of a theorist to revert to pre-scientific theological dogma, but simply because he finds the descriptive utility of material and efficient causes to be limited when it comes to the human condition.

What is fascinating about the behaviorist's presumption that he, by efficiently causing (manipulating) certain environmental stimuli to vary *solely* determines the behavioral responses of his subject, is that both historical and hard research evidence have steadily eroded this position. In the present section we take a look at this erosion from the perspective of what it means to be free in a behavioral sense (as opposed to political freedom). Because natural science advanced a strict or "hard" (100%) determinism of an efficient-cause type, the early tough-minded psychologists in this century found the concept of freedom to be totally incorrect (see, e.g., Kuo, 1928). Gradually, as the "accounting for" proclivities of functionalism were enlarged upon, a position on this conception of freedom in behavior was delineated. D. O. Hebb (1974) summarizes this view colorfully:

I am a determinist. I assume that what I am and how I think are entirely the products of my heredity and my environmental history. I have no freedom about what I *am*. But that is not what free will is about. The question is whether my behavior is entirely controlled by present circumstances. Heredity and environment shaped me, largely while I was growing up. That shaping, including how I think about things, may incline me to act in opposition to the shaping that the *present* environment would be likely to induce: And so I may decide to be polite to others, or sit down to write this article when I'd rather not, or, on the other hand, decide to goof off when I should be working. If my past has shaped me to goof off, and I do goof off despite my secretary's urging, that's free will. But it's not indeterminism (p. 75).

When Hebb states that he is a determinist, we know that he means to say a material- and efficient-cause determinist. As a Lockean thinker he would not consider it proper to assign a determination to formal and final causes in behavior. So he is brought to a conception in which freedom means somewhat free from today's material- and efficient-cause determinations but 100% determined by yesterday's material- and efficient-cause determinations. Bandura's (1969) view of freedom is comparable, although he bases his argument more clearly on mediational theory:

The process of behavioral change will be conceptualized quite differently depending upon whether one assumes that responses are regulated predominantly by external stimulus events or partly by mediating symbolic events. In nonmediational interpretations, learning is depicted as a more or less automatic process wherein stimuli become associated with overt responses through differential reinforcement. By contrast, in mediational formulations the learner plays a far more active role and his responsiveness is subject to extensive cognitive determination. On the basis of salience of environmental events and past learning experiences persons select the stimuli to which they will respond; environmental events are coded and organized for representation in memory; provisional hypotheses regarding the principles governing the occurrence of reinforcement are derived from differential consequences accompanying overt behavior; and after a given implicit hypothesis has been adequately confirmed by successful corresponding actions, the mediating rules or principles serve to guide the performance of appropriate responses on future occasions (p. 45).

We presented several arguments in Chapter 5 for why this "accounting for" mediational conception is inadequate to teleological description (see especially pp. 201–217). Bandura has improved on Hebb's informal account by placing greater emphasis on the formal-cause meaning, speaking as he does of the coding and organizing of environmental stimuli. But there is no more willingness to acknowledge a final-cause determination in his than in Hebb's formulation.

Indeed Bandura makes clear that: ". . . behavior comes to be regulated by antecedent stimulus events that convey information about probable consequences of certain actions in certain situations" (ibid., p. 19). Of course, since the past input information can influence present circumstances, Bandura like Hebb, can speak of a reciprocity between what the person brings forward (mediationally) as determinant influences and what the current environment asks of him: "Psychological functioning . . . involves a continuous reciprocal interaction between behavior and its controlling conditions. Although actions are regulated by their consequences, the controlling environment is, in turn, often significantly altered by the behavior" (ibid., p. 46). Hence: "Some degree of freedom is possible within a deterministic view if it is recognized that a person's behavior is a contributing factor to subsequent causal events" (ibid., p. 88). A person is free to the extent that he can "partly influence future events by managing his own behavior" (ibid., p. 88).

Though Hebb and Bandura are agreed and present us with what is surely the going interpretation of freedom in the behavioristic camp, the humanist cannot accept a characterization of behavior that puts the source of determination solely in the unidirectional control of the environment—whether we think of this environment as taking place yesterday and now reciprocally interacting with the present environment or not. The person, not the environment, always makes the difference in what eventually happens behaviorally. Humanists believe that to speak of efficient-cause determinism after the fact or in the abstract is easy. However, when dealing with people in the spontaneous, informal, nonexperimental atmosphere of everyday life, the telic side to behavior is always more evident. This is probably why psychotherapy practitioners have traditionally been more prone to embrace teleological theories than have experimentalists. As an historic case in point, we can even use a half-decade from the life of Bandura to show how the humanity of people can intrude on the most self-assured interpretations of the lab scientist.

In his 1969 book *Principles of Behavior Modification* Bandura took up the famous confrontation between Carl Rogers and B. F. Skinner (1956), "Some Issues Concerning the Control of Human Behavior." In this debate the humanist Rogers differentiated between various types of control, two of which were *external control* and *influence*. Bandura (1969) discussed the merits of this humanistic distinction:

In the first category [of control], designated as *external control*, person

A [a prison warden?] creates conditions that alter person B's behavior without his concurrence [a prisoner?]. The second and presumably more humanitarian form, labeled *influence*, involves processes in which A [warden] arranges conditions that modify B's [prisoner's] behavior, to which he gives some degree of consent. This distinction between external control and influence, however, is more apparent than real. In many instances certain conditions are imposed upon individuals without their agreement, knowledge, or understanding, from which they can later free themselves by willingly changing their behavior in a direction subtly prescribed by controlling agents. Thus, for example, persons who have been legally committed to mental hospitals or penal institutions may voluntarily enter into treatment programs to acquire the types of behavior that will improve their living circumstances in the institution and ensure a speedy discharge. A more fundamental ethical distinction can be made in terms of whether the power to influence others is utilized for the advantage of the controller or for the benefit of the controllee, rather than in terms of the illusory criterion of willing consent (p. 82).

In the April 1974 issue of the American Psychological Association's *Monitor* (a newspaper), Bandura's illusory criterion had come back to him with a vengence, for in a front page story entitled "Behavior Modification under Fire" it was reported that two United States Federal Agencies had just announced that they were ceasing to fund behavior-modification projects. The government actions were prompted by congressional inquiries, pressure from civil rights groups, and a recent court victory in which a group of prisoners had successfully blocked a behavior-modification program in their penal institution. We put the words *Warden* and *Prisoner* in the above quotation from Bandura's writings to underscore the parallel between what he had to say vis à vis Rogers' humanistic concerns in 1969 and what he now was to say in 1974. In the *Monitor* (1974) issue under discussion we read that Dr. Albert Bandura, then President of the American Psychological Association, advocated a "rigorous public scrutiny" of all behavior modification programs in the climate of that period. Bandura is quoted as saying: "Society has no moral or legal right to force an individual to change. If I am black and am put in a prison because I'm opposed to the political and social system in this country I sure as hell wouldn't want behavior modification forced on me" (p. 4). Bandura went on to advocate that the prisoners be granted permission to run their own program of behavior modification, saying: "There are risks in granting more responsibility but we must take those risks" (*ibid.*).

Now aside from the obvious point that this is *precisely* what

Rogers was getting at in the first place and why he felt it necessary to distinguish between external control and influence, the talk of moral and legal rights by Bandura can surely not be subsumed by his theory of efficient causation in human affairs. A moral principle embodying a right is nothing but an input X in the mediating processes of a person or a people who have been shaped into holding to this X rather than, let us say, Y or Z. If we are to speak of truly moral rights in behavior we must find a grounds in some universal (or absolute) on which to base this morality, as in the precedents for which philosophers since the beginning of recorded history have been searching (see Table 1). If Bandura really believes that human beings are determined by such considerations, his formal theory of behavior has a few missing terms—terms that can be encompassed only by a "that, for the sake of which" phrasing.

Of course because Bandura's initial theoretical position had a reciprocal relationship envisioned between the person and his environment as freedom, we might contend that all he is now doing in encouraging prisoners to design their own behavior-mod programs is to exercise this freedom. Or we might say that the prisoners' past shaping, which controls them mediationally today as "free" persons, has succeeded in controlling Bandura's behavior—as a member of the social environment of these prisoners—so that he speaks more positively today of negotiation in human relations than he had earlier. Bandura (1974) took the former view in his Presidential Address to the American Psychological Association, presenting a string of statements reminiscent of the cognitivists discussed in Chapter 5—that is, pseudotelic in intonation. But the core idea of mediational control, which in turn inevitably means yesterday's efficient-cause control of today's behavior was retained (ibid., p. 876).

Stepping back from this historical vignette, what are we to make of it? A theorist who is prepared to employ final-cause determinants in his account would find all of this reciprocity business a routine confounding of theory and method. We are back to Mischel's thinking (refer above, p. 232), in which one varying fluctuation of an efficient-cause nature pushes another about and vice versa, so that a patterning emerges and we call variations in this efficiently caused pattern freedom. This extraspectively framed give-and-take is not so absolutely wrong as a characterization as it is simply incomplete. The abstraction is too rarified, so the heart of the matter has been lost to methodological analogues. We have to assume the introspective perspective in theoretical description and look at this in human terms. What happened in the prison was that a group of human beings, who reason "for the sake of" certain assumptions about who they are and what their rights are in a culture founded by people like them, "stood up for" these rights. They could have conformed, because they actually control what is or is not going to be a successful behavior-mod program. But instead they rebelled (see our discussion of freedom vis à vis Skinner's theory, below). The prisoner said: "Look, I don't have to go along with this silly program of handing me chits everytime I meet some institutional requirement. In fact, I don't think this sort of program is proper and humane treatment to begin with. Even if some of these other men agree to go along with it, they shouldn't. It's not right! Let's see what the courts have to say about this."

Doubtless there were all manner of unnamed motivations prompting the prisoner's rejection of behavior modification. We are not so naive as to assume that they were all uniformly concerned with abstract universals of a humane nature. Some were doubtless out to get back at their imprisoners in any way open to them. But such considerations are irrelevant to the point under consideration, which is: We make far better sense out of considering the final-cause determinations in this behavior than we do in clinging to the method analogues of a reciprocal relationship between two kinds of variables or yesterday's inputs versus today's inputs, all somehow totaling to predictable interactions *without* telic considerations entering into them. No psychologist has done more for the promotion of behavior modification than B. F. Skinner, who achieved this feat through a remarkable redefinition of what it meant to respond. We now turn to Skinner's innovation and what it masks.

## B. F. Skinner and the Efficient-Cause Reversal

There has been general consensus among behaviorists concerning the locus of a response on the time dimension. Based on analogies to the reflex arc, theorists since the days of Watson have assumed that the stimulus occurs first (afferent stimulation) and the response occurs second (efferent responsivity). The reflex-arc concept was the *sine qua non* of natural-science description, combining as it did the material-cause meaning in the very "meat" of the nervous tissues and efficient-cause meaning in the electrical energy that sent the impulses on their way over time. Behaviorists may have left this literal model, but they still harbor the "in-principle" view that there is a one-to-one relationship between behavior as observed and the existing physical equipment of the behaving organism. In the mid-

1970s, D. O. Hebb (1974) could say with confidence: *"Psychology is a biological science"* (p. 72). In the first half of the twentieth century this biological emphasis was to be seen in the drive-reduction theories that flourished. Body-tissue needs, acting in consonance with other stimuli in the environment, combined to motivate behavior and, when satisfied (drive-reduction), stamped in the S-R regularity known as a habit. We can picture this sequence as follows:

TIME DIMENSION: (SOONER)————————————————→(LATER)

DRIVE *STIMULUS*————————→ENVIRONMENTAL *STIMULI* ——→
*RESPONSE*(S)————————→DRIVE REDUCTION (REINFORCEMENT)

The drive reduction achieved over time supposedly led to a reinforcement, or an adding to of the behavioral sequence (S-R regularity) that preceded it in the time sequence (English & English, 1958, p. 452). Subsequent modifications of this general model did not alter the sequence of responses occurring after stimuli. For example, in the mediation model of Dollard and Miller (1950) a response that occurred earlier in time could subsequently act as a cue (stimulus) of later behavioral responsivity. This was called a "cue-producing response" (*ibid.*, p. 98), and because of this theoretical maneuver we preserve the proper order of things in a mediation model, as follows:

TIME DIMENSION: (SOONER) ————————————————→(LATER)

DRIVE & ENVIRONMENTAL *STIMULI* ————————————→MEDIATING
*STIMULI* ————→OVERT *RESPONSE*(S) ————→REINFORCEMENT

The reason having a stimulus coming first on the time dimension is so important is because, as an efficient cause, the antecedent must—by definition (see Table 3)—push or impel the consequent. Something later in time cannot logically efficiently cause something taking place earlier. Around the turn of the twentieth century Ernst Mach was waging a war on Newtonian conceptions of the universe as supposedly underwritten by not only atoms, but by efficient causes (see our discussion of his influence on Einstein above, p. 239). He was instrumental in cementing the view of modern physics that Dirichlet's function which connected observed dependent to independent variables, was *not* the efficient cause that the Newtonians had made it (see pp. 22 and 49). Mach asked that scientists look at causes *not* as compelling efficient causes, but as *functional* formal-cause patterns of antecedents to consequents. In 1931 the young Skinner, impatient with classical views on the nature of a response, employed Mach's name and arguments in calling for a view of causation in psychology whereby "explanation is reduced to description and the notion of the function [is] substituted for that of [efficient] causation" (Skinner, 1931, p. 446). In his book *The Behavior of Organisms* Skinner (1938) again refers favorably to the "modern theories of causality in which the correlational aspect is emphasized" (p. 443).

Skinner's call for a functionalistic causation would seem to have been welcomed by the functionalistic psychologists forming ranks in the 1930s and 1940s. Unfortunately, the functionalist attitude (see Chapter 4) was of a different type than the Machian functionalism. Recall that the functionalists honestly believed they were observing the literal push of consequents by antecedents in the IV-DV regularities of their experiments. Although he felt his terminology was reflective of a difference from this S-R psychology, Skinner was to prove no exception to this rule. His Machian functionalism did not run very deep. The *formal* opposition to functional causation in psychology was articulated in Spence's (1956) subsequent distinction between so-called *R-R Laws* (response-response or, in our terms, formal-cause laws) and *S-R Laws* (stimulus-response or, in our terms, efficient-cause laws). This was a blatant hypostatization of a methodological term into a theoretical usage, but Spence left no doubt as to where the more functional R-R law fell on the Lockean hierarchy of things: "These R-R laws represent only one small segment of the total framework of a science of behavior, and unfortunately not a very basic one at that" (*ibid.*, p. 9). Thanks to writings such as these, by the 1950s and 1960s, whereas the rest of modern science had become Einsteinian-Machian, psychology had reaffirmed Newtonianism!

Skinner was only too ready to promulgate this antitheoretical outlook, which viewed anything less than a direct manipulation of reality below the efforts of science. As he said during the 1950s: "When we have achieved a practical control over the organism, theories of behavior lose their point" (Skinner, 1956, p. 231). What Skinner had actually sought a generation earlier, and the reason he invoked Mach on those occasions, was a *reversal* of the typical S-R sequence over time. As is well known, Skinner distinguished between the elicited response traditionally employed in behaviorism and his conception of the emitted response, the so-called *operant* response. The core distinction to be drawn here involves placement of the response on the time dimension:

To distinguish operant from an elicited reflex, we say that the operant response is "emitted." (It might be better to say simply that it appears, since emission may imply that behavior exists inside the organism and then comes out. But the word need not mean ejection; light is not in the hot filament before it is emitted). *The principal feature is that there seems to be no necessary prior causal event* [italics added] (Skinner, 1974, pp. 52–53).

This would of course require a revolutionary view of the causal sequence, for if a response has no prior cause, it is a "before" on the time dimension and not an "after." This means it cannot be an efficient cause, and it meets the requirements of functional causation by Mach; to that extent one is left to his theoretical predilections to fill in the details of what is essentially a formal-cause description of *patterns* over time (called schedules by Skinner). Of course when Skinner chooses a phrasing like "there seems to be no necessary prior causal event," we are not sure what he really believes, particularly when he goes on to speak of "the *apparent* [italics added] lack of an immediate cause in operant behavior . . ." (*ibid.*, p. 53). What is seeming or apparent can mean that if we knew more we could discern "the" cause after all.

The picture is further clouded by the fact that in other contexts Skinner clearly states that operants are indeed more like causes than effects—that is, they are something other than efficiently caused responses:

I prefer to use the word "operant" in the sense of behavior which operates on the environment and produces reinforcing effects. You define an operant in terms of its *effects* [italics added], and study it by means of its effects on your apparatus. Operant behavior, as I see it, is simply a study of what used to be dealt with by the concept of purpose. The purpose of an act is the consequences it is going to have (Evans, 1968, p. 19).

Skinner calls the effected consequences *contingencies*: "I use the word 'contingencies' to describe the conditions which prevail at any given time and which relate a bit of behavior to its consequences" (*ibid.*, pp. 19–20).

If the operant *operates* as a purpose does on the environment to produce consequences (effects) and if the relationship between this antecedent operant behavior and the eventual consequents is termed a contingency, Skinner clearly has *reversed* the traditional S-R sequence, as follows:

TIME DIMENSION: (SOONER) ─────────────────────────→(LATER)

OPERANT *RESPONSE* [BEHAVIOR]──────→CONTINGENT *STIMULI* AS CONSEQUENCES ──────────────────→REINFORCEMENT  EFFECTS

If the operant response did not act on the environment to effect a change in some way, reinforcement could not follow. If this action leads to a contingent circumstance that increases the probability of of subsequent responding, we can speak of reinforcement taking place. If not, no reinforcement develops. That Skinner sees the parallel between his concept of operant responding and purposivity is fitting, because as we noted in Table 1, the notion of a contingent cause was employed by John Duns Scotus and other medieval thinkers as due to a final-cause determination in which the line of efficient causation was *predetermined* by the patterned intentions of the actor (see Chapter 7, p. 294). This was viewed as something *other* than mere efficient causation. Moral decisions were said to depend upon a person's preliminary examination of the likely consequences of his act. To this extent man was free to act (free will), and the determinism achieved when a course was settled on was "softer" than the actions of noncontemplated, subhuman, or inanimate events.

If we now put the concept of contingent cause together with that of a functional cause in observed events, we could readily understand how even very predictable events of a lawful nature might be accounted for in other than efficient-cause ways (see Table 3). A person's observed behavior could be the (later) contingent effect of an (earlier) operant response termed an *intention*. If Skinner really means that operants are *not* efficiently caused by some antecedent connection thrusting them or eliciting them, his formal theoretical position admits to such a telic formulation!

## The Hidden Teleology of Operant Conditioning

Although Skinner may have defined his operant response as producing reinforcing effects, his behavioristic commitment to nontelic description never left him for a moment. It therefore did not seem circular for him to say: "I view the study of operant behavior as essentially an exploration of the effects of all of the contingencies of reinforcement which are around in daily life or can be created in laboratories" (Evans, 1968, p. 20). Now we have the effect of an operant response as supposedly the cause of subsequent operants! Skinner has performed a theoretical maneuver here paralleling Dollard and Miller's cue-producing response, which amounts to a form of mediational role for the contingent stimuli, as follows:

TIME DIMENSION: (SOONER) ————————————————→(LATER)

OPERANT *RESPONSE*————————————→CONTINGENT *STIMULI*
REINFORCEMENT————————————————→INCREASED OPERANT

Skinner conveniently overlooks the fact that he (as theorist) *begins* this sequence over time with an operant response. This means he must believe that either (1) there was a previous stimulus efficiently causing the initial operant response after all, or (2) something that occurs later in time can cause something that happened earlier to increase its occurrence. But how could the latter take place in an efficient-cause frame? In this case we retain the efficient-cause order so that contingent stimuli would be acting as cues triggering operant responses. Skinner has permitted a "kind of" previous-stimulation explanation to sneak into his theory of causation because of what is called the *discriminative stimulus*. Bandura (1969) has also been influential in this development—for example, when he notes: "The discriminative stimuli simply modify the probability that a given response will occur, but they do not elicit it" (p. 25). Skinner's (1974) reference to this possibility goes as follows: ". . . a stimulus present when a response is reinforced acquires some control over the response. It does not then elicit the response as in a reflex; it simply makes it more probable that it will occur again . . ." (p. 74).

When Skinner says: "It [discriminative stimulus] makes it more probable that it [operant response] will occur again" we know that he is confounding method (observed differences in response level) with theory (his behavioristic account of this observation). He does not want to make the discriminative stimulus an efficient cause of the operant level, and we can appreciate this reluctance for it surely cannot be so on his basic theoretical stand. Why not? Because he has already told us that without the emitted operant, *no such stimulus would exist*! If the operant response creates the reinforcing contingent circumstances, *pari passu* it creates the discriminative stimulus which is present when a response is reinforced.

Skinner has tried from his early Machian overtures to bring off an altered (revolutionary?) view of the response in psychology, but he is not fully cognizant of the final-cause possibilities in this move. He seems to have believed that he could subsume these telic factors by what he considered to be a more scientific formulation, one that retained the efficient cause as exclusive in all behavior. How did he achieve this? Over the years Skinner avoided the teleological phrasing of events that was implicit in his theory by analogizing to the style of explanation used in Darwinian evolutionary theory.

If one looks at behavior exclusively on the basis of an extraspective perspective, one can see such events occurring over time as if they were discrete units, aligned in a row much as we might align a series of children's building blocks. This is a reflection of the demonstrative unipolarity common to Lockean formulations. Because behavior is now seen to occur in distinct units over time, one can analogize between the development of organic changes in evolution over time and the successive changes to be seen in the course of these units of behavior over time. In other words, what survives in behavior is what has led to a viable outcome, a good "after" situation for the organism in question. The animal which evolves physically to a point where, for example, following some environmental shift in climate, it continues to survive the change, is in a sense rewarded by contingent circumstances just as the animal which turns over the right stick in the forest is rewarded by a lode of nutritious insects. This is the parallel Skinner (1974) draws; his core argument runs as follows:

Darwin's theory of natural selection came very late in the history of thought. Was it delayed because it opposed revealed truth, because it was an entirely new subject in the history of science, because it was characteristic only of living things, or because it dealt with purpose and final causes without postulating an act of creation? I think not. Darwin simply discovered the role of selection, a kind of causality very different from the push-pull mechanisms of science up to that time. The origin of a fantastic variety of living things [as units] could be explained by the contribution which novel features, possibly of random provenance, made to survival. There was little or nothing in physical or biological science that foreshadowed *selection as a causal principle* [italics added]. . . . There are certain remarkable similarities between contingencies of survival and contingencies of reinforcement. . . . Both account for purpose by moving it after the fact [on the time dimension], and both are relevant to the question of a creative design. When we have reviewed the contingencies which generate new forms of behavior in the individual, we shall be in a better position to evaluate those which generate innate behavior in the species (pp. 36 and 40).

Skinner's contention that Darwin discovered a new causal principle is most assuredly incorrect, because the point of natural selection as a theoretical construct is to suggest that efficient causation
can account for improvement and advance through serendipitous
and other chance occurrences without invoking final causes (God's
intentions) or even formal causes (God's plan)—although there is a
definite patterning to be seen in the course of organic structures over
time. Having once studied to enter the clergy, Darwin was well
aware of the concepts of causation and thoroughly familiar with
what *natural selection* meant in these classical descriptive terms. As
is well known, Darwin was to base his concept of morality on the
role of culture in human life, rather than directly on a moral form
of behavior evolving in the very substance of man's physical structures. Skinner employs this cultural natural-selection idea as a corollary to his belief that the environment, not the person, controls the
contingencies and hence the behavior to be seen emitted over time.
He likes to cite passages from Darwin's (1952) *The Descent of Man*
which emphasize the fact that nations which produced the most
citizens of intelligence, bravery, patriotism, and moral benevolence
through natural selection were those that survived and even pre-
vailed over the less favored nations (see Skinner, 1974, p. 205). But
he *fails* to cite the more paradoxical passages in which Darwin is
contemplating—now from a more introspective perspective—the
involutional side to evolutionary advance:

We civilised men . . . do our utmost to check the process of elimination
[natural selection]; we build asylums for the imbecile, the maimed, and the
sick; we institute poor-laws; and our medical men exert their utmost skill to
save the life of every one to the last moment. There is reason to believe
that vaccination has preserved thousands, who from a weak constitution
would formerly have succumbed to small-pox. Thus the weak members
of civilised societies propagate their kind. No one who has attended to the
breeding of domestic animals will doubt that this must be highly injurious
to the race of man (Darwin, 1952, p. 323).

Even when we can see how our vaccination practices and related
physical therapies are keeping individuals alive who might otherwise succumb, the contingent circumstance here is not so reinforc-
ingly well defined a unit as Skinner would have us believe. Though
physical controls can be introduced through eugenics, abortion, and
euthanasia, there is hardly agreement on the consequences of such
selective acts—whether of positive- or negative-reinforcing value in
the long run. But more fundamentally, so long as people do—as did

Darwin—anguish over the implications of their grasp of nature and its evolving status, these studied appraisals cannot be explained in the same way that natural selection is explained. These are clearly ruminations about contingencies *before* they happen, purposive examination of what to do. Efficient causation as the vehicle of natural selection is not the *only* causal determination at play in the evolution of mankind. In truth such introspective concerns cannot be properly analyzed by way of the natural-science theorizing that Skinner has retained.

If we could think of behavior in introspective as well as extra-spective terms, the functional cause which Skinner began his career defending is capable of subsuming a *final*-cause meaning as well as the other three meanings (see discussion of introspective perspective and teleology in Chapter 1, pp. 35–39). One could not claim through mere observation that he was seeing an antecedent thrusting or cueing or in any way *necessarily* bringing about a consequent simply because there was a patterned regularity in the course of events being looked at. The observer might even entertain the possibility that an organism behaving over time could bring to bear some "before" unit of behavior "for the sake of which" an "after" unit of behavior followed to effect changes of a contingent variety. But in this case the contingency effected had been known beforehand by the behaving organism. Skinner is surely wrong when he holds that purposes are after the fact on the time dimension (see above quote). One does not look extraspectively *at* an intended purpose *after* some course of behavior has taken place. One looks *through* an intention *before* this eventual behavior occurs—or fails to do so! Skinner's purpose construct is like that of Tolman's (see Chapter 4)—that is, only if behavior actually eventuates in reinforcement or facilitation to some end can it be said to be purposive. An intention that goes awry or a purpose that is not facilitative (Tolman's docility) fails to qualify as either of these terms *by definition*. But is the statement true that man never aspires for the unattainable or, at the very least, the highly doubtful eventuality?

Consider the following quotations taken from Skinner's interview with Evans (1968) from an introspective perspective. Skinner begins with a typical mediational supposition: "As a determinist, I must assume that the organism is simply mediating the relationships between the forces acting upon it and its own output, and these are the kinds of relationships I'm anxious to formulate" (p. 23). He is even willing to characterize his own behavior in these extraspective terms: "I regard myself simply as an organism responding to its environment. This is my environment. It's designed to bring out my verbal behavior with maximal efficiency" (ibid., p. 65). He is not an originating source of control, but is under the control of environmental contingencies. Skinner next opines that a form of reciprocity a la Bandura's argument (refer above) takes place in the operant conditioning of behavior: "Man can control his future even though his behavior is wholly determined. It is controlled by the environment, but man is always changing his environment" (ibid., p. 107). But in elaborating on this reciprocity, Skinner next offers this rule of thumb in how to approach a problem solution: "If you are faced with two courses of action, check off all possible foreseeable consequences [italics added] before making a choice" (ibid., p. 109). If a consequence is foreseeable, it cannot be something that occurs only after the fact, and even if erroneous projections were made leading to no reinforcement following this purposive examination, we would still have to recognize the existence of this initial intentionality of the behaving organism. The capacity to project possible outcomes as contingent circumstances if "such and such" behavior were instituted is precisely what Duns Scotus meant by contingent causation (Table 1). This projection did not exist in the unidirectional immutable controls of the environment, but in man's ability to judge for himself and thereby act for the sake of certain moral principles. Nothing in Skinner's theory negates this kind of behavior from actually taking place.

Thus we can see how Skinner has a hidden teleology in his theory. If organisms are telic, then all that Skinner has experimentally observed in his many studies could still hold. Operant conditioners may be controlling people's behavior today based on what they take to be the nontelic manipulations of an efficiently caused environmental input, while in fact they may be capitalizing on the teleological proclivities of human beings. Control may reflect cooperation, conformity, or submission to authority (scientific and otherwise!). Skinnerian theory is an unknowing teleology. The arguments for environmental control are circular, and even the empirical evidence to which we next turn fails to support the image of man that Skinner demands.

Awareness and the Nature of a Contingency

We know from our study of paradigmatic innovations and revolutions (Chapter 5) that evidence can be adduced for some position only if the precedent theoretical paradigm allows for this alternative in the first place. Evidence is always on the side of an affirmed consequent; without a proper antecedent theoretical stance, one cannot always see even that which is there for the seeing. Operant conditioners, like many other tough-minded psychologists, have reflected this theory-blindness concerning the mounds of evidence accruing in support of the role of awareness in both operant (instrumental) and classical conditioning (see reviews of this work in Bandura, 1969, Chapter 9, and especially Brewer, 1974, which is a most stunning indictment of both classical and operant conditioning on this question). Confining our comments to the operant-conditioning approach, whereas Greenspoon (1955) had claimed that his subjects were unaware of the experimental manipulation (contingent reinforcement) of saying "mmm hmm" following each operant emission of a plural noun, studies by De Nike (1964), Dulany (1962), and Spielberger et al. (1963) were to suggest quite the opposite. The lion's share of the predicted variance was due to those subjects who could identify *not* the contingent discriminating stimulus (see above) of "mmm hmm" but the pattern of "if I say a plural noun then he (the experimenter) hums." *All* subjects hear the contingent stimulus (this can be established with electrical equipment attuned to their inner ears if necessary) but only some of them turn it into a "discriminative" stimulus (or whatever) by catching onto the *pattern* (formal cause) of certain befores (plural nouns) leading to certain afters ("mmm hmms") over the experimental period.

This awareness factor has had several counters by the Lockean establishment in experimental circles. We mention only a few. One of the first denigrations of awareness in operant conditioning was based on Farber's (1963) finding that a significant number of aware subjects never showed a change in their behavior—that is, they failed to emit more plural nouns even when they knew that this was expected of them. Operant conditioners saw in this finding an opportunity to revive the classical distinction between learning and performance, suggesting that because performance was what counted, simply being aware was not always enough to affect overt behavior. That this nonperformance was likely to be evidence *for* rather than against telic behavior was subsequently established by Page (1972), who showed how certain subjects do indeed see the response-reinforcement contingency but who do not necessarily then conform to experimental expectations. Having first established a means for identifying these two classes of subjects—those who were aware and conformed versus those who were aware and did not conform—Page simply stopped the experiment in midrun and asked these subjects to make him (the experimenter) *do the opposite of what* he was then doing ("make me say 'mmm hmm' " or "make me stop saying 'mmm hmm' "). On the *very next trial* these two conditions crisscrossed their so-called emission rates perfectly so that statistical tests were not needed to demonstrate differences. As predicted, the subjects who were not cooperating to that point had the experimenter verbally expressing the contingent reinforcement, whereas the cooperating subjects had him cease this verbalization. And the unaware subjects continued fumbling along at about the same level at which they had been performing to that point.

Another counterargument is to claim that awareness obviously cannot function in response acquisition, although it may be important in response selection. To learn new responses is vitally important, hence here again awareness is secondary in importance to conditioning which shapes actual behavior. Bandura (1969) resorts to this argument in the following: "Acquired insights, no matter how valid they may be, have limited utility for individuals who lack the necessary performance skills. The case is analogous to informing English monolingual students in verbal conditioning experiments that the criterion responses are Hindustani adjectives" (p. 579). The question of what is or is not a limited utility is all important here. Assuming that the base rate of emission for Hindustani adjectives to this point in the experiment was zero, an astute subject, following Bandura's instruction, could increase his rate by 100% through repeating the word *Hindustani.* Furthermore, by simply playing word-rhyming games, he could concoct a series of "ani" endings and thereby further increase the chances of stumbling onto another member or two of this verbal class. Of course this says nothing about the understanding of the language in question; but when we speak of awareness, we do not necessarily mean understanding in this sense either. The operant conditioning of meaningful topics or involved language expressions has been notoriously unsuccessful—for example, that in use by psychotherapists. And the plural nouns (or other words) being emitted in these experiments are hardly meaningfully connected. What we prove in awareness research generally is that a subject must contribute something to the experiment for it to "work," and, he *has an option* to do as he pleases in this regard.

Operant conditioners staunchly deny that the subject has a true option here. The experimental evidence is simply not taken in this way. A common gambit is to "define away" the entire problem of awareness through an S-R-bind kind of reasoning, as follows:

. . . "awareness" must be a defined concept. Ordinarily, its antecedent conditions are the stimulus contingencies relevant to learning while its consequent conditions are verbal reports, behavior, which refer to those antecedent conditions. To be useful, to be a significant concept, "awareness" defined in this manner must be lawfully related to other kinds of behavior (Maltzman, 1968, p. 329).

This places awareness on the "effect" side, a verbal report under the stimulus control of contingencies, and guided by those laws of learning to which behaviorists are so fond of referring. Apparently Skinner (1974) would account for awareness in this way, for he has stated: ". . . the basic fact is that when a person is 'aware of his purpose,' he is feeling or observing introspectively a condition produced by reinforcement" (p. 57). In other words, if a person is aware of the response-reinforcement contingency and then purposively decides to meet the experimental instructions (or not to do so), *this* aspect of his behavior is *itself* produced by previous contingencies. Skinner's confidence in citing this as a "basic fact" in light of the awareness research evidence is clear testimony to the Kuhnian position on what is possible to prove in science and what is not at any one time in its history.

## The Overlooked Operant in Operant Conditioning

In psychology teleologists are often pictured as defensively rigid individuals who are unable to face research data objectively because "the facts" can be expected to explode their cherished beliefs in selves or souls. Yet the unabashed confidence the behaviorists express in experimental findings on both classical and operant reinforcement is more dangerous to the integrity of psychological science than any telic hypothesis the humanist might submit to test. Indeed there is reason today to question the objectivity of behavioristic psychology, so ingrained have the S-R bind, theory-method confound, and related "accounting for" maneuvers (see Chapter 4) become in its style of scientific description. As a case in point we present the overlooked albeit empirically demonstrable operant response going unnamed in a host of modern operant-conditioning experiments.

Let us assume from the outset that Skinner is entirely correct in his theory. We do not now hold that he is capitalizing on the human's telic capacity to prove erroneously that all behavior is efficiently caused. But in taking him at his word, we are going to be extremely rigorous and totally empirical. We begin with his definition of the operant response as "behavior which operates on the environment and produces [empirically observable] reinforcing effects" (Skinner, as quoted in Evans, 1968, p. 19). With our construct in mind we next go to the literature or conduct a series of experiments on this question of awareness in operant conditioning.[1] We evaluate the total body of findings *strictly* in terms of what is operationally definable (awareness defined as the subject's overt capacity to emit responses indicating the nature of the response-reinforcement contingency), observable (we can electronically record a subject's emitted plural-noun production and the experimenter's "mmm hmm" reinforcer), and reliable (the record of crossvalidation on awareness findings is second to none in the psychological literature).

Note that we are taking stock of a class of operant responses that is left unmentioned in the operant-conditioner's account. We make no distinction between the operant responses called *awareness* (what subjects tell us about what is going on) and the operant responses called *plural nouns* in the experimental procedure. *All* language expressions are taken as operant responses in the Skinnerian outlook so how could we do otherwise? It is not for us to say what is or is not "the" operant lawfully related to the production of a subsequent, contingent circumstance like the reinforcer ("mmm hmm"). If we are truly rigorous we let the facts determine this for us. This is especially true when we can demonstrate that awareness-operants (as we might call them) are unquestionably under emission during the ongoing data collections of operant conditioning. That is, subjects *do* make these statements preliminary to manifesting learning, if only *given the chance*. They begin giving hypotheses about what the study involves and *then* bring their "learning curves" up in objective manifestation of learning (see Brewer, 1974, for a survey of such findings).

When we take a properly rigorous view of the operant conditioning experiment, we can say with assurance that *only* the awareness-

---

[1] W. T. Roberts (1974), then a graduate student working under the writer, did his master's thesis on the topic of awareness in operant conditioning, following and crossvalidating Page's (1972) work. We note this so that the reader can be assured that the writer has had some firsthand experimental as well as literature-review experience in the topic under discussion. Even if sufficient evidence accrues in the next few decades to negate the current findings on awareness in operant conditioning, the present discussion is still relevant and historically pertinent to the science of psychology. The point of this section is that a vast body of rigorous empirical evidence now exists which readily relates to the theory generating the research but is reinterpreted beyond recognition because of its injurious implications for the model on which the whole approach rests.

operant can be shown literally to produce the experimenter's "mmm hmm" contingent reinforcer. Whatever else it may be, the plural-noun "response" is *not* an operant because—taken alone—it *fails* to produce the "mmm hmm" contingent circumstance. Though they are instrumentalities, the plural nouns *per se* operate on nothing! Contrary to Skinner's (and other's) contention that the reinforcement produces the awareness, the *observed* evidence leaves no doubt that awareness produces reinforcement (i.e., the "reinforcer" of mmm hmm).

How can Skinner say such things, which clearly depart from the facts as observed? He can do this only by leaving the rigor of experimentation to fall back on theoretical speculations about supposed reinforcements that took place in the *unobserved* past of any single organism's life history, thereby retaining awareness as an effect rather than as a cause in the theory espoused. Would it not be more parsimonious at least to begin with the assumption that the proven law of learning (i.e., awareness operants produce reinforcements more efficiently than other operants) holds at *all* times? Why should this law *not* hold early in life as well? We know that if it would indeed hold, the Skinnerian-Lockean paradigm faces a serious Kuhnian anomaly, for awareness is clearly more akin to the Kantian category of understanding than it is to the Lockean building block (see Chapter 2).

The most telling opposition to reasoning from present data to earlier behavior stems from an argument based essentially on intimidation! The operant conditioner points to the fact that both very young humans, who have not yet achieved speech, and lower animals, who cannot achieve speech, *do* reflect operant conditioning. Therefore awareness operants cannot be established in these organisms—that is, we are unable to interview them—and *this* is the kind of parsimony to which the proper psychological scientist is supposed to aspire. Why postulate two kinds of operants, one for humans and one for lower organisms (as well as infants, etc.)? Does the critic of operant conditioning wish to anthropomorphize lower animals? This natural-science admonition is usually enough to end all debate, not on evidential grounds but purely on theoretical grounds. Ironically this weight of influence from the institutionalized Lockean model is itself a clearly formal-final cause type of determinism (see Table 3).

There was a time in psychology's not-too-distant past when such nonempirical contortions of the observed facts to meet a desired belief would have been likened to the vitalist's relying on souls or guardian angels to account for the unpredictable or inexplicable in human behavior. We now find in modern times our foremost champions of scientific rigor reverting to their own type of "guardian-angel" theory. The Divine Plan seems to have been replaced by the reinforcement history.


## Summary

Chapter 6 begins with an array of terms that can mean either theory, method, or both in psychological accounts. Examples are given of how psychologists such as Underwood and Mischel denigrate theory in favor of methods by turning their methods into pseudotheories of behavior. The variable concept is particularly misused in this sense. Mathematical formulations also help to restrict theoretical developments by confounding the meaning of prediction as methodological activity with prediction as an actuarial responsibility. In opposition to the views of Cronbach, we argue that psychologists need not be actuarians, with the social responsibility of literally predicting what people will or will not do in life. The remainder of the first half of Chapter 6 deals with the role of dialectical conceptualization in both psychological and physical science. Dialectical propensities in Machian physics and the actual use of a dialectical formulation in the theorizing of Niels Bohr highlight this discussion.

The second half of Chapter 6 is devoted to a detailed consideration of determinism. To determine is to set limits on something, and we show how the antecedents to this limitation vary depending upon which of the four causes we are concerned with in the theoretical description under espousal. In discussion of the law construct we show that lawful determination does not necessarily mean efficient-cause determination. Laws are best understood in a methodological context where they draw their meaning more from the formal than any other causal meaning. The widely heralded generalizations of psychological knowledge are theoretical in nature and not literal—entitized—laws spreading across the landscape. Campbell and Stanley are seen to confound theory and method vis à vis generalizing lawfulness in this sense.

The behavioristic conception of freedom, as represented in the thinking of Hebb and Bandura, amounts to a claim that if the individual is not under the total control of present stimuli (input), but can modify this influence based on past shaping (mediators), he is to that extent "free." The efficient-cause nature of this argument is underscored, and the whole position is found wanting. Whether the unidirectional control of today or the unidirectional control of yesterday is determining behavior makes no difference; neither instance can represent a proper psychological conceptualization of freedom. In the closing sections of Chapter 6 on determinism we discuss the reversal that Skinner effected in the S-R construct, making it an R-S succession of events whereby the possibility exists that something other than an efficient-cause antecedent may be at play in the observed regularities of behavioral emission. Skinnerian theory is shown to contain a hidden teleology and to capitalize on the conforming tendencies rather than on the controlled characteristics of human beings in operant-conditioning experiments. The experimental evidence on awareness in support of this suggestion is pointed to, and some of the more prevalent disclaimers made by operant conditioners are reviewed and found wanting. Chapter 6 closes with a discussion of the overlooked operant in operant conditioning.

## References

Bakan, D. Learning and the principle of inverse probability. *Psychological Review*, 1953, **60**, 360–370.

Bakan, D. Clinical psychology and logic. *American Psychologist*, 1956, **11**, 655–662.

Bandura, A. *Principles of behavior modification.* New York: Holt, Rinehart & Winston, 1969.

Bandura, A. Behavior theory and the models of man. *American Psychologist*, 1974, **29**, 859–869 .

Bergmann, G., & Spence, K. Operationism and theory in psychology. *Psychological Review*, 1941, **48**, 1–14.

Brewer, W. F. There is no convincing evidence for operant or classical conditioning in adult humans. In W. B. Weimer & D. S. Palermo (Eds.), *Cognition and the symbolic processes.* Hillsdale, N.J.: Lawrence Erlbaum Associates, 1974.

Burtt, E. A. *The metaphysical foundations of modern physical science* (rev. ed.). Garden City, N.Y.: Doubleday, 1955.

Campbell, D. T., & Stanley, J. C. *Experimental and quasi experimental designs for research.* Chicago: Rand McNally, 1963.

Cronbach, L. J. Beyond the two disciplines of scientific psychology. *American Psychologist*, 1975, **30**, 116–127.

Darwin, C. R. *The descent of man.* In R. M. Hutchins (Ed.), *Great books of the western world* (Vol. 49). Chicago: Encyclopedia Britannica, 1952.

DeNike, L. D. The temporal relationship between awareness and performance in verbal conditioning. *Journal of Experimental Psychology*, 1964, **68**, 521–529.

Dollard, J., & Miller, N. E. *Personality and psychotherapy: An analysis in terms of learning, thinking, and culture.* New York: McGraw-Hill, 1950.

Dulany, D. E. The place of hypotheses and intentions: An analysis of verbal control in verbal conditioning. In C. W. Eriksen (Ed.), Behavior and awareness: A symposium of research and interpretation. Durham, N.C.: Duke University Press, 1962. Pp. 102–129.

Einstein, A. Ernst Mach. Physikalische Zeitschrift, 1916, 17, 101–104.

English, H. B., & English, A. C. A comprehensive dictionary of psychological and psychoanalytical terms. London: Longmans, Green, 1958.

Evans, R. I. B. F. Skinner: The man and his ideas. New York: Dutton, 1968.

Eves, H. An introduction to the history of mathematics (3rd ed.). New York: Holt, Rinehart & Winston, 1969.

Farber, I. E. The things people say to themselves. American Psychologist, 1963, 18, 185–197.

Feuer, L. S. Einstein and the generations of science. New York: Basic Books, 1974.

Frank, P. Philosophy of science. Englewood Cliffs, N.J.: Prentice-Hall, 1957.

Greenspoon, J. The reinforcing effect of two spoken sounds on the frequency of two responses. American Journal of Psychology, 1955, 68, 409–416.

Hebb, D. O. What psychology is about. American Psychologist, 1974, 29, 71–79.

Jung, C. G. Psychology and alchemy. In H. Read, M. Fordham, & G. Adler (Eds.), The collected works of C. G. Jung (Vol. 12). Bollingen Series XX.12. New York: Pantheon Books, and London: Routledge & Kegan Paul, 1953.

Jung, C. G. Psychology and religion: West and east. In H. Read, M. Fordham, & G. Adler (Eds.), The collected works of C. G. Jung (Vol. 11). Bollingen Series XX.11. New York: Pantheon Books, and London: Routledge & Kegan Paul, 1958.

Kausler, D. H. Continuity of processes across variants of recognition learning. In R. L. Solso (Ed.), Theories in cognitive psychology: The Loyola symposium. New York: Wiley, 1974. Pp. 45–75.

Kuo, Z. Y. The fundamental error of the concept of purpose and the trial and error fallacy. Psychological Review, 1928, 35, 414–433.

Levy, L. H. Psychological interpretation. New York: Holt, Rinehart & Winston, 1963.

MacCorquodale, K., & Meehl, P. E. On a distinction between hypothetical constructs and intervening variables. Psychological Review, 1948, 55, 95–107.

Mach, E. The science of mechanics. Chicago: Open Court, 1893.

Maltzman, I. Theoretical conceptions of semantic conditioning and generalization. In T. R. Dixon & D. L. Horton (Eds.), Verbal behavior and general behavior theory. Englewood Cliffs, N.J.: Prentice-Hall, 1968. Pp. 291–339.

Mancuso, J. C. Dialectic man as a subject in psychological research. In J. F. Rychlak (Ed.), Dialectic: Humanistic rationale for behavior and development. Basel, Switzerland: S. Karger AG, 1976. Pp. 113–125.

Mischel, W. Toward a cognitive social learning reconceptualization of personality. Psychological Review, 1973, 80, 252–283.

Monitor, April 1974, 5 (4). Washington, D.C.: American Psychological Association, 1974.

Oppenheimer, R. Analogy in science. American Psychologist, 1956, 11, 127–135.

Osgood, C. E., Suci, G. J., & Tannenbaum, P. H. The measurement of meaning. Urbana: University of Illinois Press, 1957.

Page, M. M. Demand characteristics and the verbal operant conditioning experiment. Journal of Personality and Social Psychology, 1972, 23, 304–308.

Piaget, J., Inhelder, B., & Szeminska, A. The child's conception of geometry. New York: Harper Torchbooks, 1964.

Rieff, P. Freud: The mind of the moralist. New York: Viking, 1959.

Riegel, K. F. Dialectic operations: The final period of cognitive development. Human Development, 1973, 16, 346–370.

Roberts, W. T. Instrumental effects of causal constructs. Unpublished master's thesis. Lafayette, Ind.: Purdue University, 1974.

Rogers, C. R., & Skinner, B. F. Some issues concerning the control of human behavior: A symposium. Science, 1956, 124, 1057–1066.

Rychlak, J. F. A philosophy of science for personality theory. Boston: Houghton Mifflin, 1968.

Rychlak, J. F. The multiple meanings of dialectic. In J. F. Rychlak (Ed.), Dialectic: Humanistic rationale for behavior and development. Basel, Switzerland: S. Karger AG, 1976. Pp. 1–17.

Sherif, M., & Hovland, C. I. Social judgment: Assimilation and contrast effects in communication and attitude change. New Haven: Yale University Press, 1961.

Skinner, B. F. The concept of the reflex in the description of behavior. Journal of General Psychology, 1931, 5, 427–458.

Skinner, B. F. The behavior of organisms: An experimental analysis. New York: Appleton-Century, 1938.

Skinner, B. F. A case history in scientific method. American Psychologist, 1956, 11, 221–233.

Skinner, B. F. Beyond freedom and dignity. New York: Knopf, 1971.

Skinner, B. F. About behaviorism. New York: Knopf, 1974.

Spence, K. W. Behavior theory and conditioning. New Haven: Yale University Press, 1956.

Spielberger, C. D., Berger, A., & Howard, K. Conditioning of verbal behavior as a function of awareness, need for social approval, and motivation to receive reinforcement. Journal of Abnormal and Social Psychology, 1963, 67, 241–246.

Suppes, P. The place of theory in educational research. Educational Researcher, 1974, 3, 3–10.

Thurstone, L. L., & Chave, E. J. The measurement of attitude. Chicago: The University of Chicago Press, 1929.

Underwood, B. J. Individual differences as a crucible in theory construction. American Psychologist, 1975, 30, 128–134.

Wightman, W. P. D. The growth of scientific ideas. New Haven: Yale University Press, 1951.

# CHAPTER SEVEN

## A Teleological Interpretation
## of Human Behavior

### In Search of New Descriptive Terminology

If we are to effect a revolution in the way human behavior is to be explained, a new terminology is required. Although some psychologists distinguish between *description* and *explanation*, an explanation is always a further description of some item or phenomenon, bringing to bear a construct system removed from the latter but aimed at clarifying it (Rychlak, 1968, p. 46). To explain behavior is to describe fully the conditions under which it may be seen to vary or remain constant. Theoretical descriptions come first, and then with proper foreplanning we can even predict the course of this variation in an experimental context. We want to avoid the tendency to accept what we observe and record in the experimental context as *necessarily* explaining (complete description) what is taking place. Henceforth we call this the *empiricist's error*. In other words, we shall always try to keep our methodological descriptions separate and distinct from our theoretical descriptions, although in certain instances the two lines of explanation will be highly similar if not identical. But they do not *have* to be identical.

Psychologists are understandably reluctant to admit new terminology to their specialty, particularly if such terms seem to indicate a reversal to an age of prescientific thinking. The institutionalized Lockean model encourages psychologists to believe that they already have the conceptual tools to "account for" any type of behavioral description (see Chapter 4). We have tried to show that such accounts do not in fact convey the meaning of what they are designed to stand for. Another reason for trying new terminology is because only in this way can we teach ourselves anything. We fashion a new term to frame concisely what we want to develop as a precedent meaning (see Table 1). Because there are always more implications in a new conception than even the innovator is aware of at the outset, the fruitfulness of new terminology is found in the range of explanation afforded as we bring such terms to bear in an ever-widening arc of theoretical description.

The precedent meanings that have been furthered again and again in psychology have devolved exclusively from the institutionalized Lockean paradigm (see Chapter 4). What is needed are terms and background explanations drawn from a more Kantian, dialectical, teleological frame of reference. In this Chapter we aim at doing precisely this.

## A Dialectical Conception of Change in Behavior

As a first step in developing a telic account of behavior, we must take a more sophisticated view of stability and change in events. We have seen in Chapter 6 the basic strategy of explanation employed by the behaviorists, who relying as they do on efficient-cause links called habits, use the time dimension as a baseline to all of their explanations. We cannot overestimate the importance of the time dimension to explanations of behavior proffered by the learning theorist (which includes not only S-R but cybernetic and information-processing accounts as well). The very meaning of behavior is as a flow over time, an efficiently caused sequence of what is first change and second a fixing of this change into set patterns or habits that can be neatly graphed as a curve of learning (Kintsch, 1970, p. 61). Note that in this explanation of behavior what is fixed is made secondary, meaning that the pattern of habitual behavior is determined by the antecedent efficient-cause "shaping" of events. Except for biological limitations (e.g., a dog cannot be shaped to fly) the behavior is determined by change rather than *vice versa*. Change is assumed and behavioral regularity is what must be accounted for. This view is consistent with post-Galilean thought, and to that extent it might be said to be "modern" (Wightman, 1951, p. 68). Pre-Galilean thought had taken behavior as the fixed pattern, and change was what had to be accounted for. Natural science reversed this ordering and modern psychology has followed this general lead.

However, if Newton's account of the universe took on motility as a precedent assumption, as noted in Chapter 1 (pp. 47–48), it *also* framed a stability in the mathematical assumptions of Cartesian geometry. Points move in Cartesian geometry whereas they were fixed in Euclidian geometry, but these moving points *do* have patterns which they define albeit in a moving sense (i.e., straight lines, circles, arcs, etc.; see our continued discussion of this below, p. 290). The obvious question implied here is: What is more important to our understanding, the *motion* of the point or the *fixed* pattern it defines in mathematical space? This question can be raised about all so-called *ideas*. That is, can the logos-pattern be explained via motion or must we acknowledge a role for the pattern *qua* pattern in human understanding?

We are reminded here of the ancient debate between the Heraclitians and the Parmenidians, with the former claiming that all in life is change and the latter contending that change is illusory (Table 1). However, this characterization of the disagreement is oversimplified, for it glosses over the core issue here of dialectical versus demonstrative differences in the view of change. Heraclitus was a dialectical theorist; though he said that no one can step into the same river twice, what he was actually getting at was the continuity and identity in events (the river remains a river) even though there is constant change (as the water flows [one-and-many thesis]) (Magill & McGreal, 1961, p. 16). Seeing flux (dialectical opposition) in all things, Heraclitus marveled at the *logos* (rationale) or pattern of recurring continuity (a form of fixity) in all things. Hence this historic debate is not a foolish exercise in primitive thinking. These human beings, as all of the great thinkers cited in Table 1, were contending something that had to do with their very nature, with what we call mentality or the recognition, creation, and maintenance of fixed patterns within lived events.

If fluctuating changes are continually taking place within the fixity of a logos, what then could constitute a change for the dialectician? This would be a matter of altering the given *pattern* in events. Such changes would take place entirely independently of time flow, and as a matter of fact even this conception of time would be the result of some noticeable reordering of events. Something happens and then something else happens. Extending the meaning of the (now quantified) first event to the second event, we can say that a time period has passed because there is a meaningfulness (meaningful relationship) across ordered events, each of which is patterned (into meaning) and the totality of the sequence is itself therefore patterned (made meaningful). There are psychologists who believe that we will always have to explain behavior in terms of time flow (Wolman, 1971), but history records that dialectical thinkers have not accepted this inevitability.

In Chapter 6 (pp. 240–241) we noted the influence of Kierkegaardian thought on the atomic theory of Niels Bohr. We can now appreciate that Kierkegaard's qualitative leaps across the fixed *stadia* of life were dialectical conceptions of change. The aesthetic, ethical, and religious styles of living are like Heraclitian rationales, each quite different from the other, an altered pattern which, when taken on, qualitatively alters all that follows. Kierkegaard interpreted change as dialectically generated through the opposition of an either/or, calling for a decision or commitment to one life course rather than another (Lowrie, 1961, p. 135). This concept of a discontinuous leap, of a nonincremental sequence resulting in qualitative changes across *stationary* states is what Bohr then used to account for the change of orbits open to an electron moving around the nucleus of an atom. Newtonian physics had accepted the quantified view that any of an infinity of possible orbits with different radius values would be possible. Bohr reversed the sequence, suggesting that only *certain* patterns would hold. That he suggested the atom in a stationary state possessed a "free choice" as to the transition it might follow in moving to the next stationary state is of more than passing interest to us. This is precisely the kind of explanation which is made possible when we take a dialectical view of the nature of change.

The dialectician begins with the assumption of an order in events, a stationary state or fixed pattern that transcends the flux of moving events at any one point in time. *Every* fluctuation in behavior is not change! The etymological roots of the word *change* imply a form of bartering in which there is a give-and-take resulting ultimately in a reordering of possessions across the two (or more) sides doing the bargaining. If this interplay is seen properly as a dialectical matter and if it is understood that without a reordering (repatterning) there is *no change*, we arrive at a more useful conception of change for the description of human behavior than heretofore available.

## Tautology as Psycho-Logic Sans Time

If we were to select a term that might capture the opposite meaning of change or difference we could find no better choice than *tautology*. The dictionary definition of this term focuses on redundancy or needless repetition in the meaning of words. Although correct enough in certain circumstances, this definition is surely inadequate to the broader meaning of tautology, and it completely underrates the importance which something like a mental tautology plays in the psychology of human beings. We now propose to raise the *Principle of Tautology* to a status second to none, paralleling it in importance to such classical psychological principles as contiguity, (law of) effect, association, frequency, and isomorphism.

To aid in our understanding of the tautology we must return to the discussion of meaning as a relational term begun in Chapter 2 (pp. 55–59). We defined *meaning* there as a term referring to the relations between items and their referents as well as to the relations between a user of such meaningful ties and the items he employs for the understanding of experience. This definition encompasses a distinction between the extraspective and the introspective theoretical perspective, a distinction we want to emphasize in the present context. Thus when we say that the item (word) *bread* means what it relates to—such referents as flour, oven, milk, butter, and so on—the relational ties can be framed entirely extraspectively, much as we define words in a dictionary by relating them to other words. But what if we were to relate the word *bread solely* to *bread*? In this case the relation would be one of identity or sameness (bread is bread), and as the definition referred to above suggests, we have expressed a tautology. This redundancy is empty only when the question of existence is not at issue. Saying, "That is bread," while looking at a referent in experience is not a needless expression when one is hungry and attempting to define the edibles in proximity to his personal identity. But the phrase, "That is bread," is actually a variant form of tautology meaning "Bread is bread" or "That is that (which I seek)."

Note however that in this latter instance we are speaking of a tautology as it would be expressed from the *introspective* perspective. We are no longer speaking about dictionary definitions, about relations between items and their referents alone, but about the relation between the user of such items (a hungry person) and the item designated (the bread). The tautological expression is made in a psychological fashion, as reflecting what the person is bringing to bear in organizing his experiences. Having a psychological view of the tautology is quite different from having simply a logical view. Classical logicians, who rarely take seriously the importance of dialectical logic due to its sophistical potentials, are prone to think of tautologies primarily in the more extraspective sense. Following Kant, they are likely to say that a tautology is an analytically true statement, which means that it is true by definition. If we analyze the statement "All bachelors are unmarried males," we can determine that it really states "All bachelors are bachelors" or "All unmarried males are unmarried males" because the definition of the antecedent term is contained in the consequent term. This is obviously comparable to our dictionary definition, a relational identity between terms.

If we are *psychologicians* and accept the view that human beings do follow something like a logic of tautology in their reasoning, would there be any difference between "All bachelors are unmarried males" and "All redheads are hotheaded" in the reasoning of a human being? Surely the latter statement can be shown extraspectively to be nontautological. The definition of *redhead* does not include the concept of hotheadedness, much less equal it identically. As psychologists, can we overlook this fallacious tautological relation an individual is drawing between redheadedness and hotheadedness (based presumably on a limited tautological identity of redness and fire, etc.)? To ask us to do so is like asking a physician to deny the usual digestive process when a patient under his treatment has swallowed a handful of sand, which is clearly in violation of the metabolic processes moving nutritious foodstuffs through the body. Erroneous mental conceptions, like bad foodstuffs in the digestive tract, do not alter or negate the process by which such meanings are extended and seen to work an influence on behavior.

We are seeking the process here and want to capture the Heraclitian identity within change. By looking at meaning through the conceptual eyes of the individual who brings such meanings to bear (i.e., introspectively), the concept of tautology permits us to take both a dynamic and a static view of behavior at the same time. There is order in life, because the person can bring certain givens (meanings) forward, tautologizing them from circumstance to circumstance (each redhead encountered is made hotheaded by definition). The very concept of *idea*, which draws historical precedence from logos, rests on the assumption of a tautologizing capacity in mind so that an X can be brought to bear as X repeatedly, even though circumstances always differ. Plato's realm of Being was a comparable notion of timelessness, from which beautifully perfect and unchanging universal ideas threw forth their variegated (imperfect) meanings, as shadows jumping about on the wall of a cave rest upon some more stable form existing between the wall and the light source. This belief in fixed universals was to dominate thought up to the rise of modern science.

Though he no longer sees the patterns of nature being determined by the prepatternings of universals, the modern scientist did find his universal assumptions in the realm of mathematics. Gödel's proof (Nagel & Newman, 1958) has weakened the earlier confidence in the fixed order of mathematics, but scientists still retain a self-assured attitude regarding quantitative arguments—particularly because these arguments do stand up to the empirical tests of validation. But what is not sufficiently appreciated here is that the psychology of mathematics *itself* draws heavily from the tautological reasoning capacities of the mathematician (Eves, 1969). In his *Introduction to Mathematical Philosophy* Bertrand Russell (1919) went into some detail concerning how tautological reasoning seems fundamental to the human mentality (pp. 204–205). As humans we somehow know by the logical order of a syllogism that it is correct, simply through an examination of its internal meaning structure (coherence theory of truth). Russell confessed that to define the tautology was difficult, but he affirmed a conviction that the farthest reaches of knowledge are fringed by such an intrinsic human capacity to know with certainty once a given pattern falls into order. Without this capacity there could be no mathematics and no science. Russell's analysis in this context is purely introspective and—we would add—psychological.

In their *Principia Mathematica* Whitehead and Russell (1963) also proved through extraspective analysis that mathematics and logic were tautological activities. In this case we are not speaking about the psychology of the human being, but of the capacity to translate mathematical symbols into logical symbols (see our discussion of the double-duty character of mathematics in Chapter 1, p. 36). Russell has shown that mathematics *per se* reduces to tautological statements of the analytical variety (i.e., All X is X). In this case we return to a more introspective formulation; for clearly when a mathematician uses the logic of mathematics, the ultimate conviction he personally senses in his *proof* emanates from the fact that he can show how the left-hand side of his equational development is identical to the right-hand side. We overlook the fact that the equation sign in mathematics signifies a tautological identity. In a psychological sense mathematical arguments are like grand analytical propositions, highly complex but subject to definitional analysis in which the left-hand member (analogical to the antecedent) turns up identical to the right-hand member (analogical to the consequent of an if . . . then . . . proposition) even though several transformations have been made.

Ironically, although statistical conceptions such as the Central Limit Theorem or a finding of unity in $F$- or $t$-tests are clearly based on tautologies, no psychological learning theorist to date has employed the tautology to explain how human beings learn. The rigorous psychologist who makes use of quantitative measures learns whether he has found something other than a redundancy of "no difference" in the relational ties of an *F*-test carried out on his data. But his experimental subject is said to learn exclusively on the basis of a frequency thesis or a principle of contiguity. We therefore have at least two theories of learning being advanced in most empirical researches, and no one currently acknowledges the principle of tautology which surely enters into at least one of them.

Skinner (1974) has observed: "All sciences simplify . . ." (p. 231) in propounding knowledge, but he failed to enlarge on precisely what this involves. Ultimately, the simplification achieved through both philosophical and scientific analysis rests upon man's ability to see identities across seemingly disparate events. Euclidian geometry is premised upon only five axioms and five postulates (Eves, 1969, pp. 121–129). Table 1 demonstrates that the four causal meanings can be seen covering centuries of human conceptualization, and the search for unchanging precedents is simply another manifestation of man's tautological capacity in reason. The history of science provides many clear examples of this human ability—for example, when Hooke tautologized between the concepts of sound and light, attributing thereby the known wave properties of the former to the latter as an hypothesis (Wightman, 1951, p. 130). This led to speculations of an ether, which would presumably undulate and thereby bring about the waves of light. Maxwell's theorizing was based upon an equation of electricity with magnetism (*ibid.*, p. 313). Hertz then did experiments to prove his contention that there was an "identity of light, radiant heat, and electromagnetic wave action" (*ibid.*, p. 315). Even Stahl's discredited phlogiston theory rested upon a commonsensical equation drawn between the giving off of a fiery substance by a burning body and the burning of a candle or the calcination of a metal (*ibid.*, pp. 180–183). The conservation of energy principle in science can be viewed as a grand tautology in which there is a fixed constant within change (*ibid.*, p. 279). It is fascinating to observe in Einstein's theoretical development a definite series of tautological extensions, identifying matter as energy (Kondo, 1969 p. 45), inertia as gravity (pp. 69–70), and gravity as curved space (p. 78).

The reader may object to some of these examples because they are more properly analogies than tautologies. This brings up an important feature of the principle of tautology, for we would now point out that what makes an analogy come about is the *identity* found between the two points of the relation—for example, when Copernicus once argued that the sphere was a "natural" shape because as with a drop of water, the sun, moon, and planets assumed this form spontaneously when left to "their own accord to limit themselves" (Schwarts & Bishop, 1958). A tautology is a relation of identity, and an analogy is a relation of likeness short of identity in meaning formation (patterning). Analogies are always based on dialectical reasoning, for beginning our parallel with what is identical across referents, we can then base our understanding on what is not the same—that is, in the disanalogy. Other so-called figures of speech, such as the metaphor (e.g., a ship plows the sea), allegory (a lengthy metaphor in story form), or synecdoche (e.g., a person typified as a "cutthroat") are the same. Beginning with a purely psychological principle, we are thrust into the entire panoply of studies subsumed by such specialties as psycholinguistics, concept-formation, creativity, and language development.

It is important to grasp that all such tautological derivatives are timeless theoretical constructions. They occur immediately, in the very delineation of the patterns of meaning premised or predicated, which is why the Kierkegaardian leap becomes qualitatively different so suddenly. This alteration of meaning is not pushed steadily along by efficient causation, but dramatically shifted through the abrupt changes of formal-final causation as when we move along the gallery of an art museum in which each new painting observed is based on its own unique set of premises. The earlier observations do not prepare us or (telically) determine for us what the next aesthetic experience will be although most assuredly we will sense a change in our awareness as we stroll along.

This timeless quality of patterns can be seen to occur in the mathematical tests to which we submit our data in experimentation. Once a psychologist has gathered his data on a sample of subjects, the very instant he concludes "this is my sample," the pattern of scores he has derived from his measurements exists as a quasi-stadia so that any of the resultant statistical tests he performs on the data are already determined via formal-cause determinism (Chapter 6). He has to spend time calculating these scores and submitting them to a computer, but the pattern of statistical treatments we know as the correlation coefficient or the analysis of variance is already fixed without regard to such time considerations. By shifting assumptions (formal-final cause determinations) the psychologist can of course alter his tests and thereby the possible meaning of what his data represent. But this "quantum jump" is again entirely outside of time considerations, because whatever rescorings or statistical revisions this may involve *must* be fixed by the patterning of the original array of subjects.

There is no more handicapping theoretical maneuver possible than to require a teleologist to use the language of stimulus and response in his description of behavior. *Response* in particular has been tautologized by rigorous psychologists with *behavior*, so that it is always thought of as motion over time even when this motility is "shaped" into a recurring pattern. We noted in Chapter 5 that not even the modern efforts to cognize psychology avoid the efficient-cause formulation implicit in this view of behavior as motion. Mediation theory simply puts a kind of pulley-and-gears system between yesterday's pushes and today's shoves. To capture the nature of humanity we advocate the coining of a new term, one that infers behavior as manifesting a stability "for the sake of which" motions are *then* seen to take place. Basing our definition on the Greek concept of *telos* as an end or reason for which behavior is to be manifested, we now propose that psychology accept the fact that certain behaviors are *telosponsive* in nature. This construct may be defined as follows:

A *telosponse* is the person's taking on (premising) of a meaningful item (image, word, judgmental comparison, etc.) relating to a referent acting as a purpose for the sake of which behavior is then intended. The *purpose* of the meaningful item can be assumed without question, as in observing factually that "the door out of the room is over there" or it can be difficult to ascertain as in the subtlety of a dream content. When the individual behaves "for the sake of" this purpose he is telosponding or acting intentionally, although this may be exclusively at the level of understanding and not seen in his overt actions. In this sense, concepts have purpose and human beings intend.[1]

In distinguishing between *understanding-intentions* and *action-intentions* we ensure that our outlook does not fall into the empiri-

[1] Since introducing this concept the writer has been—quite properly—criticized by even friendly colleagues for the "bastard form" of combining Greek (*telos*) and Latin (*spondere*) language roots. It is hoped that this scholarly failing over precedents on the writer's part may in time be forgiven, since the intent here was to coin a succinct word that would closely parallel the widely used *response* yet keep *telos* in the forefront. As with many bastards in history, our concept began life with decided handicaps—some of which even outweigh the matter of genetic lineage. Judging from the relative ease with which students and colleagues catch onto our meaning, however, the future looks reasonably good. The telosponse may yet achieve legitimacy in proper psychological society.

cist's error (p. 274). Psychologists have for too long accepted the naive functionalist dictum "All we can objectively observe is overt behavior, so all we can talk about is overt behavior." Surely the extensive work done on awareness in psychological experimentation (see Chapter 6, pp. 264–267) should convince us that some *unobservables* in the actual course of an experiment are more important than that which we can literally see in overt behavior. Einstein continually thought about physical phenomena in ways that could not be put to test through literal observations. What is the advantage to so limiting our intellectual scope?

Only a meaning-processing animal can telospond. We discuss the so-called lower animal in organic evolution below, but a conception of the person in which inputs and outputs are not contingent upon the *introspective meaning* as contained in mental conceptions would fall short of telosponsive description. Of course certain behaviors of an organism can be explained telosponsively, but others are not amenable to this type of description. A human being's stomach may undulate and secrete fluids, hence move or "behave," completely without telosponsivity. Various other reflexive behaviors of the organism, such as eyeblinking to certain stimuli, wincing in some circumstances, or the tensing of a muscle under psychological pressure might be said to occur in the classical sense of a stimulus-response regularity. But insofar as we begin to think of *mental* behavior, including those areas of study such as psycholinguistics, mentioned above (see p. 282), we would begin to touch upon the telosponsivity of human behavior.[2]

An important term in the above definition is *premise*. Logicians are likely to define this as a proposition on which, at least in part, the conclusion of an argument is based. This signifies that there are presumptive meanings embraced by a thinker that enter into the beliefs at which he ultimately arrives. What we learn is therefore always a function to some extent of what we have begun with (using function now in a formal-cause, patterning sense). The writer uses the word *premise* in this predicating sense, except that more referents than merely verbal propositions are included. An image can be

---

[2] We begin now to introduce new terminology over this and the next chapter at an increasing rate. To aid the reader's grasp and for quick reference we have provided a glossary of the most unique and repeatedly used terms (please see pp. 499–508). We have tried to elaborate on the definitions of these constructs in the glossary, interweaving meanings a bit more than is possible in the textual presentation.

thought of as a premise, as can the judgmental comparison of saying "X is better than Y" as an opening presumption to meaningful relationships between the evaluator (the person doing the premising) and X or Y. If Kuhnian paradigms (Chapter 6) predetermine to some extent what a scientist can learn about his area of interest, then either a formalized *verbal* statement or a rough analogy between some *visual* occurrence, such as a wave on a lake's surface and the flow of light under study, can serve as such a paradigmatic premise.

Other central terms in the definition of a telosponse include *purpose* and *intention*. These terms are often used interchangeably and so to draw hard and fast rules for distinguishing between them is probably unrealistic. The reader can probably accept the distinction drawn in the above definition, which points out that although one can speak of the purpose of almost anything, we reserve the meaning of intentionality for a living being—usually a higher animal. In Chapters 1 (p. 32) and 2 (p. 56) we indicated that a pattern of events or a pattern of letters called a word lacked purpose. We meant, of course, that in the extraspective use of the meaning concept, a telic possibility does not exist. A word *qua* word has no purpose. A plan *qua* plan has no purpose. However, when an intelligence (introspectively framed) makes use of a plan or word to extend the meaningful implications contained therein, we *do* see the purpose of the plan or word made manifest. Following Kant, we can say that a concept (plan, word) contains its purpose when an intelligence employs it in conceptualization. The concept *pencil*—either as a word or in a visual-image sense—when grasped by a meaning-processing intelligence expresses its purpose as something that can be used for writing, drawing, and other marking activities. The definition of *pencil* is tautologized with this meaning per our discussion above. The pencil, which is defined purely extraspectively, does not know of its purpose. There is no telosponsive intelligence attributed to the pencil as there is no life at all. Human beings, who concocted a symbolizing procedure and now require a means of utilizing this expressive scheme, intend the purpose of the pencil.

We often see or know the purpose of a concept but do not intend that the purpose contained therein be actualized in overt behavior. We do not pick up each pencil that comes into our cognizance and begin writing with it. What actually takes place in overt behavior depends upon a broader conceptualization of the life circumstances made by the individual—that is, the other meanings he is intending at the time. A premise in which pencil markings are part of the organization (pattern)—such as the realization, "I must get a note off to my stockbroker"—brings about the instrumentality of pencil writing in short order. The person might not even say this to himself, but simply picture himself drafting a note to his broker (image as a premise). However, granting this premising necessity, the purpose of the pencil will be actualized in the total pattern (the full meaning) of a person's intentional behavior.

Therefore we must distinguish between action and understanding intentions. If we think of the purpose of a concept as the *aim of the meaning* involved, not all purposes are aimed at overt action even though they *do* play a role in behavior. If we walk into an attractive room, we might be impressed by the decor without necessarily expounding on this pleasant experience. Or we glance out the window while typing letters to friends and see a robin searching for worms on our lawn. This momentary experience is most assuredly meaningful for some of us, but there is nothing called for in this understanding-intention that requires an action-intention on our part. The meanings here of *robin, grass, worm, nature,* and so forth are part of our experience but they need not relate directly to our ongoing letter typing.

In other circumstances the conceptual understanding afforded by telosponsive intelligence does relate to overt behavior. We must leave the room in order to go to our appointed destination and "there is the door." Doors as conceptual items have purposes, hence we behave "for the sake of" this door-purpose and leave the room through an action-intention. Based on our recognition above that dialectical changes take place only when a pattern alters, the present analysis suggests that meaning—an organizational conception *par excellence*—only bears on overt behavioral changes over time when the total emerging pattern calls for it. This pattern can be properly-understood only through an introspective perspective theoretical analysis of the behaving human being.

For example, not every statement made on the order of "I intend to do that" results in the end that has been projected. People aspire to college degrees who never complete their first semester of study, even though they had sincerely intended to do so. There are many reasons why this inability to actualize the aim of the meaning *higher education* comes about, and we do not wish to oversimplify things, but clearly not until we know what the individual really *was* intending can we take every statement as expressed in a literal sense. In the same way that recognizing and naming (intending) a pencil does not mean the person will necessarily actualize the pencil's purpose in behavior, so too just because the person stipulates the intention to achieve some end in life does not mean that he will actualize the purposive meaning of the words "I intend to complete college." This may simply be an understanding-intention and not an action-intention, or even as an action-intention, it might never be carried to the complete end projected.

What then determines when an intention—action or otherwise—will really eventuate in the goal projected? We will be elaborating on this issue throughout the remaining pages of this volume, but surely a good point at which to begin formulating an answer would be by looking at the totality of purposivity in the individual's psychic outlook. Along with questions of native endowment, physical health, and unforeseen setbacks, there well may be telic factors at variance with college success—such as "I intend to earn my way in college by working 60 hours weekly in an all-night restaurant" or "I expect college to be about as easy to get through as high school, which only called for a few minutes of preparation daily." Looked at totally, such ancillary intentions might be militating against successful completion of college. Without intending to fail, the person might be intending behaviors that will ensure failure.

Even if the premising purpose is quite clear—for example, seeing with one's own eyes that "the door is over there"—we are still prepared to call this a premise—as opposed to, for example, a fact of reality. We thus draw a sharp distinction between the way in which humans telospond and the contents of the premises on the basis of which they do so. Whether something exists independent of the premise and whether it is accurately framed in the premise is totally irrelevant to the dynamics of telosponsivity. One of the great misunderstandings of teleology in psychology is that a telic account supposedly deals with ends that literally exist or eventually happen in the future. In Chapter 6 (p. 263) we attributed something like this to Skinner's position, noting that he fell into this erroneous conception because of a confound between efficient and final causation. But the teleologist does not have to put his goals as literally existing down the road of time or as supposedly drawing the human being to them through a force of suction from out of the future (which is tantamount to a "reversed" efficient cause). Future goals, like present sightings of doorways, *both* come into play at the point of a premise—that is, encompassed in the meaning taken on. The process, "for the sake of this, that follows," stamps a mentality as telic, *not* the fact that it has future goals or expectations in mind toward which it works.

Another suggestion in the above definition is that some premises that the individual might take on are removed from clear under-standing—for example, in the case of dream contents (symbols, etc.). This leaves open the possibility of dualities in consciousness or a conscious-unconscious "split" in mind. Nothing in the concept of telic behavior would contradict the possible role of unconscious influences in behavior. Many dream interpretations are overdrawn analogies on the part of imaginative analysts, but there are also valid examples of a dream symbol serving a purpose in the context of meanings as understood by the individual concerned (i.e., reflect-ing his understanding-intentions but in a more analogical fashion, distorted by dialectical oppositionality, and so forth). By taking the proper introspective perspective and being sensitive to this idio-graphic meaning complex, a premising attitude at variance with the conscious outlook of the person may well be discernible. Dialecti-cians are not stymied by the fact that people hold contradictory views on life.

There are three more descriptive terms to define before a com-plete accounting of the telosponse has been rendered. The first has to do with the fact that a premise comes first, containing some meaningful item; and then flowing from this as meaning-extensions, we have the possibility of intentional behavior developing. It has been customary to speak of the "firsts" or "befores" in psychology as *antecedents* and the "seconds" or the "afters" as *consequents* (see Chapter 6, p. 245). However, due to the identification of antecedent-consequent with the time dimension we have found it desirable to use the terms *precedent* and *sequacious* to describe the order of telosponsive events. These terms make reference to the ordering of meanings, and they are totally outside the time dimen-sion except in the sense that as terms which describe *order* they could well imply "sooner" and "later," as by analogy between the ordering of meanings and the presumed flow of time.

A *precedent* meaning is one that goes before others in order or arrange-ment and establishes the course and nature of the meanings which follow it. Though it is often manifested first on the time dimension, a precedent meaning is not to be thought of as related to or a function of time passage. Order, not time flow, identifies the precedent meaning.

A *sequacious* meaning is one that follows or flows from the meanings of precedents, extending these in a *necessary* sense according to the principle of tautology. Though often manifested second on the time dimension, a sequacious meaning is not to be thought of as dependent upon time flow. Order, not location in time, identifies sequacious meanings, which are always slavishly compliant to the meanings established by precedents.

We now see that the premise is brought to bear as a fixed precedent meaning, which in turn influences the sequacious meanings that may develop as the individual advances on life. His concepts (which have purposes) are more than simply predeterminers of meanings; they literally create the sequacious line of meaning-extension which is constantly taking place in life. Human beings are not shaped or otherwise conditioned via past mediators into quasi-intentional animals (see Chapter 5). Humans are intentional organisms by fundamental nature because meanings flow from precedent to sequacious orderings. There is always more meaning in a precedent than initially grasped or circumscribed. There is always a further implication, suggestion, possibility, negation, and so forth, which the sequacious line of meaning-extension in human reason necessarily (telic determinism) enlarges upon. Thus we find that human beings constantly look for the relevance, portent, or significance of life events, often terming these insights, omens, hunches, lucky developments, and so on. The bipolarity of meaning fosters such lines of development, because given that we grasp the precedent X, we must immediately open up the possibilities: So what? or What next? or Well, sometimes not-X might happen too. A precedent meaning is impossible without a sequacious line of development following, although admittedly sometimes the implications are carried out in the dream world. Because we want to emphasize the fact that precedent premises are conceptual (formal-final cause) determinants taking place outside of time it is helpful to speak of the protopoint in this sequence, as follows:

The *protopoint* is always the first point in an ordering of meanings, although it may itself be predicated by other (including unnamed precedent) meanings. We use the term *protopoint* to emphasize that this is the first ordering in a line of meaning-extension or development *without* reference to the passage of time. Premises are brought to bear at protopoints, acting as precedents, and are then tautologized as sequacious meaning-extensions in the course of telosponsivity.

The survey of Table 1 taught us that scholars across history have tried to name the precedents to their current thinking, which was often found to be a sequacious line of development from some highly abstract universal. Plato reified these precedent meanings in his realm of Being. The ideal of universal lawfulness in science also takes inspiration from this search for an overriding precedent which sequaciously determines all else. Whether human beings will ever rise intellectually to name a protopoint level so abstract yet determinately relevant to *all* of thought or experience is an open question.

Most modern thinkers have rejected this possibility, believing as they do that the ladder of abstract conceptualization has no ceiling.

We must not equate such meaning-extension with *deduction*. It is tempting to see in our formulations a justification solely for deductive reasoning, particularly because premises are usually put in the deductive syllogistic frame of "major-premise *to* minor-premise *to* conclusion." Though this is entirely consistent with our theory of meaning-extension, we must not forget that *induction* also demands a precedent meaning-frame "for the sake of which" a generalization is then made. Inductive reasoning is just as premised as is deductive reasoning. The question of paradigms discussed in Chapter 5 is concerned with the inductive possibilities open to one based upon the precedent meanings encompassed in his paradigm. One does experiments to fill out a precedent paradigm in normal science (Kuhn, 1970, p. 23) *not* because this is a peculiarity of the scientific enterprise, but because this is a reflection of the *general human tendency* to extend meanings both inductively and deductively according to a sequacious line of development.

## Cognitive Association versus Conceptualization in Human Behavior

By introducing the construct of telosponsivity in human behavior we are seemingly returning to the pre-Galilean form of thought mentioned at the outset of this chapter, and this has particular relevance to the concept of motion in behavior. In the ancient view—for example, as typified in the philosophy of Aristotle—a precedently fixed order was postulated and then all sequaciously derived motions to be seen in nature were presumed to be aimed at restoring this harmony in organization (Frank, 1957, Chapter 4). The order was separate and distinct from the motion, but it determined the course of the motion. This preexisting fixedness was also to be seen in Euclidian geometry, where motion was not conceived as directly in the nature of a spatial distribution of lines and points. A point was defined as that which has no part, and a straight line was then readily seen as the direct distance between two such points. Points and lines were thus separate and distinct conceptions.

This view sufficed through the medieval period, but as noted in Chapter 1 (p. 47), with the advent of Cartesian geometry Newton succeeded in joining mathematics to motion in his assumption that a body (a point) which is not obstructed by another will move with a constant speed along a straight line into the infinite (Burtt, 1955, pp. 208 and 240). As a naive realist, Newton viewed all natural objects in this fashion, so that if a pattern existed in reality, it had to have been fixed in the material substrate of nature or, if manufactured by human effort, the result of modifying and altering the unidirectionality of motion into the observed pattern. Newton was not trying to explain human behavior, of course, but this general style of explanation takes us directly to the behavioristic assumption that behavior flows over time and then *secondarily* gets its patterning after a manipulated intervention. There is growing recognition in recent years of the importance of organization in mental activities such as memory, but the definitions advanced continue to stress the mediational process. For example, Voss (1972) defined organizational processes which supposedly result in memorial clusters, "chunks," or concepts as follows: "Organization is a process that intervenes between input and output in such a way that input is increased in its systematization and in such a way that there is not a 1:1 input-output relation" (p. 176). The basic idea of an individual altering or influencing the order of input to output is compatible with the present chapter's arguments, but the unidirectional (demonstrative) view of behavior reflected in this extraspective mediational model leaves all of our questions raised in Chapter 5 unanswered.

Because our view of the human being emphasizes predicating rather than mediating abilities, we propose that mentation be viewed in terms of the ability to conceptualize life experience. A *conceptualization* does not intervene, but actively creates by organizing experience from the outset (i.e., from the protopoints of mentation). Though the reader may believe that the present chapter is developing a cognitive theory, the writer would prefer to think of it as a conceptual theory of behavior, because as we saw in Chapter 5, the modern usage of *cognition* has been preempted by the Lockean-model advocates. In the style of Kant, we are now suggesting that input *itself* is precedently framed, ordered, patterned, clustered, and so on, and rather than simply intervening, such conceptualizations make the input aspects of mentation possible in the first instance.

Returning to the historical view of motion, there is more evidence for precedent organization in the thinking of Newton than the first law of motion might suggest. To relate his concept of motion to some (precedent) standard against which an object could (sequaciously) be said to move, Newton accepted the idea of absolute space, which amounts to the system of fixed stars (Frank, 1957, p. 106). Some of the Newtonians based motion on a change of location in relation to a fixed mass of "ether" (Kondo, 1969, p. 38). The logical necessity here is the same in both cases: If something is said to move, it must be said to do so in relation to a fixed standard. What Einstein and other physicists did was to challenge this notion of an absolute space (ether theory was discarded on several counts). Suppose that we have two planets, both seeming to move in a straight line relative to each other, as Newton would have it, but far out in space where there are no fixed star coordinates within which to base our claim that motion is taking place. These two planets are passing by each other and drawing farther and farther apart as we observe them. Now, which planet is moving? Are both planets moving? There is no way to answer such questions, for the motion of one body must be judged against the other. Either or both planets could be moving in relation to some third point acting as a (fixed) standard.

Does this mean that Einstein's theory of relativity could do without an anchoring of some sort against which to assess concepts of space, time, and motion? No. He too needed a precedent standard against which to sequaciously develop relational ties of object to object in a relative sense, and he found this in the (constant) speed of light (186,000 miles per second). A similar necessity for human reason to be anchored or grounded in fixity is to be seen in Heisenberg's Principle of Indeterminacy. Looked at psychologically, this amounts to a recognition that if we precedently take an interest in (the meaning of) an electron's position, we sequaciously influence (the meaning of) its velocity and vice versa (Feuer, 1974, p. 176). Hence the speed and direction of an electron are intrinsically (organizationally) related!

What does all of this teach us? For one thing, it suggests that when Newton formulated his laws of motion, laws which were subsequently to track literal events in observed reality, he was *not* basing these on motion over time but on motion *as conceptualized* within what we have termed at other points in this volume (see Chapter 1, p. 48, and Table 1) mathematical space (space without literal extensionality so that motion is *not* literally occurring). Just as one can think of a straight line or circle without introducing a time factor—that is, these forms are visualized "all at once"—so too can one visualize a straight line or a circle being defined by a *moving* point (the Cartesian geometric innovation). But note: We have the *form* of these images in mind precedently, and the moving point is incidental to a description of the form ultimately defined by its motion. Trying to visualize a moving point without putting it in some patterned form is difficult, but who would claim that once a pattern emerges in the imagined moving point, the initial motion of the point is what created the pattern? So although in actual lived reality Newtonian physics *did* accept the laws of (efficient-cause) motion as primary and the (formal-cause) patternings in events as secondary, in the *psychological conceptualizations* of the human being named Newton we see quite a different ordering taking place. Considered psychologically, Newtonian motion is a formal-cause construct first (where geometric relations are assumed) and an efficient-cause construct second (where moving points trace out the precedent geometric forms sequaciously).

The second lesson is comparably psychological, for it speaks to the question of how human beings apply their intentions. Even should we wish to view the person as behaving via what is called a free will, this *cannot* mean free from the necessity of framing his understanding in some way. As Kant appreciated, to understand is to ground one's judgments within a fixed frame (categories of the understanding). Telic determination results *after* such grounding takes place. We understand (limit the alternatives concerning) which of our two planets moves after we have framed the grounds against which we can (meaningfully) relate them. If we want to describe the mind as capable of willing (free) alternatives, this theoretical account will have to be done in light of the fact that mentality *also* works within a fixed and unchanging (determinate!) framework.

## The Conservative Role of Meaning and Mind on the Time Dimension

Now that we have a few new terms we can define *mind* and then consider several topics that relate to mental activity. The procedure we follow—as is true of all instructive efforts—is first to put down precedent terminology which then sequaciously extends the meaning encompassed therein to subsequent arguments. Taking the premise of our terminology, the meanings which then flow (extend) do so *necessarily*. To discredit the line of development one must discredit the premising terminology.

### A Definition of Mind

Considering the generations of dispute in psychology over this issue, not to mention the centuries of philosophical debate, to propose a definition of mind may be both foolhardy and impertinent. However, we cannot hope to promote a humanistic science by avoiding this technical requirement. This is *not* something that can be dealt with methodologically. We face a theoretical issue here, and, theoretical formulations can always be changed if they prove uninstructive. Our definition of *mind* would be:

*Mind* is the innate capacity to telospond in relation to patterns of meaning in experience as well as to create these patterns anew through dialectical reasoning. Patterns of meaning are conceptualized through purely sensory experience such as seeing figural shapes, hearing rhythmic sounds, feeling symptomatically, and so on, but they are also the essence of mentation, orient the patterning of precedent-sequacious meaning-extensions, and thereby constitute the rational order of logic as well as the illogic of sophistry. Mind is fundamentally conservative, so that the flux of experience is fixed at the protopoint in conceptual premises which are then tautologized through telosponsivity in upcoming experience. The patterned effort to fix experience into certainty or knowledge is called thinking, and the conceptualizations employed are called ideas.

The humanist customarily argues—and we have so argued at various points in this volume—that human mentality is an *active* process. Yet in the above definition we claim that mind serves a conservative role on the time dimension, trying in this sense to keep things constant, certain, *known*. To appreciate what is meant we must focus on the premising protopoint, for it is here that the active intellect takes root. To *conceptualize* is to put a frame (order, organization, etc.) onto experience, and as such, the frame *fixes* that which can be known—at least insofar as the frame has what William James (1952) called a "cash value" in its organization. George Kelly's (1955) personal constructs or Kuhn's (1970) paradigms reflect this same tendency for organization to precede the behaviors made possible by the conceptualization afforded. This is the conservative tendency of mind—that is, to fix a knowing premise and extend thereby the range of understanding (Kuhn), predictability (Kelly), or practicality (James).

The reference to innate capacities for telosponsivity should not be taken as some kind of innate-ideas theory in the Lockean vein (see our discussion in Chapter 2, pp. 91–92). What is held to be innate is the capacity to recognize or create patterns (meanings), and when in due time the conceptualizations resulting achieve a certain organization, we can speak of them as ideas or idea-units. We therefore follow the Kantian interpretation of ideas as *pro forma* causes of organization rather than as *tabula rasa* effects of (input) organization.

## Dialectic as a Logic of Implication, and, Affirmation

To qualify as a genuine teleology a theory must allow for the possibility of behavior to occur in an *arbitrary* fashion. The term arbitrary has been so identified with unreasonableness and caprice that one might erroneously believe it refers to unpremised behavior. Yet what arbitrariness actually signifies is that the grounds for the sake of which behavior is telosponded have shifted. For example, after claiming that no partiality would be shown in hiring practices, an employer places on his payroll a clearly unqualified family member. This is an arbitrary move, in which the grounds of impartiality have been superseded by some unnamed "blood is thicker than water" assumption. To find the precedents of arbitrary actions may be difficult, particularly because they often have such personal involvements, but they are present if we are privy to all of the thinking involved in an individual's actions.

Where does this capacity for arbitrariness in behavior come from? Is it due to the functioning of discriminative mediational aids or to the operation of a variable ratio in the contingent reinforcement circumstances of each situation? The present view would trace it to the human's dialectical intelligence, which always sees a myriad of possibilities in the continually arising experiences of life. Mind works within this flux of possibility and seeks to stabilize it in conceptual regularities. There is a sense of personal control in such stabilization, even if the order applied is inconsistent. Dialectical orders are not necessarily consistent because the bipolarity of meaning suggests alternatives at every turn. One might think of dialectic as a logic of implication. There is always more in sensory experience than meets the conceptual eye.

This quality of open alternatives in experience demands that the human being affirm some protopoint meaning at the outset for the sake of which behavior might then take place (telosponsivity). We can define *affirmation* as a telosponse in which one pole of a bipolar conception is precedently framed (held to be the case, presumed, believed in, chosen, etc.). Affirmation also encompasses the framing of meaningful unipolarities in sensory experience by tautological means. ("That is that." "That is a tree." "I recognize that face.") This affirmative necessity is another one of those active roles assigned to mind by humanists, because which pole of a bipolarity is affirmed or which item of unipolar experience is singled out for identification is up to the individual and *not* to the environment (see discussion of decision-making below). But having affirmed some premise, the individual has possibilities of affirming other premises at the same time. Indeed, it is often *necessary* that he see such alternative possibilities for affirmation due to the reverse meanings of a dialectical dimension of meaning (i.e., an implication which occurs to him via dialectical insight).

Why is it likely that the individual reasoner *will* see the reverse implications to his affirmations in a dialectical complex of meanings? *Because the dialectical relationship in this case is tautological!* Affirming one pole of a dialectical relationship tautologizes with the meaning at its opposite pole. Jung's (1953, pp. 65–66) treatment of the personal unconscious is much like this, in that what is affirmed behaviorally as persona and ego in consciousness dialectically defines what is implied as a potentially conscious behavior in the unconscious as an opposite identity—the shadow complex. Recall from Chapter 3 (p. 128) that Freud's very first theoretical attempt to explain the neuroses—long before he could be called a psychoanalyst —relied upon a similar idea. Referring to antithetic ideas and a counter will in the psyche, Freud (1966, p. 124) argued that whenever we intend to do one thing ("I must be quiet") the antithetic idea springs to mind ("I won't succeed, I'll make a noise") and that in neurotics this latter, reverse affirmation takes over because of fatigue and other unknown factors. There is a remarkable similarity here between Freud's explanation of hysterical symptoms and Jung's account of complex formation, with both theories relying on the surfacing of such reverse affirmations in overt behavior.

But the opposite of every affirmation is not necessarily *ipso facto* made into an unconscious premise. We are often only too aware that our behavior is arbitrary and that we *could* be proceeding according to a different logical position, attitude, or even lifestyle. Why we do not behave more inconsistently than we do is an involved question. One of the primary roles of mentality is to find stable grounds as so-called reasons for why we behave as we do. The same human nature that prompts us to search for precedent universals (Table 1) prompts us to ground behavioral patterns in reasoned or principled actions. Even when there may be no apparent reason for behavior, the human being would often like to know "Why did I do that?" The framing of reasons for behavior reflects an effort on the part of the human being to find the stable, recurring, predictable patterns of existence. And reasoning, or to reason, is in part an effort to find such grounds for the sake of which it can be said that things happen or behaviors occur. This effort could well help stabilize behavior as the person then continues to behave for the sake of such reasons (grounds).

Our definition of *affirmation* is consistent with the classical logical problem of affirming the antecedent or consequent of an *If . . . then . . .* proposition, which played such a central role in the arguments of Chapter 5 (p. 181). There is a precedent-sequacious relation within these propositions, because antecedents always frame consequents. We also have the bipolarity of antecedent and consequent, either of which may be affirmed in the course of reasoning (*sans* time). Specific contents are put into this organizational frame, so that rather than saying, "If antecedent, then consequent," we say "If a man, then a mortal." But the logical frame is still dialectical and which pole here is affirmed determinately influences what can be concluded as a necessity (precedent-to-sequacious) and what can be merely held to as a belief short of conviction.

Terms like *belief* and *conviction* signify the confidence we have in our affirmations. It is as if the human intelligence, knowing intuitively of the bipolarities in meanings, requires this sense of conviction as a reflection of its tautologizing nature. To hold to a factual belief is more reassuring than to confront life on the basis of premises that are "merely" opinion or hypothetical. Yet the present view would suggest that, psychologically considered, the only real difference between the hypothetical and the factual is this sense of conviction achieved through the exercise of an evidential test which is somewhat different mentation from theory. The hankering after truth is due to the recognition that we do *not* know assuredly that which we affirm in one side of a dialectical opposition. The so-called need for faith (religious or otherwise) is similarly an effort to believe in something that *ought* to be true, no matter what the provable facts may dictate. All such human behaviors reflect the important role of conviction in mental life—another form of fixedness reflecting the conservative role of mind on the time dimension.

## Conceptualization as Memory

Concepts of mind have always been closely tied to the role of memory in intelligence. The Lockean theorist, viewing ideas as receptacles, is prone to speak of "memory stores" (Kintsch, 1970, p. 142) in which the material input can be retained for a short-term or long-term period. When subjects are then found to organize their learnable items the Lockean theorist is likely to interpret this organizing capacity as a learned intervening process coming between input and output. One cannot properly name historical developments in less than a generation of time passage, but the writer feels that the reason we find the term *cognitive* virtually preempted by mechanistic theories today—that is, theories which found this term anthropomorphic in the 1930s and 1940s (see Chapter 5)—is because the vast preponderance of evidence has made it clear that human beings *do* organize their so-called input information, and hence a formal-cause emphasis in human learning theories was inescapable.

The present theoretical account of memory follows directly from our view of conceptualization, because it should make no difference whether the stabilizing role of mind is brought to bear in the present, to orient the future, or to turn around and look to the past. In both cases conceptualization at the protopoint and precedent-sequacious meaning-extension takes place. Experience is always more fraught with such logical considerations than classical sensation and perception theory has implied. We now attempt to provide a beginning theory of how logical considerations of inference (implication) enter into both original experience with objects in experience and, thereby, with the memory of such objects.

Limiting our example to visual memory, we begin by observing that visual perception, far from being a question of *tabula-rasa* input, is a matter of *pro-forma* conceptualization involving predications and inferences from the outset. Thus as infants, we all simply infer that the visual field on either side of our eyeblinks is tautologically identical without being taught to do so. This need not be the case, of course, because an apparatus is possible that could slip in a highly similar but not identical picture during the fraction of a second needed to blink one's eye. Yet in the "postblink" (sequacious) position we would simply presume that the pattern observed in the "preblink" position was identical (experienced as a continuation of the precedent pattern). Even in our very first looks at life we are, due to the continuing inferences made concerning the identity of that which is perceived, reconceptualizing our visual field again and again. In one sense we never simply conceptualize anything but always reconceptualize that which we perceive (usually called recognition). In the *act* of placing such fixed identities onto experience we come to know it. Of course the inferences made in such reconceptualization takes place so quickly or concurrently with our visual awareness that we do not think of this time lapse across eyeblinks as a problem in *memory*. However, assume now that we were to extend this lapse of time period across conceptualization or reconceptualization (we use these two terms interchangeably in the remaining pages of this volume). We would *ipso facto* be confronted with the question of so-called memory retention over short or long time periods (Kintsch, 1970).

But we have argued that tautologies function outside of time. What then would be involved in the accuracy of reconceptualizations, either here in the present moment as we look at something before us or as we try to recapture it from a more distant past? Logical learning theory would suggest that we consider this in terms of the relationship between just how reconceptualization at the protopoint was carried out as a precedent, making possible in turn a sequacious meaning-extension to the past—termed *memory*. How much actual organization was framed initially in the conceptualization (the more organization, the richer the meaning-extension, hence the better the memory, etc.)? What other premises are currently being affirmed by the individual in his memory efforts, and how well do these coalesce (pattern) with the organization being sought in recall?

Perfect visual memory would be like standing at a window and verbally describing what one sees on the other side. Yet even if one were to do this, there would be a host of bipolar meanings calling for affirmation in the scene observed on the other side of the windowpane. Hence, if a third party were to (extraspectively) test the accuracy of one's perception in the present, he could well disagree on the essential affirmations of what was being reported as observed through the window. This would not be taken as a problem in memory, of course, because it would be conducted in the immediate present. But what if the person were asked to describe yesterday's window scenes today? The (extraspective) observer might indeed attribute one's arbitrary reconceptualizations to some *failure* in memory.

One might argue that in the typical learning experiment the subject has to meet a criterion of learning, so that the experimenter has assured himself that the subject does indeed see what the experimental task demands that he see. Hence any memory deficit in this previously learned criterion is a real loss and not simply a question of some problem with the original conceptualization. Yet precisely how a subject manages to achieve the experimental learning criterion is not always clear and it need not even mean that he *has* learned anything in the sense of conceptualization. For example, if a subject *now knows* some mnemonic scheme that he can precedently bring to bear as heuristic aid, he might achieve the experimenter's learning criterion (*sic*) without having learned anything about the material being organized by his already extant mnemonic device. The items the experimenter presumed *were* seen by the subject might have no meaning (not really seen) without this predicating mnemonic scheme.

We can concretize the speculative argument now under development as follows: Assume that there are two points on the time dimension, with A taking place before B. Something takes place at point A, and the individual who witnesses this occurrence is asked to recall it at point B. According to the present view, what A would mean to the individual *at* time A would depend upon the precedent meanings he had affirmed and telosponded to. That is, if a purpose had been intended in the understanding of the individual at A, this would ensure that a precedent-sequacious line of meaning-extension would occur, and therefore the likelihood of recalling the incident would be high. As we have suggested above, memory is tied to the sequacious extension of meanings affirmed as precedents. Binswanger (1963) would suggest that the individual at point A endowed his experience with meaning, and such meanings then frame subsequent reconceptualizations as memories. For perfect memory to occur the individual would have to affirm the *identical* premise at point B. Anything short of this tautological identity across premises at points A and B adversely affects the individual's memory (reconceptualization).

Such tautological identities are difficult to draw across times A and B because circumstances change, so that what has followed in life always influences the grounds for the sake of which one telosponds, both forward *and* backward in time. The meaningful relation between the individual and what he has been asked to recall at B may be lacking or be purely incidental to what he had been intending at A. This is what the gestaltists felt was involved in the Hoffding function (Koffka, 1935, p. 561). Very often the organization resulting from telosponsivity at A has been reoriented or dropped altogether because it was not useful or instructive to the individual as he came to order his life in the intervening period (James's cash value thesis). Finally, memory itself is always inferential, so that just as we distort what is seen presently, we must of necessity distort what we are asked to see in the past.

## The Psycho-Logic of Language and the Mind-Body Problem

Our arguments rest heavily upon the concept of meaning and how extensions of meaning may be said to occur in human experience—

bringing more and more of such experience under the range of convenience of some given conceptualization. We have the relational ties of meaning extending tautologically in a precedent-sequacious fashion, and in certain contexts a dialectical opposition as a tautology enters to make diversity out of identity (many in one). Symbols as precedents are expressive of meaning like this because of the analogical variation of the tautology permitting something to stand for something else, to capture the essence of what it is like, but not exactly. The logic of dialectical implication can even turn the "is" into the "is not" in a dream sequence or possibly the supposedly illogical thinking of a psychotic person. To speculate on such matters without confronting the inevitable role of language in human behavior is difficult, and thus we must consider the relationship between what we have called our "psycho-logical" theory of behavior and the human's use of language. We do this even as we recognize that telosponsivity is *not* limited to verbal behavior. Images and affective assessments can act as protopoint premises to influence behavioral patterns in a telic fashion (see Chapter 8).

The Lockean theorists Dollard and Miller (1950) give language a major role in bringing about that human form of behavior known as logic (using the term now in its exclusively demonstrative sense —that is, without regard for the possibility of a dialectical logic). Language (words, sentences, etc.) is another way of speaking about the cue-producing response in mediation (*ibid.*, p. 87), and an individual who lacks such mediational aides is at the mercy of environmental events without being capable of discriminating the useful from the nonuseful. He is likely to behave inconsistently and reflect a "lack of conformity to the rules of logic" (*ibid.*, p. 220). The correction for this state of affairs is proper learning of language, as new input (*ibid.*, pp. 45–46). This view of language as the input materials on which logical orderings are said to depend is another source of the claim made by humanists that mechanists assign no active role to mind. Rather than placing language first and mind second, the humanist believes that mind comes first and language is itself a reflection of the logical patterning of mind. This is, of course, a variation on the theme discussed at the outset of this chapter concerning the proper location of pattern in the changing sequences of behavior. Language reflects the order of mind; it does not make this order possible.

Even a superficial study of word roots and slang expressions teaches one that words are products of the tautological (analogical, metaphorical) capacities of the human mind (via meaning-extensions). The word *attic* devolves from the style of ancient Grecian architecture in Attica. The word *chauvinism* has its basis in an analogy drawn to Nicolas Chauvin, whose showy patriotism and attachment to Napoleon delineates the meaning of this word today as an excessive commitment to one political point of view. The affective side of meaningfulness is reflected here, as it is even more crudely in the slang word *shyster*, which takes meaning from the German-Yiddish word for excrement! Psycho-logically considered, there is no difference between the meaning-extension of a word, relying as it does on some precedent concept which sequaciously extends to other referents (enriching them with this meaning) and the abstract precedents searched for by the thinkers cited in Table 1. The historical thinkers worked back from sequacious extensions to find the abstract precedents, but the general structure of meaning is the same. Both such abstract conceptions and the humblest words bring forward meanings as symbolical expressions, as dialectical implications, or as the grounds for the sake of which further understanding is made humanly possible.

The present view therefore holds that a word is coined to express something—the precedent-sequacious line of development—and it subsequently is used as a convention. That which it expresses is a patterned order (meaning), and this order again comes precedently to engender the coining of the word. Words—maybe most words used by people—lose their precise designation in actual language expression. We have all been surprised by the correct meaning of certain words we use routinely. Most of us fumble along in generalities without grasping the precise meaning of words used by others as well as by ourselves. This is possible because of our analogical capacities to take the circumstances of a communicated statement into consideration and therefore understand (intend) the purpose of another person's statements and vice versa. Hence, even if we do not understand the complete usage or realize that certain usages are literally incorrect but still globally descriptive by strained analogy, we can continue a conversation. Of course misunderstandings also result from such analogical (vague) discourse.

None of this is an argument against the fact that words *follow* logical implications (meaning-extensions). Humans are symbolizing animals because they are tautologizing animals. Mind orders experience through affirming premises at a protopoint and extending tautologically thereby the meaning of the premise to include those experiences that sequaciously follow. This is why in a certain sense *we can only know what we already know!* This theoretical outlook represents a logical and not a sensory phenomenology (Rychlak, 1973, pp. 203 and 513–514). The gestalt psychologists—Wertheimer, Köhler, and Koffka—thought of the Kantian categories of understanding as sensory frames (see Chapter 4). In opposing themselves to Lockeanism the gestaltists took an interest in how humans literally see, hear, and orient themselves by way of native physical equipment to experience reality. But because the gestaltists lacked a dialectical formulation in their construct of proximal stimulation (which might have been thought of as a protopoint needing organizing by mind) there was no real arbitrariness in their theories of mentation. Visual experience as brain physiology itself followed gestalt laws of organization. Since we speak of *grounds* for the sake of which decisions are made in telosponding, the reader may think that the present theory is a form of sensory phenomenology akin to gestalt psychology, which made much of the figure-ground construct. Actually this would be an incorrect characterization.

As a *logical* phenomenology, the present theory considers the Kantian frames of reference (the grounding categories) to function at the level of mind *qua* mind, which is not a process needing housing within the brain structure. The so-called mind-body problem arises in psychology because of the traditional reductive strategies of natural science in which there is an effort to bring all things down to some material- and efficient-cause substrate. A parallel here can be drawn to the phenomenal experience of color vision. We know that colors do not exist *in* things but in our perception of various wave lengths as reflected by the things we perceive. Yet who would deny that as a logical ordering in phenomenal experience things surely are taken as if they were indeed colored. Grass *is* green (to those not color blind), and to stumble onto a field of orange-colored grass would most assuredly upset the logical arrangement within which we move each day. Have the findings on color's source in any way affected the findings of naive experience as ordered according to color? Doubtless our grasp of scientific principles would temper our alarm if a field of orange grass were suddenly to materialize. We would look for possible atmospheric disturbances, or contaminations that might have bent our light source to alter coloration, or whatever.

But the altered meaning of *orange-colored grass* is incidental to the phenomenal necessity of reordering (reconceptualizing) experience according to the perceived coloration. Even when we find the physical reason accounting for the aberration we continue to order and reorder according to the experience of coloration with which our quandary had begun. Nothing has changed, for the logic of fixed color arrangements continues to order our experience regardless of what explanations we arrive at for any changes observed. This is like retaining the structure of a syllogism even though the specific terms we place into this frame as contents can change (see Wittgenstein's propositional variable in Table 1). The question of mind is a comparable one. We must look for the organizing capacities of mind not in the architectonic structure of the brain nor in the pattern of electrical firing of neurons in the brain, but in the logic of experience *as* organized, *as* conceptualized, *as* framed meaningfully—which are different ways of expressing the same thing. The mind need not follow the brain, because as a dialectical process, its ordering can be diametrically opposed to the demonstratively framed brain structures (see Penfield, 1975, for clinical-experimental evidence supporting this suggestion; see also Chapter 11, pp. 485–486). Mind is logic, both demonstrative and dialectical logic *in action*. We therefore suggest that the present view is a logical phenomenology, one that recognizes the physical or "body" side to experience but does not expect to find the realm of meaning-extension in such palpabilities except insofar as they enter as meaningful premises into the organizing reconceptualizations of mind (i.e., as contents within these reconceptualizations).

How can psychological science have a mind concept floating above the body in this dualistic fashion, as if it were a stable "meatless" organization directing the palpable cells of the brain "from above" like some grand spiritual force? Tough-minded psychologists dearly love to paint theorists who would see mind independent of body in this manner as misdirected clerics, searching for a concept of soul in the wrong circles. Yet to find theoretical justification for mental conceptualization as something other than brain structure is not difficult if we but add the dialectical conception to the theory of organic evolution. We saw in Chapter 6 how Skinner has used Darwinian theory to justify his operant-contingency theories (p. 261). To see dialectical reasoning as having evolved, through mutation or whatever, to turn the human being back on nature and allow him to affect that environment that used to mold him so exclusively is equally plausible.

As the mechanists now claim, up to some point in the evolutionary ladder an animal may have behaved entirely demonstratively, including following the input-mediation-output sequence at the more advanced levels. Insofar as meaning existed for this animal it was exclusively unipolar as a *sign* function in events. But, when the nervous tissue evolved to some needed level of complexity certain animals could recognize (conceptualize) that they were acting out a sequence of behavior which *could go another way*, even in direct opposition to the so-called natural prompting! Indeed the awareness of alternatives *began* in such opposition. At this point meanings of a bipolar nature arose, and the animal became a symbol-creating rather than a sign-mediating organism. Arbitrariness was born! This development removed the animal from a direct (unipolar) dependence on physical substrates, because the meanings germinating in awareness were no longer one to one with brain physiology but were opened by the immense diversity of dialectical possibilities.

This opening of the mind threw its conceptual abilities into disarray, since an awareness now of many different implications in events existed, essentially forcing the animal to affirm some one among the many possible premises available to it. This made innovations in behavior over the course of life more likely. For example, the animal which was being naturally prompted (efficiently caused) to forage for food in trees or alongside a river bank recognized in this *very prompting* (akin to the Hegelian account of inner contradiction) the alternative possibilities of descending to the ground or moving off into a plain away from the river. In other words, the alternative behavior was *not done* serendipitously; the natural selection at this point was *not* achieved gradually; but it could have been done abruptly (Kierkegaardian leap) and with a cognized plan as an intention—a plan suggested from what was occurring to what could be occurring by way of dialectical or oppositional reasoning.

The necessity of having to predicate its behavior was forced onto this animal in order to stabilize its grasp of events which suddenly took on a myriad of possibilities, bringing its identity as decision-maker into the ongoing process of existence as never before. Experience became premised experience, and behavioral arbitrariness was now always possible because the affirmation of premises was not fixed by body tissues alone but relied upon an understanding of external circumstances, including the attitudes and opinions reflected in the behavior of others. The human person is said to be a social animal, but the reason this is so is because the human intelligence absolutely must have a confident premise on which to proceed—that is, to telospond. The social norm is not some grand input likelihood, which gets funneled into the heads of the masses through external manipulations and reinforcements. The social norm is a mutual "that for the sake of which" (premise) employed in common affirmation by all members of a discernible group (small-to-large in number), lending them a common sense of identity and commitment in life. Because of the fact that norms act as premises, some social theorists have been able to speak of group mentalities, as in *Zeitgeists* and so forth (Becker & Barnes, 1952). In a certain sense this formulation is correct, but we must recognize that group intellects, *which bring on group manipulations*, occur because of the *conformity* of human intelligence to the premises which all individuals in a given group take to be collectively advantageous or the "right way" to look at things.

Norms are not poured into human mental receptacles like milk into a glass. The human intelligence is only too quick to seek and conform to what it wants to presume is a normative certainty. The intelligence opened by dialectical alternatives in evolution wants to close again in the (fixed) certainty of the scientifically truest, best, most beautiful, Divinely revealed, least assailable, and so forth, premises imagineable. Once having fixed such a premise in mind the individual is surely *determined*, as if by the proverbial "Law of Nature." But this taking on or conforming to the premises of normative behavior is *not* a reflection of efficient-cause determinism (see Chapter 6, pp. 243–249). Such behavioral controls are purely telic phenomena, reflecting the dialectical development of peoples, moving from one point of advantage to the next, seeking ever to obtain gains over nature, over others, over themselves.

Thus, although John Watson (1913) recognized "no dividing line between man and brute" (p. 158) in founding behaviorism, we now suggest that there *is* a basis for distinguishing between the lower and higher animals. When this dialectically reasoning animal "emerged" in evolution, it was a mixed blessing—as much an involution as an evolution in nature—for this animal had acquired the capacity to turn back on nature and direct rather than be directed by nature's uniform and graduated course. This transcending capacity, which we know as dialectical reasoning, allowed the higher animal for the first time to *create* alternatives by design, alternatives which were not always to the best end so that the phenomenal possibility of error and failure as well as accuracy and success arose. To call this transcendent judgmental capacity a homunculus or to force it into a spiritual phrasing is to construct a straw-man argument. There is nothing spiritual or mysterious in assuming that a realm of understanding relying upon patterned meanings functions through a form of dialectical logic that is not itself effected by some physical cause in the bodily substrate. We must first understand how this logic is reflected in behavior and then examine its role without prejudice.

## A Psychological Conception of Free Will

A psychological interpretation of free will is now possible. We emphasize the psychological here, because too often in discussions of freedom questions enter of physical impossibilities, politics, and the like. We are not free to walk through walls, and in certain political environments we are not free to elect our leadership. But these are not proper topics for a psychological analysis. We have seen in Chapter 6 the behavioristic interpretation of freedom, which amounts to saying that if the individual is not under the total control of present stimuli (input) but rather can modify this current influence thanks to the mediational aids of past stimuli (mediators), he is to that extent "free." We found this efficient-cause account wanting and now offer the following definition:

Freedom of the Will: A popular way of referring to the capacity that human beings have dialectically to alter the meaning (pattern, order, logos, etc.) of premises which are affirmed at the protopoint. Once a premise has been affirmed, the precedent-sequacious meaning-extensions may be adhered to by the individual with rigidity ("will power") so that freedom of the will and (soft) determinism are entirely compatible conceptions.

Although the phrase freedom of the will is not a technical description of mental action, we feel it has been sufficiently important in the history of thought to define and discuss it quite openly and in the context of our evolving terminology. The concept of freedom here means free to alter (hence determine) the meanings predicated when confronting environmental circumstances. The concept of will has been tied to such telic concepts as wish, purpose, and desire—usually with the implication of a power exerted to attain the desired end (will power), on the order of our action-intention. There is also the idea of a self-directed effort implied so that a willed behavior is not something done aimlessly (although one can forego such willful intention).

Skinner (1971, p. 14) has argued that a free behavior would be one that had no antecedent cause, but this formulation of the question is wrong on at least two counts. First, there are several types of antecedents; therefore if the humanist argues for teleology in behavior, he not only can but must do so based on the play of certain kinds of antecedents (precedents) in behavior (see our discussion in Chapter 6, Table 3, p. 245). Second, and more to the point, every exercise of will seems to be prompted by some environmental "thesis" against which the individual now decides or chooses to press a variant "antithesis." This initial thesis is most assuredly a form of cause (patterning of meaning), although it is not *exclusively* an efficient cause. The antithesis arrived at is not made to happen in a unipolar sense, but it is an essential ingredient in the chain of cause-effect for the human involved. The antithesis affirmed could be in direct opposition to the meaning of the thesis or merely be an alternative formulation. Alternatives are always born in the pole of opposition. We do not simply move back and forth between the extremities of two diametric opposites in behavior. There are gradations of alternatives in between.

As noted in the previous section dealing with the evolution of dialectical reasoning, such an emergence would not have occurred without decided environmental circumstances against which or in support of which an affirmation had to be made. Similarly, we probably come upon our personal willful prerogatives in maturation when we confront environmental circumstances within which we feel a personal inclination to contribute to the patternings of meaning. One has to feel the weight of the given before a willful act can be initiated. The alternative projected might simply be an understanding-intention so that we imagine ourselves in a phantasy existence achieving some end not now "in reality." But fantasied acts of freedom are not action-intentions and so remain mere possibilities until actualized.

Even so, the essential requirement here for a theory of free will is that the person does indeed reason dialectically. If so, a precedent premise that *is* affirmed need not be thought of as the *only* affirmation possible (necessarily affirmed). This is what *soft determinism* means—something less than 100% "cause-effect" in the course of behavior when considered in exclusively efficient-cause steps across time. Demonstrative positions have no need of an affirmation construct, because they hold that all premises are themselves input through and carried along exclusively on the basis of efficient causation. They therefore generate a hard determinism, or so-called 100% determinism, in which no freedom is possible in the sense of "free from necessarily affirming one and only one meaning for the sake of which behavior eventuates."

If we trace the roots of hard determinism in the history of thought, we arrive at two sources: see Becker & Barnes (1952) and Rychlak (1968). The first comes from material-cause theories in which something constructed of a material was recognized to necessarily reflect this material's qualities, as in the case of a wooden versus a marble bench or the offspring of a given animal would have the flesh qualities of that animal, and so on (see Chapter 6, p. 245). The second and more important source of a belief in hard determinism issues from *telic* precedents! As noted in Chapter 1 and also in other sections of this volume, the belief in geometric harmony, the faith in natural lawfulness, and even the confidence in accounting for events through reliable cause-effects over time, stems from the theological view that a Perfect God made this, a perfect universe—albeit one in which we do not always understand everything as it was intended to be. If we now apply the teleological theory of behavior being propounded in this chapter, we would describe this theology as follows: God freely decided to create a universe. He affirmed a plan at the protopoint as a precedent premise that in turn sequaciously (*necessarily*) determined what the world and universe would be like. As a Perfect Being did this designing, the laws promulgated were perfect in their *fixed* regularity (conservative function of the divine intellect, which effectively tautologized the regularities to be seen in its creation). Natural laws are the sequacious enactments of the perfection affirmed by the Deity at the protopoint of His creation!

Modern physics has challenged this precedent theological "myth," so that if a contemporary physicist contends that the world of motion *is* 100% determined, he is likely to be accused of projecting religious prejudices onto his area of study. There is no need to assume such hard determinism in modern physics. The paradoxical reverse is to be seen in modern psychology, where if a contemporary psychologist argues *against* 100% determinism and speaks of freedom in behavior, *he* is likely to be accused of projecting religious prejudices (free will) and mythologies onto *his* area of study. The paradox disappears when we realize that both accusations rest upon the possible use of a teleological conception by the scientist in question. If the physicist places his emphasis on the perfection of events, he appears to be reverting to the sequacious directedness of events believed in by earlier thinkers as supposedly following the creative affirmations of a God. If the psychologist places his emphasis on the arbitrary preliminaries *before* such an affirmation is made, he too appears to be reverting to prescientific accounts—accounts which were earlier combined into such theologies as the one conjectured above.

If we get our theories down properly, there is every justification for saying that a psychologically free being becomes rigidly determined once a premise is fixed. There can be material- and efficient-cause determinisms in behavior as well, of course (see Capter 6). What we can do in life is dependent upon our physical capabilities, natural endowments, and so forth. There is no need to dismiss such verities from our psychological accounts, for they clearly limit the meaning contents of the premises that are brought forward in life. But an interpretation of psychic determinism does *not* require a denial of psychic freedom. Skinner (1971, p. 20) is prone to speak of Freud as a determinist, equating his own operant theory with the determinism of psychoanalysis. Yet nothing could be further from the truth.

Freudian theory rests in part on a dialectical conception of mind as capable of affirming more than one premise for the sake of which behavior might then be intended. Through compromises of such differences, a course of symptomatic behavior is arrived at. But—and this is the important point—psychic determinisms directing such behavior are *without doubt* telosponses! Symptoms take on meanings, for they sequaciously reflect the symbolic expression of a precedent fixation point in psychic development (with a repetition compulsion ensuing). Freudian theory is a telic theory (see Chapter 3, pp. 123–132). Although Skinner's theory also brings in telic factors as reinterpreted mechanisms (see Chapter 6, pp. 255–267), the form of determinism elaborated by operant conditioning—as supposedly rooted in the environment rather than in predication—is entirely on the side of efficient causation. Random behavior issues (is emitted), and the environment supposedly patterns it (in that post-Galilean fashion discussed at the outset of this chapter). This is *diametrically opposite* to the view of behavioral determinism held to by Freud (which was more in the spirit of pre-Galilean description, with precedently fixed patterns determining the libidinal flow of mental energy rather than *vice versa!*).

**Summary**

Chapter 7 opens with a series of new descriptive terms, which are needed to alter the image of human behavior now in primacy in psychology. A Kierkegaardian conception of change is contrasted with the more customary unidirectional view held to today. This dialectical conception is more qualitative than quantitative, placing emphasis on the stationary and the fixed rather than on the fluctuations in events. The psychological principle selected to account for this fixed aspect of experience is the *tautology*, or a relation of identity in meaning. The analogy and metaphor, as relations of likeness (partial identity), are special cases of the tautology. The role of tautology in human reason is fully discussed.

As an alternative to "response" in behavioral description, we present a definition of the *telosponse*, which is the person's taking on (premising) of an item (image, word, judgmental comparison, etc.), relating to a referent acting as a purpose for the sake of which behavior is then intended. Purpose is the aim of the meaning reflected by an item, as in the point of a definition. An intention is the conceptual understanding of a purpose, which can take the form of a determination to actualize this purpose in behavior or not (understanding-intentions versus action-intentions characterize this difference). Concepts have purpose and human beings have intentions. Meaning-extensions take place in human affairs, and how the order of this extension follows a precedent-to-sequacious succession is shown. A *precedent* meaning goes before others in arrangement, and a *sequacious* meaning is one that flows or extends slavishly the meanings of precedents—as implications, inductions, deductions, and so forth. This ordering of meaning-extension is *not* dependent upon time. Precedent meanings are brought to bear as fixed premises, invoked or affirmed at a protopoint. Mind is then defined as an innate capacity to telospond in relation to patterns of meaning in experience.

Mind serves a conservative role on the time dimension in that the flux of experience is fixed at the protopoint as conceptual premises that are then tautologized through telosponsivity in upcoming experience. The patterned effort to fix experience into certainty or "knowledge" is called thinking, and the conceptualizations employed in this regard are called ideas. To conceptualize is thus to put a frame onto experience, and as such, the frame fixes that which can be known. Dialectic is shown to be a logic of implication, as the diversity it affords in the upcoming experiences of human beings demands that they affirm some given premise for the sake of which they then telospond. Dialectical opposites, in which one pole defines its reverse, are special cases of such tautological identity! Terms like *belief* and *conviction* signify the confidence we have in our affirmations.

The problems of memory are then considered in light of conceptualization. Memory is seen as inferential in the same way that sensory perception is inferential. Time passage is not considered a necessary cause of memory recognitions or reconceptualizations. The central problem is that of reconceptualizing at the protopoint so that what flows sequaciously in meaning-extension recaptures the full experience as memory. Various reasons why reconceptualization (recognition, recall) into the past proves difficult to attain are discussed.

We then consider the role of logic in behavior and how some of the logical principles such as tautology play a role in language expression. Language terms (words) are shown to be reflections of precedent-sequacious meaning expression. Logic comes first and language terms follow, not as some behaviorists claim, in the reverse order. A speculative argument is presented which traces how dialectical reasoning might have emerged in the course of organic evolution. The chapter closes with a discussion of free will, which is defined as a popular way of referring to the capacity human beings have dialectically to alter the meaning of premises which are affirmed at the protopoint. Once a premise has been affirmed, the precedent-sequacious meaning-extensions may be adhered to by the individual with rigidity so that freedom of the will and (soft) determinism are entirely compatible conceptions.

## References

Becker, H., & Barnes, H. E. Social thought from lore to science (2 vols.). Washington, D.C.: Harren, 1952.

Binswanger, L. Being-in-the-world (trans. and with a critical introduction by J. Needleman). New York: Basic Books, 1963.

Burtt, E. A. The metaphysical foundations of modern physical science. Garden City, N.Y.: Doubleday, 1955.

Dollard, J., & Miller, N. E. Personality and psychotherapy: An analysis in terms of learning, thinking, and culture. New York: McGraw-Hill, 1950.

Eves, H. An introduction to the history of mathematics (3rd ed.). New York: Holt, Rinehart & Winston, 1969.

Feuer, L. S. Einstein and the generations of science. New York: Basic Books, 1974.

Frank, P. Philosophy of science. Englewood Cliffs, N.J.: Prentice-Hall, 1957.

Freud, S. A case of successful treatment by hypnotism. In J. Strachey (Ed.), The standard edition of the complete psychological works of Sigmund Freud. (Vol. I). London: Hogarth, 1966. Pp. 115–128.

James, W. The principles of psychology. In R. M. Hutchins (Ed.), Great books of the western world (Vol. 53). Chicago: Encyclopedia Britannica, 1952.

Jung, C. G. Two essays on analytical psychology. In H. Read, M. Fordham, & G. Adler (Eds.), The collected works of C. G. Jung (Vol. 7). Bollingen Series XX.7. New York: Pantheon Books, 1953.

Kelly, G. A. The psychology of personal constructs (2 vols.). New York: Norton, 1955.

Kintsch, W. Learning, memory, and conceptual processes. New York: Wiley, 1970.

Koffka, K. Principles of gestalt psychology. New York: Harcourt, Brace, 1935.

Kondo, H. Albert Einstein and the theory of relativity. New York: Franklin Watts, 1969.

Kuhn, T. S. The structure of scientific revolutions (2nd ed.). Chicago: The University of Chicago Press, 1970. (1st ed., 1962.)

Lowrie, W. A short life of Kierkegaard. Garden City, N.Y.: Doubleday, 1961.

Magill, F. N., & McGreal, I. P. (Eds.), Masterpieces of world philosophy (2 vols.). New York: Salem, 1961.

Nagel, E., & Newman, J. R. Gödel's proof. New York: New York University Press, 1958.

Penfield, W. The mystery of the mind: A critical study of consciousness and the human brain. Princeton, N.J.: Princeton University Press, 1975.

Russell, B. Introduction to mathematical philosophy. London: Allen & Unwin, 1919.

Rychlak, J. F. A philosophy of science for personality theory. Boston: Houghton Mifflin, 1968.

Rychlak, J. F. Introduction to personality and psychotherapy: A theory-construction approach. Boston: Houghton Mifflin, 1973.

Schwarts, G., & Bishop, P. W. Moments of discovery: The origins of science. New York: Basic Books, 1958.

Skinner, B. F. Beyond freedom and dignity. New York: Knopf, 1971.

Skinner, B. F. About behaviorism. New York: Knopf, 1974.

Voss, J. F. On the relationship of associative and organizational processes. In E. Tulving & W. Donaldson (Eds.), Organization of memory. New York: Academic, 1972. Pp. 167–194.

Watson, J. B. Psychology as the behaviorist views it. Psychological Review, 1913, 20, 158–177.

Whitehead, A. N., & Russell, B. Principia mathematica (3 vols.; 2nd ed.). Cambridge: The University Press, 1963.

Wightman, W. P. D. The growth of scientific ideas. New Haven: Yale University Press, 1951.

Wolman, B. B. Does psychology need its own philosophy of science? American Psychologist, 1971, 26, 877–886.

# CHAPTER EIGHT

## Foundations for a
## Logical Learning Theory

We come now to the framing of a new approach to human learning, based on the teleological image of the person presented in Chapter 7. Although this approach is called *logical learning theory*, we include *both* demonstrative and dialectical forms of logic in this designation. That we believe humans to be logically "correct" or cybernetic in their approach to life should not be presumed. Much of human behavior consists of the so-called illogic of dialectical reasoning. What makes this theory logical is the belief that human beings *do* behave for the sake of an order (logos) which predicates their behavior in a determinate sense. But we also believe that they can effect this ordering of premises *from birth* (circa); if mind is *tabula rasa* at the outset, what is subsequently etched upon it does not rest solely with the hand of experience. The human being helps write the scenario and thereby is necessarily a contributing agent to what will be enacted.

### A Neo-Kantian Category of the Mind
### for Modern Psychology

If logical learning theory is to constitute a Kantian revolution in the Lockean climate of theory which now permeates psychology, it must come forward with a theoretical construct that acts as Kant had his unlearned categories of the understanding acting in mind. We require some aspect of behavior that can be thought of and then proven to be *pro forma* rather than strictly *tabula rasa*. We need not take over Kantian philosophy *per se* as our psychology, but we must show how in adapting Kant's theoretical style to our own approach, an instructive series of humanistic explanations will follow. In this first section of Chapter 8 we propose one such neo-Kantian category and then relate it to the experimental context.

## Emotion versus Affection

No other aspect of behavior has engendered more speculation than emotion. The early psychologists were particularly drawn to the role of what they variously called emotion, feeling, or affection on behavior, as seen in the writings of Brentano (1973), James (1952), or Wundt (1907). Often relegated to a secondary "motivating" function —especially in the drive-reduction learning theories which flourished in the first half of this century—emotions were likely to be given a physiological emphasis because of their tie to bodily sensations (Arnold, 1960, 1970). Yet, at least in the case of human beings, there is often a further motivation to stimulate emotional reactions that are not initially active—for example, in the aesthetic efforts people make via the arts. What then can be said to motivate a motivation for an unrealized emotion? To suggest that this involves yet other emotions merely compounds an already muddled picture. Furthermore, to the human animal an emotion is something beyond simply a physiological reaction or a heightened sense of activation in bodily tempo. *Emotions signify imports.* Even after the flow of a physiological reaction has passed, the recollected (reconceptualized) "feeling" is retained with vividness. One does not need to have love tingling in his breast this moment to say that he does indeed love his child with a total commitment.

Obviously the mind-body issue enters here. We all can think back to some tender period of life and in that very recollection obtain a good feeling. What is the cause here of the engendered mood (body) if not some complex of patterned meanings (mind) as so-called ideas? Even more complexly, how can one be feeling a deep emotion signifying one thing—let us say, hatred—and yet at the very same time *also* feeling either satisfaction or misery in the fact of having such animosity uppermost in one's awareness? Not all individuals enjoy entertaining certain emotions equally well. For some a sexual impulse is sheer joy anytime, while for others it is an embarrassment if not an actual annoyance "depending upon the circumstances." Theories of emotion that rely exclusively on physiological explanations have even more difficulty accounting for such twists and turns of our emotional reactions than they do in accounting for just how many "basic" emotions there supposedly are nestled among the body's organic machinery (love, hate, jealousy, etc.).

How might a Kantian theorist proceed on this question of the emotions? Because there *is* a mind-body feature involved, he would first take a position on where the emotions might be said to issue from. One must of course be cognizant of one's feelings to experience an emotion; to that extent, emotions make themselves known in mind. They are like characterizations of our feelings. We do not call all mental representations (images, ideas) emotions, nor do we feel emotional in every moment of our waking awareness. Many theorists claim that we are always emoting, in the sense that we constantly feel something in relation to what we know. But at least in commonsensical parlance, to feel an emotion is distinct from, for example, losing oneself in an abstract intellectual activity. Possibly this is merely a question of the extent of one's emotions at the moment. Whatever the case, a Kantian position might suggest that emotional feelings originate in the body and that, insofar as mental activity is concerned, not until the meaning as endowed by mind in the act of conceptualization takes place can we speak of an emotion taking place. In this sense the problem of how many emotions we have or how complexly we "feel" in relation to the circumstances of life depends entirely on the meanings generated in telosponsivity. Conceptualizing stimulations emanating within the body's physiological mechanisms are no different from conceptualizing stimulations emanating from without the body's dermal limits. Indeed the *very same* physiological stimulations may be conceptualized differently—be "felt" as different emotions—based on the extra-bodily situation in which the individual finds himself (i.e., the meanings he actively conceptualizes).

The drift of this Kantian line surely demands that we have some *mental* way of referring to the emotional experience or to whatever it is that gets confused with emotional experience. Logical learning theory suggests that we distinguish between affection (mind) and emotion (body). There is a precedent for this in the writings of Titchener (1909), who early distinguished between affection as the "characteristic element in emotion" (p. 277) and emotion proper—which would include all of those distinctive feeling states we name anger, joy, and so forth. Continuing in the vein of his teacher, Wundt, Titchener held that there are only two forms of affections: Either they are *pleasant* or they are *unpleasant* (ibid., p. 226). Though he theorized extraspectively and in no way intended a dialectical meaning, the implications for us are clear. Titchener called the pleasant or unpleasant affections sensed in relation to experience "qualities," suggesting thereby that they were reflective of or a part of sensory stimulation, much as varying wavelengths strike us with different hues of color. Although he included judgment in his psychology, Titchener failed to subsume the emotions by this evaluative concept. Logical learning theory does consider affection to involve judgment, as does all telosponsivity, and as a dialectical process, to be seen active in all mental activity. Affective assessments are considered the most abstract of mental telosponsivity possible, as follows:

*Affective assessment* in its purest manifestation is a transcendental telosponse—that is, an innate capacity to judge (via dialectical division) the meanings of one's concepts, premises, and even telosponses, characterizing them either positive or negative in meaningfulness. Affective assessment is, however, embodied in *all* telosponsivity, rendering the implicit connotative meaningfulness of the specific (denotative) meanings being extended in mental activity. Affections are purely mental phenomena, ultimately *arbitrary* and up to the person who levels such idiographic judgments from his or her (introspective) perspectives on life. Because the assessment is dialectical, there is no indifference point on the dimension of affective assessment, although there may be ambivalence.

We borrow the concept of transcendence from Kant (1952, p. 229), who in accounting for self-reflexivity in mind held that a human being could turn back on the activities of mind and examine the working of his understanding through the use of a *transcendental dialectic*. Mind could double back on itself, so to speak, and to that extent evaluate its own evaluating capacities. In like fashion, all of those meanings being actively brought to bear in telosponsivity can be evaluated according to a dialectical either-or assessment of positiveness or negativeness. This self-reflexive act is *also* a telosponse, with *its* premising task being that of intending the positive or negative purpose of the mental contents (meanings) under affirmation, conceptualization, and telosponsivity. To say that we can "telospond our telosponses," is therefore not redundant or circular for this is what self-reflexivity implies, as in knowing that we can know (see our discussion of Descartes on this point in Chapter 8, p. 353). Of course there is usually no need to telospond our telosponses because the positive or negative nature of the latter is inherent in our affirmative grasp. We are constantly affectively assessing in reasoning—we know our likes and dislikes without having to enumerate them through a self-reflexive effort. But when asked to assess specifically anything in his or her experience as to its affective quality, the human person can be shown to do so fairly easily. Indeed most people take this process for granted.

There is a Kantian recognition in this construct of affective assessment to the effect that meanings and meaningfulness always "devolve from above" in mental acts (Rychlak, 1973, p. 11). That is, the positiveness or negativeness of meanings being affirmed in telosponsivity are themselves sequaciously determined by the *even more abstract* precedents of affective assessment. If we are now telosponding in some fashion regarding the meanings of symphonic music, for example, we would be cognizant of this or that specific musical theme as it is played. Liking symphonic music in general, we may or may not appreciate the present piece we are listening to. How are we to characterize this personal appraisal? Our definition suggests that it requires a transcendental telosponse to rise above (transcend!) the ongoing telosponsivity of, for example, "I am listening to this symphonic music over the radio" and reveal the precedents which act as background assessments to color our judgment of "I find that I like this piece" or "I find this piece uninteresting." The precedent affection sequaciously colors our continuing experience of listening to the musical score—that is, literally determining our enjoyment of the music. We need not state these assessments, because the routine act of telosponding the musical score "connotes" intrinsically what we think of the piece. We often confuse this connoted significance with an emotional reaction, but logical learning theory contends that emotions are not telosponses. The *meaning* of an emotion is framed telosponsively, but emotion *qua* emotion is not a mental phenomenon; it is physical.

Emotions are rooted in the body. They are triggered by life circumstances quite automatically, and only subsequently do we realize the characterizations this stimulation has put onto our life. It is rarely appreciated that the central point of the James-Lange theory was that having first reacted organically and automatically, we *then* characterize our circumstances via a process termed "the emotions" (see James, 1952, p. 743). Arnold (1970) has termed the emotions "physiological appraisals" (p. 174) of the circumstances in which we find ourselves. An appraisal is a judgment, and so we can say that from birth the child has an unlearned potential to put experience to telic consideration because of his emotional equipment— but not *solely* on the basis of this equipment.

The infant who is pricked by a diaper pin even before language acquisition has an "experience," but the essence of this externally provoked event is that it forces him to judge, to appraise his circumstance. No one denies the truth of an unlearned emotional appraisal in human behavior, because we *do* have innate feelings of a positive or negative quality vis-à-vis environmental conditions. But is this unhappy event of a painful physiological appraisal the *cause* of subsequent appraisals made by the child in relation to sharp objects? As this child goes through life confronting nails and thumb tacks and even forks, will he assess the sharpness of such objects due solely to this earlier event with a diaper pin in which he literally felt an emotion of pain or fright and now retains it in an "affective memory" [Arnold, 1970, p. 173]? This is not how we would conceptualize the matter. Affection is something completely different from the physiological reaction of emotion, and comes into play entirely independent of it. A definition of emotion follows:

*Emotion* refers to the pattern of feelings experienced physiologically by individuals, usually in relation to certain environmental circumstances that seem to provoke them. Insofar as they are physiological appraisals of these life circumstances, emotions are *not arbitrary* but are rather forced onto the individual by the mechanisms of the body. Various emotional moods may be brought about artificially through physiological stimulants (drugs, etc.) or through capturing the environmental situation that naturally provokes them. Emotions are given meaning by the telosponding intellect that conceptualizes and names them. They sometimes provide the basis for and are often confused with affections.

Logical learning theory would therefore hold that even as the child experienced the physical feeling (crude emotion) of pain he was *ordering* (conceptualizing) this experience through an entirely independent, psychological, affective assessment—and that in this ordering of (re)conceptualization the possibility of memorial retention was *created* (see Chapter 7). In other words, the affective assessment acts as a precedent which then sequaciously determines the known through its organizational capacities, aligning meaning-extension accordingly. Assuming now that a child could have conceptualized the meaning of *sharpness* (however idiosyncratically), in his subsequent life he would premise tautologically identical circumstances as affectionally negative. Furthermore he could through analogical forms of meaning-extension, "project into" other life experiences the meaning of sharpness as a kind of negative con-

struct because of some tangential similarity—for example, as between the diaper pin (placed at hip level) and a belt (worn at hip
level).

As we do not need to learn what a positive or negative feeling
(emotion) *is* we do not have to be instructed in how to behave affectionately. Experience does *not* teach us how to assess affectively,
although it does influence the grounds for the sake of which we
make our affective assessments. Children reared in culture A eat
whale blubber with relish, while children in culture B are revolted
by the thought. Even so, this does not prove that the assessment
capacity itself is shaped by such cultural considerations. As an aspect
of the telosponse, affective assessment begins *with birth*, if not
shortly before. Gardner Murphy (1947) tried to make a similar point
in his "canalization" (p. 193) construct. Cultures "condition" children
in definite ways, but the fact that preferences arise is due to an
innate canalizing ability akin to what we have been calling affective
assessment in telosponsivity.

Another feature of the affection-emotion distinction is that although these two forms of judgment (mental and physiological) can
be concordant, they can *also* be seen to bear an oppositional relationship, one with the other. An unpleasant circumstance, once
meaningfully framed, often teaches us to do what is necessary to
make it pleasant. The concept of emotion, based as it is on a demonstrative formulation involving unidirectional promptings, fails to
capture what actually takes place in behavior of this more dialectical
variety. For example, if an individual is "blue" or depressed in the
physical sense of a literal feeling, he can reason to the opposite of
what is surely now reality and think, "Why not play my favorite
music on the stereo? That'll cheer me up." There is no need to have
a fleeting emotion—a slight dash of "good feeling"—or a concrete
recollection of how once in the past listening to music cured his blue
mood before this individual can arrive at his projected intention.

Can we be indifferent toward some item of our experience and
to that extent refrain from making an affective assessment of it
altogether? As a dialectical conception, affective assessment is not
geared to denying this possibility *in principle*. However, as a practical matter, this failure to assess affectively would seem to occur
rarely. The affirmation of. a premise in conceptualization demands
that we take a position concerning the positiveness or negativeness
of this premised meaning. Meanings simply *do* take on positive or
negative connotations, often revealed in their expressed intonations
when the individual speaks about them. What we probably mean

by indifference concerning some item of our experience is that we are either not conceptualizing it or that, though conceptualized, it is employed as an understanding-intention and not as an action-intention. But if forced to relate behaviorally to the item in question, we would soon enough be involved in an affective assessment. For example, we are indifferent to the existence of a discarded fishing pole, lying alongside the outer garage wall in our backyard until our beach ball is trapped beyond reach in the limbs of a tree. Suddenly the discarded and indifferent (to us) bamboo shaft takes on a positive valence, as it would have taken on a negative valence were we accidentally to run our power lawnmower into its protruding end. Do these examples establish a unidirectionality in affection, since retrieving beach balls or fouling up lawnmowers are events "in reality" and to that extent unipolar facts?

No. Because the empirical facts are unipolar does not mean we have to think of the reasoning organism as unipolarly directed "by" these facts. We can easily show how the environment influences us by choosing the right examples. Positive and negative reinforcements "in" the environment are especially easy to point to when we choose the extremes. Getting hurt is negative, so think about the times in the past when you were injured, spanked, failed a test, or were fired from a job. Being pleased is positive, so think about the times in the past when you were shown love, scored an academic triumph, or ate a marvelous meal. There are no equivocations about these affective ends of the behavioral dimension, as there are none about our fishing-pole alternatives. But now, what of all the other times? What of all those "in-between" times when the high and low points are not so easily delineated? This is where we usually spend our lives. Can the reader honestly believe that the environmental circumstances were *clearly* positive or negative as he or she went to school, met some new people, spent an evening alone at home, woke up one morning, took a day off, or had a lot to do? If they were not, how can we limit our descriptions of human behavior exclusively to these extrapersonal "facts?"

## Reinforcement Value as a Subject-Contributed Variable

Thus far we have been speaking of a theoretical construct in our consideration of affection. A major argument of Chapters 5 and 6 is that we must always have both a theoretical and a methodological grasp of that which we hope to study scientifically. How then are we to put affective assessment to empirical test, and what methodological construct would suffice to reflect this human capacity? We propose the term *reinforcement value* for this methodological duty, as follows:

By *reinforcement value* is meant the operationalizing of affective assessment through asking subjects in experiments to prerate for likability materials (verbal, pictorial, etc.) which they may be asked to learn or otherwise deal with in an experimental context. We assume that a rating of liking reflects positive affective assessment and a rating of disliking reflects a subject's negative affective assessment.

In Chapters 9 and 10 we trace the development of an extensive research program which was an attempt to establish the validity of affective assessment in human behavior through this operationalized measure of it. The concept of reinforcement is discussed below in Chapter 8 (p. 327). In the present context we want to discuss another aspect of the reinforcement-value variable, for it can be considered as a methodological construct. Whenever we use the term *reinforcement value* we are referring to the context of proof. It is a sequacious derivative of the affective-assessment precedent, reflecting thereby the proper course of scientific development—that is, from theory *to* method (see Chapter 5, pp. 191–192). We have tried to show in previous chapters how classical learning theories have been cast in exclusively extraspective terms (see Chapters 4, 5, and 6). We have also argued that this one-sided theory receives much encouragement from the confusion of methodological test with theoretical explanation. When the traditional experimentalist enters into a relationship with his subject it does not—or it has not typically— occurred to him that this may be a "two-way street" and that just as *he* is "manipulating variables," the subject too may be "manipulating variables."

The canons of scientific objectivity have lent an unreal air of antiseptic unidirectionality to the influences exerted on the psychological experiment. Yet we have ample evidence from decades of experience and many explicit studies of the question (e.g., Orne, 1962; Rosenthal, 1966) that *both* experimenter and subject make contributions to the observed outcome of the study being conducted —contributions that are never characterized as design factors but could easily be put in such terms. The subject is virtually always thinking about his role in first-person terms, asking himself questions like: What is he (the experimenter) up to? What's he trying to get me to do? What am I getting into here? What's the worth of all this? What's the trick? But after he conceptualizes in this intro-spective fashion and completes the research task for the experi-menter, his telic performance is taken as further proof of the exper-imenter's third-person nontelic account of behavior. Logical learning theory holds that the only way in which to rectify this situation and to bring before all psychological researchers the necessity of having to encompass the introspective side of behavior is to formalize an evaluative (hence intentional) variable and assert that it is at play in *every* experimental study done on human beings. This is how we now view the reinforcement-value variable.

Logical learning theory therefore frankly admits that both the experimenter and the subject make significant contributions to the variables of the experimental relationship. The variables being manipulated by the experimenter can be considered experimenter-contributed variables, and the variables under the manipulation of the subject may be considered subject-contributed variables. Subject-contributed variables can be turned into experimenter-contributed variables, of course, but in making this effort we should never presume that we have exhausted the play of subject-contrib-uted variables in our experiment, and we should never "account for" these introspectively framed variables in an extraspective theoretical description after the fact of data collection. The natural stance of a subject can be framed only in an introspective terminology, whereas experimenters can frame their accounts either introspectively or extraspectively.

But at another level, even the experimenter's experience as a human being conducting research can be understood only intro-spectively. He brings a theoretical point of view to the data-collecting situation, and though the construct he may be putting to test is extraspective, when we look at him as a logically construing human being we *must* perforce assume the introspective perspective to see things as he does. To assume, as many experimenters do, that the subject's conceptions of the experimental purpose (the design, the experimenter's "game plan") are "chance variations," to be cancelled out by another subject's conceptions is pure fiction. A major aspect of the learning going on in all experiments on humans has to do with the informal study being conducted by the subject as to "what this is all about." The logical learning theorist wants to put the experimenter and the subject on an equal footing, as two human beings participating in a human relationship! In doing so, the account of each participant to the relationship will necessarily be framed from an introspective theoretical perspective because this is the only way that logic can ultimately be said to take place. Logic is not an inevitability; it is not fluctuating "out there," as natural laws are supposed to be doing. Logic is something that is brought to bear out of the thinking of a human being. Logic calls for the logician!

## Logical Learning Theory

We next turn to a series of topics relating to logical learning theory. Although of necessity sketchy, the hope is that the reader will find this first formulation of the view stimulating, if not fully instructive.

### Learning as Meaning-Extension and the Nature of Reinforcement

Logical learning theory is founded on the unalterable assumption that human beings are meaning-processing animals. Hence at this point in the presentation we once again give the definition of *meaning* and *meaningfulness* already advanced in Chapter 2 (p. 55), elaborated somewhat by our newer terminology:

*Meaning* refers to the relations between items and their referents as well as to the relations between a user of such meaningful ties and the items he or she employs for the understanding of experience. An *item* can be a verbal language term (letter, word, sentence, etc.) or a purely sensory image (visual, auditory, etc.); its relation to a referent signifies (points to as a purpose) something of import, relevance, or general understanding to the person involved—including conscious and unconscious significations. *Meaningfulness* describes the extent of significance, import, or general understanding that an item has for the individual who intends its purpose. Intended meanings can be grasped conceptually and no more (understanding-intention), acted upon overtly (action-intention), or both.

Meanings are relational ties between items, but logical learning theory insists that such ties are effected not only by chance association, mere repetition, or happenstance. There is a style or strategy in the process of relating one item to a host of others. This notion of meaningful relations, reaching out from one item to make conceptual contact with other items, is captured in the construct of *meaning-extension* (see Spinoza's conception of intelligible extension in Table 1). We have used this term previously without specifically defining it, but now offer the following explanation:

*Meaning-extension* refers to the precedent-sequacious flow of meaning in the conceptualizations of telosponsivity, commonly referred to as the inductive and deductive knowing of experience. Meanings are extended from premises, framed at fixed protopoints which determine what can be known by the individual based on a psychological principle of tautology [introspectively conceived]. As meaning-extension proceeds, the knowledge framed by the premised meanings of telosponsivity extends its range, and through the tautological identity of dialectical oppositionality as well as through analogical variations, it also changes and alters relations between items and referents as the individual comes to know more about the various meanings of his life experience.

Logical learning theory emphasizes the direct, firsthand acquaintance an individual has with the items—both palpable and abstract—of his life experience. To *know* is to have conceptualized—that is, actively to have put some meaning to use in framing experience. Meanings framed at protopoints and the knowledge framed thereby do not remain unchanged, although a remarkable range of knowledge does seem to have this Parmenidean sameness over the course of a lifetime ("The more things change, the more they remain the same!"). Our knowledge of experience need not be "true," in the sense of meeting some independent criterion of "this, and only this, meaning is the correct one to entertain." Knowledge is earned through actively applying meaningful premises; at this point we can speak of learning taking place.

Since the advent of behaviorism learning has been conceptualized as occurring only when there is an alteration of overt performance, which means that some experimentally preconceived criterion of performance has been attained by an animal or human being. Tied closely to this view is the concept of reinforcement in learning theories. Pavlov's (1927) initial terminology suggested that salivatory behaviors were "made conditional upon" the administration of food powder to the animal in an apparatus designed to evoke and measure the extent of salivation. Reinforcement was subsequently wedded to the habit and drive theories such as those of Watson (1924) and Hull (1952), with the assumption being that habitual behavior was made conditional upon the reduction of drives following behavior's elicitation. Even Skinner's alteration of the response concept (see Chapter 6) did nothing to change this idea of a reinforcement as something that is other than the given behavior under observation but leads to an increased probability that this behavior will be seen to occur. As extraspective formulations, these behavioristic positions have therefore managed to deal with reinforcement concepts which have no basis in meaning or meaning-extension. They have managed to do this because of their tendency—discussed in Chapters 5, 6, and 7—to confound their methodological procedures with their theories of learning (resulting in frequency and contiguity principles being used as the major basis for explanation).

Keeping now strictly on the side of theory (as opposed to method), logical learning theory suggests that to learn is to extend meanings conceptually through what in Chapter 7 (p. 291) we called a conceptualization. To conceptualize is actively to organize experience in some way, to meet it at the level of sensation (input) with a creative capacity to order it via patterns that constitute meaning and meaningfulness. A learning trial is not a true trial unless the subject has actively employed that which he is attempting to know or put to memory in some organizing fashion. We can see such organizations emerging in the most simple forms of learning, which are just as often not truly new learnings. That is, we can employ an organizing scheme that we have already learned and then submit other items to this frame as if they were under spontaneous ordering when they are not. Probably the most simple ordering here is to employ a sing-song rhythm as precedent in sequaciously organizing a series of items in so-called rote-memory fashion. There are far more intricate memory schemes, of course, which rely upon previously memorized cue words or even the active construing of materials in what William James (1952) called an "ingenious" (p. 437) fashion and in the more popular vein of "memory strengtheners" can even take on bizarre orderings (see, e.g., Lorayne & Lucas, 1974).

From the viewpoint of logical learning theory, when a precedent scheme of this sort is being used, learning may or may not actually eventuate. That is, the sing-song rhythm or the previously learned memory devices are being tautologized—used identically (one) over many different occasions (many)—but not until the individual actively employs that which can be so memorized in a conceptual fashion would new learning be said to have emerged. Memorizing a list of names through a known conceptual scheme is one thing. Coming to know the people who carry these names and meaningfully endowing them with personal understanding and assessments so that they take on significance in one's life is quite another. We address ourselves to the latter form of (meaningful) learning when we say that learning involves active conceptualization and the attendant meaning-extensions of coming to know anything.

What would a reinforcement be in this view? As with our distinction above between affective assessment and reinforcement value, the position of logical learning theory is that reinforcement is a *methodological* construct. We have had theories of reinforcement, of course, as mentioned above. However, the early efforts in psychology to think of reinforcers as bonding agents, somehow cementing the stimulus and response engrams of the nervous system into a chemical unity, have long since fallen from view, and today one is more likely to see the reinforcement construct being used purely as a description of what goes on in the experimental apparatus. So long as the stimulated reinforcement is seen to manipulate the behavior as designed for in the experiment, no further analysis of the reinforcement theory under use is attempted. There may be an implied acceptance of some neo-Hullian drive-reduction thesis or a Skinnerian empirical law of effect, but the major use an experimenter is making of the reinforcement construct is as a gauge of his experimental manipulation. Behavior that can be seen to alter levels is reinforced behavior. Logical learning theory would define learning and reinforcement as follows:

*Learning* eventuates when through conceptualization a meaning-extension occurs and the individual has more knowledge—that is, an enriched or embellished understanding of the meaning realm initially premised. This knowledge may or may not be "true," as assessed by independent criteria, and it may or may not actually be manifested in overt behavior by the individual learner. Error can be learned! Truth and error are judgments placed upon the learning attained, either by the learner himself or by some other individual, based on some accepted criterion or standard against which what has been learned can be assessed. *Reinforcement* is best thought of as a methodological construct, but theoretically it can relate to the fact that affirmed premises which must then conceptualize meaning actually *do so.* When understanding or action-intentionality is made conditional upon a premise that truly conceptualizes for the individual employing it, we have a reinforcement of this premise. It is likely to be used again and therefore enriched or embellished. Because the premise can entail either positive or negative meanings, the nature of a reinforcement will follow accordingly. Positive reinforcements further meanings that are rooted in positive premises, and negative reinforcements further meanings rooted in negative premises.

Note that we have given a telic interpretation of reinforcement here, essentially equating the phrase *made conditional upon* with *that for the sake of which.* Also, there is a recognition that learning and failing to learn are extraindividual judgments put on a subject's performance in some task situation and that the more accurate truth of the matter could well be that the subject has learned error in seeming not to learn. Based as they are on a demonstrative assumption, the classical learning theories of psychology have always dealt with what *was* learned in behavior—and never with what was *not* learned. Error variance in a methodological test of learning is therefore to be considered the lack of something (control, acquisition, habit formation, etc.). At this point logical learning theory employs its dialectical rationale to suggest that—even acknowledging such things as errors of measurement and fatigue factors in human performance—not all errors reflect a lack of learning on the part of a subject. If a subject can learn to meet the criterion of a teacher or an experimenter, he should also be able to learn *not* to meet it. We do not ordinarily think of such things as misunderstanding directions, failing to follow instructions, or getting the point of a sentence confused as reflecting learning. But just as individuals can reason to unsound albeit "known" conclusions without thereby abandoning logic, so too does logical learning theory contend that they can learn error without abandoning learning (see Nietzsche's notion of the value of *untrue* ideas in Table 1). In fact learning how *not* to learn may be one of the major premises of so-called unmotivated student populations.

It would therefore be wrong for us to conclude that since a premise leading to a successful outcome in actual practice is reinforced (enriched and extended), one that leads to an unsuccessful state of affairs must necessarily be unreinforced (diminished or weakened). If an individual premises a situation as different, strange, impossible, or unknown even if in the abstract he might be capable of doing what is called for, the premise itself can be getting enriched and enlarged (meaning-extension) as the individual does in fact "not know" how to meet the demands of the situation. We could have a case of effective conceptualization through *negative* reinforcement. To consider these failures in performance an instance of nonlearning would be to misconstrue what was taking place from the introspective perspective of the individual learner, even though it met the theoretical understanding of the teacher or experimenter observing the individual perform (refer to our discussion of experimenter-versus-subject-contributed variables). Paraphrasing and enlarging on William James, our theory of reinforcement holds that this is the "cash value" of a premise, paid in positive or negative coin, depending upon the initial investment.

If a subject's premise encompasses meanings that can be considered positive according to *his* (introspective) standards of judgment, the sequaciously flowing reinforcement (effective meaning-extension) will be more likely to be of a positive nature. Negative reinforcements (e.g. criticisms, failures, "bad" outcomes) will not work so effectively in meaning-extension as positive reinforcements. Conversely, if a subject's premises encompass negative meanings (as judged by him), meaning-extension (reinforcements) of a positive type (e.g., compliments, successes, "good" outcomes) will be less likely to affect his performance in the meaning realm defined by those premises. What does "no reinforcement" amount to on this view? This would result when a conceptual profit is not forthcoming. This does not imply that a second-order negative reinforcement need develop through some loss of predictability in the individual's behavior sequence. Certain losses of predictability in this sense can ultimately be elating—for example, when after convincing oneself of the certainty of a serious personal illness, one learns from a physician that all is well.

In such situations the individual will often "not hear" the good news or fail to understand precisely what this entails in his case. Sometimes the patient even feels that the doctor is not telling him the truth. The meaning-extension along a positive line here proves difficult, but once it "sinks in," a changed conceptualization of the future occurs and the patient becomes more open to positive reinforcements as his mood swings upward. This dramatizes our belief that in circumstances where a premise no longer leads to either positive or negative reinforcement in line with the meaning precedently framed, a new conceptualization is likely to take place. This different conceptualization is carried out abruptly (the Kierkegaardian leap) at the *precedent* side of the precedent-sequacious ordering of experience, and a new round of meaning-extension with the attendant reinforcements is then made possible. Logical learning theory holds that reinforcement always follows sequaciously from some precedent *affective* assessment.

## Affective Assessment in Premise Affirmation at the Protopoint

In Chapter 7 we saw how, because meanings in life are often bipolar, the individual must affirm some one protopoint meaning at the outset for the sake of which his behavior will then take place. Affirmation is like taking a position on the meanings of life, which in another sense represents an *ordering* (conceptualization) of experience. Affirming "There is the door," we have precedently arranged the direction to be taken when we leave the room and will sequaciously take this route (action-intention) when the time comes. Affirming "That is an act of cowardice and not an act of bravery," we have precedently taken on several implications concerning the individual whom we believe has acted in a cowardly way. Once again we have ordered our experience. Though we are less likely to see heroism in the behavior of those whom we typify as cowardly, a coward may after all someday do something heroic; there is always the possibility that such a dialectically opposite meaning-extension will take place as a changed conceptualization.

In both instances were we to be asked, we could probably cite the grounds or reasons for our judgments "There is the door" or "That is an act of cowardice." In formal (demonstrative) logic the ideal is to have such grounds well in mind before rendering a judgment—for example, in knowing what a doorway or a cowardly act means. In actual practice, as humanistically oriented psychologists like to point out, people do not always have such clear grounds for their estimates and beliefs. They frequently act impulsively, let their heart not their brain do their thinking, and to that extent behave emotionally. There are surely times in which an ascendant emotion influences our behavior—literally controls our behavior unidirectionally. However, insofar as a true affirmation has taken place, it is based not on emotion but on affection. By a "true" affirmation we mean one in which the position taken, the grounds cited, the alternative selected, could have gone another way. We are back to the issue of arbitrariness in behavior discussed in Chapter 7.

We presume that there is a "two-step" feature in human learning. There is the (1) sensational input which via innate sense organs can be ordered or patterned into images and sounds, and there is the (2) active conceptualization of this input through affirmation. This means that sensory input per se fails to take on significance until the person has used it as a grounds for the sake of the second step —affirmation in conceptualization. The second step is where affective assessment always enters so long as a conceptualization does actually take place. That is, we hold open the possibility that an individual might simply not conceptualize some aspect of his potential experience.

Traditional learning theories have referred to this as "attending to" stimulus input, and usually there has been some discussion here of the motivation involved in such attention, suggestions of an incidental form of learning occurring, and so forth. This view of attention is as a nontelic response, a reaction either directly to the stimulus attended to or due to some other stimulation (e.g., a drive stimulus). Logical learning theory contends that the individual really can attend or not attend—be arbitrary hence telic in his behavior by actually choosing the alternative to be affirmed.

What is frequently meant by emotional reasoning is not involved with the emotions at all, but with the affective assessments of affirmed premises. The individual likes to believe X, so he affirms X and not not-X. Granting X, certain meanings follow and as is so often the case in social situations, we interpret things to meet our so-called self-fulfilling prophecies (in this case the meanings implied in premise X). Another form of emotional reasoning involves the finding of reasons after the fact—that is, after we have already taken a position on some question. This is not always so illogical as it may appear initially. If one is truly under the grip of an emotion, taking premises impulsively might indeed lead to illogical or undesired outcomes. But often in interpersonal behavior and even in abstract problem solutions we sense a "feeling" of the right direction to take even though we cannot justify the grounds on which to do so. We "let ourselves go" and proceed intuitively. Here again, rather than emotive feelings prompting this intuition, logical learning theory suggests that the judgment "This feels the right way" is based exclusively on affection. There is no literal feeling emanating from the body to stimulate such lines of intuition, but the "feeling" referred to is like feeling one's way along a darkened passageway, knowing that although one cannot see everything clearly, he is on the right track. Once at the desired goal we can always retrace our steps and find a more thorough justification for how we got there.

The reader must appreciate the Kantian emphasis of logical learning theory. The affective assessment is *not* "out there" in the stimulation of the environment, but rather "in here," in the assessment of that stimulation at the point where a conceptualization or ordering of experience is taking place in the very act of affective assessment! Because an extraspective observer, looking at the individual making affective assessments, can readily guess that he will prefer ice cream to spinach, it is extremely tempting to see the stipulated preference not in the individual's assessment but in the objects assessed. Logical learning theory is an introspective account of behavior, and there is no small amount of confusion generated when we try to make our thinking clear to such extraspectively oriented theoreticians. Although empirical measures of reinforcement value are fairly simply obtained (see Chapters 9 and 10), the extraspective theoretician cannot fathom how one can be scientifically precise about such "unobservables" as a person's unique judgments *vis à vis* the stimuli that confront him throughout the days and nights of his life.

The role of affective assessment in learning might be likened to a puzzle solution. When we solve a puzzle the problem is one of identifying the pattern that is at first unconceptualized. Once the pattern *is* conceptualized, there is no need for practice to learn it further. We might spend several trials coming to the solution of the puzzle, trials that could have been cut short if someone had told us what the required pattern had to be. This preliminary knowing of a patterned organization is made possible by affective assessment. When the meaning of an upcoming situation is liked, we have in the very assessment at point 2 already solved our life puzzle. We have taken a position, ordered experience, and now *know* by the very act of assessment what we will affectively know in the meanings of the situation as they unfold. We can of course be completely wrong about what we know here, and we can alter our affective assessments of the meanings as events unfold (though this happens more rarely than most people appreciate). But for the present at least, we have identified the pattern for the sake of which meaning will then be most likely to extend. This pattern is not fixed immutably in the efficient-cause substrate of a material reality. It is at least to some extent up to us how things will eventuate in the ever-recurring puzzles of life.

## Active Association in Meaning-Extension

The humanistic psychologist's reference to an *active* role for mind in human behavior frequently prompts the mechanist to exclaim in rebuttal: What can that mean other than the fact that all behavior involves action or motion? As a Lockean, the mechanist does not see the point of calling one view of mind active and a second passive if a principle of association is being employed in both views. But this is what logical learning theory does indeed contend, and we can better understand what is meant here by considering the familiar concept of *association* as employed in psychology. It was adopted from the philosophy of British Associationism as exclusively a question of contiguity and frequency (see David Hume, Table 1; also, Chapter 3). Items that are frequently close together in time become bonded in association and are thereafter seen to occur together. Fundamentally the principle of association has been based on an efficient-cause meaning, as a sort of "hookup" of antecedent-to-consequent which invariably translates into stimulus-to-response (see, e.g., Dollard & Miller, 1950, p. 59). In discussions of meaning the meaningfulness of an item is said to be dependent upon the number of associative ties (frequency thesis) some item has to other items in the "verbal repertoire" of the individual concerned (Underwood & Schulz, 1960, p. 9).

This mechanical—often purely accidental—bonding of one item to another is what humanists consider to be a passive characterization of mental associations. Freud (1960, p. 43) used the concept of association in his therapeutic investigations, but it is totally incorrect to equate his usage with that of the behaviorists. Freud's construct of the mental mechanism was *telic*. Rather than being determined by the frequency or contiguity of this or that input experience, Freudian *psychic* determinism is generated by the telosponsivity of one side of mind which is at all costs seeing that some given purpose (wish) be intended as a form of meaning-extension, even if this extension occurs purely in the symbolical realm (understanding-intention). This is the kind of "action" the humanist wants to capture in speaking of an active intellect.

In an effort to broaden the concept of association in psychology, logical learning theory recommends that we elevate the formal causation that is apparent in all such relational ties and no longer think of this bonding as only occurring across time in antecedent-to-consequent fashion. Associations do not now and never have fortuitously happened through contiguity in human learning. There is always a pattern, a matrix of meaning within which items are brought together. Furthermore not all relations among items can be characterized extraspectively. The concepts of practice and repetition engendered by behavioristic accounts have masked the fact that a subject is not simply "being rehearsed" in the learning context. If learning is a function of practice, we must take a closer look at what is occurring over at the subject's (introspective) perspective in these learning trials. When we take this slant we always find evidence suggesting that the subject who learns is actively bringing to bear on a trial the material we have asked him to learn either as a precedent frame *per se* or as content within some other precedent frame of his preference.

Logical learning theory suggests that there are at least four types of associative bondings that take place in human telosponsivity:

*Unqualified Affirmation:* The case in which an associative bonding between items is unidirectionally related or one end of a bipolarity is universally identified with some other referent—for example, "X is always Y, X means Y, X is the cause of Y."

*Qualified Affirmation:* The case in which an associative bonding is said to occur but without uniformity or universality—for example, "X is some-times Y, X is occasionally related to Y, X in some circumstances causes Y."

*Negative Affirmation:* The case in which an associative bonding is uni-versally denied—for example, "X is never Y, X is unrelated to Y, X never causes Y."

*Oppositional Affirmation:* The case in which an associative bonding is universally related through dialectical contradiction—for example, "X is the reverse of Y, X has a meaning diametrically opposed to Y, X contra-dicts Y."

Though classical Lockean psychology has recognized that "be-haviors" such as negation and qualification occur, the technical explanation used to account for such associations always comes down to underlying, unqualified affirmations. Unqualified affirmation is naturally compatible with the demonstrative outlook, because it reaches for the clarity of unipolarity (X is X), and the direct com-munication of what is rather than what is not, is sometimes or is the opposite of. If we look at the experimental relationship through the eyes of the typical learning psychologist (i.e., introspectively), we are likely to see him using unqualified affirmation as his sole principle of theoretical explanation. Of course he externalizes this affirmative tie through an extraspective theory—that is, the univer-sality of affirmation is put not in mind, but in external events that through the contiguity and frequency principles supposedly move the person's associative processes along as the wind blows the in-tentionless sand across the beach. Yet once we have acknowledged that human beings can bring to bear "associations" of such diverse varieties, the likelihood of mechanizing mentality is greatly dimin-ished.

There are other indications of active intelligence that go unrecog-nized by psychologists, one type of which we would like to point to in closing this section. We refer here to the common request made by a listener for an example of what a speaker is talking about. The student asks the teacher to concretize what he is saying by citing an example. Logical learning theory would view this as a reflection of the sequacious ease with which meaning is extended once a pre-cedent frame is provided for the learner, who then engulfs the ex-ample which is provided in terms of his extant knowledge and goes from there to analogize and disanalogize through our four types of affirmation until he has satisfied his communicant that he un-derstands what the latter is attempting to convey. As this active learning process goes on, the individual can even sense that his conceptualizations are taking hold. He might say, "I am catching on," and if the insights of such conceptualization are especially instructive he might even add, "You have taught me something" or "You have convinced me." If there is no such successful meaning-extension the individual would have failed to learn (in method-talk, fail to have been reinforced). Sometimes this is not the fault of the instructor, of course, because the listener must actively bring his precedents to bear on the topic for meaning to be extended. And, as discussed above, if the affection here is negative, the outcome of the learning may also be negative—that is, not successful (see Chapter 10).

## Possibility, Choice, and Psychic Determinism as "Motivation"

Because premises are affectively assessed and in this same process affirmed at a protopoint, the question naturally arises: How does the person come to change his premises? What are the determining factors of choice at the protopoint? Questions such as these are customarily entertained under the concept of motivation, and they are often followed up with queries such as: How do we get the person to change his premises, as in psychotherapy, education, and behavioral manipulation generally? Many psychologists, taking the *control* of the phrase *to control and predict* as a sanction, actually believe that psychology has a social responsibility to devise ways in which to manipulate the behavior of human beings. Logical learning theory interprets the *control* in *control and prediction* as a purely methodological requirement and *no more.* The only social responsibility to be seen here is to submit one's theoretical formulations to proper empirical test! Of course the more we know about human behavior, the greater is our likelihood of influencing people's actions. But the decision actually to influence in this way is extrascientific, and it can be made by any professional group that has some claim on the power structures of social relations (e.g., political leaders, church officials, etc.). Psychological knowledge is not exclusively for psychologists.

The purpose of logical learning theory is to represent a teleological description of behavior which is sufficiently abstract to subsume other theories of behavior, such as those of Freud, Adler, Jung, Rogers, Binswanger, and Boss (see Rychlak, 1973). Just as Dollard and Miller (1950) were able to subsume Freudian conceptions by Hullian learning theory, so too is logical learning theory capable of subsuming other theories of this lower level of abstraction. We have argued in other contexts that Dollard's and Miller's translations of Freudian theory into S-R theory were inadequate (Rychlak, 1973, pp. 387–390), because they took the basically telic meanings of Freud's outlook and twisted them into purely efficient-cause renderings. Due to space considerations we cannot here show how the above humanistic theories are better served by subsumption under the rubrics of logical learning theory, but we do contend that this is the case. And if this be true, there are already a number of ways in which to conceptualize change in behavior through the classical insight and relationship therapies listed. Even so, we must deal with the questions raised in this section in order that the reader understand the general direction taken by logical learning theory on these matters.

Behavioral motivations are to be seen as precedents—the meanings encompassed as so-called grounds for decisions to act. A ground (basis, reason, etc.) for behavior is simply another way of speaking about the premise(s) employed in telosponsivity. If we turn to a consideration of the classical distinction between motivation and learning, a rather interesting aspect of this dichotomy can be delineated. In describing the behavior of lower animals classical learning theorists like Tolman and Hull (see Chapter 4) were always dealing with a literal existing goal. A rat was placed in a T-maze, and while "under motivation" (or not), had to learn to run to the goal box. Behavior was the instrumental motion an animal manifested to attain the goal, and learning constituted a performance in which this goal attainment was actually achieved. There was no need to speak of motivation in the same breath as learning because what was there to be learned at the goal *was* "there for the learning." The goal box was not and never can be a mere possibility in the behavior of the rat, as something that is encompassed in the rat's anticipations (premises) and keeps him going, though it may actually never be there when he winds his way down the maze. *This* kind of motivation, which must of necessity be thought of as defining the end sought, was never to be encompassed in classical learning theory except by way of weak analogies to the T-maze circumstance. The upshot was that hours of food deprivation as a motivation and goal attainment as learning criterion could be kept separate in the thinking of rigorous psychologists.

But how appropriate is it to speak of human beings as either motivated or not motivated to achieve goals in life, as if such goals literally existed down some maze-run of lived time? Trying to make a business run successfully or to cultivate a successful marriage is anything but a sure thing for the person involved in these activities. As we emphasized in Chapter 7 (p. 287), there is no literal end "there" in the telic behavior of human beings, who premise their ends and then create them as they work toward them or fail to do so. People even work for ends they know to be impossible of attainment, as in the ethical principles of self-actualization (i.e., we never achieve complete self-realization yet work to do the best we can for such perfection).

Logical learning theory considers false the view of human motivation—nurtured as it is by the chimerical, the risky, the "impossible dream"—as something other than and independent of telosponsiveness. Motivation must be seen as implicit in the conceptualization process, contained in the very premise being affirmed by the individual as he moves toward the ever-recurring future of his life. Motivations are shot through with possibilities, which can be thought of as premised goals that are affirmed tentatively (via qualified affirmation), difficult to conceptualize, or exaggerated in their alternative quality from the more usual goals affirmed. We employ the term goal here, but recognize in this usage simply the idea of an end, a "that for the sake of which" reason which is affirmed at the protopoint. We do not contend that all goals exist independently of the motives that prompt them or that motives (drives, impulses, etc.) are what generate the actions in the organism making the attainment of independently existing goals possible. As a clarification of logical learning theory's position on motivation, we offer the following definition:

Motivation: An evaluation or estimation of the relative advantage that a premise (encompassing an intended goal) makes possible in life, leveled by the person affirming this premise or by an observer who presumes to know what is being intended. To understand a specific motive (premised advantage) one must know the meanings encompassed in the affirmed premise (predication), how these relate to other people, what the person has affectively assessed in the circumstance, and so on. Advantages for one person in life often hurt other people, and the individual can even consider self-destruction an advantage in some instances. Motivations vary in extent of awareness concerning the person involved. Only a telic animal can be cognizant of motivation in behavior.

We are prompted to speak of our motives in life because of the many possibilities that constantly arise in our experience. The very openness to alternatives in living induces us to affirm a habitual course of behavior (see our related discussion on organic evolution and dialectical reasoning, Chapter 7, pp. 304–305). Having to select among the open possibilities of the future is unsettling so we are "motivated" from the very nature of our dialectical mentality to seek that fixedness of routine termed habit, which itself gives us a certain advantage over the chaos of disorder. A *choice* is an intrusion on this regularity, the necessity of having to take into consideration some break in the pattern of our behavior. Another way of putting this is that the possibilities of existence surface and we must affirm one alternative over another, and naturally wish to maximize our advantage in this affirmation. We are free to see a movie film this evening; now, which one shall it be? When we have settled on one possibility over the other(s), we refer to this as a *decision*, which comes down to an unqualified affirmation of the course of behavior we will follow (often with "second thoughts," to be sure).

Certain behaviors may be engaged in based on an affective assessment to which no verbal justification can be given. We behave and then find the reasons for our behavior afterward. This is not a strike against teleological theory. When choices and decisions are discussed we often put things in an intellectualized either-or phrasing whereby the alternatives are rationally circumscribed. We speak of the choice between movie A and movie B, as if this decision were made solely on the basis of the meaningfulness of the verbally describable content of these films. The person is construed as a kind of cybernetic machine, weighing alternatives. But logical learning theory does not view all choices and affirmed decisions in this light, because the point of affective assessment is to suggest that human beings are often moved by telic evaluations of a sort that are not expressible except in the personal statement, "I just *want* to do this!" or "I do this because it suits me" or "I like doing this." An organism that behaves this way is still a telic organism.

William James (1952, p. 381) properly recognized that purpose and interest are related questions. Every affirmation of the purpose of a concept encompasses the interest we have in this item at the time. In many cases we can stipulate the interest an item holds for us—for example, when we ask that the butter be passed to coat our waiting slice of bread. Yet on other occasions we cannot put our interest value clearly into words, except to say that our preference is to do this or that thing at the time. Our grounds are purely affective assessments, but as telosponses these still reflect a telic line of behavior. There is a logic in affection, a judgment rendered, and behavior that flows thereby is being sequaciously determined for the sake of this precedent affective assessment encompassing the interest of the individual in that which is unfolding and being carried forward.

The image mechanists seem to have of the teleologist is that of a highly idealistic person, one who is overly trusting of rational intelligence and committed to the view that the person is always free to choose spontaneously the course his behavior is to take. Yet, as our discussion of the relationship between freedom and determinism made clear (see Chapter 7, pp. 307–310), there is no need for a telic theory to hold that all people can choose freely to behave spontaneously in *every* circumstance. We must never forget that the determinism of final causation can be just as rigidly determinate as the determinism of efficient causation. When a decision is made, or put in terms of affective assessment, when a telosponsive affirmation of either a positive or negative quality is rendered, there is *no turning back.*

We cannot always intend away "intellectually" a premise that we have affirmed affectionately. We construe the situation facing us negatively, and no amount of self-reproach or coaxing by others can get us to "change our minds" about the likely outcome. This is what we find taking place in so-called psychic determinism (Chapter 6) as well as in the realm of attitude and prejudice formation (Rokeach, 1973). Such biases are usually said to be based on emotion (emotional reasoning), which would make them an efficient-cause determinism. However, logical learning theory contends that it is affective assessment, an arbitrary action *before* being rendered, which fixes the immutability of such conceptual meanings in the course of behavior *after* it has been made. This final-cause determinism is basic to all human behavior, accounting for much of what we call the predictability of behavior.

How then can we "get people to change?" Logical learning theory leaves it up to them, but however they may be said to do so, the mental process will follow the Kierkegaardian leap (Chapter 7). Only through a reordering, reconstruing, reconceptualization, and so forth, which includes an affective reassessment of the meanings to be extended can the individual be said to change his behavior. Alter the precedent meanings (which includes affection), and the sequacious meaning-extensions will take care of themselves. The adage that "time heals all wounds" is a reflection of how altering circumstances can sometimes do this redefining for one. An extended vacation can aid in this reconceptualization. As to psychotherapy, logical learning theory views this as a means through which the individual learns explicit rules of thumb to follow in dealing with a symptom, models the behavior of an affectively positive therapist, or acquires a doctrinaire redefinition of who he or she is as a person. In this connection we must not forget the role of self-conceptualization in psychotherapy (see below). Unsuccessful therapy eventuates when the client's affective assessments of the relationship or the personality theory being used to characterize him are not conducive to learning. Also, emotional promptings enter in to confound the outcome of many therapy series (see Rychlak, 1973).

## Some Classical Learning Terminology as Viewed by Logical Learning Theory

In this section we sample a handful of terms taken from the classical behaviorist and gestalt learning theories, giving the interpretation logical learning theory would have of them. The concepts of operant (p. 259), reinforcement (p. 327), motivation (p. 337), association (p. 333), and habit (p. 338) have essentially already been given such translations.

*Repetition, Practice, and Similar Terms.* Most behaviorists have assumed that repetition permits the behaving organism to *acquire* learnable materials, usually framed as a new habit formation. Logical learning theory, however, views repetition in terms of the subject's effort to *retain* and extend that which he already possesses. Each trial is an opportunity to bring to bear the already known in order to know further that which is being confronted. Viewed introspectively, repetition is always a continuation, and because the learning criterion is fixed by the experimenter in the nature of the task put to the subject, whether merely one trial (Guthrie, 1952) or several are necessary to accomplish the task makes no difference. At the point when the subject's precedent conceptualization either begins to or does frame-in the task completely, we have learning occurring. Ordinarily the more clear-cut the patterning of the task, the easier is such learning reconceptualized on subsequent occasions; thus a puzzle-solution, whether found in one or several trials, is more easily remembered than a rote task or some less structured task.

*Trial and Error.* Logical learning theory interprets this introspectively to mean "do something else this time," an inclination the individual may or may not verbalize but is due to his dialectical reasoning capacities. The telosponse here is to behave for the sake of "something else," and these alternatives always begin in the poles of construct opposition. Continuing with our view of repetition, trial and error as practice is what allows such alternatives to take place, even serendipitously.

*Generalization.* Principles of generalization have been analogized to humans from work on lower animals, in which behavioral responses are extraspectively described as being learned more or less probably to a dimension of stimulation, or stimulations are attached more or less probably to a dimension of responsivity. In this formulation the spread of behavior can always take place automatically, so long as a reinforcing bonding nurtures the generalization along. The behaving organism does not generalize its behavior. Logical learning theory views generalization as a reflection of the principle of tautology in behavior, with the conservative function of mind manifest in this tendency to bring behaviors forward by direct or analogical meaning-extensions across more and more of life's situations.

*Discrimination.* The principle of discrimination has been used as the obverse of generalization; it also relates to repetition, for the assumption here is that because of repeated trials, a better perception of the stimulus or response is obtained, or depending upon the distribution of reinforcements (frequency thesis), a differential responsivity is established (in time) between two stimuli or two responses. This demonstrative formulation makes discrimination appear to be a linear phenomenon, occurring as generalizations along a unidirectional dimension of difference. Logical learning theory has it that discrimination—as the seeing of differences in events—is best understood in a dialectical either-or framework. Indeed, although not true dialectical reasoning, this is why the logic of the computing machine is binary. Human reason can greatly multiply and contort this either-or divisiveness and even make discriminations in events when objective evidence would suggest that none exists.

*Law of Effect.* Thorndike (1898) made the consequences of an act appear to be somehow independent of the intentions that might have preceded this act. In looking at behavior exclusively through the extraspective perspective we can usually convince ourselves of the legitimacy of such independence. However, in logical learning theory the point is stressed that all consequences as projected possibilities are contained in the premise at the outset. Any "effects" to be seen in the course of events as a result of such behavior are therefore directly related to the premise as framed. The reformulation of the law of effect by Thorndike clearly supports logical learning theory, for though positive consequences are likely to stamp in habits, negative consequences *do not* always stamp them out. An even more dramatic alteration of the so-called law of habit formation—which was based on the law of effect—was Dunlap's (1928) discovery that a correct response could be learned by practicing the incorrect response (in this case, practicing one's typing errors). Only if we appreciate the dialectical logic in human behavior can such findings make ready sense in our theories of learning.

*Principle of Contiguity.* This concept has done more than any other to ensure psychology's faith in the role of time on behavior. Items experienced contiguously in time or place (i.e., identical time periods) are associated together more readily than more disparate items. Logical learning theory substitutes the conception of tautology here, insisting on the importance of meaning-extension in both these circumstances. That is, items which follow each other *over time* are not simply being "hooked up" in efficient-cause tandem. They are being patterned as an event or experience by the individual who recalls, "Yes, I remember now. We turned left back there and now we are to follow this road for about a mile and then we will turn right." He might not even recall things explicitly but "feel" (affective assessment) his way forward because he has patterned things in other than purely verbal terms. Similarly, two items experienced immediately together in time are also actively patterned in the telosponsivity of the individual, who readily recalls the totality as, "Oh yes, I remember that vividly because I was just starting my first job when it happened." Logical learning theory discounts the sheer contiguity of such events and emphasizes the obvious formal causation in *both* such incidents.

*Needs, Drives.* Such constructs are subsumed by the role of emotions and affective assessments in behavior. No one can deny the immense importance of those physically based hedonic tones we all sense as emotions, needs, drives, and so on. However, insofar as they take on distinctive meanings (love, desire, respect, retribution, etc.) logical learning theory suggests that they are conceptualized by the individual's mentality rather than delineated by separate physical mechanisms. The very same hedonic equipment may signal two entirely different emotions, depending upon the individual's characterization and affective assessment of these physical promptings.

*Expectancy.* The expectancy or level of aspiration construct is interpreted as a premise by the logical learning theorist. Individuals are assumed to be able to  see possibilities in events and they can therefore project aspirations or intentions in line with this knowledge. As the meaning of telic suggests, the thrust of mind is ever forward, and human beings therefore quite naturally frame expectancies as a reflection of this telosponsivity.

*Transfer.* This is usually defined extraspectively as the facilitative (positive) or inhibitory (negative) effect of an antecedent event on a consequent event (considered across time). Theories of (specific) transfer vary, with generalization entering into several of the explanations (Chaplin & Krawiec, 1960; see Chapter 10, pp. 426–434 for a discussion of nonspecific transfer). Logical learning theory views transfer introspectively, in terms of precedent-sequacious meaning-extension based on tautology. If events can be brought together into identity (tautology) or partial identity (analogy), obviously a previous circumstance can facilitate behavior in a later circumstance. The latter become a patterned continuation of the former.

*Figure and Ground.* The remaining concepts in this section are in the realm of gestalt psychology. Viewed in terms of a logical and not a sensory phenomenology (see Chapter 7, p. 303), figure-ground is simply a manifestation of the precedent-sequacious directional flow of meaning. For example, in the work by Rubin on contour, figural contour was found to serve a one-sided function (Koffka, 1935, pp. 181–184). A figure is a figure at the level of proximal stimulation because the ground properties of one's perception always define it inwardly. Grounds define figures but figures never define grounds. Logical learning theory merely extends this into the realm of mental telosponsivity so that, for example, in affirming the antecedent of an *If. . .then. . .* proposition we *necessarily* determine the conclusion drawn as if we were framing the shape of such a figure through its surrounding ground. This is why we chose the language of precedent meanings and their slavishly compliant (sequacious) extensions.

*Set, Einstellung, Aufgabe.* These gestalt constructs obviously relate to the same issues mentioned above under the expectancy construct. Though they formulated a more introspective theory than the behaviorists, the gestalt psychologists did not capture the element of arbitrariness in thought that logical learning theory does. One is *made* to take on sets based on the organization of his perceptual field—as in Lewin's (1935) demand character conception, for example. And Watt's work on *aufgabe* was typified by a contentlessness, a lack of appreciation for the *meanings* a subject might be dealing in as he approached the task (see Boring's discussion, 1950,

p. 404). Logical learning theory places more emphasis on the arbitrary aspects of set than the gestaltists would have agreed to.

*Closure, Good Shape, Good Continuation, and Pragnanz.* Laws of organization such as closure, good shape, good continuation, and so on are related to the general principle of *pragnanz*, which states that all patternings tend to become as well articulated, homogenous, and simple as possible. The view of logical learning theory here would suggest that through tautology and the continuation of a fixed conceptualization to be seen across repetitions, a simplification and clarification would probably occur in meaning-extension. As a conservative aspect of behavior, mental organization in telosponsivity is oriented to fixing the most stable and well-delineated items of knowledge or perception possible. Affirmation might thus very well take this course of clarifying the pattern in its most stable, hence simple, outlines.

*Isomorphism.* Logical learning theory interprets this construct as something required by the gestalt psychologist to cement his psychological theory to an assumed underlying reality. That is, the gestaltist here tautologizes across the phenomenal and noumenal realms, claiming that the very activities of the electrons in the nervous tissue of the CNS can be said to follow gestalt principles. This is not a proper principle of learning so much as it is an extraspective theory purporting to unite the mental with the physical. As such, it is a daring tautology.

One last point must be added to this limited survey of the directions being taken by logical learning theory. Many of the concepts taken from classical learning theory, such as generalization, discrimination, transfer, practice, and so forth, are strictly speaking, not theoretical but methodological concepts. The close identity of theory and method in classical learning theory has made this appear to be a virtue. But the truth is that there is a greater understanding of these concepts when we are speaking of them in experimental-design terms than when we are speaking of what may actually be taking place in the psychology of the subject under study. The practice has been to consider the concept and neglect the subject. So long as the concept is operationalized, there is no responsibility to consider the subject-contributed variables that may or may not be at play in the experiment. Operational definitions are often weak substitutes for hard and clear thinking. Logical learning theory encourages the psychologist to cultivate his theoretical grasp along with his research expertise and never to let his experimental operations limit his conceptual understanding.

## Developmental Factors in Learning: Norms of Behavior

In recent decades the interest in developmental psychology has increased dramatically. There are many who feel that a theory of learning is static or at least not complete unless its formulations are based on a developmental thesis. Psychologists often claim that rather than speculating on the nature of human learning, what we ought to do is study how people *do* learn over the course of the full life span and then we would know about such things firsthand. A popular champion in recent times has been Jean Piaget, who has studied the development of causal conceptualization in children (1930) as well as several other logical features of human beings (e.g., 1952, 1957). Is this not the proper source from which to learn about learning?

Although plausible at first consideration, what this argument overlooks is that certain precedent (model) assumptions are required to organize the developmental theory propounded just as precedents are required to organize *any* theory. A theory of developmental stages that progress one from another is still a *single* viewpoint and to that extent just as static as a theory of learning which attempts to account for learning without introducing developmental conceptions. There is no magic whereby developmental accounts can circumvent the necessity of presuming via a model that the child's learning is either molded exclusively by environmental input, contingent upon successively maturing biological mechanisms, or as in the case of logical learning theory, due to the active intellect that organizes experience from birth. We can find evidence for each of these views, not to mention combinations of these and others as well. To presume that Piaget's data support *only* Piaget's theory is to commit the empiricist's error (see Chapter 7, p. 274). Our hope that logical learning theory will be capable of subsuming other theories of behavior applies equally well to theories of development. Thus when we take an interest in the way that theorists have theorized about development, there will be a need to analyze the theory constructed in terms of some uniform, heuristic, *non*developmental frame of reference. Precisely here is where logical learning theory can provide the scholar with an alternative to the Lockean formulation.

In presenting logical learning theory, certain speculations about the course of learning over the earliest years of life have been necessary, and thus we might do well to enlarge on a few points. There are noteworthy parallels between logical learning theory and the view of mind held to by William James in his *Principles of Psychology*. Although James (1952) is known for his "stream of thought" (p. 146) ideas and the supposed blooming buzzing confusion of initial experience (p. 318), he also emphasized the "sense of sameness" (p. 299) in conceptualization. Concept-formation, said James (*ibid.*, p. 300), would be impossible without the individual's capacity to see identity in experiences; and he noted that the basis for such principles of identity was at least partially due to the capacity for tautology in human thought (*ibid.*, p. 299). To think of mental concepts as "developing" in some staged or steadily unfolding way was for James an erroneous theory. Developmental advance was always heralded through new conceptualization and not through some kind of development of older conceptions (*ibid.*, pp. 302–303). If we now add to this the Kierkegaardian view of change (refer to Chapter 7, p. 282), logical learning theory's conception of development would be fairly well cricumscribed.

That is, insofar as stages of development can be seen in the conceptual maturation of the child and adult, they would be seen as sequaciously following from the altered premises that growing experience makes possible; and these stages would occur abruptly, as developmental quantum leaps. At the outset of life the infant is probably in a conceptual state of understanding, not unlike what H. S. Sullivan (1953, p. 26) called the prototaxic mode (comparable to the Jamesian blooming and buzzing). However, Sullivan's Yankee Lockeanism encouraged him to view the subsequent stages of verbal-meaning development (parataxic and syntaxic) more in a sociocultural input sense than as a manifestation of the active telosponsivity of the child, who must infer and analogize and extend from rudimentary beginnings to encompass the broader ranges of meaning which life can make available (see Rychlak, 1973, Chapter 8).

Logical learning theory would contend that the early years are notoriously sketchy and difficult to recall (reconceptualize) *not* because of some paucity of input. They are poorly recalled by each of us because this is a period of poor grounding—that is, inadequately framed premises for the sake of which meaning can then be extended in that two-step procedure which we take to be learning (see above). The earliest premising is quite primitive, based primarily on the telosponsivity of raw affective assessments. Emotions move the child, and doubtless there is considerable agreement between the tone or mood of an emotion and the affective assessment made of it in the earliest months of life. But as time passes (irrelevant as it is to learning *per se*), the natural opportunity for increased meaning-extension takes place so that not only does knowing increase dramatically, but a certain leeway develops between the evaluations of one's experience engendered by the emotions and the affective assessments made of the emotions. Put another way, the meanings encompassed in telosponsivity gradually rely less on emotionality and more on affective assessment.

Over this course of development the telosponsive mind of the child is ordering experience (endowing it with meaning). Practice in extending meaning involves not only the exposure to items, but also the "second" step of active conceptualization in extending this meaning (which makes for learning). Such practice is more like noticing experience than it is inputting meanings from experience. Returning to a metaphor employed in Chapter 7, if one sits at a window and gazes at some scene outside, so long as there is an intention to see things outside, there is more and more to be noticed even if the scene is unchanging (e.g., in looking at some complex mural painting through a window—one is enriched by the "practice" of looking at it even though there is a fixed pattern of unchanging meaning depicted there). Similarly, with maturation the child can always notice more and enlarge more on what he can know by way of what he already knows.

Most theories of development point to the influence of the environment by way of sociocultural artifacts such as modeling the "normative" behavior of others (whether in a subcultural identity or more generally among the full culture). Logical learning theory stresses the heavy contribution of conformity to premise affirmation, hence learning among humans. The very openness of conceptualization naturally frightens the child into wanting to know from parents and others what *is* the case in life. Children are also negativistic, of course. But there is a kind of miniature reenactment of what we suggest took place in the developing organisms that came to be human beings, as they sensed their dialectical intelligence emerging in the course of organic evolution. Children take on *most* of the premises of their parents, quite by inferential design. The conformity to such premises by the child is generally apparent until the advent of the teen-age years, at which time a new source of so-called influence often emerges in the peer group. Peer influences are dialectical examinations of the "other side" of the meanings then in preferred ascendance among the parental culture (including most often tastes in music, dress, and heterosexual activities, although many other issues arise as well). The onset here is abrupt, as the so-called developing child can change into a "contradictory" teenager overnight.

Logical learning theory interprets the norm construct in terms of an intrinsic rather than an instrumental value system (Rychlak, 1968, p. 146). Lockean theories invariably press an instrumental value conception in accounting for conformity. The suggestion here is that people of all ages conform to norms because these culturally defined actions are rewarded. A person is repetitively open to reinforcements that occur contiguously to certain of his behaviors, and in this instrumental fashion he is molded according to a statistically frequent habitual pattern of behavior in the society—which is then called the norm of behavior for that particular group.

In opposition to this statistical view of the normal, logical learning theory contends that the person needs and seeks the norm, for it acts as a codified premise for the sake of which he behaves. Norms are intrinsically important to the human situation, for they serve as grounding premises providing not only an ordering for the individual—an important motivation in life—but a sense of identity (a special case of the tautology) for a body of people. The total effect here is a great sense of reassurance and certainty in one's affirmations, a structuring of that openness which is experience that begins in childhood and continues throughout life. From the viewpoint of logical learning theory there is no psychological difference between the scientist's seeking of truth and the average layman's seeking of the latest fashion in clothing or food. Both scientist and layman are trying to ground their premises in the most reassuring (convincing, certain, acceptable, etc.) method possible. Societies do not "program" norms into people. People need these norms as they need the protopoint premises that permit them to behave telosponsively. Of course one can find norms of behavior in other than current cultural products—the Bible, for example—and in basing his or her behavior on this more transcendent, intrinsic grounding, stand against certain conformity pressures of the popular moment. But then, the conformity to religious sanctions must be recognized in such "inner directed" (Riesman, 1953) behavior. In any case the empirical findings of a statistical nature merely reflect the facts of normative influence on behavior. They do not tell us what a norm means to the individual and how it actually enters into his behavior.

The final question we might consider in this section is: What has logical learning theory to say of the undoubted physical changes that take place in maturation and have a bearing on behavior. We have already taken the position that organic evolution, which is surely a type of physical development, probably proceeded in a demonstrative (unidirectional non-Kierkegaardian) fashion until such time that a dialectical intelligence emerged. We see nothing inconsistent in accepting this more conventional view of development as a steady progression through periods or stages in the physical realm of maturation. Of course, insofar as the maturational changes that occur influence the person's conceptualization of his life, we can expect these to engage behavior at the protopoint in the customary fashion. Obviously, due to their immature physical stature and limited experience, children have a narrowed range of alternative premises they might entertain compared to the average adult. The physically handicapped person has special problems of premise affirmation, and so on.

As a psychological theory, logical learning theory cannot presume to speak for theories of physical development. The danger is that we permit physical constructs to limit our thinking concerning what any one individual or class of individuals is capable of achieving in life—whether that be gifted versus retarded or male versus female. There is surely ample evidence from the great number of individuals who have perfected themselves in athletic, artistic, and other intellectual attainments which seem to have been beyond their native endowment to convince us that desire and aspiration are an important ingredient in all types of human performance. Logical learning theory holds that desires as needs and drives are telic factors in behavior, encompassed as such in the premises of telosponsivity, *not* in the physical substrate *per se*.

## A Concept of the Self in Human Behavior

We noted above in discussing subject-contributed versus experimenter-contributed variables that a logic calls for the logician. To speak of logical extensions in meaning does not make much sense unless we acknowledge that there is an identity employing these assumptions, inductions, deductions, and conclusions. Thus logical learning theory, like all humanisms, must speak of something called the self.

## The Meaning of Self

The word *self* has Anglo Saxon roots meaning the "same" or "iden-tical;" when we say something is self-induced or self-motivated, we usually imply that the same organism did something today along the lines of what it did yesterday. The action may have varied a bit across time (the many), but there was a recognizable continuity nevertheless (the one). The logical learning theorist believes that psychology has erred in trying to construe selves as total organisms (persons), employing thereby all four of the causal meanings in this description. Very likely this is the heritage of the distinguished psy-chologist Gordon Allport (1937), whose influential trait theory fixed things in the neural substance so that now we feel that a self must also be constituted of something or other. Another problem is that we erroneously believe we must account for the self in efficient-cause terms—which are of course *not* well suited to the description of continuity in events but rather to the change in events.

Mention the term *self* in a conversation among psychologists today and you are likely to prompt questions like: What antecedent factors caused this self to form in the first place? This is frustrating to the self-theorist because one cannot express the meaning of "that which brings to bear an effect" by saying "that which is shaped by antecedent circumstances." Logical learning theory holds that the self is a kind of "logical thrust" from the side of conceptualization which organisms under our observation bring to bear as they "come at" the world in that formal-final-cause sense of the Kantian model. So long as there *are* premised assumptions, biases (Rokeach, 1973), personal constructs (Kelly, 1955), institutionalized paradigms (Kuhn, 1970), and so on, being affirmed by an identity, logical learning theory would argue that they are being expressed by a self. Organisms that bring meaningful premises to bear like this are usefully designated as contributing a self-influence to the course of events, particularly so when they realize that they *are* doing so. With these provisos we can now offer a definition of the self, as follows:

The *self* may be defined as a construct enabling the theorist to con-ceptualize the contribution made to behavior by an organism which brings meaningful premises to bear from a protopoint. *Behavior* in this context is overt action or covert understanding which has been predicated and styled through self-expression. The term *self* captures the impact or "logical weight" of a precedent meaning (premise), conveying sequacious implica-tions, inductions, deductions, and so on, in the act of telosponsivity. To the extent that a behaving organism *does* (1) precedently and arbitrarily formulate meaningful premises at a protopoint for the sake of which it sequaciously behaves, (2) is conscious of doing so (i.e., has self-awareness), and (3) seeks to improve on the advantages gained from the use of such premises—to that extent can it be said to be self-enhancing in behavior or to be promoting self-realization.

We must move beyond point 1 because we have nothing here different from the usual telosponsivity of human behavior. At this point *self* is a concept more for the observer than for the actor. Infants and very young children are probably telosponding at about this level, and not until later do they begin to be aware of a continuity in such actions and seek thereby to gain some advantage (motivation) in furthering their selves (e.g., goals). Note that there is nothing in this definition to suggest that a something exists to be called the self in the sense that an organ called the liver exists. Nor do we contend that the self acts according to principles that are emergent or otherwise mystical and unamenable to description. The self concept is presented as an introspective formulation, reflecting that sense of orientation and *identity* in behavior which mechanists are prone to consider illusory experience (Immergluck, 1964; Lefcourt, 1973). Just as motion (efficient causality) is not required for the successions of logical or mathematical responding to follow, so are the effects of self-implications on behavior free of impetus considerations, drawing their rationale solely from the patterns and intentions of psychic life. These self-induced features of behavior have a *logical impact* on events.

Of course as selves we are cognizant of the passage of time because of our recognition (reconceptualization) of altering patterns. The seasons of the year present us with an altered patterning of the landscape, as does the shifting location of the sun across the skies each day. We order our lives in terms of such time changes, yet not without also retaining a sense of personal identity and hence continuity at the protopoint of our telosponsivity. Logical learning theory views this capacity to know one's self in the continuity across time as a special case of the principle of tautology. Things may change around us, we may grow wrinkled and grey, yet a kernel of self-identity is tautologized across such ravages of time to reassure us that we are the same person as always. Doubtless at some point self-identities are buttressed by group identities. Knowing who one's group is and its goals can be as important as knowing who one's self is; indeed the individual's selfhood can even be lost in the cohesiveness of group identity (see Table 1, Mead's use of the self-construct).

When we speak of the weight of logic in self-expression, we of course mean *both* dialectical and demonstrative logical progressions. Much of what is called the unreliability of traits or self-concepts in predicting across different situations (Mischel, 1968, 1973) stems from the dialectical ability of the individual to press more than simply one premise at the protopoint in any given circumstance. The next time he comes at the same situation or one similar to it, the individual can precedently switch premises (Kierkegaardian leap), and what sequaciously follows appears as a lack of predictability and hence a strike against the integrity of self-theory. The extraspective theorist presumes that what must be identical across situations is the observed behavior and not some premising identity guiding even differential behaviors from circumstance to circumstance. To prove the latter would require a *post hoc* discussion with the subject, and such after-the-fact examination of what we have called above subject-contributed variables strikes the extraspectionist as an inappropriate scientific procedure. But if we can predict from the outset of our study that what subjects do contra the experimental hypotheses can subsequently be rationalized via a well-controlled interview with them following initial data collection, this prediction is in the spirit of validating evidence. We might thus prove that even though unpredictable in some cases the course of behavior is always self-directed (see Bowers, 1973, for some excellent arguments along this and other lines).

Note that a certain level of self-development is implied in the definition at points 2 and 3, because one can have a greater or lesser awareness of one's function as a premising organism. Though this may be related to the question of development discussed above, logical learning theory does not contend that there need be a uniform progression in this development; also, such a progression can reverse itself and the individual can feel more at sea in life than he had previously. Alfred Adler's (1964) conception of the self emphasized the working-toward-a-goal feature that we have incorporated into our definition. This idea of self-enhancement or self-realization has been central to the ethical theories of history. As scientists, we need not let this tie of self to ethics disturb us, because a mentality that becomes aware of its own influence on the course of events should in time consider the likelihood of improving the relative standing it enjoys among changing circumstances, as per our definition of motivation (refer above). Concepts of perfection no doubt stem from this capacity for human beings to see how their aspirations and directed efforts can improve the quality of life. Of course this does not mean that selves must *always* seek the "higher" or more noble aims of life. Whether all people can work to become whole, self-consistent (Lecky, 1969), or congruent (Rogers, 1961) is an open question. Logical learning theory frankly recognizes that improving one's relative standing among an environment full of possible advantages is hardly limited to brotherly-love behaviors. Surely sometimes this self-induction also takes on a truly "selfish" quality, which means the individual intends to injure or otherwise demean a fellow human being.

The reader must appreciate that logical learning theory does not claim that all behavior is self-induced. The nonteleological formulations of a modern functionalist might hold for much of behavior (see Chapter 4). The presumption is that, as we ascend the phylogenetic scale, a greater likelihood for self-induced behavior is the case. This is due to the increasing employment of dialectical reasoning among higher animals. Stimulus-response psychology seems to fit lower organisms reasonably well, with their more demonstrative behavioral patterns. In light of our history concerning the anthropomorphizing of lower animals, to speak of self-induced factors in subhuman behavior seems a bit foolish. But it is not excessive, and we should not be too intimidated by our history to suggest that the self aspects of behavior could extend below the human level—although surely the telosponsivity here would be limited.

## Self-Awareness and Consciousness

The historical search Descartes (1952) made to find the grounds on the basis of which to believe in his own existence is well known. After dismissing various other justifications, he arrived at the famous presumption "I think, therefore I am" (*Cogito ergo sum*). As a mathematician, Descartes' attitude toward the dialectic was very negative (*ibid.*, p. 17), and hence it is not surprising to see that his framing of a self-evident belief in his personal existence was demonstratively phrased. That is, although there is the suggestion here of transcendence in the self-reflexivity of knowing that one thinks, the emphasis is still exclusively on the act of thinking and not on the multiplicity of things that might be thought about *at the same time*. Consequently, as critics have long noted, the precedent meaning encompassing "I think" sequaciously implies that *thinking* exists more clearly than that "I" exist. One might as well say, "I breathe, therefore I exist." Even as a mediating animal, man could be made aware through some form of serendipitous input that his thinking capacity existed without thereby implying that a self-identity in control of this process *also* existed.

However, had Descartes argued dialectically "I think, and realize that I could be thinking quite the reverse many times over, therefore *I* exist" he would have put a more convincing case. In this phrasing the emphasis is taken off thinking *per se* and is placed on the duality of thought management dependent upon the "I." We have argued that a true free will is born in this arbitrary capacity to see alternative assumptions and implications in events. It is the logical weight of a self that chooses (decides, opts, etc.) to affirm "this" alternative rather than "that" alternative—or that has this option in principle—that makes a teleology possible in human behavior. Reasons are then sometimes found after the fact of deciding which direction thought is to take, although as we suggest above, this does not mean a teleology is lost. Here is where affective assessment enters. We could in this case say, "I affectively assess the meaning confronting me positively and realize that I could be assessing it negatively, therefore *I* exist." The affective assessment and the "feeling tone" [sic] this affords acts as a freely willed reason (grounds) for the behavior.

In line with our evolutionary speculations of Chapter 7 (pp. 304–305), we might define *awareness* psychologically as "appreciation of the arbitrariness in experience" or "knowing that something else might be taking place in a life circumstance" (see Table 1, Ducasse's definition of freedom). Simply registering inputs as stimuli and behaving in relation to these promptings does not mean that the animal is aware of its circumstances. Perception is not enough for awareness. To have a grasp of what is taking place demands a broader frame of reference, within which we see not only that which stands before us as reality but (at least some of) the possibilities and likelihoods not yet "there" for perceptual delineation. Telic animals are aware animals because they are constantly looking forward to such nonliteral aspects of experience. And of course even a potentially telic animal is unaware when he cannot organize the developing and unfolding possibilities of a situation in which he finds himself. But through a dialectical intelligence awareness is born.

The consciousness construct has been difficult to agree on in psychology because of a tendency to lump together simple responsivity and awareness into a common designation. If an animal is not asleep and therefore is responsive to external stimulation, it is considered by many to be conscious. There can be no great quarrel with the utility of this description because surely animals reflect altered states of vigilance and responsivity, and therefore a conscious-unconscious distinction seems plausible. However, due to the demonstrative bifurcation (i.e., acceptance of the law of contradiction) this led to, it became theoretically impossible to have these two states in any way *identical* (one among the many). Unconsciousness was now considered a *lack* of consciousness, and an animal was either in one or the other of these two states, but never in both at the same time.

Logical learning theory does not suggest that awareness is something limited to the self. One might be made aware of alternatives in life that have no focal point on selfhood. The person who looks to the skies and sees sunshine but considers the likelihood of rain based on subtle cues in the clouds rimming the horizon is reflecting an awareness, though the point of this is not selfhood. Whether aware or unaware, a person may be functioning consciously; even when aware of certain things, the individual may be unaware of his *self*-contribution in events. Unawareness of this type does not by itself necessarily signify unconsciousness. So long as a person is taking on premises and behaving for the sake of these predications he would be manifesting what our definition would call a self—that is, the weight of logic in a self-induced line of meaning-extension. But note: The definition has this framed as a construct for the utility of the observer. It says nothing about the self literally existing at the point of such telosponsivity in the behavior of others. For the person to develop a self-concept or self-awareness, he must see the contributions he *makes to* experience, depending upon what sort of meanings are affirmed at the protopoint. In this sense the self must be *intended*—that is, the purposive meaning of *self* must be brought to life by the individual, who cultivates it and furthers it *or not*. Not every conscious being has a high level of self-cultivation.

The more self-awareness an individual has, the more likely is he to appear conscious of his environment. People with so-called strong personalities, who are in command of their faculties, are of this type. They might also be self-centered and even selfish. But consciousness in the sense of vigilance and responsivity is not determined by self-awareness *per se*. We can be conscious without having a high level of self-awareness, and the problem of unconsciousness is therefore a separate issue.

## Self-Control, Awareness, and Unconsciousness

We have been arguing for an image of humanity in which there is a self-contributed factor acknowledged in the course of any human behavior. In one sense there is almost no disputing this fact. Even

the behaviorists today like to speak of self-control, by which they
mean something akin to a Skinnerian view of environments that
have been manipulated by persons and in turn control these very
same persons. Here is a fine example of this kind of statement, one
that shows the typical mediation gambit and theory-method confound as well: "Self-control is exhibited when a person engages in
a behavior whose previous probability has been less than that of
alternatively available responses. . . . Self-control patterns are usually mediated by symbolic processes and ultimately maintained by
external variables" (Thoreson & Mahoney, 1974, p. 22). The person
is ultimately controlled by independent variables in the external
environment, but he is under self-control insofar as he is aware of
these variables (sic) and arranges them to control himself. There is
no point in repeating our Chapter 7 discussion (pp. 307–310) except
to note that in logical learning theory when we speak of self-control
we mean self-control. If a self is in control, the ultimate role for
external factors (not variables) is as encompassed in the premise
which the self conceptualizes, affirms, and telosponds in terms of.
There is nothing in the research literature to counter such an interpretation of human behavior.

Can we telospond at two or more levels in mind? Can there be
unconscious selves that direct the behavior of an individual from
outside of self-awareness as most of the classical personality theories have contended? We have already taken a position on this in
Chapter 7: dream symbols and themes (p. 289) as well as the dialectical opposite of affirmed meanings (p. 296) can be thought of as potentially exerting an influence on our behavior. However, because the
definition of self given above emphasizes the eventual development
of self-awareness, we would not refer to such unconscious identities
in the personality as alternate selves. In fact, for an unconscious
affirmation to attain the level of internal consistency and continuity
(identity) that the self demands, would be highly unlikely if not
impossible. Almost by definition the "other side" of conscious affirmations or the working to consciousness of visual analogues (symbols) in dreams would have to be lacking in that alternativeness that
we have said is characteristic of awareness. The telosponsivity of
unconsciousness is therefore a kind of mirror-image of conscious
affirmation. In the unconscious state we have lost the general awareness of conscious mental states as well as the self-awareness within
consciousness.

Of course the meanings thus telosponded in unconsciousness
can germinate and order into story lines and clearly intentional

manifestations of some "hidden" premise which consciousness may have considered and discarded or never have considered at all. It is hidden because the meaning precedently affirmed in unconscious telosponsivity cannot be sequaciously enriched by consciousness any more than what person A thinks can be sequaciously enriched by person B. Not until B takes on the premises of A can this occur, and not until consciousness takes on the premises of unconsciousness can the single person come to understand what meaning is being expressed in his own unconscious mind. It is as if there is an internal semaphore communication being attempted, with the unconscious sphere sending precedent meanings, but the conscious receiving not a sequacious extension of meaning but a flurry of flags, the coding of which has not yet been deciphered by consciousness. Unconscious thoughts are lacking in the quality of awareness, hence they take on a more (hard) deterministic quality. We might say that the unconscious is on the "after affirmation" side of psychic determinism *in every case*—that is, having the quality of determinism following a decision because these contents are always nondecisions, disliked alternatives, and so on, whereas in consciousness we do at times see the "before affirmation" arbitrariness of free will in operation. The unconscious is rigid and unyielding because it is always dealing in post-affirmational materials!

For example, the directing force of hallucinations or delusional systems can be said to take away from self-control in deference to a person's fantasy life. This imaginary material has not always lacked awareness from the outset. Sometimes it can even begin in a self-aware effort to flee the dull routine or the anxiety of an unhappy life. Gradually, however, the person can lose self-awareness—that is, stop conceptualizing his role in the creation of his chimerical fantasies. Sometimes he is in a twilight state on the question, knowing that he had begun all of this "imagined nonsense" but is now losing control over it. To reverse the process and gain self-control involves the cultivation of (1) awareness in consciousness generally and (2) self-awareness in particular. Psychotherapy is aimed at achieving these ends, and even the behavior therapies necessarily devote considerable effort to showing the person how he or she can successfully alter the course of events in daily life. Telling the person that the environment controls his behavior hence he had best look carefully at this environment is surely conducive to both types of awareness. The role of awareness in behavioral manipulation is of primary importance.

Why does mind have such levels of awareness? This question

cannot be answered with assurance, but as a dialectical theory of mentality, logical learning theory would suggest that unconsciousness is a necessary corollary of the affirmation that brings about consciousness. Consciousness telosponds by premising what we think we must do, prefer to do, and so on, and unconsciousness telosponds by premising the reverse—what we must not do, what we "disprefer" to do, and so on. In the same way that we can learn error, mentality can entertain meaning that has *not* been affirmed. That alternatives which were open to behavior and yet not affirmed continue in mind and reappear as viable albeit often troublesome possibilities is probably conducive to survival in the human species. Such unaffirmed alternatives populate our dreams, although quite often what is called a dream is a self-aware affirmation of some wished-for eventuality.[1]

Can there be a direct unconscious affirmation of meaning to parallel the affirmation process that logical learning theory postulates in consciousness? Most of the theoreticians who have accepted the construct of unconsciousness have kept this possibility open, requiring thereby that they have a parallel identity to the self in unconsciousness (e.g., an id, alter-ego, shadow, etc.). Because logical learning theory essentially holds that self-awareness is made possible in the preaffirmation arbitrariness of decision-making, it does not seem consistent to speculate on unconscious identities that supposedly affirm points of view but do not advance self-awareness in so doing. Human beings can always take the opposite position (or an alternative thereby) on *any* question facing them. The unconscious identities that speak out—for example, cases of alternating or multiple personality—invariably show us this clinical picture.

---

[1] Although not suitable for presentation at this point in its speculative development, logical learning theory entertains the possibility that self-awareness may not be limited to consciousness. If we can distinguish between conscious-unconscious as levels of vigilance and responsivity (presumably based on biological factors) *and* conscious-unconscious realms of mental telosponsivity, each with its dialectically arrayed forms of premises readied for affirmation, then what we have termed "awareness in consciousness generally" may simply involve the more reality-bound type of premise—the one likely to be affirmed in the state of vigilance and responsivity (consciousness). Reverse affirmations would then occur in nonvigilant states (unconsciousness) and the self-identity would have altered levels of awareness in the two realms of mentation. In dream states, for example, for the person to ascertain the grounds for the sake of which certain actions are being carried out is difficult but not impossible. Without reality-bound grounds a more bizarre precedent-sequacious line of meaning-extension is enacted. But occasionally one *is* aware that he is having a dream, and to this extent we can appropriately speak of self-awareness.

The emergent personality is dialectically opposite to the original personality, and variations on this theme proceed as new identities multiply. What does this signify? Are these variations on the original personality (i.e., the premises that characterize the original personality) separately affirmed outlooks, or are they dialectically generated developments from the initial conscious affirmation? Logical learning theory takes the latter stance, at least for the present and finds it unfruitful to reify cohesive identities at an unconscious level.

We cannot overestimate the importance logical learning theory places on the human being's capacity to learn that which he does not prefer to learn (i.e., which he has affectively assessed negatively), the learning of error, the processing of information that is unpopular and distasteful even to the self, and so forth. Affirmation at the protopoint is not the end of things but the beginning. Affirmation tells us what direction will be taken (psychic determinism), but awareness demands that the nonaffirmed be known as well. Possibly this is the reason for unconscious behavior (understanding- and action-intentions) emerging. The burden of knowing all that is possible to know, such as the not to be, the unpreferred, the likelihoods but uncertainties, is simply too much for a well-ordered conceptualization to eventuate in conscious thought. Hence certain of these —shall we say too complex, unhappy, defensive, threatening—possibilities are no longer conceptualized, leading to a loss in awareness. Even so, these meanings are not lost to the telosponsivity of mind, and they come back as those one-sided and opinionated views that Jung (1960) called complexes or the undesirable antithetic ideas that Freud (1966) as neophyte theoretician described so well.

## Summary

Chapter 8 begins with a distinction between emotion and affection. Although both are evaluations, emotions are seen as rooted in the body and hence best conceptualized in demonstrative terms. Affections are dialectical, completely psychological assessments. Another way of speaking about affective assessment is as a transcendental telosponse—that is, a telosponse in which the individual turns back on his mental processes and evaluates their content in terms of positiveness or negativeness. Affective assessments are arbitrary before being made, whereas emotions are never arbitrary. The methodological counterpart of affective assessment is reinforcement value, which is an operational measure of likability made by the subject of various materials he may be asked to learn or otherwise deal with. A distinction is then drawn between experimenter-contributed and subject-contributed variables, with reinforcement value said to be a subject-contributed variable that usually is uncontrolled in the typical experimental study.

The next topic considered is that of meaning-extension, which refers to the precedent-sequacious flow of meaning in the conceptualizations of telosponsivity. Learning involves the extension of meanings conceptually, and a reinforcement—although best thought of as a methodological construct—can be viewed as successful meaning-extension. When a premise truly conceptualizes experience for the individual, a reinforcement of this premise may be said to have taken place. There are essentially two steps in learning: (1) sensory input as ordered into images, sounds, and so forth by innate sense organs, and (2) the active conceptualization of this input through affirmation. Logical learning theory holds that affective assessment always enters at the second step of this sequence, assuming that the conceptual act does in fact occur.

To bring home the importance of active intellect on behavior, we next introduce a refinement in the concept of association by noting that there are four types of affirmations involved in the association of ideas. These include unqualified, qualified, negative, and oppositional affirmations. We show how a simplistic view of association makes every such bonding of meaningful items in experience an unqualified affirmation when in fact the associative powers of human mentality are not this limited. The problem of motivation, as it relates to the concepts of possibility, choice, and psychic determinism, is discussed. Motivation is defined as an evaluation of the relative advantage a premise affords the individual affirming it. Logical learning theory rejects the classical distinction between learning and motivation. Motivations are always encompassed in the individual's premises, which in turn enter into learning; these are different aspects of the same process and cannot be separated except artificially for the purposes of descriptive analysis.

Classical learning-theory terminology is surveyed, reinterpreting these by way of the rubrics of logical learning theory. Constructs such as trial and error, generalization, discrimination, law of effect, expectancy, figure-ground, and isomorphism are discussed. A major feature of this reinterpretation is evident in that logical learning theory places an introspective theoretical perspective into each of these classical terms. A discussion about the possible role of development factors in learning follows. Although logical learning theory is not formed developmentally, there are certain implications for its tenets in the developmental concept, and these are reviewed. The role of norms on behavior is analyzed in terms of intrinsic versus instrumental value theories. Logical learning theory looks at norms in terms of an intrinsic theory of value.

The final major division of Chapter 8 takes up the question of self-identity in human behavior. The self is defined as a construct enabling the theorist to conceptualize the contribution made to human behavior via a "logical weight" brought to bear on events, one that takes on a continuity and a conscious self-enhancing direction (i.e., seeks advantages) in the flow of life experience. This logical weight involves both dialectical and demonstrative implications, deductions, assumptions, and so forth, brought forward from proto-points and encompassed as premises. Awareness is defined as the appreciation of arbitrariness in experience, and the self-aware individual is said to be the one who knows that he could be thinking (hence doing) otherwise in life, but does as he does for the sake of certain reasons. The closing themes of Chapter 8 include the question of consciousness versus unconsciousness, how this relates to self-awareness, and the role of such factors in self-control.

## References

Adler, A. Social interest: A challenge to mankind. New York: Capricorn, 1964.

Allport, G. W. Personality: A psychological interpretation. New York: Holt, 1937.

Arnold, M. B. Emotion and personality. New York: Columbia University Press, 1960.

Arnold, M. B. (Ed.), Feelings and emotions. New York: Academic, 1970.

Boring, E. G. A history of experimental psychology. New York: Appleton-Century-Crofts, 1950.

Bowers, K. S. Situationism in psychology: An analysis and a critique. Psychological Review, 1973, 80, 307–336.

Brentano, F. Psychology from an empirical standpoint. New York: Humanities, 1973.

Chaplin, J. P., & Krawiec, T. S. Systems and theories of psychology. New York: Holt, Rinehart & Winston, 1960.

Descartes, R. Rules for the direction of mind and Discourse on method. In R. M. Hutchins (Ed.), Great books of the western world (Vol. 31). Chicago: Encyclopedia Britannica, 1952.

Dollard, J., & Miller, N. E. Personality and psychotherapy: An analysis in terms of learning, thinking, and culture. New York: McGraw-Hill, 1950.

Dunlap, K. A revision of the fundamental law of habit formation. *Science*, 1928, **67**, 360–362.

Freud, S. *The psychopathology of everyday life*. In J. Strachey (Ed.), *The standard edition of the complete psychological works of Sigmund Freud*. (Vol. VI). London: Hogarth, 1960.

Freud, S. A case of successful treatment by hypnotism. In J. Strachey (Ed.), *The standard edition of the complete psychological works of Sigmund Freud* (Vol. I). London: Hogarth, 1966. Pp. 115–128.

Guthrie, E. R. *The psychology of learning* (rev. ed.). New York: Harper, 1952.

Hull, C. L. *A behavior system*. New Haven: Yale University Press, 1952.

Immergluck, L. Determinism-freedom in contemporary psychology: An ancient problem revisited. *American Psychologist*, 1964, **19**, 270–281.

James, W. *The principles of psychology*. In R. M. Hutchins (Ed.), *Great books of the western world* (Vol. 53). Chicago: Encyclopedia Britannica, 1952.

Jung, C. G. *The structure and dynamics of the psyche*. In H. Read, M. Fordham, and G. Adler (Eds.), *The collected works of C. G. Jung* (Vol. 8). Bollingen Series XX.8. New York: Pantheon, 1960.

Kant, I. *The critique of pure reason*. In R. M. Hutchins (Ed.), *Great books of the western world* (Vol. 42). Chicago: Encyclopedia Britannica, 1952. Pp. 1–250.

Kelly, G. A. *The psychology of personal constructs* (2 vols.). New York: Norton, 1955.

Koffka, K. *Principles of gestalt psychology*. New York: Harcourt, Brace, 1935.

Kuhn, T. S. *The structure of scientific revolutions* (2nd ed.). Chicago: The University of Chicago Press, 1970. (1st ed., 1962.)

Lecky, P. *Self-consistency: A theory of personality*. Garden City, N.Y.: Doubleday, 1969.

Lefcourt, H. M. The function of the illusions of control and freedom. *American Psychologist*, 1973, **28**, 417–425.

Lewin, K. *A dynamic theory of personality*. New York: McGraw-Hill, 1935.

Lorayne, H., & Lucas, J. *The memory book*. New York: Ballantine, 1974.

Mischel, W. *Personality and assessment*. New York: Wiley, 1968.

Mischel, W. Toward a cognitive social learning reconceptualization of personality. *Psychological Review*, 1973, **80**, 252–283.

Murphy, G. *Personality: A biosocial approach to origins and structure*. New York: Harper, 1947.

Orne, M. T. On the social psychology of the psychological experiment: With particular reference to demand characteristics and their implications. *American Psychologist*, 1962, **17**, 776–783.

Pavlov, I. P. *Conditioned reflexes: An investigation of the physiological activity of the cerebral cortex* (trans. by G. V. Anrep). New York: Oxford University Press, 1927.

Piaget, J. *The child's conception of physical causality*. London: Kegan Paul, Trench, Trubner, 1930.

Piaget, J. *The child's conception of number*. London: Routledge & Kegan Paul, 1952.

Piaget, J. *Logic and psychology*. New York: Basic Books, 1957.

Riesman, D. The lonely crowd. Garden City, N.Y.: Doubleday, 1953.

Rogers, C. R. On becoming a person: A therapist's view of psychotherapy. Boston: Houghton Mifflin, 1961.

Rokeach, M. The nature of human values. New York: Free Press, 1973.

Rosenthal, R. Experimenter effects in behavioral research. New York: Appleton-Century-Crofts, 1966.

Rychlak, J. F. A philosophy of science for personality theory. Boston: Houghton Mifflin, 1968.

Rychlak, J. F. Introduction to personality and psychotherapy. Boston: Houghton Mifflin, 1973.

Sullivan, H. S. The interpersonal theory of psychiatry. New York: W. W. Norton & Co., Inc., 1953.

Thoreson, C. E., & Mahoney, M. J. Behavioral self-control. New York: Holt, Rinehart and Winston, 1974.

Thorndike, E. L. Animal intelligence: An experimental study of the associative processes in animals. Psychological Review Monograph Supplement, 1898, No. 8.

Titchener, E. B. A text-book of psychology. New York: Macmillan, 1909.

Underwood, B. J., & Schulz, R. W. Meaningfulness and verbal learning. Chicago: Lippincott, 1960.

Watson, J. B. Behaviorism. New York: Norton, 1924.

Wundt, W. Lectures on human and animal psychology (4th ed.). New York: Macmillan, 1907. (1st ed., 1894.)

# CHAPTER NINE

## Case History of a Revolutionary Effort in Psychology: Basic Conceptual Matters

We have argued that a scientific revolution always takes place in theory and not in method. Of course if an advance in technology occurs and some new apparatus enables a scientist to do new things in his field of interest, the rapid advance of theory that flows from this entirely mechanical innovation can be called revolutionary. The telescope advanced astronomy and the microscope was of immense technical importance in the development of the biological sciences. There is a reciprocal relationship between theory and method so that advances on one front naturally call up advances on the other. Things such as telescopes and microscopes are, strictly speaking, advances in *design* rather than advances (or changes) in methodology, because the strategy of obtaining research evidence—the methodological steps—never changes even as new equipment is employed in garnering it. In psychology we occasionally see a new test instrument, as the F-scale (Adorno, Frenkel-Brunswik, Levinson, & Sanford, 1950) or the Manifest Anxiety Scale (Taylor, 1953) dominate our research efforts for a decade. Due in large measure to the underlying Lockeanism to be found in the thinking of test constructors, neither of these instruments brought about a noticeable change in the predominant paradigm of psychological science (though surely the authoritarian-personality group made a valiant effort in this direction).

What seems to be a revolutionary development in some research strategy is often no more than a new data-collecting gimmick, one that is made popular by the ease it affords the user to delineate problems and obtain the samples to test his hypotheses. Rather than confronting the inconsistencies of the predominant Lockean para-

digm in the sense of a Kuhnian anomaly, such gimmickry furthers
its ascendance by treating all such problems as puzzles which
Lockeanism can eventually solve, if everyone does his job of data
collection properly and stops all of the carping about the inappro-
priateness of the basic outlook under test. Since problems are presumed to exist "out there" in the "empirical facts," the prevailing
view in psychology is that new devices, new designs, technological
equipment (often borrowed from other sciences), and so forth carry
the hope of revolutionary advance because only through such
changes can we—quite literally—"find the answers."

The position advanced here is that it makes no difference what
methodological design or technical innovation is employed. If we
want to find teleological factors in behavior, we must begin with
the assumption that they are (or are possibly) at play in these patterned regularities and then predict where we expect them to surface in a controlled context. We can therefore take the most out-
dated, primitive, unrevolutionary research equipment available and
demonstrate the role of humanistic factors in how a subject accom-
plishes the negotiation he is asked to engage in with a fellow human
being (the experimenter). If one looks only at the efficient-cause
steps of a mechanical process the likelihood of finding formal- and
final-cause determinism in the sequence of predicted outcomes is
foredoomed "by definition." But if one approaches the experimental
situation as a negotiation between equally conceptualizing organisms, exchanging their views and preferred actions in light of
sequentially ordered hence seemingly mechanical steps, the effects
of such conceptualization—both the experimenter's and the subject's—should become apparent.

Everyone readily admits that experimenters conceptualize in
doing the business of science.That is, they employ statistical assumptions, formulate experimental hypotheses, and evaluate the outcomes
of a predetermined (by them) ordering of events by putting such
possibilities to predictive test in relation to an arbitrary standard of
validity. But the man in the apparatus is rarely given such conceptualizing prerogatives. The control in his case is not formal-final but
efficient because he is literally "methodologized" into a mechanical
sequence of events in the name of proper science. Should anyone
now call for a "new look" at these old research designs in terms of
a telic prediction, the feeling is that some form of distortion is
underway. Even those who applaud telic description sometimes
believe that it is wrong if not impossible to find a humanism in the
"lab methods" (designs) of traditional psychology. Facing this tech-

nical impasse, the only alternative for a sagacious humanist is to forge ahead in any case and see what he might come up with. Can he really invade the mechanist's home ground and stake out a claim on the basis of which a fair and open paradigmatic battle might then be waged?

Logical learning theory (LLT) holds that for the humanistic critic of modern psychology to delineate the historical and philosophical roots of mechanism in this scientific enterprise is not enough. He must point to an alternative course and take some of the first steps in this new direction as example to others. If the new path proves instructive, in time it will be trod by others. Hence, as an alternative to Lockeanism in psychology, LLT has consistently worked to demonstrate in empirical actuality what the intellectualized arguments of this volume say is true. If the thinking cannot be translated into research methods, LLT is nothing more than another reactionary discourse on the displeasures of a minority in psychology. But if we can make the thinking "work" in overt contexts of data collection, the broader community of psychology must in time give us the recognition our polemic deserves.

Thus, in Chapter 9 we begin a "case-history" account of the researches conducted on one aspect of LLT—*affective assessment* (theory) and its operationalized measure, *reinforcement value* (method). We continue this case history in Chapter 10, showing how LLT has applied affective assessment to various aspects of human behavior. Logical learning theory did not emerge as a totality first, with the research series following through on formal implications by way of deductions from known principles. Science rarely—we think never—proceeds quite this orderly. Only Kuhnian "normal science" can happen when scientists work from completely known propositions, deducing so-called theorems from them to be put to the test of falsification and so on. But the totality of science is a patchy business. It works by fits and starts, through steps and re-steps, not to mention the serendipitous and the frankly lucky occurrence.

However, if one is working along empirically, construing data from a different perspective than his colleagues, he always senses the total validity of his outlook so long as it continues to organize his observations in an instructive fashion (procedural evidence); further, he knows that in time a terminology will be coined to deal with the details he is only now hazily beginning to bring into conceptual relief. And so it was with LLT. The Kantian-Lockean contrast between how we viewed data and how the majority of our colleagues did was always evident, and over the years in conjunction with empirical investigations, a number of terms were suggested to elucidate and clarify the differences in outlook. What follows now is an overview of the empirical work, which has thus far amounted to approximately 60 data collections. In the interest of space a less detailed description of the experiments and the resultant data will be given than we might have preferred. We will also try to recreate the evolution of LLT as honestly and openly as possible, as befits a case history. At the same time, we will never forget that the *primary reason* for engaging in this research program was to test a single hypothesis: Teleological theory is entirely compatible with research designs that have been initially framed to test non-telic theory.[1]

**The Basic Dimension**

The first study in LLT was conducted in 1959.[2] Trained as a clinical psychologist, the writer was then trying to bring together his Ph.D. education as a research scientist with his experience as a fellow human being engaged in psychotherapy with a series of clients. Having graduated from The Ohio State University a few years earlier, the writer found that the theoretical orientations of Julian B. Rotter (1954) and George A. Kelly (1955)—both of whom taught there—provided an excellent contrast for the theoretical and research effort LLT required. Although he spoke of expectancies and in his clinical work viewed human beings from an introspective perspective, Rotter (the writer's major professor on the Ph.D. degree) was in the final analysis a neo-Hullian mediation theorist (Lockean). Kelly, however, was a thoroughgoing Kantian. Both men had the knack of relating their theories to the methodological context, and they did it so well that we who were fortunate enough to study under them graduated without feeling a sense of incompatibility between our clinical work and the kind of science then being practiced. Once in

---

[1] We assume that the reader is familiar with the earlier chapters of this volume, particularly with Chapters 7 and 8. Technical terms that were covered in these earlier sections will be introduced below without concern for definition or elaboration (see Glossary as well, pp. 499–508). Also, in the interest of space, detailed statistical treatments are not given for data which have been published in psychological journals. All data that have not previously been published are given a more detailed statistical presentation.

[2] Portions of this experiment were supported by Grant M-4777 (A) from the National Institute of Mental Health, United States Public Health Service.

the field, however, an immediate conflict was generated as we confronted individuals who based their image of man on a—what seemed to us—less sophisticated view of the experimental context.

This and earlier volumes (Rychlak, 1968, 1973) trace the writer's philosophical-historical efforts to make sense of the seeming contradiction between viewing a client in therapy or oneself in telic terms even as we "account for" (sic) this kind of behavior in other than telic description when we don our scientific robes. Paralleling these strictly intellectual arguments, a decision was made to conduct a research program in conjunction with the developing teleology. Kelly served as a model here, for in his personal construct theorizing he contended that he would give the research to flow from this view a "10-year try" and then, if it did not prove instructive, he would drop it entirely and try something else. Why not therefore define a telic theoretical construct which could be operationalized into the most unlikely realm of experimentation imaginable, to see if it could be kept alive and prove instructive concerning humanism over a 10-year period?

The area of research turned to was that of verbal learning, a helter-skelter collection of intricate experimental designs in which a common theme is truly difficult to find except in its general reliance on contiguity and frequency to account for learning. Few if any investigators in this field circa 1950–1960 professed to speak for teleology and their research strategies were no more accommodating to a Kantian epistemology than was Ebbinghaus' original work (see Chapter 3). Many psychologists had already begun to question the relevance of verbal learning for anything having to do with human education or even behavior in general. The studies conducted were invariably "tight" as to design, and the statistical assessments of the results were admirable in their sophistication. But the total effect of these disconnected—often pointless insofar as consistent theory is concerned—investigations of paired associates and serial learning seemed more often motivated by career considerations than anything else. Following a detailed review of 540 such studies (drawn primarily from the 1967–1969 period), two leaders in the field once observed that for at least 90% of them: "They make one wish that . . . [these] writers, faced with the decision of whether to publish or perish, should have seriously considered the latter alternative" (Tulving & Madigan, 1970, p. 442). To demean an accepted area of investigation in psychological science is not our purpose. We simply want to establish that, as a congenial testing grounds for humanistic psychology, the arid plain of verbal learning was a most unlikely candidate.

Its one saving characteristic was that verbal learning theories purported to relate to meaning and meaningfulness (via mediation concepts), and all humanistic accounts place central emphasis on these aspects of behavior. Here there seemed an opening for the teleologist if he wished to confront the mechanist with a teleological theory and then put it to test via the common designs of verbal-learning research. As a psychotherapist, the writer knew from first-hand experience how easy it was to guess a person's commitment to some aspect of life by asking him general questions of the sort: And, how did you feel about that? or How did that make you feel? Based on an analogy to emotional reactions, such questions were in fact unrelated to feelings *per se* (see Chapter 8). They signified a kind of "psychological tone" or mental outlook, one that in time we were to call an affective assessment. Sometimes the verbal expressions of a client as he discussed personal problems indicated that his *real* attitudes concerning some topic were in diametric opposition to what his expressed opinions implied. People did not always grasp their affective assessments, probably because though they constantly made them *vis-à-vis* life's contents, there was no literal feeling going on at the time. When prompted to make such evaluations concerning a realm of understanding (i.e., meanings in their experience), they could always do so even though the grounds for such assessments were unknown. Why not apply the same principle to a verbal-learning experiment? Why not ask subjects to affectively assess consonant-vowel-consonant (CVC) trigrams (formerly termed non-sense syllables) like HIB, LAT, POX, SUL, and so on, and then see if this evaluation would have a predictable influence on their learning style?

At about this time Irwin A. Berg (1957) had been doing some interesting work on the Deviation Hypothesis.[3] Berg asked subjects to look at a number of abstract designs printed on a so-called Perceptual Reaction Test and rate each along a four-step dimension of preference—i.e., like much, like slightly, dislike slightly, and dislike much. He found that abnormals deviated from normals on such ratings even as they deviated on other test items that were more to the point of measuring abnormality—such as MMPI items, for exam-

[3] The writer would like to thank Irwin A. Berg for his helpful suggestions, permission to reproduce his designs, and the general encouragement he has given to LLT over the years.

ple. In other words, abnormals tended to answer all kinds of items atypically or deviantly. They "zigged" when everyone else was "zagging" even when the nature of the test items seemed totally unrelated to personality or adjustment. We did not follow up on the Deviation Hypothesis *per se*, but the use of a four-step rating with no intermediate zero point interested us because of its dialectical implications. One essentially forced the subject here to take a stand, to judge one way or the other, even as there was some effort to dimensionalize (i.e., slightly, much) the direction of this either-or decision. Because this was compatible with our dialectical theory of affection, we decided to follow Berg's rating procedure (design) and have subjects affectively assess CVC trigrams for what by now we had named reinforcement value (RV) as a methodological term. We viewed RV as a dimension of meaningfulness as well as a variable that could be used in an experimental setting to signify the direction of a person's affective assessment (positive or negative) concerning the material he was being asked to learn, recognize, discriminate, recall, retrieve, and so forth. We began with the paradigmatic assumption that RV would have relevance for *all* such traditional research topics of the verbal-learning laboratory.

The first step seemed to be to identify a pool of trigrams that might reflect reliably different ratings for RV if administered to groups of people. We turned to Archer's (1960) norms, which contain all of the CVC trigrams that can possibly be constructed. Archer flashed these trigrams on a screen at two-second intervals to groups of at least 200 subjects, whose task it was to check Yes if the trigram was a literal word, looked like a word, reminded them of a word, or, if it could be used in a sentence. Each trigram was then assigned a meaningfulness value based on the proportion of subjects who associated a verbal (wordlike) quality to it. Thus if 10% of the subjects answered Yes the so-called association value (AV) of such a trigram (e.g., FAJ) was considered lower (less meaningful) than a trigram to which 50% (e.g., VOD) of the sample had answered affirmatively. A trigram having an AV of 90% (e.g., GOP) would be considered even higher on the dimension of meaningfulness. The AV measure is obviously based on a frequency thesis, and this purely empirical definition of meaningfulness has a long history in psychology going back to the work of Glaze (1928). Although no more than a mathematical fiction, it is easy to see the underlying theory on which this measure rests—that is, "so many" associated connections tying into verbal units to enrich them with meaningful significance. These contiguous ties are considered nontelic and thus efficiently caused.

We have here the heritage of British Associationism (theory) made manifest in an empirical measure (method).

Three hundred trigrams were selected from the middle (44–78%) range of Archer's lists and submitted to groups of subjects as a Phonetic Preference Inventory (PPI), in which they were to read each trigram to themselves. Based on how it "sounded" (in their mind's ear), if no direct idea emerged as to what it could mean, they were to rate each trigram on the four-point scale of like much, like slightly, dislike slightly, and dislike much. We were beginning on the assumption that it made no difference whether a subject rated the trigrams *per se* or he was rating some image or idea suggested by the trigram as a word-fragment. Because the affective assessment was thought to be in the subject's conceptualizing abilities and *not* in the stimulus being assessed (which is where verbal learning theories invariably place it), the precise item under assessment was irrelevant. Since we could objectively stipulate the beginning grounds on which a subject's assessment processes were brought to bear—that is, a trigram presented by the experimenter—a way was made possible for the rigorous study of self-determined preferences in human learning.

Between 30 and 40 subjects rated each trigram in this fashion on two occasions, with one week intervening. A chi-square was then run on each trigram to determine if it was rated comparably on the two occasions. The 140 trigrams that reached the .05 level of significance or greater were retained as reliable items and thus constituted the PPI. We have used this pool of items repeatedly over the years, but this is only for convenience, because the test-construction approach on which the PPI was initially based no longer holds our interest or complete support. Any other 140 trigrams from the Archer norms serve the same purpose in LLT research, including those we discarded initially as unreliable. The reasons for this view will soon be made clear. But, it was probably unfortunate that we began with such a test emphasis, because this has since confused colleagues who expect that a test will arrive at the measurement of some "one thing" (e.g., RV) in a "total score" of likes or dislikes. The focus of a test is on the *nomothetic* score achieved, disregarding the contributor to this score—that is, the *idiographic* course of behavior we call "the person" who responds uniquely to each of the items so calculated into a totality. We were in LLT research actually interested in this idiographic aspect of the test and not in some uniform test construct which it supposedly sampled nomothetically, even though affective assessment can surely be thought of in *both* senses.

The assessment was viewed as an instrumentality permitting us to delineate the specific meaningfulness an item (e.g., trigram) held for the person and *not* as an end in itself to be studied as variously distributed across groups of people.

These idiographic biases of LLT were to salvage the beginning research line, for we discovered when we returned to new samplings of subjects with the 140 trigrams that about one-third of these previously reliable items were no longer to achieve the .05 level of significance in a one-week test-retest. If one reasoned here according to nomothetic principles it would follow that the construct under development lacked general reliability hence it should probably be discarded. However, in thinking about the nature of affective judgment, aesthetic preference, and so forth, to find such idiosyncratic differences seemed perfectly natural. We were in danger here of "throwing out the baby with the bath water." There is an unfortunate contradiction between the view of human beings as idiographically unique and certain sampling theories that are aimed at the construct being sampled rather than at the variations within the persons who are asked to perform in relation to this construct's meaning. As presumed sources of error, individual differences on the construct being sampled are therefore dismissed in the name of objectivity and construct generalization.

Unique variations are consequently viewed as necessarily prompting subjective measures so even though we can objectively state how we arrive at some measurement, which as a total score changes considerably in the sample of human beings under study, the view is that our idiographic measurement is necessarily lacking in scientific value. Yet the mathematics of statistics are not inherently on the side of nomothetic thinking, and even though it did not meet the ideal of a perfect variable in the lexicon of psychological research, we decided to stick with RV by adopting the general procedure of measuring affective assessment on *two* occasions and selecting from among the ratings proffered by subjects those that we knew to be reliably liked and/or disliked. The PPI has therefore always been administered on two occasions, with from one hour to one week intervening between ratings (the most usual time period between testings has been 48 hours). Trigrams are classified for idiographically positive, negative, or ambivalent (changing signs) RV.

The first study conducted using RV in a learning task was patterned after the unconscious mediated association design of Bugelski and Scharlock (1952). The use of *unconscious* here attracted the writer initially, but he soon learned that this had little to do with the meaning assigned to this term by personality theories (see Chapter 5 on mediation theory). Bugelski and Scharlock had adapted a design of Peters (1935) in which subjects learned three successive lists of paired-associates trigrams, as follows: A-B, B-C, A-C. One string of trigram pairs in such a sequence might be MAB-DOH, DOH-PAQ, and MAB-PAQ. Because DOH here acts as a mediator, the prediction is that it will facilitate the learning of MAB-PAQ at the A-C list when compared to an A-C list that has not had the benefit of the previous mediation. There was only weak support for this prediction in Bugelski and Scharlock's original study, and we decided to put RV into the B-mediator to see if this might not make a difference. We simply contrasted this sequence when all of the trigrams were positive, negative, or ambivalent in RV. There was no A-C condition *without* a common B-mediator in this original RV study, although subsequently Laberteaux (1968) did reproduce the Bugelski and Scharlock design with no better success. Basing our prediction on the clinical experience referred to above, we hypothesized that the sequence along positive RV would show facilitation at A-C, whereas along the negative-RV line it would not.

We now discuss the general design followed in the learning tasks of RV research, so that in referring to other studies in the remainder of Chapter 9 and in Chapter 10—except in unusual cases—no such description will be necessary. As already noted, a subject's list of learnable items is made up of his reliably liked and/or disliked trigrams (the early work also included ambivalently rated trigrams). We eventually introduced words to these lists as well as the Berg (1957) designs, pictures of faces, abstract paintings, and so forth. At times such materials are flashed onto a screen before the subject by a slide projector, but memory drums are also used in many studies. Groups of subjects can be given the slide-projection procedure, as a recognition task where first paintings, designs, or faces are flashed for RV ratings, and then on a second administration during the same testing hour, subjects are asked both to rate for RV and indicate whether they have seen the face, painting, or design presented earlier (with unfamiliar items introduced to make this a recognition task on the second presentation). If a paired-associates tactic is employed, the order of pairs is randomized from trial to trial so that serial-position cues cannot be used to facilitate learning. In the case of paired-associates the subject is asked to read trigrams aloud each time they are presented and to relate them as pairs by saying "goes with" between their individual appearance—for example, "HIB . . . goes with . . . LAT." The subject is instructed to learn the pairs as such and to disregard the order of a list's presentation. The method of anticipation is followed, in which a subject must call out the second member of a pair before it is flashed or makes its appearance in the memory-drum window. Correct anticipations are called "hits," and incorrect or failures in anticipation are called "misses."

In other studies a free-recall format is followed whereby subjects are given not pairs of trigrams but a single list, within which, for example, are mixed both liked and disliked (reliably rated as per above) words or trigrams. The subject is again asked to read a trigram aloud each time it makes its appearance and then, following presentation of several items (up to 40 words in some studies), he is asked to record those he remembers in writing. In a few instances where short lists (8 or 10 words) are used we have simply asked the subject to give his recollections orally, and the experimenter records the answers between presentations of this list.

The criterion of learning attainment—that is, whether one or two consecutive recollections of a paired-associates list or simply the number of recognitions among one list of designs, and so forth—varies according to the study undertaken. There are two basic scoring methods used, one of which is called the *trials* and the other a *percent-hits* score. The former is simply the number of trials a subject takes to come to the stipulated criterion of learning. For example, in learning the pair TIB-SOQ a subject might reach the criterion of two consecutive hits at trial 6 and then hold this knowledge until trial 12, at which point he correctly anticipates all 10 of the pairs he is asked to learn for the second time in a row. Another pair, such as LAZ-GOC might not have achieved the criterion of two consecutive correct anticipations until trial 12. The trials score for the first pair is therefore 6 and for the second, 12. Assume that this subject's list of 10 pairs included five liked and five disliked pairings. The trials score for each of these RV sublists could be obtained by totaling the trials at which the subject achieved criterion for each of the pairs represented therein.

Note, however, that the trials score does not give complete weighting to all of those correct anticipations (hits) that are given by the subject and then not repeated. Assuming that 12 trials had been necessary for the subject to achieve criterion for a full list of 10 pairs, five liked and five disliked, we could then say there were 60 chances for hits in each of the sublists (5 pairs × 12 trials). If we now total the *actual* number of hits recorded for the liked and disliked sublists, and using this value as a numerator, divide it by the denominator of 60, we arrive at the percent-hits score. This ratio is usually highly correlated (.70 or greater) with the trials score, and it has never been known to reverse the direction of (statistically significant) findings to be seen in the trials score. The reason for using two scores is because they give emphasis to different aspects of the learning task and because occasionally one will give a better reflection of the hypotheses under test than the other (e.g., obtain a greater significance level, bring more variables into play in the statistical analysis, etc.). Psychologists are sometimes charged with thinking up their scoring procedures after the data have been collected so they can then judge how best to make them bring about significance in the statistical tests to follow. In using two scores we might be accused of doing something like this, but to deny these two obvious ways of looking at the data seems unrealistic, and we never depart from these two scorings in RV researches. There is one exception to the latter point, having to do with "clustering" scores in free-recall research. Because this is a special topic we reserve our presentation of this scoring procedure until clustering research is taken up in Chapter 10.

Returning to the initial RV study, 20 high school students (10 males, 10 females) were asked to learn their A-B lists of 15 paired associates (five pairs each of liked, disliked, and ambivalent trigrams) on one day, return in 48 hours to learn their B-C list, and in another 48 hours return a final time for their A-C list. In this case, overlearning was judged important so a criterion of five consecutive trials was employed. Figure 1 presents the graphed trials scores of this initial experiment.

As can be seen in Figure 1, subjects learned their RV-positive (liked) trigrams significantly more readily than their RV-negative (disliked) or RV-ambivalent (unreliable) trigrams *on all three days* ($p < .01$). There were no significant differences between liked and ambivalent sublists, so the predominant factors seem to be between the clearly liked and clearly disliked sublists. Although there was some evidence in the significantly reduced variance at A-C learning for liked trigrams that the predicted facilitation had taken place, the clearest finding of our initial experiment was that affective assessments facilitated learning right from the start. We immediately broadened our thinking on the topic and tried to determine how well affective assessment could stand up in the face of the questions that arose in the minds of our Lockean colleagues, who were only too ready to account for RV in nontelic ways.

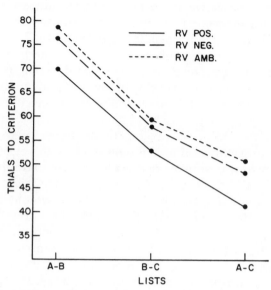

**Figure 1**   Mean trials to criterion on three paired-associates lists (A-B, B-C, A-C) learned by subjects on three successive days, with 48 hours intervening. Trials to criterion are graphed according to the RV of the CVC trigrams learned.

## The Construct Validity of Affective Assessment

Although Cronbach and Meehl's (1955) classic paper on *construct validity* discussed this form of procedural evidence (face validity) in terms of test constructs (tied through measurements to nomological nets, etc.), the phrase has come to subsume all types of theoretical constructs. There is a suggestion of parsimony here, a desire to keep one's conceptual schemes close to the context of validation in such a way that it all hangs together without introducing excess theoretical baggage. In this sense even though the PPI does not get at some "one" test construct, we can speak of the construct validity of affective assessment. Critics who viewed the findings of our first RV study raised the question of whether there *was* an affective assessment going on in this learning. And even if there was something of the sort taking place, they suggested that the reason for this was the control exerted by the trigram stimuli, a control that not only determined the initial liking or disliking but also could account for the differential learning rate observed. In almost every instance the alternative explanations they proffered reduced RV to a frequency-contiguity (AV) explanation. To answer these alternative explanations required four general counterdemonstrations. We review the four counters in the present chapter and then go on to the applications of affective assessment in various basic learning and personality researches in Chapter 10.

## Reinforcement Value in a Learning Context

One of the first steps taken in our efforts to test the construct validity of affective assessment focused on the learning context. Could we find RV differences even when the *same* trigrams were being learned by subjects who rated these positively or negatively? This would counter the suggestion that RV was somehow stimulus determined. We therefore had 20 high school subjects (divided equally by sex) learn identical paired-associates lists (i.e., same trigrams in every subject's list). There were 12 pairs of trigrams in a list, half of which were ambivalent for all subjects, and half of which were either liked or disliked depending on the subject concerned (i.e., 10 subjects liked and 10 disliked the *same* six pairs). The common ambivalent trigrams thus acted as a control sublist against which to compare learning rates for the liked or disliked sublist. We found that liked trigrams were learned significantly more readily than ambivalent trigrams, but disliked trigrams did not reflect such a difference (Rychlak, 1966). There were no sex differences. Because subjects were matched according to common stimuli, these findings were difficult to justify in terms of a stimulus pull thesis.

There is a large body of research on the question of likability (pleasantness versus unpleasantness, etc.) in learning, trailing back to Wundt's laboratory, and we have in different contexts thoroughly surveyed this literature (see in particular Rychlak, 1966; Rychlak, Tasto, Andrews, & Ellis, 1973; and Tuan, 1974). Various studies have supported the view that subjects learn liked materials more readily than disliked because they have had more exposure to the words or word-fragments (trigrams) which they rated positive in pleasantness than they have had with materials rated negatively. Researchers in the RV line could not find conclusive or even convincing evidence to this effect in the total findings of the studies surveyed, but we can surely attest to a positive and high correlation between the self-styled rigor of a psychologist and his conviction in the unassailability of this view that direction of affect can be reduced to frequency of contact. In the interest of space we do not go over this large body of research, but merely observe that what it comes down to is that there seem to be clear influences for *both* AV and RV meaningfulness in human learning.

Returning to the actual studies conducted by LLT researchers, trigrams were next taken from low (10–20%), medium (45–55%) and high (80–90%) AV levels of the Archer norms, submitted to subjects who rated them for RV, and then were entered into paired-associates lists for these subjects to learn (Abramson, 1967). There was a significant main effect for nomothetic level of AV on the trials to criterion. The high-AV (80-90%) trigrams were easier to learn than the low-AV (10–20%) trigrams, but neither of these extremes differed significantly from the medium-AV (45–55%) trigrams. This finding is common in AV studies of a nomothetic nature, where one must take a rather broad difference across levels of meaningfulness to achieve significant experimental findings. Even so, *within all three levels* of nomothetic AV a significant difference for RV was found (i.e., RV and AV did not interact in the statistical test). Simple-effects tests demonstrated that liked versus disliked trigrams accounted for the findings and that the ambivalent trigrams failed to differ between either of these two conditions at any level of AV. We soon dropped the use of ambivalently rated trigrams in RV studies, because they were unnecessary to the development of LLT. Whatever was at play for AV across nomothetic levels, *within* these levels of meaningfulness RV was bearing a uniform and predictable role—that is, liked trigrams were reaching criterion more readily than disliked trigrams.

One would expect that if RV were merely a variant frequency estimate of meaningfulness, by increasing the levels of AV the contribution of such increased meaningfulness to RV in learning should also be increased. As verbal units become *more* meaningful (word-like), two estimates of the same thing should reveal an increasing affinity for each other and thereby contribute to the rate of learning differentially across levels of meaningfulness. The fact that this was not the case lent support to our view of the independence between AV and RV. We also began to appreciate the methodological issue in so-called idiographic versus nomothetic measures.

These terms are best employed methodologically, and to mix them into one's theory leads to confusion when we get down to the actual verbal materials (trigrams, words) that people employ in a learning task. There is no point in speaking of a meaningfulness "as contained in" the Archer tables—as if these actuarial distributions related meaningfully to the world. This is absurd, of course, but even in the absurdity one can see that nomothetic AV measures are simply numerical abstractions, floating about in tables without theoretical underpinnings—which is why the theories of mathematics take over so readily to turn our subjects into cybernetic machines, manipulating probabilities. Just as we do not find married couples living in our suburbs with 2.3 children in their family, we do not find 90% of a trigram meaning nestling in the mind of a subject answering the Archer instructions. The subject associating to a trigram is just as empty of meaning if 50% or 99% of his peers see it as wordlike and *he does not*. All we are left with here is a kind of bet that, as this subject goes along he will in time be more likely to generate an associate for the 99% item than for the 50% item. But note: This statistical theory says nothing about why this will occur. Indeed, this is no theory of meaningfulness at all, but rather a theory about the probabilities of meaningfulness being expressed *by* people.

For this reason we have never constructed nomothetic tables for RV—a routine effort, easily accomplished. Though some benefit might accrue, to construct such tables did not meet our introspective *theoretical* interests. Also, we felt that in a true sense Osgood's (1952) marvelous work was examining RV at a nomothetic level and that his pervasive findings on Evaluation (see Snider & Osgood, 1969) supported the theoretical view that affective assessment was reflected in all language systems of mankind—a possibly immodest but hardly unfounded suggestion, considering Osgood's results. Of course Osgood's *theory* of meaning relies on the typical mediation-model approach we reviewed in Chapter 5. Thus he considers meaning to be a mediational process typified as (1) a fractional part of the total behavior that some stimulus complex in experience might have elicited in the individual and (2) a kind of running feedback self-stimulation that has an impact on the organized response eventually made by the individual, but one different from that which would have been made without the intervening fractional process mentioned in point 1 (*ibid.*, pp. 9–10). That this mechanistic theoretical account relies on a certain (British Empiricistic) philosophy and image of man is entirely clear to Osgood (see his remarks to this effect in Osgood, 1969). And when we now claim his findings as *also* supporting affective assessment, we do so in full cognizance of our right to bring alternative theoretical descriptions to bear concerning the results of experiments conducted by an incompatible outlook (see Chapter 5, pp. 180–184).

To test our growing awarness of the idiographic-nomothetic distinction as purely methodological, we decided to select trigrams from the limited 45–55% range of Archer's norms and then to ask subjects to rate these for both AV and RV. In other words, we would disregard the actuarial (nomothetic) value of AV and put Archer's instructions directly (idiographically) to subjects, half of whom could be expected to see these trigrams as wordlike and half of whom would not. Then on a second occasion we would get our usual RV ratings. If our thinking was sound, not only could we show AV differences in learning within an extremely narrow range of nomothetic AV, but we should also be able to show independent RV influences in the subject's learning if these were indeed separate dimensions of meaningfulness. A subject was therefore asked to learn a list of 12 paired associates, four of which fell into each of the following designations: Yes-AV, Like-RV; No-AV, Like-RV; Yes-AV, Dislike-RV; and No-AV, Dislike-RV (Tasto, 1967).

Twenty college subjects (equated for sex) were put through the typical paired-associates procedure and a 2 (sex) × 2 (AV) × 2 (RV) factorial analysis of variance (ANOVA) was run on their trials scores. The first is a between-subjects factor, and the latter two are within-subjects factors. Both AV ($p < .05$) and RV ($p < .07$) were at play as main effects in the usual fashion, with no significant statistical interactions between them and no sex differences. The RV measure fell a bit short of significance (a one-tailed assumption salvaged the findings in a technical sense), but our idiographic-nomothetic line of thinking was clearly supported. The array of means in this study is of some interest, as follows (low scores signify better performance): Yes-AV, Like-RV (Mean [M] = 31.70, Standard Deviation [SD] = 15.26); Yes-AV, Dislike-RV (M = 34.55, SD = 10.35); No-AV, Like-RV (M = 35.65, SD = 14.50) and No-AV. Dislike-RV (M = 39.75, SD = 16.62) (see Abramson, Tasto, & Rychlak, 1969). Only the extremes of this array proved significantly different in tests of simple effects. Henceforth we were to employ AV in a strictly methodological sense, to mean the value (Yes, No) that a subject assigned to a verbal item based on his judgment of its wordlikeness. Idiographic AV obtained when we focused on "a" subject and the more customary reference to tables such as those of Archer's was distinguished as nomothetic AV. The same applies to RV, although in point of fact we have never conducted researches on nomothetic RV.

Another concept that was advanced in time by colleagues to account for RV findings was that of imagery, which Paivio (1971) defines as relating to the nonverbal memory representations or modes of thcught, particularly as unrelated to the verbal symbolic processes that are concerned with the auditory-motor speech system (p. 12). Because concrete words (*horse, chair, apple*) with high imagery are easier to learn than abstract words (*respect, truth, ambition*), the suggestion was advanced that RV might possibly be a special case of imagery. Liked materials could have high imagery and disliked materials could have low imagery, thus accounting for the typical findings by LLT researchers. Although there are good reasons for dismissing this parallel on other grounds (e.g., the RV-reversal findings, see Chapter 10, pp. 411–426), a direct test of RV and imagery akin to the RV-AV confrontations was surely in order.

We did at one point hold the imagery of words constant in a learning study having to do with our self-assessment line of research (see Chapter 10, pp. 418–419) and found the predicted RV regularities occurring even when *only* very concrete words were employed (August, Rychlak, & Felker, 1975). However, a direct confrontation of the two dimensions was designed in a free-recall study. Forty college subjects (equated for sex) rated words for RV that had been taken from the extremes of an imagery-concreteness table (Paivio, Yuille, & Madigan, 1968). Half of these words were therefore high in imagery (e.g., *garden, elbow, engine*) and half were low (e.g., *rating, gist, occasion*). The ratings on RV distributed in both the positive and negative direction across these levels of concreteness, and four words in each of the possible imagery-RV combinations (high-liked, high-disliked, low-liked, low-disliked) were presented to the subjects in an individual free-recall learning task (16 words in all). Words were presented by memory drum, set on a two-second exposure cycle. The data thus lent themselves to a factorial ANOVA having the characteristics of a 2 (sex) × 2 (high versus low imagery) × 2 (liked versus disliked), with the first a between-subjects factor and the latter two within-subjects factors.

A main effect was found for RV trials scores with subjects learning their liked ($M = 21.97$, $SD = 11.87$) more readily than their disliked words ($M = 24.01$, $SD = 13.76$) ($F = 9.33$, $df = 1/38$, $p < .01$). No such differences emerged in the comparison between high-imagery ($M = 23.35$, $SD = 13.81$) and low-imagery words ($M = 22.63$, $SD = 12.94$) ($F$ less than unity, N.S.). There were no significant interactions between RV and imagery ($F$ less than unity) and no sex differences. Hence the two bits of evidence we have thus far accumulated indicate that RV cannot be reduced to or accounted for by imagery.

This is a good point at which to consider the theoretical problem that arose early in RV research, having to do with how we explained the actual learning process. Chapters 7 and 8 have gone into the LLT concepts which evolved over several years. But at the out-

The Psychology of Rigorous Humanism

set we faced a great void when we tried to remove the frequency and contiguity principles from our theoretical explanations. The writer clearly recalls a day when in a telephone conversation Don Tasto put the obvious question: "What am I going to tell my [thesis] committee 'caused' this learning if it wasn't the accumulated practice across trials?" We had been employing the language of efficient cause-effect without appreciating how it bound us to an unacceptable paradigm. We spoke of the effects of RV on learning, as if affective assessments were units of influence which, along with AV and practice and trials and warming up, and so forth, all somehow add up to something called learning. This was the Lockean model. We did not hold to it in theory, but what could take its place? We needed a different principle of explanation. Falling back on Kant's discussion of analytical propositions in which he noted the role of tautology, the writer suggested in semi-jest to Tasto: "Say that the practice trials reflect what is known at the outset, so that we are not watching subjects 'acquire' meanings so much as they are 'extending' what they already know. It follows that they would achieve a criterion more quickly if they know more about one sublist [liked] than another [disliked]."

Because this was said jokingly, poor Tasto, gasping at the other end of the line, was not required to take this rationale before his committee. But in time the joke could not be laughed off. Clearly, the logic of experimentation was severely prejudicial to a humanistic account so long as a distinction between theory and method was not drawn. The formal-cause organizations of mathematics (statistics) were obviously active in the experimenter's head, but what he ascribed to the activity of the learner's head was nothing more than a frequency distribution of efficient-causes, as if one reified the numerical values in Archer's tables and saw them coalescing in the trials to criterion. If there was an organization of such incidents in the mediation interval between inputs and outputs, this depended solely upon the earlier input incidents that somehow shaped the present outputs into form. No responsibility was assigned to the learner *qua* human being in this organization.

Yet for us the RV measure was seen as a subject-contributed variable, an *active* organization of the material to be learned rather than merely a statistical fiction in the experimenter's head. And so we began to advance the tautological principle in LLT with all seriousness. The beginnings were crude. For example, we tried to clarify the theoretical development by pointing to the Anglo-Saxon roots of *like* as meaning *both* similarity in form (a variant tautology) *and* preferential value. If a subject says that he likes some object, he could well be aligning the pattern (form, organization) of this perceived item (trigram, word, picture) in terms of some already known and also preferred pattern through which he now aligns an identity. Parallels were drawn to puzzle solutions and one-trial learning.

We know that although it takes a subject on certain tasks several trials to learn what is required of him, other tasks are learned immediately. For example, if he catches onto the principle or "trick" of a puzzle-solution, we observe the phenomenon of one-trial learning taking place. What if all learning is actually like this, with the observed "acquisition" over trials simply a reflection of the successive premises (formal causes, puzzle solutions) being brought to bear in what is called trial-and-error but is actually intention-and-confirmation? Each trial was an attempt to fit the intended meaning to the task at hand, improving on the strategy until the correct solution is finally achieved. Indeed, a major aspect of this learning is simply determining *what is required* of the learner—the grounds of the task put to him. In the case of a preliminary affective assessment, the person can be said to order things to his advantage when he likes the material he is asked to learn, because he aligns the material to be learned with what he knows (i.e., what it is "like"). The subject organizes a possible solution and *then* practices rather than *vice versa*. As he traverses the trials, he is on the cause, not the effect side of a cause-effect tandem.

This preliminary effort was to suffer from its simplicity and the lack of proper theoretical terminology. Not until we had formalized the telic flavor of LLT in the telosponse construct did any theoretical headway develop. The principle of tautology was a boon to LLT, even though it was an abomination to more than one experimental-psychology journal reviewer of the period, one of whom asked in a mood of astonishment and frustration: "And as for this 'tautology' business, I have but one question: *What is it?*" We responded: "It is, among other things, the F-ratio of unity on which you base your statistical reasoning." Our hope was to show this tough-minded individual that he used tautological learning principles in his research role as a scientist. If his F-tests proved tautological, he concluded that he knew what he already knew but that he had *not learned* anything else in his data collections (i.e., he could not reject the null hypothesis of no differences [see Chapter 7, pp. 277–281]). Though *he* proceeded on such a theory of knowledge, *our* use of an identical rationale to account for a subject's learning was seen by him as confused and obscure. We refused to be intimidated by such poorly reasoned allegations and continued on to other proofs for the construct validity of affective assessment.

### Reinforcement Value and Continuous Association

Noble (1952) introduced an alternate frequency conception, one that was based not on the proportion of a sample answering Yes to the question of possible wordlikeness, but on the continuous associations a subject makes to the *same* verbal item over a fixed interval of time (e.g., 60 seconds). The implication for RV was that, even though a subject may be dealing with trigrams low and/or high in AV via the Archer's lists, in his own unique case he could simply have more personal associates to liked than to disliked items. Thus showing an independence between AV and RV in the Archer sense does not rule out a second type of frequency operating. Two studies were conducted to examine this possible source of explanation for the RV findings (Kubat, 1969).

In the first effort 27 high school students (13 males, 14 females) rated trigrams from three levels of the Archer norms for RV: low AV (10–20%), medium AV (45–55%), and high (nomothetic) AV (80–90%). An exhaustive matching procedure was followed through use of an electronic computer to match nine subjects on the *same* *five trigrams* at each of these three nomothetic levels of AV. Three of these nine subjects had rated these five trigrams as liked, three as disliked, and three as ambivalent (nine subjects at each of three levels, hence $N = 27$). Noble's (1952) procedure was then employed, in which subjects were given several 3 × 5 index cards, which had printed on them the following: "_____ reminds me of _____." The experimenter hand-printed in characters approximately 1.25 mm in height the relevant trigram on the left before administering a series of such cards to the subject, who was to complete the association called for on the right. For example, a subject's card might read: "___LAS___ reminds me of _____." The subject was asked to take a card, complete it, and then take another, repeating this process until told to stop (after two minutes had elapsed). We were hoping to avoid chain associations in having the continuous-association to a trigram broken up by individual cards. A chain association is where the subject associates to the previously given word-associate (assume it was *girl* to LAS) rather than to the original trigram (LAS). When a trigram had been associated to for two minutes, the subject was given a second trigram, then a third, and so forth until all five trigrams were put through this so-called *production method* of verbal association.

The words that were thus associated (*girl* in the above example) were then transferred from the right-hand side of the index cards to a specially prepared rating form. A subject was next instructed to rate his word-associates for RV along a seven-point scale, from like very much (1 point) through undecided (4 points) to dislike very much (7 points). This is one of the few instances in which we have permitted subjects to take an indifferent stance in relation to the material being judged affectively. Two scores were derived for each subject. An association score reflected the mean number of word-associates a subject proffered to his five trigrams, and a likability score indexed the number of words associated to liked, disliked, or ambivalent trigrams as *divided into* the summated seven-point scale values subsequently assigned to these word-associates. For example, if a subject had associated 15 words to his five liked trigrams, he was given an association score of 3 for RV-positive materials. If these 15 words received a total of 22 points on the seven-point scale, his likability score would then be 1.47.

Before turning to the findings, we can bring in the second experiment as well. This was a cross-validation of the first effort in every way but one. That is, 45 high school subjects (22 males, 23 females) were put through precisely the same procedure with the only difference being that subjects at each of the nomothetic levels were *not* associating to the same five trigrams. There were 15 subjects at each of these nomothetic AV levels, but the extensive matching on trigrams was not carried out. The findings of the two studies were identical, however, and hence in Table 4 we present the association and likability scores for the combined samples. For the association score, the higher this value, the more words that were associated to the trigrams involved. For the likability score, the lower the value, the more positive is the rating of the trigrams concerned.

As can be seen in Table 4, there were no significant findings on the association score. There was not even a consistent trend in the rank order of associates across nomothetic AV level so that, for example, at the 80–90% level the *disliked* trigram suggested most word-associates to the subject (insignificant finding). Hence subjects did *not* associate more words to liked than to disliked or ambivalent words over the two-minute interval. Turning to the likability score on the word-associates, there was no significant main effect for the nomothetic level of trigrams associated to; subjects were *not* more likely to assign positive RV to word-associates of trigrams that were at the 80–90% than at the 10–20% level of nomothetic AV. However, at *every* such level they did assign significantly more positive ratings

**Table 4**  Mean and Standard Deviation of Association
and Likability Score for Combined Sample

| Level of Nomothetic AV | RV Value | Association Score | | Likability Score | |
|---|---|---|---|---|---|
| | | Mean | S.D. | Mean | S.D. |
| 80–90% | Liked | 5.30 | 1.77 | 3.27 | .131 |
| | Ambivalent | 4.83 | 1.29 | 3.13 | .319 |
| | Disliked | 5.63 | 3.76 | 4.11 | .219 |
| 45–55% | Liked | 6.10 | 1.89 | 2.54 | .640 |
| | Ambivalent | 5.90 | 1.51 | 3.13 | .495 |
| | Disliked | 4.55 | 1.55 | 3.61 | .803 |
| 10–20% | Liked | 4.92 | 2.55 | 2.54 | .521 |
| | Ambivalent | 4.13 | 1.28 | 3.43 | .887 |
| | Disliked | 4.43 | 1.74 | 4.02 | .591 |

Note: (a) Factorial ANOVA for independent and combined samples on
association score N.S. for main effects and interaction. (b) Factorial
ANOVA for independent and combined samples on likability score N.S.
on main effect for levels of AV. But the main effect for RV was significant
in both samples and in combined analysis ($p < .01$).

to the word-associates that had been suggested by liked than by
disliked trigrams ($p < .01$). This same finding obtained to a statistically significant degree in each sample studied (thus our combining
of samples in Table 4 is merely a space-conservation measure).

The proposal that a continuous association form of frequency
can account for RV findings has been invalidated by these data.
The fact that in one of our samples subjects rated *identical* trigrams
at a given level of nomothetic AV lent great credence to the view
that RV was not "in" the stimulus-trigram, but rather it was "in"
the subject's personal assessment of this stimulus. We are dealing
entirely with the subject's phenomenal reality at this point. The
meaning imputed by the subject's understanding, not the trigram,
is what is under learning (extension), and RV is a measure of the
relative significance of this meaning in a positive-negative *dialectical* sense. This Kantian style of thought has not been easy to convey to Lockean colleagues, who have said with great personal conviction that it is the trigrams that are being learned, not ratings of

affect or meanings indexed thereby. They can manipulate the trigrams as variables, hence to admit to a subject-contribution to the process strikes them as departing from "the observed" (see our discussion of subject-contributed variables in Chapter 8, pp. 322–323).

## Reinforcement Value and Association Value: Group Rating Issues

We next turn to a number of studies confronting RV with AV in the group-rating context. Can RV be reduced to or accounted for by the frequency factors in group ratings which provide the rationale for AV? What are the respective reliabilities of an AV and an RV measure? Can RV be capitalizing on the error of measurement in an AV procedure? These and other problems of measuring the RV dimension are discussed. In the first study 30 college subjects (15 males, 15 females) first rated trigrams for RV and were subsequently administered 10 each of a liked, disliked, and ambivalent sublist (Rychlak, 1966). Trigrams were presented, and a subject was asked to judge their word quality via the typical Archer instruction. With 30 subjects and 30 trigrams for each, there were therefore 900 possible judgments of wordlikeness, 300 in each of the RV classifications (liked, disliked, and ambivalent). What was the distribution of wordlikeness across these classifications? We found that 169 liked, 128 disliked, and 135 ambivalent trigrams were checked Yes as to word quality, but this difference proved insignificant ($p > .20$) when tested via the Friedman two-way ANOVA by ranks (Siegel, 1956, p. 166).

The next study examined the 140 trigrams of the PPI by having 46 college students (20 males, 26 females) rate these on two occasions for *both* AV and RV, with one week intervening between testings (Nishball, 1966). This permitted both a nomothetic and an idiographic analysis. Considering the proportion of these subjects who answered Yes to an AV instruction (i.e., saw the trigram as wordlike) and the proportion who saw it as positive in RV (liked it) as a score for the trigram, the 140 trigrams could be intercorrelated at test and retest. This nomothetic approach revealed a Pearsonian correlation of .85 ($p < .01$) for AV and .54 ($p < .01$) for RV. This suggests that subjects as a group tend to rate this fairly narrow range of nomothetic AV (44–78%) somewhat more consistently for AV than RV. However, the trigrams were already selected via the Archer values to favor a rank ordering for AV over RV, and this nomothetic approach is really of secondary importance to affective-assessment research in any case. What we really want to find out is how a *specific* person rates his verbal materials. How much change do we see in the protocol of 140 trigrams by a subject, not how much change do we see in a score leveling all subjects as if they were secondary in importance to the value of the average.

To achieve the latter objective, a chi-square analysis of the trigrams was conducted. In this case we determine how many subjects changed their ratings across the two testings (using McNemar tests for the significance of changes; see Siegel, 1956, pp. 63–67). Nineteen subjects made significant ($p < .05$ or greater) changes in their AV ratings of the 140 trigrams over the two occasions (moving from yes to no or *vice versa*), and 13 subjects made significant changes in their RV ratings (moving from like to dislike or *vice versa*).

The next study in this line asked 100 college subjects (55 males, 45 females) to rate the 140 trigrams of the PPI on *one* occasion for both AV and RV (the order of these ratings was counterbalanced in subgroupings of subjects put through the rating task). Each trigram was then analyzed via a 2 × 2 chi-square which compared Yes-No and Like-Dislike ratings made by the same subjects ($N = 100$). It was found that 35 of the 140 trigrams on the PPI were significantly confounded ($p < .05$ or greater) in the sense of a yes rating (trigram has word quality) going along with like rating (positive RV) and *vice versa*. When the ratings of these 100 subjects were considered proportion scores for each trigram—that is, proportion answering yes and proportion answering like—a Pearsonian correlation between the two nomothetic measures was found to be .45 ($p < .01$). Considered in light of a coefficient of determination ($r^2$) and in line with the idiographic findings on these ratings, 20–25% of the ratings made by these 100 subjects would appear to be confounded. This is of course hardly convincing evidence that the two ratings are getting at the same thing.

An unexpected finding emerged in this study, suggesting that even this fairly modest contamination of trigram ratings occurred at the *lower* nomothetic AV levels of the PPI. Recall that the PPI covers the Archer ranges of 44–78%, and when the data were looked at in decile steps, more confounding of ratings seemed to be taking place at the 44–50% level than at the 64–70% level. We therefore conducted another study in this line which assessed the full range of Archer's (1960) decile values in light of AV and RV (Tenbrunsel, 1967).

One hundred college students (29 females, 71 males) were asked to rate 10 trigrams from each of the deciles of the Archer norms— that is, spanning the 0–10% through the 90–100% range of nomothetic AV. Subjects rated these 100 trigrams for *both* AV and RV (with order of trigram presentation randomized across subgroups of the 100 subjects) on *two occasions,* with one week intervening. Once again, both nomothetic and idiographic analyses were conducted on these data. Taking up the proportion scores on AV and RV first— that is, where the percentage of 100 subjects answering yes and/or like to a trigram is its score—we found the following test-retest Pearsonian correlations: $AV = .97$, and $RV = .94$ ($p < .01$ for both). This large increase in $r$ values over what we had found on the PPI is doubtless due to the increased range of nomothetic AV, a range that spuriously inflates the correlational values. When AV and RV are intercorrelated on the proportion scores we find the following $r$ values: .84 on initial testing and .93 on retesting ($p < .01$ for both).

To demonstrate that AV and RV were more confounded at the low than at the high levels of nomothetic AV, the proportion scores were divided in half, at the 50% point, and Pearsonian correlations were then run between AV and RV on the low (0–50%) and high (51–100%) trigram levels separately. On initial testing the 0–50% trigrams correlated .73, and the 51–100% trigrams correlated .57 (this difference in $r$-level is significant, $p < .05$). On retesting, these values of $r$ increased to .91 for the 0–50% trigrams and to .72 for the 51–100% trigrams (this difference in $r$-level is *also* significant, $p < .01$).

Turning to an idiographic assessment of the data, a $2 \times 2$ chi-square analysis was performed on each of the trigrams in turn, contrasting yes-no (AV) and like-dislike (RV). It was found that 33 of the 100 trigrams were significantly confounded (i.e., rated yes and like or no and dislike) on original testing, and on retest this number jumped to 66 ($p < .05$ for both testings). The experimental hypothesis held that most of these idiographic confoundings would occur at the low ranges of nomothetic AV (as previously defined by the Archer tables). To present the findings on this hypothesis graphically, adjoining deciles of the trigrams were combined into fifths (moving from 0 to 100% in 20% steps), and then the percentage of 20 trigrams reflecting a significant chi-square *within each fifth* was graphed along a rising scale of Archer's nomothetic AV. Figure 2 contains these significant percentages of idiographic AV-RV confoundings (or relationships), graphed across the Archer ranges of nomothetic meaningfulness, for both test and retest (Tenbrunsel, Nishball, & Rychlak, 1968).

Note in Figure 2 that the experimental hypothesis was substantiated in that at the highest levels of nomothetic meaningfulness,

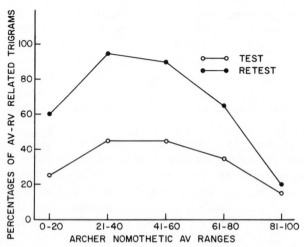

**Figure 2** Test and retest percentages of CVC trigrams found (via chi-square) to be related at the .05 level or greater across the Archer (1960) nomothetic AV range. Percentages are based on trigrams grouped in fifths, across the Archer nomothetic AV values.

we find the *least* confounding of the AV and RV ratings. The graphed curves were not entirely as expected, however, for when we come to the lowest levels of nomothetic AV (0–20%), the percentage of related AV-RV trigrams again drops off. A sign test (Siegel, 1956, pp. 68–75) was performed between the data of our two curves, and a significant increase ($p < .01$) *did* take place across the testings. Subjects were getting even more confused on retest than they were on original testing, so their ratings ran together. The interesting thing about these additional confoundings, however, is that they *did not take place* at the highest levels of nomothetic AV! Even the low range (0–20%) more than doubled the percentage of related AV-RV trigrams on retest. But the highest nomothetic range (81–100%)—where if Archer's procedure is sound, the trigrams are *most* wordlike—remains essentially unchanged at retest. We can expect about one trigram in five to show a significant idiographic relationship between AV and RV at the highest levels of nomothetic meaningfulness, even when subjects repeat the two ratings a second time.

Logic would dictate that if idiographic AV and RV are two ways of measuring the same thing, at the highest level of cultural meaningfulness (i.e., actual words are at the 100% level) we should find the *greatest* tendency for a relationship to occur between these variations on a common theme. The fact that this expectation was reversed in the findings lends further support to the view that though confounded, AV and RV are not getting at the same thing in the conceptual activities of the subject. If a subject has no basis on which to relate meaningfully to a trigram—if he is looking at so-called low levels of nomothetic AV—he would seem more likely to say that he dislikes it or dislikes the circumstance of being rootless in the realm of meaning *per se*. Surely this phenomenal experience is familiar to all of us who have been in similar circumstances, as in studying school subjects in which we are poorly instructed. But it does not follow from this weighting of confounded measures at the low nomothetic levels that the RV and AV ratings are redundant, particularly when the Pearsonian correlations which are reported in such nomothetic efforts rely on the full range of word recognition and to that extent are always spuriously inflated in any case.

There is another rather subtle point that has been raised against the RV rating procedure having to do with possible errors of measurement in the selection of trigrams from the PPI. Because we identify trigrams idiographically, avoiding a total PPI score in favor of a "hunt and peck" tactic, to select from among the 140 PPI items only those that fall into our designations of AV Yes, RV Disliked, etc., cannot we capitalize on the errors of measurement covertly to use a nomothetic AV as if it were idiographic RV when it was not? For example, a subject might say "No, it is not a word, but I like the sound of reading LOF" and "Yes, I think it could be used in a sentence but I dislike the sound of MUY." In actuality Archer's (1960) norms reveal that LOF is at the 70% and MUY the 45% level of nomothetic meaningfulness. If now the subject memorizes LOF more readily than MUY, is it the RV rating or the covert functioning of nomothetic AV that accounts for the difference? Even though we have shown RV differentially at play in lists which are identical as to the trigrams rated by all subjects, at least some of the RV findings could possibly be due to such errors in measurement. Because this criticism was used quite frequently by critics, we decided to do a rather thorough study of the precise levels of nomothetic AV at which the critical ratings of this type occurred.

That is, based on the researches already presented, we expect that a Yes-Like [AV-RV combination] trigram will occur more often as we ascend the deciles of Archer's norms. Conversely, we expect that the proportion of trigrams that are rated No-Dislike will increase as we descend this scale. There is no concern over these two cases, and no problems arise in selecting such trigrams from the PPI. The error-of-measurement criticism implies that a trigram which is idiographically disliked may actually be one that is *low* in nomothetic AV—where it is selected even though it is seen as wordlike by the subject—and a trigram which is liked is actually *high* in nomothetic AV even though the subject may not see the word quality idiographically which is "there" for emergence as learning proceeds (actuarially considered).

This criticism hinges on the probability that subjects are indeed likely to confound idiographic disliking with nomothetically low AV and idiographic liking with nomothetically high AV. To counter it, we must show that Yes-Dislike trigrams are more probable in the ratings of subjects at high nomothetic levels than they are at low nomothetic levels of AV. If it is more likely for a subject to say "That is a word and I dislike it" at a high than a low level of nomothetic AV, the expected probability of confounding disliking with low nomothetic AV is countered by the empirical facts. Similarly, if the No-Like trigrams occur more frequently at the low than at the high nomothetic AV levels, the chances of a subject saying "That is not a word and I like it" *diminishes* as we ascend the nomothetic levels, contradicting thereby the likelihood that this judgment of positive RV is due to covertly high nomothetic AV.

Eighty-six college subjects (51 males, 35 females) were asked to rate 20 trigrams at each of the steps from 1–5%, 6–10%, and so forth, up to 96–100% nomothetic AV level of the Archer's norms (400 trigrams in all). Subjects were asked to make both AV and RV judgments at the same time, thereby essentially placing a trigram in one of four categories: Yes-Like, Yes-Dislike, No-like, and No-Dislike. The experimental hypothesis held that Yes-Dislike trigrams would be *positively* correlated with Archer level, and No-Like trigrams would be *negatively* correlated with these increasing levels of nomothetic AV. This is exactly what was found, with the Pearsonian values for these correlations as follows: Yes-Dislike .70 and No-Like −.17 ($p < .01$ for both, $N = 400$). The other two categorizations reflected the expected directions as follows: Yes-Like .87 and No-Dislike −.97 ($p < .01$ for both) (Tuan, 1974). Figure 3 graphs the two crucial curves, reflecting the percentage of subjects at each level of Archer's norms who placed a trigram in the Yes-Dislike or the No-Like category.

Note in Figure 3 that even with the curvilinearity of No-Like trigrams, the empirical facts counter the suggestion that errors of measurement in selecting trigrams could lead to a covert nomothetic

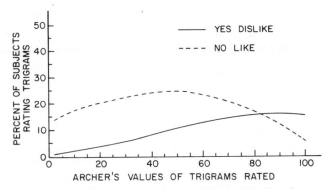

**Figure 3** The percentage of subjects (ordinate) who placed trigrams from across the Archer (1960) nomothetic AV range (abscissa) in either the Yes-Dislike or the No-Like category.

AV accounting for the findings on RV. The nomothetic range represented by the PPI (i.e., 44–78%) is particularly supportive of our experimental hypotheses. We conclude that for a subject to say that he dislikes a wordlike trigram is more likely at the *high* nomothetic levels than at the low and that he likes an unwordlike trigram at the *low* nomothetic levels. Hence, once again a frequency interpretation of the RV findings proved to be invalid.

## Reinforcement Value and the Factor Analyses of Sundry Ratings

The final tactic employed in an effort to test the independence of AV and RV was that of factor analysis. Several colleagues pressured us to put RV ratings to the test by way of this approach, in which various other types of ratings can also be employed (e.g., a common suggestion was that maybe rather than affective assessments, what the RV rating reflected was the subject's judgment of easy versus hard items to learn "for him"). The factor-analytic approach has had its ups and downs in the affections of psychologists. Judging from the ease with which a critic can find some point over which to anguish in the typical factor analysis, the effort once accomplished sometimes seems more an irritant than an aid. Even so, we decided to respond to the pressures and submit RV to factor analysis, taking this opportunity to *also* explore our belief that Osgood's Evaluation and RV were probably swimming in common waters. Two experiments were conducted along this line. In the first 44 college students (26 females, 18 males) were asked to rate 100 trigrams drawn randomly from across the 20–90% range of Archer's norms.

A subject made seven either-or ratings, three of which were hypothesized to load on a common AV factor, three of which were hypothesized to load on a common RV factor, and the last rating of meaningful versus nonmeaningful was included without prediction concerning the factor it would load on. The hypothesized AV instructions were as follows:

Yes versus no. Does this trigram look like a word, remind me of a word, or can I use it in a sentence?
Easy to pronounce versus hard to pronounce. Is this trigram easy for me to pronounce or is it hard for me to pronounce?
Easy to learn versus hard to learn. If I had to learn a list of such trigrams, would this particular one be an easy one to learn, or would it be a hard one to learn?

The hypothesized RV instructions were as follows:

Like versus dislike. The typical RV instruction.
Good versus bad. Does this trigram strike me as being good, or as being bad (cited by Snider & Osgood, 1969, p. 48 and p. 296 as the purest measure of Evaluation)?
Happy versus sad. Does this trigram strike me as being happy, or sad (an alternative form of Evaluation measure)?

The order of these six instructions was counterbalanced, and the 100 trigrams rated according to them were randomly reordered before being presented to the same subject over the six experimental days (48 to 72 hours intervening between ratings). Trigrams were projected onto a screen before the group, and each was exposed for two seconds with a two-second delay between presentations for ratings. On the sixth experimental day a second run-through of the 100 slides was carried out with the following instructions:

Meaningful versus Nonmeaningful. Is this trigram meaningful to me? Does it have meaning for me, or does it lack meaning for me?

The seven rating scales were correlated over subjects and trigrams, utilizing the tetrachoric correlation coefficient. This correlation matrix was then factor analyzed using the centroid method of rotation (Thurstone, 1947) with commonality estimates (highest coefficient in a column) inserted in the diagonal, and two factors were extracted and rotated to simple structure. Both factors reached significance when tested by Humphrey's rule ($p < .05$) (Fruchter, 1954). The correlation between the two extracted factors was .311, and together they accounted for 84% of the variance. A third factor was also extracted, but it proved uninterpretable and was taken as an error factor.

Table 5 presents the rotated factor matrix for our first factor analysis (Flynn, 1967). Note that, except for pronounceability, the instructions loaded as predicted. Asking a subject to sound out a trigram and rate it for this characteristic would appear to pick up on the pronounceability dimension. It should be emphasized, however, that RV influences are found with both easy and hard to pronounce materials, with words, and even with pictorial materials (see Chapter 10). Hence we could not conclude from this modest overlap that RV is a function of pronounceability. The tetrachoric correlations on which the factor loadings of Table 5 are based were all rather modest (as were the loading values). But the clearest difference of two factors emerging as predicted was an impressive finding in favor of our independence thesis (RV versus AV). Furthermore, there was at least preliminary evidence here that RV and Evaluation were related conceptions. Finally, though a subject's estimation of general meaningfulness was related to both of the factors which were extracted, it is significant that a subject was more likely to tie this instruction to an RV-Evaluation factor than to an AV factor. Few learning theories in this area of investigation give independent recognition or even credence to an affective dimension of meaningfulness in their theoretical accounts. Yet from the subject's perspective, such a dimension may be of great significance.

The second factor analysis focused even more specifically on the relationship between RV and Osgood's theory of meaning[fulness], for it included all three of his dimensions. Ed Flynn (1969) continued his excellent work on this aspect of LLT, essentially devoting his total graduate research effort to the question of AV-RV indepen-

**Table 5**   Rotated Factor Matrix of the First Factor Analysis

| Instructions to Subjects | Loadings on Factors Extracted | |
|---|---|---|
| | I | II |
| Yes versus no | .62 | .02 |
| Easy versus hard to pronounce | .06 | .28 |
| Easy versus hard to learn | .63 | −.03 |
| Like versus dislike | .05 | .27 |
| Good versus bad | .07 | .38 |
| Happy versus sad | −.03 | .40 |
| Meaningful versus nonmeaningful | .20 | .38 |

dence and the relationship of RV to Evaluation. Forty-three college students (24 females, 19 males) were asked to rate 25 trigrams, five paralogs (e.g., Gojey, Sagrole, Bodkin, etc., from Noble, 1952), and 20 words randomly selected from the Thorndike-Lorge (1944) lists. The paralogs were viewed as a kind of bridge item, a near-word that subjects would not find familiar but yet closer to their speech forms than the trigrams. The plan of the second study called for the 25 trigrams and the 25 words-paralogs to be analyzed separately. Henceforth we simply refer to the latter (words-paralogs) as *words*. To meet the demands of the Tucker (1964, 1965, 1966) three-mode factor analysis which was employed in this cross-validation effort, a certain adjustment had to be made in the ratings used. Thus rather than making dichotomous judgments, subjects were asked to mark an X in one of six answer boxes, arranged along dimensions of from "very" (much, often, fast, good, etc.) or "definitely" through modifiers like moderately and slightly to another "very" (seldom, unfamiliar, bad, slow, hard, etc.) or "definitely not." As in the first factor analysis, three instructions were devised which were expected to load on an AV dimension. But in this study rather than using two forms of the single Evaluation dimension, all three of the Osgoodian dimensions were employed—that is, Evaluation (good-bad), Potency (strong-weak), and Activity (fast-slow). Once again, the adjectives selected to define the ends of a dimension were based on recommendations taken from Snider and Osgood (1969, pp. 48 and 296). The usual RV instruction was also employed, and it was predicted that of the three Osgoodian dimensions *only* Evaluation would load on a factor in common with RV; of course neither would the AV instructions load on this factor.

The identical instructions for AV could not be used across both trigrams and words, because there is no point in asking a subject if a word (e.g., doctor, feather, tent) looks or sounds like a word. Nor could we use a pronounceability instruction because even the most abstract words employed (e.g., *symphony, council*) were pronounceable. Because many verbal-learning theorists take a measure of familiarity as reflecting meaningfulness, this measure was substituted for pronounceability. The instructions used in the second factor analysis will now be given, beginning with the postulated AV dimensions:

*Trigram frequency.* Does this trigram remind me of a word?
*Word frequency.* How often do I use this word?
*Trigram and word learnability.* If I had to learn a list of (trigrams/words), would this particular one be easy or hard?

*Trigram and word familiarity.* Is this particular (trigram/word) familiar or is it unfamiliar to me?

The Osgoodian dimensions were introduced as follows:

*Trigram and word evaluation.* Does this (trigram/word) strike me as being good or as being bad?

*Trigram and word Potency.* Does this (trigram/word) strike me as being strong or as being weak

*Trigram and word Activity.* Does this (trigram/word) strike me as being active or as being passive?

The RV instruction was as follows:

*Trigram and word RV.* Do I like this (trigram/word) or do I dislike it?

Once again the instructions and order of the verbal materials were randomized across administrations. Response set was countered by having the direction of the six-point continua varied, occasionally going from right to left and then moving in the opposite direction. Words and trigrams were flashed on a screen for three seconds, and a three-second delay between flashes permitted subjects to make their rating. Subjects were tested over a two-week period, with 48 to 72 hours intervening between the various instructions. The Tucker procedure enables one to examine the factor structure of each of the three classifications (subjects, verbal materials, and rating scales) independently of each other and also to permit the construction of a three-dimensional core matrix which simultaneously reveals the interrelations of all the factors in each of the modes.[4] Turning to the rating-scale factor analysis on the trigrams, Table 6 reflects the three factors that were rotated and considered interpretable (a fourth was dismissed as error).

The first factor (I) of Table 6 is obviously defined by some kind of familiarity with the materials. The Activity dimension loads negatively on factor I, as indeed it does on all three of the factors extracted—making it difficult to interpret. Factor II in Table 6 is clearly a cross-validation of the RV-findings on trigrams noted in the first factor analysis. Finally, factor III is also a cross-validation for the AV instruction but the easy-hard judgment on learnability did not load on this as expected. Note that familiarity loaded negatively on both factors II and III. This suggests that in such subword materials

[4] The writer is indebted to Gary Burger, University of Missouri at St. Louis, for his assistance in supervising the Tucker factor analysis.

**Table 6**   Rotated Factor Matrix on Trigrams of the Second Factor Analysis

| Instruction to Subjects | Loadings on Factors Extracted | | |
|---|---|---|---|
| | I | II | III |
| Wordike—unwordlike | −0.13 | −1.03 | 5.14 |
| Easy—hard to learn | 0.19 | −0.59 | −0.32 |
| Familiar—unfamiliar | 4.62 | −1.74 | −1.16 |
| Good—bad | 0.28 | 3.13 | −0.34 |
| Strong—weak | −0.38 | −0.99 | −0.86 |
| Active—passive | −3.89 | −2.45 | −2.02 |
| Like—dislike | −0.69 | 3.67 | −0.45 |

a familiarity in the procedure might have taken on demand characteristics for this instruction. The word materials are not so situation-specific (i.e., they have a broader referent in the subject's life) and, as we see in Table 7, no familiarity factor emerged.

Table 7 presents the three factors that were extracted from the 25 words. In this case factor I is positively loaded by a frequency or AV instruction—that of how often a subject believed that he used a word—and *also* loaded heavily in a negative direction by the Potency factor. Indeed, when plots were drawn of factor I against II and III, the strong-weak instruction was situated more precisely on factor I than was the word-frequency instruction. Factor II in Table 7 is once again the RV-Evaluation factor, clearly demonstrating the pervasiveness and even ascendancy of an affective dimension in the realm of human meanings and/or meaningfulness. Note the heavy negative loading of word frequency (AV) on factor II. When factors I and II were plotted, a clear bipolarity for AV and RV-Evaluation was not found; but the fact that such a disparity between these two instructions existed lends considerable support to our claim of a *conceptual* difference existing between frequency and affective factors in human understanding. Factor III in Table 7 is clearly the Osgoodian dimension of Activity, with every other instruction loading negatively on it.

These are all the data worthy of presenting from the Tucker procedure. A core-matrix analysis was not necessary because both the verbal materials and the subjects' variables proved to be unidimensional. Thus construction of the core would be of no interpretative value but would have merely completed the model in a mathematical sense (see Flynn, 1969, for a more detailed presentation). The main reasons for conducting the second factor analysis were achieved in any case. That is, we had successfully demon-

**Table 7**  Rotated Factor Matrix on Words of the Second Factor Analysis

| Instruction to Subjects | Loadings on Factors Extracted | | |
|---|---|---|---|
| | I | II | III |
| Often use—rarely use | 2.44 | −3.87 | −2.21 |
| Easy—hard to learn | 0.16 | −0.22 | −0.06 |
| Familiar—unfamiliar | 0.98 | −0.93 | −0.78 |
| Good—bad | 0.56 | 3.36 | −0.76 |
| Strong—weak | −5.09 | −0.80 | −0.31 |
| Active—passive | 0.23 | −0.75 | 4.84 |
| Like—dislike | 0.73 | 3.21 | −0.73 |

strated that (1) RV and AV loaded on different dimensions; (2) RV and Evaluation loaded on a common factor; and (3) RV proved highly pervasive, a metric which was equally relevant to the change in verbal materials—from trigrams to words—as was AV.

### Conclusion

We have detailed studies of the work done to establish the construct validity of affective assessment to show the almost dogged determination of LLT's advocates to prove beyond reasonable doubt that this dimension cannot be subsumed conceptually by accounts relying on sheer frequency or derivatives of such frequency explanations. Several of the studies reported to this point were suggested by critics. As objections were raised, we simply did the study that was called for in an open and unbiased fashion. Taken together, we believe that the facts have supported LLT's contention that affective assessment is at play in *all* types of human learning. We further contend that it is unnecessary to learn "how to" affectively assess, and that human beings are therefore contributors to the input organizations which they learn as well as simply mediators of such organizations.

It is important to approach an area of study with a common experimental attack. In our reviews of the literature on affect and learning we found that the studies were so varied in design that it was extremely difficult extrapolating findings from one study to the next (see especially Rychlak, Tasto, Andrews, & Ellis, 1973; Tuan, 1974). Even so, our combined survey and first-hand experience with a consistent methodological approach for almost a generation permit us now to conclude the following: *There is no convincing body of scientific evidence which establishes that affective assessment can* be accounted for solely on the widely accepted principles of contiguity and frequency currently ascendant in psychology thanks to its institutionalized Lockean model. In RV we have a dimension of meaningfulness that can and does reflect idiographic (not subjective) aspects of behavior, allowing for a thoroughly rigorous albeit more humanistic account to emerge in the description of experimental findings. In Chapter 10 we continue our case-history account by showing the many uses of affective assessment in both basic and applied aspects of psychological science.

## Summary

Chapter 9 begins an overview of a case history in which advocates of logical learning theory (LLT) have attempted to further their conceptual revolution in psychological theory by putting their ideas to test in a rigorous context. After first choosing the abstruse and notoriously arid area of verbal learning as a target realm of investigation, the LLT researchers set out to demonstrate that a humanistic conception like affective assessment could be shown to make a contribution to empirical findings, once we paradigmatically assume that it is active. We also predicted that the contribution made to learning by the subject's affective assessment could not be empirically reduced to or otherwise accounted for by constructs relying upon the frequency or contiguity principles.

Chapter 9 is a narrative account of how the affective-assessment conception was first suggested and how, through its operationalization in reinforcement value (RV), the researchers in LLT have been able to establish conceptual independence from association-value (AV) measures of meaningfulness. After first discussing the initial work on a Phonetic Preference Inventory (PPI), which encompasses the typical manner in which RV is measured, several empirical tests of the construct validity of affective assessment are presented. Reinforcement value is shown to be at play independently of AV in various learning studies, bringing about the positive-RV effect—that is, the tendency to learn liked more readily than disliked verbal materials. This takes place even when subjects learn identical lists of consonant-vowel-consonant (CVC) trigrams, which they have rated at opposite ends of the RV dimension.

This superiority of liked over disliked trigrams cannot be reduced to more frequent associations being produced by the former than by the latter. Nor are idiographic RV and nomothetic levels of

AV systematically related. Indeed, the more wordlike a trigram is judged by a subject to be, the more probable is it that he will make clear distinctions between this verbal item and the affective quality he assigns to it. Findings on RV cannot be explained away as due to fortuitous errors of measurement in the selection of trigrams for study. The test-retest reliability of trigrams rated for RV matches or exceeds the test-retest reliability of AV, if we consider these trigrams singly, in an idiographic fashion—that is, look at each trigram rated in turn rather than at the pooled proportion of trigrams judged one way or the other (liked versus disliked) in a nomothetic fashion. When both AV and RV are treated via such proportion scores and correlated, the resultant value of r is .54. This parallels findings of a nonparametric sort which suggest that subjects will confound RV ratings (like-dislike) with AV ratings (wordlike-nonwordlike) in 25–33% of the cases, and especially so when the trigrams are very unlike the standing language structure. Finally, in cross-validating factor analyses we found that AV and RV rating instructions load on completely different factors. Osgood's Evaluation and AV were found to load on completely different factors. Evaluation and RV are found to load on a common dimension in both studies, however, a fact that lends great generalizability to RV learning style if we appreciate the vast applicability Evaluation has been shown to have in the languages of mankind.

Considering both the series of investigations conducted by LLT researchers, and also the extant literature on the topic of affect and frequency dimensions, there is no convincing body of scientific evidence to establish the claim that affective assessment can be accounted for solely on the principles of contiguity or frequency currently ascendant in psychology's institutionalized Lockean model. A Kantian formulation stands up well to the empirical data.

## References

Abramson, Y. *Reinforcement value: An idiographic approach to meaningfulness.* Unpublished doctoral dissertation. St. Louis: St. Louis University, 1967.

Abramson, Y., Tasto, D. L., & Rychlak, J. F. Nomothetic vs. idiographic influences of asociation value and reinforcement value on learning. *Journal of Experimental Research in Personality*, 1969, **4**, 65–71.

Adorno, T. W., Frenkel-Brunswik, E., Levinson, D. J., & Sanford, R. N. *The authoritarian personality.* New York: Harper, 1950.

Archer, E. J. Re-evaluation of the meaningfulness of all possible CVC trigrams. *Psychological Monographs*, 1960, **74**, No. 10 (Whole No. 497).

August, G. J., Rychlak, J. F., & Felker, D. W. Affective assessment, self-concept, and the verbal learning styles of fifth-grade children. *Journal of Educational Psychology*, 1975, **67**, 801–806.

Berg, I. A. Deviant responses and deviant people: The formulation of the deviation hypothesis. *Journal of Counseling Psychology*, 1957, **4**, 159.

Bugelski, B. R., & Scharlock, D. P. An experimental demonstration of unconscious mediated association. *Journal of Experimental Psychology*, 1952, **44**, 334–338.

Cronbach, L. J., & Meehl, P. E. Construct validity in psychological tests. *Psychological Bulletin*, 1955, **52**, 281–302.

Flynn, E. *The factor analysis of meaning in CVC trigrams rated for association value and reinforcement value.* Unpublished master's thesis. St. Louis: St. Louis University, 1967.

Flynn, E. J. *Beyond frequency: A two-dimensional theory of verbal meaningfulness.* Unpublished doctoral dissertation. St. Louis: St. Louis University, 1969.

Fruchter, B. *Introduction to factor analysis.* New Jersey: D. Van Nostrand, 1954.

Glaze, J. A. The association value of nonsense syllables. *Journal of Genetic Psychology*, 1928, **35**, 255–269.

Kelly, G. A. *The psychology of personal constructs* (2 vols.). New York: Norton, 1955.

Kubat, W. J. *The reinforcement value of associations made to CVC trigrams.* Unpublished master's thesis. St. Louis: St. Louis University, 1969.

Laberteaux, T. E. *The influence of positive versus negative reinforcement value on mediated paired-associate learning.* Unpublished master's thesis. St. Louis: St. Louis University, 1968.

Nishball, E. R. *A comparison of meaningfulness and intensity in CVC trigrams.* Unpublished master's thesis. St. Louis: St. Louis University, 1966.

Noble, C. E. An analysis of meaning. *Psychological Review*, 1952, **59**, 421–430.

Osgood, C. E. The nature and measurement of meaning. *Psychological Bulletin*, 1952, **49**, 197–237.

Osgood, C. E. On the whys and wherefores of E, P, and A. *Journal of Personality and Social Psychology*, 1969, **12**, 194–199.

Paivio, A. *Imagery and verbal processes.* New York: Holt, Rinehart & Winston, 1971.

Paivio, A., Yuille, J. C., & Madigan, S. A. Concreteness, imagery, and meaningfulness values for 925 nouns. *Journal of Experimental Psychology Monograph Supplement*, 1968, **76**, 1–25.

Peters, H. N. Mediate association. *Journal of Experimental Psychology*, 1935, **18**, 20–48.

Rotter, J. B. *Social learning and clinical psychology.* Englewood Cliffs, N.J.: Prentice-Hall, 1954.

Rychlak, J. F. Reinforcement value: A suggested idiographic, intensity dimension of meaningfulness for the personality theorist. *Journal of Personality*, 1966, **34**, 311–335.

Rychlak, J. F. *A philosophy of science for personality theory.* Boston: Houghton Mifflin, 1968.

Rychlak, J. F. *Introduction to personality and psychotherapy: A theory-construction approach.* Boston: Houghton Mifflin, 1973.

Rychlak, J. F., Tasto, D. L., Andrews, J. E., & Ellis, H. C. The application of an affective dimension of meaningfulness to personality-related verbal learning. *Journal of Personality,* 1973, **41**, 341–360.

Siegel, S. *Nonparametric statistics for the behavioral sciences.* New York: McGraw-Hill, 1956.

Snider, J. G., & Osgood, C. E. *Semantic differential technique: A sourcebook.* Chicago: Aldine, 1969.

Tasto, D. L. *The influence of meaningfulness as measured in terms of frequency and intensity on rate of acquisition.* Unpublished master's thesis. St. Louis: St. Louis University, 1967.

Taylor, J. A. A personality scale of manifest anxiety. *Journal of Abnormal and Social Psychology,* 1953, **48**, 285–290.

Tenbrunsel, T. W. *A study of the relationship of association value and reinforcement value at various levels of nomothetic association value.* Unpublished master's thesis. St. Louis: St. Louis University, 1967.

Tenbrunsel, T. W., Nishball, E. R., & Rychlak, J. F. The idiographic relationship between association value and reinforcement value, and the nature of meaning. *Journal of Personality,* 1968, **36**, 126–137.

Thorndike, E. L., & Lorge, R. *The teachers word book of 30,000 words.* New York: Columbia University Press, 1944.

Thurstone, L. L. *Multiple factor analysis.* Chicago: The University of Chicago Press, 1947.

Tuan, N. D. *Changes in associative and affective meaningfulness as a function of frequency and intensity factors.* Unpublished doctoral dissertation. Lafayette, Ind.: Purdue University, 1974.

Tucker, L. R. The extension of factor analysis to three-dimensional matrices. In N. Frederiksen & H. Gulliksen (Eds.), *Contributions to mathematical psychology.* New York: Holt, Rinehart & Winston, 1964.

Tucker, L. R. Experiments in multi-mode factor analysis. *Proceedings of the 1964 invitational conference on testing problems.* 1965, **14**, 46–57.

Tucker, L. R. Some mathematical notes on three-mode factor analysis. *Psychometrika,* 1966, **31**, 279–311.

Tulving, E., & Madigan, S. A. Memory and verbal learning. In P. H. Mussen & M. R. Rosenzweig (Eds.), *Annual review of psychology* (Vol. 21). Palo Alto, Calif.: Annual Reviews, 1970. Pp. 437–477.

# CHAPTER TEN

## Case History of a Revolution Continued: Applications to Human Behavior

The value of a theoretical conception is its potential instructiveness in the realm of study to which it is aimed. Though, as Chapter 9 reveals, we had devoted considerable effort to establishing the integrity of affective assessment as measured by RV, our task was now to show how this construct might relate to various topics of interest to the psychologist. Over the years we have applied affective assessment to several problem areas, and in Chapter 10 we survey five of these to demonstrate that LLT can indeed teach us something about behavior without sacrificing a humanistic phrasing of the rigorously based empirical findings.

### A Metric of Meaningfulness in Personality

One of the first claims made for the RV measure was that it reflected the subject's basic dialectical (either-or) estimate of meaningfulness concerning whatever it was that he placed under affective assessment. As such, RV can be said to be a metric of meaningfulness (i.e., the extent of significance which any given meaning has for the individual; see Chapter 2, pp. 55–58 and Chapter 8, pp. 324–325). Some meanings extend in a positive and others in a negative (meaningful) direction, depending upon the judgment rendered at the protopoint in precedently arraying a premise. The view held by LLT was that the person tautologized the meaningfulness (liked, disliked) of a self-evaluation with the meaningfulness (liked, disliked) of the meanings under extension. The tautology here occurred because, in arraying materials (trigrams, words) for learning via the initial affective assessment (precedent), the average person, liking himself, extended liked more readily (sequaciously) than disliked meanings in the task to follow. He premised the task in such a way as to ensure this patterning of affective learning style.

This logic of explanation suggested that RV indexed what was significant to the self-structure or personality. This metric of meaningfulness should be applicable in a personality study, where such stylistic ordering of meanings in line with a subject's personality style can be expected to surface. How might RV relate to such considerations?

We hypothesized that if subjects with a certain personality style (so-called trait) were asked to learn verbal materials having the meanings of this style, the RV dimension would be reflected in the ordering of their learning, whereas it might not be expected to be reflected in the opposite meanings to their personality designation. For example, a masculine individual learning masculine verbal materials should reflect a clear RV-positive effect, because he or she would tautologize most readily along the liked masculine meaning of these materials (i.e., the most meaningful). Because he or she would not exhibit this tautologizing propensity for feminine materials, we would not expect as large an RV-positive effect in this opposite meaning realm. Feminine individuals (of either sex) should reveal a pronounced RV-positive effect in learning feminine verbal materials. Two studies were conducted on this topic.

The first employed trigrams as verbal materials, which allowed us to remove frequency considerations from the items subjects were asked to learn (Tasto, 1968). Though Chapter 9 surveys a host of studies proving that RV-effects cannot be accounted for by frequency or contiguity factors, we had nevertheless to control for possible frequency explanations of the findings on affective assessment. Two hundred trigrams in the 44–56% range of Archer's (1960) norms, which did not have sex differences in the original AV ratings, were presented to 122 college subjects (equally divided by sex) on a specially prepared form, with spaces for making one of two ratings for each trigram. A subject was asked to read each trigram "to yourself, as if aloud in your 'mind's eye' " and then rate whether it "looks and sounds masculine or whether it looks and sounds feminine." Trigrams were then given a percentage-of-sample score value based on the proportion of subjects rating it *masculine* in meaning. Trigrams reflecting significant sex differences in masculinity scores were dropped from the study.

Some examples of these trigrams, with the percentage scores in parentheses follow: RUK (90%), JOP (82%), GUK (81%), YUC (81%), SAH (20%), NIM (21%), WYM (25%), GEY (29%). To identify

50 masculine and 50 feminine trigrams, all those with a percentage score above 65 were considered masculine and those falling below 44 were considered feminine in meaning. These 100 trigrams (along with 40 filler trigrams of intermediate percentage scores) were then administered to 114 female nursing students and 97 male fraternity members, who rated them on two occasions for RV. In addition, the nursing students and fraternity members had been given the Masculinity-Femininity (M-F) scale of the Minnesota Multiphasic Personality Inventory (MMPI) (Dahlstrom & Welsh, 1960). Subjects were considered masculine in personality if they fell in the upper third of their MMPI M-F distribution and feminine if they fell in the lower third of their distribution. That is, each sample (men and women) was arrayed separately, and identification of personality style was accomplished within a particular sexual identity. The terms *masculine* and *feminine* must be free to modify sex type, personality type, or trigram-meaning in the present discussion.

Forty female nursing students were selected, half of whom were identified as masculine in personality and half as feminine; 32 fraternity members were similarly selected, equally divided as to masculine and feminine personality tendencies. All subjects were then put through a free-recall task, in which they were asked to learn 10 trigrams, five of which were liked and five of which were disliked. Some subjects were dealing with masculinely connoting trigrams and others with femininely connoting trigrams. To summarize, this design involved 10 nursing students (females) and eight fraternity members (males) performing in each of four free-recall conditions: (1) masculine personality type recalling masculine trigrams (five liked, five disliked, as in each of the following); (2) masculine personality recalling feminine trigrams; (3) feminine personality recalling masculine trigrams; and (4) feminine personality recalling feminine trigrams. There were thus three between-subjects factors (sex type, personality type, and trigram meaning) and one within-subjects factor (RV). A $3 \times 1$ factorial analysis of variance (ANOVA) was run on these data.

Table 8 presents the means and standard deviations of the free-recall score (trials to criterion), broken down by personality and trigram meaning. The lower the score in Table 8, the better the learning. A triple interaction in the ANOVA on these data merely approximated significance ($p < .08$), but note that the array of means is as expected. Masculine personality types (of both sexes) who learned masculine meanings have a larger RV-positive effect ($M = 7.46$ on positive, $M = 9.13$ on negative) than they do when learning

**Table 8** Experiment 1: Mean and Standard Deviation of Free Recall
Score, Broken Down by Personality and CVC-Trigram Meaning[a]

| CVC trigram meaning | Masculine Personality | | | | Feminine Personality | | | |
|---|---|---|---|---|---|---|---|---|
| | Positive RV | | Negative RV | | Positive RV | | Negative RV | |
| | Mean | SD | Mean | SD | Mean | SD | Mean | SD |
| Masculine | 7.46 | 3.53 | 9.13 | 2.17 | 8.23 | 3.43 | 9.14 | 3.77 |
| Feminine | 10.29 | 4.49 | 10.18 | 3.62 | 8.51 | 3.48 | 10.25 | 4.15 |

[a] Factorial interaction on these data, $p < .08$.

feminine meanings ($M = 10.29$ on positive, $M = 10.18$ on negative). Conversely, when feminine personality types learn feminine trigrams, their RV-positive differential is greater ($M = 8.51$ on positive, $M = 10.25$ on negative) than it is when they learn masculine trigrams ($M = 8.23$ on positive, $M = 9.14$ on negative). There were no other personality-to-learning style findings in these data. Affective assessment did indeed seem to reach beyond the verbal-learning laboratory, to unite with personality factors, but a more convincing demonstration was surely in order.

In the second study actual words were selected from the Thorndike-Lorge (1944) norms—that is, 300 nouns from a high rate of occurrence in the standing language structure (100 times per million) and 300 nouns from a low rate (5 times per million) (Andrews, 1972). This allowed us to study nomothetically high versus low AV meaningfulness in conjunction with RV meaningfulness. These nouns were administered on mimeographed forms to 78 college subjects (36 females, 42 males), who were asked to read each and to check whether its meaning suggested an *ascendant* or a *submissive* characteristic, if it were used to describe a person. The definitions of ascendant and submissive were taken from the Guilford-Martin (1948) personality scale, which was to be used to identify subjects for a subsequent RV-learning task. Only those nouns on which 75% of the subjects agreed were retained, and indeed, over two-thirds of the nouns retained had better than 90% agreement among the 78 raters. This reliability check pared the acceptable words to 250, falling into the following designations (example nouns given in parentheses); 53 high AV ascendant nouns (*chief, nature, club, dare, love*); 62 low AV ascendant nouns (*czar, piston, brawl, sleet, ammonia*); 66 high AV submissive nouns (*salt, knee, fish, hall, shade*); and 69 low AV submissive nouns (*turban, marrow, doughnut, dimple, cowardice*).

From a separate pool of 93 subjects who took the Guilford-Martin Inventory (1948), 20 subjects were identified as either ascendant or submissive (10 males, 10 females in each category), based on whether they fell one standard deviation above (ascendant) or below (submissive) the mean score of the ascendant-submission scale on this instrument. These 40 subjects were administered the 250 words and asked to rate them for RV (on two occasions, with 48 hours intervening). Paired-associates lists were then constructed for each subject in which 16 pairs were arranged as follows (two pairs in each of eight combinations): high AV, ascendant, RV positive; high AV, ascendant, RV negative; low AV, ascendant, RV positive; low AV, ascendant, RV negative; high AV, submissive, RV positive; high AV, submissive, RV negative; low AV, submissive, RV positive; and low AV, submissive, RV negative.

Once again the prediction was that RV-effects would be most noticeable in the personality-to-word meaning alignment. If tautological factors enter into human learning, a subject who is learning words in line with his self-affirmed personality style should reflect greater meaning-extension along this direction than when he learns words at variance or in opposition to his personality. The experimental design lent itself to a factorial ANOVA in which the data were grouped as follows: 2 (sex type) × 2 (personality type) × 2 (word meaning) × 2 (RV) × 2 (AV). The first two are between-subjects and the last three within-subjects factors. The method of anticipation was employed in the learning task, with trials to criterion taken as the measure of learning (a lower score reflects better learning than a high score). Table 9 presents the means and standard deviations of the trials scores broken down by personality, word meaning, and RV.

Table 9 is assembled exactly like Table 8, so that the reader can directly compare the findings of the two studies. The triple inter-

**Table 9**  Experiment 2: Mean and Standard Deviation of Paired-Associates Trial Scores, Broken Down by Personality and Word Meaning[a]

| Word meaning | Ascendant Personality | | | | Submissive Personality | | | |
| | Positive RV | | Negative RV | | Positive RV | | Negative RV | |
| | Mean | SD | Mean | SD | Mean | SD | Mean | SD |
|---|---|---|---|---|---|---|---|---|
| Ascendant | 3.95 | 1.61 | 4.45 | 1.49 | 4.08 | 1.68 | 3.90 | 1.45 |
| Submissive | 3.73 | 1.72 | 3.95 | 1.52 | 3.45 | 1.34 | 4.13 | 1.68 |

[a] Factorial interaction on these data, $p = .02$.

action on which the data of Table 9 were based achieved a satisfactory level of significance ($p = .02$). Note that, once again, ascendant personalities (combined sexes) learning ascendant words have a larger RV-positive effect ($M = 3.95$ on positive, $M = 4.45$ on negative) than they do when they learn submissive meanings ($M = 3.73$ on positive, $M = 3.95$ on negative). Conversely, when submissive personality types learn submissive meanings, their RV-positive differential is greater ($M = 3.45$ on positive, $M = 4.13$ on negative) than it is when they learn ascendant meanings ($M = 4.08$ on positive, $M = 3.90$ on negative). No such findings emerged for the triple interaction in which AV meaningfulness was employed (see Rychlak, Tasto, Andrews, & Ellis, 1973, for a more thorough presentation of these findings). The RV metric had made its first successful step outside the artificial environment of the laboratory.

There are two points to be made concerning the data of Tables 8 and 9, the first of which has sometimes been the basis of criticism for LLT research. Note that occasionally a group that is said to be less affected by RV-positive actually *does better* on the absolute score of the RV-positive sublist than does the group that is said to be more sensitive to RV-positive in its learning. In Table 8 we find this true when we compare the feminine personality learning masculine-liked trigrams ($M = 8.23$) with this group's learning of feminine-liked trigrams ($M = 8.51$). In Table 9 this seeming inversion obtains when we look at the ascendant personality learning ascendant-liked nouns ($M = 3.95$) in comparison to submissive-liked nouns ($M = 3.73$). Because the Lockean theorist views positive and negative RV as two different things, this seems to go against the claim made that a positive RV effect is being depicted in our respective tables. If subjects are tautologizing along a liked course of meaning-extension in congruence with their personality style, as LLT contends, why are not these mean scores in the *reverse* direction?

The obvious answer here would be to point out that these instances reflect between-subjects differences and hence to expect data across different groups of people to array perfectly is unrealistic. However, we do sometimes note comparable situations even when there is a within-subjects analysis under consideration. The more relevant point seems to be that as a dialectical conception, affective assessment and its RV measure must be thought of in relationship (bipolar) terms—that is, the relation between positive and negative values—rather than in absolute (unipolar) terms. Much of the disenchantment in psychology with laboratory methods like paired-associates or free-recall lists stems from the fact that learning rates in an absolute sense do not predict to performance in the school classroom (McKeachie, 1974). The LLT research line has emphasized the interactive factors within such lists or across unmixed lists without expecting the absolute scores to reflect what is most important about a subject's performance. Lacking the frequency bias of Lockeanism, we do not look for how fast the job is done as the most important dependent variable in every instance. The ideal array of means often occurs, of course, but we never lose sight of the forest for the trees.

The second point we would like to bring to the reader's attention deals with the direction of this very relationship between positive and negative RV meaningfulness. Note in Table 8 that the masculine personality learning feminine items and in Table 9 the submissive personality learning ascendant items *reverse* the expected rankordering of affective assessment. In these instances the subjects learn their disliked material more readily than their liked material. On first impression one could think of these minor fluctuations as due to error variance. However, in the second experiment (Table 9) we found a significant quadruple interaction ($p < .01$) when sex was brought into the picture. It was *only* the submissive males of our sample learning ascendant nouns who reversed in this fashion; submissive females learned ascendant words according to the typical RV-positive effect (we shall be using this term *effect* throughout Chapter 10 advisedly, in a strictly methodological sense, without implying efficient causation). A similar breakdown of Table 8 by sex revealed that it was the masculine female of our first experiment who accounted for the reversal to be seen in the learning of feminine meanings; masculine males did not reverse the rank ordering of RV (this analysis failed to reach statistical significance).

This common drift of our experimental data proved fascinating, because it suggested that human beings may learn affectively in *either* of our two relative directions—positive or negative—depending upon their frame of mind (their *premise*) concerning the meanings they were being asked to deal with. Male chauvinism aside, at the time of these studies (mid to late-1960s) and considering the background of these subjects (middle-class young adults), we thought we might be seeing here a form of rejection of the traditional role by masculine females and submissive males, who had affirmed a pole of meaning in direct opposition as their self-identity. Viewed clinically, this could even suggest a degree of maladjustment in sex role. Events taking place concurrently in RV studies on maladjusted subjects were to strengthen this line of theoretical development.

## Abnormal Behavior, Self-Evaluation and
## Affective Learning Style

A theoretical position sometimes implies something that its advocates find conceptually risky to contend but nevertheless are forced to predict solely on the implications (meaning-extensions) of their already affirmed formal position. So it was with LLT in the case of what we eventually called diminished RV-positive effects and/or RV-reversal effects. In contending that subjects tautologized a positive self-evaluation with trigram meanings, which they considered positive in RV more readily than with materials they considered negative, we were necessarily put in the position of contending the reverse. It followed that subjects who evaluated themselves negatively or who were sufficiently maladjusted in life to be considered neurotic or psychotic should *reverse* and tautologize negative self-evaluations along a negative meaning-extension. In the years since Yitz Abramson, Bill Schneider, and Doug McKee conducted the first studies on this topic we have refined our thinking considerably. But the first RV-reversal research was (almost reluctantly) predicted purely on theoretical grounds. Frankly, we approached the work with "one foot out the door," wondering how to patch up the tenets of LLT if abnormal subjects were even *more* reliant on RV-positive effects than normal subjects.

We first put a group of psychotics through the production method as outlined in Chapter 9 (pp. 384–387) to establish that they performed comparably to normals (i.e., did not rely on frequency factors in their RV ratings). Twenty schizophrenic patients from a state hospital (10 males, 10 females) were studied, with 20 neuropsychiatric (Np) aides matched for sex and social class acting as controls. Once again, no significant differences emerged in the number of word-associates (AV meaningfulness) to the CVC trigrams for either the abnormals or the normal controls. However, when we examined the RV-ratings of the words that had been associated to the trigrams, a cross-validation of our earlier findings emerged. Thus *both* normals and abnormals ascribed positive RV to the word-associates of liked trigrams and (relatively) negative RV to the word-associates of disliked trigrams (p < .01; see Rychlak, McKee, Schneider, & Abramson, 1971). Two concurrent investigations were initially conducted on the learning style of abnormals.

One of these studies was done at a state hospital, using 16 chronic Np patients (primarily schizophrenics) and 16 Np aides as matched

controls (age, sex, social class). All patients were taken off psycho-
tropic drugs for three days preceding their participation in the study.
As a side effort, we ran these subjects on RV-tasks both on and off
medication, finding no systematic differences. Subjects in this study
made idiographic ratings of CVC trigrams on two occasions for *both*
AV and RV, and the typical procedure of employing only reliably
rated trigrams in constructing the learning-task lists was followed
(see Chapter 9). Every subject had a list of six pairs for *each* of the
following AV-RV combinations: AV yes, RV liked; AV yes, RV disliked; AV no, RV liked; and AV no, RV disliked. These were presented as four different learning tasks (unmixed lists), with the
order of presentation counterbalanced across subjects to offset the
effects of transfer. Method of anticipation was followed, and the
learning criterion was two consecutive correct anticipations of the
entire list.

Once again AV meaningfulness *failed* to distinguish our experimental conditions. There was, however, a significant interaction
between experimental condition and RV-learning style ($p < .01$). As
predicted, normals learned their lists with a clear RV-positive effect,
but the abnormals slightly reversed this direction and actually
learned along a negative more readily than a positive meaning-
extension. Separate analyses conducted on males and females further
established that the males of our sample accounted for the outright
reversal (*ibid.*). We interpret such reversals as simply a more pronounced experimental effect than the diminution in the RV-positive
effect. To establish an outright reversal in learning style is not always necessary to show that a subject is less sensitive to the liked
meanings in the task at hand. Figure 4 presents the trials-to-criterion
data for our subjects, broken down by sex and experimental group.
Note that the female psychotics show a pronounced diminution in
the RV-positive effect, and the males show a reversal.

The companion study in this opening work not only studied
RV-effects, but tried to get at the claims of LLT that subjects extended meaning more readily along one affective direction than
another. If this active process of learning were true, we should be
able to show in the patterns of *errors* made by subjects that abnormals would not only diminish or reverse the RV-positive effect, but
that they would actually make more erroneous efforts to anticipate
in the realm of negative RV than in the realm of positive RV. Spence
and Lair (1964) had called a subject's verbalized but incorrect anticipation of the second member of a pair *an error of commission* because he had, after all, made the overt effort to form a connection

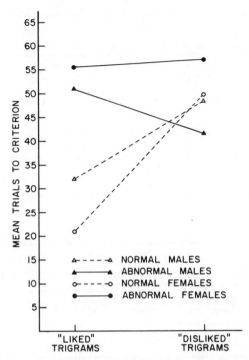

**Figure 4**  Trials to criterion in the paired-associates task are graphed according to positive RV (liked trigrams) and negative RV (disliked trigrams), broken down by the sex and mental-health status of the subjects. (The solid line reflects the performance of chronic neuropsychiatric patients in a state hospital, and the broken line represents the performance of normal psychiatric aides, matched for chronological age and social-class level.)

between trigrams rather than remain silent to see what would eventuate. Both remaining silent and making an incorrect statement constitute errors in the typical scoring procedure. But if we took note of these verbalizations, would they occur more frequently in the negative than the positive RV realm among our psychotics? This is what we predicted, along with the expected RV-diminution or outright reversal of the RV-positive effect in the learning data.

We obtained the services of 32 newly admitted patients in acute stages of schizophrenia (divided equally by sex) from a city hospital but were not permitted to use Np aides as controls (McKee, 1969). Because at the time we were obtaining considerable evidence in support of the RV-positive effect on normals, the study was carried on without a control group. The typical AV and RV rating procedures were followed. Twelve pairs of trigrams were arrayed for each subject, with three pairs in each of the four possible AV-RV combinations (mixed lists). This proved a very difficult task for the subject to complete in the testing time allotted by the hospital. Hence we followed the procedure of giving subjects a warm-up series of four trials on a different list of four pairs and then running a subject for 15 trials on his 12-pair experimental list, at which time the testing was terminated. A subject's learning score is the mean number of hits on trials 14 and 15 on each of the AV-RV combinations in his list (i.e., AV yes, RV liked; AV yes, RV disliked, etc.). A second score for each subject was also determined called the errors of commission score. The latter measure was simply a count of the number of times over his 15 trials that a subject had vocalized an *incorrect* anticipation of the second member of a pair in each of the four AV-RV list combinations.

Taking up the learning scores first (and without citing actual means), we found that both AV ($p < .01$) and RV ($p < .05$) influenced meaning-extensions in coming to the learning reflected at trials 14 and 15. The acute patients found it easier to learn trigrams they had rated as having word quality (AV yes) than trigrams they had rated as lacking word quality (AV no). But they *also* learned trigrams they disliked (RV-negative) more readily than trigrams they liked (RV-positive), thereby cross-validating our findings on the state hospital chronic patients. There was no significant interaction between AV and RV in the factorial ANOVA done on the learning scores, nor were there any sex differences in these data. Turning to our test of the meaning-extension theory, Table 10 presents the means and standard deviations of the errors-of-commission scores over the 15 trials (these are given in raw-score values, but a ratio score of errors-of-commission to the total-errors-made factorial ANOVA was also conducted with identical findings).

**Table 10**   Mean and Standard Deviation of Errors of Commission over Fifteen Trials[a]

| Sublist Breakdown on AV and RV | Mean | SD |
|---|---|---|
| AV yes, RV positive | 4.66 | 4.08 |
| AV no, RV positive | 7.75 | 2.84 |
| AV yes, RV negative | 6.06 | 3.28 |
| AV no, RV negative | 9.22 | 3.76 |

[a] There were significant main effects for AV ($p < .01$) and RV ($p < .05$), with no significant interaction between factors.

A factorial ANOVA was run on the data of Table 10, with both AV ($p < .01$) and RV ($p < .05$) reaching significance as main effects without a significant interaction occurring between them. Note that the trigram which lacks word quality (AV no) produces more errors of commission than the trigram which has word quality (AV yes). This makes good sense, suggesting that a subject is trying to formulate associative ties across relatively meaningless verbal materials but not doing so well as when he deals with materials that are idiographically meaningful to him. The learning-score data already referred to establish that these subjects were indeed doing more poorly on AV-no than on AV-yes trigrams. However, what do we make of the fact that in Table 10 the RV-disliked trigrams brought on more errors of commission than RV-liked trigrams? In this case not only did the psychotics learn RV-disliked trigrams more readily than RV-liked trigrams, but they made more errors of commission along the former than the latter!

We had by this time also begun to make up for our lack of a control group on the study just described. Ten Np male patients and 10 matched controls were put through a 12-pair list of paired-associates, six of which were liked and six disliked (AV was not involved). The 15-trial cutoff procedure in the learning task was followed. The normals both learned along an RV-positive direction and *also* made more errors of commission on RV-negative trigrams; the abnormals showed a significant diminution of the RV-positive effect and *also* made significantly more errors of commission on disliked than liked trigrams ($p < .01$ on both factorial ANOVAs). Even more interesting was the fact that when these subjects were retested one week later the flattening of the RV-positive effect and the errors of commission on disliked trigrams by the abnormals proved *greater* on retest than on original testing! Normals continue to learn along the positive and misfire along the negative in life, but our abnormals reflect a fascination with the negative which increases with a "second look."

Although we had used subjects to this point who might be considered negative self-evaluators, we had not measured this aspect of a subject's behavior to relate it systematically to his RV learning style. Bob Lappin and Gertrude Boland gave this aspect of LLT its first direct tests. Both researchers employed the Block (1965) Ego Resiliency and Control Scale (p. 142), which was based on a factor analysis of MMPI items; it presumably measures the individual's level of psychological adjustment and impulse control. This is a good point at which to emphasize that, though we naturally want to use the best scale available in our researches, LLT does not distinguish between the various self-identity names that test constructors assign to their scales. It makes little difference whether we are measuring something called the ego, the self, the personal value system, or whatever. Just so long as a subject is being asked to assess his introspectively sensed *identity* on the scale in question, we are prepared to predict the RV effects under consideration in the present section. As the weight of logical meaning-extension, the self construct employed in LLT is not to be entitized into some one thing, measured by a single instrument.

Both Lappin (1969) and Boland (1970) studied high school students who were classified as either high or low in ego strength based on their extreme scores on the Block (1965) scale in an extensive pretesting of their classmates. Trigrams were then rated idiographically for both AV and RV, and experimental subjects were put through a mixed-list format of paired-associates learning, using the familiar combinations of our two metrics of meaningfulness (AV yes, RV liked; AV no, RV liked, etc.). Boland (1970) found a trend ($p = .11$) in the interaction between ego strength and RV in which the data arrayed themselves as predicted with high ego-strength subjects showing a weak RV-positive effect and low ego-strength subjects showing a weak RV-negative effect. No such trends were noted for the AV metric. Lappin's (1969) findings were more powerful, emerging in a triple interaction between AV, RV, and ego strength ($p < .01$). That is, only when we look at the AV-yes trigrams did the low ego-strength subjects learn their disliked trigrams ($M = 33.95$) more quickly than they learned their liked trigrams ($M = 34.43$), and the high ego-strength subjects learned their liked trigrams ($M = 32.13$) more quickly than their disliked trigrams ($M = 36.13$). When AV-no trigrams were considered, there was a slight RV-positive effect to be seen in the learning of both high and low ego-strength subjects.

Nancy Carlsen (1970) then predicted that she could cross-validate Lappin's findings, using the Tennessee Self-Concept Scale (Fitts, 1965) as the measure of self-evaluation. Carlsen also wanted to see if these diminutions or reversals in the RV-positive effect could be due to a subject's typical school performance. The AV dimension was not included in her study. Forty high school females were identified as either high or low self-evaluators based on pretesting with the Tennessee Scale, and within these extremes the girls were also selected on the basis of having either a high or low grade-point average (roughly upper or lower thirds of class grade-point distribution). Subjects rated the PPI on two occasions, and a free-recall list of five liked and five disliked trigrams was administered to each as the experimental task. There were no significant findings for grade-point average. However, true to LLT predictions, the high self-concept girls learned their liked trigrams ($M = 3.65$) more readily than their disliked trigrams ($M = 4.55$), whereas the low self-concept girls learned their disliked trigrams ($M = 4.00$) more readily than their liked trigrams ($M = 4.40$) (interaction significant, $p < .01$). Affective learning style was being established as a phenomenon independent of school ability, and although occasionally dependent upon the word-quality of learnable items, it was reflecting something characteristic of human learning that could not be captured by the AV-based theories of the verbal-learning laboratory.

We next decided to extend our developing theory to the performance of children. Of course an even broader question is involved here—that is, the range which affective assessment may be said to have in learning styles across the life span. It is the position of LLT that affective assessment is innate (see Chapter 8, p. 317). Although it was not used in the research on self factors, we did eventually design a survey procedure that enabled us to study very young children on the RV dimension (see Rychlak, 1975a). Slides of the original Berg (1957) designs and also of abstract paintings obtained from the Museum of Modern Art collection were employed as items to be recognized by the children in a test-retest format. These slides were projected onto a screen before 169 children (both sexes) selected from the first six grades of two elementary schools. The children rated these designs and paintings on two occassions during the same testing hour.

The first time through, they rated them for RV; and during a readministration of the same slides (mixed in among unfamiliar slides), they were asked to rate for RV a second time and to judge whether they had rated these previously. We could therefore obtain reliable RV ratings as usual and see if children recognized liked slides more often than disliked slides. A uniform RV-positive effect ($p < .01$) was indeed found across all six grade levels. First graders, and particularly the boys at this level, seemed even more sensitive to RV in their recognition of designs and paintings than the older children (grade level $\times$ sex $\times$ RV interaction significant, $p < .01$). Kay Woodward (1973) has used this group procedure successfully with high school students and, at least for the females of her sample, was able to show that learners identified as positive or negative in the group task learned in similar fashion when asked to take an individual task. Thus we have obtained evidence for RV effects across the age span of roughly six to past 60.

Returning to the question of RV-positive diminutions or reversals in young children, we have frankly had more failures than successes in this research. In the first study attempted (Rychlak & Saluri, 1973), 40 fifth and sixth grade children (both sexes, approximately 10 to 12 years of age) were selected from the ends of a distribution of 164 children who had been administered the Piers-Harris (1964) Children's Self-Concept Scale. All these children attended the same rural elementary school. Unfortunately, we could not counterbalance for IQ, so children identified as high in self-concept (positive self evaluators) were also significantly higher in intelligence than children low in self-concept. As a learning task, subjects were given a list of 100 names (50 male, 50 female) and asked to rate them for RV in the usual fashion. A list of five liked and five disliked names was then administered to each subject in a free-recall format (subjects wrote down recalled names on a paper form between trials of list presentation).

The predicted RV-diminution or RV-reversal for low self-esteem subjects failed to materialize. Both groups of subjects reflected a positive RV-effect, and indeed the low self-concept children actually obtained a larger RV-positive effect ($M = 84.86$ on liked, $M = 74.88$ on disliked [percentage-hits scores]) than the high self-concept children ($M = 87.57$ on liked, $M = 84.81$ on disliked; factorial ANOVA interaction significant, $p < .05$). Essentially the same design was followed at a second elementary school, with the exception that as a learning task, four liked and four disliked CVC trigrams were employed (Byron, 1972). Once again the 20 low self-concept children as identified on pretesting by the Piers-Harris Scale were significantly lower in IQ than the 20 high self-concept children, and the low self-concept children reflected a larger RV-positive effect than the high self-concept children.

The relationship predicted by LLT between self-concept and affective learning style did not seem to hold for children. Some psychologists believe that children lack the self-awareness to be considered appropriate subjects for a study of this sort, but we remained skeptical, particularly because there were extraneous factors such as IQ-level that might well have accounted for our inability to show the self-phenomenon. Gerry August then conducted two helpful experiments in which he focused on several aspects of LLT, and although he did not completely resolve the question, he did provide data largely consistent with the developing line of theory (August,

1975; August, Rychlak, & Felker, 1975). August's work was more broadly based than our two initial efforts, sampling from many schools across an urban population.

In the first study, 134 white fifth grade children (72 girls, 62 boys) were selected from a sampling of hundreds of children from three large schools of generally middle-class status (August, Rychlak, & Felker, 1975). Children were assigned to high, medium, and low self-concept experimental conditions, based on their scores on the Piers-Harris which was administered in pretesting. Significant differences in IQ across these levels did not obtain. As a learning task, eight paired-associates were arrayed employing nouns that had been taken from the fifth grade spelling book these children used and equated on measures of imagery, meaningfulness, and word frequency (based on the Paivio, Yuille, & Madigan, 1968, norms). Half of the pairs were liked, the other disliked; learning criterion was the usual two consecutive correct anticipations of the complete list. Reinforcement value and level of self-concept interacted significantly ($p < .01$). True to predictions, the high self-concept subject of both sexes learned liked sublists more readily than disliked, and the low self-concept subject of both sexes reflected an RV-reversal. However, at the middle self-concept level August found that the boys reversed, learning along the negative; the girls at this level learned their list along a positive-RV direction.

In his second study August (1975) sampled widely across both white and black communities to classify 132 white (both sexes) and 64 black (both sexes) fifth graders as either high or low in self-concept based on their Piers-Harris scores. An immediate problem in design developed when we learned that the black children as a group ($M = 54.20$, $SD = 10.77$) were *lower* in self-concept than the white children ($M = 59.35$, $SD = 12.08$) ($t = 2.86$, $p < .01$). Special measures therefore were taken to equate high and low self-concept subjects across racial identity on the Piers-Harris Scale even though as a total group the blacks appeared to be more negative in self-evaluation than the whites. Once again nouns were used as task materials, and great efforts were taken to keep the pool of nouns common in the lists of whites and blacks. Only 20 nouns were actually used (e.g., *army, book, king, dust, game, doctor, dress*), all of which were adjudged as high frequency (AV meaningfulness) by both the Thorndike-Lorge (1944) and the Kucera-Francis (1967) norms. August used a free-recall procedure in this study in which a child memorized five liked and five disliked nouns.

Whereas whites as a group (132 subjects) learned their liked nouns ($M = 25.73$, $SD = 10.75$) more readily than their disliked nouns ($M = 29.15$, $SD = 11.53$), blacks as a group (64 subjects) *reversed* and extended meanings more readily along the disliked ($M = 28.88$, $SD = 14.14$) than the liked ($M = 31.72$, $SD = 13.91$) direction. This was particularly significant, because as we demonstrate below, blacks typically reflect a *larger* RV-positive effect than whites. If we are prepared to *discount* the matching done in equating white and black children on the Piers-Harris after a significant difference in their mean scores was found and view the sample as simply different as to level of self-concept, these findings are consistent with LLT. If, however, we argue that the matching was effective in delineating the high and low self-concept child within the albeit relatively low-scoring black population, our findings on self-concept reflect an inconsistency. Figure 5 presents the data on our white and black fifth-graders, broken down according to high and low self-concept.

Note in Figure 5 that although the white subjects follow experimental predictions, the black subjects do not. Low self-concept white children show a pronounced diminution in the RV-positive effect relative to high self-concept white children. Not only do both high and low self-concept black children show a predilection for

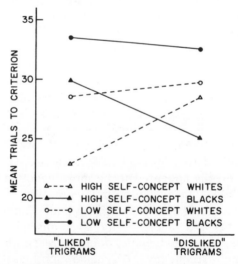

**Figure 5** Trials to criterion in the free-recall task are graphed according to positive RV (liked trigrams) and negative RV (disliked trigrams), broken down by the race and self-concept level of the subjects. (The solid line reflects the performance of black fifth grade children, and the broken line represents the performance of white fifth grade children.)

the negative meanings in their lists, but the high self-concept child actually shows a more pronounced RV-reversal than his low self-concept counterpart (the factorial ANOVA interaction between race, self-concept, and RV was significant, $p < .05$). There are good reasons to view this atypical finding on the black subjects as something other than simply error or a disconfirmed LLT hypothesis. That is, August and his assistants thought that they had sensed a reluctance on the part of many of the black children to perform in the experiment. Although none of the whites terminated the experiment, a handful of black children refused to cooperate in the task and had to be dropped from the data analysis. None of our experimenters were black; although this did not seem to make a difference in other work, the truth is in this particular community there had been some interracial conflict, and the children seemed to be reflecting a mood of the times.

The ideal of science is to rise somehow above such historical (idiographic) factors and examine lawful relations that are not subject to them. The teleologist, however, is unable to dismiss such factors simply because they may be unpleasant to cite or otherwise difficult to encompass in one's explanation of the findings. The essential point is that the implications be carried forward to even further research. Joe Marceil (1975) therefore conducted a study in which he tried to determine whether the subject's attitude toward the task *per se* could influence his affective learning style.

Marceil studied 60 white high school students (evenly divided by sex), selected from a larger pool of 120 students who had been shown a memory-drum, paired-associates task in class as a demonstration. Students were asked to rate how much they would like to be a subject in such a task. Based on these ratings, subjects were identified as either positive or negative in RV for the memory-drum task. Marceil then assigned *both* positively and negatively disposed subjects to the experimental task. As items to be learned, each subject was administered a list of six liked and six disliked trigrams taken from the PPI, which had also been administered in pretesting. He could thus examine the RV of the task in conjunction with the RV of the verbal materials. If our thinking about the black sample in the previous study was correct, we expected to find that subjects who disliked the paired-associates task might diminish or reverse the positive-RV effect when subsequently asked to perform on the memory drum. This is precisely what Marceil found. Those subjects with a negative task premise flattened the RV-positive effect and learned their disliked trigrams ($M = 36.73$, $SD = 13.66$) as readily as their liked trigrams ($M=36.30$, $SD=12.99$), whereas those subjects with a positive task premise extended meanings more readily along the positive ($M=27.40$, $SD=11.38$) than the negative ($M=32.80$, $SD=13.40$) ($F=3.77$, $df$ 1/48, $p=.055$).

There is the possible suggestion here that RV-effects are mere experimental artifacts. Subjects may be capable of changing their positive or negative RV-learning styles at whim. Obviously we had to consider the question of just how much subjects could manipulate their RV-learning propensities through the design of an experiment specifically testing this point. We therefore made the next methodological step.

After prerating CVC trigrams for both AV and RV, 100 college students (equally divided by sex) were assigned randomly to a free-recall task, taken under one of five experimental instructions. The list to be memorized contained 12 trigrams, three of each in the four typical AV-RV combinations (i.e., AV-yes, RV-liked; AV-yes, RV-disliked, etc.). Recollections were recorded in writing between list presentations. One group of 20 subjects was given the routine free-recall instructions. This group acted as a control on the remaining four groups, each of which was given additional instructions to try to order their learning by picking up either AV (yes, no) or RV liked, disliked) items first. There were 20 subjects in each of these four groups. Just before turning to his 12-trigram list following warm-up, a subject was instructed as follows (specific AV or RV "set" in brackets):

One last point. When you memorize these syllables [trigrams] we have found that a good tactic is to try and learn those you [think are wordlike, think are not wordlike, like, dislike] first. Please try to use this tactic because it will help you to learn the whole list more quickly. Never refuse to write something down. Always record every syllable you remember. But make a special effort to get the [wordlike, non-wordlike, liked, disliked] syllables down first. OK?

The basic research design lent itself to a 2 (sex)×5 (experimental instructions)×2(AV)×2 (RV) factorial ANOVA, with the first two factors between subjects and the last two within subjects. The data were analyzed in terms of our customary trials (raw) and percent hits (ratio) scores. Both of these scores require the subject to come to a full learning criterion of some sort (e.g., two consecutive correct recollections of a full list or "so many" trials for all subjects in the study, etc.). But we also thought it would be interesting to score the number of hits made on simply the first three trials, where subjects had the clearest opportunity to put our experimental instructions into effect by focusing on only certain types of trigrams.

For the first three trials on these percent-hits scores one of the instructions did trend to a near-significant interaction in the factorial ANOVA ($F=2.11$, $df$ 4/90, $p=.08$). Subjects who were asked to learn AV-yes trigrams ($M=4.95$) before AV-no trigrams ($M=3.70$) followed instructions, and subjects who were asked to learn AV-no trigrams ($M=4.70$) before AV-yes trigrams ($M=4.57$) also followed instructions. The control group reflected the expected AV-yes ($M=4.03$) over AV-no ($M=3.70$) advantage, as did both of the RV-instruction groups. It thus appeared that the usual AV-yes over AV-no direction of learning efficiency could be reversed through establishing the proper set (LLT would say premise) in the subjects being tested. The interaction of experimental instruction with trigram-RV over the first three trials was insignificant ($F=.08$, N. S.), with all subjects learning liked more readily than disliked trigrams.

Turning to our conventional scorings over all trials, there were no significant findings on the percent-hits scores for either AV or RV. However, acceptable findings did emerge on the trials scores for the AV-instruction, where we found a significant triple interaction between sex, experimental instruction, and trigram-AV ($F=2.39$, $df$ 4/90, $p=.05$). In the interest of space we will simply note that the above cited trends on hits for the first three trials combining sex were found to hold only for the males. Once again there were no significant findings on RV in the trials-score data. In no instance was the usual RV-positive effect reversed in this study, whether data were looked at as a total group or broken down by sex. Thus our confidence in the difficulty of manipulating RV effects was strengthened. As a sidelight, when we mentioned these findings to a colleague, his response was: "You have hard evidence here for behavioral determinism. How do you square this with your belief in free will?"

The answer, of course, hinges upon one's interpretation of determinism. Logical learning theory contends that people are under determination in RV-learning style but that this is a telic determination, fixed by their affective assessment of the task confronting them. Freedom of will comes in before this affirmation is rendered (see Chapters 7 and 8). The evidence we have is that conceptual manipulations can sometimes be made by the subject that will alter his pattern of learning along AV. This is based on the assumption that a subject is willing to go along with the experimenter's requests—an assumption which is not always warranted (Page, 1972). But once an affective assessment has been rendered, the premised (RV) mean-ingfulness that is sequaciously extended is (telically) determined. The very meaning of sequacious subsumes determinism, because it refers to a slavish compliance on the precedent meanings affirmed and extended in telosponsivity. It serves no purpose to obscure terminological distinctions and say that because we have demon-strated something experimentally this proves only a nontelic form of determinism.

Here is precisely where we invoke our revolutionary call for the necessary distinction between theory (subjects determine their own behavior via affective assessments which align precedent meanings that are sequaciously extended) and method (we can ask subjects to disregard how they have affectively assessed materials in extend-ing their meanings [control] and show [predicted outcome] that this effort is unrelated to the meaning-extensions that actually occur). The former presumes a telic determination on the part of the sub-ject, and the latter presumes an efficient-cause mechanical manipu-lation on the part of the experimenter who sets the scene for the human drama. But we are surely naive if we think as scientific stagehands that our arrangements of the circumstances are the only causes of the form our play takes on.

Up to this point in our researches we had generally assumed that the role of self-evaluation in affective learning style was an overall tendency. Some individuals—negative self-evaluators— were seen as prone to learn along the negative in every aspect of life's meanings, while others were assumed to be strictly positive learners. However, as we contemplated the drift of our earlier find-ings, we could no longer accept this simplistic view, and even more importantly, the tenets of LLT did not demand such a global inter-pretation. The masculine women and submissive men of our work on personality might be seen as modestly out of kilter with their social roles, but this surely did not mean that they were on a par with our hospitalized Np patients as negative learners in life. Is it not more reasonable to believe that RV reversals or diminutions may occur by degree in the learning of everyone, depending upon the particular premise under affirmation in the upcoming situation facing the individual? Even judgments of the likability of the task per se can enter into this premise affirmation, as Marceil's (1975) data suggested. Presumably, a maladjusted person would simply be ex-tending meanings in more of life's areas than would a normal person.

There is another reason to expect self-contributions to learning in one situation and not in another. This has to do with the LLT contention that individuals learn by relating what they are currently organizing into knowledge *vis-à-vis* some standard for the sake of which they ground their understanding (see Chapter 7). The individual must *begin* his (protopoint) understanding of that which he is expected to learn in a fixed meaningful premise. If what he is learning about can be delineated as some organized sphere of information—as, for example, either baseball or tennis—what the person may think of *himself* in these circumstances is relatively less important. The self in this case is not needed as a ground against which to extend meanings. Premising baseball as positive, we would expect him to extend meanings in this sphere along the positive. And premising tennis as negative, we would expect him to order (meaningfully) hence learn more of what he dislikes about this sport than what he likes (leading to diminutions of the positive RV effect and possibly even a reversal). Only if the person is "put on the spot" and brought into the situation as a self-identity would we expect his self-evaluations to intrude in this meaning-extension. For example, the "unconfident" person (negative self-evaluator), placed in a contest where he had to reveal the vast knowledge he had of baseball (his favorite sport) in competition with others, might indeed reflect a decrement in performance and generate meanings in the circumstance that he would *not* prefer to happen (mistakes). Or even if he did well in the competition, he might later speak of his "miserable performance" because each of his mental slips would count more heavily in his recollections (reconceptualizations) than his accuracies.

Because much of our research was conducted on nonsense material (CVC trigrams) or unrelated words, we made it likely that self factors would enter into the affective learning style manifested. There was no other uniform grounding possible! But what if we were to delineate clear areas of meaning and select human subjects who found one area positive in meaningfulness and the other negative? Could we show a more restricted RV-reversal taking place in the learning of a subject within the negative area of meaning even as this *same* subject learned along the positive in an alternative area of meaning? This intriguing possibility formed the basic strategy of our next study (Dunning, 1973). Sixty-four college students (divided equally by sex) were identified as either high or low in ego-strength, based on a pretesting of 350 students who were administered the Barron's (1953) Ego-Strength Scale. These subjects were asked to rate words for RV that had been identified through preratings by other students, 80% or more of whom agreed that they bore either an *aggressive-competitive* meaning (e.g., *incentive, decisively, proficient, bloodthirsty, enslave, scandalize*) or a *passive-intimate* meaning (e.g., *sensual, sympathetically, reverent, heartbreaking, unending, and pamper*). The 64 experimental subjects were also selected because each one had named one of these areas of interpersonal relations as being a personal "hang up" area and the other an area of competence. That is, some subjects had difficulty dealing with interpersonal aggression, and others judged being intimately at ease with other people a serious problem.

Based on their idiographic ratings, a 12-word free-recall list was constructed for each of the 64 subjects in which half of the words were aggressive-competitive and half passive-intimate in meaning. Three of the words in each of these meaning realms were rated as liked and three as disliked (mixed lists). Trial scores and the criterion of two successive complete recollections of a list were employed. The experimental design thus lent itself to a factorial ANOVA having the characteristics of a 2 (sex) $\times 2$ (high versus low ego-strength) $\times 2$ (problem versus competency area) $\times 2$ (aggressive-competitive versus passive-intimate words) $\times 2$ (RV). The first three are between-subjects factors and the last two are within-subjects factors.

The ego-strength manipulation failed to enter into any of the findings. However, RV did interact with the sublists a subject learned, based on the problem versus competency distinction ($F = 3.91$, $df = 1/56$, $p < .05$). When learning competency-area sublists (whether aggressive-competitive or passive-intimate in nature), the subjects acquired their liked sublists ($M = 10.04$, $SD = 2.83$) more readily than their disliked sublists ($M = 10.93$, $SD = 4.60$). However, when the sublists (aggressive-competitive or passive-intimate) were problem areas for the subjects, a facilitation of disliked lists ($M = 9.84$, $SD = 3.53$) over liked lists ($M = 10.11$, $SD$ 3.48) was found to be the case. An interesting but unexpected finding ($p < .05$) was that *all* of our subjects tended to learn passive-intimate word meanings along the positive, and *reversed* in RV on the aggressive-competitive words (see Rychlak, Carlsen, & Dunning, 1974, for a more thorough presentation of these findings).

### The Ordering of Affective Preference:
### Transfer Effects

Having just completed a survey of research in which we were forced (telically determined) to make certain predictions based on our theoretical premises, we appropriately move on to RV-effects that were discovered by accident. One is reminded here of Skinner's (1956) informal case-history analysis of his scientific-research progress in which he essentially maintained that *all* of his discoveries were of this nature. Although serendipity, accident, and luck have their place in science, as they do in all of life, a certain kind of intellect is required to recognize and benefit from such occurrences. Without some premising frame against which to assess the "lucky break" and capitalize on it, we do not see how it would be possible to speak of the help received from a fortunate turn of events. In this sense, as the saying goes, we all must "make our own luck."

The lucky break for LLT occurred when Tom Tobin decided to apply LLT to the learning styles of differential achievers in high school. Based on his experience as a teacher, Tobin (1969) predicted that underachievers would reflect a larger RV-positive effect in their learning style than overachievers. He did in fact validate this prediction, but subsequent efforts to build on his work have been unclear and thus we will not develop this aspect of RV research except to note that here is an area in which the findings have not been consistently instructive (see Jack, 1974; Lappin, 1969; Rychlak & Tobin, 1971).

When Tobin began his study we had not yet answered all of the questions raised concerning the role of affective assessment in mixed versus unmixed lists and so on. To circumvent possible criticism that an artifact accounted for the RV-positive effect (e.g., that subjects merely employed a strategy of learning their liked trigrams first) Tobin decided to use an unmixed-lists procedure. Each subject was required to learn *two* lists of eight paired-associate trigrams, one of which was liked and the other disliked. A routine counterbalancing of order was then followed in which half of the 64 (male) students tested learned their liked before their disliked, and half learned their disliked before their liked paired-associates. Nothing was expected to develop from the order of counterbalancing *per se*. However, after Tobin had begun to sense a differential change in level of performance among his subjects, depending upon the order in which they learned their lists, we decided to put this factor into the data analysis.

Tobin had, of course, inadvertantly constructed an A-B, C-D transfer design (each letter designates a different CVC trigram in a paired associate, as in learning DIB-LAT and HEB-SOQ in sequence; eight such pairings in each list had to be learned). The A-B, C-D design generates positive transfer effects—that is, the subject typically does better on the second list (C-D) than the first (A-B)—which are then termed *nonspecific* because the lists have nothing in common (e.g., they might have been A-B, A-C whereby a subject would follow the sequence of DIB-LAT, DIB-SOQ; in this case a specific anchoring point in DIB could be said to account for the transfer effects). Theories of nonspecific transfer typically rely on some variant of the frequency thesis, as in contending that it is warm-up or learning-to-learn on the first list that facilitates acquisition of the second list (Kintsch, 1970,pp. 35–36). If the C-D list were to be *lower* in trials-to-criterion scoring than the A-B list, this would of course represent a *negative* nonspecific transfer because in this case an earlier task had in some way adversely affected performance on a later task. Positive transfer calls for a facilitation across successive tasks.

Tobin was to find a dramatic interaction between list order and RV ($p < .01$), which suggested that when a subject moved from disliked to liked lists, he generated *positive* transfer across lists, but in moving the opposite way a *negative* transfer was likely to take place. All 32 of those subjects who followed the disliked-liked sequence reflected a positive transfer in their individual learning sequences, whereas only 13 of the 32 subjects moving along a liked-disliked sequence reflected positive transfer.

Another way of underscoring the facilitation effect of negative-to-positive RV sequencing is to calculate a percentage of increase in efficiency of learning list 2 over list 1. The difference between lists is first determined (positive or negative direction) and then the trials of list 1 are divided into this difference score. For example, moving from 10 trials on the first list to eight trials on the second represents a 20% improvement across lists. This score is negative when the second list takes longer to learn than the first (negative transfer). After adding all changes algebraically we can determine an improvement rate for the 32 subjects in one or the other of our two RV sequences. When the order was positive to negative RV, the nonspecific transfer amounted to 9%. However, when the order was negative to positive RV across lists, the nonspecific transfer amounted to 38% (see Rychlak & Tobin, 1971, for a more detailed presentation of these findings).

Ray Trybus (1969) next looked at nonspecific transfer in the A-B, C-D design in a slightly different way. Rather than studying the contrasting directions of positive or negative transfer across lists that *differed* in RV, Trybus looked at two successive lists in which subjects were moving along *common* liked-liked or disliked-disliked sequences *while at the same time* doing this along either an 80% nomothetic AV level (based on Archer's, 1960, norms) or a 20% AV level. Would there be more positive nonspecific transfer along AV with RV counterbalanced out of the picture, or would RV reflect transfer effects with AV held constant? He employed a "savings" score to measure the extent of improvement across lists. Both AV and RV achieved a trend ($p = .08$) in the data analyses. That is, subjects tended to reflect more positive transfer along 80–80% than 20–20% nomothetic AV list sequences. And they showed more positive transfer along liked-liked than disliked-disliked lists of trigrams. Although this study complemented the Tobin work, it did not allow for the most potent conditions of liked-disliked and disliked-liked lists to take effect. Also, the design suffered from the fact that we were comparing nomothetic AV measures with idiographic RV measures. This promising research line called for a fully balanced confrontation between idiographic AV measures and idiographic RV measures. Such a study was therefore designed and carried out.

Sixty-four college students (divided equally by sex) rated the PPI trigrams for AV on two occasions, with 48 hours intervening. One week following this testing they again rated the PPI on two occasions, with 48 hours intervening, but this time it was for the RV of the PPI items. Only trigrams rated reliably for AV *and* RV were used. A series of eight experimental conditions were then arranged, which perfectly counterbalanced AV and RV across two entirely different six-pair paired-associates lists. Subjects were randomly assigned to these eight conditions. In list 1, a subject might thus learn six pairs having the idiographic quality of AV-no, RV-liked and then follow this with a list 2 of AV-no, RV-disliked. Positive RV would have been removed from the materials to be learned in the second list. In another instance the subject might move across lists having the characteristics of AV-no, RV-disliked to AV-yes, RV-disliked. AV meaningfulness would have been "added into" the second list. Both paired-associates members had identical meaningfulness qualities (i.e., we were not involved with what has been called stimulus versus response meaningfulness [sic]).

Lists were presented by memory drum via method of anticipation, and two consecutive recollections of the full list taken as learning criterion. To test the role of sequence on transfer a factorial ANOVA having the characteristics of 2 (sex) $\times$ 4 ($+ +$, $+ -$, $- +$, $- -$ for AV or RV) $\times$ 2 (lists 1 and 2) was run for both RV and AV, which effectively held one measure constant while the other was being studied. That is, we could first assess the role of AV-yes ($+$) to AV-yes ($+$), AV-yes ($+$) to AV-no ($-$), AV-no ($-$) to AV-yes ($+$), and AV-no ($-$) to AV-no ($-$) with RV held constant across these sequences. Then a second run of the 2 × 4 × 2 ANOVA would establish these identical patterns of liked (+) versus disliked (−) RV with AV held constant. Table 11 contains the means and standard deviations of AV and RV across lists in terms of the order sequences outlined.

The crucial test of the hypothesis depended upon interaction effects between the four order sequences and the two lists. This interaction failed to reach significance for AV ($F = 1.69$, $df = 3/56$, N.S.). However, it did achieve significance for RV ($F = 3.15$, $df = 3/56$, $p < .03$). There were no sex main effects or interactions. Note that the condition accounting for maximum (positive) nonspecific transfer was when the subject moved from negative RV to positive RV and that the condition reflecting the least nonspecific transfer was when the subject moved from positive RV to negative RV. This phenomenon has since appeared so frequently in other aspects of LLT research that we now consider it one more way in which to assess the RV-positive effect.

The final study we wish to mention in this section was an attempt to determine if RV-effects occurred over *four* successive lists rather than simply two. A lower socioeconomic group of 16 adults (equated for sex) was paid to spend up to one and one-half hours taking a series of four six-pair lists, one after the other, with suitable rest breaks between list mastery.[1] Subjects had prerated trigrams for both AV and RV in the usual fashion, and their series of four lists

**Table 11**  Mean and Standard Deviation of Association Value and Reinforcement Value Meaningfulness Scores Across Two Lists

| Order of Meaningfulness across Lists 1 and 2 | Association Value | | | | Reinforcement Value[a] | | | |
|---|---|---|---|---|---|---|---|---|
| | List 1 | | List 2 | | List 1 | | List 2 | |
| | Mean | SD | Mean | SD | Mean | SD | Mean | SD |
| + to + | 15.37 | 8.01 | 8.69 | 3.57 | 14.63 | 5.12 | 8.44 | 3.74 |
| + to − | 15.06 | 5.33 | 11.88 | 4.53 | 14.31 | 6.19 | 11.19 | 5.28 |
| − to + | 16.69 | 6.71 | 9.31 | 3.69 | 19.18 | 10.00 | 9.68 | 4.37 |
| − to − | 18.13 | 10.47 | 12.19 | 5.41 | 17.13 | 6.74 | 12.75 | 3.75 |

[a] Order and list interaction, on RV, $p < .03$.

[1] This experiment and the one preceding it (Table 11 data) were supported by Grant 5-71-0039 (509) from the U.S. Office of Education, Department of Health, Education, and Welfare. The writer would like to thank Sherry L. Felbain and Marshall R. Schmidt for their assistance in data collection.

was arranged to vary sequentially in idiographic AV-RV combinations. At times AV-yes would be in (+) the list, but RV-positive would be out (−). At other times the presence of AV-yes and RV-positive would be reversed, or both would be in (+) or out (−) of the list. Due to budget and time limitations a perfect counterbalancing of all possible meaningfulness combinations over the four lists was not achieved. However, there were three critical circumstances in which subjects were moving from lists in which the RV sequence was + to −, but the AV sequence was − to +. In this confrontation a theorist relying on AV meaningfulness predicts positive nonspecific transfer across lists and a theorist relying on RV predicts negative transfer. This is the most stringent test possible for RV, because the expected course of nonspecific transfer when it occurs is always positive—the direction AV was capitalizing on in this confrontation.

There were four lists and four combinations of AV-RV in this study, so that to test the hypothesis required a 4 × 4 factorial ANOVA (earlier analyses had established that there were no sex differences). This analysis reached significance ($F = 2.72$, $df = 9/36$, $p < .05$). By examining the graphed sequences of subject performance across the four lists we could then determine just how long the transfer effects held up. There were clear indications of transfer effects occurring over all four of the lists, but due to the imperfect counterbalancing, we had only the three critical comparisons already mentioned to decide whether it was RV or AV that accounted for these findings. Inspection of the crucial graphs established that in all three instances a negative transfer took place (i.e., the curve of learning was negatively accelerated), supporting RV as influential and not AV (see Rychlak, Tuan, & Schneider, 1974).

These nonspecific transfer effects are interpreted by LLT as due to subject reconceptualization (Kierkegaardian change). When the subject completes a task he has found affectively to his liking, only to move into a succeeding task he considers negative, it is comparable to beginning a new, different, hence difficult, task after having just mastered something that is easy by comparison. The relative diminution in performance due to RV differences on the second task is due to what we called in Chapter 8 the possibility of learning error (p. 328)—not only extending the negative meanings and partial meanings of verbal materials (words, trigrams), but also literally doing more poorly on the total task. Predicating the task as difficult the person "makes it so" in his learning. Conversely, when the subject completes a disliked task and moves into a liked task the reconceptualization is comparable to moving into an easy area after having just completed something difficult. Predicating the new task as easy the person "makes it so" in his learning.

The inability of AV measures to show interlist effects in empirical research is not exactly unheard of in the verbal-learning literature. After extensive and well-controlled work on the topic, Noble (1961) summarized his efforts with the confident statement: "Meaningfulness [i.e., AV] facilitates rate of acquisition but has no influence upon [nonspecific] transfer of training" (p. 209). What then are we to make of the fact that affective assessment *has* been shown to influence learning rate across nonspecific lists? For one thing, it is now theoretically necessary to change the conception of nonspecific transfer to conform with the more popular experimental topic of specific transfer. Since Thorndike (1914), the tradition has been to say that transfer (the effect of an earlier task on a later task) takes place in either a positive or a negative sense. Nonspecific transfer is always defined as the *improvement* in performance to be noted across tasks independent of task content (Kausler, 1966, p. 361). There is no allowance made here for a negative nonspecific transfer. This seeming oversight is actually the heritage of Thorndike and Woodworth's (1901a, 1901b, 1901c) experimental attack on the *formal discipline* theory in education.

The study of transfer originated in this debate over whether, as the advocates of formal discipline contended (see, e.g., Morgan, 1906, p. 192), the training of a student in Latin was capable of developing his faculties for comparison and generalization, which in turn would redound positively on his learning of English. If such faculties could be sharpened in practice on unrelated materials, nonspecific transfer would be taking place. The work of Thorndike and Woodworth supported a specificity thesis, suggesting that only those aspects of Latin which directly related to English as stimuli (e.g., word roots, etc.) could be given credit for improvements to be noted in a subject's performance across tasks. Unrelated tasks, such as learning arithmetic to improve grammar, were not found to enter into a transferred facilitation across areas of study (see Thorndike, 1914, p. 268). If the specific factor learned earlier worked *against* what was to follow on a later task—for example, having to shift from learning a paired-associate like DIB-LAT to a second pairing of DIB-SEQ, in which case LAT and SEQ would be confounded—a harmful or negative transfer was likely to occur. Otherwise, earlier *specific* factors in learning which could be transferred to later tasks were helpful, or positive. The proven fact that there is indeed a facilitation across even unrelated tasks was later called nonspecific transfer, and it was justified as due either to specific, but so-called incidental learning, or to warm-up, learning-how-to-learn, and the like. The possibility of a *negative* nonspecific transfer therefore did not arise in theory, and decrements in tasks across time were traced to strictly motivational fluctuations, such as fatigue and boredom.

The interesting thing about formal-discipline theory for LLT is that when one sets aside the Lockean interpretation of this view as analogous to "muscle training" (frequency of practice in Latin builds mental muscles for learning mathematics) and looks more closely at some of the writings of the advocates of formal discipline, a Kantian theme is occasionally seen to shimmer through their presentation. Formal discipline held that the subject "comes at" the new learning task with a more or less well-developed capacity to influence the outcome of what is eventually learned. If highly developed, this capacity (faculty) leads to improvement; if poorly developed, a relative detriment in learning is likely to be the case (Roark, 1895, pp. 277–279). But can the teacher (through repetitious presentations of an earlier subject like Latin) bring about or manipulate this "capacity to learn" in the student which is then transferred to upcoming subjects (e.g., mathematics)? Actually the proponents of formal discipline usually held that a teacher could *do nothing* for the student, who had to bring about his own (faculty) development or suffer the consequences (*ibid.*, p. 278).

In other words, the analogy to muscle-training was drawn along the lines of active intentional use and not merely along the lines of power through mere repetition. A student could be shown the way by the teacher and be aided when questions arose, but simply to force meaningless repetitions on him in hopes of furthering his "mental muscle" was not exactly a tenet of formal-discipline theory. If we now look more critically at the classroom observations on which formal-discipline theory was based can we see how it might have arisen in the teacher's *accurate* perception of a classroom phenomenon—a phenomenon that involved affective assessment in the learning styles of students? Assuming that the teacher has contrasted the student's performance in Latin, which either preceded the English lesson or followed it, a fluctuation in general level of learning (interest, motivation, insight, etc.—all those terms used to describe rising or falling performance) might indeed have been the case, assuming *only* that most students preferred English to Latin! And if the *rise* in performance from Latin (RV negative) to English (RV positive) prompted or at least supported the view of a generalized capacity to learn, we can now in retrospect perhaps better understand why the sensitive classroom instructor began to speak of a "developing" faculty of learning. His empirical observations may well have been correct.

Not until we can test affective assessments in the actual classroom will this question be properly researched. We once had a school system interested enough to consider a program of arranging the school day according to liked and disliked school subjects, varying the time spent in each, and so forth, but the threat of departing from tradition here as well as the effort this would require led to a cancellation of the study before it was proposed to the parents of the students. Yet LLT holds that some of the benefits of so-called working at one's pace or self-selection of study topics in open classrooms are due in *fact* to the transfer effects of affective assessment. Children are probably given an opportunity to delve lightly into a disliked study topic (possibly by way of a teacher's suggestion or example) and then to devote considerable subsequent effort to a preferred study task, thus maximizing positive nonspecific transfer for the latter, which continues to be easy by comparison to the former as greater gains are made and the teacher is pleased at the child's "talent" for the maximized subject. Or the student may devote his entire time to various liked subjects, which is a sequence that our studies show also results in greater positive nonspecific transfer. As the total school effort is arranged to maximize facilitation of learning, the child may even come to reevaluate his formerly disliked subjects and place them in a more positive light. Having said this, we hasten to add that by arranging circumstances for the child to reevaluate, we would *not* be efficiently causing his reevaluation to happen. The control of behavior is telic (based on the child's idiographic reassessment of the new circumstances which have been arranged in response to his active conceptualization and initial assessments of what his school environment is like).

## Affective Assessment and Conceptual Processes

We noted in Chapter 5 that the term *cognitive* no longer bears the Kantian meaning it once signified in psychology. To keep LLT entirely free of identification with the Lockean interpretation of cognition we have preferred to speak of a subject's *conceptualization* of experience, by which we mean an active process bringing forward some affirmed premise to order what can be known by way of telosponsivity. We have made many claims over the earlier chapters (especially Chapters 7, 8, and 9) concerning this active process, through which the individual is said to predicate his experience rather than mediate it. In this section we survey a number of studies that were aimed at demonstrating the role of such conceptualizing capacities in the behavior of human beings.

Osgoodian Evaluation and Reinforcement Value in a Learning Study.

As one aspect of the construct validity of RV we presented in Chapter 9 (pp. 393–400) data on cross-validating factor analyses which showed that both RV and Osgood's (1952) Evaluation load on the same factor. Though we do not thereby claim an identity in these two conceptions, we do suggest that we can "borrow" the worldwide findings on Evaluation and use them in partial support of LLT (with the affirming the consequent of an If . . . then . . . proposition in mind; see Chapter 5, pp. 181–182). If we can demonstrate that Evaluation performs in learning tasks comparably to RV and that Potency and Activity do not, the findings across the many language systems that Osgood's group has studied would have at least some relevance for affective asssesment. We would be placing a different interpretation on the research findings Osgood gathered in support of an altogether different conception of behavior.

With this strategy in mind, 64 high school seniors (divided equally by sex) were therefore randomly assigned to one of four experimental conditions in which they were instructed to read each trigram on the PPI in turn and decide whether its meaningfulness for them was best typified as one of the following (i.e., 16 subjects rated trigrams under each of these instructions): RV (like-dislike), Evaluation (good-bad), Potency (strong-weak), and Activity (fast-slow).[2] Based on these ratings, a list of 12 trigrams was assembled for each subject, six of which were idiographically rated by him at one pole (liked, good, strong, fast) and six of which were rated at the other (disliked, bad, weak, slow). Hence the overall design adapted itself to a 2 (sex) × 4 (rating instructions) × 2 (opposite ends of bipolar ratings) factorial ANOVA, with the first two factors between-subjects conditions and the third a within-subjects condition. The 64 subjects were then put through a typical free-recall learning task.

When this factorial ANOVA was carried out, a significant interaction between instructions and oppositionality of ratings was

[2] The writer would like to thank H. Case Ellis and J. William Townsend for their assistance in data collection on this project.

found ($F$ = 7.50, df = 1/56, $p$ < .01). Inspection of the percent-hits scores revealed that the subjects had a higher proportion of correct anticipations in coming to criterion on their liked (78%) than their disliked (67%) trigrams as well as on their good (72%) over their bad (65%) trigrams. However, subjects learned their strong (72%) and weak (70%) as well as their fast (71%) and slow (70%) trigrams much more comparably. The trials scores paralleled these findings but were not statistically significant. When each of the experimental conditions was analyzed separately (N = 16), only RV ($p$ < .01) and Evaluation ($p$ < .05) achieved a significant difference on the percent-hits scores. Reinforcement value also achieved significance ($p$ < .05) on the trials scores in the individual analysis, reflecting the usual superiority for liked over disliked trigrams. There were no sex differences. Hence to this point in time nothing has happened in our researches to challenge our theoretical assumption that Osgoodian researches have relevance for LLT.

Affective Quality of a Premise and Meaning-Extension.

Nate Keedy (1975) conducted a story-completion study in which he sought to test the LLT claim that individuals do extend premised meanings along a positive or negative affective direction, depending upon their assessment at the protopoint. Forty-eight college subjects (both sexes) were administered a form on which various life situations were presented such as "You are driving a car on a long trip" or "You are just getting up in the morning" and asked to rate these for RV in the typical fashion (two administrations, with 48 hours intervening, and so forth). Three reliably liked and three reliably disliked situations were then selected for each subject and taken as an operational definition of their premised affective assessment for the situational meanings concerned. Logical learning theory holds that, should these subjects be asked to extend these meanings in a story-completion format, positive premises will lead to positive story themes and vice versa.

Subjects were next given these six situations one week later in random order and asked to write a brief narrative, with the statement previously rated for RV acting as the opening line of their story. These stories were subsequently judged by three readers who knew nothing of the study's purpose. They were asked to judge whether the general story theme was positive, negative, or neutral (undecided). Their percentage of perfect agreement (agreements divided by total comparisons) was 70; each completed narrative was then categorized as positive, negative, or neutral, based on two or more of the readers agreeing on the designation. Six chi-squares on these ratings were then run, having the characteristics of a 2 (like-dislike RV) × 3 (positive, negative, neutral story) array. All six of these tests reached significance ($p < .05$), and examination of the arrays supported the view that positively premised situations were more likely to result in positive stories being written and vice versa.

## Affective Assessment: Perceptual Defense or Conceptual Enhancement?

Two studies conducted by Karla McFarland (1969) and Judy Rumsey (née Galster, 1972) constitute a provocative cameo area of LLT research. McFarland's study established that subjects (50 high school girls) could be given a paired-associates task, with the characteristics of a Berg (1957) abstract design paired to a trigram. The design was flashed onto a screen, followed by the trigram, and a subject's job was to anticipate the trigram that followed a given design (method of anticipation). Both designs and trigrams were either liked or disliked (i.e., there was no pairing in which one or the other aspect of the pair differed in RV from its mate). McFarland found that her subjects reflected the typical RV-positive effect when this procedure was followed ($p < .05$). Indeed, this finding was cross-validated when subjects were permitted to name their own designs initially. Names assigned to liked designs were recalled accurately more often than names assigned to disliked designs when the designs were subsequently presented for recognition ($p < .05$) (see Rychlak, Galster, & McFarland, 1972).

Rumsey next substituted pictures of male and female faces for the designs and names for the trigrams to see if RV effects could be related to "naming faces." The paired-associates were not necessarily uniform—that is, a liked name could be assigned to a disliked face and vice versa. Forty college students (divided equally by sex) were then asked to rate the names and faces for RV. The faces rated were selected from college yearbooks, so the subjects were essentially rating the "looks" of peers. Each subject was then asked to learn a 12-pair list of face-name combinations having the within-lists characteristics of (based on his or her idiographic ratings): liked name to liked face; liked name to disliked face; disliked name to liked face; and disliked name to disliked face. Ten subjects (five males, five females) were assigned to each of four experimental conditions: (1) male subjects learning to associate male faces to male names; (2) male subjects learning to associate female faces to female names; (3) female subjects learning to associate male faces to male names; and (4) female subjects learning to associate female faces to female names. Subjects were shown faces and names via carousel projection with a four-second flash cycle. Learning criterion was extended to four consecutive correct recollections of a name-face combination so that we would be sure that a subject could be moved on to the next phase of the experiment.

Upon reaching criterion, a subject was put through a tachistoscopic procedure in which his or her list of faces was presented in a graduated series of exposures—1-100, 1-50, 1-10, and 1-5 seconds—and the request made to identify the "person" by name as soon as possible. A score here was the total trials needed to identify the six liked or disliked faces. The more trials taken, the greater the exposure time needed to identify a face (all subjects identified their complete list of faces by the 1-5-second trial). The basic design of this experiment, whether considering original learning or tachistoscopic presentation was suitable to a factorial ANOVA having the characteristics of 2 (sex) $\times$ 2 (male versus female materials) $\times$ 2 (RV of faces) $\times$ 2 (RV of names). The first two are between-subjects factors and the last two are within-subjects factors.

In original learning (trials scores) liked names ($M$ = 19.70, SD = 5.51) were learned more readily than disliked names ($M$ = 22.41, $SD$ = 6.68), no matter whether these had been conjoined to liked or disliked faces ($F$ = 8.99, $df$ = 1/36, $p$ < .01). There were no significant RV effects for faces in original learning. Hence what the subject had to verbalize in the task (the name and not the face) seemed to take precedence. However, when the task shifted to identification of faces tachistoscopically, exactly the reverse occurred. At least in the case of a triple interaction between sex of the subject, sex of the learning materials, and RV of the faces, a significant level was achieved ($F$ = 6.24, $df$ = 1/36, $p$ < .01). Male subjects were found to recognize both their liked male and female faces according to an RV-positive effect. This was our experimental prediction. Female subjects, however, displayed an interesting RV-reversal in one aspect of their recognitions. Whereas they recognized their liked female faces ($M$ = 6.10, SD = 2.45) more easily than their disliked female faces ($M$ = 7.15, $SD$ = 3.00), the females of our sample reversed and actually recognized their disliked male faces ($M$ = 7.35, $SD$ = 2.18) more readily than their liked male faces ($M$ = 9.15, SD = 2.85).

One study and a few subjects does not constitute an important finding. However, as a form of demonstration, we would like to contrast how LLT might explain such a finding with how it might have been accounted for according to the perceptual defense thesis (Bruner & Postman, 1947). As is well known, this once important area of research has gone into decline, if for no other reason than the difficulty in dealing with sensitive perceptions which are then selectively defended against. What can we mean by defense? Those who might believe that our females were under threat in having to identify sexually attractive versus unattractive males and hence failed to see what was "there" as a defensive maneuver would have a heavy burden of theoretical description and methodological validation to bear. Logical learning theory would begin from its already established position that, depending upon how a subject premises a task, meaning-extensions along the positive or the negative would follow. In other words, rather than a perceptual defense taking place, we would suggest that there is a (relative) conceptual enhancement occurring. The females simply premised the male-identification task negatively. If one now wishes to say this enhancement along the negative stems from the defensiveness manifested in "not liking" having to pick out males from a group on the basis of sexual attractiveness, then so be it. But LLT would add that this hardly needs to be an unconscious or even truly defensive form of behavior.

Meaning-Extension: Reinforcement Value and the Frequency Thesis

In some of the most sophisticated and important work done on LLT, Nguyen Duc Tuan (1974) set out to test the frequency thesis against our claim that affective assessments are the source of at least some of the meaning-extensions that take place independent of sheer repetition. A frequency theory would suggest that a trigram like YIJ to which the subject has no word associate (AV-no) can gain in meaning only through association with a trigram such as DOL which he reads as "doll" (AV-yes) and not through association with a trigram such as ZOS which lacks a word meaning for him (AV-no). Put succinctly, two items lacking in meaning cannot generate meaning; it takes meaning to induce meaning. But the question remains: How is this meaning eventually ascribed to YIJ by the subject achieved? Is it rubbed off from DOL because of so many associative linkings as input engrams of a DOL-YIJ unit as opposed to a ZOS-YIJ unit? Or is it extended to DOL via the person's conceptualizing abilities as an aspect of his continuing ordering of experience (meaning-extension), an ordering that is reflected in RV learning styles? Tuan thought that the associative linking theory was inadequate to account for what we were finding in RV research, but that a more explicit study of meaning-extension was needed.

Logical learning theory would suggest that though frequency over time may indeed clock or measure changes in meaning, the prime reason for such change is not repetition but rather the *ordering* of meanings that take place as the subject actively tries to make sense out of the task facing him. The familiar tendency for subjects to employ so-called mediators (*sic*) is in fact a reflection of the predicating organizing-into-premises role of mind; and if LLT is correct, the *direction* the meaning-extension should take will follow positive RV over negative RV. That is, if we were to give subjects trigrams which *lacked* a word-associate (AV-no), the frequency of exposure to trigrams which did have word-associates (AV-yes) would enrich these nonwordlike trigrams *predominantly* along RV-positive lines (so long as we employed normal subjects).

The basic strategy of Tuan's work involved first identifying a pool of trigrams that lacked idiographic meaningfulness in AV and also reflected a negative RV. These were termed *unenriched* trigrams. Meaningfulness (AV-yes) had not been extended to them, although each one had been exposed to the subject on two occasions and an opportunity had been given to rate them for word value. The use of RV-negative in addition to AV-no in the unenriched trigrams merely emphasized the fact that there was little or no actual meaning in these verbal units. Strictly speaking, a trigram with RV-negative qualities is not lacking in meaningfulness. However, considering all of the difficulties reviewed in Chapter 9 concerning the possible functioning of AV-yes as a covert positive-RV estimate, we wanted to leave no doubt but that our unenriched trigrams had *neither* of these meaningfulness incidences. If, however, such unenriched (AV-no, RV-negative) trigrams were to acquire associative ties to words through an experimental manipulation, they were termed *enriched* (i.e., word-meaning had been extended to them). The question posed in this research was: What determines the associative enrichment?

Tuan framed three hypotheses: (1) Meaning-extension will be more likely through association with trigrams high in nomothetic AV than with trigrams low in nomothetic AV; (2) meaning-extension will be more likely through association with trigrams rated idiographically meaningful (AV-yes) than through association with trigrams rated idiographically unmeaningful (AV-no); and (3) meaning-extension will be more likely through association with trigrams idiographically rated as positive in RV than in trigrams rated negatively. In this research we were essentially using the term *enrichment* to signify meaning-extension.

Fifty subjects (male-to-female ratio of approximately one-to-three) were selected from a sampling of several hundred college students who had rated trigrams idiographically across the full Archer (1960) range for both AV and RV. These trigrams were grouped in 20-percentile steps (1–20%, 21–40%, etc.). A list of 12 paired-associates was then assembled for each subject, with both trigrams of a pair at one of these five nomothetic levels. In each of these pairs an unenriched trigram (AV-no, RV-disliked) was paired with a *standard* trigram which had one of the familiar characteristics of our four idiographic combinations (AV-yes, RV-liked; AV-yes, RV-disliked; AV-no, RV-liked; and AV-no, RV-disliked). Because these four idiographic conditions obtained in the standard trigrams at each of the 20-percentile steps, we could examine both idiographic and nomothetic AV in the meaning-extension behavior of the subjects. The design lent itself to a factorial ANOVA having the characteristics of a 5 (nomothetic AV) × 2 (idiographic AV) × 2 (idiographic RV) factorial ANOVA, with the first factor a between-subjects and the latter two factors a within-subjects array.

Subjects were asked to learn their 12-pair lists in 16 trials or less, with the position of the standard trigram and the unenriched trigram *changing* placement in the paired-associates as printed on the memory-drum paper (four-second exposure cycle). The unenriched trigram appeared (randomly) as a left-hand member on eight trial-presentations and as a right-hand member on eight trial-presentations. This procedure was followed to circumvent so-called stimulus versus response learning (*sic*) (see Kintsch, 1970). The method of anticipation was not used. Extensive pretesting fixed this 16-trials limitation as suitable to time limitations; also, due to the difficulty of the task, Tuan felt compelled by morale considerations to instruct his subjects that they would be finished in 16 presentations of their list even if they had not mastered it fully

Hence over the 16 presentations of paired trigrams, the subjects said nothing. They were given three one-minute rest periods between certain trials. Following this trigram-presentation phase, a subject was given only the 12 *standard* trigrams on an answer sheet and asked to record in writing any of the paired members he could recall (which were his unenriched trigrams). Finally, the subject was put through a production method (see Chapter 9, pp. 384–387) on each of his unenriched trigrams (spending 1½ minutes in associating to each of these). Through this latter procedure we could determine whether a trigram had become enriched (extended a word meaning).

Tuan found that the only factor influencing learning was nomothetic AV ($p < .01$)—that is, subjects recalled more unenriched trigrams from the higher ranges of Archer's norms than from the lower ranges. Neither idiographic AV nor idiographic RV significantly affected recall. Turning to the findings on the production method, Tuan found that both the nomothetic AV level ($p < .025$) and the idiographic RV of the standard trigrams ($p < .05$) significantly influenced the number of associates a subject extended to his previously unenriched trigrams. Idiographic AV *failed* to influence meaning-extension to a significant degree. The more wordlike a trigram pair is in the normative sense of a base rate (Archer norms), the more likely is it that a subject will enrich it over a course of 16 exposures. This is consistent with LLT in that an organization of meaning here is more likely when we begin with materials that have a greater likelihood of being seen as a meaningful organization by most people. However, within this increasing probability of a meaningful organization and *even when it is low*—even when the paired-associates are not very wordlike in a base-rate sense—the idiographic RV metric reflected a subject's telosponsive orderings of the task which resulted in meaning-extensions via the customary RV-positive effect.

There is an alternative form of the frequency argument in meaning-extension, which suggests that trigrams take on meaning simply through increasing exposure. The more times a subject sees a trigram, the more words should he associate to it in the subsequently administered production method (this rate was held constant at 16 for all trigrams in the experiment just discussed). Tuan (1974) challenged this view, suggesting that increasing exposures to an initially *disliked* trigram might have little effect on meaning-extension, whereas the enrichment to be observed along liked trigrams might be considerable (in the interest of space we are not reviewing the extensive literature on this topic; see Tuan, 1974, for a thorough presentation). Until we have accurately gauged the subject's precedent preferences we cannot state that meaning-extension (enrichment) is a function of mere exposure to verbal materials. This problem seemed well suited to a free-recall format, so Tuan designed a second experiment in which he carefully controlled for nomothetic AV, idiographic AV and RV, and the frequency of trigram exposure to the experimental subjects. His prediction was that meaning-extension would *not* be uniform across frequency of trigram exposures when RV is taken into consideration.

Trigrams were once again taken from the 20-percentile steps of the Archer norms. Ten subjects (sex ratio similar to first study) learned trigrams at each of these nomothetic AV levels. A subject in this study worked with a list of 24 trigrams, six in each of the customary AV-RV combinations (AV-yes, RV-liked; AV-yes, RV-disliked, etc.). The lists were based on idiographic preratings made by subjects, exactly as in Tuan's first study. There was no standard trigram because this was a free-recall study (in which each trigram is recalled without regard for a pair and in any order). The measure against which trigram enrichment was to be assessed was the number of times a trigram was presented to the subject. In his 24-trigram list a subject had six trigrams in each of the (four) AV-RV combinations. One might think of these as four sublists of six trigrams each. Two trigrams within each of these six-item sublists were presented to the subject only once; two were presented five times; and two were exposed for his viewing on 10 trials. Trigrams were presented by memory drum, with randomized orders, on a four-second exposure cycle. In other words, a subject did not see all 24 trigrams on the 10 trial exposures of the experiment. Some trigrams always appeared in the memory-drum window; others were exposed only half the time; and still others appeared only once. The order was randomized so that there was no opportunity for a subject to delineate the number of appearances of any one trigram, but subjects were aware that some appeared more often than others. The subject was instructed to memorize as many of these trigrams as possible over a 10-trial course of presentation (he was *not* told about the different trigram-exposure rates).

After 10 trials in the exposure phase of the study, subjects were asked to record in writing all of the trigrams they could recall. Next they were put through a production method exactly as in the first experiment. The basic design thus lent itself to a factorial ANOVA with the characteristics of 5 (nomothetic AV) $\times$ 2 (idiographic AV) $\times$ 2 (idiographic RV) $\times$ 3 (1, 5, and 10 trigram exposures). The first was a between-subjects factor, and the remaining three factors were within-subjects.

Subjects again recalled trigrams from the higher ranges of Archer's norms more readily than trigrams from the lower levels ($p < .01$); they also recalled trigrams increasingly better as the number of exposures increased (1 to 5 to 10) ($p < .01$). Finally, there proved to be an interaction between idiographic AV and idiographic RV ($p < .05$)—that is, other factors held constant, those trigrams rated AV-yes, RV-liked were more readily recalled than trigrams falling into the remaining three AV-RV combinations.

Turning to the word-association data obtained via the production method, if the frequency thesis holds in its most simple form, as we move across increasing levels of trigram exposure (1, 5, 10), our subjects should proffer more of these word-associates as the frequency increases. Actually there was no main effect for the frequency of trigram exposure (F less than unity). Neither was there a significant main effect for nomothetic AV in the production-method data (this fails to cross-validate the earlier findings; refer above). However, a main effect for idiographic AV *was* found: Subjects proffered more words to trigrams they had rated initially as AV-yes than to trigrams they had initially rated AV-no (p < .01). No such difference was found for RV. At first glance this might appear to be a negative finding for LLT, but the meaning-extension hypothesis under test was gauged against the frequency of trigram exposure, and consequently it had to be tested in the interaction F-tests. The cited main effect for idiographic AV merely demonstrates that if we disregard (or collapse) considerations of nomothetic AV, idiographic RV, and frequency of trigram exposure in the total data, our subjects were more likely to offer additional idiographic associates to trigrams they had initially considered wordlike than to trigrams they had initially considered nonwordlike.

The proper way in which to evaluate the data of Tuan's second study is to ask: Which factors did the frequency of trigram exposure interact with, and what did these interactions suggest? The frequency of trigram exposure (1, 5, 10) was found to enter into *three* statistically significant interactions. The first involved a triple interaction with both nomothetic AV and idiographic AV (p < .01). The AV-yes trigrams were more readily enriched than the AV-no trigrams in four of the five nomothetic-AV steps investigated (i.e., 1–20%, 41–60%, 61–80%, and 81–100%). Only at the 21–40% level did the idiographically AV-no trigram receive slightly greater enrichment (approximately 3 word-associates) than the AV-yes trigram (approximately 2.9 word-associates). At every other nomothetic level the AV-yes trigram was decidedly superior, and at the 81–100% level the difference between AV-yes (approximately 5.3 word-associates) and AV-no (approximately 4.1 word-associates) trigrams was the most pronounced of all. Due to this uniform tendency of AV-yes trigrams to generate word-associates in the production method more readily than AV-no trigrams and to do so increasingly across the levels of nomothetic AV, we interpreted this as a kind of "pooling" of frequency considerations in the actuarial description of meaning-extension. The slight aberration at the 21–40% level did not seriously challenge the view that if a given subject employs a trigram with a high base rate of word quality and if he personally sees this as a word, through increased presentations of this trigram he will indeed be seen to "generate meaning as a function of trigram exposure."

The second interaction of trigram exposure rate was with RV ($p < .05$). In this case, however, *no uniform tendency* to generate word-associates was found. Thus, at the single-exposure level, both liked and disliked trigrams prompted about 3.5 word-associates in the production method; by the five-exposure level the disliked trigram reflected a rise in word-associates (to approximately 3.7), and the liked held steady (remaining at 3.5); and at the 10-exposure level this order had *reversed* so that liked trigrams were now suggesting *more* (approximately 3.8) and disliked trigrams *fewer* (approximately 2.8) word-associates. One realm of affective assessment (liked) seemed to be enriched with frequency increments, and a second realm (disliked) seemed to be literally decreasing with exposure. In contrast, *both* AV-yes and AV-no trigrams were increasingly enriched over these differential trial exposures (the former more so than the latter, of course).

The third significant interaction for trigram exposure brought nomothetic AV into the picture along with the RV pattern already described ($p < .05$). That is, the pattern of declining enrichment for disliked and increasing enrichment for liked trigrams was especially true at the highest nomothetic AV levels (81–100%). This is of theoretical importance because it suggests that the inability of mere trigram exposure to enrich disliked meanings and its success in enriching liked meanings is not an artifact of using verbal materials that are far removed from actual words. The aberrance noted at the 21–40% level on AV was probably due to such an artifact. Hence Tuan was to conclude that affective assessment influences the literal meanings taken on by initially nonmeaningful verbal materials and that it does so *independent* of frequency considerations. Though a frequency explanation has merit concerning AV meaningfulness, it cannot account for the data generated by RV meaningfulness.

Reinforcement Value and the Ordering
of Verbal Materials in Recall

A major tenet of LLT is that affective assessments enter into behavior determination by ordering meanings as premises and extending tautologically what has been framed by such premises to what therefore can be sequaciously known. To know is to order (create meaning) and thence "behave for the sake of" (see Chapter 8). It follows that we should be able to demonstrate in RV-learning styles what verbal-learning psychologists call the clustering of verbal materials. This experimental phenomenon dates from the work of Bousfield (1953), who presented subjects with a list of 60 nouns, 15 of each in the linguistic categories of animals, human names, professions, and vegetables. Although he administered them in random order, Bousfield found that subjects tended to group these nouns into clusters as they memorized them, reflecting in any one grouping the noun category to which it belonged (e.g., animals with animals, vegetables with vegetables, etc.). This was termed categorical clustering. Tulving (1962) subsequently established that so-called subjective clustering occurred in lists of words that had no discernible linguistic categorization in common. Several studies have been done on clustering, but we must forego a review in the interest of space (see Kintsch, 1970, pp. 247–261).

The first test of RV as a possible basis for clustering in free recall was conducted as a "side issue" by Ron Jack (1974), who was actually studying over- and underachievement. In addition to using trials scores as a recall measure, Jack employed a cluster-scoring method on his data (recalled nouns and paralogs). He found that subjects not only learned along an RV-positive direction but that they also clustered more frequently on liked than on disliked verbal materials (measured on the final, or criterion, list). This would be an example of subjective clustering, although LLT did predict and objectively measured the direction of this idiographic tendency to order memory. Michele Nguyen (1975) then decided to give the RV metric a proper test by reproducing as closely as possible Bousfield's (1953) experiment, with the exception that she added RV into the picture and predicted that *both* RV and linguistic categorization would be reflected in the free-recall clustering data.

Forty-two college students (equally divided by sex) were administered 180 nouns, half of which fell in the linguistic category of work specialization or professions (e.g., *rancher, plumber, soldier, physician, bartender,* etc.) and half of which fell in the linguistic category of animals (e.g., *pony, turtle, eel, swallow, fox,* etc.). All nouns were equated as closely as possible for occurrence in the language structure (via the Kucera & Francis, 1967, tables). Subjects rated these nouns (randomly mixed on a single form) for RV in the typical fashion. A list of 48 words was then arrayed for each subject, 12 of which were liked and 12 disliked in each of the linguistic categorizations. Subjects were tested individually, and following

Bousfield's original procedure, administered the 48 words in random order by having the experimenter read them aloud. A subject listened to the 48 words and then recorded in writing all those that he or she could recall. This process was repeated four times, with the order of the 48 words randomized across these trials.

We did not detail the clustering measure employed by Jack because it was different from Bousfield's procedure. However, Nguyen patterned her scoring method directly on Bousfield, and it went as follows: A cluster was defined as a *pair* of consecutive words having the same linguistic categorization (e.g., *bartender, plumber* or *fox, swallow*) and/or the same RV (e.g., liked, liked or disliked, disliked). The subject's recorded words were identified in pairs like this (requiring two scoring passes through the data, one on linguistic category and one on RV), and then each cluster was given a rank-order score with the *last* cluster recorded by the subject assigned the value of 1. Thus a subject's first recorded clusterings in recall had higher rank-score values than those he recorded last.

This allowed two scores for each subject's performance: a raw-cluster score, which was the number of clusters that fell under one of the four designations (professions, animals, liked, and disliked), and a ranked-cluster score, which was the total of rank-orderings attained by each of these four designations. The higher this total of ranked-cluster scores, the sooner was a subject recording the cluster in his written list (professions before animals or vice versa; and liked before disliked or vice versa). Based on previous research as well as the assumption that subjects will record what is most meaningful to them first, Nguyen predicted that RV-positive words would cluster more and also rank higher in the lists than RV-negative words. She had no basis on which to predict direction of recall for the linguistic categories, nor did she expect consistent differences in this regard.

To assess possible differences in clustering across the four trials, Nguyen clustered recall data on both the first and fourth trial. The experiment thus lent itself to a factorial ANOVA having the characteristics of a 2 (sex) × 2 (linguistic categories *or* RV) × 2 (first versus fourth trial). The first factor is a between-subjects, and the latter two are within-subjects factors. In the raw-cluster score analysis a trend was found in which liked clusters ($M = 7.38$, $SD = 2.36$) were a bit more frequent than disliked clusters ($M = 6.70$, $SD = 2.41$) ($F = 3.06$, $df = 1/40$, $p = .10$). This main effect did not interact with the (first and fourth) trials factor, although subjects did reflect significantly (p < .01) more raw-clusters on the fourth than on the first trial. The linguistic categories failed to reflect a main effect or to interact with trials; there was no difference between animal words (M=8.31, SD=3.10) and profession words (M=8.34, SD=2.92) on the cluster scores. Males produced significantly (p < .05) more raw-cluster scores than females.

On the ranked-cluster scores a highly significant difference was found between liked words (M=69.27, SD=36.54) and disliked words (M=55.80, SD=29.28) (F=10.48, df=1/40, p < .01). Once again the ranked-cluster scorings increased significantly over the first and fourth trials (p < .01), but this rise did not interact with RV. Males also produced significantly (p < .01) higher ranked-cluster scores than females. And once again there was no significant main effects noted between the ranked-cluster scores of animal words (M= 91.10, SD=52.27) and profession words (M=98.38, SD=71.13) (F less than unity); nor did these categories interact with trials. Nguyen was to conclude that though clustering occurred according to both linguistic category and RV, RV alone permitted the experimenter to predict the *direction* of a subject's conceptualizing activities. In a sense LLT had successfully predicted the affective clustering of a total list, because the ordering followed customary findings on affective assessment. We have since adopted clustering as another important dependent variable in RV experiments, using it along with trials-to-criterion and transfer effects to measure predicted differences in human behavior (see below, p. 452 where clustering is employed to distinguish between the learning styles of whites and blacks).

Reinforcement Value and Reinforcement

We would prefer to keep both RV and reinforcement in the realm of methodological terminology. The reinforcement concept proves an embarrassment to LLT because it is borrowed from an efficient-cause psychology and is basically unfriendly to a teleology. This is why we rephrased "made conditional upon" to express "for the sake of" in our theoretical definition of reinforcement (albeit reluctantly proffered). When a person's affirmed premises concerning his upcoming life experience make sense and hence successfully extend meaning then we can speak of reinforcement. The reinforcement is of the *premise* that then endows even further experience with meaning along this line. If the premise is positive, and situational factors are positively in line with these premised meanings, we would expect to witness a flow of more positive than negative meaning-extensions. If the premise is negative, and the situational factors meet these meanings, the reverse should occur. Theoretical difficulties arise for us here, because we have to answer questions such as which is more important, the initial premise or the reinforcing circumstances within which such premises are brought to bear? The LLT position favors the former, and some preliminary findings on this topic have been delineated.

John Muller (1975) worked out a procedure for reinforcing subjects in the paired-associates task by sounding a muffled chime each time they either correctly anticipated the second member of a pair (positive reinforcement) or failed to do so (negative reinforcement). Muller reasoned from LLT principles that in the positive-reinforcement condition subjects should extend meaning more readily along the positive than the negative RV line, and vice versa for a negative reinforcement condition. The reinforcement would signify what the nature of the task was to be—that is, a task in which either one's errors or one's achievements are noted. Given these circumstances, Muller predicted that a subject would frame the tasks accordingly, and the contrasting meaning-extensions would be seen in their learning styles. In a condition that lacked the chime entirely, he expected to see the usual RV-positive effect. The major test of reinforcement would come in altering the usual positive course of learning along negative lines based upon sounding the chimes after a subject missed his opportunity to anticipate the second member of a pair.

Thirty college subjects (16 females, 14 males) learned a 10-pair mixed list of CVC trigrams that had been idiographically prerated for RV in the usual fashion. Five of these pairs were liked and five disliked. Ten subjects learned their lists under conditions of positive reinforcement; 10 learned under negative reinforcement; and 10 were given no reinforcement (i.e., served as a control group). The study thus lends itself to a 2 (sex) × 3 (positive, negative, and no reinforcement) × 2 (RV) factorial ANOVA, with the first two factors between-subjects and the third a within-subjects factor. Muller found a significant interaction between reinforcement condition and RV ($F = 6.33$, $df = 2/24$, $p < .01$), which is diagrammed in Figure 6.

Note in Figure 6 that, as predicted, the positive-reinforcement condition shows a clear RV-positive effect and the negative-reinforcement condition shows a clear reversal. However, the control condition failed to conform to earlier findings on RV and actually reflected a slight RV reversal. There is no way to account for this,

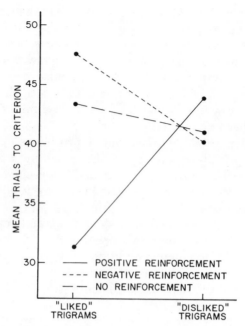

**Figure 6** Trials to criterion in the paired-associates task are graphed according to positive RV (liked trigrams) and negative RV (disliked trigrams), broken down by positive, negative, and no-reinforcement condition.

of course, though several speculations could be advanced based on the findings cited above in Chapter 10 concerning self evaluation and task premise. An interesting sidelight in this study developed when Muller had his subjects rerate their trigrams for RV following the experiment. An additional 10 subjects were used to control for only the test-retest aspect of the study—that is, these 10 subjects did not take the paired-associates task but simply rated trigrams for RV on two occasions. *All* subjects, whether in the task or not, under one sort of reinforcement or the other, rated their liked trigrams as *more* liked and their disliked trigrams as *more* disliked on rerating (48 hours intervening). This reminds us of Tuan's (1974) findings on trigram exposure at the higher nomothetic levels.

The effect of participating in the experiment seemed greatest regarding the increasing negativity of disliked trigrams. Simple-effects analyses of the data established ($p < .01$) that whether given either positive or negative reinforcement, a subject disliked his trigrams more at rerating than at original rating simply by being put through the task than did subjects who rated the trigrams twice without taking the task in the interim. As events were to develop, this was probably not an aberrant finding. Muller conducted a second study in which he tried without success to cross-validate the findings of Figure 6 when subjects were learning unmixed lists (all liked or all disliked trigrams in a list). Difficulties arose as subjects could not complete the task in the allotted time and percent-hits scores, which were then used on truncated learning performances, failed to reflect interactions between RV (which reached significance as a main effect) and reinforcement condition.

Two other studies to which we have already referred above were also concerned with the possible relationship between reinforcement and RV (both used mixed lists). August (with Rychlak & Felker, 1975) tried to introduce the chime procedure in his study of fifth grade children. He could not find any reinforcement effects in his learning data. The chime following hits or misses in the task distracted the children, who became fascinated with the source of the sound rather than with its significance to the meaning of the procedure. Children under *either* positive or negative reinforcement performed more poorly on the experimental task than children in a no-reinforcement control condition. At about the same time Marceil (1975) was also finding no effect for the chime-procedure in his sample of high school students. Marceil actually confronted the subject's task premise (whether liked or disliked) and reinforcement condition, and as noted above, found evidence to support the former but not the latter. He suggested that Muller's finding on changes in RV ratings may have been due to the subjects' task premises. That is, assuming that subjects generally did not like having to learn verbal materials which they considered negative in RV, no matter whether Muller reinforced them positively or negatively in the learning task, they continued to evaluate these items negatively and even more so than initially due to the enforced exposure as whatever enrichment in their meanings took form. These findings were comparable to Tuan's findings on exposure to disliked trigrams at the higher nomothetic AV levels.

But Muller's work has not been totally without cross-validation. Bill Apao (1976) decided to see if our AV-RV combinations entered into the reinforcement phenomenon. Sixty college subjects (divided equally by sex) were administered an eight-pair (mixed) list of CVC trigrams taken from the PPI, three pairs of which fell into each of our familiar designations based on idiographic subject ratings (AV-yes, RV-liked; AV-yes, RV-disliked, etc.). Twenty subjects were assigned to each of three reinforcement conditions: positive reinforcement, negative reinforcement, and no reinforcement (controls). The study thus lent itself to a factorial ANOVA having the characteristics of a 2 (sex) $\times$ 3 (positive, negative, and no reinforcement) $\times$ 2 (RV) $\times$ 2 (AV). The first two factors are between-subjects and the last two are within-subjects factors.

Apao found a triple interaction between reinforcement condition RV and AV ($F=3.05$, $df=2/54$, $p=.05$). Also reminiscent of Tuan's findings, this interaction suggested that the "Muller effect" could be cross-validated only when AV-yes trigrams were being memorized by the subjects. If we cast the RV-positive effect in difference (D) scores (the greater this value in the positive direction the more decidedly is a subject learning his liked over his disliked trigrams), we find the following mean values for the AV-yes trigrams: positive reinforcement, $+3.75$; negative reinforcement, $-3.45$; and no reinforcement (controls), $+5.50$. Looking at these same conditions when we have AV-no trigrams involved the mean D-scores array as follows: positive reinforcement, $-1.85$; negative reinforcement, $+2.65$; and no reinforcement, $-1.25$. The ordering of D-scores along AV-yes materials meets experimental predictions perfectly; the findings of AV-no materials are mirror opposites to expectations.

Such findings lend support to the LLT view that a subject's conceptualization of the task is probably important, and in these studies on reinforcement it may be of paramount significance. The studies by August and Marceil employed subjects who were unsophisticated about psychological experimentation, something that is not true of the older college subjects employed by Muller and Apao. Because in LLT a reinforcement is taken as that conceptualization that "works" for a subject, the younger subjects probably were never really being reinforced, because they did not conceptualize the task in the way that the experimenter had expected them to. Possibly a more explicit experimental instruction might have helped. But this correction in design would simply "reinforce" what we already premise in LLT: Reinforcement is secondary to and possibly incidental to the premised meaning and resultant meaningfulness in human learning.

## Minority Groups, Social Class, and Affective Learning Style

The final application of RV to human behavior presented here began in Larry O'Leary's speculations concerning the possible differences between white and black subjects on the RV dimension. As a humanistic approach to psychology, LLT views all persons as learning in terms of affective assessment. Other things equal, the direction of liked over disliked should be no different whether whites or blacks are studied. But what if we contrasted learning along RV with learn-ing along AV? This shifted the focus of interest to our companion dimension of meaningfulness. Logical learning theory holds that affective-assessment capacities are not learned. The human being is said to be innately capable of this telic activity which he employs to order his experience meaningfully. But what of AV? Surely there is every reason to believe that AV characteristics are more susceptible to sociocultural influences than RV characteristics.

That is, a word is only "wordlike" because of the culture that sustains this particular referent as a collection of letters having a consensual meaning. There is also the additional factor of social-class level to consider, because words vary in usages across income and educational levels. Basing his reasoning on the view of AV as a sociocultural dimension, O'Leary (1969) predicted that whites would reflect a greater influence of AV *relative to* RV in their learning styles and blacks would count more heavily on RV *relative to* AV.

This prediction was also based on O'Leary's belief that blacks have not had that sense of (self) "identity" (tautological significance) in the broader, white-dominated culture which named the intellec-tual discriminants that go to make up AV measures of meaningful-ness. Not only the wordlike items themselves but the very style of seeking to order the world in terms of such intellectualized discrimi-nants has not been cultivated by the black community. Of course this is changing and one of the ways in which to measure this pos-sibly increasing role of AV in black learning style is to include a social-class factor. O'Leary suggested that there might be an inter-action here between race and social class. Not only is it likely that middle-class blacks are more influenced by AV relative to RV than lower-class blacks, but lower-class whites are more influenced by RV relative to AV than middle-class whites. Given these social-class differences, O'Leary was still predicting that blacks as a total group would reflect a more pronounced RV-positive effect relative to AV than whites. He based this on the fact that even when blacks are more acculturated via rising education and income level, they are still as identities somewhat more marginal in cultural identity than are whites. In one sense the white-black issue is like a caste rather than a social-class distinction, and blacks continue to suffer from discrimination even though they do achieve higher socioeconomic levels. This discrimination keeps them more removed from AV considerations, and hence they fall back relatively more on RV in their learning styles.

As it developed, O'Leary could not study social class satisfac-torily because he could not identify a suitable middle-class black sample in the junior college in St. Louis, Missouri, from which he drew subjects. This was not a unique problem in racial studies conducted during the mid-1960s. Seventy-five subjects (both sexes) prerated trigrams for AV and RV, and were then put through a paired-associates task that used a (mixed) list of 16 trigrams (four pairs in each of the AV-RV combinations). The data were submitted to a factorial ANOVA having the characteristics of a 2 (sex) ×2 (race) ×2 (RV) ×2 (AV), with the first two factors between subjects and the last two within-subjects factors. O'Leary found a trend ($p = .10$) in the triple interaction between race, RV, and AV. In line with his prediction, the blacks (both sexes) reflected a larger mean difference favoring RV-positive over RV-negative than they did a mean difference favoring AV-yes over AV-no, and the whites *reversed* this ordering of relative facilitation.

The next effort in this area benefitted greatly from the hard work of Bill and Jean Hewitt (see Rychlak, Hewitt, & Hewitt, 1973). We had by this time stumbled upon the transfer effects discussed above and decided to design a study in which not only would AV and RV be perfectly counterbalanced *within* a list, but also perfectly counterbalanced *across* two lists. It would add much to our argument if we could show that blacks *transfer* more across nonspecific lists in terms of RV-over-AV than do whites. The subjects of this study were 128 female junior college students (64 blacks, 64 whites). Mean-age level was approximately 20, and the social-class factor was held constant at roughly the lower-middle to lower-class levels. Subjects rated CVC trigrams from the 65–75% nomothetic AV level for both idiographic AV and RV (Archer, 1960). Two six-pair lists were then arrayed for each subject which combined AV and RV in a specific fashion. That is, a series of eight groups was assembled (16 subjects per group) in which AV and RV were perfectly counterbalanced *across* lists:

| | Paired-Associates Lists (Six Pairs in Each) | |
|---|---|---|
| Subjects | List 1 | List 2 |
| 16 | AV-yes, RV-liked | AV-yes, RV-disliked |
| 16 | AV-yes, RV-liked | AV-no, RV-liked |
| 16 | AV-no, RV-disliked | AV-yes, RV-disliked |
| 16 | AV-no, RV-disliked | AV-no, RV-liked |
| 16 | AV-yes, RV-disliked | AV-yes, RV-liked |
| 16 | AV-no, RV-liked | AV-yes, RV-liked |
| 16 | AV-yes, RV-disliked | AV-no, RV-disliked |
| 16 | AV-no, RV-liked | AV-no, RV-disliked |
| N=128 | | |

Half of the subjects in the above eight conditions were whites and half blacks, assigned in random fashion once they had rated enough trigrams reliably to meet experimental demands. The usual method of anticipation and learning criterion was used. When list 1 had been learned a subject was given a brief respite to attend to personal needs, and then list 2 followed immediately. Testing time ranged from 45 minutes to three hours. Trials scores were analyzed via two types of factorial ANOVAs. Lists 1 and 2 were analyzed separately via a factorial ANOVA having the characteristics of a 2 (race) × 2 (AV) × 2 (RV), with all factors between subjects. All subjects learned their AV-yes trigrams more readily than their AV-no trigrams on both lists ($p < .02$ for both). But AV did not interact with race in either analysis. The RV metric failed to achieve significance on list 1, but the usual RV-positive effect was found on list 2 for all subjects ($p < .03$). Reinforcement value reflected a near-significant interaction with race on list 1 ($p = .067$) and a significant interaction with race on list 2 ($F = 5.16$, $df = 1/20$, $p = .02$). Finally, although there was no triple interaction noted in list 1, list 2 did reflect the race × AV × RV interaction ($F = 3.59$, $df = 1/20$, $p = .05$).

This triple interaction on list 2 revealed that when AV-yes materials were under consideration, the blacks reflected a slightly larger (mean) D-score of $+3.38$ than whites, who obtained a D-score value of $+1.62$ (a larger D-score signifies greater RV-positive effects in subjects' learning style). But when AV-no trigrams are considered the D-score on blacks jumps to $+17.13$ whereas for whites it actually reverses slightly to a $-2.24$. Quite clearly, our black girls were more sensitive to the RV-characteristics of the trigrams they had rated than our white girls (the meaningfulness here is not in the trigrams of course, but in the subject's conceptual assessment of the trigram).

To test for transfer across lists a 2 (race) × 8 (experimental sequence) × 2 (Lists 1 and 2) factorial ANOVA was run, with the first a between-subjects and the last two within-subjects factors. The crucial triple interaction in this analysis failed to reach significance ($F = 1.62$, $df$ 7/112, $p = .13$), but we would draw the reader's attention to these data in Table 12 in any case. An impartial survey of Table 12 must surely arrive at the conclusion that the black subjects were learning more along an RV than an AV sequence, and the opposite tendency was true for the whites. Note condition 2, in which subjects were moving from a list with AV-yes, RV-liked to a second list having AV-no, RV-liked. This takes AV meaningfulness out of the second list while retaining RV meaningfulness intact. Under this

**Table 12**  Eight Experimental Conditions Across
Lists for Blacks and Whites

| AV-RV conditions, List 1 to List 2 | n | List 1 Mean | List 1 SD | List 2 Mean | List 2 SD |
|---|---|---|---|---|---|
| 1. AV-yes, RV-liked to AV-yes, RV disliked | | | | | |
|     Blacks | 8 | 38.13 | 7.66 | 32.88 | 11.15 |
|     Whites | 8 | 40.88 | 14.87 | 27.13 | 5.06 |
| 2. AV-yes, RV-liked to AV-no, RV-liked | | | | | |
|     Blacks | 8 | 45.00 | 15.95 | 35.00 | 10.75 |
|     Whites | 8 | 33.38 | 9.94 | 39.25 | 24.71 |
| 3. AV-no, RV-disliked to AV-yes, RV disliked | | | | | |
|     Blacks | 8 | 52.00 | 19.29 | 37.38 | 15.33 |
|     Whites | 8 | 45.88 | 15.16 | 29.00 | 9.80 |
| 4. AV-no, RV-disliked to AV-no, RV liked | | | | | |
|     Blacks | 8 | 59.00 | 18.37 | 32.13 | 13.46 |
|     Whites | 8 | 46.25 | 17.66 | 33.13 | 7.75 |

sequence the eight white girls demonstrated a decline in learning efficiency, and the eight black girls continued to improve on their second list, outperforming their white counterparts on list 2.

We find a comparable development in condition 4, where subjects moved from AV-no, RV-disliked to AV-no, RV-liked. Although the eight black girls in this condition began with a 13-trial deficit on list 1, at list 2 they had achieved a one-trial advantage over the white girls. Note further that in conditions 1 and 8, where RV is changing from positive to negative, the blacks reflect the *least* gain from the first to the second list. There are four instances of black superiority in performance over whites in the learning data (conditions 1, 2, 4, 6), and in *each* case—whether these are first or second list advantages and regardless of whether AV was in or out of the list—the common denominator is that RV-liked *was* present. The meaning-

Lists for Blacks and Whites (continued)

| AV-RV conditions, List 1 to List 2 | n | List 1 Mean | List 1 SD | List 2 Mean | List 2 SD |
|---|---|---|---|---|---|
| 5. AV-yes, RV-disliked to AV-yes, RV liked | | | | | |
| Blacks | 8 | 51.13 | 17.80 | 31.75 | 11.62 |
| Whites | 8 | 40.63 | 9.64 | 24.37 | 4.75 |
| 6. AV-no, RV-liked to AV-yes, RV-liked | | | | | |
| Blacks | 8 | 52.50 | 18.40 | 31.75 | 11.32 |
| Whites | 8 | 59.88 | 15.03 | 28.50 | 8.47 |
| 7. AV-yes, RV-disliked to AV-no, RV-disliked | | | | | |
| Blacks | 8 | 67.38 | 27.28 | 51.63 | 16.40 |
| Whites | 8 | 44.38 | 13.30 | 32.00 | 10.68 |
| 8. AV-no, RV-liked to AV-no, RV-disliked | | | | | |
| Blacks | 8 | 54.38 | 28.09 | 49.75 | 22.96 |
| Whites | 8 | 49.00 | 21.14 | 35.88 | 14.64 |

fulness afforded by AV-yes when RV was negative *always* favored the white subjects (conditions 3, 5, 7). Even though we did not reach significance in the triple interaction of the second factorial ANOVA, based on the findings of the first ANOVA as well as this review of Table 12, we contend that black subjects order and "create meaningfulness" more along an RV than an AV dimension and that this tendency is *not* so characteristic of white subjects.

If this is true, we should be able to demonstrate that blacks cluster more along RV-positive than do whites. An experiment was planned to test this, in which 80 college subjects (divided equally by sex and race) were put through a free-recall task in which they memorized a list of 12 trigrams. Based on their idiographic ratings of the PPI, three of these trigrams fell in each of our familiar AV-RV combinations. A unique feature of this study was that white experimenters gathered data from white subjects, and black experimenters gathered data from black subjects.[3] Subjects recorded their trigram recollections in writing, and they were taken to full criterion of two consecutive correct trials for the complete list. We decided to examine clustering at both the initial and the final trials so that we could essentially see how subjects order their trigrams on the first pass through the task and also after they had clearly demonstrated mastery of the material. Cluster scores were obtained separately for AV and RV, following Michele Nguyen's (1975) procedure; in a sense we had merely substituted AV for the linguistic category of her study. This experiment lent itself to a factorial ANOVA having the characteristics of a 2 (race) ×2 (sex) ×2 (first versus last trial) ×2 (two levels of either AV or RV).

Taking up RV on the raw-cluster scores first, all subjects were found to cluster more on liked than disliked trigrams, and this tendency was somewhat greater on the first than the last trial ($p < .01$). Black subjects ($M=1.93$) clustered more overall in their learning than whites ($M=1.64$) ($p <.02$), but race did not interact with RV in the raw-cluster scores. However, this interaction was found when we look at the ranked-cluster scores—which weight the trigram-clusters for appearance in the list. We found as a main effect that all subjects record their liked trigram clusters ($M=6.12$) before they record their disliked trigram clusters ($M=4.80$) ($F=9.43$, $df= 1/76$, $p < .01$). However, within this proclivity, blacks are found to cluster liked trigrams ($M=7.34$) decidedly higher than disliked ($M= 5.21$), and whites show only a modest difference favoring liked ($M=4.90$) over disliked ($M=4.39$) ranked clusters ($F=3.49$, $df=1/76$, $p=06$).

This near-significant finding was brought into significance via a triple interaction between race, RV, and list. That is, whereas the white subjects moved from a clear RV-positive effect on their first list ($M=2.15$ for liked, $M=.60$ for disliked) to a slight reversal on their criterion list ($M=7.65$ for liked, $M=8.18$ for disliked), black subjects reflected the positive RV-effect on their first list ($M=2.38$ on liked, $M=1.13$ on disliked) and then *increased* this differential (raw-score difference) on their criterion list ($M=12.30$ on liked, $M= 9.30$ on disliked) ($F=6.15$, $df=1/76$, $p < .01$). When these data were reclustered and analyzed according to idiographic AV, *no significant findings* emerged in the racial comparisons. Once again an affective assessment dimension of meaningfulness permitted analyses of

[3] The writer would like to thank Joanne Alder, Cassandra Cox, Leonard Kirklen, Cheryl Langford, and Diane Netzel for their assistance in data collection on this study.

interest which the traditional measure of meaningfulness in verbal learning failed to identify.

We had not yet tackled the problem of social class in affective learning style, and because our view of why blacks learn more along RV than AV seemed definitely tied to the argument that blacks were not so middle-class identified as whites, we decided at least to try to bring *both* social class and race into a single experiment. Hence our next experiment involved 160 seventh grade children (divided equally by sex and race), half of whom were drawn from a junior high school situated in an inner city, which was a decidedly lower-socioeconomic area, and half of whom were selected from a junior high school situated in the outskirts of the city (Indianapolis, Indiana).[4] Great pains were taken to establish that we had a definite social-class contrast of the "ghetto versus suburbia" variety based on the occupational and educational level of a child's parents or guardians (see Rychlak, 1975b). The children were administered words from fifth grade spelling books (i.e., two grade levels below their own) and asked to rate them for RV (e.g., *cat, nose, milk, grass, rain, shoe,* etc.). An additional independent variable of this study was intelligence (Otis IQ), although IQ ranges could not be equated across the two schools because the middle-class sample had significantly higher IQs than the lower-class sample.

Because of this IQ disparity and evidence from pretesting in which some of the lower-class children found the task too difficult if more than eight words were used, differential list lengths were employed in the two schools. That is, lower-class children were asked to memorize two eight-word lists and middle-class children memorized two 10-word lists in a free-recall format. Percent-hits scores were then used to examine RV-differences across samples (i.e., the *higher* a score, the *better* is the subject's performance). In other words, this study used unmixed lists, in which a counterbalancing of liked to disliked and vice versa across the total sample enabled us to examine transfer effects as well as simply trials to criterion in the learning of blacks and whites. Words were presented by memory drum, set on a four-second exposure cycle. The children

[4] The writer would like to express his appreciation to the teachers and student body of the Indianapolis Public Schools. Special thanks are extended to Paul F. Brown, Stanley C. Campbell, William Delph, Alfred Finnell, Jr., Karl Kalp, and Owen B. Keene for their cooperation in making this research possible. Grateful appreciation is also extended to the following individuals for their help in data collection: Kelly Brownell, Charles Coleman, Daniel Hibshman, Arthur Kozumplik, Charles Salley, Scott Van Buskirk, and Gerald Yelusich.

were not required to write down their recollections but merely stated them aloud, and an examiner recorded the hits on each trial. The study was analyzed through various factorial ANOVA combinations, with between-subjects factors (two levels of each) being race, sex, social class, IQ-level, and order of lists (liked-disliked, disliked-liked). The within-subjects factors were RV and repeated measures (lists 1 and 2).

The expected nonspecific transfer effects were found for all subjects ($p < .01$). But this across-lists factor also interacted with race ($F = 4.10$, $df = 1/144$, $p = .04$). White children reflect positive nonspecific transfer across lists regardless of whether they are moving from positive to negative ($M = 85.13$, $SD = 5.51$ to $M = 86.73$, $SD = 5.89$) or negative to positive ($M = 85.43$, $SD = 6.16$ to $M = 87.15$, $SD = 6.38$) levels of RV. Black children reflect a *negative* transfer when moving from positive to negative ($M = 86.18$, $SD = 6.28$ to $M = 84.85$, $SD = 6.34$) and a positive transfer when moving from negative to positive lists ($M = 87.47$, $SD = 6.16$ to $M = 89.03$, $SD = 5.61$).

A significant triple interaction was found between social class, list order, and RV ($F = 8.45$, $df = 1/144$, $p < .01$). Middle-class children reflect positive nonspecific transfer across lists regardless of whether they are moving from positive to negative ($M = 85.15$, $SD = 5.38$ to $M = 85.65$, $SD = 4.43$) or negative to positive ($M = 87.45$, $SD = 6.73$ to $M = 89.92$, $SD = 6.01$) levels of RV. Lower-class children reflect a slight *negative* transfer when moving from positive to negative ($M = 86.15$, $SD = 6.03$ to $M = 85.93$, $SD = 5.40$) and a positive transfer when moving from negative to positive lists ($M = 85.45$, $SD = 6.88$ to $M = 86.25$, $SD = 6.12$). The IQ and sex factors did not enter into the significant findings.

Both a sociocultural and a racial difference appear to exist in affective learning style. We have been unable to demonstrate that simply by becoming "middle class," blacks forego their affective learning style. The problem of just how middle class a black can become in the American culture at this point in history is brought into question. Furthermore, an argument can be made that groups which perpetuate their own *cultural* world views can go on with affective learning styles more typical of a lower-class sample even though they have become upwardly mobile. In other words, rather than tracing RV-learning style to some basic unlearned capacity to fall back on affective assessments when the acculturated discriminations of an AV metric are not salient to the learner, we might argue that the findings reflect a straightforward cultural difference.

The blacks have a culture emphasizing an affective learning style, and whites have a culture emphasizing a less affectively oriented style of learning. This is the view Ray Garza (1975) took, and he predicted that if he were to study a group of Mexican-Americans in relation to Anglo-Americans he would find the same RV differences we had been finding on whites and blacks.

Sixty-four college subjects (32 Mexican-Americans, 32 Anglo-Americans, balanced for sex) were equated for grade-point average at a Southwestern university. These subjects rated trigrams from the middle ranges of Archer's (1960) norms for both AV and RV, and then a free-recall (mixed) list of 12 trigrams was arrayed, three trigrams falling in each of the four AV-RV combinations. Subjects were presented these trigrams by memory drum (two-second exposure cycle) and asked to record their recollections in writing between presentations. Garza also looked at the influence of grade-point average on performance in the free-recall task. Hence this study lends itself to a factorial ANOVA having the characteristics of a 2 (sex) × 2 (ethnic group × 2 (high versus low grade point) × 2 (RV) ×2 (AV). The first three factors are between subjects and the last is a within-subjects factor. Garza found no main effects for ethnic identity, grade-point average, or AV. He did find that his female subjects learned their task more readily than males ($p = .04$), and there was also the familiar RV-positive effect reflected in the learning data for all subjects ($p < .01$). But the test of importance came in the significant interaction between ethnic identity and RV. As predicted, Mexican-American subjects showed a large difference in trials scores (lower mean score signifies better performance) between their liked ($M = 14.69$, $SD = 7.37$) and disliked ($M = 18.23$, $SD = 8.12$) trigrams. Anglo-Americans reflected a comparable albeit significantly lessened difference between their liked ($M = 18.27$, $SD = 10.03$) and disliked ($M = 19.50$, $SD = 10.06$) trigrams ($F = 4.83$, $df = 1/56$, $p = .03$).

We were pleased with the Garza findings, as with those on the lower socioeconomic class in general, because we had no desire to be misunderstood in the use of the phrase *racial learning style*. The LLT position is drawn from formal- and final-cause considerations rather than from material- and efficient-cause considerations. We are *not* making a genetic or "blood-line" argument. Our expectation would be that other minority groups in the American culture, such as American Indians, should learn according to RV in the way that we have now seen blacks, Mexican-Americans, and Anglo (as well as black) lower-class subjects learning. This reliance on RV is a reversion to a kind of naturalistic propensity, an unlearned "basic" capacity to order experience affectively instead of relying on discriminant cues of a purely sociocultural variety. This is not to deny the likely additional role of sociocultural forces, such as what priorities are put upon memorization of intellectualized tasks in black, Mexican-American, and lower-class social environments. Garza's argument is surely tenable. But it is almost too easy to think of RV as a sociocultural product, as a kind of manipulation that is related to the cultural milieu and not actually rooted in the individual's conceptual abilities.

Cultures surely influence the *grounds* for affective assessment (influencing what is considered proper, good, beautiful, etc.), but the RV phenomenon *per se* is no more a cultural product than is the individual's ability to recall in memory that which he sets his mind to remembering. Some cultures surely emphasize memorization as a prized facility more so than others; but is this to say that memory *per se* is a cultural product? Obviously not. This is how we prefer to speak about RV: a factor in human predication *not* mediation!

The last research project we mention in this chapter is in some ways the most exciting and surely the most ambitious effort yet made to extend the findings on affective assessment to a practical realm of behavior. Judy Rumsey (1975) with help from Kay Woodward and Anita Jones (1974) managed to get this study completed. There has been considerable debate over the supposed lower intellectual ability of blacks relative to whites in recent decades, particularly since the publication of Jensen's (1969) paper on the topic. The usual interpretation of lowered IQ scores for blacks is that there is a genetic involvement of undetermined mechanism causing the decrement (a difficult extrapolation to make, considering that the evidence is purely actuarial). Yet if RV can be shown to influence IQ test performance, what happens when we calculate IQ scores in terms of positive or negative RV? Will white superiority on IQ tests be sustained equally across liked and disliked subtests? Or because we know that blacks are more sensitive to RV in learning style than whites, will this disparity in IQ between racial identities diminish when *only* liked tests are used to calculate the IQ? The latter situation would preclude attributing white-black differences to genetic roots.

Rumsey first obtained permission from the Psychological Corporation to make a (black-and-white) movie of the procedure employed in administering the Wechsler Intelligence Scale for Children (WISC).[5] Pseudo-WISC subtests were designed by Rumsey, and a movie made of two female administrators—one white and the other black—giving the test instructions to viewers as if they were about to take the WISC. The head of the female administrator was not on camera as it panned down from slightly above shoulder level to reveal a torso with arms presenting items, a test manual, and a stop watch resting on the felt-covered table top where all demonstrations were made. Presentation of verbal subtests was accompanied by expressive arm and hand movements to keep the viewer's interest. When the white administrator was on camera the black administrator's voice was used to give instructions, and vice versa. The WISC subtests were ordered randomly to intersperse verbal and performance subtests (all 12 were demonstrated, with the torso-voice counterbalanced equally across subtests). Each subtest demonstration ended with the examiner asking a viewer how much he or she would like or not like doing a task of the type presented. Viewers were requested to make their judgments known via a special answer form on which was printed the four-step rating for RV—like a lot, like a little, dislike a little, and dislike a lot.

Subjects were seventh and eighth graders (CA 12 to 15 years) attending lower-class and middle-class junior high schools similar to those mentioned above, in the free-recall study. Initially, there was a pool of 270 children who were shown the WISC film, and then 96 students (divided equally by sex, race, and social class) were selected to fill experimental conditions. Each of these children had rated *at least* two subtests reliably as liked and two as disliked. Some children had rated all 12 subtests as reliably liked, and they could not be used as subjects because we were trying to find a contrast in IQ value across the same subjects through the use of prorated scores. Subjects were then administered the 12 subtests of the WISC individually, using both white and black examiners of both sexes (examiners were counterbalanced across experimental conditions). The experiment thus lent itself to a factorial ANOVA having the characteristics of a 2 (sex) ×2 (race) ×2 (social class) ×2 (RV), with the first three factors between subjects and the last a within-subjects factor.

There were many findings, but the central interest for present

[5] The writer would like to thank the Psychological Corporation, manufacturer of the WISC, for permitting us to make this film.

purposes has to do with the main effect on RV and any interactions with the remaining factors. There *was* a significant main effect on Full Scale (prorated) IQ for the sample as a whole. Subjects did indeed earn higher IQs on their liked ($M$=96.26, $SD$=14.04) than their disliked WISC subtests ($M$=91.54, $SD$=14.25) ($F$=9.52, $df$ =1/79, $p$ < .01). However, the interaction of RV with race and /or social class did not materialize. The blacks as a group obtained a significantly lower IQ ($M$=89.21, $SD$=12.88) than the whites ($M$= 99.05, $SD$=10.25) ($F$=16.18, $df$=1/79, $p$ < .01). There were some trends on RV ($p$=.10) in certain of the subscale analyses which suggested that blacks were indeed more susceptible to an RV-positive effect in their total IQ than whites (especially on the Performance subscale). But none of these findings can be cited as satisfactory support of the thesis that racial disparities wash away when only RV-positive subtests are taken into consideration.

However, we do take satisfaction in the significant main effect on RV. The critic probably can dismiss a five IQ-point superiority of liked over disliked subtests as due to motivational factors— for example, the children "tried harder" on subtests they liked. The IQ test suffers from some of the same theory-method problems we have discussed in other contexts (see Chapter 5). It is easy enough measuring "something" and predicting to "something" like school performance with reliability after sufficient effort is expended. But does this mean we have an understanding (theory) of what is so rigorously controlled and predicted (method) in our samplings of subjects? Who is to say precisely where in a subject's performance that so-called motivation enters? The dozens of studies surveyed over Chapters 9 and 10 have not required a construct of this type to explain the observed findings. Hence we do not accept an easy dismissal of Rumsey's noteworthy demonstration that affective assessment reaches into the very core of a child's intellective processes.

Returning to the overriding prediction made at the outset of Chapter 9 (p. 367), we conclude that it *has* been validated. That is, *teleological theory is entirely compatible with research designs that have been initially framed to test nontelic theory.* And we further suggest what used to be called a *Law of Learning: All human behavior receives an idiographically generated influence from the individual's affective assessment of that which he is both seen to learn and not to learn.* The constructs of LLT and the findings of its researches fill in how and in what variations this influence may be said to take place.

## Summary

In Chapter 10 we continued the case history of a revolutionary theory of behavior begun in Chapter 9 by covering five broad areas of research in which affective assessment was put to test via the RV measure. The first area establishes that RV, as a measure of meaningfulness, relates personality style to the learning of verbal material bearing the meaning of these personality styles. Thus, for example, masculine personalities learning masculine verbal materials reflect a larger RV-positive effect than when learning feminine materials. And feminine personalities reflect a larger RV-positive effect when learning feminine than when learning masculine meanings.

The next area surveyed has to do with the reversal or diminution of RV-positive effects. Abnormals and normals with weak self-images are found to reverse the typical RV learning style and actually learn along affectively negative lines more readily than along the positive. Although initially taken as a global propensity, this is traced through a series of experiments to a combination of factors. Thus, for example, the *same* person can extend meanings along the positive more readily than the negative in one sphere and reverse this customary finding in another sphere of experience. Combining all factors examined to date, to the extent a subject predicates an area of meaning negatively, dislikes the task to be accomplished *per se*, and evaluates himself critically as a person, the RV-positive effect can be expected to diminish or reverse entirely.

The next area of RV research dealt with order effects. Quite by accident we discovered that moving from a disliked to a liked task facilitated positive nonspecific transfer, but moving in the opposite direction resulted in less positive and occasionally even negative transfer taking place. This order effect holds even when a subject is taken across several paired-associate lists. This effect has been found so often that it is now used routinely as a dependent variable in RV researches on various populations of interest.

The fourth area of research surveyed has to do with affective assessment in conceptualization. Osgoodian ratings on Evaluation parallel RV in actual learning situations. The meaning-extension of liked premises is shown to be positive in a story-writing task, and negative premises lead to negative meaning-extensions. A unique application to the perceptual defense thesis is presented. In two rather intricate experiments the extension of meanings from one CVC trigram to another is shown to be greatly influenced by RV. Reinforcment-value effects are then shown to appear in the clustering of free-recall lists, with positive RV more likely to appear first in the ordering of lists. The relationship between reinforcement and RV is then discussed, and some preliminary evidence is presented which suggests that while under positive reinforcement, subjects may extend liked meanings more readily than disliked, and vice versa for negative reinforcement. The picture is clouded by a subject's task premise—whether positive or negative—so that we have not yet clarified the importance of reinforcement *per se* in affective learning style.

The final research area presented has to do with minority groups and social class. Based on theoretical grounds it was predicted and established that blacks as a group and lower class subjects of both racial identities, rely more on RV than AV in their learning styles. A similar finding obtained when Mexican-Americans were compared to Anglo-Americans. The black subject's sensitivity to positive RV in learning style has been established in several studies, employing both mixed and unmixed lists (i.e., utilizing transfer effects as a dependent-variable measure) as well as the clustering phenomenon. Probably the most ambitious of all RV studies attempted to date revealed that higher IQ scores are obtained on liked than on disliked subtests of the Wechsler Intelligence Scale for Children. When RV is taken into consideration, the hypothesized washing away of racial differences on IQ tests failed to materialize.

Chapter 10 closed with the conclusion that teleological theories could indeed be put to test via research designs which had initially been used to test nontelic theory. A new law of learning was suggested, which holds that all human behavior receives a contribution from idiographically generated affective assessment. The person influences his course of learning at least as much as extrapersonal factors do.

# References

Andrews, J. E. *The effect of word meaning on the affective learning styles of ascendant and submissive subjects.* Unpublished master's thesis. Lafayette, Ind.: Purdue University, 1972.

Apao, W. *Reinforcement and two kinds of meaningfulness measures in paired-associate learning.* Unpublished master's thesis. Lafayette, Ind.: Purdue University, 1976.

Archer, E. J. Re-evaluation of the meaningfulness of all possible CVC trigrams. *Psychological Monographs*, 1960, **74**, No. 10 (Whole No. 497).

August, G. J. *Affective meaningfulness, self-concept and the verbal learning styles of white and black children.* Unpublished doctoral dissertation. Lafayette, Ind.: Purdue University, 1975.

August, G. J., Rychlak, J. F., & Felker, D. W. Affective assessment, self-concept, and the verbal learning styles of fifth-grade children. *Journal of Educational Psychology*, 1975, **67**, 801–806.

Barron, F. S. An ego strength scale which predicts responses to psychotherapy. *Journal of Consulting Psychology*, 1953, **17**, 327–333.

Berg, I. A. Deviant responses and deviant people: The formulation of the deviation hypothesis. *Journal of Counseling Psychology*, 1957, **4**, 159.

Block, J. *The challenge of response sets.* New York: Appleton-Century-Crofts, 1965.

Boland, G. C. *The relationship of personality adjustment to the learning of material having connotative and associative meaningfulness.* Unpublished doctoral dissertation. St. Louis: St. Louis University, 1970.

Bousfield, W. A. The occurrence of clustering in the recall of randomly arranged associates. *Journal of General Psychology*, 1953, **49**, 229–240.

Bruner, J. S., & Postman, L. Emotional selectivity in perception and reaction. *Journal of Personality*, 1947, **16**, 69–77.

Byron, R. E. *Learning of "likes" and "dislikes" in high and low self-esteem children.* Unpublished master's thesis. Lafayette, Ind.: Purdue University, 1972.

Carlsen, N. L. *The effect of high and low self concept on learning along an intensity dimension of meaningfulness.* Unpublished master's thesis. Lafayette, Ind.: Purdue University, 1970.

Dahlstrom, W. G., & Welsh, G. S. *An MMPI handbook: A guide to use in clinical practice and research.* Minneapolis: University of Minnesota Press, 1960.

Dunning, L. P. *The effects of reinforcement value on the learning of words varying in positive and negative meaningfulness for subjects high or low in ego-strength.* Unpublished master's thesis. Lafayette, Ind.: Purdue University, 1973.

Fitts, W. H. Tennessee Department of Mental Health Self-Concept Scale. Nashville: Counselor Recordings and Tests, 1965.

Galster, J. M. *Affective factors in paired-associate acquisition and tachistoscopic recognition of faces and names.* Unpublished master's thesis. Lafayette, Ind.: Purdue University, 1972.

Garza, R. T. *Affective and associative meaningfulness in the learning styles of Chicano and Anglo college students.* Unpublished doctoral dissertation. Lafayette, Ind.: Purdue University, 1975.

Guilford, J. P., & Martin, H. G. Guilford-Martin Inventory of Factors GAMIN: Manual. Beverly Hills, Calif.: Sheridan Supply, 1948.

Jack, R. M. *The effect of reinforcement value in mixed and unmixed lists on learning style of overachieving and underachieving female college students.* Unpublished doctoral dissertation. Lafayette, Ind.: Purdue University, 1974.

Jensen, A. R. How much can we boost IQ and scholastic achievement? *Harvard Educational Review*, 1969, **39**, 1–123.

Jones, M. A. *The role of racial identity, sex and social class in the affective* assessment of subtests on the Wechsler intelligence scale for children. Unpublished master's thesis. Lafayette, Ind.: Purdue University, 1974.

Kausler, D. H. Readings in verbal learning. New York: Wiley, 1966.

Keedy, N. S. The relationship between the affective quality of a premise and meaning-extension based upon its affirmation. Unpublished manuscript. Lafayette, Ind.: Purdue University, 1975.

Kintsch, W. Learning, memory, and conceptual processes. New York: Wiley, 1970.

Kucera, H., & Francis, W. N. Computational analysis of present-day American English. Providence, R.I.: Brown University Press, 1967.

Lappin, R. W. Meaningfulness, deviant achievers, and personal adjustment. Unpublished doctoral dissertation. St. Louis: St. Louis University, 1969.

Marceil, J. C. The role of the person in the psychology experiment: A reappraisal of the problems of reinforcement, response set and volunteer error. Unpublished master's thesis. Lafayette, Ind.: Purdue University, 1975.

McFarland, K. K. The influence of reinforcement value and school achievement on a "pictorial-verbal" learning task. Unpublished master's thesis. St. Louis: St. Louis University, 1969.

McKeachie, W. J. The decline and fall of the laws of learning. Educational Researcher, 1974, 3, 7–11.

McKee, D. B. Connotative and associative meaningfulness and their influence on schizophrenic learning. Unpublished master's thesis. St. Louis: St. Louis University, 1969.

Morgan, C. L. Psychology for teachers. New York: Scribner, 1906.

Muller, J. B. The effects of differential feedback and reinforcement value on the acquisition of trigrams: A conceptual theory of reinforcement. Unpublished doctoral dissertation. Lafayette, Ind.: Purdue University, 1975.

Nguyen, M. L. Clustering in terms of categorization and reinforcement value in randomly arranged associates. Unpublished master's thesis. Lafayette, Ind.: Purdue University, 1975.

Noble, C. E. Meaningfulness (m) and transfer phenomena in serial verbal learning. The Journal of Psychology, 1961, 52, 201–210.

O'Leary, L. R. The effect of idiographic meaningfulness on the learning of subjects from different racial backgrounds, social classes, and ability levels. Unpublished doctoral dissertation. St. Louis: St. Louis University, 1969.

Osgood, C. E. The nature and measurement of meaning. Psychological Bulletin, 1952, 49, 197–237.

Page, M. M. Demand characteristics and the verbal operant conditioning experiment. Journal of Personality and Social Psychology, 1972, 23, 304–308.

Paivio, A., Yuille, J. C., & Madigan, S. Concreteness, imagery, and meaningfulness values for 925 nouns. Journal of Experimental Psychology Monograph Supplement, 1968, 76, (1, Pt. 2).

Piers, E. V., & Harris, D. B. Piers-Harris Children's Self-Concept Scale: Manual. Nashville: Counselor Recordings and Tests, 1964.

Roark, R. N. Psychology in education. New York: American Book, 1895.

Rumsey, J. M. G. Affective assessment in intelligence testing of black and *white, middle- and lower-class adolescents.* Unpublished doctoral dissertation. Lafayette, Ind.: Purdue University, 1975.

Rychlak, J. F. Affective assessment in the recognition of designs and paintings by elementary school children. *Child Development*, 1975, **46**, 62–70. (a)

Rychlak, J. F. Affective assessment, intelligence, social class, and racial learning style. *Journal of Personality and Social Psychology*, 1975, **32**, 989–995.(b)

Rychlak, J. F., Carlsen, N. L., & Dunning, L. P. Personal adjustment and the free recall of material with affectively positive or negative meaningfulness. *Journal of Abnormal Psychology*, 1974, **83**, 480–487.

Rychlak, J. F., Galster, J., & McFarland, K. K. The role of affective assessment in associative learning: From designs and CVC trigrams to faces and names. *Journal of Experimental Research in Personality*, 1972, **6**, 186–194.

Rychlak, J. F., Hewitt, C. W., & Hewitt, J. Affective evaluation, word quality, and the verbal learning styles of black versus white junior college females. *Journal of Personality and Social Psychology*, 1973, **27**, 248–255.

Rychlak, J. F., McKee, D. B., Schneider, W. E., & Abramson, Y. Affective evaluation in the verbal learning styles of normals and abnormals. *Journal of Abnormal Psychology*, 1971, **77**, 11–16.

Rychlak, J. F., & Saluri, R. E. Affective assessment in the learning of names by fifth- and sixth-grade children. *Journal of Genetic Psychology*, 1973, **123**, 251–261.

Rychlak, J. F., Tasto, D. L., Andrews, J. E., & Ellis, H. C. The application of an affective dimension of meaningfulness to personality-related verbal learning. *Journal of Personality*, 1973, **41**, 341–360.

Rychlak, J. F., & Tobin, T. J. Order effects in the affective learning styles of overachievers and underachievers. *Journal of Educational Psychology*, 1971, **62**, 141–147.

Rychlak, J. F., Tuan, N. D., & Schneider, W. E. Formal discipline revisited: Affective assessment and nonspecific transfer. *Journal of Educational Psychology*, 1974, **66**, 139–151.

Skinner, B. F. A case history in scientific method. *American Psychologist*, 1956, **11**, 221–233.

Spence, J. T., & Lair, C. V. Associative interference in the verbal learning performance of schizophrenics and normals. *Journal of Abnormal and Social Psychology*, 1964, **68**, 204–209.

Tasto, D. L. *Meaningfulness and the masculinity and femininity personality factors as related to rate of acquisition.* Unpublished doctoral dissertation. St. Louis: St. Louis University, 1968.

Thorndike, E. L. *Educational psychology: Briefer course.* New York: Columbia University Press, 1914.

Thorndike, E. L., & Lorge, I. *The teachers word book of 30,000 words.* New York: Columbia University Press, 1944.

Thorndike, E. L., & Woodworth, R. S. The influence of improvement in one mental function upon the efficiency of other functions. I. *Psychological Review*, 1901, **8**, 247–261. (a)

Thorndike, E. L., & Woodworth, R. S. The influence of improvement in one mental function upon the efficiency of other functions. II. The stimulation of magnitudes. *Psychological Review*, 1901, **8**, 384–395. (b)

Thorndike, E. L., & Woodworth, R. S. The influence of improvement in one mental function upon the efficiency of other functions. III. Functions involving attention, observation, and discrimination. *Psychological Review*, 1901, **8**, 553–564. (c)

Tobin, T. J. *The effect of reinforcement value on the learning of overachievers and underachievers.* Unpublished master's thesis. St. Louis: St. Louis University, 1969.

Trybus, R. J. *The effects of reinforcement value and association value on nonspecific transfer.* Unpublished master's thesis. St. Louis: St. Louis University, 1969.

Tuan, N. D. *Changes in associative and affective meaningfulness as a function of frequency and intensity factors.* Unpublished doctoral dissertation. Lafayette, Ind.: Purdue University, 1974.

Tulving, E. Subjective organization in free recall of unrelated words. *Psychological Review*, 1962, **69**, 344–354.

Woodward, K. E. *Affective learning style across race: Group and individual identification procedures.* Unpublished master's thesis. Lafayette, Ind.: Purdue University, 1973.

# CHAPTER ELEVEN

## Summations, Reactions, and Reaffirmations

In this closing chapter of the volume we summarize what has transpired over the preceding ten chapters. Because there are objections to the general thrust of humanistic psychology, we then take up some of the reactions and questions most often called to our attention. The volume is brought to a close by delineating the tenets of a rigorous humanistic psychology.

### What Have We Accomplished?

The chapters of this volume began with a review of Western intellectual history in terms of the four causes, a metaphysical frame which we found emerging quite spontaneously in the knowledge of mankind. Aristotle gave these concepts a name, but he did not have to "think them up." The ideas presented in Table 1 were then taken as the data of a study in which our goal was to capture the kind of organism which could have proffered them, keeping as close to the meaning of these formulations as possible. That is, we took what was included in Table 1 *seriously*, feeling that a psychology should not dictate what was or was not characteristic of its data.

We found that there were many ideas in Table 1 that simply could not be expressed without the full panoply of causation subsuming their meaning. No psychological scientist who wishes to speak for the organism of Table 1 can do so if he limits his conceptualization to one, two, or even three of the *four* causal meanings. Even if such limitation is called for in the descriptive explanations of natural science, to limit the causal meanings employed by the human beings cited in Table 1 in explaining *their* behavior is consciously and arbitrarily to distort psychology's professional calling. The problem facing us, then, was to frame a psychology which could subsume the humanly generated concepts of Table 1.

We discovered that to do so involved a recognition of the precedents in thought. If we took these to be predicate assumptions, then it was possible to think of human behavior in telic terms. Surely Table 1 establishes that teleological formulations are heavily represented in the history of thought. Having committed ourselves to *all* of the ideas in our historical survey, we had to find some of our own precedents which might help aid our understanding of the telic intelligence. An analysis of meaning soon established that a belief in the human person's dialectical (in addition to demonstrative) reasoning ability could help in this effort. The remarkable fact that not only the causal meanings but the demonstrative-dialectical contrast in meaning could be found in Eastern as well as Western thought, with *no evidence of cultural transmission,* lends an historical weight of conviction (procedural evidence) to our efforts. Surely there is nothing here to weaken the contention that human beings reason *by nature* in a dialectical fashion.

While developing these themes we also established why neither the dialectic nor the final-cause description of human behavior which it makes possible is employed in modern natural science. Due to historical confrontations between deity teleology and the empirical approach of science, a Baconian restriction was put on the causes of Table 1—first, in the description of nonhuman events and then of human events as well (even though Bacon never intended to dismiss formal-final cause description in art, ethics, metaphysics, etc., each of which can be thought of as a manifestation of human behavior). The concurrent rise of mathematics with its attendant law of contradiction further served to remove dialectical formulations from the list of acceptable theoretical precedents in the conceptualization of the human condition. The inevitable (because sequacious) outcome of these ground-rule restrictions was a mechanistic cybernetic human image.

We traced the course of this development in psychology, contrasting the leading thinkers of our profession in terms of so-called Lockean-Kantian models—models named because these two philosophers typified the contrast in outlook which we have seen across the ages and in different cultural milieus. There can be no doubt but that psychology has accepted as its institutionalized paradigm the Lockean model. Even the historical debate between structuralism and functionalism in psychology was found to be a pseudo-confrontation insofar as the basic paradigm of these two schools is concerned. The naive empiricist attitude which Lockeanism has encouraged in psychology has led to a serious confounding of what is literally observed with how one accounts for what is observed. Rather than looking at the full panoply of human behavior in Table 1, psychology has cast its lot with the sociohistorical demands of the seventeenth century, accepting the solutions of this period concerning its science for all time. Indeed modern physical science has conceptually passed psychology by.

In opposition to this outmoded view of science and the image of humanity it prompts, we next called for a revolution in *theory* but not in *method*. A psychology of rigorous humanism was held possible if we retained the classical and unchanging logic of validation in science but altered the form of the hypothesis put to test by this method. Taking essentially a "middle road," we spurned both efforts to change the control-and-prediction methods of science and the almost more pernicious, because insidious, efforts to account for telic behavior in nontelic theoretical formulations. A sensible revolution was called for, in which we would strive to keep our theoretical terminology clear and distinct from our methodological terminology. Several examples of this terminological confusion are given, and an effort was made to get clearly in mind what we mean by determinism and freedom in human behavior. In this discussion we suggested that the evidence now accruing in rigorous experimentation does *not* validate an exclusively efficient-cause interpretation of determinism. If the telic hypothesis is put to the data on conditioning now issuing, there is no doubt but that the latter confirm the former!

We next moved into a teleological interpretation of human behavior, in which it was necessary to introduce some new terminology, the most important of which was probably the *telosponse*. It seems absolutely essential to find a term that contradicts the simplistic meaning of *response* without denying the fact that behavior takes place. Telosponsive behavior takes place, but it works at the initiating point of a course of events, moving precedently and sequaciously across the passage of time without itself being a function of time. Using this basic concept, we then could subsume all of the behaviors represented in Table 1, as well as the core argument in the Kuhnian conception of a scientific revolution. Such revolutions occur conceptually, brought on initially when some phenomenon cannot be understood as a sequacious meaning-extension from the precedent paradigm (i.e., it "doesn't follow"), and hence a new precedent must be delineated more in consonance with the observed facts, which in turn are themselves created (made possible) by the new conceptualizations of the changed paradigm.

This process is merely one example of the general fact that human beings order their understanding of experience in terms of something else. They must have and constantly seek the grounding frame for the sake of which their behavior takes place or can be rationally understood, altered, reinterpreted, and so on. In the same way that scientists may disagree over what they empirically see taking place in their most rigorous experimental framework, so too do humans constantly diverge and take contrasting positions on the "right" way of viewing things, behaving, handling their interpersonal relations, and so on. The most difficult aspect of human relations must surely be finding a common ground on which to proceed. Morale suffers among group members to the extent that a family, professional society, or a nation lacks such predications in common.

As an initial statement of a humanistic psychology to accomodate this view of the person we then moved into a description of logical learning theory (LLT). It is sufficiently abstract to subsume both the mechanistic and the telic formulations of behavior *as proffered by* the scientists who propound them. It has no quarrel with mechanistic formulations of inanimate nature, but does suggest that there are many hidden telic behaviors going on within the experimental designs of classical laboratory psychology. We can understand both historically and practically why a behavioristic psychology uses cybernetic and related machine *metaphors* (in LLT terms, variants of the tautology) to explain behavior. They proceed on the misguided precedent assumption that this is what they *must* do to be scientific, and they find a common language syntax with many of their colleagues in the physical sciences.

The irony in this is that someone like Kuhn (1970)—a historian of science—is needed to paint an image of the scientist that is *more human* (because telic) than the image being propounded in the science of psychology. Compounding the irony, behaviorists then accept his characterization of their behaviors "as scientists," without seeing the anomaly in the fact that their formal theory of behavior is unable to capture what Kuhn's analysis is all about. Logical learning theory *is* capable of subsuming this analysis, as it is capable of taking the concepts across history reflected in Table 1 at their own level of significance and treat them with the dignity they deserve.

The book contents then move into a series of experiments, undertaken specifically in an area of study (verbal learning) which has been saturated with nontelic theoretical formulations. As a case in point of the type of revolution needed in psychology, the prediction is made that teleological formulations based on LLT can be brought to bear in research designs which have been initially framed to test nontelic theory and, even on such unfriendly ground, *proven* to hold. After more than 15 years of empirical study based on this predication, the advocates of LLT conclude that it has been confirmed. In recognition of our affirming-the-consequent of an If . . . then . . . proposition fallacy, we should perhaps conclude that a null hypothesis of "no unique RV effects" in the data gathered can be rejected at a satisfactory level of statistical significance.

The human image which validly emerges in research on affective assessment is that of a telosponsive organism, capable of both arbitrariness and rigid determinism in its behavior, furthering meanings for the sake of which it behaves in both preferred and nonpreferred directions. Life experience is ordered by an identity known as the person or self, actively conceptualizing from the protopoint. Much of what is predictable in this organism's behavior stems from the fact that these introspective orderings into meaning are either known or can be guessed at by an extraspective observer who, for the sake of this insight, forecasts its direction. The individual's telic determination is graphed or tracked by the mathematical (formal-cause) determinism of statistical prediction. But by not letting such methodological tracking serve as our theory of explanation, we can appreciate the *self*-determined nature of behavior which makes such regularities possible. Furthermore we see in the error variance a "something" and not a "lack of something." Error is not *only* chance fluctuation from a substrate hence predictable reality. Error has as much subject-contributed determination as does the performance tracked and then predicted (see Rychlak, 1976b, for a discussion of tracking versus identity in human behavior).

If the lessons of history have been taken correctly and if our recommended solutions are reasonably sound, we can call this approach to psychology "revolutionary." What has been our experience with this self-styled revolution?


## The Convolutions of Our Revolution

No one can step up and proclaim a revolution in the conceptual realm of science. As presented by Kuhn, a scientific revolution should evolve or be forced upon a school of thought gradually as the inconsistencies within a paradigm become apparent. But what happens when a body of scientists does not acknowledge such inconsistencies (as seen by other scientists?) or acknowledging them, takes as a professional aspiration to live within them? This is what seems to be happening in psychology. To say "Look, your conception of humanity is at variance with the human image as known since the beginnings of thought" is hardly to suggest an anomaly to the psychologist who prides himself on being tough-minded. He replies: "Well, so what? That is what science is *supposed* to do—strip man of his fancied achievements and present human behavior in its true fashion, unadorned by anthropomorphic claptrap." Psychologists are not all this outspoken concerning their commitment to nontelic description. Most have not thought about it, which means, however, that practically speaking they continue to support a tradition of nontelic human description.

If one gauged a revolution by its overt impact on the profession, surely to this point in time LLT or telic psychology of any other variety would be adjudged completely *non*revolutionary. As we discussed in Chapter 5, the institutionalized mechanistic outlook has been able to give its Lockeanism the "sound" of intentionality in so-called cognitive psychology. Because of this adaptation, the current *Zeitgeist* seems to view such cognitive formulations as revolutionary, and no amount of shouting from this rather dark and lonely corner of the profession is going to change things. We do not flatter ourselves into believing that LLT is revolutionary in anything but a conceptual sense. Telic psychology is a hoped-for revolution yet to be activated and extended to the field as a whole.

There are those who, hearing a psychologist speak this way—as if the ideas (theory) must first be *accepted* and *then* evidence in support of the view might be possible—believe that the cart is being put before the horse. They say: "Let the evidence speak for itself"; or "rather than fixing our minds first let's look at the results of experimentation;" or "this calls for a new experiment to be done, not a new theory." We have tried to demonstrate why this naively empirical approach to science is *invalid*. We cannot find something unless we are willing to predicate its possible occurrence before we begin our empirical search. The writer began RV research in 1959, believing that should an experiment be designed "tightly" and evidence garnered rigorously, a professional peer would entertain the theory put to test without preconceived bias. And even if such bias existed, surely as more and more data were added to the evidential support of a theory, the referees of our profession who sit on journal or granting boards would take the necessary time to understand what a peer was driving at, would examine the entire approach and line of empirical data, and so forth.

How naive this view is! How right Kuhn is in his analysis! What one *actually* learns is that a scientist trained in one school of thought finds it professionally impossible to look at things another way. One would hope that psychological science could emulate the profession of law on this matter. Although there are surely rigid or convinced lawyers who cannot entertain a position in opposition to their own, the ideal of the legal profession is to be capable of viewing the fact pattern of a case in terms of several grounding lines of precedence. The effective courtroom lawyer is surely that person who can argue the case from both his and an opponent's theoretical legal precedent. Indeed, should he know the opponent's case better than the opponent, there is every expectation that the outcome will favor the more comprehensive outlook he embraces. This does not mean he is "right" for all time of course. The opponent may be defending the more viable legal alternative. Once the case is closed, the opponent may even be taught the lines of argument open to him on which he had failed to capitalize.

We may be criticized here for using an adversary-procedure analogue to relate to science, but in the spirit of our views on revolutionary innovation it does not seem inappropriate. Unfortunately, the courtroom for the professional psychologist is that thin but hard line of professional-journal and granting-agency referees who must necessarily set themselves up as guardians of the scientific trust. And when they—for any of a number of reasons—are unable to prepare themselves in an alternative line of thought, the situation becomes dispiriting for anyone who speaks from a different frame of reference. It is tempting to review for the reader a series of—occasionally humorous—circumstances faced by the writer over the years in publishing LLT phraseology or trying to get funding to pursue its implications. Much of the responsibility lies with the theoretical outlook and terms selected *per se*. Surely the language is unfamiliar to most psychologists, including those who would like to see a change in how behavior is to be accounted for. In fact, we eventually despaired of getting our preferred theoretical phrasing into research publications and—by sticking primarily to methodological lingo—relegated LLT to footnote references in which the reader was encouraged to send for the "broader theory" which was "too involved" to present "in the interest of space," and the like. This made the journal referee's life a little easier and increased the

chances that our researches would see the light of day in the literature—although, in truth, even this maneuver did not help in many
instances.

Doubtless the use of the term *reinforcement* in operationalizing
affective assessment was partially at fault for the difficulty in understanding the drift of LLT researches. Though we still believe that it
is acceptable as a methodological construct, the mythology in psychology is that one theoretical outlook really understands how
another outlook employs this term. Hence, to speak of reinforcement "values" and *not* mean some level of food reward, shock, or
empirically tracked fluctuations in performance—even though all
of these are methodological (tracking, design) factors—is to tamper
with a hallowed theoretical (*sic*) construct. We have no one to blame
for this aspect of the innovation difficulties but ourselves.

However, an unexpected source of confusion and disagreement
stemmed from the use of verbal-learning experimental designs and
paraphernalia. Though we entered this area believing that it was an
acceptable (if complex) branch of psychological science, we were
shocked to learn that so many—even tough-minded—psychologists
were prepared to dismiss evidence issuing from a paired-associates
study. Memory drums are horse-and-buggy devices in this age of
computers. No amount of talk about proving man to be human can
assuage the shudder of horror sent up the spine of some psychologists when they hear those words *verbal learning*. One is pictured
more the Don Quixote than the Sir Galahad, riding into the arid land
of irrelevance. To force these psychologists to think beyond the
apparatus selected is literally impossible. There can be *no worthwhile evidence* issuing from such experimental designs *ever!*

As if this were not trouble enough, the psychologists who typically
embrace verbal-learning data found it impossible to accept RV as anything short of all those things we tried to prove (see Chapter 9) it was
*not*—that is, frequency related, experimental artifact, redundant
measure of "something else," and so on. Even when we presented evidence to the opposite and referred the journal referee to our earlier
work, we found that such "verbal learning psychologists" or "experimental psychologists" (note that RV publications appear only in personality and clinically related journals) simply dismissed all that had
gone before and raised old questions again and again. One particularly
obstinate editor never *did* get past the "How can you be sure this
isn't a frequency factor?" stage. We have no doubt that if we referred
him to Chapter 9 of this volume he would still consider the picture
dark enough on this question to turn back an RV-study. Another

editor, with a sense of humor, actually admitted that some of the problem with letting the LLT viewpoint stand "as is" in a write-up stemmed from the "negative RV" his journal referees' had for the constructs involved. We both had a good laugh over that irony. There is nothing *personal* in such editorial decisions; these editors and their staffs were doing the best job possible under the circumstances and given their paradigmatic assumptions.

Of course occasionally the machinations of an editorial policy have proven personally frustrating. For example, an editor of one of the leading experimental journals once rejected an RV study, basing his grounds in part on the fact that we had supposedly confounded so-called stimulus- and response-meaningfulness in the paired-associates tandem. Foolishly believing that this was stated sincerely, as if it made a difference in theory, we then spent one year conducting a series of experiments to show that RV seems to work more at the stimulus *(sic)* half of the S-R pairing than it does at the response *(sic)* half—at least it does when both members of a pair are *pronounced* by the subject (this aspect of RV research was not discussed in Chapters 9 and 10). When drafted and resubmitted over a year later to this same journal the rejection came back placing great emphasis on the fact that this research was dated, that it was anachronistic, that it was irrelevant and not in tune with what was then a "hot issue" in the literature, and so forth. As the rejected suitor, who is told anything just to be gotten rid of, we finally caught the drift that no amount of data would ever legitimize the RV construct for the members of this editorial board. To believe in a Popperian principle of falsification while living through such circumstances is *really* to take on a quixotic world outlook.

There is no single study in psychology that—totally by itself—is worth singling out as an unassailable collection of facts establishing some theoretical position *all at once.* We can fault the design, results, or interpretation of *any* research report. This fact is magnified for the more innovative research line because the referee is naturally brought up short as the theoretical language and conceptualization begins to shift from the familiar to the strange. In the case of RV research, we heard many times of the supposed research design not *necessarily* testing the theory lying behind it. This is actually a principle of LLT, in recognition of the affirming-the-consequent of an If . . . then . . . proposition fallacy. But to the critic this seems to be grounds for dismissing the evidence actually accrued out of hand. If the evidence *could be* accounted for another way it *must be* so accountable; hence the theory as espoused (being unusual) is unreliable if not flatly invalid! At the very least, this would dictate that the "going paradigm" should not be tampered with, because there is strength in numbers and why not stay with the predominant position? This is the way in which many of our critics seemed to have reasoned. It is especially easy to think this way when the findings of any one study on RV are not immense, in the sense of a mean difference between experimental conditions, or the p-level cited is not extreme.

The sheer power of a score value in the mean difference between groups can sometimes bear a hypnotic influence. Better to have a 10-score-points mean difference at the .05 level than a 2-score-points mean difference at the .01 level of statistical significance. But even this is not infallible, for there are tough-minded psychologists who make a virtue of the p-level per se. It is not unusual for a psychologist to consider .05 findings "weaker" than .01 findings, which in turn are considerably "weaker" than .001 findings. This reification of the logic of statistics is very pernicious, so if a critic has both the mean-difference and the p-level to consider, through a self-styled claim of "rigor" he can say "These are not very impressive findings," when in fact neither of these purely methodological instrumentalities are "the findings." Experimental findings always wait upon the theory that lends them meaning, and because we in science do accept the control-and-prediction standard (correspondence theory of truth), so long as these mean differences array as predicted and attain the acceptable level of significance, their merit lies not in such arbitrary instrumentalities but in the theory to which they point and from which they take meaning. But if as is so often the case today, a theory-method confound obtains in the critic's awareness, leading to a Lockean world view on all things, important theoretical implications can easily be rejected by adding his own type of rigor (sic) to the observed facts.

This unimaginative approach is impossible to sustain when we enter the more subtle areas of research, as outlined in Chapter 10. We must of necessity look for cross-validation of small but significant differences, which may not look like much standing alone but which gain in merit—and statistical significance—due to the consistency reflected over a series of developing researches. We easily forget that a p-level is not a probability statement of the likelihood that findings will cross-validate in the real world of data collection. Experience with a series of studies on some topic soon teaches the researcher that .001 level findings often fail to cross-validate at this or any conventional level of significance, whereas a .05 finding which stands up at even the .10 level (or vice versa) across different samplings has much more to say for the theory under test in the long run.

All of this brings us back to the fact that a revolutionary or innovative line of thought demands assessment at a broader level than simply "study-by-study" examination without regard for the full line of investigation and the subtlety of the research design in question (though such individual examination has its place of course). Hence any one reviewer of a single LLT research effort would understandably have difficulty grasping precisely what is involved and under test. Now that we have put the full body of work forward with a theoretical discussion preceding it, we hope the convoluted ups and downs of our—if not a revolution or an innovation—then at least alternative view of the human person will be smoothed into a more direct ascent in the psychological literature of the future.

## Reactions and Questions

Over the years a number of objections have been raised and observations rendered concerning the shortcomings of LLT. In this section we review 10 of the more commonly heard reactions and objections. The format followed is to state a reaction or objection and then to answer it.

1. *This view is based on a circularity, because it contends that learning is possible only after it has already taken place.*

This objection rests on the assumption that learning occurs in the process of acquisition as graphed in a curve of learning. Logical learning theory contends that the process being graphed reflects the conceptualization which is brought forward as a fixed given over (and within) time. The experimenter defines what (the criterion of) learning is, but since much of the subject's performance within the so-called error variance of the graphing procedure is premised behavior, it is held by LLT to be just as much a part of the learning process as is the line eventually traced. One of the first things the subject must learn (premise) is the ground rules the experimenter expects him to follow and then to comply with these or not. The graphing of such learning is "after the (conceptual) fact," but this does not make the explanation of learning circular. The measurement process must be decided on beforehand in line with experimental predictions, but in the scientific method data are necessarily recorded in *post hoc* relationship to what has occurred in learning, after sampling has been completed according to plan, subjects have attained their arbitrary criterion levels, and so forth.

2. *Why would learning ever take place, if people have fixed premises that endow their experience with meaning? Would not all people be rigid and inflexible?*

Research evidence over the developmental years or through the course of psychotherapy is hardly indicative of a great changeability in the behavior of human beings. Logical learning theory contends that insofar as people *are* unchangeable this rigidity is due to the telic determinism made possible through fixed premises, premises that have endowed life with meaning and therefore are very difficult to dismiss without some dramatic quantum leap taking place in experience. Whether a person changes or not, the contention of LLT is that we can determine the reasons for such eventualities only through a proper understanding of the premises being affirmed at the period of life under consideration. Psychologists who deny the role of premises in behavior have serious theoretical and methodological problems to confront, because the unequivocal drift of findings on human behavior demonstrates that awareness is a central feature of this process, that even erroneous predications are brought to bear in experimental efforts with success, and hence to continue pretending that telosponsivity is not a proven fact seriously distorts what we have already proven many times over.

Those individuals who change more have probably *already* affirmed premises which sequaciously imply that adaptation, innovation, and creative alternatives are natural in life. This kind of individual moves through life ready to use an analogue, draw a parallel, make the dialectical reversal of from affirming what is certainly true to affirming what is not true but might be possible, and so on. Factors such as talent, the cooperation of others, and even so-called luck enter into the equation as well. But our Kierkegaardian conception of change keeps LLT anchored in the protopoint "given," because we hold that behavior is predicated and not merely mediated. We also insist on looking at the predications of the theorist who claims that changes are or are not taking place in the lives of people. What does this theorist precedently take to be a change? Surely his framing predications sequaciously determine what he will then count a change in the behavior of others. Whether we consider subjects or experimenters who make claims for the subjects,

LLT pushes the issue back to the precedent meanings being sequaciously conveyed by the identity (self) taking a position on what occurs in human behavior.

3. *Is it good to base a psychology on innate factors such as affective assessment? Isn't this a concession to material-cause determinism? How can a free-will conception be based on physical determinism?*

One should not confuse the structural ordering of physique, including all aspects of genetic patterning, with the ordering and patterning of mentality. As a *logical* theory of behavior, LLT is contending that human intelligence lends pattern and order to events based on an inherited capacity to behave in this way. The logic (*logos* = order) made possible by the innate physical structure is no more determined solely by this palpable structure than is the patterning of human behavior determined solely by the fact that all people have the same general physical structure. There are vast differences in the way people walk, talk, in what they do, how they play out their lives, and so on, both intra- and interculturally. Saying that people innately affectively assess the experiential contents they bring into premises concerning the meaning of life is not to say that the resultant orders (meanings) are *themselves* innately determined. The determination here is not primarily material-formal but formal-final, albeit granted that the reason a body which can make judgments (orderings) of this sort exists is due to the material-cause determination of biological heredity.

4. *Where do affective assessments come from?*

This is the most frequent question raised by colleagues. What it *really* asks is "Can you explain affective assessment in efficient-cause terms?" or "Could you tell us the efficient cause of the judgments made in affection?" To answer No to this reformulated question is a simple matter, believing as we do that a final-cause construct is a legitimate explanation unto itself. But when one frames the issue in these terms, he seems to be saying to the critic: "No, I don't know where these assessments come from; they are a mystery." Rather than take the more frank and sophisticated route and cast the issue in theory-construction terms, we have learned from experience the best way to deal with this question is by answering in the following vein: We are born with the innate capacity to affectively assess, as we are born with the capacity to remember what we input from experience. Experience influences the *grounds* for making affective assessments. In this sense we can say that affective assessments come from "past experience." The only point LLT wants acknowledged in this phrase is that from the very out-set of lived experience as conceptualized in memory the individual (self) is structuring or ordering what will be perceived initially, retained conceptually, and recovered as grounds for the sake of which current behavior is telosponded. An identity factor (self) transcending simply input-output takes a position vis-à-vis the strictly mechanical processes of the body and adds to the structuring and ordering (meaning) of *all* experience, past and present.

5. *Isn't the dialectic unamenable to physiological and biological investigation? Physical theory is virtually 100% demonstrative in tone.*

Although biological explanation has traditionally followed natural-science description in the demonstrative material- and effi-cient-cause sense, there are some interesting developments taking place in brain research that offer hope for a change. Surely there is nothing in the split-brain research findings to discourage an inter-pretation of behavior in terms of dialectic (Gazzaniga, 1967; Sperry, 1964). Finding that the two halves of the brain can get somewhat different slants on the nature of perceived reality, leading at times to disagreements or conflicts over how to accomplish either a lan-guage expression (left hemisphere) or artistic performance (right hemisphere), hardly strikes a death blow to dialectical formulations. Quite the reverse! We view Ornstein's (1972) highly original—if occasionally strained—efforts to draw parallels between brain re-searches and dialectical world views like Zen Buddhism as unwitting indications that dialectic plays a role in human behavior at the biological level.

Spinelli and Pribram (1967) electronically recorded cells in the frontal cortex of the brain while simultaneously stimulating the retina with input and found that the patterning of the receptor field on the retina was altered by the cells of the brain. Thus retinal recep-tion can be altered from moment to moment based on a selective and directive brain process. Is it plausible to believe that this direc-tive capacity is *learned*? Or is it more reasonable to presume that this capacity is part of the innate machinery brought to bear in life as experience unfolds? We think the latter theory is at least as sen-sible as the former. All we need do is consider the possibility that this reordering of retinal stimulation follows oppositionality—as the findings on dream distortion suggest, where perceived things and people often run to their opposites in appearance and behavior—and we have the beginnings of a dialectical biological theory. Some of our leading brain authorities have taken theoretical stances that are less Lockean than the leading behavioristic psychologists discussed in Chapters 4, 5, and 7. Thus Karl H. Pribram (1971) has acknowledged the neo-Kantianism of his "biologist view" in which mental activity is said to be "constructional" (p. 34).

But the most striking evidential support for dialectical formulations is found in the interpretation of mind advanced by the eminent neurosurgeon and brain authority, Wilder Penfield (1975), who did his work at McGill University, Montreal, Canada. Though he does not use the language of dialectic, Penfield's experience with brain stimulation of epileptic patients who were conscious during implantation of an electrode in their exposed brain presents us with several images for a beginning dialectical biological theory. There is the image of the patient, lying on the operating table in a state of astonishment because he was *both* laughing with his cousins on a farm in South Africa and being operated on in Montreal at the same time (*ibid.*, p. 55). There is the image of the patient who, when made to vocalize by electrical stimulation reported: "I didn't make that sound. . . . You [Penfield] pulled it out of me" (*ibid.*, p. 76). And there is the image of the patient who under stimulation to move an arm, reached over with his free arm and held the moving limb in place against the dictates of the electrical charge (*ibid.*, p. 77). To imagine any more concrete empirical evidence permitting a *rejection* of the law of contradiction in human behavior would be difficult. Here we have human beings (psychically) in two places at once, rejecting responsibility for what they are now saying, and opposing through counteraction what they are now doing!

Though we cannot now presume to do so, for an investigator to begin using a dialectical rationale to describe the nature of neuronal activity in the brain would obviously be easy. Penfield continues to speak in a quasi-biological vein, referring to the "two essences" (*ibid.*, p. 62) of mind and body. Though his willingness to accept dualism is more encouraging to a humanistic than a mechanistic psychology (see Penfield's comments on mechanism's inability to account for mind, *ibid.*, p. 46), there may be other ways of describing mind short of entitizing it as a presumed second realm of energy expenditure. Thus if meanings (energy organizations, in physical terms) are indeed dialectical, we can find a duality in the one realm of (energic) existence without postulating a separate and distinct realm (many-in-one thesis). Penfield has the brain a computer, and the mind is said to be the programmer of this purely instrumental mechanism (ibid., p. 85). This metaphor of the programmer makes it appear that meanings from one realm (mind) are brought into another realm (brain) which is separate and distinct on the question of meaningful (energy) organizations from the first. The dialectic as metaconstruct permits us to suggest that a single identity, defined oppositionally in relation to input experience ("me" versus "not me" or "that, which is input") affirms a course of meaning-extension with awareness that things could be otherwise (exactly as witnessed in Penfield's clients). This is not unlike Fichte's development of self-definition (see Table 1), except that we do not base the dialectical self-definition on an idealism. The dualism resulting rather than involving two realms of energy source would be due to the separate organizations of that which is physically input and that which is logically predicated. The former (brain tissue) would not directly and simply account for the latter (mind).

What is needed now is a theoretician working in the biological-physiological realm to begin with the possibility that some cells in the brain—or some forms of cellular organization in the brain—permit not simply the unidirectional passing of messages through an input-output series (with memory storage intervening), but an actual self-reflexivity in the potential to know that knowing is occurring *from the very first* brain action. As with Penfield's patients, if such neural tissue permits the person-identity to take a stand on its input, rather than simply to respond to it, we have the biological justification for believing in the telosponsivity of behavior. Self-reflexivity would replace feedback as a theoretical term in this view. As Penfield was to learn over a distinguished career of some 40 years, there is always a transcending identity to acknowledge, independent of the physical processes of the computer-brain, with the capacity to judge and decide on the validity and import of the electrical input as it was taking place. Brain stimulation could not bring his patients to such decisions and beliefs (ibid., p. 77). This capacity of an identity, which was not itself input, to comment on the passing physical scene, to view the humor or irony in a situation, and to retain an integrity distinct from the brain's mechanisms, led Penfield to conclude: "A man's mind . . . is the person" (ibid., p. 61).

Our answer to the question posed is that dialectic is not unamenable to physiological-biological research, though the theory it generates will depart from the traditional reductive material-efficient cause descriptions of the classical medical model. We can only hope that the future will see a humanistically oriented neurophysiologist take a dialectical conception seriously enough to use it heuristically in his research efforts (see Rychlak, 1976a, for various uses of the dialectic in psychology, especially pp. 135–139 for the reasons usually given in its rejection).

6. *How do other sciences view the prospects of a teleological description of behavior? Don't we run the risk of being ostracized from the scientific community if we reintroduce final causes?*

We have at various points throughout this volume presented evidence from other sciences which suggests that our fellow scientists might be more ready to accept teleology than we now appreciate. The final answer probably comes down to who shall decide what the definition of science is. We have noted how Bacon's restrictions in natural-science description were extended from inanimate to animate nature. Yet Bacon also said that final causation *was* relevant to theoretical description in metaphysics, the arts, ethics, and so on. But this is precisely the responsibility of a psychology of human behavior, to account for an animal in nature which reflects interests in artistic creations, morality, and the play of ideas in thought.

If a natural scientist dismisses psychology as nonscientific because it deals with telic behaviors and then additionally dismisses teleology, he is surely open to challenge. He had better have a defensible position on the nature of *nontelic* behavior in human beings. Stating this position, a humanistic psychologist can then challenge his arguments, citing empirical evidence to the opposite whenever possible. In other words, no matter what this critic may regard as science or nonscience, he cannot circumvent the responsibility of all scholars to make his thinking clear and to confront arguments and evidence to the opposite. In the final analysis definitions of science are mere conventions. A scientist who lets convention rather than argument and evidence dictate his professional activity is hardly someone to emulate or to be concerned about.

A generation ago Robert Oppenheimer (1956) spoke directly to psychologists at an American Psychological Association convention. One can only surmise what his attitude toward our theories of behavior was at the time, but he selected as his theme the use of analogy in science (in LLT we view the analogy as a partial tautology). His essential argument was that psychology continued to analogize its science on a Newtonian (Lockean) mechanism, when in fact at least physics had moved beyond this paradigm. Oppenheimer's concern about the human image was made clear when he said: "I think that, especially when we compare subjects in which ideas of coding, of the transfer of information, or ideas of purpose, are inherent and natural, with subjects in which these are not inherent and natural, that formal analogies have to be taken with very great caution" (p. 134). He was not speaking of mediation theory. His trailing comments clearly indicate that he would have welcomed a psychology more open to the conceptualizing ability of the human being. The changes called for in this volume meet Oppenheimer's criticisms and suggestions directly. They also mesh perfectly with the explanation of scientific behavior proffered by Kuhn (1970). We therefore cannot see how ostracism is sure to follow if psychology takes the lead in describing behavior humanistically—or, that most horrid of all terms, *anthropomorphically.* Why not anthropomorphize the anthrop-? Surely this tautological characterization is a logical first step to take if our interest is the description of human behavior.

7.   *By acknowledging the affirming-the-consequent of an If . . . then . . . proposition fallacy in science, you must now admit that the RV research conducted proves nothing with certainty for all time. Why then should we bother doing research at all?*

The reason we do research is not simply to counter the views of our theoretical opponents in the description of behavior. We always appreciate that though we have evidence for our theory, the "other side" could probably explain it away in some fashion (and this goes both ways of course). But validation is important within our own line of thinking. It is important because only through such evidence can we become assured that our ideas actually stand up when we are not there to twist and contort them into the flow of behavior as if they were relevant when they were not. But even more importantly, if we want others to begin looking at events as we do, we have a responsibility to transfer our ideas into methodological designs so that they can "get their hands wet" by plunging into the practical demonstration of that which we contend. Nothing is more convincing to our potential supporters than seeing that what we predict will happen actually comes about.

In LLT we say that a scientist is someone who moves to validate his or her theoretical contentions "some of the time," leaving open how often this is done (sometimes 100% and sometimes only 5% of the time, "depending"). Obviously someone else—a student or colleague—could also accomplish this empirical testing for the theoretical scientist concerned. But if such tests are never made and if the results of such tests do not influence the theoretical generation under development, we would contend that this person is *not* scientific though he or she may be of immense importance in other realms of knowledge. Harking back to point 6, the types of *evidence* (and not the theories) used stamp a body of knowledge as either scientific or nonscientific.

8. *Humanistic psychology alienates comparative psychology.*

If this is true, and we do not believe it to be so, the blame should be laid at the feet of those natural scientists who insist on keeping all behavioral description uniformly efficiently causal. This reductive requirement was taken as a predication because it seemed to promote a parsimonious line of theoretical description in psychology. We suggest an alternative principle of parsimony below. But more fundamentally, we wonder if a telic account at the human level downgrades the importance of comparative psychological study. If one looks into the literature of comparative ethology, for example, one can see that there is just as great a range of attitude concerning the acceptability of telic description in this speciality as there is in psychology (see Lorenz', 1970, critical analysis: pp. 351–370). If there are no telic comparative psychologists today and there are telic ethologists, this is surely an historical curiosity. But to say that a telic human psychology must *necessarily* alienate theories of lower animal behavior is most surely incorrect. The humanist can only wonder why psychology has *no* telic formulation at the subhuman level (if this is indeed the case). Rather than alienate, the humanist would be delighted to encourage such formulations, if they ever arise.

9. *You employ an ad hominem argument when you insist on looking at the theorist's predications, the assumptions made by his school of thought, and so forth. Scientists cannot be concerned with such "personal" factors. They must deal in hard evidence alone.*

An *ad hominem* argument is one in which a position is rejected because of extraneous and irrelevant factors concerning the opponent "as a person." For example, if moved by religious considerations to argue for free will, the free-will argument fails because of this biasing motivation. A critic who believes that we employ *ad hominems* in LLT would presumably hold that in challenging the material-efficient cause predications of natural scientists as we do, we are discrediting what they have accrued as hard data simply because they refuse to see but *two* causal meanings in the play of these data. It is being claimed by the critics of LLT that so long as

evidence is accrued for what these theories suggest, we have to deal
with the empirical data as recorded and not dispel them by arguments from the precedent assumptions made before data were
sought.

If all LLT did in challenging traditional natural-science description was to dismiss its evidence based on the narrow range of causation predicated in such study, this criticism would have merit. But
if, as we have done in this book, the evidence proffered by natural-
science psychologists can be shown to subvert telic proofs (see our
discussion in Chapter 4, pp. 172–174) and if a body of alternative
data are presented to challenge such nontelic accounts of behavior
(see Chapters 9 and 10), to contend that we are waging an *ad
hominem* argument is entirely erroneous. The scientist who holds
that the data speak for themselves has probably already lost the
case for humanism, because as we have seen, the scientific method
*per se* is a poor analogue for the "discovery" of anything but efficient-
cause regularities (the S-R bind).

In another sense, however, we must admit that humanistic psychologists cannot entirely avoid an interest in the *ad hominem* tactic.
Bias, sophistry, and related human characteristics of this variety are
surely not to be defined out of existence in humanistic psychology.
We do not want to employ such arguments in our psychological
experimentation, but neither do we want to pretend that they do
not take place or that scientists in their personal outlooks are free
of such irrelevancies. Humanistic psychology will always take a
deep interest in the "hominem."

10.   *Logical learning theory is unable to predict the direction an
intention will take. Simply calling one intention understanding and
a second action does not salvage the inability of LLT to predict behavior. How can we have a science that admits its inability to predict
from the outset?*

The last question we consider is probably taken by the critics of
teleology as the *coup de grace* for this approach to behavioral study.
It is based on a definition of science which stresses prediction above
knowledge. We have tried to show that scientists often can predict
something which they fail to understand (see Frank, 1957, Chapter
2, for the best discussion of this point in the literature). If prediction
is an aspect of evidential demonstration—for example, in the control and prediction of validation—there is no need for any science
to presume from the outset that it will someday predict everything!
A science which takes as a premise that everything is predictable has

already precluded the possibility that some things may *not* be predictable or that there are different forms of prediction possible (some call these "levels" of prediction, but we dislike the implied rank ordering in speaking of levels and prefer the "forms" usage). Such a science would not be objective, for it would be blind to certain alternatives the data might suggest.

In psychology those who believe that their mission is to "predict all behavior, all of the time" do so because they elevate their methodological skills above their responsibilities as theoreticians. They have turned psychologists into actuarians and have succeeded in propounding the mythology that actuarial prediction suffices for scientific evidence, when it clearly *does not!* As discussed in Chapter 6, one can study the identity within the actuarial rule and find thereby that the reason the rule "works" is because of the premises this identity (self) brings forward, given the logic of the situation being faced (final-cause determinism).

We do not deny that our willingness to assign responsibility to the individual means that at some point in the course of behavioral description we may say that the behavior is up to the person, and although we can give the odds that he will choose this way or that, what he actually "does" is *in principle* not determined by our actuarial rule but by *his* decision. There is no other way for a free-will psychology to operate. Either one accepts a final-cause construct as the legitimate cause of behavior in at least some situations, or he does not. If the person can pattern his brain processes, conceptualizing that which he then "behaves for the sake of" and the only way in which we can predict his behavior is to know what other people do in his situation or to know the likely advantages to be gained through this or that option, we must hold open the possibility that any one person may order the meanings (energic brain processes) *against the observed odds.* Put in other terms, he may frame the situation in which we have empirically garnered the base rates as a "different" situation, thereby invalidating our base rates. If we knew his framing, we could of course then approximate a prediction of his behavior; but we cannot know his framing beforehand so long as he is a dialectical reasoner and can indeed order (Penfield's "program") his precedent premises.

Practically speaking, the loss in prediction here is more than offset by the benefit received in knowing what "most people" will premise in this or that situation (we feel that psychometric tests capitalize on this factor as well). The unusual orderings (premises) are swallowed up in the error variance. As a rigorous humanistic

psychology, LLT does not have to admit an *inability* to predict behavior. It expects to predict about as much behavior as the mechanistic psychology. But some of the predictions made by the humanistic
psychologist in the experimental context will be of the variety: We
predict that the person will base his course of behavior—whether
this way or that way—on an idea (predication) about what should
be done in this experiment, even when what he then does is incorrect. Mechanists think that prediction always means something like:
We predict that the subject is likely to do this and *not* likely to do
that. If one is trying to approximate the role of actuarian, the latter
type of prediction is considered essential because a practical outcome is expected (who buys the soap, how many accidents eventuate, which students actually graduate, etc.). But in a *science of the
person* predictions can be of the former variety as well. Since it is
*not* theoretical activity *per se,* the scientific method cannot tell us
which of these two types of prediction should be put to test. Logical
learning theory is interested in the "nonactuarial" prediction at least
as much as it is interested in the actuarial variety.

## Tenets of a Psychology of Rigorous Humanism

It is important to appreciate that LLT is only one of several humanistic psychologies possible. We feel that as a first effort in the
direction of humanizing the person, this learning theory deserves
consideration by psychologists. But even if its constructs prove
unworthy of further development, there are certain tenets upon
which most (maybe all) humanistic psychologists who wish to be
part of the scientific endeavor can probably agree. In this closing
section of the volume we crystallize 10 position points on rigorous
humanism and thereby reaffirm our commitment to this much needed
expansion of psychological science.

   1.  *The precise nature of theory is different from the nature of
method, and to attain the former from the latter is impossible in
principle.*
   Unless we take as precedently true that theory and method are
two somewhat different enterprises, the efficient-cause frame of
scientific method will continue to be entitized into our theoretical
descriptions of behavior. Once this distinction is accepted, the
responsibility of the psychological scientist broadens. Not only must
he garner scientific evidence, but he must also continually refine his

thinking and examine his assumptions concerning any "empirical account" he proffers concerning such data.

2. *Extraspectively framed methods are compatible with theories that are framed introspectively.*

The attitude of "I can only say in my scientific account what I have observed in my method" has led to a tautological rephrase of the experimental design in the discussion to follow. Though admirable as a starting point, "sticking to the facts" can mean that one refuses to get over into the perspective of the facts to see what may be going on there. Although improper for some aspects of scientific description, one can frame introspective theoretical formulations to describe the human being. It is perfectly logical to frame first-person accounts of behavior as we observe this behavior from a third-person perspective aimed at removing our influence in what transpires. We can look at "that behavior, over there" for evidential reasons but explain the predicted course of events as "my" behavior in a theoretical sense (i.e., what *I* would do in *that* circumstance).

3. *It is profitable to view two or more identities—the experimenter's and the subject's—in every experiment on human beings.*

If we conceptualize a subject in an experiment as a noncontributing agent in the course of events, obviously a humanistic account of his behavior will be difficult if not impossible to attain. Experimental evidence now establishes beyond doubt that this passive view of the subject is fallacious. We must accept the fact that in *every* experiment on humans there is an identity, bringing forward what we have called subject-contributed variables to the course of events. Recognizing the identity of the experimenter is also important, because in this way we remind ourselves that experimenters speak from certain points of view, that they have paradigmatic presumptions about what they can possibly see in their data, and the like. Research experimentation on human beings is therefore a *relationship* between two identical organisms, each of whom has a "say" in the outcome. This takes us into our next point.

4. *Considered on introspective theoretical grounds, the principle of parsimony dictates that any descriptive formulation applicable to the experimenter must be applicable to the subject and vice versa.*

Psychologists are wont to speak of the importance of a parsimonious explanation of behavior, never realizing that parsimony in the physical sciences relates exclusively to *extraspective* accounts.

Considered extraspectively, it makes good sense "parsimoniously"
to describe human behavior in identical terms to the behavior of
lower animals—which translates into material- and efficient-cause
concepts. But what of introspective theory? In this case we must
obviously relate the (human) experimenter to the (human) subject
and insist that the behavioral account of one person match up with
the behavioral account of the other. If we look at how all experimentalists speak about *their* (introspectively framed) scientific behavior,
what do we find?

The experimentalist thinks of himself as proceeding on the basis
of hypotheses which he draws analogically from models of this or
that type, and then he puts these hypotheses to test through a series
of rigorously prearranged steps which meet his evaluative standards,
submitting the resultant data to mathematical tests that rest on self-
evident assumptions (e.g., the central limit theorem), and the p-level
he employs is entirely arbitrary. The experimentalist is only too
willing to describe his behavior in this manner. Yet when he records
his description of the empirical facts under his observation, we hear
nothing about analogical assumptions, prearrangements, evaluations,
or arbitrary standards of judgment. The human organism "in the
apparatus" or "in the research design" comes out as the tail end of
an efficiently caused reinforcement history! Surely this is a most
*unparsimonious* manner in which to behave. Henceforth, humanists
will ask on the grounds of introspective theoretical parsimony that
psychologists describe both their and their subject's behavior in
identical fashion.

5.   *There are, in principle, N possible explanations for any observed factual pattern—experimental or otherwise.*

Though almost no theoretical physicist today is naive enough to
assume that an *experimentum crucis* is possible, much less desirable,
too many psychologists still harbor this eighteenth-century dream.
Method will never suffice for theory, and though we may put down
rules of thumb for theoretical descriptions such as our "new parsimony," no psychologist should delude himself into believing that
a method can be devised that will allow him to settle, once and for
all time, which theory is representative of *the* nature of anything!
More than one theory can and always will be true about the same
thing.

6.   *The word* control *in the phrase* control and prediction *refers
to both the logic of experimental design and the subsequent manipulations carried out in the experimental context.*

The concept of controlling behavior has been given too narrow a definition in discussions of method. It is presumed that only an efficient-cause control is meant, when in fact the *logic* of scientific discovery—that is, the aligning of premises, the seeking of measurements, the testing of predicted results, and the drawing of conclusions—is heavily weighted with the meanings of formal and final causality. Even if the scientist denies that he reasons teleologically (employing final causation in the meaning of his behavior), he surely cannot deny that he follows ordered steps of logic, and logic is *not* an efficiently caused succession of events. Hence at least *some* of the control in our control-and-prediction definition of validating evidence is *logical* control. This simply means we are never observing only efficient causes in our scientific procedures. We are observing what we have logically prearranged to see, and this is a succession of events that might easily be influenced by both our own and our subject's (precedent-to-sequacious) logic.

7. *To encourage broader conceptualizations by psychological theorists, it would be helpful to lengthen the line of development from theory to methodological test.*

Psychology suffers as much from a conscious effort to *avoid* conceptualizing data as it does from so-called loose conceptualization in wild theorizing. If there was a time when psychologists theorized wildly (and we doubt it), that time has surely long past. A conceptual research effort cannot be done successfully unless the psychologist and those who later review his work for publication outlet accept the fact that a *logical line of development* is possible from the background conceptualization to the empirical test generated. This line can be lengthened a bit, so long as our logical controls remain clear and rigorous. By trying to see theory in method—in the experimental design—psychology has guaranteed that conceptual innovation will never take place. It is not legitimate to dismiss a study on the grounds that it failed to test its entire paradigm "at once" or that only a logical derivative of the background paradigm was tested in the actual experiment. Since validation is patterned on efficient causality, all that one can "see directly" as a paradigm in this ordering of events is the precedent Lockean model. To claim that this paradigm is the only one possible in evidence generated by scientific method is to *forego* true objectivity!

8. *Confine the use of variable to methodological discussion and remove it entirely from theoretical discussion.*

We must flatly deny that psychologists study variables. They study that which their theoretical predilections suggest are relevant to their professional interests, and once they have moved to the job of proving that which they believe, their theoretical ideas are brought to evidential life as variables. To speak of our constructs as variables once we have left the methodological context serves no purpose and is actually very sloppy usage.

9. *In the realm of theory, readmit formal- and final-cause constructions as legitimate explanations in their own right.*

Humanistic psychology is simply impossible without teleological description of behavior. This requires that we return to a style of description that has been disowned and ridiculed in natural science for over three centuries. Scientists threw out telic description 350 years ago for good and proper reasons. It created problems it could not solve, and those it did solve were achieved repressively. But we are untrue to our mission as twentieth-century scientists if we must, like sheep, herded along by the weight of seventeenth-century history, continue to press a restriction on our theoretical descriptions which has been negating man's humanity in the face of rigorous evidence to the opposite. The dialectic as metaconstruct provides a useful rationale for the telic description of human behavior (Rychlak, 1976a).

10. *Distinguish between humanistic and humanitarian approaches in psychology.*

The growth of humanism in psychology would be encouraged if we could—once and for all time—dispel the view that one must be a humanitarian to propound a humanistic psycholgy. Because teleology has been associated in the history of thought with theology, moral philosophy, and ethics, an unfortunate development we see taking place in the present is to presume that a humanist *must* argue for the more uplifting quasi-religious side to man. Some psychologists who might honestly prefer to give a humanistic theory serious consideration in their work are dissuaded from doing so because of the "goody-goody" connotation of humanism. Humanism has been identified with encounter groups and social reforms of various types —often framed in an emotionalized manner by dewey-eyed advocates ready to press the *purity criticism* (Chapter 5, p. 193) on any characterization put forth by an observer of behavior.

It therefore appears to a listener when we speak of humanistic psychology that we are asking him to "view thy brother human being as worthy of respect and help" or some such. Desirable as this

might be for a general approach to human relations, such ethical pronouncements are unquestionably harmful to an objective assessment
of the data we must examine as scientists. They arise as short-cut
solutions to the problems discussed in the present volume. Not understanding that man's dehumanization is due to technical questions
in theory construction, this kind of humanistic (sic) advocate thinks
he can force his fellow psychologist into presenting mankind teleologically by going to telic pronouncements on how one "ought" to
view man as a higher being. This is a misguided effort. Much better
to follow the Jungian insight that human beings are no more elevated
than they are submerged.

As we propose to use the term, humanism in psychology is a
purely technical aspect of any theory under espousal. Humanists
employ teleology in their description of a person's behavior. Mechanists do not bring such final-cause conceptions into their explanations. Humanitarians, however, whether of a humanistic or a
mechanistic persuasion, are in the profession of psychology at least
in part to improve man's lot—either by raising his level of self-worth
in a conceptual sense (e.g., Rogers, 1961) or by raising his level of
material satisfaction in some managed fashion (e.g., Skinner, 1971).
This distinction between humanitarian and humanist has the advantage of removing those unfair ad hominems Skinner and other behaviorists have had to confront such as fascist or cruel or enemy of
man's dignity. One may disagree with the image of man underwriting operant conditioning in behavioral modification, but surely the
intent of such efforts is no less humanitarian than the sharing and
caring of an encounter-group interaction. In fact, behavior modification advocates often use the term humanistic to modify their approaches when they should more properly be using the term
humanitarian (see Chapter 6). But the point is that one can be a
humanist without having to bear the weight of sociopolitical or
psychotherapeutic advance on one's shoulders.

We do not ask the reader to accept any type of humanitarian
premise in order to do the work of a humanistic psychologist. We
welcome the iconoclast and the misanthrope, so long as these individuals are prepared to submit their notions to rigorous empirical
test. The aim is to be tough-minded without being close-minded. Let
no one badger, cajole, or intimidate us into basing our theories on
anything but what we personally take to be a suitable beginning
model for the human condition. The scientific methodological devices are "there" for those who are ready to put forward the effort
to prove what they theoretically believe in, and we hope that this

book aids the humanistic cause by framing a more satisfactory language of description to be used in this regard.


## Summary

Chapter 11 is a summary of the book's total argument. We offer an interpretation of what has probably been accomplished, respond to several questions raised concerning the shortcomings of LLT, and then reaffirm those tenets of rigorous humanistic psychology that have emerged in the preceding chapters.


## References

Frank, P. Philosophy of science. Englewood Cliffs, N.J.: Prentice-Hall, 1957.

Gazzaniga, S. The split brain in man. Scientific American, 1967, 216, 24–29.

Kuhn, T. S. The structure of scientific revolutions (2nd ed.). Chicago: The University of Chicago Press, 1970. (1st ed., 1962)

Lorenz, K. Studies in animal and human behavior (Vol. 1). Cambridge: Harvard University Press, 1970.

Oppenheimer, R. Analogy in science. American Psychologist, 1956, 11, 127–135.

Ornstein, R. E. The psychology of consciousness. San Francisco: Freeman, 1972.

Penfield, W. The mystery of the mind. Princeton, N.J.: Princeton University Press, 1975.

Pribram, K. H. Languages of the brain: Experimental paradoxes and principles in neuropsychology. Englewood Cliffs, N.J.: Prentice-Hall, 1971.

Rogers, C. R. On becoming a person. Boston: Houghton Mifflin Co., 1961.

Rychlak, J. F. (Ed.) Dialectic: Humanistic rationale for behavior and development. Basel, Switzerland: S. Karger AG, 1976. (a)

Rychlak, J. F. Personality theory: Its nature, past, present and—future? Personality and Social Psychology Bulletin, 1976, 2, 209–224. (b)

Skinner, B. F. Beyond freedom and dignity. New York: Knopf, 1971.

Sperry, R. W. The great cerebral commissure. Scientific American, 1964, 210, 42–52.

Spinelli, D. N., & Pribram, K. H. Changes in visual recovery functions and unit activity produced by frontal and temporal cortex stimulation. Electroencephalography and clinical neurophysiology, 1967, 22, 143–149.

# GLOSSARY

**Affective Assessment, Affection:** A transcendental telosponse—an innate capacity to judge (via dialectical division) the meanings of one's concepts, premises, and even telosponses, characterizing them as either positive or negative in meaningfulness. In contrast to emotions, affections are purely mental phenomena, ultimately *arbitrary* and up to the person who levels such idiographic judgments from his or her (introspective) perspective on life. Because the assessment is dialectical, there is no indifference point on the dimension of affective assessment, although there may be ambivalence. *See also:* emotions, meaningfulness, telosponse, transcendental dialectic.

**Affirmation:** A special case of the telosponse in which one pole of a bipolar conception is precedently framed (presumed, held to be the case, "believed in," chosen, etc.). Affirmation also encompasses the framing of meaningful unipolarities in sensory experience by tautological means ("That is that." "That is a tree." "I recognize that face."). Affirmation can be further analyzed into unqualified, qualified, negative, and oppositional varieties. *See also:* meaning-extension, premise.

**Affirming the Consequent of an If, . . . Then . . . Proposition:** A (demonstrative) logical fallacy in which what is affirmed as the case (i.e., necessarily true), being more broadly distributed than that which we are interested in relating to it, fails *necessarily* to support the relationship suggested. An example of this fallacy would be: "All men [antecedent] are mortal [consequent]. This is a mortal. Hence, this is a man." This fallacy obtains in the theory-to-method sequence of scientific activity; hence for any empirically demonstrable fact pattern there will always be *in principle* N theories to account for "the findings" observed. *See also:* method, theory.

**Arbitrary Behavior:** Behavior which is telically determined due to frequent or unexpected shifting of the grounds "for the sake of which" action is then intended. Behavior continues to be premised but the meaning under affirmation and extension has been changed.

*See also:* awareness, dialectical change, freedom of the will, proto-point.

**Association Value:**  A metric of meaningfulness based on a frequency theory of some form—for example, the number of associative bondings connecting to a verbal item or the number of people in a population who recognize an item as wordlike. *See also:* reinforcement value.

**Awareness:**  Appreciation or cognizance of the arbitrariness in experience—knowing that something might be taking place in a life circumstance other than what is now occurring. *See also:* arbitrary behavior.

**Behavior:**  A global reference to the overt and covert activities of organisms, including the various physiological and biological functions of life. Behavioral descriptions in psychology vary: Some employ predominantly material- and efficient-cause meanings, and others introduce the formal- and final-cause as equally important. *See also:* logical learning theory, meaning, teleology.

**Cause(s):**  A highly abstract formulation (concept, model, "paradigm," etc.) which, acting as a precedent, sequaciously determines the descriptive account a theorist gives of his area of interest. There are *four* causal meanings, named by Aristotle as the material, efficient, formal, and final causes. Roughly equivalent parallel meanings would suggest substance, impetus, pattern, and intention in the description of anything hypothesized or known.

**Choice:**  A nontechnical way of referring to the affirmation of bipolar conceptions. Arbitrariness and alternatives in behavior must necessarily arise due to the nature of telosponsivity. *See also:* affirmation, freedom of the will.

**Conceptualize:**  Actively to organize experience in some way, to meet it at the level of sensory input with a creative capacity to *order* it via patterns which constitute meaning and meaningfulness. *See also:* affirmation, meaning, meaning-extension, meaningfulness, *pro forma.*

**Decision:**  According to logical learning theory, decision is an unqualified affirmation in which the individual comes down to a specific course of (purposive) behavior which he then intends (action-intention). *See also:* affirmation, intention.

**Demonstrative:**  A global reference to the fact that the study of meaning reflects unipolarity not only in reasoning but also in the theoretical constructs that reasoners have proffered in their conceptualization of experience. The core features of a demonstrative conception include singularity, linearity, unidirectionality, and non-contradiction. *See also*: dialectic, law of contradiction, meaning, tautology.

**Determinism:** Refers to the limitation or setting of limits on events, including behavior. Framed in terms of antecedents (or precedents) and consequents (or sequacious events), *four* types of determinism can be described, depending upon which of the causes we wish to emphasize in our accounts. *See also*: cause.

**Dialectic:** A global reference to the fact that the study of meaning reflects bipolarity not only in reasoning but also in the theoretical constructs reasoners have proffered in their conceptualization of experience. The core feature of dialectic is oppositionality, so that not only conflict and dynamic alternatives are generated within the totality of such descriptions, but there is a uniting of these contradictory poles into a unitary significance once we properly understand them from this (dialectical) viewpoint. *See also*: demonstrative, dialectical change, meaning, one and many thesis, tautology.

**Dialectical Change:** Oppositional alteration of the pattern of precedent events, thereby effecting changes in meaning "for the sake of which" sequacious events occur. This can be contrasted with the linear unidirectional change of efficient causation. *See also* demonstrative, dialectic.

**Emotions:** Bodily feelings that can act as physiological grounds for the appraisal of an organism's circumstances at any given point in time. Emotions are never arbitrary and can be thought of in nontelic terms. *See also*: affective assessment.

**Empiricist's Error:** The tendency to accept what we observe and record in the experimental context as *necessarily* explaining (completely describing) what is taking place there. The most serious outcome of this error is when a scientist confounds his method with his theory. *See also*: method, theory.

**Extraspective Theoretical Perspective:** Description of events in the third-person, from the convenience of an observer. *See also*: introspective theoretical perspective.

**Freedom of the Will, Free Will:** A popular nontechnical way of referring to the capacity human beings have dialectically to alter the meaning (pattern, order, logos, etc.) of premises which are affirmed at the protopoint. Before affirmation we can speak of freedom, and after the protopoint affirmation, we can speak of will(power). *See also*: affirmation, dialectical change, protopoint.

**Ground(s):**   The reference point or "that on the basis of which" or "for the sake of which" a telosponse is enacted. Grounds are necessary aspects of, but not sufficient to, telosponsivity, which is made possible when the person who, utilizing such grounds, assesses (evaluates, judges, assumes, believes, etc.) and then behaves accordingly. *See also:* premise, telosponse.

**Humanism:**   A theory of behavior in which—knowingly or unknowingly—the theorist employs telic constructs. This is purely a *technical* theory-construction matter to be decided upon by analysis of the theory under consideration. *See also:* humanitarianism, mechanism.

**Humanitarianism:**   Theories of *either* a mechanistic or a humanistic cast which seek to improve man's lot by raising his level of selfworth in a conceptual sense, or, by raising his level of material satisfaction in some (scientifically) managed fashion. *See also:* humanism, mechanism.

**Idea:**   A repetitive patterning of meaning brought forward tautologically to extend what is predicated. This is essentially a Kantian view of the idea in which it is said to be *pro forma,* in opposition to the Lockean idea of a receptacle of the mind beginning in a *tabula rasa* state and then being "ordered from without." *See also: pro forma, tabula rasa.*

**Intention:**   Behaving "for the sake of," hence enlivening or creating the purposive meaning of a concept in words, images, intellectual or affective assessments, and so on. Such intended meanings can relate to overt behavior (*action-intentions*) or be restricted to rational cognizance (*understanding-intentions*). Intentionality is as pure an expression of final-causation as possible. *See also:* cause, purpose, telosponse.

**Introspective Theoretical Perspective:**   Description of events in the first-person, from the outlook as envisioned by the identity of a person. *See also:* extraspective theoretical perspective, self.

**Kantian Model:**   The minority position in current psychology concerning a "model of man." The significant features are dialectical as well as demonstrative reasoning, *pro-forma* intellect, noumenal versus phenomenal experience, meaningful understanding, transcendence, and predication rather than mediation. *See also:* Lockean Model.

**Knowledge, Known:**   The broadly conceptualized, hence fixed and repetitive (constant), grasp of experience permitting individuals to further meanings to their advantage in life. Although usually framed in a positive sense, knowledge of the limitations facing one in life is also possible. *See also*: mind, reason.

**Law of Contradiction or Noncontradiction:** The view that "A is not not-A" or that something cannot both be and not be. This assumption predicates demonstrative reasoning. *See also*: demonstrative, one and many thesis.

**Learning:** As viewed in logical learning theory, learning eventuates when a meaning-extension is the case, and an individual thereby has an enriched understanding of experience based on the meaningful conceptualization he premised at the outset. This increase in knowledge may not be "true," as assessed by independent criteria—that is, people can "learn error." *See also*: logical learning theory, reinforcement.

**Lockean Model:** The currently ascendant paradigm or "model of man" in psychology. The significant features are demonstrative reasoning, *tabula-rasa* intellect, simple-to-complex ideas, constitutive mentality, mediation, and empirical determination of all that mind represents. *See also*: Kantian Model.

**Logical Learning Theory:** A teleological (humanistic) formulation of learning which rests on both demonstrative and dialectical types of logical explanation. The question of its application to lower (subhuman) organisms is left open, but there is no intent to deny telic behaviors below the level of man.

**Meaning:** A relationship between "poles" or points of reference, which in turn creates patterns with purpose and intentional features. Purpose obtains when, for example, we consider the relationship between items (words) and referents (the word's designated point or "aim") or between any two of these poles. When the poles of meaning are the individual (person) and the conceptual patterns he organizes to predicate his behavior, we are concerned with not only purpose but also intentionality. As a relationship, meaning can be analyzed in terms of its tautological unipolarities or bipolarities, extraspective or introspective formulations, and sign or symbolic manifestations. The necessity of having to opt for a "given" meaning to predicate within the multiplicity of experience—especially bipolar experience—gives rise to affirmation in behavior. *See also*: affirmation, intention, meaningfulness, mind, purpose.

**Meaning-extension:** The precedent-sequacious flow of meaning in the conceptualizations of telosponsivity, commonly referred to as the *inductive* and *deductive* knowledge of experience. As meaning-extension proceeds, the knowledge framed by the premised meanings of telosponsivity extends its range; and through the tautological identity of dialectical oppositionality as well as through analogical variations, it also changes and alters relations between items and referents as the individual comes to know more about the various meanings of his life experience. *See also*: dialectical change, meaning, meaningfulness, one and many thesis.

**Meaningfulness:**  The extent of significance, import, or general understanding an item or its referent has for the individual. Meaningfulness is thus a measure or metric of the extent of meaning—that is, clarity, centrality, import, value, and so on—the item holds for the individual or part-personality structure. Traditionally measures of meaningfulness have rested on the frequency thesis (association value), but there are also nonfrequency metrics of meaningfulness (reinforcement value). *See also*: affective assessment, association value, reinforcement value.

**Mechanism:**  A theory of behavior in which—knowingly or unknowingly—the theorist fails to use telic constructs. This is purely a *technical* theory-construction matter to be decided upon by analysis of the theory under consideration. *See also*: humanism, humanitarianism.

**Method:**  The means or manner of determining whether a theoretical construct or proposition is true or false. Methods follow theories, though one can work back from sequaciously defined methodological events to a new or modified precedent theory. Methods are vehicles for the exercise of evidence. There are two general types: (1) *cognitive* (or conceptual) method, which makes use of procedural evidence, and (2) *research* method, which uses validating evidence in addition to procedural. *See also*: theory.

**Mind:**  The innate capacity to telospond in relation to ["for the sake of"] patterns of meaning in experience as well as to create these patterns anew through dialectical reasoning. Mind is fundamentally conservative, so that the flux of experience is fixed at the protopoint in conceptual premises which are then tautologized through telosponsivity in upcoming experience. The patterned effort to fix experience into certainty or knowledge is called *thinking*, and conceptualizations employed in this effort are called *ideas*. *See also*: idea, telosponse.

**Motivation:**  According to logical learning theory, this is an evaluation of the relative advantage a premise (encompassing an intended "goal") makes possible in life, leveled by the person affirming this premise or by an observer who presumes to know what is being intended. To understand a specific *motive* (i.e., premised advantage, gain, reward, etc.) one must know the meanings encompassed in the affirmed premise, how these relate to other people, what the person has affectively assessed in the circumstance, and so on. *See also:* affirmation, premise, meaning-extension.

**Objective:** Refers to meanings that transcend the individual who propounds these relationships and hence may be grasped or understood by all individuals who seek to understand the meaning at issue. *See also*: meaning, subjective.

**One and Many Thesis:** The view that all events are united (ordered meaningfully) and thus must necessarily be arbitrarily distinguished, one from the other. This assumption predicates dialectical reasoning. *See also*: arbitrary behavior, dialectic, Law of Contradiction.

**Precedent:** Refers to the ordering of meaning without regard for time considerations. A precedent meaning is one that goes before others in order or arrangement and establishes via the principle of tautology the course and nature of meanings which follow it (telic determination). *See also*: protopoint, sequacious, tautology.

**Premise, Predicate Assumption, Predication:** The presumptive meanings ("that") affirmed by telosponding organisms which telically determine ("for the sake of which") in precedent-sequacious fashion what will be known (understood, learned, furthered, etc.) by these organisms. The truth-value of the premise does not alter the process, but premises held to with conviction are often called "facts." *See also*: protopoint.

**Pro Forma:** For the sake of a form, organization, order, and so on, which when considered relationally is *meaning*. In logical learning theory this phrase is used to suggest that human mentation, rather than being *tabula rasa* and hence ordered exclusively by experiential input, contributes order (meaning) "to" experience. *See also*: freedom of the will, Kantian Model, meaning, meaning-extension, precedent, protopoint, *tabula rasa*.

**Protopoint:** Refers to the anchoring point of meaning-extension at which affirmations are made. The terms *precedent* and *sequacious* refer to the ordering of meaning-extension at *any* point in the course of intentional behavior—for example, over the full course of a deductive or inductive line of thought. But the *initiating* point at which a *pro-forma* intelligence grounds its understanding or intends its purposes is the protopoint. In one sense this is the "first precedent" for any one line of intentionality, but all protopoint affirmations are sequaciously implied by ever more abstract conceptions. If there are "universals" in human intelligence, they would represent the ultimate protopoints of reason (as in Plato's Realm of Being). *See also*: freedom of the will, premise, precedent, self, sequacious.

**Purity Criticism:**   The charge that theoretical constructs sometimes force their descriptive referents into arbitrary and distorted meanings, losing the essence of that which is under description (explanation). Purity criticisms range from mere cautions of this possibility to highly aggressive rejections of "all theory" in favor of a "spontaneous illumination" sent to the unprejudiced observer by the data *qua* data.

**Purpose:**   The "aim of the meaning" of a concept, which is brought to mental existence by the intentional behavior of a living organism. Purpose focuses on the formal-cause aspect of telosponsive behavior. When such patterned organizations that have an aim (point, significance, end, etc.) are intended by a conceptualizing organism, we can speak of the combined process as a telosponse. *See also*: intention, telosponse.

**Reason, Reasoning:**   Finding the grounds "for the sake of which" behavior (events, "happenings") may now be taking place, or, "should" ("could," "might") be taking place. See also: idea, mind.

**Reinforcement:**   Best understood as a methodological procedure, but logical learning theory would consider reinforcement as occurring when the learner's affirmations are successfully extended. Thus, when understanding- or action-intentionality is made conditional upon a premise that truly (effectively, helpfully) conceptualizes for the individual employing it, we have a *reinforcement* of this premise taking place. It is likely to be used again and therefore enriched or embellished (learned). Positive reinforcements further meanings that are rooted in positive premises, and negative reinforcments further meanings that are rooted in negative premises. *See also*: affirmation, learning, premise.

**Reinforcement Value:**   The operationalized measure (metric) of affective assessment achieved by asking subjects to prerate for likability materials (verbal, pictorial, etc.) which they may be asked to learn or otherwise deal with in an experimental context. It is assumed that a rating of liking reflects positive affective assessment and a rating of disliking reflects a subject's negative affective assessment. Considered from its background theory, reinforcement value is a nonfrequency measure of meaningfulness. *See also*: affective assessment, association value.

**Self:**   A logical learning theory demands that there be a logician—

an identity—who brings forward the "logical weight" of meaning-extension in what is commonly called an inductive or deductive fashion. The *self* captures this identity feature of telosponsivity. To the extent that a behaving organism (1) *does* precedently and arbitrarily formulate meaningful premises at a protopoint "for the sake of which" it sequaciously behaves, (2) is conscious of doing so (i.e., has self-awareness), and (3) seeks to improve on the advantages gained from the use of such premises, to that extent can it be said to be self-enhancing in behavior or to be promoting self-realization. *See also*: affirmation, meaning-extension, telosponse.

**Sequacious:**  Refers to the ordering of meaning without regard for time considerations. A sequacious meaning is one that follows or flows from the meanings of precedents, extending these in a *necessary* sense according to the principle of tautology (telic determination). Sequacious meaning-extensions can be purely or partially tautological (i.e., analogical, metaphorical, etc.). *See also*: precedent, tautology.

**S-R Bind:**  Limiting one's theoretical conceptions to an efficient-cause frame. This is especially harmful to psychology when a theorist fails to distinguish between his theory and his method (of establishing proof), for then the independent-dependent variable (method) tandem is confounded with the stimulus-response (theory) tandem. *See also*: method, theory.

**Subjective:**  Refers to meanings that are somehow private, difficult or impossible to circumscribe, and hence are incapable of being extended beyond the behavior of the individual who has affirmed them. *See also*: meaning, objective.

**Tabula Rasa:**  The view that mind is as a "smoothed tablet" at birth and that all it subsequently manifests in mentation is input or etched upon it by experience. *See also*: idea, Lockean Model, *pro forma*.

**Tautology:**  A relation of identity, considered either extraspectively as redundant analytically true statements or introspectively as the premised meaning being extended from what is known to what can be known. Examples of tautology range from the repetitive rigidity of the stereotype to the partial identities of analogy, metaphor, allegory, synecdoche, and so on. Even more complexly, pure dialectical relations are tautological because one pole of the meaning necessarily enters into the definition of the other, accounting for the One and Many Thesis. *See also*: demonstrative, dialectic, One and Many Thesis.

**Teleology, Telic:**  The view that events are predicated according to

plan, design, or assumption—that is, based upon purposive meanings—and therefore directed to some intended eventuality. In psychology this generates a humanistic not mechanistic conception of
behavior. *See also*: humanism, humanitarianism, meaning, purpose,
intention.

**Telosponse:**   Taking on (premising, predicating) of a meaningful
item (e.g., image, word, judgmental comparison) relating to a
referent acting as a purpose for the sake of which behavior is then
intended. Telosponsivity is the global term, subsuming intentionality
and purposivity, which makes teleological description possible in
logical learning theory. Human beings do not "learn" to telospond.
It is an aspect of their very nature, a description of what mind *is*
rather than how it has been molded into performing from some other
innate condition. *See also*: intention, mind, purpose.

**Theory:**   A series of two or more constructions (abstractions, concepts, items, images, etc.) which have been hypothesized, assumed,
or even factually demonstrated to bear a certain relationship, one
to the other.

**Transcendental Dialectic:**   The Kantian conception suggesting that
human reason can rise above and observe its own cognitive (conceptual) processes, permitting thereby a self-reflexivity in thought.
*See also*: conceptualize, dialectic, Kantian Model, method.

**Unconscious Behavior:**   Logical learning theory views this as a kind
of mirror-image telosponsivity in which the opposite or reverse of
affirmations made with awareness are brought into play without the
benefit of such alternative understanding. This makes unconscious
behavior very literal and unbending (psychic determinism). *See also*:
affirmation, awareness, telosponse.

# BIBLIOGRAPHY

Abramson, Y. *Reinforcement value: An idiographic approach to meaningfulness.* Unpublished doctoral dissertation. St. Louis: St. Louis University, 1967.

Abramson, Y., Tasto, D. L., & Rychlak, J. F. Nomothetic vs. idiographic influences of association value and reinforcement value on learning. *Journal of Experimental Research in Personality,* 1969, **4,** 65–71.

Adams, D. K. The inference of mind. *Psychological Review,* 1928, **35,** 235–252.

Adams, D. K. Note on method. *Psychological Review,* 1937, **44,** 212–218.

Adler, A. *Social interest: A challenge to mankind.* New York: Capricorn Books, 1964.

Adorno, T. W., Frenkel-Brunswik, E., Levinson, D. J., & Sanford, R. N. *The authoritarian personality.* New York: Harper, 1950.

Alexander, F. G., & Selesnick, S. T. *The history of psychiatry: An evaluation of psychiatric thought and practice from prehistoric times to the present.* New York: Harper & Row, 1966.

Allport, G. W. *Personality: A psychological interpretation.* New York: Holt, 1937.

Allport, G. W. Personalistic psychology as a science: A reply. *Psychological Review,* 1946, **53,** 132–135.

Andrews, J. E. *The effect of word meaning on the affective learning styles of ascendant and submissive subjects.* Unpublished master's thesis. Lafayette, Ind.: Purdue University, 1972.

Angell, J. R. The relations of structural and functional psychology to philosophy. *Philosophical Review,* 1903, **12,** 203–243.

Angell, J. R. The province of functional psychology. *Psychological Review,* 1907, **2,** 61–91.

Apao, W. *Reinforcement and two kinds of meaningfulness measures in paired-associate learning.* Unpublished master's thesis. Lafayette Ind.: Purdue University, 1976.

Archer, E. J. Re-evaluation of the meaningfulness of all possible CVC trigrams. *Psychological Monographs,* 1960, **74,** No. 10 (Whole No. 497).

Aristotle. *Metaphysics.* In R. M. Hutchins (Ed.), *Great books of the western world* (Vol. 8). Chicago: Encyclopedia Britannica, 1952. Pp. 499–626.

Aristotle. *Physics.* In R. M. Hutchins (Ed.), *Great books of the western world* (Vol. 8). Chicago: Encyclopedia Britannica, 1952. Pp. 257–355.

Aristotle. *Posterior analytics.* In R. M. Hutchins (Ed.), *Great books of the western world* (Vol. 8). Chicago: Encyclopedia Britannica, 1952. Pp. 95–137.

Arnold, M. B. *Emotion and personality*. New York: Columbia University Press, 1960.

Arnold, M. B. (Ed.), *Feelings and emotions*. New York: Academic, 1970.

August, G. J. *Affective meaningfulness, self-concept and the verbal learning styles of white and black children*. Unpublished doctoral dissertation. Lafayette, Ind.: Purdue University, 1975.

August, G. J., Rychlak, J. F., & Felker, D. W. Affective assessment, self-concept, and the verbal learning styles of fifth-grade children. *Journal of Educational Psychology*, 1975, **67**, 801–806.

Bakan, D. Learning and the scientific enterprise. *Psychological Review*, 1953, **60**, 45–49.

Bakan, D. Learning and the principle of inverse probability. *Psychological Review*, 1953, **60**, 360–370.

Bakan, D. A reconsideration of the problem of introspection. *Psychological Bulletin*, 1954, **51**, 105–118.

Bakan, D. Clinical psychology and logic. *American Psychologist*, 1956, **11**, 655–662.

Bandura, A. *Principles of behavior modification*. New York: Holt, Rinehart & Winston, 1969.

Bandura, A. Behavior theory and the models of man. *American Psychologist*, 1974, **29**, 859–869.

Barron, F. S. An ego strength scale which predicts responses to psychotherapy. *Journal of Consulting Psychology*, 1953, **17**, 327–333.

Bartlett, F. C. *Remembering*. Cambridge: The University Press, 1932.

Bartlett, F. C. *Thinking*. New York: Basic Books, 1958.

Becker, H., & Barnes, H. E. *Social thought from lore to science* (2 vols.). Washington, D.C.: Harren, 1952.

Berg, I. A. Deviant responses and deviant people: The formulation of the deviation hypothesis. *Journal of Counseling Psychology*, 1957, **4**, 159.

Bergmann, G., & Spence, K. Operationism and theory in psychology. *Psychological Review*, 1941, **48**, 1–14.

Binswanger, L. *Being-in-the-world* (translated and with a critical introduction by J. Needleman). New York: Basic Books, 1963.

Block, J. *The challenge of response sets*. New York: Appleton-Century-Crofts, 1965.

Blumenthal, A. L. A reappraisal of Wilhelm Wundt. *American Psychologist*, 1975, **30**, 1081–1088.

Boland, G. C. *The relationship of personality adjustment to the learning of material having connotative and associative meaningfulness*. Unpublished doctoral dissertation. St. Louis: St. Louis University, 1970.

Boneau, C. A. Paradigm regained? Cognitive behaviorism restated. *American Psychologist*, 1974, **29**, 297–309.

Boring, E. G. Mind and mechanism. *American Journal of Psychology*, 1946, **54**, 173–192.

Boring, E. G. *A history of experimental psychology* (2nd ed.). New York: Appleton-Century-Crofts, 1950.

Boss, M. *Psychoanalysis and daseinsanalysis.* New York: Basic Books, 1963.

Bousfield, W. A. The occurrence of clustering in the free recall of randomly arranged associates. *Journal of General Psychology,* 1953, **49,** 229–240.

Bowers, K. S. Situationism in psychology: An analysis and a critique. *Psychological Review,* 1973, **80,** 307–336.

Bransford, J. D., & Franks, J. J. The abstraction of linguistic ideas. *Cognitive Psychology,* 1971, **2,** 331–350.

Brentano, F. *Psychology from an empirical standpoint.* New York: Humanities, 1973.

Breuer, J. Theoretical selection, section III. In J. Strachey (Ed.), *The standard edition of the complete psychological works of Sigmund Freud* (Vol. II). London: Hogarth, 1955. Pp. 185–251.

Breuer, J., & Freud, S. On the psychical mechanism of hysterical phenomena: Preliminary communication. In J. Strachey (Ed.), *The standard edition of the complete psychological works of Sigmund Freud* (Vol. II). London: Hogarth, 1955. Pp. 1–17.

Brewer, W. F. There is no convincing evidence for operant or classical conditioning in adult humans. In W. B. Weimer & D. S. Palermo (Eds.), *Cognition and the symbolic processes.* Hillsdale, N.J.: Lawrence Erlbaum, 1974.

Bridgman, P. W. *The way things are.* Cambridge: Harvard University Press, 1959.

Broadbent, D. E. Flow of information within the organism. *Journal of Verbal Learning and Verbal Behavior,* 1963, **2,** 34–39.

Bronowski, J. *The common sense of science.* Cambridge: Harvard University Press, 1958.

Bruner, J. S., & Postman, L. Emotional selectivity in perception and reaction. *Journal of Personality,* 1947, **16,** 69–77.

Bugelski, B. R., & Scharlock, D. P. An experimental demonstration of unconscious mediated association. *Journal of Experimental Psychology,* 1952, **44,** 334–338.

Bugental, J. F. T. Humanistic psychology: A new break-through. *American Psychologist,* 1963, **18,** 563–567.

Burtt, E. A. *The metaphysical foundations of modern physical science* (rev. ed.). Garden City, N.Y.: Doubleday, 1955.

Byron, R. E. *Learning of "likes" and "dislikes" in high and low self-esteem children.* Unpublished master's thesis. Lafayette, Ind.: Purdue University, 1972.

Caldwell, W. Professor Titchener's view of the self. *Psychological Review,* 1898, **5,** 401–408.

Caldwell, W. The postulates of a structural psychology. *Psychological Review,* 1899, **6,** 187–191.

Calkins, M. W. A reconciliation between structural and functional psychology. *Psychological Review,* 1906, **13,** 61–81.

Calverton, V. F. The rise of objective psychology. *Psychological Review,* 1924, **31,** 418–426.

Campbell, D. T., & Stanley, J. C. *Experimental and quasi-experimental designs for research.* Chicago: Rand McNally, 1963.

Carlsen, N. L. *The effect of high and low self concept on learning along an intensity dimension of meaningfulness.* Unpublished master's thesis. Lafayette, Ind.: Purdue University, 1970.

Cassirer, E. *An essay on man.* Garden City, N.Y.: Doubleday, 1944.

Cassirer, E. *The problem of knowledge.* New Haven: Yale University Press, 1950.

Chan, W.-T. Chinese theory and practice, with special reference to humanism. In C. A. Moore (Ed.), *The Chinese mind: Essentials of Chinese philosophy and culture.* Honolulu: University of Hawaii Press, 1967. Pp. 11–30.

Chan, W-T. The story of Chinese philosophy. In C. A. Moore (Ed.), *The Chinese mind: Essentials of Chinese philosophy and culture.* Honolulu: University of Hawaii Press, 1967. Pp. 31–76.

Chaplin, J. P., & Krawiec, T. S. *Systems and theories of psychology.* New York: Holt, Rinehart & Winston, 1960.

Colaizzi, P. F. An analysis of the learner's perception of learning material at various phases of a learning process. *Review of Existential Psychology and Psychiatry,* 1967, **7**, 95–105.

Colaizzi, P. F. *Reflection and research in psychology: A phenomenological study of learning.* Dubuque, Iowa: Kendall/Hunt, 1973.

Conant, J. B. *Modern science and modern man.* Garden City, N.Y.: Doubleday Anchor, 1952. (Originally published, New York: Columbia University Press, 1929).

Creelman, M. B. *The experimental investigation of meaning: A review of the literature.* New York: Springer, 1966.

Cronbach, L. J., & Meehl, P. E. Construct validity in psychological tests. *Psychological Bulletin,* 1955, **52**, 281–302.

Cronbach, L. J. Beyond the two disciplines of scientific psychology. *American Psychologist,* 1975, **30**, 116–127.

Dahlstrom, W. G., & Welsh, G. S. *An MMPI handbook: A guide to use in clinical practice and research.* Minneapolis: University of Minnesota Press, 1960.

Darwin, C. R. *The descent of man.* In R. M. Hutchins (Ed.), *Great books of the western world* (Vol. 49). Chicago: Encyclopedia Britannica, 1952.

Datta, D. M. Epistemological methods in Indian philosophy. In C. A. Moore (Ed.), *The Indian mind: Essentials of Indian philosophy and culture.* Honolulu: University of Hawaii Press, 1967. Pp. 118–135.

DeNike, L. D. The temporal relationship between awareness and performance in verbal conditioning. *Journal of Experimental Psychology,* 1964, **68**, 521–529.

Descartes, R. *Rules for the direction of mind* and *Discourse on method.* In R. M. Hutchins (Ed.), *Great books of the western world* (Vol. 31). Chicago: Encyclopedia Britannica, 1952. Pp. 1–40 and 41–67.

Dollard, J., & Miller, N. E. *Personality and psychotherapy: An analysis in terms of learning, thinking, and culture.* New York: McGraw-Hill, 1950.

Dulany, D. E. The place of hypotheses and intentions: An analysis of verbal control in verbal conditioning. In C. W. Eriksen (Ed.), *Behavior and awareness: A symposium of research and interpretation.* Durham, N.C.: Duke University Press, 1962. Pp. 102–129.

Dulany, D. Awareness, rules, and propositional control: A confrontation with

S-R behavior theory. In T. R. Dixon & D. L. Horton (Eds.), *Verbal behavior and general behavior theory.* Englewood Cliffs, N.J.: Prentice-Hall, Inc., 1968.

Dunlap, K. A revision of the fundamental law of habit formation. *Science,* 1928, **67**, 360–362.

Dunning, L. P. *The effects of reinforcement value on the learning of words varying in positive and negative meaningfulness for subjects high or low in ego-strength.* Unpublished master's thesis. Lafayette, Ind.: Purdue University, 1973.

Ebbinghaus, H. *Memory: A contribution to experimental psychology.* New York: Dover, 1964.

Eddington, A. *The philosophy of physical science.* Ann Arbor: University of Michigan Press, 1958.

Edwards, P. (Editor-in-Chief) *The encyclopedia of philosophy* (8 vols.). New York: Macmillan and Free Press, 1967.

Einstein, A. Ernst Mach. *Physikalische Zeitschrift,* 1916, **17**, 101–104.

Einstein, A. *Essays in science.* New York: Philosophical Library, 1934.

Engels, F. *Dialectics of nature.* Moscow: Progress, 1966.

English, H. B., & English, A. C. *A comprehensive dictionary of psychological and psychoanalytical terms.* London: Longmans, Green, 1958.

Evans, R. I. *B. F. Skinner: The man and his ideas.* New York: Dutton, 1968.

Eves, H. *An introduction to the history of mathematics* (3rd ed.). New York: Holt, Rinehart & Winston, 1969.

Farber, I. E. The things people say to themselves. *American Psychologist,* 1963, **18**, 185–197.

Fehl, N. E. *History and society.* Hong Kong: Chung Chi College Publications, 1964.

Fernberger, S. W. Behavior versus introspective psychology. *Psychological Review,* 1922, **29**, 409–413.

Feuer, L. S. *Einstein and the generations of science.* New York: Basic Books, 1974.

Fitts, W. H. Tennessee Department of Mental Health Self-Concept Scale. Nashville: Counselor Recordings and Tests, 1965.

Flynn, E. J. *The factor analysis of meaning in CVC trigrams rated for association value and reinforcement value.* Unpublished master's thesis. St. Louis: St. Louis University, 1967.

Flynn, E. J. *Beyond frequency: A two-dimensional theory of verbal meaningfulness.* Unpublished doctoral dissertation. St. Louis: St. Louis University, 1969.

Forbes, R. J., & Dijksterhuis, E. J. *A history of science and technology* (2 vols.). Baltimore: Penguin, 1963.

Frank, P. *Philosophy of science.* Englewood Cliffs, N.J.: Prentice-Hall, 1957.

Frazer, J. G. *The new golden bough* (abridged by T. H. Gaster). Great Meadows, N.J.: Phillips, 1959.

Freud, S. The interpretation of dreams. In J. Strachey (Ed.), *The standard edition of the complete psychological works of Sigmund Freud* (Vols. IV & V). London: Hogarth, 1953.

Freud, S. *The origins of psycho-analysis, letters to Wilhelm Fliess, drafts and notes:* 1887–1902. New York: Basic Books, 1954.

Freud, S. The psychotherapy of hysteria. In J. Strachey (Ed.), *The standard edition of the complete psychological works of Sigmund Freud* (Vol. II). London: Hogarth, 1955. Pp. 254–305.

Freud, S. On narcissism: An introduction. In J. Strachey (Ed.), *The standard edition of the complete psychological works of Sigmund Freud* (Vol. XIV). London: Hogarth, 1957. Pp. 67–102.

Freud, S. Some general remarks on hysterical attacks. In J. Strachey (Ed.), *The standard edition of the complete psychological works of Sigmund Freud* (Vol. IX). London: Hogarth, 1959. Pp. 227–234.

Freud, S. *The psychopathology of everyday life.* In J. Strachey (Ed.), *The standard edition of the complete psychological works of Sigmund Freud* (Vol. VI). London: Hogarth, 1960.

Freud, S. The neuro-psychoses of defence. In J. Strachey (Ed.), *The standard edition of the complete psychological works of Sigmund Freud* (Vol. III). London: Hogarth, 1962. Pp. 41–61.

Freud, S. The aetiology of hysteria. In J. Strachey (Ed.), *The standard edition of the complete psychological works of Sigmund Freud* (Vol. III). London: Hogarth, 1962. Pp. 182–221.

Freud, S. A case of successful treatment by hypnotism. In J. Strachey (Ed.), *The standard edition of the complete psychological works of Sigmund Freud* (Vol. I). London: Hogarth, 1966. Pp. 115–128.

Freud, S. Project for a scientific psychology. In J. Strachey (Ed.), *The standard edition of the complete psychological works of Sigmund Freud* (Vol. I). London: Hogarth, 1966. Pp. 283–397.

Fruchter, B. *Introduction to factor analysis.* Princeton, N.J.: Van Nostrand, 1954.

Galster, J. M. *Affective factors in paired-associate acquisition and tachistoscopic recognition of faces and names.* Unpublished master's thesis. Lafayette, Ind.: Purdue University, 1972.

Garza, R. T. *Affective and associative meaningfulness in the learning styles of Chicano and Anglo college students.* Unpublished doctoral dissertation, Lafayette, Ind.: Purdue University, 1975.

Gazzaniga, S. The split brain in man. *Scientific American,* 1967, **216**, 24–29.

Giorgi, A. *Psychology as a human science: A phenomenologically based approach.* New York: Harper & Row, 1970.

Giorgi, A. Toward phenomenologically based research in psychology. *Journal of Phenomenological Psychology,* 1970, **1**, 75–98.

Giorgi, A. Phenomenology and the foundational problems of psychology. In W. J. Arnold & J. K. Cole (Eds.), *Nebraska symposium on motivation* (Vol. 22). Lincoln: University of Nebraska Press, 1975.

Glaze, J. A. The association value of nonsense syllables. *Journal of Genetic Psychology,* 1928, **35**, 255–269.

Greenspoon, J. The reinforcing effect of two spoken sounds on the frequency of two responses. *American Journal of Psychology,* 1955, **68**, 409–416.

Guilford, J. P., & Martin, H. G. Guilford-Martin Inventory of Factors GAMIN: Manual. Beverly Hills, Calif.: Sheridan Supply, 1948.

Guthrie, E. R. *The psychology of learning* (rev. ed.). New York: Harper, 1952.

Haigh, G. V. Letter to the Editor. *Psychology Today*, 1969, **3**, 4.

Hebb, D. O. What psychology is about. *American Psychologist*, 1974, **29**, 71–79.

Helmholtz, H. von. Treatise on physiological optics. In T. Shipley (Ed.), *Classics in psychology*. New York: Philosophical Library, 1961.

Hess, E. H. Attitudes and pupil size. *Scientific American*, 1965, **212**, 46–54.

Hilgard, E. R., & Bower, G. H. *Theories of learning*. New York: Appleton-Century-Crofts, 1966.

Hull, C. L. Mind, mechanism, and adaptive behavior. *Psychological Review*, 1937, **44**, 1–32.

Hull, C. L. *Principles of behavior*. New York: Appleton-Century-Crofts, 1943.

Hull, C. L. *A behavior system*. New Haven: Yale University Press, 1952.

Hume, D. *An enquiry concerning human understanding*. In R. M. Hutchins (Ed.), *Great books of the western world* (Vol. 35). Chicago: Encyclopedia Britannica, 1952. Pp. 446–509.

Immergluck, L. Determinism-freedom in contemporary psychology. An ancient problem revisited. *American Psychologist*, 1964, **19**, 270–281.

Irwin, F. W. *Intentional behavior and motivation: A cognitive theory*. Philadelphia: Lippincott, 1971.

Jack, R. M. *The effect of reinforcement value in mixed and unmixed lists on learning style of overachieving and underachieving female college students*. Unpublished doctoral dissertation. Lafayette, Ind.: Purdue University, 1974.

James, W. *The principles of psychology*. In R. M. Hutchins (Ed.), *Great books of the western world* (Vol. 53). Chicago: Encyclopedia Britannica, 1952.

Jaspers, K. *The great philosophers*. New York: Harcourt, Brace & World, 1962.

Jenkins, J. J. Remember that old theory of memory? Well, forget it! *American Psychologist*, 1974, **29**, 785–795.

Jensen, A. R. How much can we boost IQ and scholastic achievement? *Harvard Educational Review*, 1969, **39**, 1–123.

Jones, E. *The life and work of Sigmund Freud: The formative years and great discoveries* (Vol. 1). New York: Basic Books, 1953.

Jones, M. A. *The role of racial identity, sex and social class in the affective assessment of subtests on the Wechsler intelligence scale for children*. Unpublished master's thesis. Lafayette, Ind.: Purdue University, 1974.

Jung, C. G. *Two essays on analytical psychology*. In H. Read, M. Fordham, & G. Adler (Eds.), *The collected works of C. G. Jung* (Vol. 7). Bollingen Series XX.7. New York: Pantheon, 1953.

Jung, C. G. *Psychology and alchemy*. In H. Read, M. Fordham, & G. Adler (Eds.), *The collected works of C. G. Jung* (Vol. 12). Bollingen Series XX.12. New York: Pantheon, and London: Routledge & Kegan Paul, 1953.

Jung, C. G. *Symbols of transformation*. In H. Read, M. Fordham, & G. Adler (Eds.), *The collected works of C. G. Jung* (Vol. 5). Bollingen Series XX.5. New York: Pantheon, 1956.

Jung, C. G. *Psychology and religion: West and east*. In H. Read, M. Fordham, & G. Adler (Eds.), *The collected works of C. G. Jung* (Vol. 11). Bollingen

Series XX.11. New York: Pantheon, and London: Routledge & Kegan Paul, 1958.

Jung, C. G. The structure and dynamics of the psyche. In H. Read, M. Fordham, & G. Adler (Eds.), The collected works of C. G. Jung (Vol. 8). Bollingen Series XX.8. New York: Pantheon, 1960.

Kant, I. The critique of pure reason. In R. M. Hutchins (Ed.), Great books of the western world (Vol. 42). Chicago: Encyclopedia Britannica, 1952. Pp. 1–250.

Kausler, D. H. Readings in verbal learning. New York: Wiley, 1966.

Kausler, D. H. Continuity of processes across variants of recognition learning. In R. L. Solso (Ed.), Theories in cognitive psychology: The Loyola symposium. New York: Wiley, 1974. Pp. 45–75.

Keedy, N. S. The relationship between the affective quality of a premise and meaning-extension based upon its affirmation. Unpublished manuscript. Lafayette, Ind.: Purdue University, 1975.

Kelly, G. A. The psychology of personal constructs (2 vols.). New York: Norton, 1955.

Kintsch, W. Learning, memory, and conceptual processes. New York: Wiley, 1970.

Koffka, K. Principles of gestalt psychology. New York: Harcourt, Brace, 1935.

Köhler, W. Gestalt psychology today. In M. Henle (Ed.), Documents of gestalt psychology. Berkeley: University of California Press, 1961. Pp. 1–15.

Köhler, W. Psychological remarks on some questions of anthropology. In M. Henle (Ed.), Documents of gestalt psychology. Berkeley: Univeristy of California Press, 1961. Pp. 203–221.

Kondo, H. Albert Einstein and the theory of relativity. New York: Franklin Watts, 1969.

Kubat, W. J. The reinforcement value of associations made to CVC trigrams. Unpublished master's thesis. St. Louis: St. Louis University, 1969.

Kucera, H., & Francis, W. N. Computational analysis of present-day American English. Providence, R.I.: Brown University Press, 1967.

Kuhn, T. S. The structure of scientific revolutions (2nd ed.). Chicago: The University of Chicago Press, 1970. (1st ed., 1962.)

Kuhn, T. S. Logic of discovery or psychology of research? In I. Lakatos & A. Musgrave (Eds.), Criticism and the growth of knowledge. Cambridge: The University Press, 1970. Pp. 1–23.

Kuo, Y. Chinese dialectical thought and character. In J. F. Rychlak (Ed.), Dialectic: Humanistic rationale for behavior and development. Basel, Switzerland: S. Karger AG, 1976. Pp. 72–85.

Kuo, Z. Y. The fundamental error of the concept of purpose and the trial and error fallacy. Psychological Review, 1928, 35, 414–433.

Laberteaux, T. E. The influence of positive versus negative reinforcement value on mediated paired-associate learning. Unpublished master's thesis. St. Louis: St. Louis University, 1968.

Langer, S. K. Philosophy in a new key. New York: Penguin, 1948.

Lappin, R. W. Meaningfulness, deviant achievers, and personal adjustment. Unpublished doctoral dissertation. St. Louis: St. Louis University, 1969.

Lecky, P. *Self-consistency: A theory of personality*. Garden City, N.Y.: Doubleday, 1969.

Lefcourt, H. M. The function of the illusions of control and freedom. *American Psychologist*, 1973, **28**, 417–425.

Levy, L. H. *Psychological interpretation*. New York: Holt, Rinehart & Winston, 1963.

Lewin, K. *A dynamic theory of personality*. New York: McGraw-Hill, 1935.

Locke, J. An essay concerning human understanding. In R. M. Hutchins (Ed.), *Great books of the western world* (Vol. 35). Chicago: Encyclopedia Britannica, 1952. Pp. 85–395.

Lorayne, H., & Lucas, J. *The memory book*. New York: Ballantine, 1974.

Lorenz, K. *Studies in animal and human behavior* (Vol. 1). Cambridge: Harvard University Press, 1970.

Lowrie, W. *A short life of Kierkegaard*. Garden City, N.Y.: Doubleday, Anchor Books, 1961.

MacCorquodale, K., & Meehl, P. E. On a distinction between hypothetical constructs and intervening variables. *Psychological Review*, 1948, **55**, 95–107.

Mach, E. *The science of mechanics*. Chicago: Open Court, 1893.

Magill, F. N., & McGreal, I. P. (Eds.), *Masterpieces of world philosophy* (2 vols.). New York: Salem, 1961.

Mahoney, M. J. *Cognition and behavior modification*. Cambridge, Mass.: Ballinger, 1974.

Maltzman, I. Theoretical conceptions of semantic conditioning and generalization. In T. R. Dixon & D. L. Horton (Eds.), *Verbal behavior and general behavior theory*. Englewood Cliffs, N.J.: Prentice-Hall, Inc., 1968. Pp. 291–339.

Mancuso, J. C. Dialectic man as a subject in psychological research. In J. F. Rychlak (Ed.), *Dialectic: Humanistic rationale for behavior and development*. Basel, Switzerland: S. Karger AG, 1976. Pp. 113–125.

Marceil, J. C. *The role of the person in the psychology experiment: A reappraisal of the problems of reinforcement, response set and volunteer error*. Unpublished master's thesis. Lafayette, Ind.: Purdue University, 1975.

Marrow, A. J. *The practical theorist: The life and work of Kurt Lewin*. New York: Basic Books, 1969.

Marx, K. *Capital*. In R. M. Hutchins (Ed.), *Great books of the western world* (Vol. 50). Chicago: Encyclopedia Britannica, 1952. Pp. 1–393.

Maslow, A. H. Eupsychia, the good society. *Journal of Humanistic Psychology*, 1961, **1**, 1–11.

Maslow, A. H. *The farther reaches of human nature*. New York: Viking, 1971.

Masterman, M. The nature of a paradigm. In I. Lakatos & A. Musgrave (Eds.), *Criticism and the growth of knowledge*. Cambridge: The University Press, 1970. Pp. 59–89.

McDougall, W. Prolegomena to psychology. *Psychological Review*, 1922, **29**, 1–43.

McDougall, W. Purposive or mechanical psychology? *Psychological Review*, 1923, **30**, 273–288.

McFarland, K. K. *The influence of reinforcement value and school achievement* on a "pictorial-verbal" learning task. Unpublished master's thesis. St. Louis: St. Louis University, 1969.

McGuire, W. (Ed.), *The Freud/Jung letters*. Bollingen Series XCIV. Princeton, N.J.: Princeton University Press, 1974.

McKeachie, W. J. The decline and fall of the laws of learning. *Educational Researcher*, 1974, **3**, 7–11.

McKee, D. B. *Connotative and associative meaningfulness and their influence on schizophrenic learning*. Unpublished master's thesis. St. Louis: St. Louis University, 1969.

Meehl, P. E., & MacCorquodale, K. On a distinction between hypothetical constructs and intervening variables. *Psychological Review*, 1948, **55**, 95–107.

Miller, D. L. The meaning of explanation. *Psychological Review*, 1946, **53**, 241–246.

Miller, N. E., & Dollard, J. *Social learning and imitation*. New Haven: Yale University Press, 1941.

Mischel, T. Wundt and the conceptual foundations of psychology. *Philosophical and Phenomenological Research*, 1970, **31**, 1–26.

Mischel, W. *Personality and assessment*. New York: Wiley, 1968.

Mischel, W. Toward a cognitive social learning reconceptualization of personality. *Psychological Review*, 1973, **80**, 252–283.

*Monitor*, April, 1974, Vol. 5, No. 4. Washington, D.C.: American Psychological Association, 1974.

Moore, C. A. Introduction: The comprehensive Indian mind. In C. A. Moore (Ed.), *The Indian mind: Essentials of Indian philosophy and culture*. Honolulu: University of Hawaii Press, 1967. Pp. 1–18.

Moore, C. A. Introduction: The humanistic Chinese mind. In C. A. Moore (Ed.), *The Chinese mind: Essentials of Chinese philosophy and culture*. Honolulu: University of Hawaii Press, 1967. Pp. 1–10.

Morgan, C. L. *Psychology for teachers*. New York: Scribner, 1906.

Muller, J. B. *The effects of differential feedback and reinforcement value on the acquisition of trigrams: A conceptual theory of reinforcement*. Unpublished doctoral dissertation. Lafayette, Ind.: Purdue University, 1975.

Murphy, G. *Personality: A biosocial approach to origins and structure*. New York: Harper, 1947.

Nagel, E., & Newman, J. R. *Gödel's proof*. New York: New York University Press, 1958.

Nakamura, H. *Ways of thinking of Eastern peoples*. Honolulu: East-West Center Press, 1964.

Neisser, U. *Cognitive psychology*. New York: Appleton-Century-Crofts, 1967.

Nguyen. M. L. *Clustering in terms of categorization and reinforcement value in randomly arranged associates*. Unpublished master's thesis. Lafayette, Ind.: Purdue University, 1975.

Nikhilananda, S. Concentration and meditation as methods of Indian philosophy. In C. A. Moore (Ed.), *The Indian mind: Essentials of Indian philosophy and culture*. Honolulu: University of Hawaii Press, 1967. Pp. 136–151.

Nishball, E. R. *A comparison of meaningfulness and intensity in CVC trigrams.* Unpublished master's thesis. St. Louis: St. Louis University, 1966.

Noble, C. E. An analysis of meaning. *Psychological Review*, 1952, **59**, 421–430.

Noble, C. E. Meaningfulness (m) and transfer phenomena in serial verbal learning. *The Journal of Psychology*, 1961, **52**, 201–210.

O'Leary, L. R. *The effect of idiographic meaningfulness on the learning of subjects from different racial backgrounds, social classes, and ability levels.* Unpublished doctoral dissertation. St. Louis: St. Louis University, 1969.

Oppenheimer, R. Analogy in science. *American Psychologist*, 1956, **11**, 127–135.

Orne, M. T. On the social psychology of the psychological experiment: With particular reference to demand characteristics and their implications. *American Psychologist*, 1962, **17**, 776–783.

Ornstein, R. E. *The psychology of consciousness.* San Francisco: Freeman, 1972.

Osgood, C. E. The nature and measurement of meaning. *Psychological Bulletin*, 1952, **49**, 197–237.

Osgood, C. E. On the whys and wherefores of E, P, and A. *Journal of Personality and Social Psychology*, 1969, **12**, 194–199.

Osgood, C. E., Suci, G. J., & Tannenbaum, P. H. *The measurement of meaning.* Urbana: University of Illinois Press, 1957.

Page, M. M. Demand characteristics and the verbal operant conditioning experiment. *Journal of Personality and Social Psychology*, 1972, **23**, 304–308.

Paivio, A. *Imagery and verbal processes.* New York: Holt, Rinehart & Winston, 1971.

Paivio, A., Yuille, J. C., & Madigan, S. A. Concreteness, imagery, and meaningfulness values for 925 nouns. *Journal of Experimental Psychology Monograph Supplement*, 1968, **76**, 1–25.

Palmer, R. E. *Hermeneutics.* Evanston, Ill.: Northwestern University Press, 1969.

Pavlov, I. P. *Conditioned reflexes: An investigation of the psychological activity of the cerebral cortex* (trans. by G. V. Anrep). New York: Oxford University Press, 1927.

Penfield, W. *The mystery of the mind.* Princeton, N.J.: Princeton University Press, 1975.

Pepper, S. C. *World hypotheses.* Berkeley: University of California Press, 1970.

Peters, H. N. Mediate association. *Journal of Experimental Psychology*, 1935, **18**, 20–48.

Piaget, J. *The child's conception of physical causality.* London: Kegan Paul, Trench, Trubner, 1930.

Piaget, J. *The child's conception of number.* London: Routledge & Kegan Paul, 1952.

Piaget, J. *Logic and psychology.* New York: Basic Books, 1957.

Piaget, J., Inhelder, B., & Szeminska, A. *The child's conception of geometry.* New York: Harper Torchbooks, 1964.

Piers, E. V., & Harris, D. B. Piers-Harris Children's Self-Concept Scale: Manual. Nashville, Tenn.: Counselor Recordings and Tests, 1964.

Polanyi, M. *Personal knowledge.* New York: Harper Torchbooks, 1964.

Popper, K. R. The logic of scientific discovery. New York: Basic Books, 1959.

Popper, K. R. Normal science and its dangers. In I. Lakatos & A. Musgrave (Eds.), Criticism and the growth of knowledge. Cambridge: The University Press, 1970. Pp. 51–58.

Pribram, K. H. Languages of the brain: Experimental paradoxes and principles in neuropsychology. Englewood Cliffs, N.J.: Prentice-Hall, 1971.

Raju, P. T. Metaphysical theories in Indian philosophy. In C. A. Moore (Ed.), The Indian mind: Essentials of Indian philosophy and culture. Honolulu: University of Hawaii Press, 1967. Pp. 19–40.

Rancurello, A. C. A study of Franz Brentano. New York: Academic, 1968.

Rieff, P. Freud: The mind of the moralist. New York: Viking, 1959.

Riegel, K. F. Dialectic operations: The final period of cognitive development. Human Development, 1973, 16, 346–370.

Riesman, D. The lonely crowd. Garden City, N.Y.: Doubleday, 1953.

Roark, R. N. Psychology in education. New York: American Book, 1895.

Roberts, W. T. Instrumental effects of causal constructs. Unpublished master's thesis. Lafayette, Ind.: Purdue University, 1974.

Rogers, C. R. Client-centered therapy. Boston: Houghton Mifflin, 1951.

Rogers, C. R. On becoming a person: A therapist's view of psychotherapy. Boston: Houghton Mifflin, 1961.

Rogers, C. R. Toward a modern approach to values: The valuing process in the mature person. In J. T. Hart & T. M. Tomlinson (Eds.), New directions in client-centered therapy. Boston: Houghton Mifflin, 1970. Pp. 430–441.

Rogers, C. R., & Skinner, B. F. Some issues concerning the control of human behavior: A symposium. Science, 1956, 124, 1057–1066.

Rokeach, M. The nature of human values. New York: Free Press, 1973.

Rosenthal, R. Experimenter effects in behavioral research. New York: Appleton-Century-Crofts, 1966.

Rotter, J. B. Social learning and clinical psychology. Englewood Cliffs, N.J.: Prentice-Hall, 1954.

Rumsey, J .M. G. Affective assessment in intelligence testing of black and white, middle- and lower-class adolescents. Unpublished doctoral dissertation. Lafayette, Ind.: Purdue University, 1975.

Russell, B. Introduction to mathematical philosophy. London: George Allen & Unwin, 1919.

Russell, B. Wisdom of the west. Garden City, N.Y.: Doubleday, 1959.

Rychlak, J. F. Reinforcement value: A suggested idiographic, intensity dimension of meaningfulness for the personality theorist. Journal of Personality, 1966, 34, 311–335.

Rychlak, J. F. A philosophy of science for personality theory. Boston: Houghton Mifflin, 1968.

Rychlak, J. F. Lockean vs. Kantian theoretical models and the "cause" of therapeutic change. Psychotherapy: Theory, Research and Practice, 1969, 6, 214–222.

Rychlak, J. F. The human person in modern psychological science. British Journal of Medical Psychology, 1970, 43, 233–240.

Rychlak, J. F. Communication in human concordance: Possibilities and impossibilities. In J. H. Masserman & J. J. Schwab (Eds.), *Man for humanity: On concordance vs. discord in human behavior.* Springfield, Ill.: Charles C Thomas, 1972. Pp. 91–101.

Rychlak, J. F. *Introduction to personality and psychotherapy: A theory-construction approach.* Boston: Houghton Mifflin, 1973.

Rychlak, J. F. Affective assessment in the recognition of designs and paintings by elementary school children. *Child Development,* 1975, **46**, 62–70.

Rychlak, J. F. Affective assessment, intelligence, social class, and racial learning style. *Journal of Personality and Social Psychology,* 1975, **32**, 989–995.

Rychlak, J. F. (Ed.), *Dialectic: Humanistic rationale for behavior and development.* Basel, Switzerland: S. Karger AG, 1976.

Rychlak, J. F. The multiple meanings of dialectic. In J. F. Rychlak (Ed.), *Dialectic: Humanistic rationale for behavior and development.* Basel, Switzerland: S. Karger AG, 1976. Pp. 1–17.

Rychlak, J. F. Personality theory: Its nature, past, present and—future? *Personality and Social Psychology Bulletin,* 1976, **2**, 209–224.

Rychlak, J. F. A humanist looks at psychological science. In W. J. Arnold & J. K. Cole (Eds.), *Nebraska symposium on motivation* (Vol. 22). Lincoln: University of Nebraska Press, 1975.

Rychlak, J. F. Is a concept of "self" necessary in psychological theory, and if so why? In A. H. Wandersman, P. J. Poppen, & D. F. Ricks (Eds.), *Humanism and behaviorism: Dialogue and growth.* Elmsford, N.Y.: Pergamon, 1976.

Rychlak, J. F., Carlsen, N. L., & Dunning, L. P. Personal adjustment and the free recall of material with affectively positive or negative meaningfulness. *Journal of Abnormal Psychology,* 1974, **83**, 480–487.

Rychlak, J. F., Galster, J., & McFarland, K. K. The role of affective assessment in associative learning: From designs and CVC trigrams to faces and names. *Journal of Experimental Research in Personality,* 1972, **6**, 186–194.

Rychlak, J. F., Hewitt, C. W., & Hewitt, J. Affective evaluation, word quality, and the verbal learning styles of black versus white junior college females. *Journal of Personality and Social Psychology,* 1973, **27**, 248–255.

Rychlak, J. F., McKee, D. B., Schneider, W. E., & Abramson, Y. Affective evaluation in the verbal learning styles of normals and abnormals. *Journal of Abnormal Psychology,* 1971, **77**, 11–16.

Rychlak, J. F., & Saluri, R. E. Affective assessment in the learning of names by fifth- and sixth-grade children. *Journal of Genetic Psychology,* 1973, **123**, 251–261.

Rychlak, J. F., Tasto, D. L., Andrews, J. E., & Ellis, H. C. The application of an affective dimension of meaningfulness to personality-related verbal learning. *Journal of Personality,* 1973, **41**, 341–360.

Rychlak, J. F., & Tobin, T. J. Order effects in the affective learning styles of overachievers and underachievers. *Journal of Educational Psychology,* 1971, **62**, 141–147.

Rychlak, J. F., Tuan, N. D., & Schneider, W. E. Formal discipline revisited: Affective assessment and nonspecific transfer. *Journal of Educational Psychology,* 1974, **66**, 139–151.

Saksena, S. K. Relation of philosophical theories to the practical affairs of men. In C. A. Moore (Ed.), *The Indian mind: Essentials of Indian philosophy and culture.* Honolulu: University of Hawaii Press, 1967. Pp. 19–40.

Sarton, G. *Introduction to the history of science* (4 vols.). Baltimore: Williams & Wilkins, 1927. (Reprinted, 1968)

Schrödinger, E. *Science theory and man.* New York: Dover, 1957.

Schwartz, G., & Bishop, P. W. (Eds.), *Moments of discovery: The origins of science.* New York: Basic Books, 1958.

Sheriff, M., Hovland, C. I. *Social judgment: Assimilation and contrast effects in communication and attitude change.* New Haven: Yale University Press, 1961.

Siegel, S. *Nonparametric statistics for the behavioral sciences.* New York: McGraw-Hill, 1956.

Skaggs, E. B. The limitations of scientific psychology as an applied practical science. *Psychological Review,* 1934, **41,** 573–576.

Skinner, B. F. The concept of the reflex in the description of behavior. *Journal of General Psychology,* 1931, **5,** 427–458.

Skinner, B. F. *The behavior of organisms: An experimental analysis.* New York: Appleton-Century, 1938.

Skinner, B. F. Are theories of learning necessary? *Psychological Review,* 1950, **57,** 193–216.

Skinner, B. F. A case history in scientific method. *American Psychologist,* 1956, **11,** 221–233.

Skinner, B. F. *Beyond freedom and dignity.* New York: Knopf, 1971.

Skinner, B. F. *About behaviorism.* New York: Knopf, 1974.

Snider, J. G., & Osgood, C. E. *Semantic differential technique: A sourcebook.* Chicago: Aldine, 1969.

Solso, R. L. (Ed.), *Theories in cognitive psychology: The Loyola symposium.* New York: Wiley, 1974.

Spence, J. T., & Lair, C. V. Associative interference in the verbal learning performance of schizophrenics and normals. *Journal of Abnormal and Social Psychology,* 1964, **68,** 204–209.

Spence, K. W. The postulates and methods of "behaviorism." *Psychological Review,* 1948, **55,** 67–78.

Spence, K. W. *Behavior theory and conditioning.* New Haven: Yale University Press, 1956.

Sperry, R. W. The great cerebral commissure. *Scientific American,* 1964, **210,** 42–52.

Spielberger, C. D., Berger, A., & Howard, K. Conditioning of verbal behavior as a function of awareness, need for social approval, and motivation to receive reinforcement. *Journal of Abnormal and Social Psychology,* 1963, **67,** 241–246.

Spinelli, D. N., & Pribram, K. H. Changes in visual recovery functions and unit activity produced by frontal and temporal cortex stimulation. *Electroencephalography and clinical neurophysiology,* 1967, **22,** 143–149.

Stevens, S. S. The operational definition of psychological concepts. *Psychological Review,* 1935, **42,** 517–527.

Sullivan, H. S. *The interpersonal theory of psychiatry.* New York: Norton, 1953.

Suppes, P. The place of theory in educational research. *Educational Researcher,* 1974, **3**, 3–10.

Suzuki, D. T. *The essentials of Zen Buddhism* (edited and with an introduction by B. Phillips). New York: Dutton, 1962.

Takakusu, J. Buddhism as a philosophy of "thusness." In C. A. Moore (Ed.), *The Indian mind: Essentials of Indian philosophy and culture.* Honolulu: University of Hawaii Press, 1967. Pp. 86–117.

Tasto, D. L. *The influence of meaningfulness as measured in terms of frequency and intensity on rate of acquisition.* Unpublished master's thesis. St. Louis: St. Louis University, 1967.

Tasto, D. L. *Meaningfulness and the masculinity and femininity personality factors as related to rate of acquisition.* Unpublished doctoral dissertation. St. Louis: St. Louis University, 1968.

Taylor, J. A. A personality scale of manifest anxiety. *Journal of Abnormal and Social Psychology,* 1953, **48**, 285–290.

Tenbrunsel, T. W. *A study of the relationship of association value and reinforcement value at various levels of nomothetic association value.* Unpublished master's thesis. St. Louis: St. Louis University, 1967.

Tenbrunsel, T. W., Nishball, E. R., & Rychlak, J. F. The idiographic relationship between association value and reinforcement value, and the nature of meaning. *Journal of Personality,* 1968, **36**, 126–137.

Thoreson, C. E., & Mahoney, M. J. *Behavioral self-control.* New York: Holt, Rinehart & Winston, 1974.

Thorndike, E. L. Animal intelligence: An experimental study of the associative processes in animals. *Psychological Review Monograph Supplement,* 1898, No. 8.

Thorndike, E. L. *Educational psychology: Briefer course.* New York: Columbia University Press, 1914.

Thorndike, E. L., & Lorge, I. *The teachers word book of 30,000 words.* New York: Columbia University Press, 1944.

Thorndike, E. L., & Woodworth, R. S. The influence of improvement in one mental function upon the efficiency of other functions. I. *Psychological Review,* 1901, **8**, 247–261.

Thorndike, E. L., & Woodworth, R. S. The influence of improvement in one mental function upon the efficiency of other functions. II. The stimulation of magnitudes. *Psychological Review,* 1901, **8**, 384–395.

Thorndike, E. L., & Woodworth, R. S. The influence of improvement in one mental function upon the efficiency of other functions. III. Functions involving attention, observation, and discrimination. *Psychological Review,* 1901, **8**, 553–564.

Thurstone, L. L. *Multiple factor analysis.* Chicago: University of Chicago Press, 1947.

Thurstone, L. L., & Chave, E. J. *The measurement of attitude.* Chicago: The University of Chicago Press, 1929.

Titchener, E. B. *An outline of psychology.* New York: Macmillan, 1897.

Titchener, E. B. A text-book of psychology. New York: Macmillan, 1909.

Titchener, E. B. The postulates of a structural psychology. Philosophical Review, 1898, 7, 449–465. Reprinted in T. Shipley (Ed.), Classics in psychology. New York: Philosophical Library, 1961. Pp. 224–243.

Titchener, E. B. Systematic psychology: Prolegomena. Ithaca and London: Cornell University Press, 1972.

Tobin, T. J. The effect of reinforcement value on the learning of overachievers and underachievers. Unpublished master's thesis. St. Louis: St. Louis University, 1969.

Tolman, E. C. Purposive behavior in animals and men. New York: Appleton-Century-Crofts, 1967.

Trybus, R. J. The effects of reinforcement value and association value on nonspecific transfer. Unpublished master's thesis. St. Louis: St. Louis University, 1969.

Tuan, N. D. Changes in associative and affective meaningfulness as a function of frequency and intensity factors. Unpublished doctoral dissertation, Lafayette, Ind.: Purdue University, 1974.

Tucker, L. R. The extension of factor analysis to three-dimensional matrices. In N. Frederiksen & H. Gulliksen (Eds.), Contributions to mathematical psychology. New York: Holt, Rinehart & Winston, 1964.

Tucker, L. R. Experiments in multi-mode factor analysis. Proceedings of the 1964 invitational conference on testing problems, 1965, 14, 46–57.

Tucker, L. R. Some mathematical notes on three-mode factor analysis. Psychometrika, 1966, 31, 279–311.

Tulving, E. Subjective organization in free recall of "unrelated" words. Psychological Review, 1962, 69, 344–354.

Tulving, E., & Madigan, S. A. Memory and verbal learning. In P. H. Mussen & M. R. Rosenzweig (Eds.), Annual review of psychology (Vol. 21). Palo Alto, Calif.: Annual Reviews, 1970. Pp. 437–477.

Underwood, B. J. Individual differences as a crucible in theory construction. American Psychologist, 1975, 30, 128–134.

Underwood, B. J., & Schulz, R. W. Meaningfulness and verbal learning. Chicago: Lippincott, 1960.

Untersteiner, M. The sophists. New York: Philosophical Library, 1954.

van Kaam, A. Existential foundations of psychology (Image Books ed.). Garden City, N.Y.: Doubleday, 1969.

Voss, J. F. On the relationship of associative and organizational processes. In E. Tulving & W. Donaldson (Eds.), Organization of memory. New York: Academic, 1972. Pp. 167–194.

Waters, R. H. Morgan's canon and anthropomorphism. Psychological Review, 1939, 46, 534–540.

Waters, R. H. Mechanicomorphism: A new term for an old mode of thought. Psychological Review, 1948, 55, 139–142.

Watson, J. B. Psychology as the behaviorist views it. Psychological Review, 1913, 20, 158–177.

Watson, J. B. Behaviorism. New York: Norton, 1924.

Watson, R. I. Psychology: A prescriptive science. *American Psychologist*, 1967, **22**, 435–443.

Watson, R. I. *The great psychologists* (3rd ed.). Philadelphia: Lippincott, 1971.

Weiss, A. P. The mind and the man within. *Psychological Review*, 1919, **26**, 327–334.

Wertheimer, M. *Productive thinking.* New York: Harper, 1945.

Whitehead, A. N. *The function of reason.* Boston: Beacon, 1958.

Whitehead, A. N., & Russell, B. *Principia mathematica* (3 vols., 2nd ed.). Cambridge: The University Press, 1963.

Wiener, P. P., & Noland, A. (Eds.), *Roots of scientific thought.* New York: Basic Books, 1957.

Wightman, W. P. D. *The growth of scientific ideas.* New Haven: Yale University Press, 1951.

Winter, J. E. The postulates of psychology. *Psychological Review*, 1936, **43**, 130–148.

Wolman, B. B. Does psychology need its own philosophy of science? *American Psychologist*, 1971, **26**, 877–886.

Woodward, K. E. *Affective learning style across race: Group and individual identification procedures.* Unpublished master's thesis. Lafayette, Ind.: Purdue University, 1973.

Woodworth, R. S., & Sheehan, M. R. *Contemporary schools of psychology* (3rd ed.). New York: Ronald, 1964.

Wundt, M. *Die Wurzein der deutschen Philosophie in Stamm und Rasse.* Berlin: Junker und Dunnhaupt, 1944.

Wundt, W. *Lectures on human and animal psychology* (4th ed.). New York: Macmillan, 1907. (1st ed., 1894.)

Wundt, W. Contributions to the theory of sensory perception. In T. Shipley (Ed.), *Classics in psychology.* New York: Philosophical Library, 1961.

Wundt, W. *The language of gestures.* Paris: Mouton, 1973.

Yerkes, R. M. Concerning the anthropocentrism of psychology. *Psychological Review*, 1933, **40**, 209–212.

# AUTHOR INDEX

# SUBJECT INDEX